Frommer's®
Alaska
13th Edition

by Kris Capps, Michael Dunham,
Charlotte Glover & David Kiffer

WILEY

John Wiley & Sons, Inc.

Published by:
JOHN WILEY & SONS, INC.
111 River St.
Hoboken, NJ 07030-5774

ISBN 978-1-118-07470-1 (paper); ISBN 978-1-118-16308-5 (ebk); ISBN 978-1-118-16307-8 (ebk); ISBN 978-1-118-16309-2 (ebk)

Editor: Anuja Madar & Michael Kelly
Production Editor: Katie Robinson
Cartographer: Guy Ruggiero
Photo Editor: Cherie Cincilla, Richard Fox, Alden Gewirtz
Design by Vertigo Design
Layout, Graphics, and Prepress by Wiley Indianapolis Composition Services

Front cover photo: Two bull moose size each other up in brilliant fall colors with Mount McKinley towering in the background in Denali National Park © Leo Keeler / Alamy Images.
Back cover photo: *Left:* Female Brown Bear with cub © Thomas Sbampato / Picture Press / Alamy Images. *Middle:* Historic "Creek Street," famous from the days of the Alaskan Gold Rush, Ketchikan © Don Klumpp / Alamy Images. *Right:* Tufted puffin (*Lunda cirrhata*), standing on rock, USA, Alaska © Blickwinkel / Alamy Images..

For information on our other products and services or to obtain technical support, please contact our Customer Care Department within the U.S. at 877/762-2974, outside the U.S. at 317/572-3993 or fax 317/572-4002.

Wiley also publishes its books in a variety of electronic formats. Some content that appears in print may not be available in electronic formats.

Manufactured in China

5 4 3 2 1

CONTENTS

6 ANCHORAGE & ENVIRONS 212

7 THE KENAI PENINSULA & PRINCE WILLIAM SOUND 278

LIST OF MAPS

ABOUT THE AUTHORS

Kris Capps is a longtime Alaska journalist who has traveled extensively throughout the state. She spends most of her time in Interior Alaska and currently lives right outside Denali National Park with her teenage daughter; this has been her home for 20 years. She writes a weekly newspaper column about the Denali area for the Fairbanks Daily News-Miner and is the author of award-winning guidebooks including the Denali Road Guide and Denali Walks.

Mike Dunham moved to Quinhagak, Alaska, on the Bering Sea, with his parents in 1955, when he was 4 years old. He has since lived and worked in Mountain Village, Togiak, Afognak, Homer, Haines, Kodiak, Kenai, Seward and Cordova—but mostly in Anchorage, where he is the Arts and Entertainment editor for the *Anchorage Daily News.* He has won numerous regional and national awards for articles on travel, art, education, food, history and humor, as well as for his work in radio. Outside Alaska he has written for publications ranging from *Orion* magazine to *Opera News.* He is among the editors of the University of Alaska's recent "Grammar of Central Alaskan Yupik, an Eskimoan Language" and suspects that he is the only non-Alaska Native in the world who has to divulge on his tax returns how much money he makes as an Eskimo dancer.

Dave Kiffer is a fourth generation Ketchikan resident on both sides of his family. A professional jazz musician with degrees in Journalism and Creative Writing, he has worked for newspapers and public radio in several states. He currently runs Historic Ketchikan, a non-profit that promotes economic development through historic preservation and heritage tourism. In addition to serving as the current Ketchikan Gateway Borough Mayor, Dave teaches music and writes humor and Alaska history columns for sitnews.us. His wife, **Charlotte Glover,** is a Youth Services librarian for the Ketchikan Public Library who has done travel research for "Alaska Best Places" and "Frommer's Alaska" for many years and contributes regularly to TripAdvisor. Their son Liam is 10 years old and is on track to win the 5K in the 2020 Olympics.

HOW TO CONTACT US

In researching this book, we discovered many wonderful places—hotels, restaurants, shops, and more. We're sure you'll find others. Please tell us about them, so we can share the information with your fellow travelers in upcoming editions. If you were disappointed with a recommendation, we'd love to know that, too. Please write to:

Frommer's Alaska, 13th Edition
John Wiley & Sons, Inc. • 111 River St. • Hoboken, NJ 07030-5774
frommersfeedback@wiley.com

ADVISORY & DISCLAIMER

Travel information can change quickly and unexpectedly, and we strongly advise you to confirm important details locally before traveling, including information on visas, health and safety, traffic and transport, accommodations, shopping, and eating out. We also encourage you to stay alert while traveling and to remain aware of your surroundings. Avoid civil disturbances, and keep a close eye on cameras, purses, wallets, and other valuables.

While we have endeavored to ensure that the information contained within this guide is accurate and up-to-date at the time of publication, we make no representations or warranties with respect to the accuracy or completeness of the contents of this work and specifically disclaim all warranties, including without limitation warranties of fitness for a particular purpose. We accept no responsibility or liability for any inaccuracy or errors or omissions, or for any inconvenience, loss, damage, costs, or expenses of any nature whatsoever incurred or suffered by anyone as a result of any advice or information contained in this guide.

The inclusion of a company, organization, or website in this guide as a service provider and/or potential source of further information does not mean that we endorse them or the information they provide. Be aware that information provided through some websites may be unreliable and can change without notice. Neither the publisher nor author shall be liable for any damages arising herefrom.

FROMMER'S STAR RATINGS, ICONS & ABBREVIATIONS

Every hotel, restaurant, and attraction listing in this guide has been ranked for quality, value, service, amenities, and special features using a **star-rating system.** In country, state, and regional guides, we also rate towns and regions to help you narrow down your choices and budget your time accordingly. Hotels and restaurants are rated on a scale of zero (recommended) to three stars (exceptional). Attractions, shopping, nightlife, towns, and regions are rated according to the following scale: zero stars (recommended), one star (highly recommended), two stars (very highly recommended), and three stars (must-see).

In addition to the star-rating system, we also use **six feature icons** that point you to the great deals, in-the-know advice, and unique experiences that separate travelers from tourists. Throughout the book, look for:

special finds—those places only insiders know about

fun facts—details that make travelers more informed and their trips more fun

kids—best bets for kids and advice for the whole family

special moments—those experiences that memories are made of

insider tips—great ways to save time and money

great values—where to get the best deals

The following **abbreviations** are used for credit cards:

AE American Express	**DISC** Discover	**V** Visa
DC Diners Club	**MC** MasterCard	

TRAVEL RESOURCES AT FROMMERS.COM

Frommer's travel resources don't end with this guide. Frommer's website, **www. frommers.com**, has travel information on more than 4,000 destinations. We update features regularly, giving you access to the most current trip-planning information and the best airfare, lodging, and car-rental bargains. You can also listen to podcasts, connect with other Frommers.com members through our active-reader forums, share your travel photos, read blogs from guidebook editors and fellow travelers, and much more.

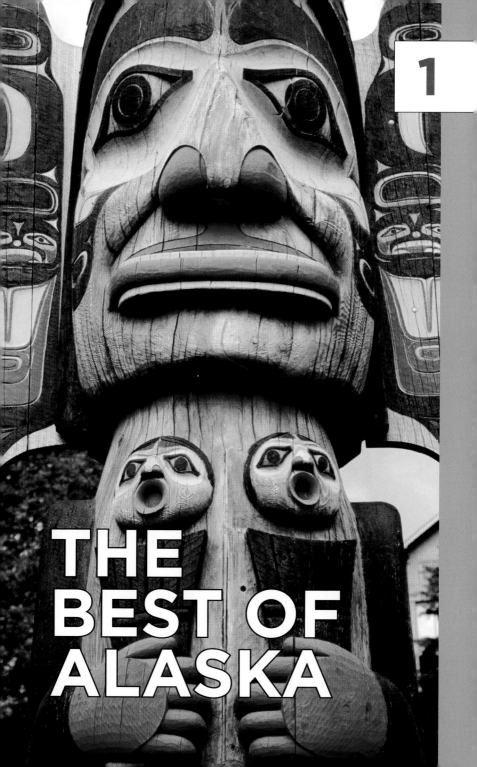

THE BEST OF ALASKA

T he works of man are not what bring visitors to Alaska. Driving into a city or town at the end of a long, empty road feels surreal because everything is, in a way, in the middle of nowhere; the fact that things have been built at all, often with heroic difficulty, makes even tiny cabins special. Alaska's real draw and glory is the works of nature, so numerous and stupendous as to make any list of "bests" a mere suggestion of where to start. Natural forces of vast scale are still shaping the land in their own way, inscribing a different story on each of an infinite number of unexpected places.

Alaska's unformed newness makes it interesting and fun. Despite the best efforts of tour planners, the most memorable parts of a visit are unpredictable and often unexpected: a humpback whale leaping clear of the water, the face of a glacier releasing huge ice chunks, a bear feasting on salmon in a river. As a visitor, opening yourself to what's new, real, and unexpected is your job, but it's an effort that's likely to pay off.

THE best VIEWS

o **A First Sight of Alaska:** Flying north from Seattle, you're in clouds, so you concentrate on your book. When you look up, the light from the window has

PREVIOUS PAGE: **Chief Johnson totem pole in Ketchikan;** ABOVE: **A grizzly bear catches salmon.**

Headed out to flightsee over Punchbowl Cove.

changed. Down below, the clouds are gone, and under the wing, where you're used to seeing roads, cities, and farms on most flights, you see instead only high, snowy mountain peaks, without the slightest mark of human presence, stretching as far as the horizon. Welcome to Alaska.

o **Punchbowl Cove (Misty Fjords National Monument):** A sheer granite cliff rises smooth and implacable 3,150 feet straight up from the water. A pair of bald eagles wheels and soars across its face, providing the only sense of scale. They look the size of gnats. See p. 110.

o **From the Chugach Mountains over Anchorage, at Sunset:** The city sparkles below, on the edge of an orange-reflecting Cook Inlet, far below the mountainside where you stand. Beyond the pink and purple silhouettes of mountains on the other side of the inlet, the sun is spraying warm, dying light into puffs of clouds. And yet it's midnight. See "Getting Outside," in chapter 6.

o **Mount McKinley from the Air (Denali National Park):** A bush pilot guides your plane up from the flatlands of Talkeetna into a realm of eternal white, where a profusion of insanely rugged peaks rises in higher relief than any other spot on Earth. After circling a 3-mile-high wall and slipping through a mile-deep canyon, you land on a glacier, get out of the plane, and for the first time realize the overwhelming scale of it all. See "Attractions & Activities Outside the Park" and "Talkeetna: Back Door to Denali," in chapter 8.

o **The Northern Lights (Alaska's Interior):** Blue, purple, green, and red lines spin from the center of the sky, draping long tendrils of slow-moving light. Bright, flashing, sky-covering waves wash across the dome of stars like ripples

Alaska

BEAUFORT SEA

C. Dalhousie

140°W

Prudhoe Bay
Deadhorse

Inuvik

Great Bear
Lake

R A N G E

DALTON HWY.

Porcupine R.

NORTHWEST
TERRITORIES

Ft. Yukon

Circle

Yukon R.

Yukon-Charley
Rivers Nat. Pres.

C A N A D A

DEMPSTER HWY.

College   FAIRBANKS
North Pole

Eagle

M A C K E N Z I E

Ogilvie Mountains

Nenana

Delta Jct.

Mertie
Mts.

Dawson

YUKON
TERRITORY

R A N G E

Tanana R.

Tok

Susitna R.

ALASKA HWY.

Talkeetna
Mts.   Glennallen

Copper R.

Wrangell
Mts.
Wrangell-St. Elias
N.P. & Pres.

KLONDIKE HWY.

Pelly   Mountains

M O U N T A I N S

Teslin R.

Palmer
Wasilla

Chugach

Kluane L.

Whitehorse ★

Watson Lake

ANCHORAGE   Valdez

Mountains

St. Elias
Mountains

Carcross

Whittier

Cordova

BRITISH
COLUMBIA

Kenai
Mts.

Seward

Prince
William Sd.   Kayak

Montague

Skagway

Haines

Atlin L.

C O A S T

Kenai
Fjords
N.P.

Yakutat

Glacier Bay N.P. & Pres.

Gustavus

★ JUNEAU

Stikine

M O U N T A I N S

G U L F   O F   A L A S K A

Hoonah

Chicagof

Admiralty I.
N.M.

Kake

Petersburg

Sitka

Wrangell

Baranof

C. Ommaney

P A C I F I C   O C E A N

Prince of Wales

Klawock
Craig

Ketchikan

Metlakatla

Dall

Dixon Entrance

Masset

Graham

Queen Charlotte

5

The northern lights create natural art against the skyline.

driven by a gust of wind on a pond. Looking around, you see that your companions' faces are rosy in a silver, snowy night, all gazing straight up with their mouths open. See p. 413.

THE best GLACIERS

More of Alaska—more than 100 times more—is covered by glacier ice than is settled by human beings.

- **Grand Pacific Glacier (Glacier Bay National Park):** Two vast glaciers of deep blue meet at the top of an utterly barren fjord. Three intimidating walls of ice surround boats that pull close to the glaciers. See "Glacier Bay National Park," in chapter 5.

- **Childs Glacier (Cordova):** Out the Copper River Highway from Cordova, this is a participatory glacier-viewing experience. The glacier is cut by the Copper River, which is ¼ mile broad; standing on the opposite shore (unless you're up in the viewing tower), you have to be ready to run like hell when the creaking, popping ice gives way and a huge berg falls into the river, potentially swamping the picnic

Childs Glacier.

Exit Glacier.

area. On one occasion, a glacier-generated wave left a salmon in a tree. Even when the glacier isn't calving, you can feel the ice groaning in your gut. See "Cordova: Hidden Treasure," in chapter 7.

o **Exit Glacier (Seward):** You can park near the glacier and walk the rest of the way on an easy, short gravel path. The vast wall of the glacier towers above like a huge blue sculpture, the spires of broken ice close enough to breathe a freezer-door chill down on watchers. See "Exit Glacier" under "Kenai Fjords National Park," in chapter 7.

o **Western Prince William Sound:** On a boat from Whittier, you can see a couple of dozen glaciers in a day. Some of these are the amazing tidewater glaciers that dump huge, office building–size spires of ice into the ocean, each setting off a terrific splash and outward-radiating sea wave. See "Whittier: Dock on the Sound," in chapter 7.

THE most beautiful DRIVES & TRAIN RIDES

You'll find a description of each road in "Alaska's Highways a la Carte" on p. 406. Here are some highlights:

o **White Pass and Yukon Route Railway (Skagway to Summit):** The narrow-gauge excursion train climbs a steep grade that was chiseled into the granite mountains by stampeders to the Klondike gold rush. The train is a sort of mechanical mountain goat, balancing on trestles and steep rock walls high above deep gorges. See p. 205.

o **Seward Highway/Alaska Railroad (Anchorage to Seward):** Just south of Anchorage, the highway and rail line have been chipped into the side of the Chugach Mountains over the surging gray water of Turnagain Arm. Farther

Driving along the Seward Highway on Turnagain Arm.

south, the route splits and climbs through the mountain passes of the Kenai Peninsula. See "Side Trips to Turnagain Arm & Portage Glacier," in chapter 6, and "The Seward Highway: A Road Guide," in chapter 7, for information on the highway, and p. 297 for information on this Alaska Railroad route.

- **Denali Highway:** Leading east-west through the Alaska Range, the highway crosses terrain that could be another Denali National Park, full of wildlife and with views so huge and grand they seem impossible. This highway is not as well maintained as other roads in the state, though, so travel with care. See p. 368.

- **Richardson Highway:** Just out of Valdez heading north, the Richardson Highway rises quickly from sea level to more than 2,600 feet, switching back and forth on the side of a mountain. With each turn, the drop down the impassable slope becomes more amazing. North of Glennallen, the highway rises again, bursting through the tree line between a series of mountains and tracing the edges of long alpine lakes, before descending, parallel with the silver skein of the Alaska pipeline, to Delta Junction. See "Richardson Highway & Copper Center," in chapter 9.

- **The Roads Around Nome:** You can't drive to Nome, but 250 miles of gravel roads radiate from the Arctic community into tundra that's populated mainly by muskoxen, bears, reindeer, birds, and other wildlife. See p. 492.

- **The Dalton Highway:** When you're ready for an expedition—a real wilderness trip by road—the Dalton Highway leads from Fairbanks across northern Alaska to the Arctic Ocean, a mind-blowing, bone-jarring drive through 500 miles of virgin country, most of it drab until you reach the Gates of the Arctic. See "The Dalton Highway," in chapter 9.

ABOVE: **Trophy salmon at the Kenai River;**
RIGHT: **Cleaning the day's catch in Homer.**

THE best FISHING

The quality of salmon fishing in Alaska isn't so much a function of place as of time. See p. 516 for information on how to find the fish when you arrive.

- **Bristol Bay:** This is the world's richest salmon fishery; lodges on the remote rivers of the region are an angler's paradise. See p. 466.

- **Copper River Delta, Cordova:** The Copper itself is silty with glacial runoff, but feeder streams and rivers are rich with trout, Dolly Varden, and salmon, with few other anglers in evidence.

- **The Kenai River:** The biggest king salmon—up to 98 pounds—come from the swift Kenai River. Big fish are so common in the second run of kings that there's a special, higher standard for what makes a trophy. Silvers and reds add to a mad, summer-long fishing frenzy and some of the most crowded fishing grounds in the state. See p. 317.

- **Homer:** Alaska's largest charter-fishing fleet goes for halibut ranging into the hundreds of pounds. See p. 337.

- **Kodiak Island:** The bears are so big here because they live on an island that's crammed with spawning salmon in the summer. Kodiak has the best roadside salmon fishing in Alaska, and the remote fishing, at lodges or fly-in stream banks, is legendary. See p. 473.

A Kodiak brown bear.

THE best BEAR VIEWING

There are many places to see bears in Alaska, but if your goal is to make *sure* you see a bear—and potentially lots of bears—these are the best places (but note that, in most cases, you have to time your trip to salmon runs, when bears are present):

- **Anan Wildlife Observatory:** When the fish are running, you can see dozens of black bears feeding in a salmon stream from close at hand. Access is easiest from Wrangell. See p. 122.

- **Pack Creek (Admiralty Island):** The brown bears of the island, which is more thickly populated with them than any other place on Earth, have learned to ignore the daily visitors who stand at viewing areas along Pack Creek. DNA research shows that these bruins are more closely related to polar bears than to the grizzlies found elsewhere. Access is by air from Juneau. See p. 172.

- **Mendenhall Glacier (Juneau):** With a group of female black bears in the vicinity, anyone who can walk to the edge of a parking lot may have the pleasure of watching them feeding on fish and rearing their young during the salmon run. Quiet, respectful behavior and no food, please, when watching the bears. See p. 165.

Black bear at the Anan Wildlife Observatory.

- **Katmai National Park:** During the July and September salmon runs, dozens of giant brown bears congregate around Brooks Camp, where, from wooden platforms a few yards away, you can watch the full range of their behaviors. Flight services from Kodiak also bring guests at any time of the summer to see bears dig clams on the park's eastern seashore. See "Katmai National Park" and "Kodiak: Wild Island," in chapter 10.

- **Fortress of the Bear (Sitka):** This nonprofit education and rescue center for orphaned brown bear cubs has two older bears in residence as well, providing hours of safe viewing from platforms into their imaginatively landscaped three-quarter acre habitats. See p. 172.

- **Denali National Park:** The park offers the best and least expensive wildlife-viewing safari in the state. Passengers on the buses that drive the park road as far as mile 63 usually see at least some grizzlies. And you don't have to worry about whether fish are running, as these bears are not focused on salmon streams. See chapter 8.

THE best MARINE MAMMAL VIEWING

You've got a good chance of seeing marine mammals almost anywhere you go boating in Alaska, but in some places, it's almost guaranteed.

- **Frederick Sound (Petersburg):** A humpback jumped right into the boat with whale-watchers here in 1995. The whales show up reliably for feeding each summer. Small boats from Petersburg have no trouble finding them and watching in intimate circumstances. See p. 133.

- **Juneau:** A mom-and-pop whale-watching operation here claims 100% success in finding whales on every tour for 5 years running. You can count on seeing humpback whales and often killer whales and spectacular Dall's porpoises. And the competition of many operators provides numerous choices and low prices. See p. 170.

- **Icy Strait (Gustavus) and Bartlett Cove (Glacier Bay National Park):** Humpback whales show up, and often orcas are present off Point Adolphus, in Icy Strait, just a few miles from little Gustavus, a town of luxurious country inns. They can also be seen in Bartlett Cove within Glacier Bay National Park. See "Glacier Bay National Park" and "Gustavus: Country Inns & Quiet," in chapter 5.

- **Sitka Sound:** Lots of otters and humpback whales show up in the waters near Sitka. In fall, when the town holds its WhaleFest, you can spot them from a city park built for the purpose. See "Sitka: Rich Prize of Russian Conquest," in chapter 5.

A killer whale heads under water in Frederick Sound.

○ **Kenai Fjords National Park (near Seward):** You don't have to go all the way into the park—you're pretty well assured of sea otters and sea lions in Resurrection Bay, near Seward, and humpbacks and killer whales are often seen in the summer, too. See "Kenai Fjords National Park," in chapter 7.

○ **Prince William Sound:** Otters, seals, and sea lions are easy—you'll see them on many trips

A sea otter in the Kenai Peninsula.

out of Valdez, Whittier, or Cordova—but you also have a chance of spotting both humpback and killer whales in the Sound. See chapter 7.

THE best ENCOUNTERS WITH NATIVE CULTURE

○ **Ketchikan Totem Poles:** The junction of three totem-making tribes—Tlingits, Haida, and Tsimshian—the island has three unique places to see totem poles: historic poles indoors at the Totem Heritage Center, faithful reproductions outdoors in a natural setting at Totem Bight State Park, and brand-new poles as they are created in a workshop at the Saxman Native Village Totem Pole Park. See p. 102.

○ **Sitka:** The Tlingits influence remains strong here, where they met Russian settlers in two battles more than 200 years ago. There are a significant number of totem poles at the Sitka National Historic Park, a grand clan house to tour, and an astonishing collection of Native art from around the state at the Sheldon Jackson Museum. See "Sitka: Rich Prize of Russian Conquest," in chapter 5.

○ **Alaska Native Heritage Center (Anchorage):** All of Alaska's Native groups joined together to build this grand living museum and gathering place, where dance and music performances, storytelling, and art and craft demonstrations happen daily. See p. 248.

○ **Iñupiat Heritage Center (Barrow):** A living museum, this is a place to meet and enjoy performances by the Native

Chief Johnson Totem Pole in Ketchikan.

people who built it, and to see extraordinary artifacts they have made and recovered from digs in frozen ground. See p. 499.

THE best MUSEUMS & HISTORIC SITES

o **Sitka National Historical Park:** The historic park, its buildings, and other structures in Sitka keep alive an alternate stream in history: one in which a Russian czar ruled Alaska and this little town was one of the most important on the west coast of North America. See p. 141.

o **The Alaska State Museum (Juneau):** This richly endowed museum doesn't just show off its wealth of objects—it also uses them to teach about the state. A visit will put Alaska's Native cultures and pioneer history in context. See p. 156.

o **Anchorage Museum at Rasmuson Center:** Alaska's largest museum has the room and expertise to tell the story of Native, non-Native, and natural history in Alaska; to showcase contemporary Alaskan art and culture; and to teach about science with fun, interactive exhibits. The Smithsonian Institution's Arctic Studies Center, on the second floor, displays a remarkable collection of historic Alaska Native Art accompanied by informative audiovisual stations. See p. 246.

o **The Pratt Museum (Homer):** The Pratt explains natural history (especially the life of the ocean) in a clear and intimate way you'll find nowhere else in Alaska. See p. 331.

o **UA Museum of the North (Fairbanks):** The spectacular university museum includes swooping and ingenious galleries that present Alaska's art, anthropology, and natural science in mixed, thematic collections that spur new ideas

An exhibit at the UA Museum of the North.

and connections for viewers. Treasures include the ancient, tiny "Okvik Madonna" and "Babe," a mummified steppe bison from the Ice Age. An audio exhibit lets you hear the invisible astronomical, seismic, auroral, and weather phenomena in real time. See p. 415.

THE best WINTER DESTINATIONS

o **Anchorage:** Anyone can enjoy the Fur Rendezvous and Iditarod sled-dog races, which keep a winter-carnival atmosphere going through much of February and March, but winter sports enthusiasts get the most out of winter here. The city has some of the best Nordic skiing in the country, close access to challenging downhill skiing, dog mushing, and groomed lake skating. See chapter 6.

o **Alyeska Resort (Girdwood):** Alaska's premier downhill skiing area has lots of snow over a long season, fantastic views, few lift lines, and the luxurious Hotel Alyeska. See "Side Trips to Girdwood & Mount Alyeska," in chapter 6 and "The Best Hotels," below.

o **Chena Hot Springs Resort:** A 90-minute ride from Fairbanks, and you're out in the country, where the northern lights are clear on a starry winter afternoon and night. The resort has lots of activities to get you into the snowy countryside, or you can just relax in the hot mineral springs. See p. 435.

o **Homer:** In March, you can fish for king salmon in the morning and cross-country ski over a high ridge with limitless ocean views in the afternoon. In the evening, check out Alaska's best art galleries and eat in its best restaurants. See "Homer & Kachemak Bay: Cosmic Hamlet by the Sea," in chapter 7.

Taking in the view at Alyeska Resort.

Cross-country skiing in Anchorage.

- **Barrow:** Go to the shore of the frozen Arctic Ocean, and you have a chance to experience the most extreme winter conditions in the world. It's dark for 65 days except for the aurora blasting across the sky. There's not much to do, but you could run into a polar bear in the street. See "Barrow: Way North," in chapter 10.

THE best HOTELS

- **Cape Fox Lodge** (Ketchikan; ✆ **800/325-4000**): Clinging to cliffs above the downtown, amid the tops of huge spruce trees, the hotel feels like a peaceful treehouse. The elegance and proportions of the understated building perfectly enhance the setting, all framed in rich cedar. The Alaska Native owners complete the experience by filling the hotel with masterpieces of their culture's art. See p. 109.
- **Hotel Captain Cook** (Anchorage; ✆ **800/843-1950**): This is the grand old hotel of downtown Anchorage, with a heavy nautical theme, teak paneling, several terrific restaurants, and every possible amenity. It remains the state's standard of service and luxury. See p. 224.
- **Hotel Alyeska** (Girdwood; ✆ **800/880-3880**): The first sight of this ski resort hotel—designed in a château style and standing in an undeveloped mountain valley—will make you catch your breath. Wait until you get inside and see the starscape and polar bear diorama in the lobby atrium, or the salt-water swimming pool, with its high-beamed ceiling and windows, looking out on the mountain. A tram carries skiers and diners to the mountaintop, and you can also ski from the back door. See p. 272.

A room with a view at Cape Fox Lodge.

○ **Land's End Resort** (Homer; *𝒞* **800/478-0400**): It's the location: right on the end of Homer Spit, 5 miles out in the middle of Kachemak Bay, where you can fish for salmon from the beach right in front of your room, or watch otters drifting by. The hotel itself is excellent, too, with a tremendous variety of rooms, some extraordinarily luxurious, and a complete spa. See p. 340.

○ **Westmark Fairbanks Hotel & Conference Center** (Fairbanks; *𝒞* **800/544-0970**): A tower rises over the flat river city of Fairbanks, a stylish and charming wing of the city's oldest modern hotel, owned by the Holland America Line, which is a center of activity downtown. See p. 426.

The deck at the Land's End Resort.

THE best WEBSITES

Many useful websites are listed throughout the book; some of the best are under "Visitor Information" near the beginning of each town section. Here's an idiosyncratic sampling of some fun or informative links.

- **www.trollart.com:** Ketchikan artist Ray Troll has created a website that carries you deep into his mind, which is full of odd and resonant humor about the evolution of fish, man, and our common relations. His vibrantly colored art makes it an aesthetic journey.

- **www.adfg.state.ak.us:** The Alaska Department of Fish and Game posts valuable information for anyone interested in fishing, hunting, wildlife-watching, or just learning about creatures. Everyone from children to wildlife biologists will find something at their level. Try **www.wildlife.alaska.gov** for information about where to go and how to see Alaska's wild animals.

- **www.gi.alaska.edu:** The Geophysical Institute at the University of Alaska Fairbanks maintains a fascinating and cool site filled with real-time earth science information about Alaska, such as aurora predictions, volcano watches, earthquake and tsunami updates, rocketry, and space science.

- **www.adn.com:** The *Anchorage Daily News* site has been widely visited since former Gov. Sarah Palin's rise to national prominence. It's the place to look for the latest on her career, the rest of the crazy Alaska political scene, and a good deal of handy travel and outdoor information as well, including blogs by writers from around the state.

- **Some of Alaska's Liveliest Current Blogs: Alaska Dispatch** (www.alaskadispatch.com), a journalist-written news channel with opinions mostly from the liberal side. **The Alaska Standard** (www.thealaskastandard.com) provides the conservative counterpoint. From Wasilla, **www.progressivealaska.blogspot.com** mixes observations on art with unabashedly controversial commentary on current events. Businessman Andrew Halcro's **www.andrewhalcro.com** often scoops local media with hard news and generally presents a firm grasp of facts and numbers.

- **Favorite Small-Town Sites:** Small-town Alaska newspapers, and people in communities too small to have a newspaper, communicate through the Internet; visitors to these sites can vicariously experience the pleasures and pitfalls of remote living, which can be touching and hilarious. Check **www.alaskanewspapers.com**, which covers several far-flung towns, Ketchikan's **www.sitnews.us**, Nome's **www.nomenugget.com**, and Kotzebue's **www.cityofkotzebue.com**.

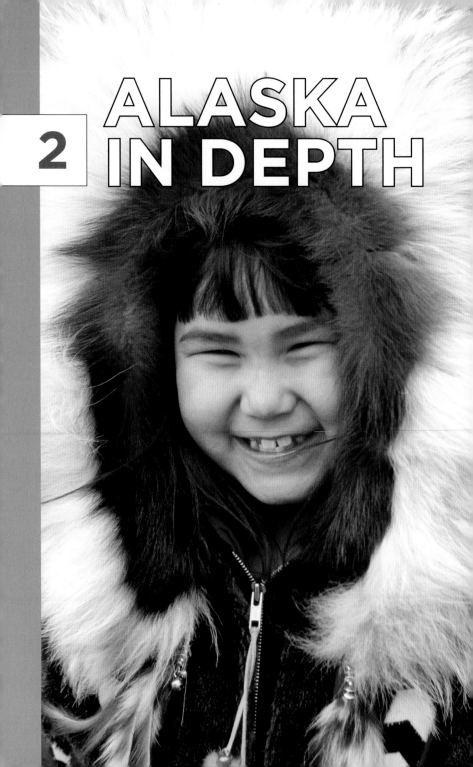

F or most people, coming to Alaska is the trip of a lifetime. For those of us who live here, we may spend a lifetime exploring our own state, knowing that no matter how hard we try, we'll see only a tiny portion of its vast landscape and attractions.

Tour guides try to get it across with statistics, and some do give you a general idea of scale. If you placed Alaska's estimated 692,000 residents an equal distance apart across the state, each would be almost a mile from any other. Of course, that couldn't happen—no one has ever been to some parts of Alaska.

But numbers are not what cross your mind when you see a chunk of ice the size of a building fall from a glacier; when you feel a wave lift your sea kayak from the fall of a breaching humpback whale; or when, after driving all day along an Interior Alaska highway, the sun still hanging high in what should be night, you realize you haven't seen anyone else in an hour.

Anyone with the time to let the place sink in can make the same discoveries—you only have to be open and able to slow down long enough to experience it.

ALASKA TODAY: WHAT IT MEANS TO BE ALASKAN

To be an Alaskan today means that, after years of benign neglect, you find yourself answering a lot of questions when you travel. When former Gov. Sarah Palin entered national politics as the Republican vice-presidential nominee in 2008,

national attention focused a bright light on Alaska—and not necessarily in a good way.

Palin has been a lightning rod in Alaskan politics since she took on the Republican political establishment and became governor in 2002. She was initially extremely popular, pushing through increased taxes on the oil industry and then spreading a budget windfall throughout the state by giving all Alaskans a bonus check to help with rising fuel prices.

But then came the 2008 presidential race, and Palin's intense partisanship began to wear on Alaskans, most of whom proudly vote for "person" before "party." Palin also began to show a face to the national media that played up an outsider's stereotypical view of Alaska. Her "folksiness" and

FACING PAGE: **An Iñupiat Eskimo bundled against the cold;** ABOVE: **A young Iñupiat Eskimo girl.**

Sunset over the Alaska Range in Fairbanks.

general lack of intellectual curiosity struck many Alaskans as both false and demeaning.

Palin resigned the governorship several months after the presidential election but continued to be a national media figure. At press time, she was still pondering seeking the presidency in 2012.

But Palin's national race was not the only item of national interest. Alleged political corruption in the Alaska State Legislature led to several prominent trials, most notably one involving Alaska's longest-lived and most powerful political figure, U.S. Sen. Ted Stevens.

Stevens, who was known affectionately as "Uncle Ted" for his ability to steer billions of federal dollars to Alaska, had been Alaska's ranking senator since the 1960s and was a major player in Washington, D.C., serving as chairman of the Senate Appropriations Committee. After a lengthy trial, he was found guilty shortly before the 2008 election and lost his seat by a few thousand votes to Democrat Mark Begich, the son of Congressman Nick Begich, who disappeared on a flight from Anchorage to Juneau in the early 1970s. But Stevens had the last laugh when his conviction was overturned in the face of significant misconduct on the part of the government attorneys prosecuting his case. Stevens later died in a 2010 plane crash in western Alaska.

Problems with prosecutorial misconduct also plagued several other trials involving state legislators, who allegedly took bribes from representatives of the oil industry.

In 2010, Alaska was back in the national spotlight because of an unusual U.S. Senate campaign. Incumbent Lisa Murkowski lost during the Republican primary to Joe Miller, a candidate favored by both the national Tea Party organizations and Sarah Palin, who had defeated Murkowski's father for the governorship nearly a decade earlier.

Murkowski then chose to run a "write-in" campaign and easily won the general election, to the surprise of many; the last successful Congressional "write in" was in the 1950s. As usual, Alaska was going its own way politically.

Alaska was also in the national news as the "poster child" for out-of-control federal spending, particularly the controversial practice of Congressional earmarking in which a legislator directs funding toward a specific project rather than just funding government agencies and letting them decide. One Alaskan earmark—a $200-million bridge connecting the city of Ketchikan with its airport on a nearby island—became known as "The Bridge to Nowhere."

Living the Seasons

The stereotype of Alaska as a land of ice and snow doesn't hold up when you look at its size—expecting a single climate in an area this large just isn't realistic.

Alaska remains a state of climatic extremes. The lowest recorded temperature in Alaska was –80°F (–27°C) in Bettles, yet occasionally temperatures approaching 100°F (38°C) have been recorded not far away in Fairbanks. Ketchikan in the southeast is one of the wettest places in the world, with more than 14 feet of rain annually, while parts of the Far North are almost desertlike, with less than 15 inches each year.

Yes, there are parts of the state (the Far North, for example) where winter descends like a black curtain, the sun barely rises above the horizon, and summer days are marked by the midnight sun, but most of Alaska has much more moderate temperatures and climates.

Aurora borealis.

How Alaskans deal with the weather is an endless source of conversation in the 49th state. Although most residents live in urban areas, there remains a frontier sense among many locals that keeps a sharp eye trained on the weather. You don't want to caught unprepared; even at the height of summer, hurricane-strength storms can brew with little warning, and in the winter, spring, and fall, deadly storms are commonplace.

The Human Landscape

Another facet of "village life" also carries through to those Alaskans who live in the "big cities." You often hear Alaskans refer to the state as a "big village," and in many ways, that's true. Even the major centers such as Anchorage, Fairbanks, and Juneau often operate like they are little more than overgrown villages, especially politically.

Although Alaskans are ruggedly independent, they also take a remarkable interest in knowing everyone else's business. For a huge landmass, it's surprising how many Alaskans keeps tabs on other parts of the state, and it seems like everyone "knows" everyone else in the state.

Politically, it's a state where everyone in every town seems to know the mayor personally, and that extends to statewide elected officials, too. Congressmen, senators, and governors are expected to visit just about every community in the state fairly frequently, and they do. When outsiders ask questions about Sarah Palin, for example, it's surprising how many residents have actually had a close encounter with her. That just doesn't happen in other states.

Of course, it's impossible to understand Alaska without knowing something about its traditional inhabitants, the numerous Native tribes of the Last Frontier. Most anthropologists believe that the first Americans crossed over a Bering Sea land bridge more than 15,000 years ago. But in recent years, other theories have been promoted, including the use of skin boats. Some scientists also surmise that it may have been possible for Natives to have crossed from Asia earlier and farther south and spread north.

At any rate, Native Americans were living in Alaska more than 10,000 years before European and other explorers arrived. The Natives spread throughout the entire continent and likely were the ancestors of all the tribes of the Americas.

Those that chose to stay in what became Alaska were the Inupiat, Yupik, Alutiiq, Athabaskan, Tlingits, Haida, and Tshimpshian. They carved out largely separate territories in Alaska, mixing only to trade and go to war.

FROM TOP: **The small Yukon River village of Stevens; The Anchorage skyline.**

The Inside Passage.

The Inupiat inhabit the north; the Yupik the southwest; the Alutiiq the Gulf coast; and the Tlingits, Haida, and Tshimpshian the southeast and the Canadian north coast. What they did share was a strong oral history and an artistic culture that passed the time when the weather or the season forced them inside.

This traditional lifestyle was disrupted when European explorers began arriving after the "discovery" of Alaska in the 1740s. The first to arrive were the Russian fur traders, who prized sea otter pelts above all. The Russians began settling the islands of the Aleutian Chain and established their largest trading post on Kodiak Island. They enslaved many Aleuts, forcing them to harvest the sea otter. They also brought the Russian Orthodox religion, which is still strong in many western Alaskan villages. By 1808, the Russians moved their "capital" to Sitka, where they would remain until the United States purchased Alaska in 1867.

By then, other nationalities had visited Alaska, some in search of treasure or fur, many in search of the mythical "Northwest Passage" through the continent to the Atlantic. Place names along the coast commemorate the Spanish, French, and English explorers who visited Alaska in those years. There was also a strong American presence with New England whaling ships discovering the vast numbers of whales in the Gulf of Alaska and the Bering Sea.

American presence increased after 1867, but it wasn't until the Klondike Gold Rush of 1897 that it picked up rapidly. Although those gold strikes were in Canada, nearly all of the 100,000 people who flooded north passed through Alaska. Many who didn't strike it rich at the Klondike stuck it out in the north, which led to later, smaller strikes in Nome and Fairbanks. Mining activity would spur most of the growth in Alaska, at least through World War I.

The boom and bust cycle of mining set the tone for nearly all of Alaska's industries to come, although one can argue that the original Russian fur industry in the late 1700s was also boom and bust, especially after the sea otter populations were decimated by the early hunters.

As mining waned in the first 20 years of the 20th century, fishing, particularly the canned salmon industry, rose to take its place. Soon, just about every large coastal bay sported a cannery village, and floating fish traps dotted the horizon. By the 1930s, coastal towns such as Ketchikan sported numerous canneries and millions of cases of salmon were sent south.

The fish traps were supposed to operate on limited hours to allow enough fish to get through and repopulate the species, but by the time World War II rolled around, it was clear that the runs were rapidly decreasing. The traps themselves became the center of a pitched political battle, fought mostly between Alaskans, who felt the traps were destroying the resource, and outsiders who controlled the cannery interests and exercised greater political pull in Washington, D.C., which called most of the shots in the territory.

The traps were one of the main issues in the statehood debate, which lasted from the 1920s until the late 1950s. Alaska residents wanted statehood in order to gain control of the fisheries and abolish fish traps, but were continually blocked in Congress. When Alaska finally became a state in 1959, one of the first actions of the new state legislature was to ban traps. By then, the salmon runs were a fraction of what they once were. It took more than 20 years before Alaskan salmon runs recovered to their original levels.

World War II provided another economic boost to the territory, with numerous military installations being built and more than 100,000 American and Canadian troops being stationed here.

Early in the war, the Japanese occupied Attu and Kiska at the end of the Aleutian Chain, and the Allied forces marshaled a significant effort to drive them out. New military bases created infrastructure in many areas of Alaska, particularly airfields that opened up many coastal areas as well as the interior.

The most significant bit of war-related construction was the Alaska–Canada (ALCAN) Highway, which ran from northern British Columbia to Alaska. Built in less than 8 months at a cost of $130 million, the 1,300-mile road became Alaska's only "hardlink" with the rest of America.

After the war, it took about 20 years before the entire ALCAN was improved enough for significant vehicle traffic. Thousands of visitors now use it to drive to Alaska.

An aerial view of Matanuska Glacier.

Kayaking in Kenai Fjords National Park.

The statewide economy diversified after the war as timber, mining, tourism, and oil production developed, though fishing remained significant in coastal communities and is still one Alaska's largest employers.

In the coastal rainforests such as the Tongass and the Chugach, the timber industry became the new "boom and bust" economy. For nearly 40 years, large lumber and pulp mills generated thousands of jobs and hundreds of millions of dollars for local economies. But the national environmental movement and the expenses involved in keeping the large plants open eventually shut down most of the timber operations in the state by the late 1990s.

By then, tourism, particularly cruise-ship tourism, had begun to dominate large portions of the state. The number of cruise visitors to Alaskan coastal communities quadrupled between 1990 and 2005, with some ports hosting up to a million visitors a year.

Even tourism paled in comparison to Alaska's "big dawg" industry: oil. Oil has been successfully drilled in Alaska since 1900, but not in quantities large enough for export. That changed in 1957 with the Swanson River oilfield on the Kenai Peninsula. By the early 1960s, a significant number of offshore oil and gas wells were operating in Upper Cook Inlet.

The big jolt came in 1967, when the massive Prudhoe Bay oilfield was discovered on the Arctic coast east of Point Barrow. The field would eventually produce more than 20% of the U.S. domestic market, and taxes on oil would provide approximately 80% of the state budget. The Trans-Alaska Pipeline was built to carry the oil some 800 miles from the Arctic Ocean to Valdez on the Gulf of Alaska, where massive oil tankers loaded the oil to be taken and refined.

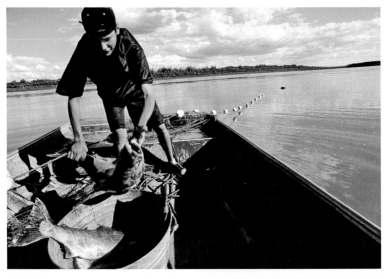

TOP: **An Athabascan young man bringing in his catch;** RIGHT: **Two Native children sit beneath a polar bear skin.**

In 1989, one of those tankers, the *Exxon Valdez,* ran aground and spilled more than 32 million gallons of oil, causing one of America's worst environmental disasters.

Production at Prudhoe Bay has been declining for several years, leading many Alaskans to wonder what the "post-oil" future of the state will bring. Efforts by the state to open up the nearby Arctic National Wildlife Refuge (ANWR) for potential drilling have been unsuccessful, as have efforts thus far to build a natural gas pipeline from the North Slope to either Valdez or central Canada.

NATURAL HISTORY: ROUGH DRAFTS & ERASURES
Glaciers

In 1986, Hubbard Glacier, north of Yakutat, suddenly decided to surge forward, cutting off Russell Fjord from the rest of the Pacific Ocean. A group of warm-hearted but ill-advised wildlife lovers set out to save the marine mammals that had been trapped behind the glacier. Catching a dolphin from an inflatable boat isn't that easy—they didn't accomplish much, but they provided a lot of entertainment for the locals. Then the water burst through the dam of ice, and the lake became a fjord again, releasing the animals anyway. In 2002, it happened again (no rescue this time). Ships were warned away as the 70-square-mile lake, having risen 61 feet above sea level, quickly drained through a 300-foot-wide channel with a whoosh. Geologists say it could happen again anytime.

Bering Glacier, the largest in North America (about 30×145 miles in area), can't decide which way to go. Surging and retreating on a 20-year cycle, it reversed course in 1995 after bulldozing a wetland migratory bird stopover, and speedily contracted back up toward the mountains. Yanert Glacier surged 100 yards a day in 2000 after moving 100 yards a year since 1942. The next year, Tokositna Glacier started galloping after 50 years of quiet. In 1937, surging Black Rapids Glacier almost ate the Richardson Highway. In Prince William Sound, Meares Glacier plowed through old-growth forest. On a larger scale, all the land of Glacier Bay—mountains, forests, sea floor—is rising 1½ inches a year as it rebounds from the weight of melted glaciers that 100 years ago were a mile thick and 65 miles long.

These new and erased lands are just small corrections around the margins compared to all the Earth has done in setting down, wiping out, and rewriting the natural history of Alaska. In the last Ice Age, 15,000 years ago, much of what is Alaska today was a huge glacier. Looking up at the granite mountains of Southeast Alaska, especially in the Lynn Canal, you can see a high-water mark near their towering peaks—the highest point to which the glaciers reached.

The living glaciers of Alaska, like living fossils from the last Ice Age, helped figure out how glaciers work. In the 1830s, scientists in Switzerland found huge rocks (now called glacial erratics) that appeared to have moved miles from where they had once been a part of similar bedrock. Scientists theorized that ancient glaciers shaping the Alps must have moved the rocks. John Muir, the famous writer and naturalist, maintained in the 1870s that the granite mountains of

St. Augustine volcano.

Yosemite National Park had been rounded and polished by the passing of glaciers that melted long ago (he was only partly right). He traveled to Alaska to prove it. Here, glaciers were still carving the land—they never finished melting at the end of the last glacial period—and Muir could see shapes, like those at Yosemite, being created. Glacier Bay, which Muir "discovered" when guided there by his Alaska Native friends, was a glacial work in progress, as it still is today.

When you visit, you'll see moraines, heavy blue ice and white snow streaked with black rock and dust, obviously gouged from mountains and left at the faces and along the flanks of the glaciers in debris piles. Today Alaska's 100,000 glaciers cover about 5% of its landmass, mostly on the southern coast. There are no glaciers in the Arctic—the climate is too dry to produce enough snow. The northernmost large glaciers are in the Alaska Range, such as those carving great chasms in the side of Mount McKinley. At that height, the mountain creates its own weather, wringing moisture out of the atmosphere and feeding its glaciers. The Kahiltna Glacier flows 45 miles from the mountain, descending 15,000 feet over its course. The Ruth Glacier has dug a canyon twice as deep as the Grand Canyon, half filled with mile-deep ice. Similarly, fjords and valleys all over Alaska were formed by glaciers that covered North America over the last 2.5 million years.

Earthquakes & Mountains

Alaska has an average of 13 earthquakes a day, or 11% of all the earthquakes in the world, including 3 of the 10 largest ever recorded. On November 3, 2002, Alaska felt the world's largest earthquake of the year and one of the largest ever in the United States. Waves slopped across the bayous of Louisiana, and geysers at Yellowstone changed their size and period of eruptions. No one died and few people were injured because the quake occurred in such a sparsely populated area, the region between Anchorage and Fairbanks in the Alaska Range east of Mount McKinley. A 140-mile-long crack appeared right across that region, running over mountains and through glaciers. The land on each side moved laterally as much as 22 feet and vertically up to 6 feet.

Sitka.

Drunken forest of spruce trees.

It's all part of living in a place that isn't quite done yet. Any part of Alaska could have an earthquake, but the Pacific Rim from Southcentral Alaska to the Aleutians is the shakiest. This is where Alaska is still "under construction." The very rocks that make up the state are something of an ad hoc conglomeration, still in the process of being assembled. The floor of the Pacific Ocean is moving north, and as it moves, it carries islands and mountains with it. When they hit the Alaska plate, these pieces of land, called terranes, dock like ships, but slowly—an island moving an inch a year takes a long time to travel thousands of miles. Geologists studying rocks near Mount McKinley found a terrane that used to be tropical islands. In Kenai Fjords National Park, fossils have turned up that are otherwise found only in Afghanistan and China. The slowly moving crust of the Earth brought them here on a terrane that makes up a large part of the south coast of Alaska.

Living in such an unsettled land is a matter of more than abstract interest. The Mount Spurr volcano, which erupted most recently in 1992, turned day to night in Anchorage, dropping a blanket of ash all over the region. A Boeing 747 full of passengers flew into the plume and lost power in all its engines, falling in darkness for several minutes before pilots were able to restart the clogged jets. After that incident, the airport was closed until aviation authorities could find a way to keep volcanic plumes and planes apart. In early 2009, the Anchorage airport repeatedly closed due to eruptions of Redoubt Volcano, stranding thousands of passengers for days. Such events underline the remoteness of Alaska—you can't just take a bus. With more than 80 active volcanoes, it could happen again at any time; your only defense is travel insurance (p. 528). Find up-to-date volcano monitoring information at the Alaska Volcano Observatory website (www.avo.alaska.edu).

Earthquakes between 7 and 8 on the Richter scale—larger than the 1994 Los Angeles quake—occur once a year on average, and huge quakes over 8 averaged every 13 years over the last century. The worst of the quakes, on March 27, 1964, was the strongest ever to hit North America. It ranked 9.2 on the Richter scale, twisting an entire region of the state so land to the west sank 12 feet, while on the east it rose more than 30 feet. More land moved laterally than in any other recorded earthquake. The earthquake destroyed much of Anchorage and several smaller towns, and killed about 131 people, mostly in sea waves created by underwater landslides. In Valdez, the waterfront was swept clean of people.

But even that huge earthquake wasn't an unusual occurrence, at least in the Earth's terms. Geologists believe the same Alaska coast sank 6 feet in an earthquake in the year 1090.

Permafrost & Sea Ice

The northern Interior and Arctic parts of the state are less susceptible to earthquakes, and since they receive little precipitation, they don't have glaciers, either. But there's still a sense of living on a land that's not permanent, since most of northern Alaska is solid only by virtue of being frozen. When it thaws, it turns to mush. The phenomenon is caused by permafrost, a layer of earth just below the surface that never thaws—or, at least, you'd better hope it doesn't. Buildings erected on permafrost without some mechanism for dispersing their own heat—pilings, a gravel pad, or even refrigerator coils—can thaw the ground below and sink into a self-made quicksand. With the climate warming, sections of the Trans-Alaska pipeline are leaning, and many miles of highway in Interior Alaska are being rebuilt each year because the ground they traverse has turned to mush.

The Arctic and much of the Interior is a swampy desert. Annual precipitation measured in Barrow is the same as in Las Vegas. Most of the time, the tundra is frozen in white; snow blows around, but not much falls. It melts in the summer, but the water can't sink into the ground, which remains frozen. Water on top of the permafrost layer creates huge, shallow ponds. Alaska is a land of 10 million lakes, with 3 million larger than 20 acres. Birds arrive to feed and paddle around those circles and polygons of deep green and sky blue.

The permafrost also preserves many things. Although few and far between, tractor tracks remain clearly delineated for decades after they're made, appearing as narrow, parallel ponds reaching from one horizon to the other. The meat of prehistoric mastodons, still intact, has been unearthed from the frozen ground. On the Arctic Coast, the sea eroded ground near Barrow that contained ancient ancestors of the Eskimos who still inhabit the same neighborhood. In 1982, a family was found that apparently had been crushed by sea ice up to 500 years ago. Two of the bodies were well preserved, sitting in the home they had occupied and wearing the clothes they had worn the day of the disaster, perhaps around the time Columbus was sailing to America.

Sea ice is the frozen ocean that extends from northern Alaska to the other side of the world. For a few months of summer, it pulls away from the shore. Then in October, icebergs floating toward land are cemented together by new ice forming along the beach. But even when the ice covers the whole ocean, it still

Taiga, a type of boreal conifer forest.

moves under the immense pressure of wind and current. The clash creates towering pressure ridges—piles of broken ice that look like small mountain ranges and are about as difficult to cross.

The National Weather Service keeps track of the ice pack and issues maps and predictions online (www.arh.noaa.gov). Eskimo hunters traveling on the ice by snowmobile need this information, as do crabbers who tempt disaster by fishing the south-moving ice edge in the fall and shippers looking for the right moment in the summer to venture north with barges of fuel and other supplies for the coast of the Arctic Ocean. Sometimes there is barely time in the summer to get there and back before the ice closes in again in the fall.

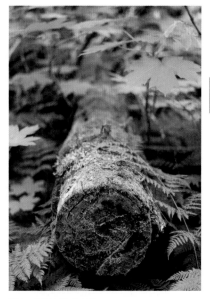

Mossy temperate forest.

Rainforest

By comparison, southern coastal Alaska is warm and biologically rich. Temperate rainforest ranges up the coast from Southeast Alaska north into Prince William Sound and westward to Kodiak Island, with bears, deer, moose, wolves, and even big cats living among the massive western hemlock, Sitka spruce, and cedar. This old-growth forest, too wet to burn in forest fires, is the last vestige of the virgin, primeval woods that seemed so limitless to the first white settlers who arrived on the east coast of the continent in the 17th century. The trees grow on and on, sometimes rising more than 200 feet high, with diameters up to 10 feet, and falling only after hundreds or even a thousand years. When they fall, the trees rot on the damp moss of the forest floor and return to soil to feed more trees, which grow in rows upon their nursery trunks.

The rivers of the great coastal forests bring home runs of big salmon, clogging in spawning season like a busy sidewalk at rush hour. The fish spawn only once, returning by a precisely tuned sense of smell to the streams where they were hatched from 2 to 5 years before. When the fertilized eggs have been left in the stream gravel, the fish conveniently die on the beach, making a smorgasbord for bears and other forest animals. The huge Kodiak brown bear, sometimes topping 1,000 pounds, owes everything to the millions of salmon that return to the island each summer. By comparison, the grizzly bears of the Interior—the same species as browns, but living on grass, berries, and an occasional ground squirrel—are mere midgets, their weight counted in the hundreds of pounds. Forest-dwelling black bears grow to only a few hundred pounds.

Boreal Forest

Rainforest covers only a small fraction of Alaska. In fact, only a third of Alaska is forested at all, and most of this is the boreal forest that covers the central part of the state, behind the rain shadow of coastal mountains that intercept moist clouds off the oceans. Ranging from the Kenai Peninsula, south of Anchorage, to the Brooks Range, where the Arctic begins, this is a taiga—a moist, subarctic forest of smaller, slower-growing, hardier trees that leave plenty of open sky between their branches. In well-drained areas, on hillsides and southern land less susceptible to permafrost, the boreal forest is a lovely, broadly spaced combination of straight, proud white spruce and pale, spectral paper birch. Along the rivers, cottonwoods grow, with deep-grained bark and branches that spread in an oaklike matrix—if they could speak, it would be as wise old men.

Forest fires tear through Alaska's boreal forest each summer. In the newly warmed climate, million-acre fires have become common. It's impossible to fight that much fire. Alaska has always allowed fire to take its course unless structures or certain resources are at risk. In most cases, forest managers do no more than note the occurrence on a map.

This is the land of the moose. They're as big as large horses, with a long, bulbous nose and huge eyes. Their flanks look like a worn-out shag carpet draped over a sawhorse. But moose are survivors. They thrive on land that no one else wants. In the summer, they wade out into the swampy tundra ponds to eat green muck. In the winter, they like nothing better than an old burn, where summer lightning has peeled back the forest and allowed a tangle of willows to grow—a moose's all-time favorite food. Eaten by wolves, hunted and run over by man, stranded in the snows of a hard winter, the moose always come back.

In the summer, moose disperse and are not easily seen in thick vegetation. In the winter, they gather where walking is easy, along roads and in lowlands where people also like to live. Encounters happen often in the city, until, as a resident, you begin to take the moose for granted, or see them as a pest that eats decorative plantings and blocks bike trails. Then, skiing on a Nordic trail one day, you round a corner and come face to face with an animal that stands 2 feet over you. You can smell the beast's foul scent and see his stress, the ears pulled back on the head and the whites of the eyes showing, and you know that this wild creature, fighting to live until summer, could easily kill you. In light of a recent attack, state wildlife biologist Jessy Coltrane said, "Assume that every moose is a serial killer standing in the middle of the trail with a loaded gun."

Light & Darkness

There's no escaping the stress of winter in Alaska—not for moose or people—nor any shield from the exhilaration of the summer. In summer, it never really gets dark at night. In Fairbanks in June, the sun sets in the north around midnight, but it doesn't go down far enough for real darkness to settle, instead rising again 2 hours later. It's always light enough to keep hiking or fishing, and, in clear weather, it's always light enough to read. You may not see the stars from early May until sometime in August (see seasonal daylight chart on p. 41). Visitors have trouble getting used to it: Falling asleep in broad daylight can be hard. Alaskans deal with it by staying up late and being active outdoors.

In the winter, on the other hand, you forget what the sun looks like. Kids go to school and come home in the dark. The sun rises in the middle of the morning and sets after lunch. At high noon in December, the sun hangs just above the southern horizon with a weak, orange light, a constant sunset. Animals and people go into hibernation.

As you go north, the change in the length of the days gets bigger. In Ketchikan, the longest day of the year, on the June 21 summer solstice, is about 17 hours, 20 minutes; in Fairbanks, 22 hours; and in Barrow, the longest day is more than 2 months. In contrast, at the North and South poles, the sun is up half the year and down the other half.

THE IDITAROD

The Iditarod Trail Sled Dog Race—a 1,150-mile run from Anchorage to Nome that takes place over 2 weeks in mid-March—is the biggest event of Alaska's year, not only in terms of sports, but also culturally and as a unifying event. The race is big news—TV anchors speculate on the mushers' strategies at the top of the evening news and break away live to cover the top finishers, regardless of the time of day or night. Schoolchildren plot the progress of their favorite teams on maps and over the Internet. Increasingly, the world is joining in. Visitors, especially Europeans, fill hotels in Anchorage and Nome for the Iditarod. Flight services drop spectators at remote checkpoints along the trail to see the mushers come through. It's a wonderful time of year to visit, with light skies, excellent late-season skiing, and winter festivals enlivening many towns. Nome goes crazy when the mushers hit. Even if the first team crosses the finish line at 3am in –30°F (–34°C) weather, a huge crowd turns out to congratulate the winner. And crowds keep turning out until the last competitor crosses the finish line.

Given all this, it's difficult to report objectively on the activities of animal rights opponents to the race, currently led by People for the Ethical Treatment of Animals (PETA). While PETA opposes all human use of animals, some mainstream animal welfare advocates also criticize the race. They charge that dogs can suffer and die on the trail and, while not racing, are inhumanely tethered in dog lots. Iditarod mushers insist that the dogs, which are worth thousands of dollars, receive veterinary care superior to the doctoring that most people get. Sick dogs have been evacuated from the trail by helicopter, and mushers who abuse dogs are kicked out of the sport.

However, harmful practices do occur in the lower ranks of mushing. For example, uncontrolled breeding by amateurs or careless professionals produces too many pups that end up being killed, and sled dogs can be tethered excessively or otherwise abused. Successful mushers—including Iditarod competitors—must give their dogs thorough exercise, as only that way can the animals perform as athletes, but there's no law limiting how many dogs an irresponsible musher or pet owner can acquire or how often they must be run.

Conservation Movement

Fewer words are more politically charged in Alaska than *conservation* and *preservation*. Alaskans of nearly all stripes agree that at least some of the Great Land needs to be "preserved" or "conserved," but what those words actually mean and how much land is involved has been at the heart of heated debates in Alaska for more than a century.

From the first efforts of President Theodore Roosevelt to limit potential mining development in Alaska to the present debate on "roadless areas" in the Tongass National Forest, the question for either development or preservation has always been, "How much is enough?" It's safe to say that most residents feel that the state should be allowed to develop its resources in a manner that it sees fit, taking into account that no one really wants to environmentally foul their own nest. But with 70% of Alaska federally owned, it's not realistic to assume that Alaskans have the final say. And many others in the rest of country realize that they do have a "say" in how Alaska is developed and are not shy in exercising it.

Of course, historically Alaska has often found itself in the unfortunate position of having its major industries (fishing, timber, tourism, oil) controlled elsewhere. Some have called Alaska an economic "colony" throughout most of its history, and it's hard to argue with that characterization.

In response to the lack of "access" to most of its land base, Alaska has accepted instead one of the highest levels of per-capita federal spending in the country. And it has celebrated leaders such as Sen. Ted Stevens, who served for more than 40 years and brought billions of federal dollars back to the state.

In truth, many Alaskans do not see the conservation debate as a zero-sum game, where one side must win and the other lose. Alaska already has more wilderness land and more national parks than any other state, and more land can be preserved without preventing the state from taking charge of its economic future. But there must also be a realization that Alaska cannot survive if the rest of the country demands it "make up" for all the environmental mistakes that America has made elsewhere. There will have to be some sort of economic development, or else Alaska will continue to have to rely on billions of dollars from the federal treasury in order to survive.

Statehood & Native Lands

The fight for Alaska's statehood was a fight for control of land and fishing resources. Except for a few homesteads and tiny towns, all of Alaska remained federally owned. The Statehood Act would transfer 103 million acres to the new state, about a third of its total landmass, to be selected over a 25-year period. Statehood leaders hoped to use these lands to produce the resource boom dreamed about since the gold rush.

The founding of the state in 1959 brought huge celebrations in Alaska cities, but worry in some Native communities. Alaska Natives had never abandoned traditional lifestyles of hunting, fishing, and gathering. Their claims to their land mostly had not been resolved, but as long as Alaska lacked property lines, it hadn't mattered much. The wording of the Statehood Act nodded to their land rights but gave no real assurance they would receive title. The threat of losing their land to the State of Alaska forced Native groups to organize and become militant in the 1960s.

Westward expansion in the rest of the United States had robbed American Indians of land, but in Alaska, they were able to stay on their ancestral land. However, the population was ravaged by disease brought in by the outsiders. Salmon canneries destroyed fish runs and starved villages. Russian fur traders and Yankee whalers depleted marine mammals Natives used for food and clothing. Newcomers introduced alcohol abuse and disease epidemics that wiped out entire villages. Christian missionaries and teachers suppressed Native languages and culture and imposed social practices and ways of life inappropriate to the Alaskan environment. Natives faced official discrimination in their own land, were denied economic opportunity, and were subject to racial segregation.

Alaska's leaders of the 1960s had little interest in a land settlement for the Natives, but new national awareness of American Indian rights had an impact in Washington, D.C. As Alaska Natives filed claims covering almost the entire state, the federal government froze release of land to the state, or to almost anyone else. Then, at the end of the decade, America's largest oil field was discovered at Prudhoe Bay, in northern Alaska, on land owned by the state. Boosters saw that, under the Native land freeze, construction of a pipeline to remove the oil could be indefinitely delayed. With the support of the oil industry, Alaska politicians lined up in support of a generous settlement of Native land claims to get things moving.

Prodevelopment Alaskans had feared that land transferred to the Natives would be used for traditional Native priorities—hunting and gathering—not for economic projects such as mining, timber cutting, or oil drilling. But the form of the Native claims settlement addressed that concern. Land was transferred into for-profit corporations owned by Native shareholders—corporations that would be forced to earn a profit and, therefore, would be motivated to develop their lands.

When the Alaska Native Land Claims Settlement Act passed in 1971, it was the largest indigenous land settlement yet in history, returning 44 million acres of land. And it initiated a new way of Native people relating to their land—not as tribes or tenants of reservations, but as corporate stockholders. Four decades later, some of these corporations had become the largest and most successful in Alaska.

Big Oil & Big Money

The completion of the Trans-Alaska Pipeline in 1977 created the biggest boom in Alaska's history, and the billions of dollars of royalty money flowing into the state coffers truly changed everything.

The boom also brought in hundreds of thousands of new residents, all looking to "make it big in Alaska." While the urban areas, most notably Anchorage and Fairbanks, experienced the seedier side of prosperity, high crime, and urban congestion, most of Alaska was initially untouched. That changed when the state decided to spread its wealth around. Soon it seemed like almost every community had new schools and other new infrastructure. Villages that had survived for decades with very limited amenities found themselves recipients of sewer systems and paved streets.

Then the state legislature went one step further by creating an oil wealth dividend program that provided a check (a percentage of the earnings from the Alaska Permanent Fund, which set aside money from the boom years to help get through the eventual lean years) of between $1,000 and $1,500 to every resident.

native art: **FINDING THE REAL THING**

Good estimates of the amount of counterfeit Alaska Native art sold annually don't exist, but authorities have put it close to $100 million. That's money taken from Alaska Bush economies where jobs in the cash economy are virtually nonexistent and prices for essentials such as fuel and housing are astronomical. Buying fake Native art is cultural and financial theft from subsistence hunters and fishermen who can least afford it.

You can avoid being scammed if you pay attention. Ask questions before you buy. Any reputable art dealer will provide you with a biography of the artist who created an expensive work. Ask specifically if that artist actually carved the piece: Some Native artists have sold their names and designs to wholesalers who produce knockoffs. Price is a tip-off. An elaborate mask is more likely to cost $1,000 than $100. Another indicator is the choice of materials; most soapstone carvings are not made in Alaska. Even relatively inexpensive craftwork should bear the name of the person who made it, and the shop owner should be able to tell you how he or she acquired the item.

Another caution, for international visitors: Do not buy products made from marine mammals, such as walrus ivory, whale bone, or seal skin. Except for antiques, export of these materials is illegal. (You may need a permit to export other wildlife items as well. See "Taking Home Wildlife Products," p. 526.)

The **Alaska State Council on the Arts** (📞 **907/269-6610**) authenticates Native arts and crafts with a **silver hand** label, which assures you it was made by the hands of an Alaska Native with Alaskan materials. But the program isn't universally used, so the absence of the label doesn't mean the work definitely isn't authentic. Other labels aren't worth much: An item could say ALASKA MADE

even if only insignificant assembly work happened here. Of course, in Bush Alaska and in some urban shops, you can buy authentic work directly from craftspeople. Buying in Native-owned co-ops is also safe.

Another program covers any item made within the state, both Native and non-Native. The logo of a mother bear and cub (www.madeinalaska.org) indicates that a state contractor has determined that the product was made in Alaska, when possible with Alaskan materials. Non-Natives produce Alaskan crafts of ceramics, wood, or fabric, but not plastic—if it's plastic, it probably wasn't made here. Again, price is an indicator: As with anywhere else in the United States, the cheapest products come from Asia.

You can learn about and buy authentic work from the **Alaska Native Arts Foundation,** a nonprofit with online shopping at www.alaskanativearts.org and a brick-and-mortar gallery in Anchorage (p. 260). **Sealaska Heritage Foundation** offers a nonprofit website selling work by Southeast Alaska Natives at www.alaskanativeartists.com. Even if you don't buy anything from these sites, taking a look will give you an idea of what real Native art looks like and how much it should cost, so you can be a better shopper when you get to Alaska.

Before the major economic crash in 2008, the Permanent Fund had reached nearly $40 billion, and Alaskans were getting more than $1,500 a year from the state in "free money."

Interestingly enough, the political compromise necessary to build the pipeline also shepherded in one of Alaska's largest conservation events, ANILCA, which puts tens of millions of additional acres into wildernesses and refuges and created several additional mammoth national parks within the state.

Since the mid-1990s, Alaskans have been wrestling with what comes after the Prudhoe Bay oil reserves run out, as they inevitably will. A great political effort has gone into getting federal approval to open up the Arctic National Wildlife Refuge to exploratory drilling, but at press time, those efforts had come to naught. In recent years, the state legislature and the administration have been also attempting to get a natural gas pipeline built south from Prudhoe Bay to deliver that plentiful commodity to market, although no one seems to be stepping up to fund the multibillion-dollar project.

In the meantime, higher-than-expected oil prices are making up for the declining amounts of oil traveling through the pipeline, so the state continues along its generally free-spending path, and the growth and largesse of the government remains a significant portion of the Alaskan economy.

ALASKA IN POP CULTURE

Alaska remains a popular setting upon which writers and directors can project their fantasies. Oddly, despite the many new movies and television programs about Alaska, few are actually produced here.

Books

The Call of the Wild, by Jack London (1903): Classic tale of the Klondike gold rush from the point of view of a dog sent to pull a sled. London published it just 5 years after giving up on the gold rush himself after suffering scurvy in a Yukon cabin (Aladdin).

Coming into the Country, by John McPhee (1976): A gifted nonfiction writer captures the spirit of Alaska during the years of transition that marked the end of the frontier. McPhee's vivid

Jack London.

portraits of backcountry personalities portray the motivations of the sort of odd people you may yet encounter (Farrar, Straus, and Giroux).

The Last Light Breaking: Living Among Alaska's Inupiat Eskimos, by Nick Jans (2007): This collection of meticulously crafted essays by a man who lived in the villages of Northwest Alaska for years provides a vivid picture of the lives of rural Alaskans (Graphic Arts Center Publishing Company).

Ordinary Wolves, by Seth Kantner (2004): This harrowing autobiographical novel is a compelling and realistic account of life in the Alaska Bush, in all its beauty and hardship. Kantner grew up in a sod hut before his rough introduction to the urban world, and many say this is the best novel to come out of Alaska (Milkweed Editions).

A Cold Day for Murder (1993): This is the first of Edgar Award winner Dana Stabenow's wildly popular Kate Shugak mystery series. A former investigator for the Anchorage District Attorney's office, Native Alaskan Shugak solves crimes all over the state. Stabenow is the most successful of Alaska's mystery writers, which include John Straley and Sue Henry (Poisoned Pen Press).

Film

Mystery, Alaska (1999): A pond hockey team from small-town Alaska gets to play the New York Rangers. Some found the film heartwarming, but more were disappointed by the clichés and lack of substance. Weekend pond hockey is a real tradition in some of Alaska's rural communities.

Insomnia (2002): A gritty police thriller set in a small town in Alaska during the summer, when the sun never sets. Al Pacino gives a brilliant performance as an ethically stained detective who can't get to sleep.

Grizzly Man (2005): Probably the best movie yet made about Alaska, Werner Herzog's documentary explores humanity's relation to nature using film shot by a misguided animal lover who ultimately was eaten by the bears he befriended.

Into the Wild (2007): Director Sean Penn's dramatization of the true story of a young wanderer who died in the Alaska wilderness, the movie is packed with spectacular scenery and was filmed on location.

The Simpsons Movie (2007): The summer blockbuster cut uncomfortably close to home with its portrayal of greedy Alaskans eager to destroy the environment. Homer seemed so darned at home here, a place where "you can never be too fat or too drunk."

Television

Northern Exposure (1990–95): The comedy series about a spoiled New York doctor forced to practice medicine in an eccentric Alaskan town remains the most perceptive screen portrayal of such places (despite the fact that it was filmed in Roslyn, Washington). It sometimes shows in reruns and is available on DVD.

Deadliest Catch: Crab Fishing in Alaska (2005–present): This surprise hit records the real-life hazards and conflicts of hard-driving fishermen as they battle the notoriously bad weather of the Bering Sea (Discovery Channel).

Northern Exposure.

EATING & DRINKING

Alaska will probably never be a food destination, but you'll find some excellent restaurants and many opportunities to dine on fresh Alaska seafood, primarily salmon and halibut.

Salmon

FREEZE AS LITTLE AS POSSIBLE Ask if the salmon is fresh (never frozen) when you order it in a restaurant, and eat as much as you can because it will never be better, except cooked on a cedar plank or driftwood fire. If you have a lot of salmon, don't overlook smoking, the traditional Native way of preserving fish for the winter. See p. 339 for information on getting your salmon frozen and smoked.

Restaurants incorporate Alaska's fresh fish in dishes.

CHOOSING THE BEST FISH The best restaurants advertise where their salmon comes from on the menu. In early summer, Copper River kings and reds are the richest in flavor; later in the summer, Yukon River salmon are best. King, red, and silver salmon are the only species you should find in a restaurant. Avoid farm-reared salmon, which is mushy and flavorless compared with wild Alaska salmon and doesn't come from here. (Fish farming is outlawed in Alaska.)

KEEP IT SIMPLE When salmon is fresh, it's best with light seasoning, perhaps just a little lemon, dill weed, and pepper and salt; basted with soy sauce; or simply grilled over alder coals. Some restaurants prepare it blackened or with a reduction sauce; their success depends on the skill of the chef, as they run the risk that the nuances of the fish's flavor will be hidden.

DON'T OVERCOOK IT Salmon should be cooked just until the moment the meat changes color and becomes flaky through to the bone, or slightly before. A minute more, and the meat becomes "fishier" and loses its texture, taking on a dry, uniform feel rather than its exquisite delicacy. That's why those huge barbecue salmon bakes often are not as good as they should be—it's too hard to cook hundreds of pieces of fish just right and serve them all hot. Japanese chefs and some trendy restaurants serve salmon raw or cured, which is delicious if the fish is good. Avoid fried salmon, which can be dry and fishy tasting.

FILETS, NOT STEAKS Salmon is cut two ways in Alaska: lengthwise filets or crosswise steaks. The filet is cut with the grain of the flesh, keeping the oil and moisture in the fish in ways steaks do not. Do not remove the skin before cooking—it holds in the oils and will fall off easily when the fish is done. If you have a large group, consider cooking the salmon bone-in (sometimes called a roast), stuffing seasonings in the body cavity. When it's done, the skin easily peels off and, after eating the first side, you can effortlessly lift out the skeleton.

Halibut

SEASONS & PROCESSING   The halibut fishery continues through most of the year, so fresh fish is usually available if you're willing to pay. Halibut are large, so if you have a successful sportfishing charter trip, you will end up with more than you can eat fresh. If properly processed—and it is well worth using a professional with the right equipment—frozen halibut will last most of the winter in the freezer and will taste almost as good as fresh.

CHOOSING THE FISH   If you are buying halibut or deciding which fish to keep while angling, consider this: The younger, smaller fish are better eating. Huge halibut make good pictures, but their flesh breaks into relatively tough chunks rather than thin, tender flakes of the under-20-pounders known as "chicken halibut." Keep the cheeks, which are prized as the best meat of the entire fish.

PREPARATION   There are a lot of good ways to prepare halibut, both simple and sophisticated, that complement its healthy, lean flavor. Halibut is wonderful fried with light batter; grilled with lemon or soy; baked in foil with olive oil, basil, and garlic; or even baked with onions and sour cream for a regional favorite called "Halibut Olympia." Fresh fish needs little help; if it has been frozen awhile, some added fat in the form of oil or butter is a good idea.

DON'T OVERCOOK IT   Because a halibut filet can be thick, it's easy to mess up the cooking time. Overcooking quickly dries the fish. When baking, use high heat and check frequently. Thinner pieces can be layered so they don't get done before the bigger chunks. Put bigger filets on first when grilling, and as soon as the flakes separate, the fish is done.

WHEN TO GO

Alaska's vastness means the seasons change at different times in various parts of the state, and as a result, sports and cultural activities take place at different times in different places.

Climate & Seasons

The weather in Alaska can be extreme and unpredictable. The state is the first to get whatever Arctic Siberia or the void of the North Pacific have to throw at North America. The extremes of recorded temperatures are a high of 100°F (38°C) and low of –80°F (–62°C). At any time of year, your vacation could be enlivened by weeks of unbroken sunny weather or weighed down by weeks of unbroken rain. All you can do is play the averages, hope for the best, and if you do get bad weather, get out and have fun anyway—that's what Alaskans do.

JUNE, JULY & AUGUST   Summer in Alaska is a miraculous time, when the sun refuses to set, the salmon run upriver, and people are energized by limitless daylight. The sun dips below the horizon in Anchorage for only about 4 hours on June 21, the longest day of the year, and the sky is light all night. Weather gets warmer, although how warm depends on where you go (see the chart below). June is the driest of the summer months, July the warmest, and August generally the rainiest month of the brief summer, but warmer than June. In most respects, June is the best summer month to make a visit, but it does have some drawbacks to consider: In the Arctic, snow can linger until mid-June; in Southcentral Alaska, trails at high elevations or in the shade may be too muddy or snowy; it's too early for prime wildlife viewing, and not all activities or facilities at Denali National Park open until late June. It's also the worst time for mosquitoes.

Alaska's Climate, by Months & Regions

	JAN	FEB	MAR	APR	MAY	JUNE	JULY	AUG	SEPT	OCT	NOV	DEC
ANCHORAGE: SOUTHCENTRAL ALASKA												
AVERAGE HIGH**	21/-6	26/-3	33/1	44/7	55/13	62/17	65/18	63/17	55/13	40/4	28/-2	22/-6
AVERAGE LOW**	8/-13	11/-12	17/-8	29/-2	39/4	47/8	51/11	49/9	41/5	28/-2	16/-9	10/-12
HOURS OF LIGHT*	6:53	9:41	12:22	15:20	18:00	19:22	18:00	15:15	12:19	9:29	6:46	5:27
SUNNY DAYS†	12	10	13	12	11	10	9	9	9	10	10	10
RAINY OR SNOWY DAYS	8	8	8	6	7	8	11	13	14	12	10	11
PRECIPITATION‡	0.8	0.8	0.6	0.6	0.7	1.0	1.9	2.7	2.6	1.9	1.1	1.1
BARROW: ARCTIC ALASKA												
AVERAGE HIGH**	8/-13	-12/-24	-8/-22	6/-14	25/-4	39/4	46/8	43/6	34/1	20/-7	5/-15	-6/-21
AVERAGE LOW**	-20/-29	-24/-31	-21/-29	-8/-22	15/-9	30/-1	34/1	34/1	27/-3	10/-12	-6/-21	-17/-27
HOURS OF LIGHT*	0:00	8:05	12:33	17:43	24:00	24:00	24:00	17:34	12:30	7:46	0:00	0:00
SUNNY DAYS†	7	18	21	18	8	9	11	5	4	6	8	4
RAINY OR SNOWY DAYS	4	4	4	4	4	5	9	11	11	11	6	5
PRECIPITATION‡	0.2	0.2	0.1	0.2	0.2	0.3	0.9	1.0	0.6	0.5	0.2	0.2
COLD BAY: ALEUTIAN ARCHIPELAGO												
AVERAGE HIGH**	33/1	32/0	35/2	38/3	45/7	50/10	55/13	56/13	52/11	44/7	39/4	35/2
AVERAGE LOW**	24/-4	23/-5	25/-4	29/-2	35/2	41/5	46/8	47/8	43/6	35/2	30/-1	27/-3
HOURS OF LIGHT*	8:05	10:10	12:17	14:36	16:32	17:25	16:33	14:34	12:17	10:04	8:01	7:08
SUNNY DAYS†	8	6	8	4	3	3	3	2	4	6	6	7
RAINY OR SNOWY DAYS	19	17	18	16	17	16	17	20	21	23	22	21
PRECIPITATION‡	2.8	2.5	2.3	2.0	2.5	2.3	2.4	3.7	4.3	4.2	4.2	3.3
FAIRBANKS: INTERIOR ALASKA												
AVERAGE HIGH**	-2/-18	8/-13	24/-4	42/6	60/16	71/22	73/23	66/19	55/13	32/0	11/-12	1/-17
AVERAGE LOW**	-19/-28	-15/-26	-2/-19	20/-7	38/3	52/11	52/11	47/8	36/2	17/-8	-5/-21	-16/-27
HOURS OF LIGHT*	5:46	9:14	12:22	15:54	19:22	21:48	19:26	15:52	12:24	9:04	5:39	3:43
SUNNY DAYS†	15	14	17	14	16	13	12	10	10	9	12	12
RAINY OR SNOWY DAYS	8	7	6	5	7	11	12	12	10	11	11	9
PRECIPITATION‡	0.6	0.4	0.4	0.2	0.6	1.4	1.8	1.8	1.1	0.8	0.7	0.8
JUNEAU: SOUTHEAST ALASKA												
AVERAGE HIGH**	29/-2	34/1	39/4	48/9	55/13	62/17	64/18	63/17	56/13	47/8	37/3	32/0
AVERAGE LOW**	18/-8	23/-5	27/-3	32/0	39/4	45/7	48/9	48/9	43/6	37/3	28/-2	23/-5
HOURS OF LIGHT*	7:31	9:55	12:18	14:55	17:11	18:17	17:13	14:54	12:20	9:49	7:27	6:22
SUNNY DAYS†	8	7	7	8	8	8	8	9	6	4	6	5
RAINY OR SNOWY DAYS	18	17	18	17	17	15	17	17	20	24	20	21
PRECIPITATION‡	4.3	3.9	3.5	2.9	3.5	3.1	4.2	5.3	7.2	7.8	5.4	5.1

	JAN	FEB	MAR	APR	MAY	JUNE	JULY	AUG	SEPT	OCT	NOV	DEC
VALDEZ: PRINCE WILLIAM SOUND												
AVERAGE HIGH**	27/-3	30/-1	37/3	45/7	53/12	60/16	63/17	61/16	54/12	43/6	33/1	29/-2
AVERAGE LOW**	18/-8	19/-7	24/-4	31/-1	39/4	45/7	48/9	46/8	41/5	33/1	23/-5	19/-7
HOURS OF LIGHT*	6:54	9:41	12:22	15:19	17:58	19:20	17:57	15:14	12:20	9:30	6:48	5:29
SUNNY DAYS†	9	9	11	11	9	8	8	10	8	8	10	7
RAINY OR SNOWY DAYS	17	14	16	14	17	15	17	17	20	20	16	18
PRECIPITATION‡	5.7	5.5	4.7	3.2	3.2	2.8	3.6	6.5	9.3	7.9	5.7	7.6

*Hours of light is sunrise to sunset on the 21st day of each month.

**All temperatures are given in degrees Fahrenheit first, with degrees Celsius after the slash.

†Sunny days include the average observed clear and partly cloudy days per month.

‡Precipitation is the average water equivalent of rain or snow.

Summer is also the season of high prices. Most operators in the tourism industry have only these 90 days to make their year's income, and they charge whatever the market will bear. July is the absolute peak of the tourist season, when you must book well ahead and when crowds are most prevalent. Before June 15 and after August 15, the flow of visitors relaxes, providing occasional bargains and more elbowroom. Real off-season prices show up before Memorial Day and after Labor Day. But the length and intensity of the visitor season varies widely in different areas: In cruise-ship ports, it's busy from chilly early May into stormy October.

MAY & SEPTEMBER   More and more visitors are coming to Alaska during these "shoulder months" to take advantage of the lower prices, reduced crowds, and special beauty.

May is the drier of the 2 months, but as you travel farther north and earlier in the month, your chances of finding cold, mud, and even snow increase. In Alaska, there is no spring—the melt of snow and resultant seas of mud are called **breakup.** Flowers show up with the start of summer. Many outdoor activities aren't possible during breakup, which can extend well into May. Except in cruise-ship towns, most tourist-oriented activities and facilities are still closed before May 15, and a few don't open until Memorial Day or June 1. Where visitor facilities are open, they often have significantly lower prices. The very earliest salmon runs start in May, but for a fishing-oriented trip, it's better to come later in the summer. Cruise ships begin calling May 1, and the towns they visit swing into action when they arrive.

Sometime between late August and mid-September, weather patterns change, bringing clouds, frequent rainstorms, and cooling weather, and signaling the trees and tundra to turn bright, vivid colors. For a week or two (what week it is depends on your latitude), the bright yellow birches of the boreal forest and the rich red of the heathery tundra can make September the loveliest time of year. Most tourist-oriented businesses stay open, with lower prices, until September 15, except in the Arctic. After September 15, it's potluck. Some areas close up tight, but the silver salmon fishing is still active on the Kenai Peninsula, and the season there continues until the end of the month. A lucky visitor can come in September and hit a month of crisp, sunny, perfect weather, and have the state relatively to him- or herself. Or it can be cold and rainy all month.

OCTOBER, NOVEMBER, APRIL   From Southcentral Alaska northward, snow and ice arrive sometime in October; in Southeast Alaska, these are the months of cold, unending rain. Winter starts in November, but you can't count on being able to do winter sports, and darkness is prevalent as the year's shortest day approaches. April is a month of waiting, as winter sports come to an end and summer activities are blocked by melt and mud (although spring skiing can still be great in high-snow years). In-town activities are down in these months, too; with few visitors, many facilities are closed.

DECEMBER THROUGH MARCH   Winter is the whole point of Alaska. This is the time to see the aurora borealis. Communities get busy with activities such as sled-dog and snowmobile races; theater, music, and other performing arts; ice-carving competitions and winter carnivals; and all the rest of the real local culture that takes a break in the summer, when most visitors come. If you enjoy winter and its outdoor activities, an Alaska visit is paradise, with superb downhill, cross-country, and backcountry skiing; snowshoeing; snowmobiling; dog mushing; ice-skating—anything that can be done on snow and ice.

By far the best time to come is late winter, February and March, when the sun is up longer and winter activities hit their peak. Anchorage's Fur Rendezvous is in late February; the Iditarod Sled Dog Race is in early March. Visiting in late March could mean thin snow at lower elevations for cross-country skiing, but downhill skiing and skiing at backcountry locations keep going strong. At Alyeska Resort, south of Anchorage, skiing is still active in April, and upper-mountain skiing sometimes extends beyond Memorial Day if there is enough interest. In Homer, you can cross-country ski and go salmon fishing on the same day in March. In Southeast Alaska, you might hit weeks of cold and clear weather.

What to Wear

Unless you're coming for business meetings, you'll find little use for a tie or any formal attire anywhere in Alaska, but you do need to prepare for broad swings in weather.

SUMMER   You're not going to the North Pole, and you don't need a down parka or winter boots weighing down your luggage. But you do need to be ready for a variety of weather, from sunny, 80°F (27°C) days to windy, rainy 50°F (10°C) outings on the water. The way Alaskans prepare for such a range is with layers. The content of the layers depends on what you'll be doing, but everyone should bring at least this: warm-weather clothes, heavy long-sleeved shirts and pants, a wool sweater or fleece equivalent, a jacket, and a waterproof raincoat and rain pants. Gloves and wool hats are a good idea, too, especially for boating trips. If you'll be camping, add synthetic thermal long underwear and wool socks, and make sure your jacket is thick synthetic fleece. Combining these items, you'll be ready for any summer conditions. For hiking, bring sturdy shoes or cross trainers.

WINTER You can be warm and comfortable no matter how cold it is. Once you know how to dress, winter is not a time of suffering, and the world of snow opens up to you. To make the dash from car to heated building, all you need is an overcoat, sweater, hat, gloves, and wool socks. For outdoor pursuits, wear synthetic thermal long underwear, synthetic fleece pants and coat, wool sweater, wind-resistant pants and jacket, wool socks and hat, warm boots with liners or covers, and lined mittens. Remove layers for warmer temperatures. For more sedentary outdoor activities, such as watching the aurora or riding a snowmobile or dog sled, you need warmer clothing. Likewise, drives on rural highways in winter require warm clothing in case of breakdowns. On guided trips or at cold-weather resorts, they'll tell you what to bring or provide or rent it to you. You don't want any skin showing while riding a snowmobile or standing in a strong wind in below-zero (Fahrenheit) temperatures. Such a get-up costs more than $500. You can buy what you need in Anchorage at **Army Navy Store,** 320 W. 4th Ave. (☎ **888/836-3535** or 907/279-2401; www.army-navy-store.com), or in Fairbanks at **Big Ray's Store,** 507 2nd Ave. (☎ **800/478-3458** Alaska only, or 907/452-3458; www.bigrays.com).

Alaska Calendar of Events

Here are some of the biggest community events of the year in Alaska's cities and towns. Event plans can change, so don't set up your vacation around any of these dates without checking for current details. Fishing derbies, which go on in almost every coastal town in the summer, are listed in destination chapters.

FEBRUARY

The Yukon Quest International Sled Dog Race (☎ **907/452-7954;** www.yukonquest.com). Many mushers say this rugged 1,000-mile race is even tougher than the Iditarod. It runs between Fairbanks and Whitehorse, Yukon Territory, trading the direction each year. Starts February 4, 2012, in Whitehorse.

The Anchorage Fur Rendezvous Winter Festival (☎ **907/274-1177;** www.furrondy.net). The citywide winter celebration includes community events, fireworks, craft fairs, dog-sled rides, and other fun.

MARCH

The Iditarod Trail Sled Dog Race (☎ **907/376-5155;** www.iditarod.com). The world's most famous sled-dog race starts with fanfare from **Anchorage;** then the teams are loaded into trucks for the **Iditarod Restart,** north of the city, the real beginning of the race,

where the historic gold-rush trail becomes continuous for the dogs' 1,000-mile run to Nome. The start and the finish in Nome are the biggest sporting and cultural events of Alaska's year, drawing world media attention and turning Nome into a huge party for a few days (they even play golf out on the sea ice). Along the way, visitors can stay in remote lodges and fly bush planes to see the checkpoints (with plenty of advance planning and a big budget). In 2012, the race starts March 3.

The Nenana Ice Classic (☎ **907/832-5446;** www.nenanaakiceclassic.com), Nenana. This is a betting pool on the date of spring breakup that has happened every year for the last 9 decades. The kick-off is Tripod Days, when a "four-legged tripod" that will mark the ice going out on the Tanana River is erected during the first weekend in March, with a celebration of dance performances, dog mushing, and other activities. The ticket buyer who guesses the minute the tripod will move, usually about 2 months later, wins the jackpot, typically more than $300,000.

APRIL

The Alaska Folk Festival (℡ **907/463-3316;** www.alaskafolkfestival.org), Juneau. April 9 to April 15, 2012. This is a communitywide celebration, drawing musicians, whether on the bill or not, from all over the state.

MAY

The Kachemak Shorebird Festival (℡ **907/235-7740;** www.homeralaska.org), Homer. The festival includes guided bird-watching hikes and boat excursions, natural-history workshops, art shows, performances, and other events. Early May.

Little Norway Festival (℡ **907/772-3646;** www.petersburg.org), Petersburg. This festival celebrates the May 17, 1814, declaration of the independence of Norway from Sweden. The town has several days of community events. The festival takes place on the third full weekend in May.

Kodiak Crab Festival (℡ **907/486-5557**), Kodiak. This Memorial Day weekend event is the town's biggest of the year, including fun events, the solemn blessing of the fleet, and a memorial service for lost fishermen and other mariners.

JUNE

The Sitka Summer Music Festival (℡ **907/747-6774;** www.sitkamusicfestival.org), Sitka. Since 1972, this chamber music series has drawn musicians from all over the world for most of June. Performances take place Tuesdays, Fridays, and Saturdays, with other events all week, over 3 weeks in June.

Midnight Sun Baseball Game, Fairbanks. A century-old summer-solstice tradition: a game without artificial lights beginning at 10:30pm. The local semipro baseball team, the Alaska Goldpanners

(℡ **907/451-0095;** www.goldpanners.com), has hosted since 1960. June 21.

The Last Frontier Theater Conference (℡ **907/834-1614;** www.pwscc.edu), Valdez. The conference brings playwrights and directors from all over the nation to the community for a week of seminars and performances. June 10 to June 16, 2012.

JULY

Independence Day. Most of the small towns in Alaska make a big deal of the Fourth of July. Seward always has a huge celebration, exploding with visitors, primarily from Anchorage. Besides the parade and many small-town festivities, the main attraction is the **Mount Marathon Race,** which goes from the middle of town straight up rocky Mount Marathon to its 3,022-foot peak and down again. **Seldovia, Ketchikan, Skagway,** and **Juneau** also have exceptional Fourth of July events. See the individual town sections for more information.

The Southeast Alaska State Fair (℡ **907/766-2476;** www.seakfair.org), Haines. Held for 4 days in late July, this is a regional small-town get-together and music festival, with exhibits, cooking, a logging show, a parade, and other entertainment.

AUGUST

The Alaska State Fair (℡ **907/745-4827;** www.alaskastatefair.org), Palmer. The region's biggest event of the year is a typical state fair in some ways, but you won't see vegetables this large anywhere else. The good soil and long Valley days produce cabbages the size of beanbag chairs. Try to imagine a 19-pound carrot. Held the 12 days up to and including Labor Day.

OCTOBER

Alaska Day Festival (℡ **907/747-8806**), Sitka. Alaska Day, commemorating the Alaska purchase on October 18, 1867, is a big deal in this former Russian and U.S. territorial capital city. The festival lasts 4 days, with exact dates changing annually.

NOVEMBER

Sitka WhaleFest (✆ **907/747-7964;** www.sitkawhalefest.org), Sitka. Over a weekend in early November, during the fall and early winter period when humpback whales congregate in Sitka Sound, experts from around the world present a 3-day symposium, and there are whale-watching tours, concerts, an art show, a run, and community events.

The Alaska Bald Eagle Festival (✆ **907/766-3094;** www.baldeagle festival.org), Haines. Five days of seminars and special events mark an annual congregation of 3,000 eagles near Haines. Mid-November.

DECEMBER

Anchorage International Film Festival (www.anchoragefilmfestival.org). As many as a dozen screenings a day feature films from every corner of the world and include the obscure, the bizarre, and the profound. Two weeks beginning December 7, 2012.

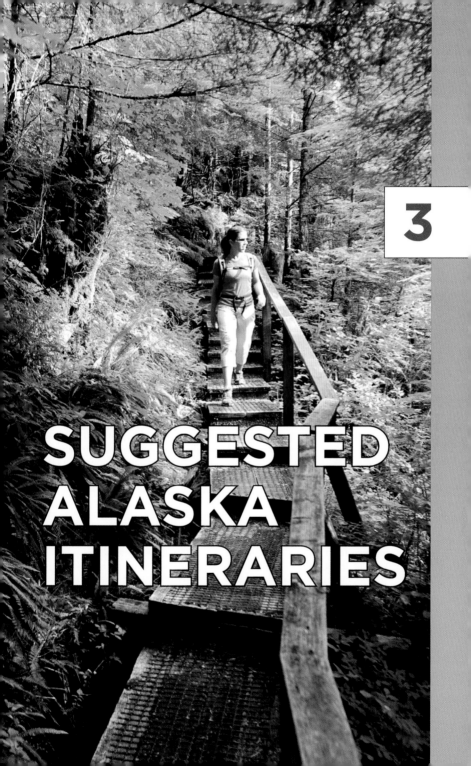

3

SUGGESTED ALASKA ITINERARIES

Alaska can be pretty daunting when you're trying to put together an itinerary. The land is immense and there never seems to be a straight line between any two points. But with a little patience and a lot of focus, you can come up with your dream itinerary.

The biggest challenge is narrowing down your choices to fit the time you have. You simply can't see it all. More than a few vacations have been ruined when people try to "capture" all the highlights and then waste valuable time traveling back and forth. Our advice is to focus on a single region and enjoy it.

Once you decide where you want to go, you can then decide how you want to get there. You can fly, drive (in some areas), or take a train, but you probably don't want to do all three. Your visit should be spent enjoying Alaska firsthand, not watching it whiz by outside your window.

You don't have to come home with all the major attractions checked off, but our itineraries will help you make the most of your time, whatever region you choose to explore.

SOUTHEAST ALASKA IN 1 WEEK

This plan takes you to the Southeast's highlights, with whales, glaciers, mountains, totem poles, and Russian-American history included. It's fast paced yet still covers less than half of this diverse and fascinating region. If you have more time, this plan would make a much more relaxing 10-day trip. Add a day each in Sitka, Juneau, and Gustavus. There's plenty to do in each town. You can extend this itinerary even more by beginning with a flight into **Petersburg** instead of Sitka. Spend a day or two there sea kayaking, hiking, fishing, or whale-watching before boarding an Alaska Marine Highway System ferry to Sitka and picking up on Day 1 of this plan.

DAY 1: Arrive in Sitka ★

Fly on an **Alaska Airlines** jet to the historic island city of Sitka, once the capital of Russian America. The town layout you see from the air is little changed from historic photographs and paintings. After settling in, take a walk along winding Lincoln Street, taking in the views from **Castle Hill** (p. 144), where the Russians handed over Alaska to the United States in 1867. Look into stately **St. Michael's Cathedral** (p. 143), and visit the **Russian Bishop's House** (p. 142), making sure to take a National Park Service tour of the extraordinary upstairs section.

DAY 2: Tlingit History & Sitka Wildlife ★★★

Start the day at the **Sitka National Historical Park** (p. 141) to see an extraordinary collection of historic and contemporary totem poles, meet Tlingit artisans at work, and learn about their culture and history. Now walk through the lovely forested totem park and battlefield sites before continuing

PREVIOUS PAGE: **Backpacker in Tongass National Forest.**

Suggested Alaska Itineraries

SOUTHEAST ALASKA IN 1 WEEK
1 Arrive in Sitka
2 Tlingit History & Sitka Wildlife
3 Juneau by Ferry
4 Juneau
5 To Gustavus/Glacier Bay
6 Glacier Bay Tour
7 Sea Kayaking in Gustavus

TWO NATIONAL PARKS IN 1 WEEK
1 Arrive in Anchorage
2 To Seward & Kenai Fjords National Park
3 In Seward
4 Denali National Park
5 Exploring Denali National Park
6 Denali & Back to Anchorage
7 Anchorage Activities

A 2-WEEK GRAND LOOP
1 Starting in Fairbanks
1 Fairbanks
3 The Richardson Highway to Copper Center
4 Kennecott
5 Kennecott to Valdez
6 Valdez to Cordova Ferry
7 Prince William Sound Sea Kayaking
8 Copper River Delta
9 Across the Sound to Whittier & Anchorage
10 Anchorage
11 Flying over Mount McKinley
12 Exploring Denali National Park
13 Denali & Drive to Fairbanks
14 Fairbanks

A WEEK IN ALASKA WITH KIDS
1 Arrive in Anchorage
2 To Seward & Kenai Fjords National Park
3 Seward
4 Homer
5 Kachemak Bay Natural History
6 Swan Lakes Canoeing
7 Anchorage

A WEEK OF ALASKA WINTER SPORTS
1 Anchorage Festivals & Sled Dog Races
2 Anchorage Cross-Country Skiing
3 Girdwood Downhill Skiing
4 Girdwood to Fairbanks
5 Museum of the North & Dog Mushing
6 Chena Hot Springs Resort
7 Fairbanks

200 mi
200 km

to the **Alaska Raptor Center** (p. 144) to see eagles being rehabilitated and learning to fly again after injuries. After lunch, join any one of the half-day **wildlife cruises** that go from the boat harbor to see otters, sea lions, and possibly whales; and, if conditions permit, the **sea bird colony** at St. Lazaria Island (p. 145).

DAY 3: Juneau by Ferry ★★

After a final goodbye to Sitka, board a ferry of the **Alaska Marine Highway System** (p. 92) for a spectacular ride to Juneau that will take much of the day. When you arrive, get a cab from the ferry dock to the airport and rent a car there. If you have enough time left in the day, you can visit **Mendenhall Glacier** (p. 165) and drive out the road (that's the common local phrase for it) for a lovely and moving walk to the tiny island of the **Shrine of St. Thérèse** (p. 166). Then settle into your lodgings.

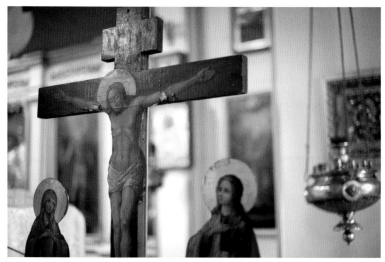

St. Michael's Cathedral in Sitka.

Snuggling up with a pup on a dog-sledding expedition.

DAY 4: Juneau ★★

In the morning, take a **helicopter flight** to the **Juneau Icefield** for a walk or even a dog-sled ride, to get a feel for the immensity of the place, and to touch glacier ice. If weather isn't promising for that, visit the **Alaska State Museum** (p. 156) or do the **walking tour** downtown (p. 158). In the afternoon, take a **hike** on one of Juneau's beautiful rainforest or mountain trails (p. 168). There are wonderful choices, such as the **Perseverance Trail** near downtown, but since you have a car, you can hike anywhere and get away from any cruise-ship crowds that may wreck the solitude on some of the paths.

DAY 5: To Gustavus/Glacier Bay ★★

Fly a prop from Juneau to Gustavus, the gateway to **Glacier Bay National Park** (p. 179), to arrive early enough to orient yourself and take a walk on the trails around the park headquarters to enjoy the shoreline and mossy forest trails. Or go bicycling on the country roads or explore the long sandy beaches in Gustavus. If you're more ambitious, the waters off Gustavus are among Alaska's best for watching humpback whales, and you'll have time today for a half-day viewing trip. You have two lodging choices here. Check in at the **Glacier Bay Lodge** (p. 183), or stay at a wilderness lodge or country inn in Gustavus (your host will pick you up).

DAY 6: Glacier Bay Tour ★★

The all-day **boat tour ride** (p. 182) leaves from Bartlett Cove and passes through humpback whale areas and other marine mammal grounds far up the bay to where two large glaciers stand like walls at the edge of the water. Be sure to bring binoculars and warm clothing, as the glaciers produce frigid downdrafting winds, even in the height of summer.

Settling in for a long ferry ride.

DAY 7: Sea Kayaking in Gustavus ★★★

We've saved some of the best for last. Your Alaska Airlines jet doesn't leave Gustavus until the evening, so you have time today for a **sea-kayaking** outing in the lovely waters of **Bartlett Cove,** where whales frequently visit (p. 183), or, if you are staying in **Gustavus,** kayak from there (p. 186) into an area where whales are virtually always seen in the summer. You can connect the flight from Gustavus through Juneau onward to home.

TWO NATIONAL PARKS IN 1 WEEK

An itinerary connecting Kenai Fjords National Park, south of Anchorage, and Denali National Park, to the north, is probably Alaska's most popular land trip for first-time visitors. That's because these parks and the area in between offer so much of what visitors come to Alaska to see, and in spectacular places: at Kenai Fjords, waterways full of whales, marine birds, and glaciers; and at Denali, broad swaths of mountain tundra frequented by bears and caribous. This itinerary is set up to do without a car. To save money and have more flexibility, do the same tour with a car rented in Anchorage.

DAY 1: Arrive in Anchorage ★★

Fly to Anchorage and move into a room in the walkable downtown area, which is near the train station, from where you will be departing tomorrow. If the weather is nice, do the **walking tour** (p. 237) to find out what the area is like, or rent a bike and hit the **Tony Knowles Coastal Trail** (p. 252) to see the waterfowl in West Chester Lagoon, the moose in Earthquake Park, and maybe even the beluga whales of Cook Inlet. You can go as far as you want: Anchorage's paved bike trails weave through the entire city on wooded greenbelts. In bad weather, or if you're not up for exercise, spend your time at the **Anchorage Museum at Rasmuson Center** (p. 246),

3

Two National Parks in 1 Week

SUGGESTED ALASKA ITINERARIES

This week-long itinerary to two national parks is fast paced. You can have a more relaxing trip and allow for more spontaneity by adding days to the stops that are already planned.

If you've still got more time after slowing down the pace, extend your trip with a visit to **Fairbanks.** Instead of taking the train back to Anchorage on Day 6, take it northward to Fairbanks. There I recommend renting a car to see the sites and perhaps explore the surrounding rural highways for a few days. (See Days 1 and 2 of "A 2-Week Grand Loop," below.)

When you're finished, fly home from Fairbanks.

Also consider adding on a **Southeast Alaska** sojourn. When you buy your ticket to Alaska, buy it from Seattle to Anchorage on Alaska Airlines and include a stopover, for a reasonable additional cost, in a Southeast Alaska town—Sitka would be my first choice. Spend time seeing the Russian-American history and Tlingit culture there, and getting outdoors (see Days 1 and 2 of "Southeast Alaska in 1 Week," p. 48), before flying on to Anchorage and beginning the itinerary listed at Day 1.

getting oriented to Alaska's history, culture, and art, and maybe even catch a planetarium show.

DAY 2: To Seward & Kenai Fjords National Park ★★★

Board an **Alaska Railroad** (p. 217) train to Seward to enjoy some of Alaska's most spectacular scenery along the cliffs and surging ocean waters of Turnagain Arm, and through the untouched mountains of the Kenai Peninsula; those who choose to drive get to see similar scenery on a slightly different route (see "Side Trips to Turnagain Arm & Portage Glacier," in chapter 6, and "The Seward Highway: A Road Guide," in chapter 7). In Seward, board a tour boat to **Kenai Fjords National Park** (see "Kenai

Sitka National Historical Park.

Fjords National Park," in chapter 7). Make sure to take a vessel headed all the way into the park so you see the best of the wildlife and get close to a tidewater glacier. Make sure also to take a seasickness remedy such as Dramamine or Bonine 2 hours before getting onboard. If the weather is bad, ask to be switched to a boat tomorrow and do tomorrow's activities today instead.

3

Kenai Fjords National Park.

DAY 3: In Seward ★★

After a couple of tiring days, this is a good day to relax in a charming little town. In the morning, join a half-day sea-kayaking paddle from Lowell Point with **Sunny Cove Sea Kayaking** (p. 301). You'll likely see sea otters, birds, intertidal creatures, and maybe spawning salmon. By going in the morning, your chances of smooth water are better. In the afternoon, see the marine life and seabirds you encountered yesterday, up close, at the **Alaska Sea-Life Center** (p. 302). Consider joining one of their educational programs to get even closer to the animals.

DAY 4: Denali National Park

Take the comfortable and convenient **Park Connection Motorcoach Service** (p. 373) from Seward straight to Denali National Park, a journey of more than 360 miles. The driver provides commentary on the highlights along the route. The bus ride takes almost 10 hours with a couple of long stops. If you drive instead, you can do it in less than 7 hours. Arriving in Denali, check into your hotel and stretch your legs, but get to bed promptly to be ready for an early start tomorrow.

DAY 5: Exploring Denali National Park ★★★

This is the primary day to see Denali and the bears, caribou, and other wildlife there. The park shuttle bus system is the key to your visit. Reserve as far ahead as possible (the previous Dec is not too soon) to get a seat on the earliest bus you can manage (reservation details are on p. 370). Wildlife tends to be more active in the morning. Ride deep into the park, taking along all your food and water, a warm jacket and raincoat, and good hiking shoes. Take a look at the suggestions for cross-country hiking in chapter 8, and then make your route choice according to how the countryside looks to

Caribous in Denali National Park.

you. This is a remarkable chance for a low-stress, low-cost wilderness experience. When you're ready to head home, just catch another bus on the way back.

DAY 6: Denali & Back to Anchorage ★

Your train back to Anchorage doesn't leave until late afternoon, giving you most of the day to enjoy the Denali park entrance area. The **visitor center** (p. 370) and **Murie Science and Learning Center** (p. 383) should not be missed: The exhibits and programs here will deepen your understanding of the natural places you have already seen. You also have time for a white-water rafting ride on the **Nenana River** (p. 386) or a relaxing walk on the nature trails and hiking trails near the **visitor center** (p. 370). Your train arrives in Anchorage in the evening.

DAY 7: Anchorage Activities ★

If you can arrange for a flight home late in the day, you'll have time for one more activity in Anchorage. Take a shuttle to the **Alaska Native Heritage Center** (p. 248) to meet indigenous people and learn about their cultures in a magnificent facility they built, own, and manage.

A native garment at the Alaska Native Heritage Center.

A 2-WEEK GRAND LOOP

This driving loop includes much of the best of the Interior, Prince William Sound, Anchorage, and Denali National Park. It allows you to end up where you started, saving money on plane tickets and car rental. And you'll see some remote and off-the-beaten-track places. Not many visitors make it to see Childs Glacier on the Copper River Delta, which is the most spectacular accessible glacier in Alaska. Likewise, a trip to Kennecott, in Wrangell–St. Elias National Park, takes you way off the grid, letting you see an amazing historical ghost town and a community of real, backwoods Alaskans.

DAY 1: Starting in Fairbanks ★

Fly to Fairbanks, rent a car, and then check into your hotel. (If you will drive the rented car on gravel roads, such as the McCarthy Rd. on **DAY 4** or the Copper River Hwy. on **DAY 8**, you will need to rent from one of the few firms that allow this, listed on p. 419.) If time permits, visit the University of Alaska campus and see the magnificent **UA Museum of the North** (p. 415) and, if you are interested in such topics, the **Large Animal Research Station** or the **Georgeson Botanical Garden** (p. 416).

DAY 2: Fairbanks ★

Take the car to explore the Chena Hot Springs Road and the boreal forest of the **Chena River State Recreation Area** (see "Chena Hot Springs Road," in chapter 9). There are several wonderful trails here with varying difficulty levels. As an alternative, arrange for a canoeing paddle on the Chena. When you've finished hiking or paddling and start thinking about sore muscles, stop at the **Chena Hot Springs Resort** (p. 435) for a soak in the natural mineral springs pond there. At the end of the day, return to Fairbanks for dinner and bed.

UA Museum of the North.

Rika's Roadhouse and Landing.

DAY 3: The Richardson Highway to Copper Center ★★

Today you will drive approximately 260 miles (driving time: under 6 hr.) through some of Alaska's most spectacular scenery. Drive east from Fairbanks toward Delta Junction; stop there, after about 2 hours, to see the historical park at **Rika's Roadhouse and Landing** (p. 448) and for lunch in the town (see "The Alaska Highway," in chapter 9). Now drive south on the Richardson Highway. The best part of the drive is here, as the highway rises up and over the Alaska Range on open tundra country, along the silver Alaska pipeline, and at the edge of a series of alpine lakes. Stop for the night in the Athabascan village of Copper Center, where there is an exceptional hotel, **Copper River Princess Wilderness Lodge** (p. 453). Be sure to stop in at the **Wrangell–St. Elias National Park Visitor Center** (p. 457) to get oriented to the park before your visit tomorrow.

DAY 4: Kennecott ★★★

Get up early to drive east about 85 miles on the Edgerton Highway to Chitina, arriving there in time for the 8:30am **Backcountry Connection shuttle** (p. 456; reserve in advance) for a ride into the park. It's a rough road over an old railroad line deep into the wilderness park to a copper mine that was abandoned in the 1930s and the ghost town it left behind; by taking the van, you save yourself the driving and the planning necessary for that tough route, and you gain a guide to show you the way (you will have to cross a footbridge at one point). In Kennecott, check into one of two **wilderness lodges** (see "Wrangell–St. Elias National Park & Kennecott," in chapter 9), and join a guided walking tour through the enormous ghost-town buildings.

DAY 5: Kennecott to Valdez ★★

You have time in the morning to relax and wander in the friendly, quiet setting of Kennecott and its funky sister village of McCarthy. If you have the energy, take a half-day guided hike on the glacier that faces the ghost town. In the afternoon, take an air-taxi flight back to **Chitina** (p. 457) to get to your car (if you ride the van back, you will get in too late; besides, the view from the plane will be fantastic). Drive back to the Richardson Highway and then south to Valdez, about 190 miles total (roughly 4 hr.). The mountain scenery is spectacular through Thompson Pass nearing the town. Dine and check into lodgings in **Valdez** (see "Valdez," in chapter 7).

DAY 6: Valdez to Cordova Ferry ★

Today you will be taking your car by ferry for a scenic trip across eastern Prince William Sound to the town of Cordova. Depending on when the ferry leaves, you may have time for a dayhike, a museum visit, or another activity in Valdez. In the evening, walk around the quaint town of Cordova; if time permits, take a look at the two small **community museums** (see "Cordova: Hidden Treasure," in chapter 7).

DAY 7: Prince William Sound Sea Kayaking ★★★

Join **Cordova Coastal Outfitters** (p. 356) for a sea-kayaking excursion, or, if you are staying at the **Orca Adventure Lodge** (p. 361), you can go with a guide there. Cordova is an exceptional spot for a day's sea kayaking because waters near town are protected and exceptionally rich in marine mammals. You're almost assured of seeing sea otters and sea lions, and very likely to see many birds and other animals as well. (See "Cordova: Hidden Treasure," in chapter 7.)

DAY 8: Copper River Delta ★★

Drive your car east from Cordova over the gravel Copper River Highway through the Copper River Delta, an immense wetland teeming with wildlife, especially trumpeter swans and other waterfowl. (If your car-rental agency doesn't allow this, you can rent a vehicle for the day in Cordova.) There are several excellent and little-used trails and bird-watching areas along the road. The destination at the far end is the Childs Glacier, an incredible wall of ice that is cut by the Copper River. From a viewing area on the other side of the river, you are remarkably close to the glacier, and in warm weather you can see huge chunks falling off and hear the groan of the moving ice. (See "Cordova: Hidden Treasure," in chapter 7.) Spend a third night in Cordova.

DAY 9: Across the Sound to Whittier & Anchorage ★

Get back on the ferry for a trip across the sound to Whittier. Again, the scenery is incomparable. **Whittier** is a strange little port town built by the military during World War II that is reached only by boat or through a one-lane tunnel almost 3 miles long (p. 291). On the far side of the tunnel, you find yourself on Turnagain Arm about 50 miles from Anchorage. Time permitting, stop in Girdwood for a meal and perhaps a hike or visit to a **historic gold mine** (see "Side Trips to Girdwood & Mount Alyeska," in chapter 6). Finish the day in lodgings in Anchorage.

Kayaking at Prince William Sound.

DAY 10: Anchorage ★★

Take in the **Alaska Native Heritage Center** (p. 248) in the morning to meet indigenous people and learn about their cultures in a magnificent facility they built, own, and manage. In the afternoon, visit the **Anchorage Museum at Rasmuson Center** (p. 246), or spend the day outdoors, hiking, mountain-biking, fishing, or bird-watching. (See "What to See & Do," in chapter 6.) At the end of this fairly low-key day, eat in one of Alaska's best **restaurants,** of which Anchorage has the broadest selection (p. 273).

DAY 11: Flying over Mount McKinley ★★★

Get an early start for the 112-mile drive to Talkeetna (about 2 hr.) so you can be there in time for a morning flight over Mount McKinley before the clouds build up in the afternoon. The flight services that carry mountain climbers to the flanks of North America's tallest peak can also take you there for a landing on a **high-elevation glacier** (p. 399). After lunch and a walk around hip and historic Talkeetna (see "Talkeetna: Back Door to Denali," in chapter 8), drive about 150 miles (roughly 3 hr.) to Denali National Park and check into your lodgings. You should have time to take in the fascinating exhibits at the visitor center, too.

DAY 12: Exploring Denali National Park ★★★

This is the primary day to see Denali and the bears, caribous, and other wildlife there. The park shuttle bus system is the key to your visit. Reserve as far ahead as possible (the previous Dec is not too soon) to get a seat on the earliest bus you can manage. Wildlife tends to be more active in the morning. Ride deep into the park, taking along all your food and water, a warm jacket and raincoat, and good hiking shoes. Take a look at the suggestions for cross-country hiking in chapter 8, and then make your route choice according to how the countryside looks to you. This is a remarkable chance for a low-stress, low-cost wilderness experience. When you're ready to head home, just catch another bus on the way back.

Exploring Mount McKinley via bush plane.

DAY 13: Denali & Drive to Fairbanks ★

The drive from Denali back to Fairbanks is only a couple of hours, so you can take your time at the park. A white-water rafting ride in the Nenana River would be exciting; a nature walk in the woods from the visitor center might be calming. Also consider an educational program at the **Murie Science and Learning Center.** (See chapter 8.) Drive to your lodgings in Fairbanks in the afternoon.

DAY 14: Fairbanks

Today you get on a plane and fly back home, but if you have time for a relaxing outing before that, stop off for a stroll in **Pioneer Park** (p. 414) to look at the historic paddle-wheeler *Nenana* and the other museums and attractions, and to soak up the small-town ambience.

A WEEK IN ALASKA WITH KIDS

Traveling with children means limiting distances and increasing time for casual fun. The best place to do that is on the Kenai Peninsula south of Anchorage. Despite being a relatively contained area, the peninsula is a microcosm of the whole state, with glaciers, mountains, trails, and rugged coastline like that found over the vast span of Alaska. Consider renting an RV, which takes the stress out of having to keep children quiet in restaurants and hotel rooms. If you prefer to sleep in a tent, rent a car and your camping equipment in Anchorage. You'll have even more flexibility and opportunities for spontaneous fun. If you can, improve on this itinerary by adding days in Homer or on the Swan Lake Canoe Route.

DAY 1: Arrive in Anchorage

Fly to Anchorage and pick up your rented **RV** (p. 216), or pick up your car and rented **camping gear** (see "Equipment," p. 251). After buying your groceries, you can get on your way south on the Seward Highway, stopping at the **Bird Creek Campground** (p. 230) or the **Williwaw** or **Black Bear** campgrounds at Portage Glacier. The children will need to burn off some energy after your flight and drive, and this stretch of the highway has some of Alaska's best hiking trails. They are all covered, along with other sites, in "Side Trips to Turnagain Arm & Portage Glacier," in chapter 6.

DAY 2: To Seward & Kenai Fjords National Park ★★★

Drive the rest of the way to Seward on the Seward Highway and get on a tour boat to see **Kenai Fjords National Park** (see "Kenai Fjords National Park," in chapter 7). Every kid enjoys a boat ride, and on this one, you're likely to see whales, glaciers, and lots of seabirds. *Note:* These vessels go into the open ocean, and seasickness is common. Everyone in the family should take a seasickness remedy 2 hours in advance (see **"Seasickness,"** on p. 524). Make sure to take a vessel headed all the way into the park so you see the best of the wildlife and get close to a tidewater glacier. After you get back on land, set up your camp: If in an RV, set up at **Waterfront Park** (p. 305), or if tenting, drive out of Seward to the **Primrose Campground** (p. 290).

DAY 3: Seward ★★

You have three choices today, depending on the ages of your children and your interests (consider splitting up, as we often do, so everyone can choose what he or she enjoys most). (1) Visit the **Alaska SeaLife Center** (p. 302), where you can encounter the marine life and seabirds you saw in the fjords yesterday up close, and join in educational programs that get you even closer. Allow half a day. (2) Sea-kayak for half the day or the whole day with **Sunny Cove Sea Kayaking** (p. 301). You'll likely see sea otters, birds, intertidal creatures, and maybe spawning salmon. (3) Take a water taxi and hike the **Caines Head State Recreation Area** (p. 300) to Fort McGilvray to explore the dark corridors of the abandoned World War II installation. (Bring a flashlight.)

DAY 4: Homer ★

Today you'll drive 135 miles from Seward to the end of the road on the southern Kenai Peninsula and the town of **Homer** (see "Homer & Kachemak Bay: Cosmic Hamlet by the Sea," in chapter 7). Allow 4 hours, with

Touch tanks at the Alaska SeaLife Center.

traffic and some stops. In Homer, you can get hookups for the RV on Homer Spit—a fingerlike point into the middle of Kachemak Bay—or in the downtown part of Homer (still near the beach). Tenters have even more choices. Spend the afternoon beachcombing and enjoying relaxed time on the many miles of pebbled shoreline. If it's raining, take in the **Islands and Ocean Visitor Center** (p. 328) or the **Pratt Museum** (p. 331).

DAY 5: Kachemak Bay Natural History ★★★

Join the nonprofit **Center for Alaskan Coastal Studies** (p. 338) for a boat ride to the far side of Kachemak Bay. Their all-day natural history outings take visitors through tide pools to see strange little creatures, through a forest of big trees and wildflowers to learn about ecology, and to an ancient Native archaeological site. Even without the guides and all their knowledge, this would still be an enchanting place to visit, with wide beaches, caves, and plenty of space for a kid's energy and imagination to run free. Bring your own lunch.

DAY 6: Swan Lakes Canoeing ★

Now it's time to start heading back toward Anchorage. Drive about 90 miles to Sterling and stop at **Alaska Canoe & Campground** (p. 324) to rent a canoe you can take down Swanson River Road to the Swan Lake Canoe Route in **Kenai National Wildlife Refuge** (see "Kenai National Wildlife Refuge," in chapter 7). Spend the rest of the day paddling in this placid network of connected lakes, where you can fish and explore in solitude. There are numerous primitive campgrounds for the RV overnight, or, if you are tent camping, you may want to paddle to a campsite among the hundreds on the lakes.

DAY 7: Anchorage

From Sterling to Anchorage is about 150 miles and will take more than 3 hours with traffic. You probably won't have extra time after returning the RV or camping equipment before your flight, but if you do, the best way to spend it is at the **Alaska Zoo** (p. 249), where you will be sure of seeing all the most popular Alaska wildlife.

A WEEK OF ALASKA WINTER SPORTS

Winter is when Alaska is at its best. The snow simplifies the scenery and makes it even more beautiful. The outdoor activities are superb: cross-country and downhill skiing, snowmobiling, ice-skating, and dog mushing. The people are especially hospitable, since visitors are rare, and the towns are alive with festivals, sled-dog races, and authentic cultural events—not just tourist stuff. There's also a very good chance you will see the northern lights.

DAY 1: Anchorage Festivals & Sled-Dog Races ★

To enjoy Anchorage fully, rent a car when you arrive. If you have planned your trip for late February or early March, you can be here when Anchorage is alive with the **Fur Rendezvous Festival,** with its dozens of events and World Championship Sled Dog Race, and the **Iditarod Trail Sled Dog Race** (both p. 221), which starts its journey across Alaska to Nome right after the festival. Local cultural institutions will be busy, too: Visit the **Anchorage Museum at Rasmuson Center** (p. 246) during the day and catch a performance in the evening at the **Alaska Center for the Performing Arts** (p. 240).

DAY 2: Anchorage Cross-Country Skiing ★★

If you've never tried cross-country skiing, Anchorage is an excellent place to give it a go. If you do ski, you can enjoy some of the nation's best trails here in many settings and varying difficulty levels, and with grooming that's world class. There are no trail fees. The very best trail system is at **Kincaid Park** (p. 254). **Ski rental** is covered under "Equipment," on p. 251. If you don't want to ski, Anchorage also has groomed ice-skating ponds; Westchester

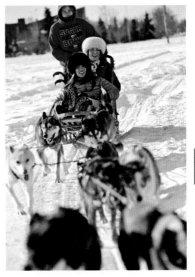

A sled ride during the Fur Rendezvous Festival.

Lagoon has more than a kilometer of **skating trails** (p. 252). At the end of the day, drive 40 miles to the **Hotel Alyeska** (p. 272) in Girdwood for the night. You will find two of Alaska's best restaurants to choose from for dinner: **Seven Glaciers** (p. 272) and **Double Musky Inn** (p. 273).

DAY 3: Girdwood Downhill Skiing ★★★

Spend the day on the slopes of Alyeska Resort, skiing near sea level, but mostly above the tree line, and with extraordinary ocean views from the slopes and lifts. Those who don't want to ski have enough to do: swimming in the saltwater pool at the hotel, visiting the spa or shops, or skating on the outdoor rink at the base of the mountain.

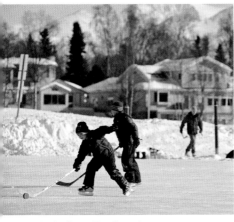

Ice hockey at Westchester Lagoon.

DAY 4: Girdwood to Fairbanks ★

Drive to Anchorage and return the car. If you have time, take the Alaska Railroad, which runs a single-car train once a week from Anchorage to Fairbanks; it's a spectacular and uniquely Alaskan ride. The most practical route is to fly from Anchorage to Fairbanks and rent another car when you arrive. That will leave you with most of the day to explore the town, including the downtown attractions and, if possible, the **World Ice Art Championships** (p. 411).

> ### Doubling Up the Seasons
>
> Here's a little-known approach to experiencing the best of Alaska: Arrive in late March and head to **Homer,** on the south end of the Kenai Peninsula, as an add-on to the above winter itinerary. The community has lengthy and spectacular cross-country ski trails that usually have plenty of snow all month. At the same time, salmon fishing gets started in March in the waters of Kachemak Bay—there's even a fishing derby joined by hundreds of boats. You can go **salmon fishing** in the morning and **ski** in the afternoon! (See "Late March Is Perfect," p. 332.)

DAY 5: Museum of the North & Dog Mushing ★★

The **UA Museum of the North** (p. 415) will engage your mind and imagination with galleries that mix art, anthropology, and science in unique and surprising ways. This is also the best place anywhere to learn about the aurora. Make a point of going for a dog-sled ride while you're here, too, with **Sun Dog Express Dog Sled Tours** (p. 422) or one of the many other operators giving rides; Fairbanks is a center for the sport, with limitless miles of trails in the hilly boreal forest that extends in every direction.

DAY 6: Chena Hot Springs Resort ★★

Drive a little more than an hour into the Bush for a visit to the hot springs, a unique resort (for example, one of the buildings is made entirely of ice) nestled in the rounded mountains of winter. **Chena Hot Springs Resort** (p. 435) has its flaws, but the experience of floating in a pond of hot artesian water on a day when the air around is below zero more than makes up for them. If you want to do more than soak, lots of activities are available, including snowmobiling and dog mushing. After dark, step outside for the unsurpassed aurora viewing out here, beyond city lights.

Chena Hot Springs.

DAY 7: Fairbanks

Today you can take one more swim or ski run before returning your car in Fairbanks and returning home by air.

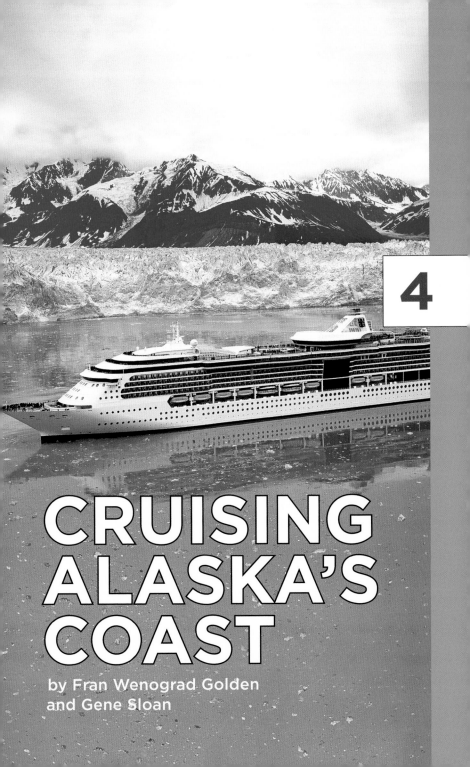

4

CRUISING ALASKA'S COAST

by Fran Wenograd Golden
and Gene Sloan

There is an optimism in Alaska this year, with state industry leaders hoping for increased good relations with the cruise lines, and cruise lines looking more favorably at the market and, in some cases, increasing capacity. This follows a contentious period centered largely on a controversial state tax on cruise passengers.

To fight the tax, Royal Caribbean, Princess Cruises, Norwegian Cruise Line, and Holland America all downsized, moving ships from Alaska to Europe and other cruise destinations, or cutting down on their numbers of Alaska itineraries in 2010 and 2011.

After much debate, filing of a federal lawsuit by the cruise lines against the state, and even a visit by Gov. Sean Parnell to the Cruise Shipping Conference in Miami, the cruise industry's annual major conference, in an attempt to make nice, the Alaska legislature in 2010 approved a reduction in a controversial $50-per-cruise passenger head tax passed by Alaska voters in 2006. The tax was originally to support the infrastructure at the ports and enforce environmental compliance, but whether it was all used for that was subject to debate.

Taking effect last year, the head tax was reduced to $35. The legislature also listened to the cruise lines in approving deeper offsets of the tax in Juneau and Ketchikan, which have their own taxes of $8 and $7 per cruise passenger, respectively, and approved more funds for tourism marketing.

But in the meantime, cruise passenger numbers in Alaska fell by an estimated 142,000 in 2010 to about 868,000 passengers. There was better news in 2011, with an estimated 933,000 cruise passengers expected.

Obviously, Alaska wants ships and cruisers back—the decline in 2010 alone meant some $150 million in lost revenue, including onshore spending. Everyone is looking forward to a more fruitful 2012.

Good news for Alaska cruising has come in several forms, including an announcement by Disney Cruise Line that it would return to Alaska for the second year in 2012. Disney debuted in Alaska for the first time in 2011 and drew much attention to the state as a family destination. (Princess launched new family programs, too.)

Market leaders Holland America and Princess Cruises have a substantial presence in Alaska this year, with seven ships each; Princess added a ship, and Holland America has 130 departures, representing a 6% capacity increase.

Two lines are leaving Alaska in 2012. Crystal Cruises will visit only briefly with its luxury product, as part of a multicountry itinerary (the line had returned last year after a 6-year absence), and upscale Oceania did its first season ever in Alaska in 2011 but is not back in 2012.

But InnerSea Discoveries, which debuted a new line of small ships last year, is back, and so is new small-ship line Alaskan Dream.

The cruise season here is dictated by the weather and generally runs from about mid-May to mid-September.

PREVIOUS PAGE: **Royal Caribbean's** *Radiance of the Seas,* **sailing near Hubbard Glacier.**

Especially for first-time visitors, a cruise is an excellent way to get the lay of the land and an introduction to Alaska. Cruise passengers visit the towns and wilderness areas of the Southeast (the Inside Passage, also known as the Panhandle) or the Gulf of Alaska by day, and burrow into their ships for effortless travel by night. The lack of roads between towns makes the waters of the Inside Passage the region's de facto highway.

Your options—apart from a somewhat limited airline schedule—are basically taking a cruise ship or the Alaska Marine Highway System (the state ferries). You have to be willing to invest more time—both for the actual traveling and for the planning—to use the ferries. And you have to be willing to give up the comforts and diversions of the average cruise ship. Then again, the ferry *does* give you unlimited stops along the way and a chance to meet Alaskan residents not only in major cruise ports, but also in smaller, less-visited communities. (See "Exploring Southeast Alaska," in chapter 5.) For most people, the luxury of cruise travel is preferable to the rough-and-ready nature of ferry transportation.

No matter how much revenue cruise passengers (and ships' crews) generate for merchants in the ports visited, some locals aren't as welcoming as they might be. Alaskans are known for their hospitality, but they have their limits. During the height of the cruise season, once-charming streets are transformed into virtual carnival midways jammed wall to wall with vacationers from simultaneous ship landings. As a result, service standards suffer somewhat—especially toward the end of the season.

Some communities feel that the cultural bulldozing brought by cruise ships is not worth the economic benefit and have placed limits on the number of ships that can come into port, in addition to taxes based on passenger count.

The cruise lines have taken the prevailing mood very seriously. Individual lines have appointed community affairs officers with orders to smarten up the public's perception of cruising and cruise operators. And the industry as a whole brought on Johne Binkley, a prominent lifelong political figure (he's a former state senator, gubernatorial candidate, and chairman of the state-run Alaska Railroad) to liaise with both the elected officials in Juneau and the voters who put them in power. In addition to the partial repeal of the head tax, the cruise lines successfully got a delay in new wastewater dumping regulations that were to take effect in 2010.

Alaska's popularity as a cruise destination is due in most part to its natural splendor. As a visitor, you can avoid much of the human congestion caused by ships by choosing a small-ship cruise that spends more time enjoying the wilderness and the small towns that big ships can't reach. On the small ships, you might visit Haines, for instance, or Cordova, or Metlakatla, and a dozen other places where the big guys don't (or, at least, seldom) go.

On the other hand, riding a megaship is a different kind of fun—the ship itself is an attraction, with far more amenities than any of the towns along the way. If you need to relax and leave all the stresses of life at home behind—and if seeing Alaska wilderness isn't the most important part of your trip—a big ship is the way to go. Plus, you can still get a taste of some wilderness areas on shore excursions.

Another way to avoid some of the disadvantages of overcrowding and service problems is to choose an early season cruise—say, the last couple of weeks in May. One other option: You can always travel independently after the cruise to the real Alaska, inland from the cruise ports. (For more on the relative benefits of big versus small cruise ships, see "Weighing Your Cruise Options," below.)

In this chapter, we'll go through the cruise options available in the state, focusing primarily on those that provide a true in-depth experience. For even more information, pick up a copy of *Frommer's Alaska Cruises & Ports of Call* (Wiley Publishing, Inc.).

WEIGHING YOUR CRUISE OPTIONS

Your three main questions in choosing a cruise in Alaska are "When should I go?," "Where do I want to go?," and "How big a ship?"

When to Go

Alaska is very much a seasonal, as opposed to year-round, cruise destination, generally open to cruising from May through September (although some smaller ships start up in late Apr). May and September are considered the shoulder season, and lower brochure rates are offered during these months (and more aggressive discounts as well; watch your local newspaper and check the Internet). Cruising in May can be extremely pleasant—the real, near-gridlock-inducing crowds have yet to arrive, and if you're lucky, the temperatures will already be warm. Locals, coming off what is usually a fairly isolated winter, are friendlier than they are later in the season, when they're tired and, frankly, pretty much ready to see the tourists go home. There is also the statistical fact that May in the Inside Passage ports is one of the driest months in the season. Late September also offers the advantage of fewer fellow tourists clogging the ports. The warmest months are June, July, and August, with temperatures generally around 50° to 80°F (10°–27°C) during the day and cooler at night. But warmer days can occur as well—and when it gets above 80°F (27°C) in, say, Juneau, you can be sure there will be plenty of local speculation about global warming. Pack a parka, but also pack some T-shirts. You will need to bring along a sweater or two, and a rain slicker is a good idea. June 21 is the longest day of the year, with the sky lit virtually all night. June tends to be drier than July and August, and April and May are drier than September (though in early Apr you may encounter freezing rain and other vestiges of winter). Somebody once said, "Everybody complains about the weather but nobody does anything about it." And that's very much the way it is in Alaska. The simple fact is that, in Alaska, perhaps more than in many other states, the weather is going to do what it's going to do. You may be forced to don a coat, hat, and gloves in July and August—theoretically, the months in which one might expect higher temperatures. On the other hand, we've also been comfortable in short sleeves on deck in Glacier Bay in May and September—when, again, theoretically it should be a little cooler. You may encounter so much wind-driven rain in Skagway that you'd think the moisture was moving horizontally. But it might also be completely dry and so sunny that you have to put on sunblock so you don't burn—and pack a bathing suit, because you may even want to take a dip in the ship's pool. In other words, be prepared for anything.

If you are considering traveling in a shoulder month, remember that some shops don't open until Memorial Day, and the visitor season is generally considered over on Labor Day (although cruise lines operate well into Sept).

Inside Passage or the Gulf of Alaska?

The Inside Passage runs through the area of Alaska known as the Southeast (which the locals also call "the Panhandle"), that narrow strip of the state—islands, mainland coastal communities, and mountains—that runs from the Canadian border in the south to the start of the Gulf in the north, just above the Juneau/Haines/Skagway area. The islands on the western side of the area afford cruise ships a welcome degree of protection from the sea and its attendant rough waters (hence the name "Inside Passage"). Because of that shelter, such ports as Ketchikan, Wrangell, Petersburg, and others are reached with less rocking and rolling, and thus less risk of seasickness. Sitka is not on the Inside Passage (it's on the Pacific side of Baranof Island), but that beautiful little community is included in most Inside Passage cruise itineraries.

The Southeast encompasses the capital city, **Juneau,** and townships influenced by the former Russian presence in the state (**Sitka,** for instance), the Tlingit and Haida Native cultures **(Ketchikan),** and the great gold rush of 1898 **(Skagway).** It is a land of rainforests, mountains, inlets, and glaciers (including Margerie, Johns Hopkins, Muir, and the others contained within the boundaries of **Glacier Bay National Park**). The region is rich in wildlife, especially of the marine variety. It is a scenic delight. But then, what part of Alaska isn't?

The other major cruising area is the **Southcentral** region's Gulf of Alaska, usually referred to by the cruise lines as the "Glacier Discovery Route," or the "Voyage of the Glaciers," or some such catchy title. "Gulf of Alaska," after all, sounds pretty bland.

The coastline of the Gulf is that arc of land from just north of Glacier Bay to the Kenai Peninsula. The Southcentral also takes in the truly spectacular **Prince William Sound;** the **Cook Inlet,** on the northern side of the peninsula; **Anchorage,** Alaska's biggest city; the year-round **Alyeska Resort** at Girdwood, 40 miles from Anchorage; the **Matanuska** and **Susitna** valleys (the "Mat-Su"), a fertile agricultural region renowned for the record size of some of its garden produce; and part of the Alaska Mountain Range.

The principal Southcentral terminus ports are **Seward** or **Whittier** for Anchorage. Ships typically carry passengers from Seward or Whittier to Anchorage by bus or train. (Getting all the way around the peninsula to Anchorage would add a day to the cruise.) Let us stress that going on a Gulf cruise does not mean that you don't visit any of the Inside Passage. The big difference is that, whereas the more popular Inside Passage cruise itineraries run 7 nights round-trip to and from Seattle or Vancouver, the Gulf routing is 7 nights one-way—northbound or southbound—between Vancouver and Seward or Vancouver and Whittier. A typical Gulf itinerary also visits such Inside Passage ports as **Ketchikan, Juneau, Sitka,** and/or **Skagway.**

The Gulf's glaciers are quite dazzling and every bit as spectacular as their counterparts to the south. **College Fjord,** for instance, is lined with glaciers—16 of them, each one grander than the last. On one cruise, Fran saw incredible calving at **Harvard Glacier,** with chunks of 400- and 500-year-old ice falling off and crashing into the water with thunderous sounds every few minutes (worries about global warming aside, the sight was spectacular). Another favorite part of a Gulf cruise, though, is the visit to the gigantic **Hubbard Glacier**—at 6 miles, Alaska's longest—at the head of Yakutat Bay (our all-time favorite, by the way—where the chunks in the water may remind you of ice in a giant punch bowl). Not to raise again the specter of global warming, but sadly, most of Alaska's glaciers are in retreat, some receding quite rapidly. On a recent visit to Sawyer Glacier, the ice face had gone so far back that the ship was unable to get closer than a mile or so. Not the best way to view a glacier.

Cruise tours combine a cruise with a land tour, either before or after the cruise. Typical packages link the cruise with a 3- to 5-night Anchorage/Denali/Fairbanks tour, a 4- to 7-night Yukon tour (which visits Anchorage, Denali, and Fairbanks on the way), or a 5- to 7-night tour of the Canadian Rockies. Holland America, Princess, and Royal Caribbean/Celebrity lead the big-ship cruise-tour market. Even if you book with another cruise line, chances are, at least some portions of your land tour will be bought from one of these operators.

Big Ship or Small?

Imagine an elephant. Now imagine your pet pug dog, Sparky. That's about the size difference between your options in the Alaska market: behemoth modern ships and small, more exploratory coastal vessels.

SMALL SHIPS   Just as big cruise ships are mostly for people who want every resort amenity, **small** or **alternative ships** are best suited for people who prefer a casual, crowd-free cruise experience that gives passengers a chance to get up close and personal with Alaska's natural surroundings and wildlife. Small ships offer little in terms of amenities: They usually have small cabins, only one lounge/bar and dining room, and no exercise facilities, entertainment, or organized activities. There are little or no stabilizers on most of these smaller ships, and the ride can be bumpy in open water—which isn't much of a problem on Inside Passage itineraries, since most of the cruising area is protected from sea waves. They are also difficult for travelers with disabilities, as none of the ships in the market have elevators. Despite all of this, they're universally more expensive than the big ships and offer fewer discounts. That's the down side.

But a big plus, thanks to their smaller size, is that these ships can go places that larger ships can't, such as narrow fjords, uninhabited islands, and smaller ports that cater mostly to small fishing vessels. Due to their shallow draft, they can nose right up to sheer cliff faces, bird rookeries, bobbing icebergs, and cascading waterfalls that you can literally reach out and touch. Also, sea animals are not as intimidated by these ships, so you might find yourself having a rather close encounter with a humpback whale, or watching other sea mammals bobbing in the ship's wake. Cruising recently in Misty Fjords, Fran and her fellow passengers watched through binoculars as a shore-side bear stood to its full height, the captain positioning the ship a safe distance from the creature for a good half-hour so everyone could take in the sight. The decks on these ships are closer to the waterline, too, giving passengers a more intimate view than they would get from the high decks of the large cruise ships. Some of these ships stop at ports on a daily basis, as do the larger ships, while some avoid ports almost entirely, exploring natural areas instead. Small ships also have the flexibility to change direction as opportunities arise—say, to go where whales have been sighted and to linger awhile once a sighting's been made.

Visitors aboard large ships have access to the real, natural Alaska, too, with frequent whale spottings. But since you are calling mostly at popular ports, to dig further, you really need to do some of the more remote (and pricey) shore excursions. Visitors aboard small ships will have simpler accommodations and not much onboard entertainment, but will get an experience that's more intimate, allowing them to really get in touch with the place they've come to see. Choose your ship accordingly.

BIG SHIPS The **big ships** in the Alaska market fall generally into two categories: midsize ships and megaships. Carrying as many as 2,670 passengers, the **megaships** look and feel like floating resorts. Big on glitz, they offer loads of activities, attract many families and (especially in Alaska) seniors, offer a large number of public rooms (including fancy casinos and fully equipped gyms and spas), and provide a wide variety of meal and entertainment options. And though they may feature 1 or 2 formal nights per trip, the ambience is generally casual (with casual buffet options now available on formal nights and some people not dressing up at all; and we've noticed a trend among those who do—fewer tuxes and ball gowns and more dark suits and cocktail dresses). The Alaska vessels of the Carnival, Celebrity, Princess, and Royal Caribbean fleets all fit in this category, as do Norwegian Cruise Line's *Jewel* and *Pearl,* Holland America's *Zuiderdam* and *Westerdam,* and the *Disney Wonder.* **Midsize ships** in Alaska fall into two segments: the ultraluxurious, such as Regent Seven Seas' *Seven Seas Navigator,* Silversea Cruises' *Silver Shadow,* and the modern midsize, such as Holland America's *Veendam, Amsterdam, Volendam, Zaandam,* and *Statendam.* In general, the size of these ships is less significant than the general onboard atmosphere. Both the midsize ships and the megaships have a great range of facilities for passengers. Cabins on these ships range from cubbyholes to large suites, depending on the ship and the type of cabin you book. Big dining rooms and a tremendous variety of cuisines are the norm. These ships carry a lot of people and can, at times, feel crowded.

The sizes of these big ships also come with **three major drawbacks** for passengers: (1) They can't sail into narrow passages or shallow-water

---

Sick Ships

Every year, hundreds of cruise-ship passengers and plenty of visitors on shore come down with vomiting and diarrhea caused by a bug now known as the norovirus. The good news is, it's rarer in summer than winter. Still, the illness is no fun. It lasts a day or two and is rarely serious, although some passengers do end up in the hospital because of dehydration. The virus is extremely contagious from the first symptoms until at least 3 days and up to 2 weeks after it clears up. Touching a contaminated handrail and then your face is enough to catch it. To minimize your chances of contracting the virus, wash your hands frequently, drink bottled water, and avoid eating raw food onboard, especially shellfish. The Centers for Disease Control and Prevention (CDC) also recommends that passengers 65 and older or those with chronic illnesses check with their doctors before taking a cruise. The CDC website (www.cdc.gov/nceh/vsp) posts sanitation inspection scores for each ship. Type "norovirus" into the search page to find a fact sheet. Most cruise lines now have hand sanitizer stations at the boarding ramp and throughout the ship—including at the entryways to the gangway, buffet area, and the dining rooms. Their use is mostly voluntary, but our advice is—do.

ports, (2) their size and inflexible schedules limit their ability to stop or even slow down when wildlife is spotted, and (3) when their passengers disembark in a town, they tend to overwhelm it, limiting your ability to get insight into the real Alaska communities. But on the plus side, they offer dozens of excursions at each port so you can get well out of town.

THE BEST CRUISE EXPERIENCES IN ALASKA

Cruise lines are in the business of giving their guests a good time, so they've all got something going for them. Here are our picks for Alaska's best, in a few different categories.

- **The Best Ships for Luxury:** Luxury in Alaska is defined in 2012 by **Regent Seven Seas** and **Silversea.** If you want a more casual kind of luxury (a really nice ship with a no-tie-required policy), the ***Seven Seas Navigator*** offers just that on an all-suite vessel (most cabins have private balconies) with excellent cuisine. **Silversea,** on the other hand, represents a slick, Italian-influenced, slightly more formal luxury experience with all the perks—big suite cabins and excellent food, linens, service, and companions. Both Regent and Silversea include fine wine and booze in their cruise fares. For the ultimate Alaska experience in a small-ship setting, check out the intimate offerings of **American Safari Cruises,** where soft adventure comes with upscale accouterments.

- **The Best of the Mainstream Ships:** Every line's most recent ships are beautiful, but **Celebrity's *Infinity*** is a true stunner, as is its sister ship, ***Millennium.*** These modern vessels, with their extensive art collections, cushy public rooms, and expanded spa areas, give Celebrity a formidable presence in Alaska. And the late-model ***Sapphire Princess*** and ***Diamond Princess*** have raised the art of building big ships to new heights. Both of these vessels will again be in Inside Passage service this year from Vancouver.

- **The Best Ships for Families:** All the major lines have well-established kids' programs, with **Carnival, Royal Caribbean,** and **Norwegian Cruise Line** leading the pack in terms of facilities and activities. **Princess** gets a nod for its National Park Service Junior Ranger Program to teach kids about glaciers and Alaska wildlife (they can even earn a Junior Ranger badge), and last year increased shore excursions geared for families. But no one can beat **Disney,** which is back in Alaska in 2012 for a second year with the *Disney Wonder.*

- **The Best Ships for Pampering:** It's a toss-up—**Celebrity's *Infinity*** and ***Millennium*** offer wonderful AquaSpas complete with thalassotherapy pools and a wealth of soothing and beautifying treatments, and the solariums on **Royal Caribbean's *Rhapsody of the Seas*** and ***Radiance of the Seas*** offer relaxing indoor pool retreats. We are also fans of the thermal suite (complete with hydrotherapy pool) in the Greenhouse Spas on **Holland America's *Zuiderdam*** and ***Westerdam.***

- **The Best Shipboard Cuisine: Regent Seven Seas** is tops in this category. And the expertly prepared and presented cuisine on **Silversea's *Silver Shadow*** must also come in for some props. While this may surprise some, of the mainstream lines, we like the buffet and dining room offerings of **Carnival**—flavorful food, well prepared. The ***Carnival Spirit*** in Alaska also boasts the Nouveau Supper Club ($30 service charge per person), where you can enjoy just about as fine a meal as you're likely to find anywhere. And **Norwegian Cruise Line**'s teppanyaki restaurant ($25 per person charge) is also an experience not to be missed—yummy food and a show by knife-wielding chefs.

○ **The Best Ships for Onboard Activities:** The ships operated by **Carnival** and **Royal Caribbean** offer a very full roster of onboard activities that range from the sublime (lectures) to the ridiculous (contests designed to get passengers to do or say outrageous things). **Princess**'s ScholarShip@Sea program is a real winner, with excitingly packaged classes in such diverse subjects as photography, personal computers, cooking, and even pottery.

○ **The Best Ships for Entertainment:** Look to the big ships here. **Carnival, Royal Caribbean,** and **Disney** are tops when it comes to an overall package of show productions, nightclub acts, lounge performances, and audience-participation entertainment (Disney with a family focus, but also offering adult entertainment options). **Princess** also offers particularly well-done—if somewhat less lavishly staged—shows. **Holland America** has not historically been noted for its entertainment package, but the company has improved considerably in the show lounge in recent years, including adding performances by magicians and comedians.

○ **The Best Ships for Whale-Watching:** If the whales come close enough, you can see them from all the ships in Alaska—Fran spotted a couple of orcas from her cabin balcony on a recent Holland America cruise, for instance. Smaller ships, though—such as those operated by **Alaskan Dream, American Safari, InnerSea Discoveries,** and **Lindblad**—might actually change course to follow a whale. Get your cameras and binoculars ready!

○ **The Best Ships for Cruise Tours: Princess, Holland America,** and the twin-brand Royal Caribbean Cruises (which owns **Royal Caribbean International** and **Celebrity**) are the market leaders in getting you into the Interior of Alaska either before or after your cruise. They own their own deluxe motorcoaches and railcars. Princess and Holland America Line (HAL) also own lodges and hotels. After many years in the business, these two really know what they're doing. Royal Caribbean is a comparative latecomer, but its land company, Royal Celebrity Tours, with some of the finest rolling stock (rail and road) around, has made huge strides. Most of the other lines actually buy their land product components from Princess or HAL. One of Holland America's strengths is its 3- and 4-night cruises combined with an Alaska/Yukon land package. The company offers exclusive entry into the Yukon's Kluane National Park, and they've added another Yukon gem—Tombstone Territorial Park, near Dawson City, a region of staggering wilderness beauty, Native architecture, stunning vistas, and wildlife. Princess is arguably stronger in 7-night Gulf of Alaska cruises in conjunction with Denali/Fairbanks or Kenai Peninsula land arrangements. Princess's Copper River Lodge is by the entrance to Wrangell–St. Elias National Park.

○ **The Best Ports:** Juneau and Sitka are our favorites. Juneau is one of the most visually pleasing small cities anywhere and certainly the prettiest capital city in America (once you get beyond all the tourist shops near the pier). It's fronted by the Gastineau Channel and backed by Mount Juneau and Mount Roberts, offers the very accessible Mendenhall Glacier, and is otherwise surrounded by wilderness—and it's a really fun city to visit, too. In recent years, an addition to the tourist attraction roster is a drive past the governor's mansion, once the residence of former Gov. Sarah Palin. Sitka's Russian architecture, historic totem pole park, and Raptor Rehabilitation Center earn it the nod here, not to mention the fact we've had very pleasant conversations with Sitka locals about topics ranging from the fishing season to local politics—when the first non–locally owned T-shirt shop was railroaded in a few years ago, the whole town was abuzz. No town in Alaska is more historically significant than Skagway, with its old buildings so quaint you might think you stepped into a Disney version of what a gold-rush town should look like. But the arrival of so many glitzy, expensive jewelry stores imported from the Caribbean has impacted our impressions of that community. Still, if you can get yourself into the right frame of mind, and if you can recall the history of the place—the gold rush frenzy that literally put the town on the map—it's easier to capture the true spirit of Skagway. For a more low-key Alaska experience, take the ferry from Skagway to Haines, which reminds us of the folksy, frontier Alaska depicted on the TV show *Northern Exposure* and is a great place to spot eagles and other wildlife. Some ships also stop at Haines as a port of call, usually for a few hours after Skagway.

- **The Best Shore Excursions:** Flightseeing and helicopter trips in Alaska are absolutely unforgettable ways to check out the scenery, if you can afford them. But airborne tours tend to be pretty pricey—sometimes approaching $600 a head. A helicopter trip to a dog-sled camp at the top of a glacier (usually among the priciest of the offerings) affords both incredibly pretty views and a chance to try your hand at the truly Alaskan sport of dog sledding. (Yes, even in summer: If there is not enough snow, the sleds are fitted with wheels.) It's a great way to earn bragging rights with the folks back home. For a less extravagant excursion, nothing beats a ride on a clear day on the White Pass and Yukon Route Railway out of Skagway to Canada—the route followed by the gold stampeders of '98. The railway a couple of years back expanded its rail system so that some of its trains go not just to Fraser at the border, but all the way to Carcross (formerly known as Caribou Crossing) in the Yukon Territory (adding more than 30 miles by rebuilding old track). While you're riding the rails, try to imagine what it was like for those gold seekers crossing the same track on foot! We also like to get active with kayak and mountain-biking excursions offered by most lines at most ports. In addition to affording a chance to work off those shipboard calories, these excursions typically provide optimum opportunities for spotting eagles, bears, seals, and other wildlife. Another, less hectic shore excursion that's become increasingly popular is whale-watching. On an evening excursion from Juneau in May, on one cruise we were on, passengers on one of the whale-watching boats got the thrill of seeing an entire pod of orcas, more than a dozen of the giant creatures frolicking well within view. For wildlife lovers, the Sea Otter & Wildlife Quest tour in Sitka guarantees you'll spot whales, bears, otters, or other impressive wildlife, or your money back.

BOOKING YOUR CRUISE

Every cruise line has a brochure full of beautiful glossy photos. You'll see low starting rates on the charts, but look further, and you'll realize those are for tiny

Shore excursions offered by the cruise lines provide a chance for you to get off the ship and explore the sights close up, taking in the history, nature, and culture of the region—from exploring gold-rush-era streets to experiencing Native Alaskan traditions such as totem carving.

Some excursions are of the walking tour or bus tour variety, but many others are activity oriented: Cruise passengers have the opportunity to go sea kayaking, mountain-biking, horseback riding, salmon fishing, and even rock climbing or zip-lining through the treetops, and to see the sights by seaplane or helicopter—and maybe even to land on a glacier and go for a walk. Occasionally, with some of the smaller cruise lines, you'll find quirky excursions, such as a visit with local artists in their studios. Some lines even offer scuba diving and snorkeling. The cruise lines vet the operators, so you do get assurance you're dealing with pros.

With some lines, select shore excursions are included in your cruise fare, but with most lines, they are an added (though very worthwhile) expense.

inside cubicles; most of the cabins sell for much more. Sometimes the brochures feature published rates that are nothing more than a pie-in-the-sky wish (most customers will pay less). The cruise lines would like you to look at the early bird savings column and book your cruise early. (The brochures come out about a year in advance and you typically have until mid-Feb for average savings of 25%–30% and sometimes as much as 50%.) In previous years, if you waited until March or April to book, you might save significantly more. This was not the case in 2011. Chalk it up to less capacity, or perhaps the increasing popularity of Alaska cruises—given natural disasters and war in some other parts of the world—but there were few last-minute bargains to be had at the start of the cruise season last year. The cheapest fares we could find in mid-April for early season cruises were $619 and $699. Compare that to 2010, when there were plenty of $399 fares in the market and even one crazy fare we spotted of $269, though that was also a year when the economic downturn caused travelers to book closer in and the cruise lines to panic about filling their ships. We don't expect many last-minute deals this year, but for those there are, it's important to remember these kinds of prices are for a limited number of cabins, and getting last-minute airfare is not always that easy. So here's our suggestion: Either book way in advance and snag an early booking deal, or decide what month you want to travel and keep careful track of what's happening in the market come mid-February into March. Check websites that track cruise sales, including Gene's own *USA Today* Cruise Log Blog (www.usatoday.com/travel/cruises). In reality, you may be able to get the cruise for 40% or 50% off, but if you don't reserve space early, you could just as easily be left out in the cold. Remember that the most expensive and the cheapest cabins tend to sell out first. The midrange rooms are by and large the last to go. Increasingly aggressive marketing by the cruise lines to previous passengers is adding to the increase in early bookings.

Book your cruise through an experienced cruise travel agent or online. Many people still turn to **travel agents** and, though the **Internet** has knocked some of those agents out of business, many of the remaining traditional travel agencies have created their own websites in an effort to keep pace.

So which is the better way to book a cruise these days? The answer can be both. If you're computer savvy, have a good handle on all the elements that go into a cruise, and have narrowed down the choices to a few cruise lines that appeal to you, websites are a great way to trawl the seas at your own pace and check out last-minute deals, which can be dramatic. On the other hand, you'll barely get a stitch of personalized service searching for and booking a cruise online. If you need help getting a refund or arranging special meals or other matters, or deciding which cabin to choose, you're on your own. In addition, agents usually know about cruise and airfare discounts that the lines won't necessarily publicize on their websites. So the best bet, to our way of thinking, is to do your research electronically and, better informed, then visit a travel agent to make the reservation.

Booking a Small-Ship Cruise

The small-ship companies in Alaska—Alaskan Dream, American Safari, Lindblad Expeditions, and InnerSea Discoveries—all offer real niche-oriented cruise experiences, attracting passengers who have a very good idea of the kind of experience they want (usually educational and/or adventurous, and always casual and small scale). In many cases, a large percentage of passengers on any given cruise will have sailed with the line before. Because of all this, and because the passenger capacity of these small ships is so low, in general, you're not going to find the kind of deep discounts you do with the large ships. Still, for the most part, these lines rely on agents to handle their bookings, taking very few reservations directly. All of the lines have a list of agents with whom they do considerable business, and they can hook you up with an agent if you call (or e-mail) and ask for an agent near you.

Booking a Mainstream Cruise

If you don't know a good travel agent already, try to find one through your friends, preferably those who have cruised before. For the most personal service, look for an agent in your local area, and for the most knowledgeable service, look for an agent who has cruising experience. It's perfectly okay to ask an agent questions about his or her personal knowledge of the product, such as whether he or she has ever cruised in Alaska or with one of the lines you're considering. The easiest way to be sure the agent is experienced in booking cruises is to work with a **cruise-only agency** (meaning that the whole agency specializes in cruises) or to find somebody in a more conventional agency who is a **cruise specialist** (meaning he or she handles that agency's cruise business). If you are calling a full-service travel agency, ask for the **cruise desk,** which is where you'll find these specialists. If the agency doesn't have a cruise desk, per se, it might be wise to check elsewhere.

A good and easy rule of thumb to maximize your chances of finding an agent who has cruise experience and who won't rip you off is to book with agencies that are members of the **Cruise Lines International Association** (**CLIA;** ☎ **754/ 224-2200;** www.cruising.org), the main industry association. Membership in the **American Society of Travel Agents** (**ASTA;** ☎ **800/275-2782;** www. travelsense.org) ensures that the agency is monitored for ethical practices, although it does not designate cruise experience.

You can tap into the Internet sites of these organizations for easy access to agents in your area.

The Cost: What's Included & What's Not

However you arrange to buy your cruise, what you basically have in hand at the end is a contract for transportation, lodging, dining, entertainment, housekeeping, and assorted other miscellaneous services that will be provided to you over the course of your vacation. It's important, though, to remember what extras are *not* included in your cruise fare. Are you getting a price that includes port charges, taxes, fees, and insurance, or are you getting a cruise-only fare? Are airfare and airport transfers included, or do you have to book them separately (either as an add-on to the cruise fare or on your own)? Make sure you're comparing apples with apples when making price comparisons. Read the fine print!

Aside from **airfare,** which is usually not included in your cruise fare (see more on air arrangements below), the priciest addition to your cruise fare, particularly in Alaska, will likely be **shore excursions.** Ranging from about $35 for a bus tour to $299 and up (sometimes as high as $600) for a lengthy helicopter or seaplane flightseeing excursion, these sightseeing tours are designed to help cruise passengers make the most of their time at the ports the ship visits, but they can add a hefty sum to your vacation costs.

You'll also want to add to your calculations **tips for the ship's crew.** Tips are given at the end of the cruise, and passengers should reserve at least $10 per passenger per day for tips for the room steward, waiter, and busperson. (In practice, we find that most people tend to give a little more.) Additional tips to other personnel, such as the head waiter or maitre d', are at your discretion. On small ships, all tips often go into one pot, which the crew divides up after the cruise.

Most ships charge extra for **alcoholic beverages** (including wine at dinner) and for soda. Nonbubbly soft drinks, such as lemonade and iced tea, are included in your cruise fare. (Regent's *Seven Seas Navigator* and Silversea's *Silver Shadow* both include alcoholic beverages in the cruise price.) You'll also want to set some money aside for optional offerings such as spa treatments, fancy dinners in your ship's alternative dining room (which may carry a price tag of up to $30 per person), shipboard photos, Internet access, and other temptations.

Money-Saving Strategies

Cruise pricing is a fluid medium, and there are a number of strategies you can use to save money on the booking price.

EARLY & LATE BOOKING

When you **book in advance,** in a typical year, you can expect to save 25% to 50% off the brochure rate if you book your Alaska cruise by mid- to late February of the year of the cruise. If the cabins do not fill up by the cutoff date, the early bird rate may be extended. We've seen starting early bird brochure prices for 2012 as low as $529 on Carnival and $459 on Norwegian Cruise Line. Princess, in April 2011, was selling 2012 Alaska cruises from $649, and cruise tours with 3 nights in Denali from $948.

If the cabins are still not full as the cruise season begins, cruise lines typically start marketing special deals, usually through their top-producing travel agents. These discounts ran as high as 50% to 75% in previous years, though not in 2011, as noted above, and may be sparse in 2012. And again, remember that last-minute deals are usually for a very limited number of cabins. Planning your Alaska cruise vacation well in advance and taking advantage of early booking discounts is still the best way to go.

SHOULDER SEASON DISCOUNTS

You can save by booking a cruise in the **shoulder months of May or September,** when cruise pricing is lower than during the high summer months. Typically, Alaska cruises are divided into budget, low, economy, value, standard, and peak seasons, but since these overlap quite a bit from cruise line to cruise line, we can lump them into three basic periods:

1. **Budget/Low/Economy Season:** May and September
2. **Value/Standard Season:** Early June and late August
3. **Peak Season:** Late June, July, and early to mid-August

DISCOUNTS FOR 3RD & 4TH PASSENGERS & GROUPS

Most ships offer highly discounted rates for third and fourth passengers sharing a cabin with two full-fare passengers, even if those two have booked at a discounted rate. It may mean a tight squeeze, but it'll save you a bundle. Some lines offer **special rates for kids,** usually on a seasonal or select-sailings basis, that may include free or discounted airfare. Norwegian Cruise Line, for one, was offering a kids' rate on Alaska cruises in 2010, from $199 (the rates apply only when kids share a cabin with two adults paying the regular fare).

One of the best ways to get a cruise deal is to book as a **group** of at least 16 people in at least eight cabins. The savings include a discounted rate, and at least the cruise portion of the 16th ticket will be free. Ask your travel agent about any group deals they may offer.

SPECIAL DISCOUNTS

Occasionally, cruise lines will do offers of two-for-one fares, free shore excursions, onboard spending credits (the cruise line gives you, say, $200 per person you can spend any way you please onboard), and offers of cabin upgrades. We can't predict which of these perks will reappear in 2012, or when. But keep an eye out, as they can amount to significant savings.

Booking Air Travel Through the Cruise Line

Except during special promotions, airfare to the port of embarkation is rarely included in the cruise rates, so you'll have to purchase airfare on your own or take advantage of the cruise lines' air add-ons, which is usually a better option. Why? First of all, as frequent customers of the airlines, cruise lines tend to get decent (if not the best) discounts on airfare, which they pass on to their customers. Second, booking air with the cruise line allows the line to keep track of your whereabouts. If your plane is late, for instance, they may hold the boat, though not always. When you book air travel with your cruise line, most lines will include **transfers** from the airport to the ship, saving you the hassle of getting a cab. (If you book the air travel on your own, you may still be able to get the transfers separately—ask your agent about this.) Be aware that once the air ticket is issued by the cruise line, you usually aren't allowed to make changes. It may pay to book your own air transportation if you are using frequent-flier miles and can get your air travel for free, or if you are particular about which carrier route you take. Or you may see a much better deal than the cruise line is offering.

Choosing Your Cabin

Cruise-ship cabins run from tiny boxes with accordion doors and bunk beds to palatial multiroom suites with hot tubs on the balcony. Which is right for you?

Price will likely be a big factor here, but so should the vacation style you prefer. If, for instance, you plan to spend a lot of quiet time in your cabin, you should probably consider booking the biggest room you can afford. If, conversely, you plan to be out on deck all the time checking out the glaciers and wildlife, you might be just as happy with a smaller (and cheaper) cabin to crash in at the end of the day. Cabins are either **inside** (without a window or porthole) or **outside** (with), the latter being more expensive. On the big ships, the more deluxe outside cabins may also come with **private verandas.** The cabins are usually described by price (highest to lowest), category (suite, deluxe, superior, standard, economy, and others), and furniture configuration ("sitting area with two lower beds," for example).

Special Menu Requests

The cruise line should be informed at the time you make your reservations about any special dietary requests you have. Some lines offer kosher menus, and all will have vegetarian, low-fat, low-salt, vegan, and sugar-free options available.

Smoking

Cruise lines have recently been reevaluating their smoking policies, and some, including Celebrity Cruises and Regent Seven Seas, have moved to ban smoking in cabins and on cabin balconies (Royal Caribbean and Disney Cruise Line do not allow smoking in cabins but do allow it on cabin balconies). Smoking is generally not allowed in shipboard theaters, show lounges, or dining rooms, and may be restricted to certain bars (many ships now have cigar lounges) or even certain sides of the ship (open decks on starboard side only on Royal Caribbean vessels, for instance). If you are a smoker, check with your line in advance. If you are not a smoker, you will no doubt be relieved policies are being enhanced.

THE SMALL-SHIP CRUISE LINES

Small ships allow you to see Alaska from sea level, without the kind of distractions you get aboard the big ships—no glitzy interiors, no big shows or loud music, no casinos, no spas, and no crowds, as the largest of these ships carries only 76 passengers. You're immersed in the 49th state from the minute you wake up to the minute you fall asleep, and, for the most part, you're left alone to form your own opinions. Personally, we feel that despite these ships' higher cost, they provide by far the better cruise experience for those who really want to get the feel of Alaska.

Small-ship itineraries can be categorized as **port-to-port,** meaning they mimic the larger ships in simply sailing between port towns; **soft adventure,** meaning they provide some outdoors experiences such as hiking and kayaking, while not requiring participants to be trained athletes; and **active adventure,** meaning the hiking and kayaking will be the real focus of the trip and may be strenuous.

On all of these types of cruises, the small-ship experience tends toward education rather than glitzy entertainment. You'll likely get **informal and informative lectures** and sometimes video presentations on Alaska wildlife, history, and Native culture. Meals are served in open seatings, so you can sit where and with whom you like, and time spent huddled on the outside decks scanning for whales fosters great camaraderie among passengers.

Cabins on these ships don't generally offer TVs or telephones, and they tend to be very small and sometimes spartan (see the individual reviews below for exceptions). There are no stabilizers on most of these smaller ships, so the ride can be bumpy in rough seas. In general, the small ships are not good choices for travelers who require the use of wheelchairs or have other mobility problems.

Note: All average prices listed below are **per night.** Multiply the per-night cost by the number of nights of the cruise for the estimated cost.

Alaskan Dream Cruises

P.O. Box 1049, Sitka, AK 99835. ✆ **855/747-8100.** Fax 907/747-4819. www.alaskandreamcruises. com.

Last year brought the debut of this small ship line, founded by the owner of Sitka-based Allen Marine Tours, owned by an Alaskan family with a long history in the boating business (including day tours and boatbuilding) in the state. The company is operating two small vessels on 7-night summer voyages out of Sitka. Both the 42-passenger *Alaskan Dream* and 78-passenger *Admiralty Dream* visit Glacier Bay National Park (for a full day), Tracy Arm, Hobart Bay, Frederick Sound, and several other landmark Southeastern Alaska locations, as well as Juneau. Hoping to fill the vacuum created by the collapse of Alaska cruise pioneer Cruise West in 2010, the line aims at the same sort of market as that company: vacationers looking for a more intimate, hands-on experience visiting Southeast Alaska than can be found traveling with one of the big ship lines. The *Admiralty Dream,* in fact, came from Cruise West (where it sailed as the *Spirit of Columbia*). Shore excursions are included in the cruise fare, as are wine and beer with dinner. Cabins come equipped with hair dryers, bathrobes, and flatscreen TVs (though reception is limited).

PASSENGER PROFILE At press time, the line was just starting up and Frommer's had yet to test out the new product, but *Alaskan Dream* is aiming at the soft-adventure market. The line is going for a friendly, casual "jeans and sweaters" ambience.

SHIPS The 42-passenger, 104-foot *Alaskan Dream* is the line's flagship, a streamlined catamaran that previously operated as the *Executive Explorer* for defunct Glacier Bay Cruiseline. The ship serves up cabins with extra-large viewing windows, twin beds that can be converted to a queen, and head-style bathrooms (the toilet and shower share a space with the sink in the main part of the cabin); and a forward-facing lounge and dining room. The 78-passenger, 148-foot *Admiralty Dream* was built in 1979 for American Canadian Caribbean Line and has a patented bow ramp, which basically allows the vessel to beach itself, disembarking passengers right onto shore in wild areas without ports. Cabins on *Admiralty Dream* are snug but comfortable, and there's a main dining room and a small lounge with a bar. On both ships, meals are open seating. The crew is all American.

American Safari Cruises

3826 18th Ave. W., Seattle, WA 98119. ✆ **888/862-8881.** Fax 206/283-9322. www.american safaricruises.com.

American Safari Cruises promises an intimate, all-inclusive cruise to some of the more out-of-the-way stretches of the Inside Passage—and it succeeds admirably. The price is considerable—but so is the pampering. The company's three small vessels carry between 12 and 36 guests, guaranteeing unparalleled flexibility, intimacy, and privacy. Once passenger interests become apparent, the expedition leader shapes the cruise around them. Black-bear aficionados can chug off in a Zodiac boat for a better look, active adventurers can explore the shoreline in one of the yacht's kayaks, and slacker travelers can relax aboard ship. A crew-to-passenger ratio of about one to two ensures that a cold drink, a good meal, or a sharp eagle-spotting eye is always nearby on the line's comfortable 120-foot ships. In 2012, the ships offer 7-night Discoverers' Glacier Bay itineraries and season-beginning and season-ending 14-night Inside Passage cruises as well. The core 7-night itinerary includes an unusual 2 full days in Glacier Bay National Park, in which passengers can hike on glaciers or in the rainforest with a park ranger, as well as stops in more off-the-beaten-path Alaskan areas such as Frederick Sound and Dawes Glacier.

PASSENGER PROFILE   Passengers, almost always couples, tend to be more than comfortably wealthy and range from 45 to 65 years of age. Most hope to get close to nature without sacrificing luxury. Dress is always casual, with comfort being the primary goal.

SHIPS   The line's newest ship, the 36-passenger *Safari Explorer,* entered service just in time for the 2008 cruise season, after a 10-month refurbishment costing $3.5 million. Add in the 22-passenger *Safari Quest* (1992) and the 12-passenger *Safari Spirit* (1991), and the fleet has three small-ship options for people looking to explore Alaska in a non–big ship environment that offers an unhurried, flexible adventure. Cabins are comfortable, and sitting rooms are intimate and luxurious, almost as if they were transported whole from a spacious suburban home. A big-screen TV in the main lounge forms a natural center for impromptu lectures during the day and movie-watching at night. A shipboard chef assails guests with multiple-course meals and clever snacks, barters with nearby fishing boats for the catch of the day, and raids local markets for the freshest fruits and vegetables—say, strawberries the size of a cub's paw and potent strains of basil and cilantro. **Sample nightly rates per person:** Lowest-price outside cabin from $699 for the 7-night cruises on *Safari Explorer;* no inside cabins or suites.

InnerSea Discoveries

3826 18th Ave. W., Seattle, WA 98119. ℰ **877/901-1009.** Fax 206/283-9322. www.innersea discoveries.com.

Looking for an off-the-beaten-path adventure in Alaska? That's what it's all about at InnerSea Discoveries, which debuted in 2011 and is back for a second year. The two-ship company focuses on getting adventure-minded vacationers into the most beautiful and wildlife-filled corners of Southeast Alaska's Inside Passage and is the brainchild of Dan Blanchard and Tim Jacox, who revolutionized luxury cruising in Alaska in 1997 with the launch of American Safari Cruises. This time around, the duo has aimed to offer a more affordable way for adventurers to explore the region. Operating as a sister brand to American Safari, InnerSea Discoveries costs less than half as much as its sibling, with pricing starting around $300 per person per day (American Safari trips often start at $850 per person, per day or more). The ships are a bit bigger than at American Safari, with room for 60 to 76 passengers, not everything is included in the price, and the crew-to-passenger ratio of about one to three is not quite as impressive. But in many ways, the concept is similar. By foregoing calls in Southeast Alaskan towns such as Skagway and Haines, InnerSea's ships will have more time to explore the many remote (and little-visited) bays, fjords, and glaciers of the region. The company says the voyages should appeal to adventurers who thrive on new experiences and want to push themselves physically, mentally, and emotionally.

PASSENGER PROFILE   The company draws a relatively young, outdoorsy type of customer—the kind of people who shop at outdoors store REI, says one manager. Most passengers will be in their mid-30s to mid-60s in age, with a smattering younger and older, and multigenerational families are expected to be a solid market, as the line won't have the age restrictions imposed at sister American Safari Cruises.

SHIPS   While the line is relatively new, its two ships aren't. In fact, the ships are quite familiar to some experienced Alaska cruisers. InnerSea Discoveries launched with the 76-passenger *Wilderness Discoverer* and the 60-passenger *Wilderness Adventurer*. Parent company American Safari acquired the vessels in 2009 from a bank that had held them since the bankruptcy of Glacier Bay Cruise Lines in 2006. The two ships, originally built for 80 and 66 passengers, respectively, have gone through a top-to-bottom overhaul over the past year. **Sample nightly rates per person:** Lowest-price outside cabin from $256 for a 7-night Inside Passage cruise on the *Wilderness Adventurer*.

Lindblad Expeditions

96 Morton St., 9th Floor, New York, NY 10014. ℰ **800/397-3348** or 212/765-7740. Fax 212/265-3770. www.expeditions.com.

Lindblad Expeditions specializes in environmentally sensitive, soft-adventure vacations that are explorative and informal in nature—what the company calls "respectful tourism." Its programs—operated since 2004 in partnership with the National Geographic Society—are designed to appeal to the intellectually curious traveler seeking a cruise that's ecologically friendly and educational, as well as being relaxing. Days aboard are spent learning about life above and below the sea (from National Geographic experts to high-caliber expedition leaders trained in botany, anthropology, biology, and geology), and observing the world either from the ship or during shore excursions, which are included in the cruise package. Educational films and slide presentations aboard ship precede nature hikes and quick jaunts aboard Zodiac boats. Flexibility and spontaneity are keys to the experience, as the route may be altered at any time to follow a pod of whales or school of dolphins.

The Alaska program of its two ships, the nearly identical 62-passenger *Sea Lion* and *Sea Bird,* includes 7-night cruises between Juneau and Sitka from May to August, and an 11-night cruise between Seattle and Juneau (including the San Juan Islands and British Columbia) in April and September.

PASSENGER PROFILE   Lindblad Expeditions tends to attract well-traveled and well-educated, professional, 55-and-older couples who have "been there, done that" and are looking for something completely different in a cruise experience—and who share a belief in the need to preserve the environment.

SHIPS   The 62-passenger *National Geographic Sea Lion* and *National Geographic Sea Bird* (built in 1981 and 1982, respectively) are nearly identical. Both are well-appointed vessels built to get you to beautiful spots and feature a minimum of public rooms and conveniences: one dining room, one bar/lounge, and lots of deck space for wildlife and glacier viewing. They have the added advantage of being accompanied throughout by historians, anthropologists, scientists, and other such specialist lecturers chosen by the National Geographic Society. Cabins are small and functional, but not inexpensive. **Sample nightly rates per person:** Lowest-price outside cabin $748 for 7-night cruises; no inside cabins or suites.

THE BIG-SHIP CRUISE LINES

The ships featured in this section vary in size, age, and offerings, but share the common thread of having more activities and entertainment options than any one person can possibly take in over the course of a cruise. You'll find swimming pools, health clubs, spas, nightclubs, movie theaters, shops, casinos, multiple restaurants, bars, special kids' playrooms, and, in some cases, sports decks, virtual golf, computer rooms, martini bars, and cigar clubs, as well as quiet spaces where you can get away from it all. Generally, you'll find lots and lots of onboard activities, including games, contests, classes, and lectures, plus a variety of entertainment options and show productions, some very sophisticated.

Note: All average prices listed below are **per night.** Multiply the per-night cost by the number of nights of the cruise for the estimated cost.

Carnival Cruise Lines

Carnival Place, 3655 NW 87th Ave., Miami, FL 33178. ✆ **800/CARNIVAL** (227-6482). Fax 305/471-4740. www.carnival.com.

Carnival is the ultimate fun-in-the-sun warm-weather line, and even in Alaska, the Caribbean-focused operator retains its "Fun Ship" philosophy. Sure, you'll be cruising past glaciers and on the lookout for whales, but you'll be doing it with people who like to take in the natural wonders with a multicolored party drink in hand. Drinking and R-rated comedians are part of the scene, as are "hairy-chest contests" and the like.

Entertainment is among the industry's best, with each ship boasting a dozen dancers, a 10-piece orchestra, comedians, jugglers, and numerous live bands, as well as a big casino. Activity is nonstop. Cocktails begin to flow early, and through the course of the day you can learn country line dancing or ballroom dancing; take cooking lessons; learn to play bridge; watch first-run movies; practice your golf swing by smashing balls into a net; or just eat, drink, shop, and then eat again. Alaska-specific naturalist lectures are delivered daily. In port, Carnival offers more than **120 shore excursions,** divided into categories of easy, moderate, and adventure. For kids, the line offers Camp Carnival, an expertly run children's program with activities that include Native arts and crafts sessions, lectures conducted by wildlife experts, and special shore excursions for teens.

Carnival's ship in Alaska cruises the Inside Passage route with round-trip departures out of Seattle.

PASSENGER PROFILE Overall, Carnival has some of the youngest demographics in the industry. But it's far more than age that defines the line's customers. Carnival executives are fond of using the word *spirited* to describe the typical Carnival passenger, and indeed the descriptor is right on target. The line's many fans increasingly come from a wide range of not just ages, but occupations, backgrounds, and income levels, but what they share is an unpretentious, fun-loving, and outgoing demeanor. On Carnival, you'll find couples, a few singles, and a good share of families, but the bottom line is, this is not your average sedentary, bird-watching crowd. Passengers want to see whales and icebergs, but they also want to dance the Macarena.

SHIPS   The 2,124-passenger megaship *Carnival Spirit* returns to Alaska in 2012. It offers plenty of activities, great pool and hot-tub spaces (some covered for use in chillier weather), a big ocean-view gym and spa, and more dining options than your doctor would say are advisable. **Sample nightly rates per person:** Lowest-price inside cabin $125, lowest outside cabin $161, lowest suite $261 for a 7-night Inside Passage cruise.

Celebrity Cruises

1050 Caribbean Way, Miami, FL 33132. (C) **800/437-3111** or 305/262-8322. Fax 800/437-5111. www.celebritycruises.com.

Celebrity Cruises offers a great combination: a classy, tasteful, and luxurious cruise experience at a moderate price—it's definitely the best in the midpriced category. The line's ships are real works of art; the cuisine is above the norm; the service first-class, friendly, and unobtrusive; and the spa facilities among the best in the business.

A typical day might offer bridge, darts, a culinary art demonstration, a fitness fashion show, an art auction, a volleyball tournament, and a not-too-shabby stage show. Resident experts give lectures on the various ports of call, the Alaskan environment, glaciers, and Alaskan culture. For children, Celebrity ships employ a group of counselors who direct and supervise a camp-style children's program. Activities are geared toward different age groups. There's a modest kids' play area and a lounge area for teens.

Celebrity, like sister company Royal Caribbean, visits the tiny port of Icy Strait Point between Juneau and Glacier Bay; the port offers a prime vantage point for whale- and wildlife-watching and easier access to the Alaskan wilderness. The company offers 7-night Inside Passage and 7-night Gulf of Alaska itineraries.

PASSENGER PROFILE   The typical Celebrity guest is one who prefers to pursue his or her R & R at a relatively relaxed pace, with a minimum of aggressively promoted group activities. The overall impression leans more toward sophistication and less to the kind of orgiastic Technicolor whoopee that you'll find, say, aboard a Carnival ship. You'll find everyone from kids to retirees.

SHIPS   Sleek, modern, and stunningly designed, the 1,814-passenger *Century* and the recently overhauled, 1,950-passenger *Infinity* and *Millennium* have a lot of open deck space and lots of large windows that provide access to the wide skies and the grand Alaskan vistas. All the ships (but especially *Century*) feature incredible spas with hydrotherapy pools, steam rooms, and saunas, plus health and beauty services and exceptionally large fitness areas. **Sample nightly rates per person:** Lowest-price inside cabin $128, lowest outside cabin $150, lowest suite $757 for a 7-night cruise.

Disney Cruise Line

P.O. Box 10210, Lake Buena Vista, FL 32830. (C) **800/951-3532.** Fax 407/566-3541. www. disneycruise.com.

When it comes to entertaining every member of a family—from the littlest children to parents and grandparents—no other cruise line has it down quite like

Disney. The 12-year-old operator has famously focused on catering as much to adults as kids, with a number of adults-only areas to balance an industry-leading array of kid's facilities and activities.

Entertainment, as one might expect from a movie-studio-owning company, is among the industry's best, with family oriented musicals featuring classic Disney characters. Dining, too, has a measure of Disney's trademark pixie dust, with an innovative system where passengers (along with their servers) rotate among three themed restaurants. And, of course, what other ship can boast Mickey, Donald, and the gang out and about to entertain passengers?

The summer of 2012 will mark the second year Disney has sent a ship to Alaska, the *Disney Wonder,* which will sail 7-night Inside Passage cruises out of Seattle (a switch from Vancouver, B.C.).

PASSENGER PROFILE Disney's ships attract a wide mix of passengers, from honeymooners to seniors, but as at the company's famous theme parks, the largest percentage is made up of young American families with children. Because of this, the average age of passengers tends to be younger than aboard many of the other mainstream ships, with many passengers in their 30s and 40s. The bulk of the line's passengers are first-time cruisers, and because the line attracts so many families, more than half of its bookings are for multiple cabins.

SHIPS The 1,754-passenger *Disney Wonder* is the line's sole ship in Alaska in 2012. It offers plenty of activities, great pools (including one shaped like Mickey Mouse's head), and the most family friendly cabins at sea (in addition to being larger than the industry average, all rooms come with pullout sofas or pull-down beds that allow, in many cases, for up to five people). **Sample nightly rates per person:** Lowest-price inside cabin $117, lowest outside cabin $193, lowest suite $407 for a 7-night Inside Passage cruise.

Holland America Line

300 Elliott Ave. W., Seattle, WA 98119. ✆ **800/426-0327** or 206/281-3535. Fax 206/286-7110. www.hollandamerica.com.

Holland America Line (HAL) can be summed up in one word: *tradition.* The company was formed way back in 1873 as the Netherlands-America Steamship Company, and its ships today strive to present an aura of history and dignity, like a European hotel where they never let rock stars register. Thanks to its acquisition over the years of numerous land-based tour operators, Holland America also has positioned itself as Alaska's most experienced and comprehensive cruise company. The company has seven ships in the Alaska market in 2012.

Though most of HAL's Alaskan fleet is relatively young, the ships are designed with a decidedly "classic" feel—no flashing neon lights here. Similarly, Holland America's ships are heavy on more mature, less frenetic kinds of activities. You'll find good bridge programs and music to dance (or just listen) to in the bars and lounges, plus health spas and the other amenities found on most large ships. Service is excellent, delivered by a crew mostly trained at the line's own schools in Indonesia and the Philippines. The line has improved its nightly show-lounge entertainment, adding magicians, comedians, and the like. Alaska Native guides are onboard most Glacier Bay–bound ships, offering their local insight. With fewer kids on these ships than some of the other mainstream lines, the Club HAL children's playrooms are small, but the program is nonetheless big on creative activities. A recently launched "as you wish" dining program allows guests to choose either a set time or anytime dining for dinner. Alaska itineraries include 7-night Inside Passage cruises and 7-night Gulf of Alaska cruises.

PASSENGER PROFILE   Holland America's passenger profile used to reflect a much older crowd. Now the average age is dropping, thanks to an increased emphasis on its Club HAL program for children and some updating of onboard entertainment. Still, HAL's passengers in Alaska include a large percentage of middle-age-and-up vacationers.

SHIPS   The 1,260-passenger *Statendam* boasts cabins with sitting areas and lots of closet and drawer space, and even the least expensive inside cabins run almost 190 square feet, quite large by industry standards. Outside doubles have either picture windows or verandas. The striking dining rooms, two-tiered showrooms, and Crow's Nest forward bar/lounges are among these ships' best features. The somewhat newer 1,432-passenger *Volendam* and *Zaandam,* the 1,350-passenger *Veendam,* and 1,380-passenger *Amsterdam,* are larger and fancier, with triple-decked oval atriums, nearly 200 suites, and deluxe staterooms with private verandas, five showrooms and lounges, and an alternative restaurant designed as an artist's bistro, featuring drawings and etchings. The smallest cabin is a comfortable 190 square feet. The *Zuiderdam* and *Westerdam,* two of the newest vessels in the fleet, weigh 82,300 tons and carry 1,916 passengers. These are sophisticated, spacious, yet intimate ships well equipped to support HAL's position as a force in the Alaska market. **Sample nightly rates per person:** Lowest-price inside cabin $118, lowest outside cabin $147, lowest suite $333 for a 7-night cruise.

Norwegian Cruise Line

7665 Corporate Center Dr., Miami, FL 33126. ℂ **866/234-7350** or 305/436-4000. Fax 305/436-4120. www.ncl.com.

Very contemporary Norwegian Cruise Line (NCL) offers an informal and upbeat onboard atmosphere on two large ships, the **Norwegian Pearl** and the **Norwegian Jewel,** both sailing from Seattle. The line excels at activities, and its recreational and fitness programs are among the best in the industry. NCL recently launched a food upgrade program—the best food is at venues where you pay an extra fee—and has what has become a very popular "freestyle" casual dining policy that allows passengers to have dinner pretty much whenever they want, with whomever they want, dressed however they want.

In Alaska, NCL offers an Alaskan lecturer, wine tastings, art auctions, cooking demonstrations, craft and dance classes, an incentive fitness program, and bingo, among other activities. Passengers can choose from a good selection of soft-adventure shore excursions, including hiking, biking, and kayaking. Entertainment is generally strong and includes Vegas-style musical productions. The top-notch kids' program includes an activity room, video games, an ice-cream bar, and guaranteed babysitting aboard, plus sessions with park rangers and escorted shore excursions. The line offers 7-night Inside Passage cruises.

PASSENGER PROFILE   In Alaska, the demographic tends more toward retirees than on the line's warmer-climate sailings, but you'll find families as well, including grandparents bringing along the grandkids.

SHIPS   One of the first ships built with NCL's trademark "freestyle" cruising in mind, the 2,376-passenger **Norwegian Jewel** has more than a dozen places where people can eat—depending on the time of day. The *Jewel* also is well equipped for the sports-minded and active vacationer—in addition to the fitness center, there are three heated pools, a jogging/walking track, and a wide array of sports facilities. The 2,394-passenger **Norwegian Pearl** is the line's newest ship in Alaska and has the most bells and whistles (including one of the only bowling alleys at sea!), providing a fun and lively Alaska cruise experience. **Sample nightly rates per person:** Lowest-price inside cabin $107, lowest outside cabin $128, lowest suite from $214 for a 7-night cruise.

Princess Cruises

24305 Town Center Dr., Santa Clarita, CA 91355. (✆ **800/PRINCESS** (774-6237) or 661/753-0000. Fax 661/753-1535. www.princess.com.

Aboard Princess, you get a lot of bang for your buck, attractively packaged and well executed. Although its ships serve every corner of the globe, nowhere is the Princess presence more visible than in Alaska, where it will have seven ships in 2012—the same as sister line Holland America. Through its affiliate, Princess Tours, it owns wilderness lodges, motorcoaches, and railcars in the 49th state, making it one of the major players in the Alaska cruise market, alongside Holland America.

Princess passengers can expect enough onboard activities to keep them going morning to night, if they've a mind to, and enough nooks and crannies to allow them to do absolutely nothing if that's their thing. Kids are well taken care of, with especially large children's playrooms. On shore, the line's shore excursion staff gets big points for efficiency. Passengers have the option of eating dinner at a set time (early and late seating) or dining in the "anytime dining" room, at any time.

Princess offers the standard 7-night Inside Passage cruises and 7-night Gulf of Alaska cruises, as well as 10-night Inside Passage cruises from San Francisco.

PASSENGER PROFILE   Typical Princess passengers are likely to be between 50 and 65. They are experienced cruisers who know what they want and are prepared to pay for it. Recent additional emphasis on its youth and children's facilities has begun to attract a bigger share of the family market.

SHIPS   Princess's diverse fleet in Alaska comprises seven ships, six of which are new since the millennium. The fleet includes the *Diamond* and *Sapphire,* which were completed in 2004; the *Coral* and *Island,* of 2003 vintage; and the *Golden* and *Star,* built in 2001 and 2002, respectively. The *Sea Princess,* which was built in 1998 and served in the British P&O Cruises fleet until joining Princess after a major refit in 2005, rounds out the company's Alaska lineup for 2012. The ships generally are pretty but not stunning, bright but not gaudy, spacious but not overwhelmingly so, and decorated in a comfortable, restrained style that's a combination of classic and modern. They're a great choice when you want a step up from Carnival, Royal Caribbean, and NCL but aren't interested in the slightly more chic ambience of Celebrity, or the luxury of Regent Seven Seas. **Sample nightly rates per person:** lowest-price inside cabin $109, lowest outside cabin $139, lowest suite $185 for a 7-night cruise.

Regent Seven Seas Cruises

1000 Corporate Dr., Ste. 500, Fort Lauderdale, FL 33334. (✆ **800/285-1835.** www.rssc.com.

Regent's guests travel in style and extreme comfort. Its brand of luxury is casually elegant and subtle, its cuisine among the best in the industry. That goes for the

Seven Seas Navigator, which is sailing in Alaska this year for a second season. The line assumes for the most part that passengers want to entertain themselves onboard, so organized activities are limited, but they do include lectures by local experts, well-known authors, and the like, plus facilities for card and board games, blackjack and Ping-Pong tournaments, bingo, big-screen movies with popcorn, and instruction in the fine arts of pompon making, juggling, and such. Bridge instructors are onboard on select sailings. The line has a no-tipping policy and offers creative shore excursions. Room service is about the best you'll find on any ship, and the cuisine is excellent. Regent recently switched to a fleetwide liquor-inclusive policy on all departures. This year, *Seven Seas Navigator* will sail primarily a 7-night Gulf of Alaska itinerary between late May and August, with two interesting 12-day itineraries between San Francisco and Vancouver, B.C., at the beginning and end of the season.

PASSENGER PROFILE Regent tends to attract passengers in their 40s to 60s who have a household income of more than $200,000 and don't like to flaunt their wealth. The typical passenger is well educated, well traveled, and inquisitive.

SHIPS Cabins on the 490-passenger *Seven Seas Navigator* are all ocean-view suites, all but a handful of which have private verandas. The standard suite is a roomy 301 square feet; some suites can interconnect if you want to book two for additional space. The Seven Seas Lounge is a comfortable, two-tiered showroom in which, despite the space limitations imposed by the ship's small size, succeeds in presenting a high level of cabaret, Broadway revue, classical music, and comedian/magic shows. Elsewhere on the ship, Star's Lounge offers dancing to the music of a DJ, from which the less hectic piano bar, Galileo's, is a welcome alternative. The Connoisseur Club is a cushy venue for predinner drinks and after-dinner fine brandy and cigars, and a smallish casino allows guests to indulge their taste for blackjack, roulette, stud poker, craps, and slot machines. The ship's Carita Paris spa, while not as extensive as those of its larger Alaska rivals, is nevertheless well equipped to provide a variety of services using a variety of herbal and water-based therapies. **Sample nightly rates per person:** Per diems for the lowest-priced suites start at $614 for the 7-night cruise.

Royal Caribbean International

1050 Caribbean Way, Miami, FL 33132. ℰ **866/562-7625.** www.royalcaribbean.com.

Royal Caribbean sells a mass-market style of cruising that's reasonably priced and offered aboard informal, well-run ships with nearly every diversion imaginable—craft classes, horse racing, bingo, shuffleboard, deck games, line-dancing lessons, wine-and-cheese tastings, cooking demonstrations, art auctions, and the like—plus elaborate health clubs and spas; covered swimming pools; large, open sun deck areas; and innumerable bars, lounges, and other entertainment centers. The Viking Crown Lounge and other glassed-in areas make excellent observation rooms from which to see the Alaska sights. Royal Caribbean spends big bucks on entertainment, which includes high-tech show productions. Headliners are often featured. Port lectures are offered on topics such as Alaska wildlife, and the line offers dozens of adventurous shore excursions. The line's children's activities are some of the most extensive afloat. The line offers 7-night Sawyer Glacier and Gulf of Alaska cruises.

PASSENGER PROFILE   The crowd on Royal Caribbean ships, like the decor, rates pretty high on the party scale, though not quite at the Carnival level. Passengers represent an age mix from 30 to 60, and a good number of families are attracted by the line's well-established and fine-tuned kids' programs (the line's ships are a particularly good bet for tweens and teens, who love such trademark Royal Caribbean desktop offerings as climbing walls and miniature golf).

SHIPS   Royal Caribbean owns the largest ships in the world, including the much-ballyhooed, 225,282-ton *Oasis of the Seas,* which set a new record for size when it debuted in December 2009. Although this groundbreaking 5,400-passenger ship—which includes such innovative design features as an open-air Central Park with live trees, an outdoor AquaTheater for water shows, and onboard zip-lining—is not in Alaska this year, Royal Caribbean does offer the very up-to-date 90,000-ton, 2,112-passenger *Radiance of the Seas,* sailing Gulf of Alaska cruises between Vancouver, B.C., and Seward. Also returning to Alaska in 2012 is the older (1997) but still up-to-date 1,998-passenger *Rhapsody of the Seas,* a Vision-class ship cruising out of Seattle. **Sample nightly rates per person:** Lowest-price inside cabin on the Radiance $78; lowest outside cabin $157; lowest suite $264 for a 7-night cruise.

Silversea

110 E. Broward Blvd., Fort Lauderdale, FL 33301. ℭ **800/722-9955.** www.silversea.com.

Silversea is one of the most luxurious—and pricey—cruise lines in the business, and it's known for exquisite service, gourmet cuisine, and spacious and elegant all-suite accommodations. The line offers an impressive enrichment program with naturalists, well-known authors, and even celebrity chefs mingling with passengers nightly. A cooking school program allows for cooking lessons at sea. Entertainment is more low-key than on the big ship lines, but the passengers seem to enjoy the cabaret-type acts. The company offers niceties including free alcohol and a fine selection of complimentary wines at lunch and dinner—and probably at breakfast as well, if you're really interested. A friend of Fran's is fond of telling about the time he ordered a late-night hot dog from room service and it came elaborately presented on a silver tray. For Alaska, the line offers 7- to 10-night Gulf of Alaska cruises between Vancouver and Seward, Alaska.

PASSENGER PROFILE   Look for the 60-something set, well heeled, well educated, and knowing what to look for when they lay out the kind of money it takes to get a place on one of this company's ships.

SHIPS   While Silversea has a growing fleet of six ships, it sends just one to Alaska, the 382-passenger *Silver Shadow.* There are no rock-climbing facilities, but there are two alternative restaurants, one of which doubles as the breakfast and lunch buffet room, and there's a small casino. There is no children's program; it's not a ship for kids. **Sample nightly rates per person:** Least expensive suite is $508 for a 7-night cruise.

The Big-Ship Cruise Lines

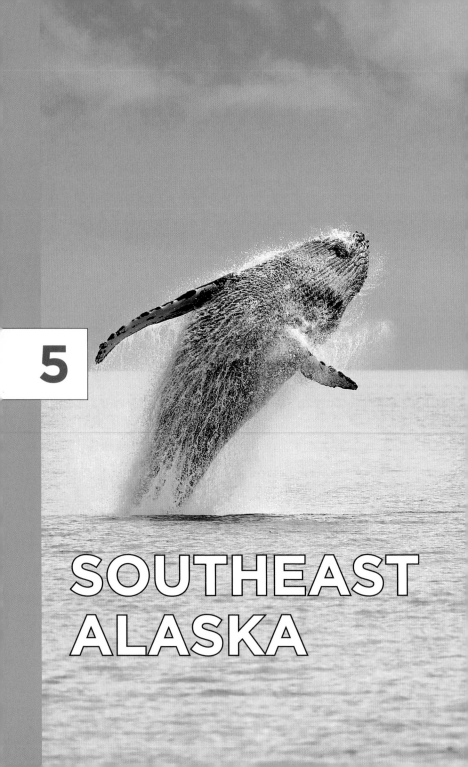

5

SOUTHEAST
ALASKA

n sharp contrast to Alaska's mythical image of a land of ice and snow, Southeast Alaska has—at least, since the Little Ice age 10,000 years ago—provided a veritable bounty for the Native tribes inhabiting it. The thousands of square miles of the Tongass National Forest are spread among mountainous stretches of the "mainland" and hundreds of islands, some larger than several Eastern states.

The rainforest itself is a dense wilderness that has only been slightly touched by the large-scale logging that took place in the latter half of the 20th century. It also remains the untouched, living forest that nurtured the Tlingit and Haida tribes over the last several millennia in which everything has living spirits and must be treated with respect and ceremony to ensure its continued bounty.

The greatest of the ceremonies have always been the "potlatches" in which the Natives showed how favored they were by giving away what they had themselves received. The potlatches not only reinforced the "communal" life of the Natives, but were also a strong showing of their belief in the future and that it would bring them more than they had given up.

The Native presence remains strong in Southeast Alaska. The bounty from the sea helped create strong, wealthy tribes, and nowhere is that more apparent than in the art created by the Tlingit, Haida, and Tsimshian tribes. Even the most utilitarian items were turned into works of art that continue to be treasured by collectors worldwide. The totem poles and long houses were spectacular community creations, and the tribal subsets, called *moeties,* were honored with beautiful masks, beadwork, and blankets.

Although Southeast Alaska has been "settled" longer than many other parts of the state, it still remains "unknown" compared to many parts of the United States. As visitors travel from town to town, they understand how the communities are "islands" in the greater wilderness, and they imagine if they were to step ashore on an isolated island or wander up into the dark woods, they could indeed be the first human being to do so. The islands themselves have mountains soaring up to 5,000 feet above sea level. When you add the density of the forest and the lack of roads, they just might be right.

The lack of roads in Southeast Alaska also creates some challenges in traversing the region. To get from Ketchikan to Juneau, for instance, you have two options, boat or plane. The airports are small, the flights are short, and the Alaska Airlines 737s are filled with local folks commuting from town to town for meetings, school events, and shopping. For those with more time, the Alaska Marine Highway System is used instead of Greyhound or Amtrak. When you ride the ferries, or "Blue Canoes," as they are affectionately called, you will find yourself sharing a ride with everyone from the governor to loggers and fishermen lugging their gear to the next job. The informal chats you will have with your shipmates will teach you more about Alaska than a library of guidebooks.

Introduction

FACING PAGE: **Humpback whale breaching in Frederick Sound.**

EXPLORING SOUTHEAST ALASKA

A unique and inviting aspect of travel in Southeast Alaska is that no roads connect most of the communities. People are forced to get out of their speeding cars and ride on boats, where they can meet their fellow travelers and see what's passing by—slowly. The islands of the region form a protected waterway called the **Inside Passage,** along which almost all of the region's towns are arrayed. Thanks to the **Alaska Marine Highway** ferry system, it's not too expensive to travel the entire passage, hopping from town to town and spending as much time in each place as you like. And if you're short on time, air service is frequent, with jets to the major towns and commuter planes to the villages.

Getting Around by Ferry: The Alaska Marine Highway

The state-run **Alaska Marine Highway System** (*©* **800/642-0066** or 907/465-3941; www.ferryalaska.com) is a subsidized fleet of big, blue-hulled ferries connecting many of Alaska's roadless coastal towns. The system mostly serves Southeast Alaska, though it does cover most of coastal Alaska, with a sailing or two a month (the *Kennicott*) connecting Southeast Alaska with the Southcentral region near Anchorage. The smaller Southcentral ferries link communities all the way out to the Aleutian chain (see chapters 7 and 10).

In the Southeast, the large, mainline ferries serve the Inside Passage. Some begin their run in British Columbia's Prince Rupert and travel about 30 hours north to Haines and Skagway. Less frequent sailings start in Bellingham, Washington, travel 37 hours nonstop to Ketchikan, then continue up to Skagway and Haines. In the summer, the large ships stop approximately daily (although sometimes in the middle of the night) in Ketchikan, Wrangell, Petersburg, Juneau, Sitka, Gustavus, Haines, and Skagway.

Getting up close to a humpback whale on Admiralty Island.

View of the landscape approaching Cordova.

The **Alaska Marine Highway** (www.ferryalaska.com) has an easy online booking system; just be sure to make vehicle and cabin reservations as early as possible. Vehicle space frequently sells out on popular routes and is expensive, so consider renting a car at your destination. If you need to talk to a real person for advice or to change reservations, the system has a toll-free number (✆ **800/642-0066**); the reservation center operates Monday through Friday 7am to 5pm. If you find yourself waiting on the state's reservation system, one way around it is to call **Viking Travel,** in Petersburg (✆ **800/327-2571** or 907/772-3818; www.alaskaferry.com), which will accept your booking before the official reservation system opens, then reserve it the first day the system becomes available; likewise, if your preferred date is booked, they'll monitor the system for cancellations to get a spot for you. They can also take care of all your air and tour connections, lodgings, activities, travel insurance, and so on.

Ferry travel is relatively comfortable. Amenities vary by boat, but each of the mainline ferries has staterooms, a cafeteria, bar, gift shop, solarium, observation lounge, and (often) a children's play area, game room, or movie theater. Passengers without cabins bring sleeping bags and enjoy the lounge chairs on the covered outdoor solarium on the top deck or the comfy chairs in the recliner lounge, or simply crash on the floors in a quiet corner of the ship. Blankets and pillows are available for rent from the purser, and the spacious common bathrooms have showers.

Getting Around by Air & Road

BY AIR Air travel is the primary link between Southeast's towns and the rest of the world. Several towns without road access have jet service provided by **Alaska Airlines** (✆ **800/252-7522;** www.alaskaair.com), the region's only major airline. Juneau is Southeast Alaska's travel hub. Ketchikan and Sitka each have a few flights a day, while Wrangell, Petersburg, and Yakutat each have one flight going each direction daily. Gustavus is served from Juneau once daily during the summer. Haines and Skagway, which have highway connections, don't receive visits from jets, but all the towns and even the tiny villages have scheduled prop service.

BY ROAD   Three Southeast Alaska communities are accessible by road: Haines, Skagway, and the village of Hyder, which lies on the British Columbia border east of Ketchikan and is accessible from the gravel Cassiar Highway through Canada. If you're driving the Alaska Highway, passing through Haines and Skagway adds 160 miles of very scenic driving to the trip, as well as a 15-mile ferry ride between the two towns (they're separated by 362 road miles). You also can rent a car from Haines or Skagway for travel to the rest of the state at the end of a ferry journey (Haines saves just 60 miles over Skagway). If you're driving the highway in winter, you should be prepared for weather as cold as 40°F below zero (–40°C). Alaska winter driving information is under "Health & Safety" in chapter 11.

Getting Outside in the Tongass National Forest

Nearly all of Southeast Alaska, stretching 500 miles from Ketchikan to Yakutat, is in Tongass National Forest. The towns sit in small pockets of private land surrounded by 17 million acres of land controlled by the U.S. Forest Service—an area nearly as large as the state of Maine, and considerably larger than any other national forest or national park in the United States. The majority of this land has never been logged, and the rate of logging has dropped dramatically in recent years, preserving one of the world's great temperate rainforests in its virgin state. It's an intact ecosystem full of wildlife, and mostly free of human development. Indeed, you quickly forget it *is* the Tongass National Forest. Since it always surrounds you when you're in this region, it's simply the land.

FOREST SERVICE CABINS

One of the best ways to get into the Southeast's wilderness is by staying at one of the scores of remote Forest Service Public Recreation Cabins. These are simple cabins without electricity or running water where you can lay your sleeping bag on a bunk and sit by a warm woodstove out of the rain. You need to bring everything with you, as if camping, but it's a good deal more comfortable than a tent. Do your research, pack carefully (take all the essentials, but little more), and spend at least 3 nights to make all the effort pay off with real relaxation.

GETTING CABIN INFORMATION   For complete information on cabins, check the Tongass website (**www.fs.fed.us/r10/tongass**) or contact the visitor centers and ranger offices listed with each town section in this chapter. The main contact point for recreation information for the whole forest is the **Southeast Alaska Discovery Center,** 50 Main St., Ketchikan, AK 99901 (© **907/228-6220**).

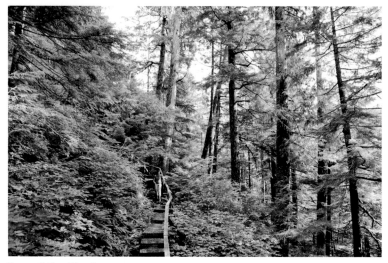
Tongass National Forest.

You'll need a good map to figure out where the cabins are, and an idea of how to get there and how much travel will cost—generally, the cost of transportation will be many times larger than the cabin rental fee of $25 to $45 a night. Few cabins can be reached without a boat or aircraft, and for all but large groups, flying is the most economical way to go. A flight service can help you choose a cabin according to your interests and how far you can afford to fly.

RESERVING A CABIN OR CAMPSITE   The cabins and some campgrounds are reserved through a national system. When you're ready to book, the easiest way is to use **www.recreation.gov**, where you can check availability dates at various places. By telephone, contact the **National Recreation Reservations Service** at ✆ **877/444-6777** or 518/885-3639.

KETCHIKAN: ON THE WATERFRONT

Not so long ago, Ketchikan was a rugged and exotic intersection of cultures built on the profits of logging Southeast's rainforest, but in 15 years, it has transformed itself into a tourist center, softening its rough edges while selling their charm to visitors. Southeast Alaska's last major timber mill—the Louisiana Pacific pulp plant in Ward Cove, north of town—closed in 1997 due in part to environmental concerns.

On summer days, the white cruise ships tower above the town like huge new buildings on the dock facing Front Street, the downtown's main drag. Each morning their gangways disgorge thousands of visitors, clogging the streets and for a few hours transforming the town into a teeming carnival. On their short visits, the passengers explore the closest of the twisting streets, see the museum at the Southeast Alaska Discovery Center, or take a tour to one of the totem pole

Ketchikan

HOTELS
Best Western Landing **1**
Cape Fox Lodge **11**
Captain's Quarters **4**
Ketchikan Youth Hostel **6**
New York Hotel **14**

RESTAURANTS
Bar Harbor Restaurant **2**
Burger Queen **5**
Diaz Café **15**
Halibut Hole **9**
Ocean View Restaurant **3**

ATTRACTIONS
Cape Fox Hill–Creek Street
Funicular **10**
City Park **18**
Creek Street Boardwalk **12**
Deer Mountain Tribal Hatchery &
Eagle Center **16**
Dolly's House **13**
Southeast Alaska Discovery Center **7**
Tongass Historical Museum **8**
Totem Heritage Center **17**

Downtown Ketchikan

see inset
at left

1/4 mi
1/4 km

TONGASS
NATIONAL
FOREST

Tongass Narrows

Pennock I.

Bar Harbor

Thomas
Basin

Ketchikan Cr.

Ketchikan
Visitors Bureau

Cruise Ship Docks

parks. Then evening comes, the streets empty, and the cruise ships slide off quietly on the way to their next port.

Then a sense of the old, misty, mysterious Ketchikan starts to return. Visitors with a little more time to spend, and the willingness to explore beyond the core tourist areas, can drink in the history and atmosphere of the place. Stay in a quaint old hotel, enjoy some fresh fish, hike a boardwalk path through the primeval rainforest, and visit the museums, clan house replicas, and totem pole parks that make Ketchikan a center of Tlingit and Haida culture.

Ketchikan also makes a great jumping-off point for some spectacular outdoor experiences, including a trip to **Misty Fjords National Monument** (p. 110). As the state's fourth-largest city, Ketchikan is the transportation hub for the southern portion of Southeast Alaska. (The nicknames "Gateway City" and "First City" refer to its geographical location and transportation function.) Seaplanes based on docks along the waterfront are the taxis of the region, and a big interagency visitor center can get you started on your explorations of the area. Ketchikan is one of the wettest spots on Earth, with rain measured in the hundreds of inches; quality rain gear is requisite for any activity, in the wilds or in the streets of town.

Essentials

GETTING THERE

BY AIR   **Alaska Airlines** (✆ 800/252-7522; www.alaskaair.com) jet service connects Ketchikan south to Seattle nonstop and north to Petersburg, Wrangell, Sitka, Juneau, and Anchorage. Commuter lines run wheeled planes and floatplanes from Ketchikan to the neighboring communities, and also offer fishing packages and flightseeing.

The airport is on Gravina Island, to which there is no bridge. A ferry runs each way every half-hour (more frequently at peak times). Believe the airline when it tells you when to catch the ferry for your plane. The fare, payable in cash only, is $5 for adults, $2 ages 6 to 12, and free 5 and under. Returning the same day is free. The fare for cars is $6 each way, no matter how soon you come back. Carts are available to move your luggage onto the boat. See "Getting Around," below, for how to get from the airport ferry dock to town and for a water taxi right from the airport (a fun option).

BY FERRY   The dock is 2½ miles north of downtown. **Alaska Marine Highway** ferries (✆ 800/642-0066; www.ferryalaska.com) run 6 hours north to Wrangell and 6 hours south to Prince Rupert, B.C. The walk-on fare from Prince Rupert is $54, from Wrangell $37. Call the local terminal at ✆ **907/ 225-6182** or 225-6181 for a recording of updated arrival and departure times.

ORIENTATION

Ketchikan is on huge **Revillagigedo Island,** popularly known as **Revilla Island.** The downtown area, pretty much taken over by tourism, is quite compact and walkable, but the whole of Ketchikan, including a second commercial area used by locals, is long, strung out between the Tongass Narrows and the mountains. A waterfront road goes under various names through town—Front Street, Water Street, Tongass Avenue—becoming North Tongass Highway as it stretches about 16 miles to the north. Saxman is 2½ miles to the south of downtown on the 14-mile South Tongass Highway.

GETTING AROUND

You can spend a day seeing the downtown sights on foot, but you will need transportation to get to the totem pole parks or airport.

BY TAXI The local taxis, mostly minivans, are convenient and usually easy to flag down on the single main road through town. Try **Sourdough Cab** (© **907/225-5544**). **Alaska Cab** (© **907/225-2133**) is another taxi company in Ketchikan. Taking a cab to the airport terminal is costly because of time that runs up on the meter waiting for and riding the ferry to Gravina Island. A better choice is to take the cab to the ferry and then walk on, using a cart to move your luggage on the ferry. On the far side, you will have to go up a long walkway to the airport terminal.

BY WATER TAXI Only in Ketchikan could you take a boat from the airport to your hotel. **Tongass Water Taxi** (© **907/225-8294**) also happens to be reasonably priced and quick. The six-passenger boat runs back and forth from near the airport ferry dock to downtown all day. The first person is $19 and each additional person $8. It also crosses the same route as the airport ferry (without going on to downtown) for $8. Several hotels are right on the water, so the water taxi can take you almost to your door. The operator holds up a sign in the baggage claim area to meet arriving flights, or you can call to arrange a pick-up.

BY BUS The least costly way to the airport or ferry dock is the **Ketchikan Gateway Borough bus** (© **907/225-8726**). To get downtown or points south from the airport costs $1. Buses come every half-hour. Your luggage must fit under the seat. A free shuttle bus runs seasonally in the downtown area, connecting all the attractions in that area three times an hour. The loop goes from cruise-ship Berth 4 to the Totem Heritage Center, stopping at the Discovery Center and library.

BY RENTAL CAR **Alaska Car Rental** (© **800/662-0007** or 907/225-5000; www.akcarrental.com) has offices at the airport or in town, and delivers vehicles to customers.

VISITOR INFORMATION

The **Southeast Alaska Discovery Center,** 50 Main St., Ketchikan, AK 99901 (© **907/228-6220;** www.fs.fed.us/r10/tongass, scroll down for the link), is much more than a visitor center. Housed in a large, attractive building of big timbers and cedar, and located a block from the cruise-ship dock, the center is the best museum in the region when it comes to illustrating the interaction of the region's ecology and human society, including both traditional Native and contemporary uses. An auditorium shows a selection of films. Admission to these facilities in summer costs $5, free ages 15 and under, with a $15 family maximum; in winter it's free. Without paying, you can get guidance about planning your time and activities in the outdoors. An information kiosk is located near the entrance, and downstairs you'll find a luxurious bookstore decorated like an explorer's private den with room to relax. The center is open May through September daily from 8am to 5pm, October through April Thursday through Sunday 10am to 4pm.

The **Ketchikan Visitors Bureau,** 131 Front St., Ketchikan, AK 99901 (© **800/770-3300** or 907/225-6166; fax 907/225-4250; www.visit-ketchikan. com), has two offices on the docks. The main office on downtown cruise-ship Berth 2 offers town information and booths where tourism businesses sell their

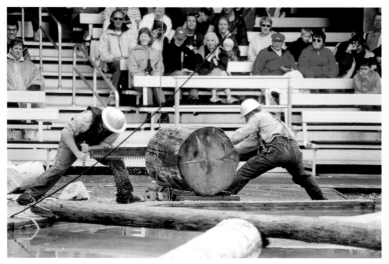

The Great Alaskan Lumberjack Show.

wares, including tickets for tours. A satellite is located on Berth 3, just north of the downtown tunnel, where you'll find a large public restroom. The bureau is open daily in the summer from 8am to 5pm and when cruise ships are in town; weekdays only in winter.

Special Events

There's a detailed events calendar at www.visit-ketchikan.com.

A variety of events are put on all year by the Ketchikan Area Arts and Humanities Council, 330 Main St. (℃ **907/225-2211;** www.ketchikanarts. org). The **Blueberry Arts Festival,** held the first weekend of August, has booths, music, and food. If visiting during the colder months, the council has much more going on. The **Monthly Grind** coffeehouse variety show happens in the Saxman Tribal House every third Saturday from September to May. The **Torch Night Performing Series** brings in well-known musicians. And the **Festival of the North** brings art to Ketchikan audiences for the entire month of February, including theater, ballet, live music, poetry readings, and a wearable art show the first weekend of the month that is a highlight of the winter.

Summer events include the **King Salmon Derby,** a 60-year-old tradition, which takes place at the end of May and the beginning of June. The **Fourth of July** celebration is huge, with a long parade on Front Street attended by mobs of locals and visitors. Don't miss the legendary **pie sale** at St. John's Church at 423 Mission St., where a slice, ice cream, and beverage is $5. Fireworks are at 11pm on Gravina Island, best viewed from the cruise-ship dock. Twice weekly through July, the **First City Players** (℃ **907/225-4792;** www.firstcityplayers.org) perform the melodrama *Fish Pirate's Daughter,* as they have for more than 40 years, and serve a crab feed at the Civic Center.

The crowd-pleasing **Great Alaskan Lumberjack Show** goes on all summer near the cruise-ship pier and Alaska Discovery Center (℃ **907/225-9050;** www. lumberjacksports.com). Canadian and U.S. professional teams of lumberjacks compete three or more times daily, mostly for an audience of cruise-ship passengers. The show is charming and intentionally a little goofy. The setting is attractive and comfortable. Tickets are $35 adults, $18 ages 3 to 12.

[FastFACTS] KETCHIKAN

Banks A bank with an ATM is at 306 Main St.; grocery stores and the visitor center also have ATMs.

Hospital Ketchikan General Hospital is at 3100 Tongass Ave. (*© 907/225-5171*).

Internet Access SeaPort Cyberstations

(*© 907/247-4615;* www. seaportel.com) is at the ship dock on the second floor at 5 Salmon Landing. The public library at 629 Dock has two free guest terminals with a 15-minute limit.

Police Call *© 907/225-6631* for nonemergencies.

Post Office There's a post office at 3609 Tongass Ave.; a more convenient downtown substation is 2 blocks from the cruise-ship dock at 422 Mission St.

Taxes Sales tax is 6% within city limits, 2.5% outside. Room taxes add another 7% to each sales tax.

Exploring Ketchikan

Pick up a copy of the **Official Historic Ketchikan Walking Tour Map,** available all over town, which has three routes to follow and loads of information about sites of both great and modest interest on the way. The town also maintains handy directional signs and maps at intersections all over the downtown area.

Many motorized tours of the town vie for customers, getting the majority of their clients from the cruise ships, but welcoming independent travelers when space is available. Tickets are for sale at the visitor center on the dock. Besides riding a tour bus through town, you can go into the woods in a Hummer or on a motorcycle, or even drive from the streets into the harbor in an amphibious vehicle. That one, painted bright yellow and called the **Duck** (*© 866/341-DUCK* [3825] or 907/225-9899; www.akduck.com), is a favorite of kids. It costs $38 adults and $24 children, and lasts 90 minutes.

Ketchikan's longest-established tour guide caters only to five visitors at a time—not ships full of clients. Schoolteacher Lois Munch, of **Classic Tours** (*© 907/225-3091;* www.classictours.com), has a fun personality and creative concept: She drives visitors around in her '55 Chevy, often wearing a poodle skirt. A 2-hour tour to the Saxman totem poles is $109; a 3-hour tour adds a natural history stop and costs $139. Rates are per person and include the admission to Saxman.

TLINGITS, HAIDA & TSIMSHIANS CULTURAL HERITAGE

The Ketchikan area has two totem pole parks and a totem pole museum, as well as a wealth of contemporary Native art displayed all over town. Notable pieces stand at Whale Park at Mission and Bawden streets and at the Cape Fox Lodge. Most of what you see in Southeast Alaska is Tlingits—the Haida and Tsimshians generally live to the south and east in British Columbia—but Ketchikan is near the boundary between the three peoples' areas, so their similar cultures mix here.

Totem Bight State Historical Park ★★★   The park presents poles and a clan house carved, beginning in 1938, by Natives working with traditional tools to copy fragments of historic poles that had mostly rotted away. The project, funded by the New Deal's Civilian Conservation Corps, helped save a Tlingits and Haida culture that had been essentially outlawed until that time. The setting, purportedly the site of a traditional fishing camp, is a peaceful spot on the edge of Tongass Narrows, at the end of a short walk through the woods, so the experience is both aesthetic and educational. The park also stands out for its excellent interpretive signs, a printed guide, and an interpretive website. There's a small park bookstore.

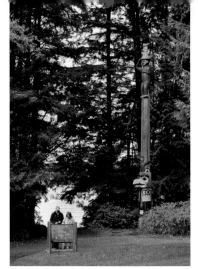

Totem Bight State Historical Park.

10 miles out of town on N. Tongass Hwy. Ketchikan Area State Park Office, 9883 N. Tongass Hwy. ✆ **907/247-8574.** www.alaskastateparks.org (click on "Individual Parks"). Free admission. Park always open.

Totem Heritage Center ★★   Located near City Park, the center contains the largest collection of original 19th-century totem poles in existence. The poles, up to 160 years old, are displayed indoors, mostly unpainted, many with the grass and moss still attached from when they were rescued from the elements in villages. Totem poles were never meant to be maintained or repainted—they generally disintegrate after about 70 years and were constantly replaced—but these were preserved to help keep the culture alive. A high ceiling and muted lighting highlight the spirituality of the art. The museum also shows changing exhibits by contemporary masters of Tlingits art. Well-trained guides are on hand to explain what you're looking at, and there are good interpretive signs.

601 Deermount St. ✆ **907/225-5900.** Admission $5 in summer, free in winter. Summer daily 8am–5pm; winter Mon–Fri 1–5pm.

Saxman Native Village Totem Pole Park ★   Saxman's park has artifacts similar to those at Totem Bight park, but with an added attraction: You can see carvers at work in the building to the right of the park, including Nathan Jackson, perhaps Alaska's greatest contemporary artist, who has even been honored by a postage stamp. Cape Fox Corp. hosts visitors at the park, catering mainly to cruise-ship passengers with its 2-hour tour, which includes entry to the clan house and a demonstration of traditional dance and song by the Cape Fox Dancers. The tour schedule is different each day, depending on the ships. Buy tour tickets in the gift store on the right as you enter the park. If you're not interested in the tour and just want to see the poles, Totem Bight is a better stop—it has a more inspiring location and better interpretive materials. On the other hand, the carving studio at Saxman is remarkable, and you can sneak in there on your own without the tour by paying the $3 park fee.

Ketchikan is overrun with as many as 10,000 cruise-ship passengers daily May through September, far more than the small visitor attractions or even the streets can comfortably handle. Independent travelers can avoid the crush by planning to visit popular spots in the afternoon. Spend the morning on an outdoors activity instead. Ships usually leave the town in early evening. If you can plan your itinerary around this issue, Saturday is usually the quietest day in Ketchikan. Check out cruise-ship schedules for the whole year at www.claalaska.com, the website for Cruise Line Agencies of Alaska.

In Saxman, 2½ miles south of Ketchikan on the S. Tongass Hwy. ℂ **907/225-4846** for tour times and tickets, ext. 100 for general information. www.capefoxtours.com. Tour $35 adults, $18 children 12 and under; unguided visits $3. Park always open. No tours Oct–Apr.

DOWNTOWN ATTRACTIONS

Ketchikan's best downtown attractions are all within walking distance of one another. See Creek Street, then walk up Park Avenue past the Ketchikan Creek fish ladder and up to lovely **City Park,** site of the Totem Heritage Center, described above. The park is among our favorite places in Ketchikan. The creek splits into a maze of ornamental pools and streams once used as a hatchery, with footbridges, a fountain, and large trees with creeping roots.

The **Creek Street** boardwalk starts at the Stedman Street bridge, running over the tidal creek. It was Ketchikan's red-light district until not that long ago; now it's a quaint tourist mall. Prostitution was semilegal in Alaska until 1952, recent enough to survive in local memories but distant enough to have made Creek Street historic and to transform the women who worked there from outcasts to icons. Dolly Arthur, who started in business for herself on the creek in 1919 and died in 1975, lived through both eras, and her home became a commercial museum not long after her death. **Dolly's House** (ℂ **907/225-6329**) is amusing, mildly racy, and a little sad. Admission is $5; it's open from 8am to 4pm during the summer and when cruise ships are in town.

Creek Street has some interesting shops, described below, but it's also fun just to walk on the creek-side boardwalk, into the forest above, and over the "Married Men's Trail"—once a discreet way for married men to reach the red-light district. The **Cape Fox Hill–Creek Street Funicular** (known as "the tram"), a sort of diagonal elevator, runs 211 feet from the boardwalk up to the Cape Fox Lodge on top of the hill. Take it up and then

Creek Street boardwalk.

enjoy the walk down through the woods. The summertime fare is $2, but if no one is around, just press the "up" button and go.

Deer Mountain Tribal Hatchery & Eagle Center ★★   This remarkable nonprofit center combines one of Alaska's best hatchery tours and a great place to see a bald eagle close up. The wooden buildings stand over Ketchikan Creek. You can see fish climbing against the current up into pools where they are sorted before being cut open to complete their biological purpose (salmon die when they spawn anyway). The hatchery tours are special for letting you get so close, right in the action, where you can feed the growing salmon fry yourself. The hatchery produces king and silver salmon and steelhead trout. Visitors can also walk right through the eagle enclosure. Remarkably, the resident pair of injured, flightless bald eagles have mated for life and built a nest where they lay eggs each year. They hunt salmon swimming naturally through their enclosure. No glass stands between you and this activity, only a few feet away.

1158 Salmon Rd. 📞 **800/252-5158** or 907/228-5530. Admission $12, ages 12 and under free. May–Sept daily 8am–4:30pm; winter by arrangement.

Tongass Historical Museum   This one-room museum is where Ketchikan talks back to itself, with well-executed revolving exhibits that have always held my interest. A small permanent area shows Native artifacts. In the same building, the attractive Ketchikan Public Library is a great place to recharge, especially in the children's section downstairs, where big windows look out on Ketchikan Creek's falls.

629 Dock St. 📞 **907/225-5600.** Admission $2 summer; free winter. Summer daily 8am–5pm; winter Wed–Fri 1–5pm, Sat 10am–4pm, Sun 1–4pm.

Shopping

The Ketchikan art scene is one of Alaska's liveliest, thanks in part to the Ketchikan Arts and Humanities Council, whose helpful staff operates the **Main Street Gallery,** at 330 Main St. (www.ketchikanarts.org). Shows change monthly.

Scanlon Gallery in Ketchikan.

Starting from Main and turning toward the mountains on Mission, here's a walk to take you to the best locally owned galleries in Ketchikan. Your first stop is for treats. **Orca Corn,** 305 Mission, has sweets and kettle corn. **Ketchicandies** is at 315 Mission, with handmade chocolates. Across the street, **Scanlon's Gallery,** 318 Mission, is the city's oldest gallery, carrying crafts and fine arts. Continue on to 605 Mission for the charming **Forget-Me-Not Sweater Shop,** which carries imported woolens from around the world, and then head next door to 607 Mission to **Crazy Wolf Studio,** where Tsimshians artist Ken Decker shows his work.

Join the pedestrian boardwalk of Creek Street. Our favorite stops are in the building at 5 Creek St., where Alaska's leading fish-obsessed artist, Ray Troll, has his small gallery, **Soho Coho.** It's worth a visit even if you aren't a shopper. The gallery shows Troll's own work and that of other Ketchikan artists from the same school of surreal rainforest humor. The gallery is open summer daily from 9am to 6pm, winter Wednesday through Saturday from noon to 5:30pm; you can also order at ℭ **800/888-4070.** Upstairs in the same building, **Parnassus Books** is a crowded browsers' paradise with a broad range of books, including many on local themes. Continuing down Creek Street, you'll find many other busy shops of varying levels of quality. Don't miss Norman Jackson's **Carver on the Creek** gallery, at 28 Creek St.

Creek Street meets Stedman at the Stedman Street Bridge. Turn left. **Ketchikan Dry Goods,** 219 Stedman, has handmade silver and beadwork jewelry and gift items, much of it made by local people. **Chinook and Company,** 307 Stedman, carries smoked salmon and Pacific Northwest clothing.

Note: Ketchikan is a shopping and art destination, but if you want something authentically Alaskan, you have to be careful. For some important tips, see "Native Art: Finding the Real Thing," in chapter 2.

Getting Outside

There's a lot to do outdoors around Ketchikan, but most of it will require a boat or plane; drive-by attractions are limited. In any event, your first stop should be the trip-planning room at the Southeast Alaska Discovery Center (see "Visitor Information," near the beginning of the Ketchikan section) for details on trails, fishing, and dozens of U.S. Forest Service cabins.

BEAR VIEWING   Salmon returning to a fish hatchery on a creek south of town have long attracted black bears. A local business, **Alaska Rainforest Sanctuary** (ℭ **877/847-7557;** www.alaskarainforest.com), takes advantage of the viewing opportunity by hosting visitors on well-made trails with guides. A tour also includes captive reindeer and an owl and bald eagle, as well as a Native carving demonstration. It's a good variety of experiences, and the tour is the right length. Most guests come from cruise ships, affecting times, so call to check for availability and scheduling. The price is $79 for adults, $50 children 12 and under. You may be able to watch the same bears from public property for free, without a guide. Drive about 10 miles south of town, beyond Saxman on the South Tongass Highway, to the Herring Cove Bridge. From here you have a viewpoint of the same estuary owned by the sanctuary and just as good a chance of seeing black bears. Bears may be present June through September, and sightings are most likely in July and August.

For more of a wilderness experience, Ketchikan is a good place to get on a floatplane, soar over water and wooded islands, and land where bears are gathering at streams where the salmon are running. Depending on where the bears are and the flight service you choose, it costs $329 to $495 per person. **Promech Air** (☎ **800/860-3845** or 907/225-3845; www.promechair.com) and **Island Wings Air Service** (☎ **888/854-2444** or 907/225-2444; www.islandwings.com) offer this service; both are described in "Majestic Misty Fjords," p. 110.

CABIN TRIPS　The U.S. Forest Service maintains more than 50 **cabins** around Ketchikan; all are remote and primitive, but at $25 to $45 a night, you can't beat the price or the settings. This is a chance to be utterly alone in the wilderness; many of the lake cabins come with a boat for fishing and exploring. For details and descriptions of all the cabins, contact the **Southeast Alaska Discovery Center** (☎ **907/228-6220**; www.fs.fed.us/r10/tongass, scroll down for link). The reservations system to use when you're actually ready to book a cabin is described in "Getting Outside in the Tongass National Forest," on p. 94.

If you stay in a cabin, you'll need all your camping gear except a tent, including sleeping bags, a camp stove, your own cooking outfit and food, a lantern, and so on. The easy way to handle this is to contact **Alaska Wilderness Outfitting and Camping Rentals,** 3857 Fairview St. (☎ **907/225-7335;** www.latitude56.com/camping), which has been supplying cabin trips for more than 15 years. They rent almost everything you need, including small outboards and life jackets for the skiffs, and deliver directly to the air taxi or water taxi.

The cabins are remote. You can hike or take a boat to some of them, but most are accessible only by floatplane (and unless you have loads of stuff, flying is probably the cheapest way to go). Expect to pay around $1,000 to $1,500 round-trip for three to five passengers. Some cabins at tidewater can be reached more economically by water taxi (see "Sea Kayaking," below). Obviously, the logistics makes sense only if you will stay for a while—we never go for less than 3 nights. For recommended air carriers, see "Majestic Misty Fjords," p. 110.

FISHING　The **Alaska Department of Fish and Game** produces a 24-page fishing guide to Ketchikan with details on where to find fish in both freshwater and saltwater, including a list of 17 fishing spots accessible from the roads. Get it from the local office of the **Alaska Department of Fish and Game,** 2030 Sea Level Dr., Ste. 205, Ketchikan, AK 99901 (☎ **907/225-2859**), or download from www.alaska.gov/adfg (click "Sport Fish," then the Southeast region on the map). More fishing ideas are under "Hiking," below, and "Cabin Trips," above. As is generally true in Southeast Alaska, most fishing takes place from boats in saltwater, for which you need a guided charter. **Ketchikan Charter Boats** (☎ **800/272-7291** or 907/225-7291; www.ketchikancharterboats.com) has a lot of experience in these waters. You can also find links to charter companies on the Visitor Bureau's website (www.visit-ketchikan.com), or contact them for a referral. The going rate for a daylong charter for salmon or halibut is around $300 per person, half-day about $150.

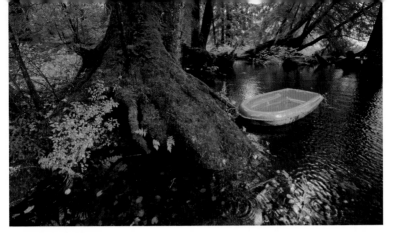
Ward Lake Recreation Area.

HIKING Eight miles out the North Tongass Highway, the **Ward Lake Recreation Area** covers a lovely patch of rainforest, lake, and stream habitat and has a picnic area, several trails, and campgrounds. Ward Creek has steelhead and cutthroat trout, Dolly Varden char, and silver salmon; check current regulations before fishing. The wide, gravel **Ward Lake Nature Trail** circles the placid lake for 1.3 miles among old-growth Sitka spruce large enough to put you in your place. For a more challenging hike, the newly refurbished **Perseverance Lake Trail** climbs through forest from the Three Cs Campground, across the road from Ward Lake, to a lake 2.3 miles away that can be reached no other way. There's a good bit of climbing to get there, but the trail is extraordinarily well maintained, without mud even in wet weather. To reach the recreation area, turn right off the highway on Revilla Road and follow the signs.

Deer Mountain Trail, right behind downtown, is a steep but rewarding climb through big, mossy trees up to great views. You can walk from City Park to the trail head, .5 mile and 500 feet higher on steep Fair Street and Ketchikan Lakes Road, but if you take a cab, you will save energy for the trail. The first mile rises 1,000 feet to a great ocean view south of Tongass Narrows, and the next mile and 1,000 feet to another great view, this time of Ketchikan. The alpine summit, at 3,000 feet, comes near the 3-mile mark. A public shelter (first come, first served) is a bit farther, and the trail continues to another trail head 10 miles away. Pick up a trail guide from the Forest Service at the Southeast Alaska Discovery Center (p. 99).

SEA KAYAKING The islands, coves, and channels around Ketchikan create protected waters rich with life and welcoming for exploration by kayak. **Southeast Sea Kayaks** (✆ **800/287-1607** or 907/225-1258; www.kayakketchikan. com) rents kayaks, provides transportation to remote areas, and guides day trips and overnights. They offer a number of half-day, full-day, and overnight tours starting at $89 per person and going as high as $1,600 per person for 5 days in Misty Fjords. A 2½-hour paddle is $89 adults, $59 children 15 and younger; kids need to be at least 6 to go along. The shop is a mile from the cruise ship dock at 1621 Tongass Ave.

ZIP-LINE TOURS The sport of zooming through the tree tops in a harness attached to a cable has become a popular visitor attraction in Southeast

5

SOUTHEAST ALASKA

Ketchikan: On the Waterfront

Alaska Canopy Adventures zip-line tour.

Alaska, but no more so than in Ketchikan, where there are three choices. **Southeast Exposure** (☎ **907/225-8829;** www.southeastexposure.com) offers the **Rainforest Ropes and Zipline,** which is like a giant jungle gym, with eight spans, suspended logs, and rope bridges. It happens at regular morning sessions, costs $99, and is only for ages 11 and older. The same folks who offer the Alaska Rainforest Sanctuary bear-viewing experience, described above, have a family-oriented zip line at that site, with a mountain slide, and a more challenging setup at the end of an all-terrain-vehicle ride. The tours each cost $179 and last 3½ hours for participants at least 70 pounds and 50 inches tall only. Book with **Alaska Canopy Adventures** (☎ **907/225-5503;** www.alaskacanopy.com).

Where to Stay

In addition to the hotels and B&Bs listed below, the **Ketchikan Reservation Service,** 412 D-1 Loop Rd., Ketchikan, AK 99901 (www.ketchikan-lodging.com; ☎ **800/987-5337** or ☎/fax 907/247-5337), books many bed-and-breakfasts and outfitted apartments, and has online availability and reservations. **Alaska Travelers Accommodations LLC** (www.alaskatravelers.com; ☎ **800/928-3308** or 907/247-7117) is a Ketchikan-based service of long standing that handles lodgings here and in Juneau.

Here are a couple of single-unit rentals in pleasant residential settings that we can recommend, each with cooking facilities: **Soaring Eagle Vacation Rental** (www.vrbo.com/162011; ☎ **907/247-1710**), a luxurious, new suite for $135 double; and **Stormy Seas Bed & Breakfast** (www.stormyseasbb.com; ☎ **907/617-1997**), a great choice for a small family, in a lovely location, for only $98 double.

EXPENSIVE

Best Western Landing ★★   This hotel offers rooms in bright colors with granite bathroom counters. Some have 9-foot ceilings and big, opening windows. Rooms are equipped with high-quality beds, cherry-wood furniture, and the latest technology. Service is warm and efficient, and the entire place is kept immaculately. The location, right across from the ferry dock, is distant from the downtown sights, so you'll need to rent a car or use the courtesy van that the hotel offers.

The **Landing Restaurant,** a fountain and grill with lots of chrome, is a local favorite and very kid-friendly. Food is consistently good year after year. Try the fresh halibut sandwich or Salisbury steak with real mashed potatoes. Lunch and dinner range from $7.25 to $25. You can order from that same steak-and-seafood menu upstairs, at **Jeremiah's** bar, which also serves sandwiches, pizza, and good pasta in a sumptuous room.

3434 Tongass Ave., Ketchikan, AK 99901. www.landinghotel.com. ✆ **800/428-8304** or 907/225-5166. Fax 907/225-6900. 107 units. High season $205–$255 double, $235–$255 suite; low season $145–$155 double, $165–$193 suite. AE, DC, DISC, MC, V. **Amenities:** 2 restaurants; bar; exercise room; room service. *In room:* TV, fridge, hair dryer, microwave, Wi-Fi.

Cape Fox Lodge ★★ This is Alaska's most beautiful hotel. It stands on a wooded pinnacle above downtown, reached from Creek Street by a funicular. The sheer drop-off and tall rainforest trees create the lofty feeling of a treehouse in the rooms and restaurant. Warm wood frames complement the stunning views out of the double-hung windows. The Cape Fox Native corporation built the hotel, and the lobby and parking area are a museum of Tlingits art masterpieces, adding to the peace and rainforest spirit. Rooms are large and airy, and all but a dozen share a view of Ketchikan and the sea and islands beyond (rooms on the opposite side are $10 less). Each room has an attractively tiled bathroom. The hotel and furniture are showing a little age, but the place is well kept. There's a good coffee shop off the lobby.

The **Heen Kahidi** restaurant has one of Alaska's most attractive dining rooms, a tall, narrow rectangle of windows with a fireplace. The furniture is notably attractive and comfortable. The setting is worth going for a meal. The food is generally quite good, worth paying prices that are higher than other choices in town. Lunch ranges from $9 to $24; dinner main courses range from $20 to $60, with most around $30. The dining room is open daily from 7am to 9pm.

800 Venetia Way, Ketchikan, AK 99901. www.westcoasthotels.com. ✆ **800/325-4000** or 907/225-8001. Fax 907/225-8286. 72 units. High season $209–$229 double, $300 suite; low season $99–$109 double, $229 suite. AE, DC, DISC, MC, V. **Amenities:** Restaurant; bar; room service. *In room:* TV w/pay movies and Nintendo rental, hair dryer, Wi-Fi.

MODERATE

Black Bear Inn ★★★ 🛏 This is a luxury inn on a large waterfront lot with extensive gardens and a trail to a private beach. The main building shows the owners' attention to detail and exquisite taste—wood floors, exceptional tile, fireplaces, the best fabrics, leather furniture, Alaskan art originals, satellite TV and radio, and so on. Each of the five units has its own covered porch, and there is a large outdoor hot tub and barbecue area, shielded from the wind and with space heaters. A cabin in a refurbished cannery building overlooks the water, with walls of whitewashed red cedar and floors of slate and porcelain. Breakfasts are self-served from a shared guest kitchen; a suite and the cabin have their own cooking facilities. The location is near the ferry terminal and airport, 4 miles north of downtown.

5528 N. Tongass Hwy., Ketchikan, AK 99901. www.stayinalaska.com. ✆ **907/225-4343.** 6 units. $160–$185 double; $215–$225 suite; $190–$200 cabin. Lower prices in winter. Extra person $25. Rates include self-serve breakfast from stocked kitchen. AE, MC, V. Children by arrangement only. **Amenities:** Hot tub; fish-cleaning and freezing facilities. *In room:* TV/DVD, fridge, gas fireplace, Wi-Fi.

MAJESTIC MISTY fjords

In Punchbowl Cove, south of Ketchikan in Misty Fjords National Monument, sheer cliffs rise 3,150 feet straight up from calm water, as high and smooth as those in the Yosemite Valley. Misty is more than twice Yosemite's size, but there isn't a single car here; there isn't so much as a mile of road—in fact, there are hardly any trails. It's something like a great national park before the people arrived.

The experience at Misty is pure geology. You go for the scenery.

Two companies currently offer boat tours to Misty's Punchbowl Cove, Rudyerd Bay, and back, and both offer meals in the price. Sitka-based **Allen Marine** (𝄞 **877/686-8100** or 907/225-8100; www.allenmarinetours.com) has some distinct advantages. The fast, quiet boat makes the round-trip in 4½ hours. All seats face forward. A knowledgeable naturalist interprets the scenery. Adult passengers can peruse regional books while children work with craft boxes and activities. Tickets are $159 adults, $109 children ages 3 to 12; 2 and under sail for free. Sailings every day in the summer coordinate with the cruise ships' dockings. A Misty Fjords tour operated by **Alaska Travel Adventures,** doing business as Alaska Cruises (𝄞 **800/323-5757;**

www.bestofalaskatravel.com), offers the opportunity to see the fjords from above by floatplane and return to Ketchikan by water for $329 adult, $289 child; taking the boat both ways is $159 adult and $106 child.

We prefer seeing the fjords on an extended floatplane flight (and we certainly recommend it for those susceptible to seasickness). Flying over the scenery is amazing, but it's the floatplane landing that really blows your mind, because then you get a sudden sense of the scale of everything you've seen from the air. The cliffs are magnified while you shrink to a speck. Go in the late afternoon, when the light is pretty and the swarms of planes carrying cruise-ship passengers are gone. Several air-taxi operators in Ketchikan take flightseeing day trips to Misty Fjords or drop clients at remote cabins.

The Narrows Inn ★ The motel buildings sit above the water, where fishing charters and floatplanes collect guests for outings. The rooms are quite small, but fresh, immaculate, and nicely decorated, with wallpaper borders. The bathrooms are large. Rooms with balconies rent for $10 more. The location is 4 miles from downtown; they have a shuttle that takes guests to the airport, ferry terminal, and sites within city limits. For flexibility, however, you may want to rent a car if staying here.

A solid kitchen staff and good service at the **Narrows Inn Restaurant** (𝄞 **907/247-5901**) make this dining room a favorite with local families, serving consistently excellent meals. Try the crab cakes. Breakfasts are generous, well prepared, and reasonably priced. The comfortable seating has a water view.

4871 N. Tongass Hwy. (P.O. Box 8296), Ketchikan, AK 99901. www.narrowsinn.com. 𝄞 **888/686-2600** or 907/247-2600. Fax 907/247-2602. 47 units. High season $140–$170 double, $230–$245 suite; low season $109–$115 double, $160–$185 suite. Extra person $10. AE, DC, DISC, MC, V. **Amenities:** Restaurant; bar; free airport transfers; courtesy shuttle; marina. *In room:* TV, fridge, hair dryer, microwave, Wi-Fi.

commentary about the fjords. We soared with Van Morrison while Michelle told us about her favorite places down below. The landing was as long as anyone needed to soak in the awesome surroundings. It felt like an outing with old friends. Masden charges $239 for a seat on a six-passenger DeHavilland Beaver for a 2-hour flight that includes 45 minutes on the ground at the fjords. She also flies guests to Forest Service cabins (many of them in Misty), places she knows intimately, and she will take the time to help you choose one that suits your interests and budget. Take a look at her informative website for a good start.

Promech Air (✆ **800/860-3845** or 907/225-3845; www.promechair.com) is a large one with many years' experience, charging about $200 for a 75-minute flight, including about 10 minutes on the water.

We prefer a smaller company, **Island Wings Air Service** (✆ **888/854-2444** or 907/225-2444; www.islandwings.com). The owner and pilot is Michelle Masden, and our flight with her was among the most memorable of the many we've taken around Alaska. She flew with a choice of music on the iPod as background to her impromptu

Visiting the fjords by kayak is a real expedition, advisable only for those who already know they enjoy this mode of travel, but we can think of few more spectacular places to paddle. **Southeast Exposure** (✆ **907/225-8829;** www.southeastexposure.com) offers guided paddles there, and has for 20 years, earning a good reputation. Their 4-day trip is $850 per person.

INEXPENSIVE

Captain's Quarters Bed & Breakfast ★ ✦   These big, spotless rooms with sweeping views of the city and ocean are a remarkable value. Those who prefer hotels to B&Bs will be happy saving here as well, as the self-serve breakfast setup allows as much privacy as you want. A charming nautical theme carries through the building. One room has a full kitchen. The house is perched in a mountainside neighborhood just north of the tunnel, where half the streets are stairs or wooden ramps. It's a significant but doable walk from downtown.

325 Lund St., Ketchikan, AK 99901. www.captainsquartersbb.com. ✆ **907/225-4912.** 3 units. High season $105–$115 double; low season $69–$85 double. Extra person $15. Rates include continental breakfast. MC, V. *In room:* TV, hair dryer.

New York Hotel/The Inn at Creek Street ★ ★ ✦   The same family operates two sets of lodgings in the center of the most historic area, offering the best value in town. The original portion is the hotel, a funny little 1924 building with a tiny lobby and charming, antique-furnished rooms. Four rooms look out on a small boat harbor, while four others, with less street noise, face the garden. None

Ketchikan: On the Waterfront

is large, but all are a good value and are constantly upgraded and refreshed. The newer part of the business, the inn, consists of seven spacious, modern individual suites above the shops on the Creek Street boardwalk. These units are downright luxurious, with kitchens, excellent amenities, and great privacy, and they sit on pilings over the flowing creek. The hotel offers a courtesy van to the airport, ferries, and hiking trails. Note that those who have trouble with stairs shouldn't consider either of these properties.

The **Ketchikan Coffee Company,** in a storefront in the hotel (✆ **907/225-2326**), is one of the town's best places to eat breakfast or lunch: inexpensive, hip, and friendly. They offer healthy, delicious food, including many vegetarian choices, such as the black bean burrito, hummus plate, or terrific soups. It's a small, bright dining room with historically appropriate furniture, including a long mahogany bar where guests order; occasional long lines to order and noisy crowds are the only downside of the restaurant.

207 Stedman St., Ketchikan, AK 99901. www.thenewyorkhotel.com. ✆ **866/225-0246** or 907/225-0246. Fax 907/225-1803. 14 units. High season $149–$169 double, $199–$219 suite; low season $89–$99 double, $119–$139 suite. AE, DISC, MC, V. **Amenities:** Restaurant; free airport transfers. *In room:* TV, hair dryer, Wi-Fi.

A HOSTEL & CAMPING

Three Forest Service campgrounds with a total of 47 sites are located at **Ward Lake.** A salmon stream runs through the middle of the lakeside Signal Creek Campground, which, along with the Last Chance Campground, can be reserved through the national system described in "Getting Outside in the Tongass National Forest," on p. 94. The camping fee at either place is $10.

Eighteen miles out North Tongass Highway, the **Settler's Cove State Park** includes a sandy beach (a good place to watch whales, beachcomb, or even swim), an accessible path to a spectacular waterfall, and a short coastal trail. There are 14 campsites, half of which will take rigs of up to 30 feet, without hookups. Camping costs $10 a night. For information, contact the **Alaska Division of Parks,** 9883 N. Tongass Hwy. (✆ **907/247-8574**).

If you need hookups for an RV, try **Clover Pass Resort,** about 15 miles north of the ferry terminal on North Point Higgins Road (www.cloverpassresort.com; ✆ **800/410-2234** or 907/247-2234). They charge $34 to $39 a night.

Ketchikan Hostel This hostel, downtown in the First United Methodist Church, has room for 19 guests in pleasant male and female dorms and allows guests use of the church kitchen, although the hostel is independent of the church. Bring a sleeping bag or rent bedding from the hostel. It is open only June through August; office hours are from 7 to 9am and 6 to 11pm. Reserve ahead to assure a bunk.

400 Main St. (P.O. Box 8515), Ketchikan, AK 99901. ✆ **907/225-3319.** $20 per person. Closed Sept–May.

Where to Eat

Besides these restaurants, see the Best Western Landing, Narrows Inn, Cape Fox Lodge, and New York Hotel, all above, for other choices that are among the best in town.

There are several good stops for light meals or snacks. The Smith family's **Alaskan Surf Fish and Chips** booth comes back to the dock every summer, to the delight of locals and cruise-ship crew members who line up at lunchtime.

The fish is halibut with beer batter, and they also serve shrimp and great clam chowder. Picnic tables are handy for seating on a sunny day. **Halibut Hole,** 7 Creek St., on the deck of the Eagles Club (✆ **907/225-5162**), serves some of the best fried fish in town, including halibut, salmon, clams, and shrimp in crispy batter, with fries and hush puppies. It's open daily 11am to 4pm in the summer and accepts cash only.

Annabelle's Famous Keg and Chowder House ★ SEAFOOD   This restaurant is on the main street, across from the cruise-ship dock, in a historic concrete building. The decor in the dining room interprets the building's past with brass, dark wood, and plush patterned fabrics; the tin ceiling is original. Fast, friendly servers bring terrific sandwiches and salads, including the standout halibut BLT. The seafood chowder is the specialty, and you can have it in a bowl made of bread that is baked in-house. In the evening, the menu includes various seafood specials. You can order the same menu in the large, festive, and sometimes smoky bar next door.

326 Front St. ✆ **907/225-6009.** Lunch $10–$17; dinner main courses $10–$30. AE, DC, DISC, MC, V. High season Mon–Thurs 10am–10pm, Fri–Sat 10am–11pm; low season Mon–Thurs 11am–9pm, Fri–Sat 10am–10pm.

Burger Queen 🍴 AMERICAN   Restaurants with the word *burger* in the name don't often get full write-ups in travel guidebooks, and this place looks unlikely for special treatment as well. But Debbie and Shawn Rahr have turned their four-table restaurant into a Ketchikan institution by doing simple food right. You certainly won't go wrong ordering a burger and milkshake here, but also consider the grilled chicken (teriyaki or barbecue), the cornmeal-breaded halibut, or the Oriental grilled chicken salad. The portions are big enough for two. Since the dining room is so small, having your meal delivered for no extra charge makes sense, or get takeout and eat in the park across the street.

518 Water St. ✆ **907/225-6060.** Lunch and dinner $6–$17. MC, V. High season Mon–Sat 11am–7pm; low season Wed–Sat 11am–3pm.

Diaz Cafe ★ 🍴 FILIPINO   In Ketchikan, the heartbeat of the Filipino community has been in this bright little diner since the early 1950s, as ownership passed from generation to generation in the same family. The place is so well loved among all in Ketchikan that its current owner is unable to change the slightest detail, so everything remains today as it was half a century ago: the Formica, worn from wiping, and the yellow and red walls. If you haven't had Filipino food, this is the place to try it. The spicy chicken adobo—a huge, delicious half-chicken bathed in gravy with rice—is $12. The sweet-and-sour halibut is memorable, too. Regulars order the "Large Guy," a bowl of sweet-and-sour rice mixed with spare ribs, which arrives instantly and costs $5.25. You can also get sandwiches, burgers (also served with rice), and Chinese food. Families with children are warmly welcomed here.

335 Stedman St. ✆ **907/225-2257.** Lunch and dinner $8–$20. No credit cards. Tues–Sat 11:30am–2pm and 4–8pm; Sun noon–7:30pm.

Ocean View Restaurante ★ 🍴 MEXICAN   This lively, festive family restaurant is loud even on an off-season weeknight—in fact, the dining room can be deafening—but few tourists know about it or make the drive a mile from downtown. The menu is long and reasonably priced, with separate columns of Mexican and Italian cuisine (and an occasional Greek item slipped into the Italian column), a page of seafood and sautéed entrees, plus chicken, veal, steak, pasta, and pizza. Variety is a common technique used by small-town restaurants to make it through the winter, as is consistent, basic cooking. The food here is inexpensive and predictable—nothing that will surprise you for good or bad. The pizza is the best in town, and delivery is available. The restaurant's popularity may require dining early on weekends to get a table; call ahead.

1831 Tongass Ave. © **907/225-7566.** Reservations recommended. Lunch $7–$9; dinner $6–$20. MC, V. Daily 11am–11pm.

WRANGELL

Wrangell, valued for its position near the mouth of the Stikine River, began as a Tlingits stronghold and trading post and became the site of a Russian fort built in 1834. The British leased the area from the Russians in 1840, and their flag flew until the U.S. purchase of Alaska in 1867. Over the balance of the 19th century, Wrangell experienced three gold rushes and the construction of a cannery and sawmill.

Then time pretty much stopped.

With little incentive for anyone to visit, Wrangell stayed as it was after a 1952 fire burned the downtown: a burly, blue-collar American logging town, simple and conservative. Wrangell cut trees, processed them, and shipped them. The bars stayed busy, and no one thought of opening a health food restaurant. As long as there were trees to saw into lumber, the future was safe in the past.

When the lumber mill closed in 1994, some feared that Wrangell would disappear. But they didn't count on the remarkable "can do" spirit of its citizens, who are slowly transforming this little lumber town into a comfortable jumping-off point for wilderness adventures on a grand scale.

Wrangell worked to improve on its positive qualities. Residents show an endearing eagerness to please. A new museum was completed in 2005, and eco-tourism operators offer kayaking paddles. Tour boats take guests up the wild Stikine River, out on the water for Southeast's great salmon fishing, and over to the mainland to see hordes of black bears at the Anan Wildlife Observatory. The U.S. Forest Service maintains gravel roads that lead to some spectacular places. The community even built a golf course to attract visitors, and **Muskeg Meadow** (© **907/ 874-4653;** www.wrangellalaskagolf. com) is truly spectacular. The townspeople are so proud of it, you'll find it difficult to turn down a round ($22–$44 per day; clubs are for rent).

The town has a nonthreatening small-scale feel that allows a family to wander comfortably and make friends.

Petroglyph Beach.

Wrangell

ATTRACTIONS
Grave of Chief Shakes **8**
Nolan Center Museum &
  Visitor Center **4**

HOTELS
Alaska Sourdough Lodge **9**
Rooney's Roost B&B **2**
Stikine Inn **1**
Wrangell Hostel **3**
Zimovia B&B **7**

RESTAURANTS
Diamond C Café **5**
Zak's Café **6**

Visitors are often invited home to dinner because, with little crime, there seems to be almost no fear of strangers. You can picnic in a totem pole park, hike in a rainforest, and look at the ancient art of Petroglyph Beach. It's clear that Wrangell still has a long way to go to catch up with the rest of the world, but that's not necessarily a bad thing.

Essentials

GETTING THERE   **Alaska Airlines** (☎ 800/252-7522; www.alaskaair.com) serves Wrangell once daily with a jet flying 28 minutes north from Ketchikan and another 19 minutes south from Petersburg, a flight that skims treetops the entire way.

 Wrangell is on the main line of the **Alaska Marine Highway System** (☎ 800/642-0066; www.ferryalaska.com). The voyage through the narrow, winding **Wrangell Narrows** north to Petersburg is one of the most beautiful and fascinating in Southeast Alaska. The walk-on fare is $37 from Ketchikan, $33 from Petersburg. The terminal is downtown (☎ 907/874-3711), a block from the Stikine Inn.

VISITOR INFORMATION   The city's **Wrangell Visitor Center** is in the Nolan Center, along with the Wrangell Museum, on the water in the heart of town at 296 Campbell Dr. (℃ **800/367-9745;** www.wrangellalaska.org). Staff from both the Nolan Center and the U.S. Forest Service are on hand to answer questions.

The Forest Service's **Wrangell Ranger District Office** is at 525 Bennett St. (P.O. Box 51), Wrangell, AK 99929 (℃ **907/874-2323;** www. fs.fed.us/r10/tongass), located on the hill behind town. Forest Service personnel here and at the visitor center have local knowledge of the logging roads and fishing holes, offer printed information on each Forest Service cabin and path, and, for $10, sell a detailed Wrangell Island Road Guide topographic map, which is printed on waterproof material. The district office is open Monday through Friday from 8am to 4:30pm.

ORIENTATION The main part of town is laid out north to south along the waterfront on the northern point of Wrangell Island. **Front Street** is the main business street, leading from the small-boat harbor and **Chief Shakes Island** at the south to the city dock and the ferry dock at the north. Most of the rest of the town is along **Church Street,** which runs parallel to Front Street a block higher up the hill. **Evergreen Avenue** and **Bennett Street** form a loop to the north that goes to the airport. The only road to the rest of the island, the **Zimovia Highway,** heads out of town to the south, paved for about 12 miles, then connects to more than 100 miles of gravel logging roads built and maintained by the Forest Service, most of which are usable by two-wheel-drive vehicles in the summer.

GETTING AROUND You can do the town on foot, but you will need wheels for the airport or Zimovia Highway. **Practical Rent A Car** is located at the Wrangell Airport (℃ **907/874-3975**). **Northern Lights Taxi** is at ℃ **907/ 874-4646.**

[FastFACTS] WRANGELL

Bank **Wells Fargo** is at 115 Front St., with an ATM.

Hospital **Wrangell Medical Center** is at 310 Bennett St. (℃ **907/874-7000**).

Internet Access At the **Nolan Center,** 296 Campbell Dr.

(℃ **907/874-3770**), access is $5 for the first 20 minutes, $10 an hour. It's free at the public library on Church Street (℃ **907/ 874-3535**).

Police For nonemergency calls, dial ℃ **907/874-3304.**

Post Office The post office is at 105 Federal Way, across from the Stikine Inn.

Taxes Sales tax is 7%. Rooms are taxed at 13%.

SPECIAL EVENTS The **Stikine Birding Festival,** held the last week in April, marks the arrival of the sea lions, hooligans (a smelt also known as eulachon), shorebirds, and a great concentration of bald eagles on the Stikine River Delta, a spring tornado of wildlife in the region's largest coastal marshes. Community activities take place in town, while jet boat and birding tours traverse the delta.

The **Wrangell King Salmon Derby,** the last half of May and first half of June, started in 1953. Contact the Wrangell Chamber of Commerce for details (© **907/874-3901;** www.wrangellchamber.org). Wrangell also puts on a classic small-town **Independence Day** celebration on July 4, with 3 days of events, including kids' competitions, a logging show, a parade, a fair, and fireworks.

Wrangell BearFest (© **907/874-2998;** www.alaskabearfest.org) celebrates the bear viewing that comes with the summer salmon runs. There are films, workshops, a symposium on bears, games, and other activities. July 25 to July 29, 2012.

Exploring Wrangell & Environs

Before white settlers arrived, the Tlingits had already warred for centuries over this strategic trading location near the mouth of the Stikine River. The first Chief Shakes was a successful conqueror who enslaved his enemies, then handed down power through the female line, in the Tlingits tradition, for seven generations. Charlie Jones was recognized as Chief Shakes VII, the last of the line, at a potlatch in 1940, but the position had long since lost most of its status. (An excellent pamphlet, "Authentic History of Shakes Island and Clan," by E. L. Keithhahn, sells at the Nolan Center Museum, described below.)

Chief Shakes Island, a tiny islet in the middle of the small-boat harbor, is the site of a Tlingits clan house and collection of totem poles constructed by Native workers, using traditional tools, in the Civilian Conservation Corps during the 1930s. This house is an exact, scaled-down copy of the house in which Chief Shakes VI lay in state in 1916. The inside of the clan house is fascinating, both in the sense it gives of the people's ways and for some extraordinary artifacts. Open hours are posted around town or on the site www.shakesisland.com. Admission is $5. Otherwise, you can pay a $25 minimum to have someone come down and show you around. Great-granddaughters of Chief Shakes VII open the house: Tis Peterman (© **907/874-3097**), or, if you can't reach Tis, Carol Snoddy (© **907/874-3538**). Even if

you can't arrange to get in, visit the island to see the totem poles and the charming setting (and, with extra time, visit the grave of Chief Shakes V, on Case Ave., just across the harbor). You can often see an otter near the island's footbridge.

The carved house posts in the clan house are replicas of the mid-18th-century originals protected by the local museum. These are probably the oldest and certainly the best-preserved Tlingits house posts in existence, still bearing the original fish egg and mineral paints, and a gash where, during a potlatch, a chief hacked off an image that a visitor admired and gave it to him—a gesture that demonstrated the extent of his wealth then, and still does.

The **Nolan Center Museum,** 296 Campbell Dr. (© **907/874-3770**),

Chief Shakes Island.

is an impressive building, with galleries devoted to natural history, logging and fishing, and Native culture. The museum owns many important early Alaska Native pieces, and a lot of just plain old stuff telling the story of Wrangell, one of Alaska's most historic towns. Admission is $5 adults, $3 seniors, $2 children ages 6 to 12; family admission is $12. The museum is open May 1 to September 30 Monday through Saturday 10am to 5pm, the rest of the year Tuesday through Saturday 1 to 5pm, or by appointment. Don't miss the shop, which has an extraordinary collection of books on Alaska and authentic Native crafts for bargain prices.

A carving at Petroglyph Beach.

The museum helped preserve an impressive set of petroglyphs that lie on the beach a mile north of town. The 50 carvings at **Wrangell Petroglyph Beach State Historic Park** probably represent the work of forgotten indigenous people predating the Tlingits and were made over a long period of time. The images, chipped into rocks, are of animals and geometric forms. Their purpose is lost to time. Walk north on Evergreen Avenue and follow the signs down to the beach (don't go within an hour of high tide). Replicas of the petroglyphs were carved so that visitors who want to take rubbings will not destroy the originals; also try not to step on them. The great pleasure here is simply to search for the carvings—they're just lying out there, and it takes some looking—and to wonder at their meaning and age.

Getting Outside

ON THE ISLAND   Wrangell Island's network of gravel roads, maintained by the Forest Service, leads to places of awesome beauty rarely visited by non-Alaskans. There are a few dayhike trails, some lovely campsites, and paths to remote shelters and fishing lakes you can have to yourself. There are also

---

Stop in for a Swim

Every time we visit Wrangell, we end up envying the people living there. The **Wrangell Municipal Pool** is one reason. It's also a good stop for visitors on rainy days (which are plentiful here). The facility, at 321 Church St., next to the high school (© **907/874-2444**), has a weight room and racquetball courts and the pool itself, which, during open swim, contains a giant inflatable dinosaur that drives children gaga. General admission costs all of $2.50 for adults, and court fees are similarly very inexpensive. Towels are for rent. It's open Monday and Friday 6am to 1pm and 4:30 to 8:30pm, Tuesday through Thursday 8am to 6pm, Saturday noon to 4pm.

Touring glaciers by floatplanes.

a couple of calm and scenic places to start a kayak paddle. The Forest Service even has a public-use cabin that you can drive to on a logging road 20 miles from town—that's rare, as most can be reached only by air or boat. (It's the Middle Ridge Cabin. Use the resources under "Forest Service Cabins," p. 95, to learn more and reserve.)

There's only one way out of town: south on the **Zimovia Highway** along narrow Zimovia Strait. The Forest Service map (see "Visitor Information," above) is helpful for anything you might want to do along this route. The first potential stop is **City Park,** just south of town. Besides having a picnic area on the shore among big trees, it's a fine **tide-pooling** spot. Go a couple of hours before a good low tide.

Five miles out Zimovia Highway, you reach the **Shoemaker Bay Recreation Area,** with a small boat harbor, campground, and picnic sites (see "A Hostel & Camping," later in this chapter). Continuing south, **Eight Mile Beach** is a good stop for a ramble, and don't miss **Nemo Point,** a high, ocean-side overlook from which you can see more than 13 miles along Zimovia Strait all the way back to town. There are eight gorgeous campsites, and a plank walk trail (described under "Hiking," below) along the road leads down to the beach.

All the way across the island, about 45 minutes from town, **Earl West Cove** gives access to the protected wilderness waters on the Eastern Passage. There's a campsite there, too.

OFF THE ISLAND   Wrangell provides a stepping-off point for vast, rich wild lands and remote fishing, rafting, sea kayaking, or wildlife-watching. I've described two of the main off-island destinations below—the Stikine River and the Anan Wildlife Observatory—but there are many more, too many to mention. To get beyond the island, you need a boat or floatplane. You can go independently, hiring a water taxi for $200 to $260 an hour; it costs more than $500 one-way to get to a remote Forest Service cabin by boat. That service is offered by various operators (see "Gearing Up," below). If you prefer to go by air, **Sunrise Aviation** (✆ **800/874-2311** or 907/874-2319;

www.sunriseflights.com) is a Wrangell-based operator offering charters and glacier flightseeing.

GEARING UP   For a lift over the water, a guide, or rental equipment, there are several long-established businesses. **Klondike Bikes,** 502 Wrangell Ave. (☎ **907/874-2453;** klondikebike.com), rents quality bikes for $35 a day. **Alaska Waters,** with a desk in the Stikine Inn, 107 Stikine Ave. (☎ **800/ 347-4462** or 907/874-2378; www.alaskawaters.com), rents equipment and offers various marine services, including fishing and tours. Check the website for monthly specials and other useful information. **Alaska Vistas,** at the city dock where the cruise ships dock (☎ **866/874-3006** or 907/874-3006; www.alaskavistas.com), started as a sea-kayaking business but now offers water taxis; guided hiking and rafting; rental of canoes, kayaks, and bicycles; and other services. You can stop in at their office on the dock for advice, books and maps, gear, and espresso. Both companies are listed below under the appropriate headings. There are other excellent charter businesses in town as well.

OUTDOOR ACTIVITIES NEAR WRANGELL

BIKING   A paved 6-mile bike trail along the water next to the Zimovia Highway leads all the way from town to the Shoemaker Bay Recreation Area. There's nothing to block the ocean views and a good destination at the end, with a well-developed picnic site and the starting point of hiking trail to a waterfall (see "Hiking," below). There are many more miles of appealing mountain-bike routes on Forest Service roads all over the island. See "Gearing Up," above, for rental information.

FISHING   Anglers can dip a line in various streams and lakes on Wrangell Island reachable by car or a drive and short hike. The Forest Service provides a list, and the **Alaska Department of Fish and Game** (☎ **907/874-3822;** www.adfg.state.ak.us, click "Sport Fish," then the Southeast region) publishes an extensive *Petersburg/Wrangell Sport Fishing Guide,* available online or in print. May and June are the prime months for king salmon fishing, silvers start in July, and halibut are available all summer. **Alaska Waters** (see "Gearing Up," above) can help you find a guide or charter boat for a fishing trip from Wrangell.

HIKING   Across the road from the Shoemaker Bay Recreation Area, the **Rainbow Falls Trail** climbs steeply for just under a mile (and 500 ft. in elevation gain) on a boardwalk with steps, up a ridge between two creeks, forested with big, mossy Sitka spruce and western hemlock. The falls seem to tumble down between the branches. From that point, you can continue another 2.7 miles and another 1,100 feet higher into open alpine terrain on the **Institute Creek Trail** to the Shoemaker Overlook, where there are great views, a picnic area, and a shelter. An additional section of the trail continues from there another 8 miles across the island.

Besides Rainbow Falls, various other walks start from the logging roads—the Forest Service can point the way. The **Nemo Saltwater Access Trail** is a well-built .5-mile plank walk leading to the beach near Turn Island, near a wonderful stand of red cedar and the Turn Island Campsite, with two wooden platforms, picnic tables, and dry firewood. An easy 1-mile **trail to Thoms Lake** was reconstructed in 2008, starting from the Nemo–Skip Loop Road (Forest Road 6267). Another good choice is the

Shakes Creek.

Salamander Ridge Trail, which leads a mile to subalpine terrain, where you can go off-trail hiking. The trail begins 27 miles from Wrangell on Salamander Road, also known as Forest Road 50050. The **Long Lake Trail** leads over a half-mile boardwalk to a public shelter and rowboat on the lake, on Forest Road 6271 (you'll need a map).

SEA KAYAKING   **Alaska Vistas** (see "Gearing Up," above) offers kayaking day-trip paddles starting from the boat harbor, longer day tours to lovely Earl West Cove on the east side of the island, or guided trips of many days.

THE STIKINE RIVER

The Stikine's gray glacial waters rush all the way from the dry Interior of British Columbia to a broad, shallow delta in the rainforest a few miles from Wrangell. It's among the fastest free-flowing navigable rivers in North America and in early gold-rush years was a route through the Coastal Range. Tours that sometimes go as far as Telegraph Creek, B.C., speed against the current with the roar of high-powered engines that send a jet of water out from under their shallow, metal bottoms. On still water, the jet boats can go as fast as a car on the highway.

The shallow delta is an exceptionally rich wildlife-viewing area, a habitat of grasslands, braided channels, and marshes populated by sea lions, eagles, and many other species of birds. In late April and early May, when the hooligan run, more than 1,500 bald eagles congregate, and some two million other birds rest on their West Coast migration. Later in the year, when summer's salmon are running, you can see them thrashing in their spawning pools. Farther upriver, tours encounter Sitka black-tailed deer, moose, brown and black bears, mountain goats, river otters, and beavers.

Traveling upriver, tours usually stop at the **Shakes Glacier** and **Shakes Lake,** where there are 3,000-foot cliffs and some 50 waterfalls. Among others, Alaska Waters and Alaska Vistas offer these outings (see "Gearing Up," above). Some trips stop at the Forest Service–owned **Chief Shakes Hot Springs,** where there's an indoor and an outdoor tub for public bathing. **Alaska Waters** goes all the way to Telegraph, B.C., 160 miles upriver, bringing travelers to a

A black bear and cub at Anan Wildlife Observatory.

remote homestead lodge. Commentary on all their trips includes natural history and Tlingits cultural traditions and legends. A 4-day, 3-night package is $1,699. The going rate for a 5-hour jet boat tour from Wrangell to the glacier, delta, and hot springs is $150 to $180.

Rafting the Stikine offers fast water, expansive scenery, and the potential for a remote, many-day journey. Alaska Vistas offers these guided trips, lasting about 9 days, for an inclusive price of around $2,600 per person. Alaska Vistas also rents rafts and other gear for floating the Stikine. (See "Gearing Up," above.)

ANAN WILDLIFE OBSERVATORY

When the pink salmon are running in July and August (peak is mid-July to Aug 20), a population of about 60 black bears and 10 brown bears gather near a waterfall on Anan Creek, on the mainland southeast of Wrangell Island, often walking close to a platform where visitors stand watching. Don't visit outside the time of this salmon run, however, unless you have it on good authority that bears are actively using the creek. Forest Service interpreters are on duty during the bear months; visitors must also follow safe bear behavior (they'll brief you when you arrive; also see "Outdoors Health & Safety," in chapter 11). Most visitors will enjoy a guided day trip from Wrangell more than going on their own. Both **Alaska Waters** and **Alaska Vistas** go by boat (see "Gearing Up," above). Expect to pay $210 to $265 per person for the hour-long run from Wrangell and at least a few hours with the bears. Both are good companies. Alaska Vistas particularly emphasizes the long day they spend with the bears and their guides' biology and game-management experience.

It's also possible to go to the Anan observatory without a guide, but you will need a pass issued by the Forest Service **Wrangell Ranger District Office,** at 525 Bennett St. (P.O. Box 51), Wrangell, AK 99929 (*©* **907/874-2323;** fax 907/874-7595; www.fs.fed.us/r10/tongass/districts/wrangell). Check the website for an explanation of the system, a calendar showing the number of permits available each day, and application forms. A total of 60 passes are allocated for each day of the period from July 5 through August 25, with 12 held back until 3 days before the visit. Passes are given out first come, first served by mail, fax, e-mail, or in person, and cost $10. There's a Forest Service cabin for rent, too, in very high demand during the bear-viewing season. The walk to the observatory is a half-mile from the shore where you land, on a good trail.

Sunrise Aviation (☎ 800/874-2311 or 907/874-2319; www.sunrise flights.com) offers charters to Anan for prices competitive with going by boat.

Where to Stay

Besides the accommodations listed in detail, families and fishing groups will enjoy **Grand View Bed & Breakfast,** at mile 1.9 Zimovia Hwy. (www.grandviewbnb. com; ☎ 907/874-3225), with lots of room, cooking facilities, laundry machines, Wi-Fi, well-equipped new rooms, and breakfast cooked to the guests' specifications. Rates are $105 to $135 double, and the B&B takes personal checks but not credit cards. You'll also find clean but basic budget rooms at **Diamond C Hotel,** 225 Front St. (www.diamondchotel.com; ☎ 907/874-3322), for $85 to $100 per room, regardless of number of guests, May through October.

Alaskan Sourdough Lodge ★   Former mayor Bruce Harding runs this hotel in the style of a fishing lodge, renting the rooms alone or as packages with trips to the Anan Bear Observatory, Stikine River tours, fishing, kayaking, rafting, and other outdoor activities. The attractive building with a wraparound porch is immaculately kept. The lodge is decorated in an outdoors theme. Most rooms are small, and some have shower stalls rather than tubs. The suite is huge and has a Jacuzzi tub. Fresh seafood dinners are served nightly, family style (you eat what they cook). Dinner prices are $19 to $24 per person; nonguests by reservation only.

1104 Peninsula (P.O. Box 1062), Wrangell, AK 99929. www.akgetaway.com. ☎ **800/874-3613** or 907/874-3613. Fax 907/874-3455. 16 units. $124 double; $209 suite. Rates include continental breakfast. AE, DC, DISC, MC, V. **Amenities:** Free airport transfers; bike rental; fish freezing; sauna. *In room:* TV, high-speed Internet.

Rooney's Roost Bed & Breakfast   A warm family has offered this old downtown house with dormer windows to guests for many years. Antiques rest on the hardwood floors in the common areas, and the four rooms, while small, are decorated according to cute themes. All have private bathrooms and four-poster beds with thick mattresses, comforters, and oversize pillows. In the summer, elaborate breakfasts with local ingredients, such as seafood or berries, are served in a sunny dining room at the guests' convenience.

206 McKinnon (P.O. Box 552), Wrangell, AK 99929. www.rooneysroost.com. ☎ **907/874-2026.** Fax 907/874-4404. 4 units. $115 double private bathroom. Extra person $25. Rates include full breakfast. MC, V.

Stikine Inn ★   The waterfront hotel has been a center of community activity for decades, and attentive owners have worked at upgrading and remodeling it a little at a time for several years. The attractive public spaces include a coffee bar and lounge, the Stik, with dark hardwood floors and a fresh but classic look. Also new, a women's salon and spa, the Parlor (☎ 907/874-3595; open Mon–Sat 10am–5pm), occupies a bright, tiled space with ocean views. The rooms are comfortable and clean and received updated furniture, fabrics, and carpet in 2009. For guests, the convenience of the location can't be better, close to the ferry dock and right on the water's edge. Rooms sharing superb water views carry an $11 to $12 premium. You can watch the sunset on the ocean and hear water lapping the shore.

The **Stikine Inn Restaurant** offers pleasant casual meals in a dining room that is noticeably clean and bright and has a terrific view. Simple local specialties, such as the halibut and chips, are done quite well and priced reasonably for the region. The salads also are very good. The restaurant serves lunch and dinner year-round. Prices range from $9 to $35.

107 Stikine Ave. (P.O. Box 662), Wrangell, AK 99929. www.stikineinn.com. © **888/874-3388** or 907/874-3388. Fax 907/874-3923. 35 units. At press time, $114–$160, but call for rates. AE, DC, DISC, MC, V. **Amenities:** Restaurant; airport/ferry courtesy van. *In room:* TV, Wi-Fi ($7 a day).

Zimovia Bed & Breakfast ★★ 🎁   The cedar-shingled house 2 blocks above Front Street contains a pair of extraordinary handcrafted rooms—one with a boat's door on the closet, garnets in the tiles, and a cedar-walled sauna; the other decorated with hand-fused glass tiles and a glass sink atop a display of coral, sand, and glass fish. Nor is the beauty skin deep. Both rooms are encased in 10-inch-thick soundproof walls and have heated floors, and the linens and beds are sumptuously first rate. Each unit has a private entrance from a riotously blooming garden outside. The hospitality of hostess Barb Rugo—with her wonderful baking—matches the attention to excellence that has been poured into creating the place. She even picks up guests on arrival and gives them a town tour.

319 Weber St. (P.O. Box 1424), Wrangell, AK 99929. www.zimoviabnb.com. © **866/946-6842** or 907/874-2626. 2 units. $100 double year-round. MC, V. Rates include continental breakfast. *In room:* TV/VCR, kitchenette, stocked fridge, Wi-Fi.

A HOSTEL & CAMPING

Wrangell Hostel is at the First Presbyterian Church, 220 Church St. (P.O. Box 439), Wrangell, AK 99929 (© **907/874-3534**). They're open Memorial Day through Labor Day; the rate is $20 a night, or $50 for a private room for couples or families; and there is no daytime lockout period.

There are several attractive campgrounds in Wrangell. We've never seen another campground in a spot like the mountaintop **Nemo Point Forest Service Campground** (see "Getting Outside," earlier in this section), but it's more than a dozen miles out of town. Five miles south of town, the **Shoemaker Bay Recreation Area** has sites by the road overlooking the boat harbor, right across from the Rainbow Falls Trail. There are free tent sites and RV sites with electric hookups for $25 a night, $15 without electric; the camping fee includes use of the town pool and its showers (see "Stop in for a Swim," earlier). Contact the **Wrangell Recreation and Parks Department** (© **907/874-2444**) for information. They also manage **City Park,** right at the edge of town on Zimovia Highway, where tent camping is permitted with a 1-night limit. For a full hookup RV site, try **Alaska Waters'** small park, at 241 Berger St. (www.alaskawaters.com; © **800/347-4462**). They charge $25 a night for rigs up to 32 feet, $30 over that length.

Where to Eat

The two hotels (see "Where to Stay," above) also offer some of Wrangell's best dining. **Alaskan Sourdough Lodge** serves meals to guests, and to others by reservation. It's a family-style dinner without a menu. The **Stikine Inn Restaurant** is a popular spot, with excellent simple meals.

You have other choices for deli sandwiches or a simple meal, including the **Diamond C Coffee Shop,** 223 Front St. (© **907/874-3350**), next to the cafe of the same name, described below. It's a typical coffee and espresso shop, with good daily sandwich specials for lunch, such as the halibut panini served the day we visited.

The deli at **Bob's IGA,** 223 Brueger St. (✆ **907/874-2341**), produces good sandwiches and also sells frozen yogurt. It is open Monday through Saturday 9am to 6pm.

Diamond C Cafe ★ DINER   This is a clean, reliable diner offering speedy, friendly service and well-done food from the grill. Indeed, it produces some of the most consistently satisfying meals in town. The day's fresh halibut, perfectly and simply grilled, comes with a generous salad and garlic bread, all for $11. The pies are delicious, too. The menu is lengthy, but all prices are reasonable and all the food familiar and done right.

215 Front St. ✆ **907/874-3677.** Breakfast $5.50–$12; lunch $7.50–$14. AE, MC, V. Mon–Sat 6am–3pm; Sun 6am–2pm.

Zak's Café ★ SEAFOOD   Options are few in the evening, but this is a good one. The owners started it partly out of frustration with the lack of fine dining in Wrangell, and their dinner menu of halibut, salmon, steaks, pasta, poultry, and stir-fry could come from many a traditional restaurant in a larger town. For lunch they serve salads, wraps, burgers, and sandwiches.

316 Front St. ✆ **907/874-3355.** Reservations recommended for dinner. Lunch $6.25–$10; dinner $13–$25. MC, V. Mon–Sat 11am–8pm.

PETERSBURG: UNVARNISHED THRESHOLD TO THE OUTDOORS

Petersburg is the perfect small town, the sort of prosperous, picturesque, quirky place that used to be mythologized in Disney films. Except that Petersburg would never let Disney in the door. Petersburg's residents are glad the big cruise ships can't enter their narrow harbor, keeping the town unspoiled by the ships' throngs of tourists and seasonal gift shops. Instead, the main street thrives with

Water-side homes in Petersburg.

family-owned grocery and hardware stores, a fish market, and other businesses. Wooden streets over Hammer Slough still serve utilitarian purposes. As you walk along Sing Lee Alley and check out the stylish little bookstore, you'll see Norwegian fishermen in pickup trucks and blond-haired kids on bikes.

Because Petersburg is small and isolated, there are wonderful trails, mountain-biking routes, and secret places where you will seldom see other people. On the water, the humpback whale-watching is as reliable as anywhere in Alaska and largely undiscovered. There's a glacier to visit, terrific fishing, and limitless sea-kayaking waters. The in-town attractions are few, a day is plenty for simple sightseeing, but Alaska's best is waiting for those willing to spend the effort to look.

Petersburg is named for its founder, Peter Buschmann, who killed himself over bad debts after living here for only 4 years. Buschmann founded a cannery on Mitkof Island facing the slender, peaceful Wrangell Narrows in what was to become Petersburg. The stunning abundance of salmon and halibut and a nearby source of ice—the LeConte Glacier—made the site a natural.

Buschmann's suicide followed his financial reverses, but the promise of Petersburg remained. The Norwegians stayed and slowly built a charming town of white clapboard houses with steeply pitched roofs, hugging the water. Their living came from the sea, as it still does. Appropriately, the downtown area doesn't stop at water's edge. Roads, boardwalks, and buildings continue over the smooth waters of Wrangell Narrows, out to the cannery buildings that survive on long wooden piers, and into the boat harbors, which branch out in a network far more extensive than the city's streets.

Today the town's economy is based on fishing and government work. The Stikine Ranger District of the Tongass National Forest is headquartered here. That makes for a wealthy, sophisticated, and stable population.

Essentials

GETTING THERE   Petersburg has the most welcoming **ferry terminal** in the system (© **907/772-3855**), with a grassy lawn and a pier from which to watch the boats and marine animals. It's about a mile to the town center. The **Alaska Marine Highway** (© **800/642-0066;** www.ferryalaska.com) connects to Juneau directly (an 8-hr. run) or by way of Sitka, far to the west. The details of the schedule are complicated and can change; your best source of information is the website. The fare is $33 from Wrangell (3 hr.), $45 from Sitka (8 hr.), and $66 from Juneau (10 hr.).

Petersburg is served by **Alaska Airlines** jets (© **800/252-7522;** www.alaskaair.com) once north and once south each day, with the nearest stops on the puddle jumper being Juneau and Wrangell. From the airport, call **Metro Cab** (© **907/772-2700**) or **Midnight Rides** (© **907/772-2222**) for a taxi into town.

VISITOR INFORMATION   The Petersburg Chamber of Commerce **Visitor Information Center,** at the corner of 1st and Fram streets (P.O. Box 649), Petersburg, AK 99833 (© **866/484-4700** or 907/772-4636; www.petersburg.org), offers guidance on outdoor opportunities, boats, lodgings, and Forest Service cabins; distributes trail guides, maps, and natural history publications; and sells useful books. The center is open in summer Monday through Saturday from 9am to 5pm, Sunday from noon to 4pm; winter Monday through Friday from 10am to 2pm.

Petersburg

The full-service **Viking Travel** agency, corner of Nordic Drive and Sing Lee Alley (℡ **800/327-2571** or 907/772-3818; www.alaskaferry. com), also specializes in booking local guides for tours, kayaks, whale-watching, flights, fishing charters, bear viewing, and other activities. Owners Dave and Nancy Berg are knowledgeable and helpful.

ORIENTATION   Petersburg is on Mitkof Island, divided from the much larger Kupreanof Island by the long, slender channel of the Wrangell Narrows. There are three small-boat harbors and so many docks, boardwalks, and wooden streets that the town seems to sit on the ocean. **Nordic Drive** is the main street, running from the ferry dock through town, then becoming **Sandy Beach Road** as it rounds Hungry Point to the north. At Sandy Beach, you can circle back, past the airport, which stands above the town, to **Haugen Drive,** which meets Nordic again near **Hammer Slough,** right in town. To the south, Nordic becomes the **Mitkof Highway,** which runs to the undeveloped balance of the island.

GETTING AROUND   You can walk downtown Petersburg, but you'll need wheels or a boat to get to most outdoor activities. The **Tides Inn Motel** and **Scandia House** (see "Where to Stay," later in this chapter) both rent cars, but not many are available in town, so book well in advance for summer.

A boat opens more of the area than any other mode of transportation, allowing exploration of Wrangell Narrows, the trails on the far side, and the opportunity for inexpensive self-guided fishing. **Jensen's Boat Rentals,** in North Harbor (📞 **877/442-4010** or 907/772-4435), offers 18-foot skiffs and a 21-foot runabout with a top, with quality outboards and trolling motors, for $135 and $300 a day respectively, including a crab pot. The firm also rents fishing and shrimping gear.

[Fast FACTS] PETERSBURG

Banks There are two banks, both with ATMs, at the intersection of Nordic Drive and Fram Street.

Hospital **Petersburg Medical Center** is at 2nd and Fram streets (📞 **907/ 772-4291**).

Internet Access Free at the public library, at

Nordic and Haugen drives (📞 **907/772-3349**).

Police Find them on Nordic Drive near Haugen; nonemergencies 📞 **907/772-3838.**

Post Office Near the airport on Haugen Street.

Trading Union Grocery

Store, 401 N. Nordic (📞 **907/772-3881**), sells stamps and has a postal drop box.

Taxes Sales tax is 6%. The tax on accommodations totals 10%.

SPECIAL EVENTS The **Little Norway Festival,** which celebrates the May 17, 1814, declaration of independence of Norway from Sweden, is an occasion for Petersburg to go wild. The 4-day schedule of events includes a street fair, food and craft booths, a luncheon and bunad-style show (a bunad is a traditional embroidered Norwegian costume), street music and dancing, and a salmon bake on the beach. The celebration is held on the third full weekend of May. The **King Salmon Derby** offers $30,000 in prizes over Memorial Day weekend. **July 4th** is a very big deal in Petersburg and lasts 2 days. The **Canned Salmon Classic** lasts from July 1 to August 15, with a first prize of up to $4,000 going to the person who guesses how many cans of salmon will be packed in Petersburg during the season. The **Festival of Lights** begins the day after Thanksgiving with an evening candlelight parade, the lighting of the Community Christmas Tree, and caroling. **Julebukking,** a Norwegian tradition, happens on Christmas Eve, when merchants offer food and drink to their customers and the streets fill with people under twinkling white lights.

For information on any of the above events, contact the **Petersburg Chamber of Commerce** (📞 **866/484-4700** or 907/772-4636; www. petersburg.org).

Exploring Petersburg

A walk around Petersburg should include the boardwalk streets of **Hammer Slough,** the tidal mouth of a creek that feeds into the waterfront. **Sing Lee Alley** leads from North Nordic Drive at the charming center of town, passing by several interesting little shops, including **Sing Lee Alley Books,** at no. 11 (📞 **907/772-4440**), where there's a good collection on natural history and local culture. Petersburg has so many thriving little shops because of its isolation and healthy economy—so far, it's been too small to attract the predation of Wal-Mart and other chains.

Large model Viking ship next to the Sons of Norway Hall.

Sing Lee Alley turns from solid ground to wooden dock before you reach the **Sons of Norway Hall,** a town center where a large model Viking ship used in the Little Norway Festival is often parked. Next door, also on pilings, is the **Fishermen's Memorial Park.** Plaques memorialize Petersburg mariners lost at sea under a bronze statue of Bojer Wikan, a fisherman and lifelong resident.

Across the street, on the outboard side, **Tonka Seafoods** (ⓒ **888/560-3662** or 907/772-3662; www.tonkaseafoods.com) is a specialty fish processor with a shop and mail-order operation; they will process your sport-caught fish, too.

Continue on to Nordic Drive and turn left, crossing back over the slough to **Birch Street,** which follows the slough's bank on pilings upstream past old, weathered houses that hang over the placid channel. Many have one door for the road and another for the water. It's a charming, authentic place. Step out of the way of cars on the one-lane dock/street.

Back down at the waterfront, stroll the harbor floats to see the frenetic activity of the huge commercial fishing fleet in the summer, then continue north on Nordic Drive to **Eagle's Roost Park,** where there is a grassy area to sit and a stairway that leads down to the water. At low tide, an interesting but rugged beach walk starts here. Another nice walk leads you on a boardwalk about a fourth of a mile over muskeg swamp from the uphill side of the elementary school, at 4th Street.

The **Clausen Memorial Museum,** at 2nd and Fram streets (ⓒ **907/772-3598;** www.clausenmuseum.org), interprets Petersburg and its history for the people who live here. The world's record king salmon is mounted here—127 pounds—landed by a Petersburg commercial fisherman. It is almost 30 pounds heavier than the record sport-caught king, in Soldotna. The museum is open in summer Monday through Saturday from 10am to 5pm; call for hours in the winter. Admission is $3 for adults, free for children 12 and under.

There are some interesting gift and art shops in town. **Wild Celery Framing Studio and Eclectic Gallery,** 400 N. Nordic, carries art and jewelry, gifts and linens, and wood carvings and turnings. **Seaport Gallery and Gifts,** 219 N. Nordic Dr., concentrates on fine art, offering ceramics, prints, oils, and locally made handcrafted jewelry.

Getting Outside

I have listed only a few highlights from Petersburg's wealth of outdoor opportunities. For other choices, many of them just as good as those we've written about here, or for the detailed trail and backcountry information you'll need, contact the U.S. Forest Service at the **Petersburg Ranger District** offices at 12 N. Nordic Dr. (P.O. Box 1328), Petersburg, AK 99833 (✆ **907/772-3871;** www. fs.fed.us/r10/tongass/districts/petersburg), or the visitor information center at the corner of 1st and Fram streets (✆ **907/772-4636**).

Some of the best places to go around Petersburg require a boat. **Viking Travel** (see "Visitor Information," above) books most of the dozen or so small charter boats that operate from the harbor at any one time, allowing them to consolidate small groups into 6- to 15-person boatloads for whale-watching, sightseeing, glacier viewing, or fishing. See p. 127 for the option of renting your own boat.

A few operators have made a specialty of natural history and environmentally responsible tours. Barry Bracken, a marine biologist, offers these kinds of trips on his 28-foot vessel. Contact **Kaleidoscope Cruises** (✆ **800/TO-THE-SEA** [868-4373] or 907/772-3736; www.petersburglodgingandtours.com). You can also set up a package with Bracken for a multiday stay in a lovely waterfront guesthouse. To get to remote cabins by air, or for flightseeing, contact **Pacific Wing Air Charters** (✆ **907/772-4258**).

SPECIAL PLACES

SANDY BEACH   The beach at City Park is an easy bike ride or a longish walk 1½ miles up Nordic Drive, around Hungry Point at the northern tip of the island, then along Sandy Beach Road to the beach and picnic area. Return by way of the airport, coming back into town on Haugen Drive. The beach itself is coarse sand and fine gravel, and you can't swim in the frigid water, but it's a lovely spot, facing Frederick Sound on the east side of Mitkof Island.

If you go at high tide, you can beachcomb and bird-watch—a great blue heron was hanging around on one visit—but a better plan is to time your visit at low tide to see the remains of an ancient fish trap and view petroglyphs carved into rocks near the traps. (Ask about the occasional Forest Service interpretive walks of the beach at the Ranger District office.) Please be sensitive to the delicate artifacts so they can last another 2,000 years, being especially careful of the fish trap stakes, which are not obvious and can be trampled.

RAVEN TRAIL & RAVEN'S ROOST CABIN   About 4 miles up the steep but spectacular Raven Trail, which begins behind the airport

Roasting a hot dog on Sandy Beach.

off Haugen Drive roughly a mile from town, the Raven's Roost Forest Service cabin sits atop a mountain with a sweeping view of the town and surrounding waters and islands. Allow 3 to 4 hours for the climb along a boardwalk, then up a steep muddy slope, then along a ridge, with an elevation gain of more than 1,000 feet. To stay at the cabin, you'll need sleeping bags, cooking gear, lights, and food. Reserve the cabin through the national system described earlier in "Getting Outside in the

A black-tailed deer.

Tongass National Forest," and check there for information sources on the other 19 cabins in the area, most of which are reached by plane or boat.

MITKOF ISLAND   The Mitkof Highway, leading south from Petersburg, opens access to most of Mitkof Island, with its king salmon fishing; views of swans, fish, and glaciers; hiking trails; lakes; and many miles of remote roads for mountain-biking. The town's swimming hole and ice-skating pond are out the road, too. Anyone can enjoy a day's sightseeing drive over the island, and if you like hiking and the outdoors, you'll find days of fun. Pick up the $9 *Forest Service Mitkof Island Road Guide* map at the visitor center or ranger office; it shows what you'll find along the way.

The **Three Lakes Loop Road** intersects with the highway twice, once 10 miles from Petersburg and again 20 miles from town. From the north intersection, the one closest to town, it's 15 more miles to the level, 4.5-mile boardwalk **Three Lakes Trail,** which circles four small lakes, each of which contains trout, and three of which have Forest Service rowboats for public use. A three-sided shelter at the smallest lake makes a good rest or camping spot. Besides the fish, the area is abundant with wildflowers and berries, and you may see deer, beavers, bear, and many birds, including seasonal sandhill cranes.

Fourteen miles down Mitkof Highway from Petersburg, a quarter-mile wheelchair-accessible boardwalk leads across the damp, hummocky ground of the rainforest muskeg to **Blind River Rapids,** a peaceful spot with a three-sided shelter where you can watch and fish for king salmon in June and silvers in September, and sometimes see eagles and bears feeding on the fish. A half-mile-long loop leads farther into the forest and muskeg.

At 17 miles, somewhat hidden in the trees on the right, a bird-watching blind looks out on **Blind Slough,** where trumpeter swans winter. Swans normally will be gone by mid-March, but later in the year, you can see bear, salmon, and eagles.

At 18 miles, you'll reach the **Blind Slough Recreation Area,** where locals go to swim in amber water in the summer. Water warms in the narrow slough, more than 5 miles from Wrangell Narrows. In the winter, much of the town congregates here for ice-skating and bonfires.

At 21 miles from Petersburg, the popular **Man Made Hole** picnic area and swimming pond has foot bridges and a pathway; it is accessible to people with disabilities.

At 22 miles, you reach the **Ohmer Creek campground** ($6 camping fee in summer), with a 1-mile trail, a floating bridge over a beaver pond, and trout and some salmon in late summer. The road continues from here along the south shore of Mitkof Island, with great ocean views, to its end at mile 32.

PETERSBURG CREEK   The lovely, grassy Petersburg Creek area either could offer an afternoon frolic among the meadows of wildflowers that meet the water, or could be the start to a challenging 21-mile, multiday hike into the **Petersburg Creek-Duncan Salt Chuck Wilderness.** The fishing is exceptional: The creek contains four species of salmon and two of trout. You'll need a skiff or sea kayak, or get a charter to drop you off, as the creek is on Kupreanof Island, across Wrangell Narrows from town; the state maintains a dock there. Sea-kayaking up the creek makes a wonderful day trip, which you can do on your own or with a guide (see "Sea Kayaking," below). A trail reaches two Forest Service cabins, at Petersburg Lake and East Salt Chuck, each with a boat for public use (reservations are required). The trail to the lake is not difficult, but continuing on to East Salt Chuck is tougher going, including wading some beaver ponds. At the lake, you can fish for trout, and odds are good of seeing ducks, geese, loons, trumpeter swans, bald eagles, or black bears. The Kupreanof dock also provides access to the 3-mile, 3,000-foot trail that climbs Petersburg Mountain, a challenging hike that has spectacular views from the top.

ACTIVITIES

FISHING   Besides the ocean fishing mentioned below, there are various fishing streams and lakes that you can reach on the roads, for cutthroat and rainbow trout and Dolly Varden char—several are mentioned above, under "Mitkof Island"—and many more lake- and stream-fishing opportunities are accessible by boat or plane. Check at the visitor center, or contact the **Alaska Department of Fish and Game** (℃ **907/772-5231;** www. alaska.gov/adfg, click "Sport Fish"). They produce updated fishing reports during the spring and summer, run timing calendars, and other useful information, all available on the website, as well as an informative *Petersburg/ Wrangell Sport Fishing Guide* that you can download or get on paper.

The boat harbor has a couple dozen licensed charter fishing boats, mostly six-passenger vessels. As elsewhere, halibut and salmon are usually the target. You can get a list of operators at the visitor center, at www.petersburg. org under "Marine Charters and Tour Operators," or book through **Viking Travel** (see "Visitor Information," earlier). Half-day salmon charters cost around $200 per person, while halibut charters or longer salmon charters are $335 per day. You can rent your own boat and gear for much less, without a guide. See "Getting Around," p. 127.

SEA KAYAKING   The waters of Wrangell Narrows are protected and interesting, with plenty to see. On longer trips of 3 days to a week, you can get out among the glaciers, Stikine River Delta, and even the whales—there's as much variety here, among these rainforest islands, as anywhere in the region. It's possible to set up a kayak trip linking some of the Forest Service cabins, too, or to use one as a base camp for a few days of exploration. (Get a copy of the free handout *Paddling the Petersburg Ranger District* from the district office, or download it from their website.) **Tongass Kayak Adventures** (✆ **907/772-4600;** www.tongasskayak.com) offers guided and unguided versions of each of these adventures (they rent equipment, too). Their 4-hour paddle crosses Wrangell Narrows from the harbor and penetrates Petersburg Creek, where they stop for a snack and often see bear and deer. No experience is required. They charge $95; reserve through Viking Travel, listed under "Visitor Information," earlier. A 3-night base camp tour costs $1,180 per person, and an 8-night version begins at $2,450; reserve those trips directly with Tongass Kayak.

WHALE-WATCHING   Most summers, Petersburg's **Frederick Sound** is one of the best places in the state to see humpbacks feeding. Whale-watching charters can go any day from May 15 to September 15, but the height is midsummer. Several charter operators offer trips in small, six-passenger boats. Some, including Kaleidoscope Cruises (p. 130), have hydrophones onboard, so you may be able to hear the whales' vocalizations while waiting for them to surface, if their feeding behavior and the water conditions are right. Book trips through Viking Travel or directly with one of the operators. Trips usually

Humpback whales feeding off Frederick Sound.

leave around 8am and stay out 6 to 10 hours, with several hours among the whales. Prices are $285 per person, with discounts for three or more. Viking Travel's conference room (at the corner of Nordic Dr. and Sing Lee Alley) houses the Petersburg Marine Mammal Center (www.psgmmc.org), where you can use a computer or talk to interns to learn more about whales.

Where to Stay

There are lots of places with character to stay in Petersburg, more than we have room to describe in full. Besides those listed below, we also recommend **Das Hagedorn Haus,** right downtown at 400 2nd St. N. (www.dashagedornhouse. com; ☏ **907/772-3775**), where a wonderfully hospitable couple rents a full apartment in their historic home for $80 to $110 high season, including amenities such as Wi-Fi, free laundry machines, and a full breakfast cooked to order. They do not take credit cards.

Scandia House ★★   Built in the town's distinctive Norwegian style, this building's solid simplicity puts it in a class by itself. White rooms with blond-wood trim are blessed with natural light. They have various configurations of comfortable beds, including rooms with kitchenettes and a magnificent fourth-floor suite with towering ceilings. Most units have only one bed, and a few have shower stalls, not tubs. The hotel has an elevator and is barrier-free. The rooms are some of the cleanest we've ever seen, over various visits. A continental breakfast is 6 to 9:30am, including fresh homemade muffins. Book well in advance for the busy summer season. The owners offer car rentals, and a hair salon is off the lobby.

110 Nordic Dr. (P.O. Box 689), Petersburg, AK 99833. www.scandiahousehotel.com. ☏ **800/722-5006** or 907/772-4281. Fax 907/772-4301. 33 units. $110–$130 double; $150 double with kitchenette; $185–$195 suite. Extra person 13 and over $10. Rates include continental breakfast. AE, DC, DISC, MC, V. **Amenities:** Free airport transfers. In room: TV.

Sea Level Bed & Breakfast ★ 🛏   Hostess Jean Ellis designed this remarkable building, which stands on pilings over the water, as a bed-and-breakfast, creating a sense of being at sea when you look out the big picture windows. At high tide, you can fish from the front deck. There are two rooms, both well equipped and tastefully decorated with soft colors and floral quilts. She serves breakfast to order in the smaller room; the other unit has a full kitchen and living area, and Jean stocks it with self-service food. Each room rents to no more than two adults, but they can be combined, and kids are welcome without charge. The B&B does not accept credit cards.

N. Nordic Dr. (P.O. Box 1068), Petersburg, AK 99833. www.sealevelbnb.com. ☏ **907/772-3240.** 2 units. High season $100–$130 double; low season $90–$120 double; $210 for both rooms. No credit cards. In room: TV, Wi-Fi.

Tides Inn Motel ★ 🚗   Few hotels in Alaska have such good rooms at such affordable prices. The kitchenette rooms are a particular bargain. The biggest difference among the rooms is the views, as all are well maintained. Those in the older part of the motel face the other building, while smoke-free units in the front of the new section get a sweeping view. We watched bald eagles doing aerobatics less than 50 feet from our front window. The motel management is efficient and committed to quality, and they keep the motel in clean, attractive condition. Besides, it's one of the friendliest places we've ever stayed—the staff makes life easy. The hotel has an Avis car-rental franchise.

307 N. 1st St. (P.O. Box 1048), Petersburg, AK 99833. www.tidesinnalaska.com. ℰ **800/665-8433** or 907/772-4288. Fax 907/772-4286. High season $90–$130 double; low season $65–$85 double. Extra person $10. Rates include light continental breakfast. AE, DC, DISC, MC, V. **Amenities:** Free airport transfers; Internet access. *In room:* TV, Wi-Fi.

Waterfront Bed & Breakfast   The attraction here is the location, on pilings over the Wrangell Narrows near the ferry dock and steps from Emily's Bakery. Rooms have Mission-style oak beds with excellent mattresses and down comforters. Each unit has individual heat control. Bathrooms have shower stalls, not tubs. Four of the rooms have one bed—two with a queen and two with a double—and one has two double beds. The communal living room is cozy and has a great view.

1004 S. Nordic Dr. (P.O. Box 1613), Petersburg, AK 99833. www.waterfrontbedandbreakfast.com. ℰ **866/772-9301** or 907/772-9300. Fax 907/772-9308. 5 units. $110–$132 double. $10 each additional adult. Rates include full breakfast. MC, V. **Amenities:** Covered outdoor Jacuzzi.

CAMPING

The closest natural camping is found 22 miles out the Mitkof Highway at **Ohmer Creek** (see "Special Places: Mitkof Island," above). **Twin Creek RV Park** is 7½ miles out the highway (www.twincreekrv.com; ℰ **907/772-3244**) and charges $28 for full hookups, $15 for tent camping. Showers are $3 extra.

Where to Eat

The talented bakers at **Emily's Bakery,** 1000 Nordic Dr. (ℰ **907/772-4555**), produce truly memorable whole-grain pastries, cookies, bars, and cakes, as well as quiche that will fill you with longing until the day you return. Also for lunch, try a loaf of whole-wheat bread with a swirl of cheese and sautéed vegetables baked inside. Hours are Monday through Friday 8am to 4pm. You'll have to take out your meal, as the bakery has no seating. **Java Hus,** by Scandia House at 110 N. Nordic Dr. (ℰ **907/772-2626**), is a bright, comfortable spot for coffee and a snack, open summer Monday through Saturday 6am to 6pm, Sunday 7am to 5pm; winter closing an hour earlier each day.

For terrific takeout pizza or calzone, burgers, fried fish, or other casual choices, try **Papa Bear's Pizza** (ℰ **907/772-3727;** www.papabearspizza.com), above Coastal Cold Storage at Excel Street and Nordic Drive. The owners are fanatics in search of the perfect pizza, and it shows. The pizzeria is open in summer Monday through Saturday 11am to 9pm, Saturday and Sunday 3 to 8pm (in winter Mon–Sat 11am–8pm, closed Sun). It is one of the better bets in town.

Helse, 13 Sing Lee Alley (ℰ **907/772-3444**), is a popular lunch spot serving soup, salads, and specials. It's open year-round Monday through Friday 8am to 5pm, Saturday 10am to 3pm.

Joan Mei Restaurant ★ CHINESE   This is a good choice for dinner. The whole family works together in a large, bright dining room, serving familiar Americanized Chinese cuisine and an appealing salad bar. Service is friendly and the food satisfying. Ask about the nightly specials. The menu also includes American items such as burgers and fried fish and a few Mexican selections. Locals come here for a nice dinner out.

1103 S. Nordic, across from the ferry dock. ℰ **907/772-4222.** Lunch $7.50–$15; dinner $10–$25. MC, V. Mon–Tues and Thurs–Sat 11am–2pm and 4–8:30pm; Sun 8am–2pm and 4–8:30pm. Closed mid-Jan to mid-Feb.

Tina's Kitchen ★ INTERNATIONAL   On a sunny summer day, this booth in an empty lot next door to the Scandia House is *the* place for a quick and tasty lunch or dinner. Picnic-style dining is outdoors or in a heated tent. The menu includes Korean, Mexican, and American choices, all for reasonable prices, all cooked from scratch. Our halibut tacos were fresh and flavorful, and the mood of the happy teens and friendly staff was infectious.

104 N. Nordic Dr. ☎ **907/772-2090.** All items $4.50–$11. No credit cards. Mon–Sat 6–9am and 10am–8pm; Sun 6–9am and 11am–7pm. Closed Oct–Apr.

SITKA: RICH PRIZE OF RUSSIAN CONQUEST

In many ways, Sitka is the quintessential Alaskan destination. Scenery, wildlife, and the small-town atmosphere that visitors crave are all here in spades. And there aren't hordes of tourists that can sometimes mar visits to other main port communities in Alaska. Sitka continues to keep an arm's length away from the cruise industry, offering a small dock for the big ships to ferry in their passengers, but not building the mammoth docks that allow Ketchikan and Juneau to berth three, four, or five of the big ships at once.

As a result, Sitka gets a fraction of the number of ship visits that the other towns do. There are some "summer" businesses in downtown Sitka, but the downtown remains a working, year-round community, much like Sitka itself, making it the perfect place to experience the "real" Alaska in an unhurried fashion.

Sitka is also the "capital" of European Alaskan history. It still proudly wears its Russian colonial history, when it was most sophisticated community north of San Francisco and was dubbed the "Paris of the North" by some visitors in the early 1800s.

Things aren't quite that hoity-toity these days, but Sitka does keeps its history alive through Russian dance programs and the annual in-costume Alaska Day transfer commemoration ceremony on the site of the Russian castle that once signaled the Tsar's "Alaskan adventure."

That transfer happened a year after the purchase in 1867; political intrigue in Congress delayed things. You may have heard all about "Seward's Icebox" and "Seward's Folly," which pretty much summed up the general American attitude toward Sec. of State William Henry Seward's decision to purchase Alaska. It wasn't until the various gold rushes of the 1880s and 1890s that most Americans began to see the wisdom of purchasing the territory for $7.2 million, a little more than 2¢ an acre.

The Russians had been in Sitka for 68 years when they decided to sell and go home. They had moved there in the 1790s, when the Russian American Company had generally depleted the sea otter stocks in northern Alaska and were looking to expand to the south. There was even interest in moving farther down the coast, into the disputed Pacific Northwest area in which neither Spain nor England had established a secure foothold. Russia even had some territorial designs on the Hawaiian Islands, and it was clear the capital of Russian America needed to be closer to the action.

As a result, Alexander Baranof began scouting better locations farther south than Kodiak. He settled on the area around what is now Sitka, an area protecting the potential harbors with a series of small islands, but providing for easy access to the ocean.

Sitka

ATTRACTIONS
Alaska Raptor Center **20**
Castle Hill **8**
Harrigan Centennial Hall
  Visitor Center **12**
The Russian Bishop's House **16**
Russian Blockhouse **5**
Sheldon Jackson Museum **18**
Sitka National Historical
  Park **19**
Sitka Tribe of Alaska's
  Community House **6**
St. Michael's Cathedral **11**
St. Peter's-by-the-Sea
  Episcopal Church **17**

HOTELS
Alaska Swan Lake
  Bed & Breakfast **1**
Fly-In Fish Inn **2**
Shee Atika Totem
  Square Inn **4**
Sitka Hotel **9**
Super 8 Sitka **15**
Westmark Sitka **13**

RESTAURANTS
Backdoor Café **10**
Highliner Coffee **14**
Larkspur Cafe **7**
Ludvig's Bistro **3**
Pizza Express **21**

> ### Thank You. No, Thank *You.*
>
> In 1867, Russia's Czar Alexander feared that he couldn't hold the unprofitable colony of Alaska and saw a political advantage in doing his American allies the favor of selling it to them. Ironically, the Americans thought they were doing Russia a favor by buying it. Congress balked at paying the $7.2 million price that Sec. of State William Seward had negotiated for this worthless waste, relenting more than a year later partly out of fear of offending the czar. Americans didn't change their dim view of "Seward's Folly" until gold discoveries decades later.

Unfortunately, the area was not uninhabited. The powerful tribe of Tlingit Indians lead by Chief Katlian were not interested in giving up their territory. Baranof initially built his small settlement—named Redoubt St. Michael—about 7½ miles north of present-day Sitka. When Baranof and most of his soldiers went back north to Kodiak 3 years later, the Tlingits overran Redoubt St. Michael, killing nearly all of its approximately 150 male residents and taking more than 100 women and children as slaves. Many were later ransomed.

Baranof returned in 1804 and returned the favor, overrunning Katlian's settlement just south of what is now downtown Sitka. The Russians then built New Archangel and made it the capital of Russian America. The Russians would remain in Sitka for the next 63 years, but it was an uneasy peace, at best, with the Native community.

Downtown Sitka retains the general shape of the Russian community, with a replica stockade building still overlooking the area where the Natives built their houses, along what is now Katlian Street. There is an old Russian Orthodox Cemetery in the woods above town.

Baranof's "castle" burned down in 1894, but the hill where it sat and where Alaska was officially transferred to the United States remains the focal point of downtown. Several other buildings from the 1830s remain, and the Russian Orthodox Church is still the town's most recognizable building, although the church is just under half a century old, replacing the original 1848 church that burned in 1966.

Besides the numerous small islands that dot Sitka Sound, the town is ringed by a variety of spectacular mountains, most notably the Mount Fuji of Alaska, Mt. Edgecombe, a dormant volcano that rises on an island just to the northwest of Sitka.

Wildlife viewing is also a major draw for the area, with seabird colonies, killer whales, seals, and sea lions all within a short boat excursion from town. Most notably, Sitka hosts large numbers of humpback and other whales from the early spring into the late fall. Whale sightings are not guaranteed, but they are frequent enough that refunds are often given by the tour boat operators.

Despite its numerous charms, Sitka remains just slightly off the tourism path. You will see visitors there in the summer, but you won't be overwhelmed by them. And you will see a bustling Southeastern Alaskan port community that has more history than nearly all the rest of the towns in the state combined.

Essentials

GETTING THERE Sitka sits on the west side of Baranof Island, a detour from the Inside Passage for the **Alaska Marine Highway System**

(📞 **800/642-0066;** www.ferryalaska.com). The ride through narrow Peril Straits and other narrows into Sitka is definitely worth the trip. The shore seems close enough to touch, and if you look closely, you can sometimes see deer. The fare from either Juneau (a 9-hr. run) or Petersburg (10 hr. away by conventional ferry) is $45, and a two-berth cabin is $58 more. The ferry dock (📞 **907/747-3300**) is 7 miles out of town.

Alaska Airlines (📞 **800/252-7522;** www.alaskaair.com) links Sitka daily to Juneau, Ketchikan, and Seattle; northbound flights continue to Anchorage.

To get to town from the ferry dock, the **Sitka Tours** (📞 **907/747-8443**) bus charges $8 each way. No reservations are needed, just climb aboard and pay the driver. **Nina's Taxi** (📞 **907/738-1931**) and **Sitka Cab** (📞 **907/747-5001**) are among five taxi companies in town; the ride from the ferry dock is around $18. See Hank's Cab on p. 141.

VISITOR INFORMATION A kiosk in the city-operated **Harrigan Centennial Hall,** 330 Harbor Dr., next to the Crescent Boat Harbor (📞 **907/747-3225**), is a handy walk-in information stop. It is usually staffed when the hall is open, Monday through Friday from 8am to 10pm, Saturday and Sunday 8am to 5pm; if no one is at the desk, inquire in the office. The town's professional visitor organization is the **Sitka Convention and Visitors Bureau,** P.O. Box 1226, Sitka, AK 99835 (📞 **907/747-5940;** fax 907/747-3739). They maintain a very useful website at **www.sitka.org**.

The **Sitka National Historical Park Visitor Center,** 106 Metlakatla St., Sitka, AK 99835 (📞 **907/747-0110;** www.nps.gov/sitk), run by the National Park Service, which maintains key historic sites in Sitka, is an essential stop to gather information and learn about what happened here. The center is open daily from 8am to 5pm in summer, Monday through Saturday from 8am to 5pm in winter. Also see "Exploring Sitka," below, for more on the park.

ORIENTATION Sitka, on the west side of Baranof Island, has only a few miles of road. The **ferry terminal** is located at its north end, 7 miles out, on **Halibut Point Road;** the site of an abandoned pulp mill is at the south end, roughly the same distance out **Sawmill Creek Road.** The town faces Sitka Sound. Across Sitka Channel is **Japonski Island,** with the **airport** (don't worry, it only looks as if your plane is going to land in the water). **Lincoln Street** contains most of the tourist attractions.

GETTING AROUND The airport has **Avis** (📞 **800/230-4898** or 907/966-2404; www.avis.com) and **North Star Rent-a-Car** (📞 **800/722-6927** or 907/966-2552; www.northstarrentacar.com).

The Visitor Transit Bus operated by the **Sitka Tribal Tours** (see "Exploring Sitka," below) makes a continuous circuit of the sites from May to September when large cruise ships are in town. The fare is $5 round-trip or $10 all day.

Bike rental makes a good deal of sense in Sitka. **Yellow Jersey Cycle Shop,** 329 Harbor Dr., right across from the Centennial Hall downtown (📞 **907/747-6317;** www.yellowjerseycycles.com), rents quality bikes for $25 a day.

[FastFACTS] SITKA

Banks Three banks are at the center of downtown, around 300 Lincoln St., with ATMs, which are also found at local grocery stores.

Hospital **Sitka Community** (☎ **907/747-3241**) is at 209 Moller Dr.

Internet Access Try **Highliner Coffee,** on Lake Street near Seward Street, or the downtown post office.

Police Call ☎ **907/747-3245** for nonemergency business.

Post Office At 338 Lincoln St.; it is open Saturday.

Taxes Sales tax is 5% October through March, 6% April through September. The tax on rooms totals 11% and 12%, respectively.

SPECIAL EVENTS The **Starring Ceremony,** January 7, marks Russian Orthodox Christmas with a procession through the streets and song and prayer at the doors of the faithful. Call St. Michael's Cathedral for information (☎ **907/747-8120**).

The **Sitka Salmon Derby** occurs at the end of May and beginning of June, when the kings are running; contact the Sitka Sportsman's Association (☎ **907/747-3469**) for information.

The **Sitka Summer Music Festival,** a chamber-music series that began in 1972, is one of Alaska's most important cultural events, drawing musicians from all over the world for 3 weeks in June. Performances take place Tuesdays, Fridays, and Saturdays, as well as other events all week. Contact the festival office for information (☎ **907/747-6774;** www.sitka musicfestival.org).

The **Sitka WhaleFest** (☎ **907/747-7964;** www.sitkawhalefest.org) takes place over a weekend in early November, during the fall and early winter period when humpback whales congregate in Sitka Sound to feed before migrating to Hawaiian waters. Experts come from around the world to present a 3-day symposium on marine mammal research, and there are whale-watching tours, concerts, a banquet, a market, a run, and other community events.

New Archangel Dancers.

Hank Moore, of **Hank's Cab** (℡ **907/747-8888;** www.hankstours.com), can drive you around, like any taxi driver, but, if you ask, he offers something more. For $25 to $35 per person, he offers a tour of Sitka's Russian and natural history, including a scenic stop where he pulls out his guitar and performs. Hank's a good blues/folk musician with two CDs out, and he can really sing.

Exploring Sitka

The **Sitka Tribe of Alaska**'s Community House is a good starting point, where you can watch Tlingits dance performances (see below), join walking or bus tours, or sign up for kayaking or other outdoor activities, including trail hikes. A 2-hour walking tour includes the town and national historic park. The house is at 200 Katlian St. (℡ **888/270-8687** or 907/747-7290; www.sitkatours.com). **Sitka Tours** (℡ **907/747-8443**) also offers tours, taking more of the Russian perspective. Prices for each choice of tour range from about $20 for a brief downtown tour to $66 for a longer town tour that includes most of the attractions and dancing; the type of dancing—Native or Russian—depends on which firm you go with. See **Sitka Tribe Dance Performances,** p. 144, for a description of the Alaska Native choice. Russian folk dance is performed by the women of the **New Archangel Dancers** (℡ **907/747-5516;** www.newarchangeldancers.com) in the Harrigan Centennial Hall, 330 Harbor Dr., next to Crescent Harbor. Performances are scheduled when cruise ships are in town, and most of the audience comes from Sitka Tours, but walk-ins are welcome; check the website or call the number above for a recorded message with showtimes. Tickets, which cost $10, go on sale a half-hour before the performance.

SITKA'S TLINGITS & RUSSIAN HERITAGE

Sitka National Historical Park ★★★
In 1799, the Russian American Company, led by Alexander Baranof, landed from their base in Kodiak, established Redoubt St. Michael (today the **Old Sitka State Historic Site,** 7½ miles north of town—just a grassy picnic area with interpretive signs), and claimed the Pacific Northwest of America for Russia. The Tlingits, sophisticated traders who had already acquired flintlocks, attacked with knives, spears, and guns, and destroyed the redoubt in mid-June 1802, killing almost all of the Russians. Tlingits warriors quickly began building fortifications on the site now within the national historical park, anticipating a Russian counterattack, which came in 1804. Baranof returned with an

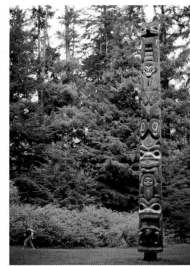

Sitka National Historical Park.

attacking force of a Russian gunship and a swarm of Aleut kayaks, which towed the becalmed vessel into position to begin the bombardment. The Tlingits withstood the siege for 6 days, then vacated their fort at night after a canoe delivering gunpowder exploded, leaving them short of ammunition. The Russians founded and heavily fortified the town of New Archangel, and in 1808 it became their administrative capital. But the Tlingits name is the one that stuck: Shee Atika, since contracted to Sitka.

The historic significance of the battle site was recognized early. President Benjamin Harrison, a friend of Alaska missionary Sheldon Jackson, set the land aside as a public park in 1890. In 1902 and 1905, a collection of totem poles from around Southeast was brought here, and in 1910, the site was designated a national monument. The park visitor center and grounds emphasize the Native perspective. There is no better place to learn about Tlingits art and history. A naturally lit hall with a 30-foot ceiling displays original poles (many of those outside are reproductions) in startlingly good condition, despite their age. Extraordinary poles by current Native artists stand outside, and within the building, artisans of the Southeast Alaska Indian Cultural Center work in a series of windowed workshops creating traditional crafts of metal, wood, beads, textiles, and woven grass. Visitors are invited to enter the workshops and ask questions. A free 12-minute video provides a good historical overview.

The outdoor totem trail and the site of the battle also must not be missed. The totems stand tall and forbidding along a pathway through massive spruce and hemlock, where misty rain often wanders down from an unseen sky somewhere above the trees. The shore-side battle site and the nearby fort site—only a grassy area now—are along the trail. While plenty of imagination is needed to place a desperate fight in this peaceful setting, it is easy to feel deep down what the Tlingits were fighting for when you stand among the trees and totems and hear the lapping sea and raven's call.

106 Metlakatla St. ✆ **907/747-0110.** Admission $4. Visitor center year-round daily 8am–5pm. Park May 1–Sept 1 daily 6am–10pm; Sept 2–Apr 30 daily 7am–8pm.

The Russian Bishop's House ★★★

Bishop Innocent Veniaminov, born in 1797, translated scriptures into Tlingits and other Native languages and trained deacons to carry Russian Orthodoxy back to their Native villages. When the United States bought Alaska in 1867, few Russians stayed behind, but thanks to Veniaminov's work, the Russian Orthodox faith remains strong in Native Alaska; today there are 89 parishes, primarily in tiny Native villages. In 1977, Veniaminov was canonized as St. Innocent in the Orthodox faith.

In 1842–43, the Russian American Company constructed this extraordinary house for Veniaminov as a residence, school, and chapel. It may have survived many years of neglect in part because its huge beams fit together like a ship's. In 1972, the National Park Service bought and began restoring the building, which is the best of only four surviving from all of Russian America (another is the gift store at 206 Lincoln St.). The Bishop's House is Alaska's most interesting historic site. Downstairs is a self-guided museum; upstairs, rangers lead tours of the bishop's quarters, which are furnished with original and period pieces. It's an extraordinary window into an alternate stream of American history, from a time before the founding of Seattle or San Francisco, when Sitka was the most important city on North America's Pacific Coast. The tour concludes with a visit to a beautiful little chapel with many of the original icons Innocent imported from Russia.

Lincoln and Monastery sts. No phone; call Sitka National Historical Park Visitor Center (☎ **907/747-0110**). Admission $4 per person or $15 per family (family admission covers both facilities). Hours depend on staffing.

Sheldon Jackson Museum.

Sheldon Jackson Museum ★★

Sheldon Jackson, a Presbyterian missionary with powerful friends in Washington, was Alaska's first General Agent for Education. As a side hobby during his travels from 1888 to 1898, Jackson gathered an omnivorous 5,000-piece collection of Native art and everyday cultural objects. That unique collection has been displayed for more than a century in a concrete building on the campus of a college that bore Jackson's name, which closed several years ago and at press time was being reinvented as the Sitka Fine Arts Camp campus and more. The museum is a jewel box of treasures, arguably the best collection of Native artifacts in the state, with more added regularly. Many drawers open to reveal more displays. Don't miss Katlian's helmet, worn by the Kiksadi clan's war leader in the Battle of Sitka in 1804; raven shaped, it is that rare piece of great history that's also great art. The gift shop contains the work of more than 100 Native artists, some of whom demonstrate their craft on summer days. Authentic Native art pieces cost more than tourist trinkets: Plan to spend more than $100 except for small, simple items.

104 College Dr. ☎ **907/747-8981.** www.museums.state.ak.us. Admission $4 adults, free for ages 18 and under. Mid-May to mid-Sept daily 9am–5pm; mid-Sept to mid-May Tues–Sat 10am–4pm.

St. Michael's Cathedral ★★

The first Orthodox cathedral in the New World stands grandly in the middle of Sitka's principal street, where it was completed in 1848. Bishop Veniaminov (see the **Russian Bishop's House,** above) designed it and oversaw construction. The cathedral contains several miraculous icons, some dating from the 17th century. The St. Michael, the farthest right of six on the front screen, was bound for Sitka aboard the *Neva* in 1813, when the ship went down some 30 miles out. Thirty days later, the icon, in its crate, washed ashore undamaged and was recovered by Sitka's townspeople. The original building burned down in a 1966 fire that started elsewhere and took much of Sitka's downtown, but the contents were saved by a human chain in the 30 minutes before the building was destroyed. Orthodox Christians all over the United States raised the money to rebuild the cathedral exactly as it had been. A knowledgeable guide is on hand to answer questions or give talks when large groups congregate. Sunday services are sung in English, Church Slavonic, Tlingits, Aleut, and Yupik. Right across Lincoln Street, stop in at the cathedral's well-stocked Archangel Michael Icons, Books and Gift Shop for souvenirs, music CDs, books, and even children's books.

Lincoln and Cathedral sts. ☎ **907/747-8120.** $2 donation requested. Generally open summer Mon–Fri 9am–4pm; however, hours change and are extended due to cruise-ship calls. Call ahead. Also call for winter hours.

A Sheet'ka Kwaán Naā performance.

Sitka Tribe Dance Performances ★   The Sheet'ka Kwaán Naa Kahidi, Sitka's community house, on the north side of the downtown parade ground, is a modern version of a Tlingits Clan House, with an air-handling system that pulls smoke from the central fire pit straight up to the chimney. The magnificent house screen, a carved wall at the front of the hall, installed in 2000, is the largest in the Pacific Northwest. Performances last 30 minutes, including dances and a story. It's entirely traditional and put on by members of the tribe. You can also sign up for tours and activities in the lobby.

200 Katlian St. ✆ **888/270-8687** or 907/747-7290. www.sitkatours.com. Admission $10 adults, $5 children. Call for times.

OTHER ATTRACTIONS IN TOWN

Alaska Raptor Center ★★   This nonprofit center takes in injured birds of prey (mainly bald eagles, but also owls, hawks, and other species) for veterinary treatment and release or, if too badly injured, for placement in a zoo or as part of the collection of 20 that live on-site. Visitors get to see the impressive birds up close in a lecture setting, through the glass wall of the veterinary clinic, and in outdoor enclosures, but the highlight is an extraordinary flight-training center, built in 2003 at a cost of $3 million. This enormous aviary is where recuperating birds learn to fly again, and visitors can walk its length behind one-way glass, watching them preen, feed, and take to the air in a peaceful setting simulating their natural habitat. Watching these giant birds fly from so close is awesome. The center's grounds also include a pleasant nature trail (accessible for travelers with disabilities) that leads down to a salmon stream where healthy eagles can sometimes be seen feeding.

1000 Raptor Way (off Sawmill Creek Blvd.) ✆ **800/643-9425** or 907/747-8662. www.alaska raptor.org. Admission $12 adults, $6 ages 12 and under. Summer Mon–Fri 8am–4pm. No admission or tours in the winter; call for winter hours.

Walking Downtown   The grassy park at Lincoln and Katlian was the site of the Russians' barracks and parade ground. Just north on Marine Street is a replica of a **Russian Blockhouse;** across Lincoln Street to the south and up the stairs is **Castle Hill,** a site of historic significance for the ancient Tlingits, for the Russians, and for contemporary Alaskans. The first American flag raised in Alaska was hoisted here in 1867. There are historic markers and cannons. As you walk east past the cathedral and Crescent Harbor, several quaint historic buildings are on the left. My favorite is **St. Peter's by-the-Sea Episcopal Church,** a lovely stone-and-timber chapel with a pipe organ, consecrated in 1899. At the east end of the harbor, there is a nice **public playground.**

Shopping

There are some good shops and galleries in Sitka, mostly on Lincoln and Harbor streets. Several are across the street from St. Michael's Cathedral. **Fairweather Prints,** 209 Lincoln St., has a fun, youthful feel; it's large and has a diverse selection, including wearable art (including T-shirts), watercolors, prints, ceramics, and cute, inexpensive crafts. Continue west on Lincoln to **Old Harbor Books,** 201 Lincoln St., a good browsing store with an excellent selection of Alaska books. Near the Crescent Harbor dock, the **Sitka Rose Gallery** occupies a Victorian house at 419 Lincoln St., featuring higher-end work, mostly local: sculpture, original paintings, engraving, and jewelry. The **Sheldon Jackson Museum Gift Shop,** 104 College Dr., is an excellent place to buy Alaska Native arts and crafts with assurance of their authenticity.

Getting Outside: On the Water

The little islands and rocks that dot Sitka Sound are an invitation to the sea otter in all of us; you must get out on the water.

SIGHTSEEING & WILDLIFE TOURS

When conditions allow, tour boats visit **St. Lazaria Island,** a bird colony where you can expect to see tufted puffins, murres, rhinoceros auklets, and other pelagic birds. Storm petrels show up by the hundreds of thousands at dawn and dusk for those who charter a boat to stay overnight at the rookery. The volcanic rock drops straight down into deep water, so even big boats can come close, but in rough weather, even they won't go to the exposed location of the island. Even then, there's plenty to see in protected waters. Humpback whales show up in large groups in the fall and are often seen by the half-dozen in the summer. There are so many bald eagles that you're pretty well guaranteed to see them (even from shore), as well as abundant sea otters. The public tubs at **Goddard Hot Springs,** 17 miles south of town, are another possible stop for charters.

The **Sitka Wildlife Quest,** operated by Allen Marine Tours (✆ **888/747-8101** or 907/747-8100; www.allenmarinetours.com), is a popular marine tour run for many years with naturalists to explain the wildlife. Tours visit St. Lazaria Island when sea conditions permit. Tours are 3 hours and run Tuesday, Wednesday, and Thursday at 1:15pm, and Saturday at 1:30pm. On weekday tours, most seats are taken by cruise-ship passengers, but Saturday voyages take more independent travelers. The cost is $120 adults, $79 children. The boat leaves from the Crescent Harbor Visitors Dock late May through early September. Call ahead for schedule changes and to reserve.

A sea otter near Sitka.

For $120 per person, you can charter a six-passenger boat for a 3-hour tour to St. Lazaria Island for whale-watching and to learn about the Sound with a married couple who are both former wildlife biologists, Kent Hall and Beverly Minn, at **Sitka's Secrets** (✆ **907/747-5089;** www.sitkasecret.com). They offer fishing charters, too.

Friendly Davey Lubin of **Esther G Sea Taxi** (see "Forest Service Cabins," below) also offers educational small-boat marine tours.

Sea Life Discovery Tours (✆ **877/966-2301** or 907/966-2301; www. sealifediscoverytours.com) offers a chance to see the rich underwater life of Sitka Sound from an extraordinary boat with big windows 4 feet below the waterline; it's really cool. They charge $86 for a 2-hour tour; call for times.

SALTWATER FISHING

Many charter boats are available for salmon or halibut. The Sitka Convention and Visitors Bureau (see "Visitor Information," earlier) keeps a detailed charter boat list online. Using the grid view (www.sitka.org/grid.html), you can compare boats, rates, and services, and link to the vessel's own home page.

Or book through **Alaska Adventures Unlimited** (✆ **907/747-5576;** www.alaskafishing-sitka.com), which has set up charters in Sitka since 1982.

If you can handle your own boat, skiffs rent for $105 half-day and up from BJ's Boat Rentals (✆ **907/738-0481**).

SEA KAYAKING

Sitka's protected waters and intricate shorelines are perfect for sea kayaking. You're almost sure to see sea otters, seals, sea lions, and eagles, and could see whales. A locally owned firm, **Sitka Sound Ocean Adventures** (✆ **907/752-0660;** www.kayaksitka.com), offers day paddles of various lengths. A 2½-hour outing is $69 for adults and $49 for children ages 6 to 12 (no children 5 and under), or take a half-day paddle for $149 and $109. Reserve ahead, then make contact at the blue bus in the parking lot of the Harrigan Centennial Hall.

Getting Outside: Onshore

FRESHWATER FISHING

Anglers should pick up the ***Sitka Area Sport Fishing Guide,*** which has lots of tips on streams, lakes, and fishing methods in the area. You can download the guide from the **Alaska Department of Fish and Game** at www.alaska.gov/adfg

---

🗒 One Halibut Per Customer

For years, ever more charter boats carried visitors to Southeast Alaska in pursuit of halibut, all chasing the same resource of fish. Although anglers take far fewer halibut than the commercial fishing industry, they have repeatedly overrun the annual limits set on their total catch. Consequently, federal fishery managers invoked a one-fish-per-day bag limit, with a size limit of 37 inches. If you enjoy fishing, the limit shouldn't stop you. A single 50-pound fish should be enough for anyone, and you can keep fishing and throwing back halibut until you decide to land and kill one. Or book a charter, in season, to fish halibut and salmon on the same day.

(the URL for the guide itself is long; to find it, click on "Sport Fish" and then the Southeast region, the Sitka area, and finally on "Additional Information"). The site also has weekly fishing updates during the summer months. The local Fish and Game office is at 304 Lake St., Room 103, Sitka, AK 99835 (✆ **907/747-5355**).

FOREST SERVICE CABINS

The **Sitka Ranger District,** 204 Siginaka Way, Sitka, AK 99835 (✆ **907/747-6671;** www.fs.fed.us/r10/tongass/districts/sitka), maintains two dozen wilderness cabins on Baranof, Chichagof, and Kruzof islands, in sea-kayaking coves and on remote fishing lakes, where rowing skiffs generally are provided. The cabins and their facilities are described in a Forest Service handout or on their website. One cabin is accessible by road from Sitka (see "A Hostel & Camping," below). You will need camping gear to use any of the cabins, and a boat or floatplane to all but that one, a much greater cost than the nightly rental of $35 to $50.

For cabins on saltwater near Sitka, the most affordable way may be a water taxi, such as **Esther G Sea Taxi** (✆ **907/747-6481** or 738-6481 cell; www.puffinsandwhales.com). Operator Davey Lubin also offers educational marine wildlife tours, beach and forest tours, and kayak drop-offs to remote shores. Ken Bellows of **Air Sitka** flying service (✆ **907/747-7920**) has been flying anglers, hunters, and cabin visitors out to remote spots around Sitka for many years. He also offers half-hour flightseeing spins for $250. His helpful office person is on duty Monday through Friday from 8am to noon, at 485 Katlian St.

Either way, allow time in your schedule in case bad weather prevents backcountry travel. Information on researching and reserving a cabin is under "Getting Outside in the Tongass National Forest," earlier in this chapter.

HIKING

Sitka is a great hiking area, with trails threading all over the mountains behind the town. There are a dozen U.S. Forest Service hiking trails accessible from the roads around Sitka and another 20 rough trails you can get to by plane or boat. A beautifully made little book, *Sitka Trails* (Alaska Geographic), covers each trail with a detailed description and fine-scale color topographic map. If you need further advice, contact the ranger district office (see the preceding section).

From downtown, the 4-mile (one-way) **Indian River Trail** is a relaxing rainforest walk rising gradually up the river valley to a small waterfall. Take Indian River Road off Sawmill Creek Road just east of the downtown. For a steeper mountain-climbing trail to alpine terrain and great views, the **Gavan Hill–Harbor Mountain Trail** is near the end of Baranof Street, which starts near the Russian Bishop's House. It gains 2,500 feet over 3 miles to the peak of Gavan Hill, then continues another 3 miles along a ridge to meet Harbor Mountain Road. The **Sitka Cross Trail** connects these trails and neighborhood streets, allowing you to start almost anywhere.

At the north end of Halibut Point Road, 7½ miles from downtown, several wonderful trails loop through the **Starrigavan Recreation Area.** On the right, the **Estuary Life Trail** and **Forest Muskeg Trail,** totaling about a mile, are well developed and accessible to anyone, circling a grassy estuary rich with birds and fish. The pleasant **Mosquito Cove Trail,** starting from within the Starrigavan Bayside Loop picnic area on the left, circles 1.25 miles along the shore to the secluded gravel beach of the cove, returning over boardwalk steps through the old-growth forest.

TIDE-POOLING & SHORE WALKS

Halibut Point State Recreation Area, 4½ miles north of town on Halibut Point Road, is a great place for a picnic, shore ramble, and tide-pooling. The Mosquito Cove Trail (above) is also promising. To find the best low tides, check a tide book, available all over town. It's best to go at the lowest tide possible, arriving on the shore an hour before the low. To identify the little creatures you'll see, pick up a plastic-covered field guide at a bookstore.

WHALE-WATCHING

Humpback whales stop to feed in Sitka Sound on their way south in the winter migration. During October, November, December, and March, you can watch from shore—the local government has even built a special park for the purpose. At the fun **Whale Park,** just south of town on Sawmill Creek Road, spotting scopes are mounted on platforms along a boardwalk and at the end of staircases that descend the dramatic, wooded cliffs. Excellent interpretive signs, located near surfacing concrete whales in the parking lot, explain the whales. The Sitka WhaleFest, in November (see "Special Events," earlier), is the best time for whale enthusiasts, as then you can watch whales in the company of cetacean scientists. For summertime whale-watching, take a boat: Choices are above under "Sightseeing & Wildlife Tours."

Where to Stay

In addition to the places below, you'll find superclean rooms with many amenities (including free Wi-Fi) in a quiet, landscaped building downtown at the **Super 8 Sitka,** 404 Sawmill Creek Blvd. (www.super8.com; ✆ **800/800-8000** for reservations, or 907/747-8804). The 24-hour laundromat is open to the public, too. We also like the **Cascade Inn,** 2½ miles from downtown on Halibut Point Road (www.cascadeinnsitka.com; ✆ **800/532-0908** or 907/747-6804), with 10 light, waterfront rooms over Sitka Sound, for reasonable prices, next to a gas station and liquor store.

The town has several good B&Bs. The **Sitka Convention and Visitors Bureau** (www.sitka.org; ✆ **907/747-5940**) has links to many on its website and can send you a printed list as well. Among them is **Alaska Swan Lake Bed & Breakfast,** 206½ Lakeview Dr. (www.sitka.org/swanlake/index.htm; ✆ **907/ 747-3917**), with rooms with private bathrooms for $100 a night in a big, white house above the lake just half a mile from the downtown area.

Fly-In Fish Inn ★★   This is a classy little boutique hotel right on the water a bit off the beaten path north of the town center. The spacious rooms, with entrances off covered walkways, have simple, elegant decoration, in sage, gold, and burgundy. High-quality mattresses are covered with down pillows and cotton comforters. Each unit has a small wet bar with a sink, microwave, and coffeemaker, stocked with snacks and supplies. Rooms renting for a $20 premium enjoy wonderful views, as does the beautifully appointed waterfront bar downstairs, with a fireplace and a mosaic behind the bar and a deck over the harbor. The included breakfast is served in the bar, cooked to order for each guest. The hotel is only a few years old, and everything has been kept so clean, it is as if you're the first guest. The name comes from the air taxi service that's on-site, which leaves from the dock.

485 Katlian St., Sitka, AK 99835. www.flyinfishinn.com. ✆ **907/747-7910.** 10 units. High season $159–$179 double, $388 suite; low season $99 double, $199 suite. Extra person no charge. Rates include full breakfast. MC, V. **Amenities:** Bar. *In room:* TV, hair dryer, microwave, Wi-Fi.

An Otter's Cove Bed & Breakfast ★   A custom-built house contains three large, well-appointed bedrooms and an attractive common room right on the ocean, with stunning views and a covered outdoor seating area, on Halibut Point Road, north of town. Newly constructed, the building has elaborate stonework and landscaping, and even the fish-cleaning area is a work of art, divided off by a stained-glass window. Guest quarters take up the entire downstairs and are entered from the far side from the family's quarters, helping create the B&B's overall sense of privacy and peace. Hostess Cheryl Jordan cooks full breakfasts and keeps the place like new.

3211 Halibut Point Rd., Sitka, AK 99835. www.ottercovebandb.com. ✆ **907/747-4529.** 3 units. High season $130–$150 double; low season $89–$109 double. Extra person $20. MC, V. **Amenities:** Outdoor Jacuzzi; barbecue; fish-cleaning/freezing facility; Internet. *In room:* TV/DVD, hair dryer, Wi-Fi.

Shee Atika Totem Square Inn ★★   This is the best large hotel in town. Owned by the local Native corporation and standing across the street from the community house, it makes full use of their Tlingits motifs and colors in its decoration—red, black, white, and earth—and employs many Natives on its staff. The service was uniformly excellent on both our recent visits, and the housekeeping spotless. The building makes use of the ocean view in two directions, and the rooms are well thought out and nicely equipped, with comfortable beds and large flatscreen TVs. Continuous upgrading for several years has kept it all like new. Common rooms include a light, spacious breakfast room, where a generous continental breakfast is served; fast, free computer terminals in the lobby; and snacks for guests available at all hours. A dock for tour and fishing charter boats is attached. The downtown location allows walking to some of the attractions, although the national historic site is a long walk.

201 Katlian St., Sitka, AK 99835. www.totemsquareinn.com. ✆ **866/300-1353** or 907/747-3693. Fax 907/747-2839. 68 units. High season $139–$179 double; low season $89–$109 double. Extra person $15. AE, DC, DISC, MC, V. **Amenities:** Free airport transfers; exercise room; Internet access. *In room:* TV, hair dryer, Wi-Fi, wired broadband.

Sitka Hotel ✍   An old building facing the parade ground right downtown contains some large, attractive rooms with large TVs and good beds for bargain rates. But the hotel is a budget choice and has its rough edges, including noisy heat and thin walls—not for the light sleeper—and casual service. The rooms vary, with those in the older section at the front relatively small and creaky, and the newer rooms, in the back of the building, larger and with added amenities, such as coffeemakers. Overall, it's a good place to save money and has always been clean on our many visits.

   Victoria's Restaurant, with about a dozen tables in the storefront downstairs, tries for a high Victorian feel, but in actuality, it's more of a friendly small-town diner, with hearty breakfasts and lunches in winter and an inexpensive fine-dining dinner menu added in the summer. The hotel has a small bar, too.

118 Lincoln St., Sitka, AK 99835. www.sitkahotel.com. ✆ **907/747-3288.** Fax 907/747-8499. 60 units, 46 with private bathroom. High season $105 double with private bathroom; low season $70 with private bathroom. Extra person $5. AE, DISC, MC, V. **Amenities:** Restaurant; free airport transfers. *In room:* TV, Wi-Fi.

Westmark Sitka ★   This hotel, above Crescent Harbor in the heart of the historic district, contains many standard rooms with sweeping views of Sikta Sound. Remodeled in 2009 with granite countertops and large flatscreen TVs, rooms have mission-style oak furniture and all the amenities expected in a corporate hotel; beds were replaced in 2010. The lobby is done up with leather furniture, the walls decorated with mounted fish.

The **Raven Dining Room** restaurant shares the hotel's view and outdoorsy decorative theme, with numerous mounted animal heads on the walls. Dark blue tablecloths accent mahogany furniture. They serve a long menu of seafood and beef.

330 Seward St., Sitka, AK 99835-7523. www.westmarkhotels.com. (℃ **800/544-0970** for reservations, or 907/747-6241. Fax 907/747-5486. 105 units. High season $189 double; low season $99 double. Extra person no charge. AE, DC, DISC, MC, V. **Amenities:** Restaurant; bar; free airport transfers. *In room:* TV, hair dryer, high-speed Internet.

A HOSTEL & CAMPING

Sitka International Hostel, 109 Jeff Davis St. (www.sitkahostel.org; (℃ **907/747-8661**), is just three buildings from Lincoln Street. The 25 beds in five gender-separated dorms are $24 per night, children are $15, and a single-family room is $60. Office hours are 6 to 10pm, and the lights are out at 11pm; lockout is 10am to 6pm. You can reserve ahead by phone or e-mail without advance payment. The hostel is open year-round and does not take credit cards.

The Forest Service's **Starrigavan Recreation Area** contains excellent campsites and a cabin at the north end of Halibut Point Road, 7½ miles from town and ¾ mile from the ferry dock. There are three loops. The Backpackers' Loop has six hike-in sites. The Estuary Loop (which joins the Estuary Life Trail), on the right, has 25 sites for RVs or tents, which are widely separated under huge trees. The Bayside Loop, at the water's edge, is the last left on the highway. Three of its sites are situated on the edge of Starrigavan Bay, creating the feeling that you're way out in the wilderness. Fees are $12 to $30 a night, or $50 for the new Starrigavan Creek Cabin, a rare road-accessible Forest Service cabin that is also fully usable by people with disabilities. Twenty-one sites and the cabin can be reserved on the national system (see "Reserving a Cabin or Campsite," p. 96). The recreation area is open all year, but vehicle access is restricted in the winter. May through mid-September, access gates are locked from 10pm to 7am.

There are two RV parks, each with water and electric hookups only, and each charging under $22: City-run **Sealing Cove RV Park** (℃ **907/747-3439;** no reservations) is near the airport and a free dump station, and **Sitka Sportsman's Association RV Park** (℃ **907/747-4712**) is near the ferry dock.

Where to Eat

In addition to the restaurants described here, and in the Sitka Hotel and Westmark Sitka, a Subway sandwich shop is at Seward and Lake streets, behind the Westmark.

The Channel Club ★★ STEAK   With an updated dining room and improved service, this is a lovely, calming place to eat, enjoy company, and take in the ocean view. The restaurant's look is simple, elegant, and spotless. The menu includes salmon, halibut, and cod, which is done well, but it's a steakhouse, and the specialty is seasoned beef grilled right. Don't miss the outstanding salad bar. The location, several miles out of town, requires you have a car or take the restaurant's free shuttle.

2906 Halibut Point Rd. (℃ **907/747-7440.** www.sitkachannelclub.com. Reservations recommended. Dinner $16–$48. AE, MC, V. Daily 5–9pm year-round.

A cool couple owns the **Backdoor Café,** in the back half of Old Harbor Books at 104 Barracks St. (☏ **907/747-8856**), the kind of place that develops a following among local poets, musicians, and the like. Besides coffee and the owners' own homemade bagels and fantastic pies, the cafe serves fresh pastries for breakfast and a single special for lunch (which can run out). It's open Monday through Friday from 6:30am to 5pm, Saturday 6:30am to 2pm. Credit cards are not accepted.

Highliner Coffee, on Lake Street just above Seward Street (☏ **907/747-4924**), is a fancier place, with free Wi-Fi (or use their computer for $4 for the first half-hour). A "highliner" is a top commercial fisherman; the name here is a bit of a boast for its fisherpeople owners, who hope to educate customers about their way of life, as well as roasting Sitka's coffee. It's open Monday through Saturday from 5:30am to 6pm, Sunday from 7am to 5pm.

For something a bit more traditional, and sweeter, stop at **Harry's Soda Shop,** in the Harry Race Pharmacy at 106 Lincoln St. (☏ **907/747-8006**), a real old-fashioned soda fountain serving sundaes, floats, cones, and shakes. It's open Monday through Friday 9am to 6pm, till 5pm Saturday, and accepts MasterCard and Visa.

Larkspur Cafe ★ CAFE   Below Sitka's public Raven Radio, in the historic cable house on the water, this is a happening coffee shop that also serves sophisticated, handcrafted food. The dining room has a small collection of funky, mismatched antique tables on a wood floor, and there's more seating outside with ocean views. That's where you'd go if you want to get away from the live music and the loud voices in the festive atmosphere inside. The menu changes daily with the availability of local food but includes items such as cold smoked lox on rye toast with cream cheese and capers, or marinated black cod with brown rice and baby bok choy. Influences are eclectic, with the common element the owners' enthusiasm and the positive scene they've created.

2 Lincoln St. ☏ **907/966-2326.** www.larkspurcafe.blogspot.com. All items specials, prices vary, approx. $5–$15. MC, V. Mon–Tues 11am–3pm; Wed–Sun 11am–10pm.

Ludvig's Bistro ★★ MEDITERRANEAN   This tiny dining room and its chef-owner, Colette Nelson, offer Sitka's first-rate cuisine, and it's a very pleasant place for a meal. She's taken a formerly grungy concrete space and filled it with charm and warmth, Mediterranean colors, wine bottles, and whimsical art. The restaurant is too small to serve many meals a night, so each one is carefully crafted, coming from a changing menu intended to stretch the chef and introduce the small-town clientele to new tastes. A recent menu included grilled marinated lamb chops, a wild mushroom ragout, and calamari. The food is truly memorable. For lunch, catch their chowder cart downtown.

256 Katlian St. ☏ **907/966-3663.** Reservations recommended. Dinner main courses $17–$34. MC, V. Daily 4–10pm. Closed Oct–Apr.

Pizza Express ✦ MEXICAN   Despite the name, this is primarily a Mexican place that also bakes pizza pies. But the pizza is good. It's where Sitka families dine. Come here when you want a filling, inexpensive meal or to take out and get a pizza without a delivery fee. The dining room is a strip mall a long walk from downtown, near the Raptor Center and across from the historical park. The menu is very lengthy and produced by Mexican-American owners who know their stuff. Takeout pizza is sold somewhat later than the dining room hours listed below.

1321 Sawmill Creek Rd. © **907/966-2428.** Main courses $9–$20. MC, V. Mon–Sat 11am–9pm; Sun noon–9pm.

JUNEAU: FOREST CAPITAL

If your time in Alaska is limited, then northern Southeast Alaska serves as the perfect microcosm of nearly all that Alaska has to offer: spectacular scenery, amazing wildlife, and miles of barely touched wilderness surrounding the isolated frontier communities that serve as "cities" in Alaska. It features the largest national forest in America, the 17-million acre Tongass National Forest, and hundreds of islands ranging in size from barely big enough to stand on to ones larger than the states of Delaware and Rhode Island.

Juneau, the state capital, holds nearly half of Southeast Alaska's 75,000 residents. It's the only state capital with no road system, though there always seems to be an expensive plan being considered to punch a road through the wilderness. It's a community with a dual personality, politics in the winter and tourism in the summer, where the residents revel in the great outdoors and enjoy fishing, hiking, and hunting most of the year.

Surrounded by tall mountains ringing the coastline, Juneau is also on the edge of the 1,500-square mile Juneau Icefield, home to more than 140 glaciers. Just a few miles north of downtown is the Mendenhall Glacier, arguably the most accessible glacier in Alaska. The coastline itself is a cornucopia of wildlife, with everything from 1,500-pound brown bears to 70-foot-long humpback whales. The Japanese current that warms the coastline also brings with it millions of salmon that return each summer to spawn in the hundreds of streams.

Because Juneau is the third-largest city in Alaska, it has a greater variety of dining experiences than most island communities in Alaska, but all are casual and fun; dressing up means a clean pair of jeans. Local favorites range from the handcrafted comfort foods at the Sandpiper Cafe to pub and pizza places such as Island Pub across the bridge in Douglas. The surf-and-turf selections on any menu are always a good choice, though Juneau also has surprisingly well-regarded

A mural in Juneau.

The Cruise-Ship Dock: Where Do You Get Off?

Cruise-ship passengers disembark in Juneau's attractive **Marine Park** waterfront area, where a kiosk dispenses information and tour operators sell their services. Downtown shops and attractions are close by. Among the most popular sights is one right at the dock, the statue of a small dog facing the ships as they come in. This is *Patsy Ann,* a bull terrier that in the 1930s always seemed to know when a steamer was arriving and faithfully stationed herself on the dock to meet the disembarking passengers. There's also a spotting scope in the park for watching mountain goats on Mount Juneau. For a quiet break, visit the beautiful library at the top of the parking garage at the south end of the dock.

Mexican and Asian restaurants. And since it is Alaska, the nightlife is hopping year-round, particularly at places such as the Hangar, the Triangle, and the legendary Red Dog Saloon.

Perhaps the best facet of Juneau is that it serves as a great home base for excursions into the heart of some of the most spectacular scenery in North America. Among the many (almost too many to choose) options are the whale-watching cruises up Lynn Canal, boat trips to the spectacular steep-sided fjords Tracy Arm/Fords Terror, and day trips into Glacier Bay National Park.

Essentials

GETTING THERE

BY AIR Jet service is available only from **Alaska Airlines** (✆ 800/252-7522; www.alaskaair.com), with several daily nonstop flights from Seattle and Anchorage and from the smaller Southeast Alaska towns. Many of the region's commuter and air-taxi operators also maintain desks at the airport and have flights out of Juneau. Among the best is **Wings of Alaska** (✆ 907/789-0790; www.ichoosewings.com).

BY FERRY All the main-line ferries of Southeast's **Alaska Marine Highway System** (✆ 800/642-0066; www.ferryalaska.com) stop at the terminal in Auke Bay (✆ 907/789-7453, or 465-3940 recording), 14 miles from downtown. The run to Haines or Skagway takes 5 hours. The passenger fare is $37 to Haines, $50 to Skagway.

GETTING INTO TOWN FROM THE AIRPORT & FERRY TERMINAL An airport shuttle may be operating when you visit. Ask at the visitor desk in the baggage claim area.

An express **Capital Transit city bus** (✆ 907/789-6901) comes to the airport every half-hour on weekdays, at 11 and 41 minutes past the hour.

Flying to Juneau

Juneau's mist-shrouded airport, wedged between ocean and mountain, has a special verb: *to overhead.* That means that when you try to fly to Juneau on a foggy day, you could end up somewhere else instead (although this now happens less frequently, thanks to new navigational technology). Planes overhead other Southeast towns, too, but more frequently in Juneau, since it is the region's travel hub, with many flights a day. The airline will put you on the next flight back to Juneau when the weather clears, but they won't pay for hotel rooms or give you a refund. Your only protection is travel insurance and a loose itinerary. This situation is such an ingrained part of Juneau's way of life that a channel on the cable TV system broadcasts the view toward the airport 24 hours a day, showing the weather over the Gastineau Channel (it's called the Channel Channel, 19 on the dial). Residents know the view so well they can tell from the silent image if they'll get out that day.

The first bus is at 7:11am, the last at 6:11pm; but there is no bus at 7:41am. Fare is $1.50. Your luggage has to fit under your seat or at your feet. Ask the driver for the stop closest to your hotel. Generally, you can walk from there.

Shuttles sometimes operate from the ferry dock downtown in the summer, but the arrangements are changeable. Ask when you arrive, or call ahead to the visitor center (below). A cab downtown from the airport will cost you $22, from the ferry dock $33. One taxi company is **Capital Cab** (*©* **907/586-2772**), which also offers tours for $55 an hour.

ORIENTATION

Juneau has three main parts: downtown, the Mendenhall Valley, and Douglas. Downtown Juneau is a numbered grid of streets overlying the uneven topography like a patchwork quilt over a pile of pillows. As you look at Juneau from the water, Mount Juneau is on the left and Mount Roberts on the right; Mount Roberts is a few hundred feet taller, at 3,819 feet. **Franklin Street** extends south of town 5½ miles to good hiking trails and the hamlet of Thane. When the city outgrew its original site downtown, housing spread to the suburban **Mendenhall Valley,** about a dozen miles north out the Egan Expressway or the parallel two-lane Glacier Highway. The glacial valley also contains the Juneau International Airport, University of Alaska Southeast, and the **Auke Bay** area, where the ferry terminal is located. The road continues 40 miles to a place known as **"The End of the Road."** Across a bridge over the Gastineau Channel from downtown Juneau is Douglas Island. Turn left for the town of **Douglas,** mostly a bedroom community for Juneau, and turn right for the North Douglas Highway, which leads to the ski area and some beautiful rocky beaches.

GETTING AROUND

BY RENTAL CAR   A car is a hindrance in compact downtown Juneau, but if you're going to any of the attractions out the road or on Douglas Island, renting a car for a day or two is a good idea. Hertz, Avis, Budget, Alamo, and National are based at the airport.

BY BIKE   If you can handle hills, bikes make good sense in Juneau, where separated paths parallel many of the main roads and downtown traffic is slow.

5

SOUTHEAST ALASKA   Juneau: Forest Capital

The 24-mile round-trip to Mendenhall Glacier keeps you on a bike path almost all the way. Bikes are for rent at the **Driftwood Lodge,** 435 Willoughby Ave. (✆ **800/544-2239** or 907/586-2280; www.driftwoodalaska.com), for $25 a day.

VISITOR INFORMATION

The **Visitor Information Center** is in the Centennial Hall at 101 Egan Dr., near the State Museum (✆ **888/581-2201** or 907/586-2201; fax 907/586-6304; www.traveljuneau.com). Operated by the Juneau Convention and Visitors Bureau, the center distributes a *Juneau Guide & Travel Planner,* online or on paper, that contains exhaustive listings of hotels and B&Bs, charter boats, tours, and other services. On-site you can use a touch-screen kiosk for information and reservations. The center is open in summer daily 8am to 5pm, and Saturday and Sunday from 9am to 5pm; in winter Monday through Friday from 8am to 5pm. The bureau also operates **information desks** at the airport in the baggage-claim area, and at the Auke Bay ferry terminal. During the summer, centers are staffed at the cruise-ship terminal and at Marine Park.

The office of the **Tongass National Forest Juneau Ranger District** is at 8510 Mendenhall Loop Rd., Juneau, AK 99801 (✆ **907/586-8800;** fax 907/586-8808; www.fs.fed.us/r10/tongass).

[FastFACTS] JUNEAU

Banks **Wells Fargo,** 123 Seward St. (✆ **907/586-3324**), is one of the many banks and stores that have ATMs.

Hospital **Bartlett Regional,** 3260 Hospital Dr. (✆ **907/796-8900**), is 3 miles out the Glacier Highway from downtown.

Internet Access Computers are easy to find downtown at coffeehouses and businesses such as **Copy Express,** at 230 Seward St. (✆ **907/586-2174**).

Police The police station is at 6255 Alaway Ave. (✆ **907/586-0600** for nonemergencies).

Post Office Downtown in the federal building, 709 W. 9th St.; and in the Mendenhall Valley at 9491 Vintage Blvd., near Carr's/Safeway supermarket. A postal contract station handier to the cruise-ship docks is at 145 South Franklin St.

Taxes Sales tax is 5%. You pay 12% tax on rooms.

SPECIAL EVENTS An events calendar is posted on the visitors bureau website: www.traveljuneau.com/discover.

The **Alaska Folk Festival** (✆ **907/463-3316;** akfolkfest.org) is the state's biggest annual coming together of musicians, at Centennial Hall. Musicians take over the town and can be found jamming in every bar and coffeehouse, or wherever a crowd gathers. The 37th annual festival is April 9 to April 15, 2012.

The **Juneau Jazz & Classics Festival** (✆ **907/463-3378;** www.jazzandclassics.org), May 4 to May 19, 2012, presents concerts and workshops in many styles of music—blues, jazz, classical, rock—at various venues, even on a boat, and at many prices—free to $60 a ticket. Most evening performances are around $25.

The **Golden North Salmon Derby** (© **907/789-2399;** www.goldennorthsalmonderby.org), held annually since 1947, targets kings and silvers, normally the first weekend in August. Unlike some other such fishing contests around the state, this isn't just a tourist thing—it brings out as many as 3,000 local fishermen and is even covered live on the radio.

Native Parade in Juneau.

Exploring Downtown

Alaska State Museum ★★★ The museum contains a large collection of art and historical artifacts, but it doesn't seem like a storehouse at all because the objects' presentation is based on their meaning, not on their value. Superb artifacts from Native cultures from around the state are presented to illustrate the lifestyle of those who made them. The ramp to the second floor wraps around the natural history display, with an eagle nesting tree, and at the top, a state history gallery uses significant pieces to tell Alaska's story. The children's area is exceptionally fun, with a ship that the kids can play in. In 2009, the museum installed "Science on a Sphere," a huge interactive globe for displaying earth science concepts, sponsored by the National Oceanic and Atmospheric Administration. Allow at least 2 hours for the museum; half a day would not be out of line. The shop off the lobby is also well worth a look. Although small, it carries lots of quality Alaska Native art and books.

395 Whittier St. © **907/465-2901.** www.museums.state.ak.us. Admission mid-May to mid-Sept $5 adults, free for ages 18 and under; mid-Sept to mid-May $3 adults, free for ages 18 and under. Mid-May to mid-Sept daily 8:30am–5:30pm; mid-Sept to mid-May Tues–Sat 10am–4pm. Closed legal holidays.

The Juneau–Douglas City Museum ★ This fun museum displays artifacts and photographs from the city's pioneer and mining history and Tlingits culture, and impressive special art exhibits that change annually. It's quite well done and holds real interest. The tiny bookshop is stocked with handy information for your visit to Juneau, including the historic hike guide booklet, free historic walking-tour map, and maps of the Evergreen Cemetery and the old Treadwell Mine. In the summer, the museum leads historic walking tours Tuesday through Thursday at 1:30pm. The cost is $10 adults, $7 ages 13 to 18, free 12 and under. Call ahead to reserve your spot, as numbers are limited.

At the corner of 4th and Main sts. © **907/586-3572.** www.juneau.org/parkrec/museum. Admission $4 adults (free in winter), free for ages 18 and under. Summer Mon–Fri 9am–5pm, Sat–Sun 10am–5pm; winter Tues–Sat 10am–4pm.

The Last Chance Mining Museum and Historic Park ★ 🎁 On the site on forested Gold Creek where gold was first discovered in Juneau, the museum preserves old mining buildings and some of their original equipment, including an immense 1912 air compressor and a layered glass map of the tunnels. The highlight is its energetic and learned guide, Renee Hughes, who lives above the compressor with her husband, Gary Gillette. Both are leaders of the Gastineau

Juneau

Mt. Roberts Trail

ATTRACTIONS

Abandoned wooden flume **5**
Alaska State Capitol **14**
Alaska State Museum **9**
Evergreen Cemetery **2**
Gold Creek **4**
Governor's Mansion **6**
Juneau-Douglas City Museum **12**
Last Chance Mining Museum **18**
Mount Roberts Tramway **29**
Patsy Ann statue **28**
St. Nicholas Orthodox Church **20**
State Courthouse **15**
State Office Building **13**
The Wickersham House State
   Historic Site **10**

HOTELS

Alaska's Capital Inn **11**
Baranof Hotel **25**
Breakwater Hotel **1**
The Driftwood Lodge **8**
Goldbelt Hotel Juneau **17**
The Historic Silverbow Inn **16**
Juneau Hotel **3**
Juneau International Hostel **19**

RESTAURANTS

The Hangar **26**
Heritage Coffee Co. & Cafe **27**
Pizzeria Roma **26**
Rainbow Foods **21**
Sandpiper Cafe **7**
Silverbow Bakery **16**
Tarantino's Italian Restaurant **23**
Twisted Fish Co. Alaskan Grill **30**
Valentine's Coffee House &
   Pizzeria **24**
Zephyr Restaurant **22**

An exhibit at the Alaska State Museum.

Channel Historical Society. Ask Renee about the cave-in of the Treadwell Mine to hear her riveting storytelling. The entrance to the site—which contains relics and buildings spread over several acres—is a bridge across the creek, which leads to a steep trail up to the buildings.

1001 Basin Rd. ✆ **907/586-5338.** Admission $4. Daily 9:30am–12:30pm and 3:30–6:30pm. Closed mid-Sept to mid-May. From downtown, take Gold St. up the hill to its end, then join Basin Rd., continuing 1 mile up the valley to the end of the road.

Mount Roberts Tramway ★   The tram takes only 6 minutes to whisk passengers from tourist-clogged Franklin Street to the clear air and overwhelming views at the tree line (1,760 ft.), a destination that used to require a day of huffing and puffing to witness. The tram can be crowded; once you're up there, the beauty hits you. The Alaska Native owners seem to understand that, and they have built a network of alpine paths that take advantage of the views. If you're energetic, you can start a 6-mile round-trip hike to Mount Roberts's summit (at 3,819 ft.), or you can hike the 2½ miles back to downtown. At the top, you'll also find a film on Tlingits culture, a gift shop, and a bar and grill serving lunch and dinner. We would choose something else to do on a day when fog or low overcast obscures the view, however, especially considering the high price.

490 S. Franklin St., at the waterfront near the cruise-ship dock. ✆ **888/461-8726** or 907/463-3412. www.mountrobertstramway.com. Full-day pass $27 adults, $14 children ages 6–12, free age 5 and under; tax included. May–Sept. Call or visit the website for hours.

WALKING TOUR: JUNEAU

START & FINISH:	**Alaska State Capitol, 4th and Seward streets.**
TIME:	**1 hour (1 mile) for standard tour; 2½ hours (2½ miles) for the extended tour, with minimal stops.**

1   The Alaska State Capitol

This structure fills the block between 4th and 5th and Main and Seward streets. Except for the marble portico on the 4th Street side, it is a nondescript brick box, probably the least impressive state capitol in the most beautiful setting in the nation. Legislators hanker for a larger, grander building, but the still-simmering desire of some politicians to move the capital nearer the state's population center has defeated plans to build here. The federal government built the Capitol in 1931, when Alaska was still a territory. Inside, some of the old-fashioned woodwork and decorative details are interesting, and the public is free to walk through. During the summer, free tours are offered Monday through Friday 8am to 5:30pm, Saturday and Sunday 10am to 4pm. Check at the desk in the lobby or call ℂ **907/465-3853** for information. The legislature is in session from January to April.

Across 4th is the:

2 State Courthouse

The statue of a bear in front defines official Alaskan taste in art: It replaced a hated abstract steel sculpture called *Nimbus* that was removed by an act of the legislature and that finally came to rest in front of the state museum a few blocks away.

On the opposite, northwest corner is the:

3 Juneau–Douglas City Museum

Stop in here to buy the Evergreen Cemetery map if you plan to include that in your walk, or get the *Historic Downtown Juneau Guide* to learn more on the whole walk. (The museum is described on p. 156.) Even if you don't stop in, take a look at a rare American flag out front. This small plaza is where the 49-star U.S. flag was first raised in 1959—they didn't make many of those, as Hawaii was admitted as the 50th state within a year, but you'll still find one flying here.

On the southwest corner of Main and 4th is the:

4 State Office Building

This building is built into the edge of a cliff that forms a major barrier through the downtown area; if you're headed for the lower land, where the State Museum and Centennial Hall are located, you can avoid eight flights of steps in between by taking the building's elevator down. In any event, visit the towering atrium, with its great views and a 1928 movie theater pipe organ that's played on Fridays at noon. The totem pole is called "The Old Witch" and was taken from Sukkum Village around 1880. The historical collections of the Alaska State Library are housed here (www.library.state.ak.us/hist), and a stop to view historic photographs and artifacts on display is well worth the effort. Visitors are welcome to browse, too; or do it from home, as thousands of pieces have been digitized at http://vilda.alaska.edu. On sunny days, the patio off the atrium is a warm place for a picnic, with a fabulous view.

The State Courthouse.

The Governor's Mansion.

Leaving again through the door that you entered, turn left and follow Calhoun Street around the curve. An outdoor staircase here leads down to the flat area of town below (but you know about taking the elevator). Those lowlands originally were mostly underwater, and this embankment stood just above the shoreline, which continued along Front and South Franklin streets. The land you see below you is made of mine tailings that were dumped in the Channel. Continue on Calhoun; the governor uses the pedestrian overpass (which we walk under) to cross Calhoun to get to the Capitol from the white, neoclassical:

5 Governor's Mansion

Located on the left, the mansion was built by the federal government in 1912 for $40,000. It isn't normally open for public tours. Our most famous governor, Sarah Palin, didn't care for it and spent little time here, but most governors who've moved in lived here full time.

Shortcut: If you don't mind missing the next stop (Gold Creek), you can save yourself some hill-climbing by continuing on Calhoun, turning right on Goldbelt Street, climbing past some beautiful houses to 7th, then picking up the tour at the Wickersham House.

Continuing down Calhoun, you'll come to:

6 Gold Creek

Juneau's founders made their gold strike in this stream in 1880. Trace it upstream through peaceful **Cope Park,** past the playground and tennis courts to the unique ball field, which is bounded by the stream's forested canyon walls.

Go all the way to your right, across the baseball diamond, to find a lovely path and public stairway through the woods steeply up to 7th Street. Seventh runs along a narrow ridge between downtown Juneau and the creek. Across the street from the top of the stairway is:

7 The Wickersham House State Historic Site

This white 1898 frame house, at 213 7th St. (© **907/586-9001;** www. alaskastateparks.org, click "Individual Parks"), was the retirement home of Judge James Wickersham, who was revered by Alaskans for bringing law to the gold rush in Eagle, Nome, and Fairbanks; for exploring the Denali area and helping to make it a national park; for helping convince the federal government to build the Alaska railroad and found the state university; and for winning Alaska's right to make its own laws when he represented the territory as a nonvoting delegate in Congress. The house was in the family from 1928 until the state bought it in 1984, so it still contains many of Wickersham's belongings, including an Edison cylinder gramophone he took to Fairbanks, and his written assignment to go to Alaska, which is signed by Theodore Roosevelt. The house badly needed repair before a recent renovation project funded in part by the National Park Service. The first floor is open May 15 to September 15 Tuesday through Saturday 10am to 4pm. Admission is free.

Continue on 7th to Gold Street, turn right, and follow it downhill to 5th, site of the:

8 St. Nicholas Orthodox Church

This small structure is a significant architectural and historic landmark. The octagonal building was built in 1893–94 by Serbian miners and Tlingits. Many Tlingits chose the Russian Orthodox faith in the late 19th century when government-sponsored Protestant missionaries arrived with authority to force Christianity on Alaska Natives. The Protestants' civilizing program entailed wiping out Native languages and culture, but the Orthodox allowed people to worship in Tlingits and to continue more of their own customs. Bishop Innocent Veniaminov had translated sacred texts into Tlingits 50 years earlier when the Russians were still in Sitka (learn more under the **Russian Bishop's House,** p. 142). Today Alaska Natives make up the bulk of Russian Orthodox congregations in Alaska, and St. Nicholas still has an active Tlingits parish. There is no admission, but a donation is requested. There is a small gift shop and museum. The church is normally open in summer daily 9am to 5pm.

The next part of this walk leads to Evergreen Cemetery and up to the top of the town and through the woods on the flume—it's a 2½-mile strenuous hike that includes some steep stairways and streets. If that sounds appealing, continue 1 block down and 2 blocks to the right. Cross the creek and stay on the same road (which goes by various names), bearing right as it becomes Martin Street. On the left is:

9 The Evergreen Cemetery

The cemetery slopes toward the ocean, opening a wonderful vista over the clear green lawn. One reason the view is so broad and open is that the markers are flush with the ground. The old Alaska Native graves are in the wooded portion on the far side. Joe Juneau and Richard Harris, the city's founders, are buried near the cross at the top end of the cemetery, close to where you arrive on the walk.

Across the road from the cross, Hermit Street reaches a little way into the mountainside. Follow the steep public stairs next to house no. 430 up to the bottom of Pine Street. This is the walk we described in the introduction. The views get better and better as you rise to the top of Pine Street, then go right on Evergreen Street, following the road to where it dissipates into a trail among shadowy spruce and western hemlock.

Continue on the peaceful forest trail among the ferns and evergreens up the valley, coming to the:

10 Abandoned Wooden Flume

Once the town's aqueduct, the flume now is maintained as a boardwalk into the forest. Since it carried water, it's nearly level, but watch your step in wet weather, as it crosses some high trestles over gullies.

At the end of the flume, cross over the valley to Basin Road and continue upstream. Stop to see:

Avoiding Cruise-Ship Crowds

On the busiest days of the summer, cruise ships bring more than 10,000 passengers and another 4,000 crew members to the docks on Juneau's Franklin Street. That's simply too many for these narrow old streets; downtown becomes a solid crush of people, and attractions are packed, spoiling the experience for everyone. The crush is largely unavoidable, with more than one ship in port every day of the summer, but normally midweek days are busiest and Fridays and Saturdays quieter, since most cruises begin on the weekend and Juneau is partway along their voyage. If you can plan your Juneau sightseeing then, you may find somewhat less crowding; also, the farther you go from the dock, the less crowding you encounter. You can find a current schedule showing how many ships will be in port each day at www.claalaska.com, the website for Cruise Line Agencies of Alaska.

11 The Last Chance Mining Museum

The museum is described on p. 156.

To the left is the Perseverance Trail, which continues up between the mountains; the Perseverance also leads to the trail head for a challenging hike up Mount Juneau (both hikes are covered below).

To get back to town, follow Basin Road 1 mile back down the valley. Taking the first right will put you at the top of Gold Street. Descend a block to 7th and pick up the walking tour at stop 7 (the Wickersham House is a block down 7th), or continue down Gold to St. Nicholas Orthodox Church, stop 8 on the tour.

Shopping

The shops near the dock cater primarily to cruise-ship passengers. After around 500 summer port calls, many close their doors. The year-round community and more local shops tend to be farther up the hill. If you're looking for authentic Alaska Native arts and crafts, be warned that counterfeiting is widespread. For buying tips, read "Native Art: Finding the Real Thing," in chapter 2.

Juneau Artists Gallery, in the Senate Building, at 175 S. Franklin (© 907/586-9891; www.juneauartistsgallery.com), is staffed by a co-op of local artists and shows only the members' work: paintings, etchings, photography, jewelry, fabrics, ceramics, and other mediums. Much of it is good and inexpensive, and the way it is displayed creates a panorama of artistic visions.

Juneau's Rie Muñoz is one of Alaskans' favorite artists for her simple, graphic, generally cheerful watercolors of coastal Alaskan communities and Native people, among other subjects. Her prints, silk screens, note cards, and the like are shown downtown at the **Decker Gallery,** 233 S. Franklin (© 907/463-5536), and in the Mendenhall Valley at the **Rie Muñoz Gallery,** 2101 Jordan Ave., across from the Nugget Mall (© 800/247-3151 or 907/789-7449; www.riemunoz.com), where you'll also find her original watercolors and stained glass.

For gifts, try **Annie Kaill's** fine arts and crafts gallery, at 244 Front St. It's a little out of the cruise-ship shopping area and gets business from locals. The shop has a rich, homey feeling, with local work at various price levels. The long-established **Ad Lib,** 231 S. Franklin St., is also a fun little shop.

Hearthside Books (www.hearthsidebooks.com) is a cubbyhole of a bookstore at the corner of Franklin and Front streets but has a good selection for its size, especially of Alaskan books and maps. (A larger branch, with a good toy department, is in the Mendenhall Valley's Nugget Mall, 8745 Glacier Hwy., a 5-min. walk from the airport.) If you're at the airport in need of reading matter, you also may want to check out **Amazing Bookstore,** in the Airport Shopping Center, 9131 Glacier Hwy. (www.friendsjpl.org/bookstore). Operated by the public library, its large used book selection is mostly priced at $1.

The most unexpected shop in Juneau is the **Observatory,** at 299 N. Franklin St. (© **907/586-9676;** www.observatorybooks.com). This browser's paradise specializes in rare maps and books about Alaska, with a large collection of antique engravings. Among the items I've seen here were huge charts drawn by the first 18th-century explorers to trace Alaska's coastline. To get the full effect, you must strike up a conversation with the shop's owner, Dee Longenbaugh. She is a fellow of the Royal Geographical Society and member of the Antiquarian Booksellers Association. One question will start a fascinating tour of Alaska history.

The **Urban Eskimo,** at 217 Seward St. (© **907/796-3626;** www.urban eskimo.com), also specializes in history, focusing on the gold-rush era with photographs, books, and ephemera, and carrying regional art and antiques.

Bill Spear sells his own brightly colored enamel pins and zipper pulls from his studio, hidden upstairs at 174 S. Franklin (© **907/586-2209;** www.wm spear.com). Alaskans collect the vividly executed fish, birds, airplanes, dinosaurs, vegetables, and many other witty, provocative, and beautiful pins, which cost from $5 to $20 each.

Taku Store, 550 S. Franklin, across the parking lot from the tram station (© **800/582-5122** or 907/463-3474; www.takustore.com), is worth a stop if you're nearby, even if you're not in the market for the pricey seafood in the case: It's interesting to watch workers fillet, smoke, and pack salmon through large windows, and to read the explanatory signs about what they're doing. They'll ship fish anywhere in the U.S.

Attractions Beyond Walking Distance

Mendenhall Glacier Transport (© **907/789-5460;** www.mightygreattrips. com) leads a 2½-hour town and Mendenhall Glacier tour for $30, or you can ride its "Blue Glacier Express" bus for $16. Generally, it runs every half-hour both directions, from the waterfront visitor center to the glacier and back, daily 9am to 6pm in summer.

Otherwise, take a rented car or, for vigorous people, bike 24 miles out to the Mendenhall Glacier and back. I've listed these sites by distance from downtown, with directions starting from there.

Alaskan Brewing Company Beer lovers and aspiring capitalists will enjoy the tour of Alaska's most popular craft brewery. Now too big to be called "micro," the brewery started small in 1986 when Geoff and Marcy Larson had the idea of bringing a local gold rush–era brew back to life. It worked, and now Alaskan Amber and several other brews are everywhere in Alaska and many places down the west coast, and the brewery has won a long list of national and international awards for its brews. The short, free tour, which starts every hour, is fairly interesting, with views of the brewing equipment behind glass and an amazing worldwide beer bottle collection, but it's the tasting that makes it fun. They serve a wide variety of free samples, often creating an impromptu party in the lobby.

Identification is required. The brewery also has a downtown gift shop at 219 S. Franklin St.

5429 Shaune Dr. © **907/780-5866.** www.alaskanbeer.com. May–Sept daily 11am–6pm; winter Thurs–Sat 11am–6pm; last tour starts at 4:30pm winter and 5:30pm summer. Turn right from Egan Dr. on Vanderbilt Hill Rd., which becomes Glacier Hwy., then right on Anka St. and right again on Shaune Dr.

Glacier Gardens This is the place to see the rainforest if you have mobility problems. The heart of the hour-long tour is a ride in vehicles similar to golf carts up a steep mountainside, past a stream and pools, to a platform with a view of the Mendenhall Valley. The gardens' trademark is upside-down trees whose roots, way up in the air, are planted with trailing flowers. An eagle nest on the grounds has been active in recent years. The garden has a hiking trail for those who don't want to ride on the vehicles, but hikers have plenty of rainforest trails to choose from without fees.

7600 Glacier Hwy. © **907/790-3377.** www.glaciergardens.com. Admission $25 adults, $16 ages 6–12, free 5 and under. Summer daily 9am–6pm. Closed Oct–Apr. Near the Fred Meyer store about 1 mile from the airport.

Macaulay Salmon Hatchery ★ The hatchery, known by locals as DIPAC (Douglas Island Pink and Chum, Inc.), was ingeniously designed to allow visitors to watch the whole process of harvesting and fertilizing eggs from outdoor decks. From mid-June to October, salmon swim up a 450-foot fish ladder, visible through a window, into a sorting mechanism, then are "unzipped" by workers who remove the eggs. Guides and exhibits explain what's happening. During that period, you can often see seals and other wildlife feeding on the returning salmon just offshore from the hatchery. Inside, large and realistic saltwater aquariums and touch tanks show off the area's marine life as it looks in the natural environment. The tour is less impressive in May and June, before the fish are running.

Mendenhall Glacier.

Juneau Beyond Downtown

0   2 mi
0   2 km

ATTRACTIONS
Alaskan Brewing Company **6**
Glacier Gardens **5**
Macaulay Salmon Hatchery **7**
Mendenhall Glacier Visitor Center **3**

HOTELS
Pearson's Pond Luxury Inn &
    Adventure Spa **2**
Frontier Suites Airport Hotel **4**

RESTAURANTS
Hot Bite **1**

At that time, visitors see the immature salmon before their release and get to feed them. The tours don't take long; allow 45 minutes for your entire visit.

2697 Channel Dr. 877/463-2486 or 907/463-4810. www.dipac.net. Admission $3.25 adults, $1.75 children ages 12 and under. Summer Mon–Fri 10am–6pm, Sat–Sun 10am–5pm; winter call ahead. 3 miles from downtown, turn left at the first group of buildings on Egan Dr.

Mendenhall Glacier ★★★   This is easily Juneau's best attraction, and one of the most rewarding in the state, with Alaska's easiest access to both a glacier and to bear viewing. Read on.

At the head of Mendenhall Valley, the glacier glows bluish white, looming above the suburbs like an Ice Age monster that missed the general extinction, a truly impressive sight. The parking and an adjacent shelter have a great view across the lake 1 mile to the glacier's face, and a wheelchair-accessible trail leads close to the water's edge. Atop a bedrock hill, reached by stairs, a ramp, or an elevator, the Forest Service visitor center contains a glacier museum with excellent explanatory models, computerized displays, spotting scopes, and ranger talks.

Beginning in August and lasting into September, the area has an extraordinary added attraction: the most accessible bear-viewing opportunity you're likely to find anywhere. Red and silver salmon spawn in **Steep Creek,** just short of the visitor center on the road, making an easy source of bear food. Around a dozen female and juvenile black bears congregate to catch and feast on the fish, all within a few yards of viewing platforms. Despite the bears' apparent docility and interest in their dinner, remember they are dangerous wild animals. Stay on the trail and give them space. Don't bring food or drink, not even coffee. For more on bear safety, see p. 521.

There are several hiking trails at the glacier, including two fairly steep hikes, one on each side of the glacier. At the visitor center and a booth near the parking lot, the Forest Service distributes a brochure that includes a trail map. The **East Glacier Loop Trail** is a beautiful 3.5-mile round-trip hike leading through the forest to a view of a waterfall above the glacier about half a mile from its face. The trail has steep parts but is doable for school-age children. You can park at the visitor center and start from there. The **West Glacier Trail,** 7 miles round-trip, is more challenging, leaving from 300 yards beyond the Skaters' Cabin and following the edge of the lake and glacier, providing access to the ice itself for experienced climbers with the right equipment. You will need wheels to get to the trailhead. Take the Mendenhall Loop Road to Montana Creek Road, turn right, and then turn right again on Skaters' Cabin Road.

The granite Skater's Cabin is also the starting point for a groomed cross-country-ski loop on Mendenhall Lake in front of the glacier. Don't go beyond the orange safety markers near the glacier's face.

At the head of Glacier Spur Rd. (right from Egan Dr. on Mendenhall Loop to Glacier Spur). Visitor center admission summer $3 adults, free children 15 and under; winter free. Visitor center ((*C* **907/789-0097**) daily in summer 8am–7:30pm; winter Thurs–Sun 10am–4pm.

What to See & Do "Out the Road"

On sunny summer weekends, Juneau families get in the car and drive "out the road" (northwest along the Glacier Hwy., as it's officially known). The views of island-stippled water from the paved two-lane highway are worth the trip, and there are also several good places to stop. To use this road guide, set your trip odometer to zero at the ferry dock (which is 14 miles from downtown Juneau).

The **Auke Village Recreation Area** is a mile beyond the ferry dock and is a good place for picnics and beach walks. Less than a mile farther is a Forest Service campground.

The **Shrine of St. Thérèse** ★ (*C* **907/780-6112;** www.shrineofsaint therese.org), 9 miles beyond the ferry dock (23 miles from downtown), rests on a tiny island reached by a foot-trail causeway. The wonderfully simple chapel of rounded beach stones, circled by markers of the 15 stations of the cross, stands peaceful and mysterious amid trees, rock, water, and the cries of the raven and eagle. Sunday liturgy services are held from June to September at 1:30pm. The shrine is part of a large retreat maintained by the Juneau Catholic Diocese, which includes a log lodge on the shore facing the island, as well as several cabins for rent as lodgings. The shrine's island is a good vantage from which to look upon

Lynn Canal for marine mammals or, at low tide, to go tide pooling among the rocks. The website covers the shrine's history and gives information on the facilities, as well as a labyrinth, a columbarium, gardens, and trails at the shrine.

Eagle Beach, 14 miles beyond the ferry dock, makes a good picnic area in nice weather, when you can walk among the tall beach grass or out on the sandy tidal flats, watch the eagles, or go north along the beach to look for fossils in the rock outcroppings.

The road turns to gravel, then comes to **Point Bridget State Park,** 24 miles beyond the ferry dock (☎ **907/ 465-4563;** www.alaskastateparks.org, click on "Individual Parks"). A flat 3.5-mile path leads through forest,

Shrine of St. Thérèse.

meadow, and marsh to the shore, where you may see sea lions and possibly humpback whales. Three public-use cabins rent for $35 or $45 a night, depending on the season; for rental information, see "State Parks Cabin Reservations," p. 283. The road ends 26 miles from the ferry dock at pretty **Echo Cove.**

Getting Outside: Onshore

BIRD-WATCHING Bald eagles are everywhere in Juneau and most common on the shoreline, especially where fish are plentiful, such as at the hatchery. For more variety, visit the **Mendenhall Wetlands State Game Refuge,** which encompasses 3,800 acres of tidal estuaries, fresh and salt marshes, ponds, sedge meadows, sandy islands, and beaches spanning the Gastineau Channel, much of it near the airport. More than 100 species of birds use the refuge, mainly during the April and May migration. Access points are on either side of the channel, including a viewing platform on the downtown-bound side of Egan Drive, at mile 6. Hike out into the refuge near the Mendenhall River to see feeding birds in the summer: Take Old Glacier Highway just beyond the airport to Berner's Avenue, turn left on Radcliffe Road, and follow it to the end. Go near low tide.

FRESHWATER & SHORELINE FISHING Juneau isn't particularly known for its stream fishing (boat charter fishing is covered below under "Getting Outside: On the Water"). But there are a few places on the road system where you can find good fishing in freshwater or even in the ocean. The advice you need is in the free **Juneau Sportfishing Guide,** available in print or online from the Alaska Department of Fish and Game, 1255 W. 8th St. (P.O. Box 115526), Juneau, AK 99811-5526 (☎ **907/465-4270;** www.alaska.gov/ adfg, click on "Sport Fish," then on the Southeast region on the map).

For a remote fly-in experience with fly or spinning gear, contact **Alaska Fly 'N' Fish Charters,** 9604 Kelly Court (☎ **907/790-2120;** www.alaska byair.com). A guided 5-hour trip is $550 per person, with a two-person minimum. The same reputable guy (Butch Laughlin) also provides flightseeing and bear-viewing air tours. **Bear Creek Outfitters** (☎ **907/723-3914;**

www.juneauflyfishing.com) specializes in catch-and-release fly-fishing only, with all gear and hand-tied flies provided. The aircraft drops off a guide with no more than five anglers for an 8-hour day for $615 per person, or 5½ hours for $400 with a minimum of three passengers.

HIKING   We've mentioned several good hikes at Mendenhall Glacier and out the road, above. More than two dozen are described in a nicely made book with detailed topographic maps of each, *Juneau Trails* (Alaska Geographic), which you can find at visitor centers. *In the Miner's Footsteps,* a guide to the history behind 14 Juneau trails, is available from the Juneau–Douglas City Museum. The Juneau city and borough **Department of Parks and Recreation** (✆ **907/586-5226;** www.juneau.org/parksrec) leads hikes (and other activities) through the year; check the website or call the 24-hour hike line at ✆ **907/586-0428.**

The **Perseverance Trail** climbs up the valley behind Juneau and into the mining history of the area it accesses. It can be busy in summer. The trail head is about 1½ miles from town on Basin Road. The trail is 4 miles of easy walking on the mountainside above Gold Creek to the Perseverance Mine, at the Silverbow Basin, a mining community from 1885 to 1921. Use caution on icy patches, as there are steep drop-offs. A well-documented historical pamphlet is for sale at the Juneau–Douglas City Museum.

Two trails start from points along the Perseverance Trail. The challenging **Mount Juneau Trail** rises more than 3,500 feet over about 2 miles from a point 1 mile along from the Perseverance trail head. Go only in dry weather, to avoid disastrous falls. The **Granite Creek Trail,** starting 2 miles in on the Perseverance Trail, climbs 1,200 feet over 1.5 miles to an alpine basin. Both are quieter than the Perseverance Trail.

Another hike right from downtown climbs **Mount Roberts**—just follow the stairway from the top of 6th Street in a neighborhood called Star Hill. The summit is 4.5 miles and 3,819 vertical feet away, but you don't have to go all the way to the top for incredible views and alpine terrain. At the 1,760-foot level, you come to the restaurant at the top of the Mount Roberts tram, mentioned on p. 158. Of course, it's easier to take the tram up and hike down. A third choice: Start from the tram and hike to the summit.

The **Treadwell Mine Historic Trail,** on Douglas Island, is a fascinating hour's stroll through the ruins of a massive hard-rock mine complex

Gearing Up for Juneau's Outdoors

You can rent the gear you need for outings on the water or to equip Forest Service cabin visits from **Alaska Boat and Kayak Center,** at the Auke Bay Harbor (✆ **907/789-6886;** www.juneau kayak.com). Besides camping and fishing gear, they rent sea kayaks ($50 a day for a single, $70 double, with multiday discounts) and will deliver the boat anywhere on Juneau's road system, to outlying areas, or to Admiralty Island. They also offer a variety of guided outings; check the website. Rent skiffs with outboard motors that you can use for fishing or exploring from **Panhandle Powerboats** (✆ **907/789-5767;** www. panhandlepowerboats.com). Prices range from $195 to $400 a day. See "Getting Around," earlier in this section, for bike rentals.

REMOTE cabins ON FOOT

Five U.S. Forest Service cabins and three Alaska State Parks cabins are accessible by hikes of less than a day on trails connected to Juneau's road system. That means that you can get to these cabins without an expensive plane or boat charter, and that's a rarity. The three Alaska State Parks cabins are at Point Bridget State Park (see "What to See & Do 'Out the Road,'" above). The Forest Service cabins include **Peterson Lake,** with lake and stream fishing for Dolly Varden char and cutthroat trout; **John Muir,** on a 1,500-foot ridge top above Auke Bay, up the Auk Nu Trail; **Dan Moller,** on Douglas Island right across from town; **Eagle Glacier Memorial,** overlooking the glacier upriver from Eagle Beach and reached by the Amalga Trail; and beautiful **Windfall Lake,** with fishing. Each cabin rents for $35 a night, and generally there's a 2-night maximum stay. All are popular and must be reserved well in advance (it's wise to book as soon as your dates become available 6 months earlier). If you can afford a charter, or if you are an expert sea kayaker, there are many more choices farther afield, especially on Admiralty Island (see below). You'll need camping gear to stay at any of these primitive cabins (see "Gearing Up for Juneau's Outdoors," p. 168). Get information on Forest Service cabins from the Ranger District (see "Visitor Information," p. 155), then reserve through the national system described in "Getting Outside in the Tongass National Forest" on p. 94.

5

SOUTHEAST ALASKA

that once employed and housed 2,000 men. A well-written guide to numbered posts on the trail is available from the Juneau–Douglas City Museum. This is a great hike for kids. To find the trail head, take 3rd Street in Douglas, bearing left at the Y onto Savikko Street, which leads to Savikko Park, also known as Sandy Beach Park. The trail starts at the far end of the park.

Another great family outing is to the **Outer Point Trail,** 1.3 miles on a forest boardwalk to a beach with good tide pooling, lots of eagles, and possible whale sightings. The trail's only drawback is crowding, especially when tour groups tromp through; avoid them by going early or late. To get there, drive over the bridge to Douglas, then right on North Douglas Highway 12 miles to the trail head.

SKIING   For **downhill skiing,** the city-owned **Eaglecrest Ski Area** (© 907/ 790-2000; www.skijuneau.com) is the large, steep home hill of Olympic silver medalist Hillary Lindh, Juneau's favorite daughter (her father helped choose the site in the 1970s). A chair goes almost to the top of Douglas Island, with expansive views and 640 acres of skiing terrain. The four lifts serve 34 runs with a total vertical drop of 1,400 feet, rated 40% expert, 40% intermediate, and 20% novice. It's only 12 miles from downtown on North Douglas Highway, up Fish Creek Road. An all-day lift ticket is $37 weekends and $42 weekdays for adults. Even among Alaskans, Eaglecrest is little known, despite being second in size and ski lift development only to Alyeska Resort, near Anchorage.

Eaglecrest has 8km of **cross-country-skiing** trail, offering the most reliable track skiing in town.

Often Juneau's warm, damp winters don't provide enough snow for good cross-country skiing at lower elevations. Many of the hiking trails into

Juneau: Forest Capital

the mountains become winter backcountry routes, however, and snow does stick up there. Before going out, always check with the Forest Service (see "Visitor Information," earlier) for advice on your route and on avalanche conditions. Several of the Forest Service cabins also serve as winter warm-up houses during the day and make good skiing destinations. If conditions permit, a network of trails is set around the Mendenhall Glacier, with parking and access from the Skaters' Cabin off Montana Creek Road (see "Mendenhall Glacier," above).

ZIP-LINE TOURS   A zip line is a cable strung between two high points from which a passenger hangs on a wheeled runner, zipping from one end to the other. Once thought the province of Special Forces training and the like, riding a zip line (with a safety harness) is now considered a cruise activity and is billed as a way of seeing the rainforest. We're aware of seven tours, in Ketchikan, Juneau, Skagway, and at the Icy Strait cruise-ship stop, but this one, on Juneau's Douglas Island, caters primarily to independent travelers, with less stratospheric prices: **Alaska Zipline Adventures** (② **907/321-0947;** www.alaskazip.com), with a tour of seven rides and a suspension bridge near the Eaglecrest Ski Area. The 3½-hour tour costs $149 adults, $99 children 12 and under, including a snack and transfer to the site. Clients must be 10 and older, fit, not pregnant, and between 70 and 250 pounds. Wear pants and shoes with closed heels and toes.

Getting Outside: On the Water

SALTWATER FISHING   Many charter boats are available for fishing excursions from Juneau. Some will also include whale-watching on a trip. **Juneau Sportfishing and Sightseeing,** 2 Marine Way, Ste. 200 (② **907/586-1887;** www.juneausportfishing.com), is one of the largest operators. They charge $395 per person for a full day of fishing for salmon, $449 for halibut and salmon; or $205 for 4 hours of fishing salmon. They charge $125 for a 2½-hour whale-watching trip and also offer booking of other local tours. See other whale-watching choices below.

SEA KAYAKING   The calm waters around Juneau appeal to sea kayakers, and the city is a popular hub for trips on the water farther afield. Besides the sublime scenery, you'll likely see eagles and sea birds, and may encounter porpoises, seals, and possibly humpback whales. **Alaska Travel Adventures** (② **800/323-5757** or 907/789-0052; www.bestofalaskatravel.com) offers 3½-hour kayak trips (half that time on the water) in Auke Bay for $89 adults, $59 children 6 to 12. The tour includes orientation for beginners, a snack, and transportation from downtown.

Another business that offers guided sea kayaking, and rents and delivers kayaks, is listed under "Gearing Up for Juneau's Outdoors" (p. 168).

WHALE-WATCHING   Whale-watching is reliable near Juneau, and many small boats are available for trips, offering a chance to experience the whales closely. You've got good chances of encountering humpback and killer whales, Steller's sea lions, harbor seals, and, perhaps most exciting, Dall's porpoises, which shoot through and over the water in packs. The Juneau Convention and Visitors Bureau maintains a list of businesses, and their website has links to each. **Harv & Marv's Outback Alaska** (② **866/909-7288** or 907/209-7288; www.harvandmarvs.com) is run with 6- and

A DAY TRIP TO tracy arm

The fjords of the Tracy Arm–Fords Terror Wilderness (part of Tongass National Forest) are relatively unknown outside the area, but the scenery and wildlife viewing easily rival those of Glacier Bay National Park. And for those not riding a cruise ship, Tracy Arm has a significant advantage over Glacier Bay: It costs less than half as much and is easier to get to. A Tracy Arm tour takes about 8 hours; going to Glacier Bay from Juneau is an exhausting day trip—it's wiser to overnight there, though that adds more to the cost.

The Tracy Arm fjord is a long, narrow, twisting passageway into the coastal mountains, with peaks up to a mile high that jut straight out of the water, waterfalls tumbling thousands of feet down their sides. At its head, Sawyer Glacier and South Sawyer Glacier calve ice into the water with a rumble and a splash. Whales and other wildlife usually show up along the way. And, as at Glacier Bay, John Muir paid a visit. No second-best here!

Adventure Bound Alaska, 76 Egan Dr., across from the Goldbelt Hotel (© **800/228-3875** or 907/463-2509; www.adventureboundalaska.com), is a family business operating a 56-foot single-hull boat to Tracy Arm every day in the summer, with deck space all the way around. The boat leaves from the downtown Marine Park by 8am. (You have to be onboard at least 15 min. earlier.) They charge $150 adults, $95 ages 5 to 17; children must be at least 5 to go.

Another way to visit Tracy Arm is to charter your own boat. Although it may cost twice as much or more per person, you can decide when and where to linger with the animals or ice. Check with the visitor center for a referral, or with **Juneau Sportfishing and Sightseeing** (© **907/586-1887**), listed in this section under "Saltwater Fishing."

12-passenger boats by a couple of lifelong Juneau residents with decades of experience, each of whom go by their high school nicknames (really they're Jay and Pete), and who are known as characters offering fun, personal whale-watching trips. They charge $149 per person for a half-day, but prices vary by group size. **Orca Enterprises** (© **800/SEE-ORCA** [733-6722] or 907/789-6801; www.alaskawhalewatching.com) is a larger whale-watching firm, with four good-size vessels, offering 3½-hour tours and free transfers from your hotel. The cost is $119 adults, $89 ages 5 to 12, and $59 ages 4 and under.

Getting Outside: On the Ice

More than 36 major glaciers around Juneau flow from a single ocean of ice behind the mountains, the 1,500-square-mile **Juneau Icefield.** You can land on it in a helicopter just to touch the ice or to take a nature hike or dog-sled ride. It's expensive, but there are few other places to see, let alone explore, the kind of ice sheet that carved North America in the last Ice Age. From the air, glaciers look unreal, like creations by a graphic artist, their sinuous lines of blue and white ice striped with darker gray gravel debris. Only standing on the ice, which on closer inspection resembles the crusty compressed snow of springtime snow berms, do you get a clear sense of this entirely unfamiliar kind of terrain.

It's worth noting that these tours have had some major mishaps. While the accidents represent a tiny fraction of all the safe flights, they're a reminder that flying a helicopter to a glacier is not like flying an airliner.

Era Helicopters (☎ **800/843-1947;** www.eraflightseeing.com) is a respected operator. Their 1-hour glacier overflight with a 20-minute landing on Norris Glacier costs $279 per person. They also offer a program of **dog-sled rides** on the ice, a chance to try a winter sport in the summer. That excursion includes the four-glacier overflight and adds about an hour at a sled-dog camp on a glacier with a ride

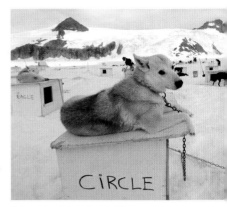
Taking a break from dog-sledding.

behind the dogs. It costs $489 per person. ***One caveat:*** Poor or even overcast weather makes it difficult to see the ice clearly, but if you wait for a sunny morning, all seats will likely be booked. They have a 48-hour cancellation policy, so you have to gamble to some extent on good viewing conditions. Of course, they don't fly in unsafe conditions.

NorthStar Trekking (☎ **866/590-4530** or 907/790-4530; www.north startrekking.com), another company with its own helicopters, specializes in hiking and teaching about glaciers. Their small groups (a maximum of 12, with two guides) go on ice-hiking excursions of up to a few miles, with the speed determined by the group. Various tour lengths are offered, with 1 to 3 hours spent on the ice. The 4¼-hour trip, which includes 2 hours on the ice and half an hour in the air (the balance is getting to the helicopter and gearing up), costs $399 per person.

Wings Airways (☎ **907/586-6275;** wingsairways.com) offers glacier overflights by floatplane and flightseeing tours to the remote Taku Lodge, where they land for king salmon for brunch, lunch, or dinner. It's a great opportunity to see bears, which snoop around the lodge. The cost is $280 adults, $225 ages 12 and under.

Getting Outside: On Admiralty Island

Beyond Douglas Island from Juneau, near the entrance to Gastineau Channel, is 1-million-acre Admiralty Island, one of the largest virgin blocks of old-growth forest in the country. The vast majority of the island is the protected **Kootznoowoo Wilderness.** Kootznoowoo, Tlingits for "fortress of bears," is said to have the highest concentration of brown bears on Earth. Despite the town of Angoon on the western side of the island, there are more bears than people on Admiralty. The island's **Pack Creek Bear Viewing Area** is the most famous and surefire place to see bears in Southeast. The area has been

Bear cub on Admiralty Island.

managed for bear viewing since the 1930s, when hunting was outlawed. Visitors come to see bears up close as they feed on salmon spawning in the creek in July and August. Peak viewing occurs in the middle of that period. The bears generally pay no attention to the watchers, who mostly gather on a gravel bar with no barriers between people and bears. There's good bird-watching here, too, with an extraordinary abundance of bald eagles.

Only 25 miles from Juneau, Pack Creek is so popular that the Forest Service uses a permit system to keep it from being overrun during the day (9pm–9am, no humans are allowed). The great majority of people go for only a few hours. There are no facilities in this wilderness area, and you can't even camp without some kind of water craft to get to a designated area. The easiest way to go is with a tour operator who has permits. The Forest Service District Ranger Office can give you a list of guides.

Alaska Fly 'N' Fish Charters (✆ 907/790-2120; www.alaskabyair.com) has permits for its naturalist-guided, 5½-hour fly-in Pack Creek visits, which cost $600 per person, with everything you need included. Twelve permits per day go to the commercial operators, but there are permits for unguided private parties, too. The Forest Service is considering changes to the permit system, using a national reservation system; check for changes, but here's how it works at press time. Daily, 12 permits are allocated to people who go without any guide; 8 of those 12 can be booked in advance with the Forest Service beginning on March 1, and the other 4 are available 3 business days before the date on which they're good, the previous Friday for Tuesday and Wednesday, at 9am at the Juneau Ranger District Office. In the peak season, July 5 to August 25, permits cost $50 for adults, $25 for those ages 16 or under or 62 and over. Lower prices and easier availability prevail outside the peak, but then you might not see any bears. After you have the permit, you'll still need a way to get there, plus your own gear (including rubber boots and binoculars). The Forest Service lists air taxi operators on its website (see the next paragraph).

Protected **Seymour Canal,** on the east side of the island, is good for canoeing and kayaking, and has two other sites besides Pack Creek where bears often show up: Swan Cove and Windfall Harbor. For information on the island, its 15 Forest Service cabins, and an excellent $4 map, contact the **Admiralty Island National Monument,** 8510 Mendenhall Loop Rd., Juneau (✆ 907/586-8800; www.fs.fed.us/r10/tongass/districts/admiralty).

Where to Stay

Lodging rates are high and room reservations tight in Juneau. The Juneau Convention and Visitors Bureau's *Juneau Guide & Travel Planner* and website contain listings of the hotels and B&Bs with links (www.traveljuneau.com; ✆ 888/581-2201).

Near downtown, but a long walk from the sights, try the **Breakwater Hotel** (www.breakwaterinn.com; ✆ 800/544-2250 or 907/586-6303) to save money on a clean standard room. The rectangular building overlooks the boat harbor. Rates are $89 to $119 double in the high season.

VERY EXPENSIVE

Alaska's Capital Inn ★★★   This scrupulously restored 1906 mansion half a block from the Capitol Building offers authentic antiques and period detailing combined with modern comfort for an unforgettable stay. There are many large rooms with high ceilings, good views, fireplaces, claw-foot tubs, and real elegance. The best asset of all, however, may be the warmth and fun of the inn. The common rooms are conducive to socializing, and the hosts, Linda and Mark, love to connect with guests and strive to accommodate their needs. Breakfast is wonderful (served at 8:30am), the cookie jar never runs out, and everyone gathers for wine and snacks in the afternoon. A Scotty dog patrols throughout.

113 W. 5th St., Juneau, AK 99801. www.alaskacapitalinn.com. © **888/588-6507** or 907/586-6507. Fax 907/586-6508. 7 units. High season $259–$339 double; low season $139–$259 double. Extra person $25. Rates include full breakfast. AE, DC, DISC, MC, V. Children 10 and under not permitted. **Amenities:** Shared computer w/Internet access; Jacuzzi. *In room:* TV, Wi-Fi.

Pearson's Pond Luxury Inn and Adventure Spa ★★★   This retreat of superbly appointed rooms, packed with every conceivable amenity, is on grounds that create the illusion of being in a fairyland somewhere in the Alaska wilderness—there's even a private pond with a rowboat—although it really lies in a residential subdivision near the Mendenhall Glacier. Rooms have kitchenettes, feather beds, and wonderful bathing facilities, and the inn offers massage and a sauna. Run by a three-generation family, it has warm hospitality that includes afternoon gatherings in the lounge and a well-stocked fridge. They also plan custom tour packages; sample itineraries are on the website. Book their Web specials to save something on the very high rates.

4541 Sawa Circle, Juneau, AK 99801. www.pearsonspond.com. © **888/658-6328** or 907/789-3772. Fax 907/789-6722. 5 units. High season $279–$449 double; low season $149–$399 double. Extra person $50. AE, DC, DISC, MC, V. Rates include full breakfast summer, continental breakfast winter. **Amenities:** Concierge; fitness room; 2 outdoor Jacuzzis; massage; sauna; free loan of kayak, rowboat, paddleboat, fishing gear, and bike. *In room:* TV/VCR and DVD, CD player, hair dryer, kitchenette, Wi-Fi.

EXPENSIVE

Goldbelt Hotel Juneau ★   This is a solidly built business hotel on the waterfront amid the sights downtown. The full lobby is filled with superb Tlingits art presented by the Goldbelt Native Corporation, which owns the hotel. The clean, geometrical lines of the building are carried throughout, including large rooms with high ceilings. But on our last visit, rooms were ready for renewal, with fabrics and carpet, although clean, showing wear. Rooms with the water view cost $10 more. The best in the house are on the corners, with even more space and light.

The restaurant off the lobby, **Zen,** is beautifully decorated in a fully realized Asian theme in shades of green. Tables are widely separated. The Asian fusion cuisine includes items such as ginger halibut and black cod for $24 to $29. That part of the menu is some of the best in town, but the inexpensive portion of the menu doesn't deliver the same standard of excellence.

51 W. Egan Dr., Juneau, AK 99801. www.goldbelttours.com. © **888/478-6909** or 907/586-6900. Fax 907/463-3567. Summer $179–$209 double; winter $139–$164 double. Extra person $15. AE, MC, V. **Amenities:** Restaurant; lounge; airport shuttle. *In room:* TV, coffeemaker, Wi-Fi.

The Historic Silverbow Inn ★★   This quirky little downtown hotel has an oddly pleasing, slightly frayed style and warm, casual hospitality. The 1914 building, with wood floors, bare brick, and stained glass, is decorated with a stylish, contemporary mode that nonetheless captures the warmth of a B&B. Downstairs is the Silverbow, a popular local gathering place with terrific bagels, spreads, and hearty sandwiches. That space, and the lounge, where the proprietors and staff hold a free wine tasting for guests in the summer months and show films and other cultural events in the winter, adds to the sense when you stay here that you've been adopted into a friendly community scene.

120 2nd St., Juneau, AK 99801. www.silverbowinn.com. ☏ **800/586-4146** or 907/586-4146. Fax 907/586-4242. 11 units. High season $179–$209 double; low season $119–$149 double. Extra person $20; $20 surcharge for 1-night stays in high season. Rates include full breakfast. AE, DISC, MC, V. **Amenities:** Restaurant; Jacuzzi; sauna. *In room:* TV, hair dryer, Wi-Fi.

Juneau Hotel ★★ 🍴   The remarkably comfortable suites in this downtown waterfront hotel offer a terrific bargain for families—rates are for any number of guests in the unit. The tidy but blocky red building stands next to Egan Drive and the bridge over Gastineau Channel. Every unit has a separate living area and a fully equipped kitchen with in-room laundry machines free for guest use. We were impressed by the many newly remodeled rooms with new appliances and flooring, and by the extraordinary housekeeping. The best of the lot are on the upper floors, which have water views. Art is Alaska themed, but the decoration in general is generic. Many suites have flatscreen TVs and all have wired broadband Internet; a guest computer is in the lobby, too. The courtesy van to the airport and ferry terminal saves additional money.

1200 W. 9th St., Juneau, AK 99801. www.juneauhotels.net. ☏ **800/544-2250** or 907/586-5666. 72 units. High season $189–$199 suite; low season $109–$129 suite. AE, DISC, MC, V. **Amenities:** Free airport and ferry transfers; fitness room. *In room:* TV/DVD and HBO, Internet, kitchen.

MODERATE

Baranof Hotel ★   The Baranof is the only lodging in Alaska with the pedigree and style to pull off the role of the old-fashioned grand hotel. The structure feels historic, in part, because the concrete construction limits modernization—bathrooms and many bedrooms will always be small. In some places, past efforts at renovation have made the most of the classic features, retaining glass doorknobs and pressed-tin hallway ceilings, while in other spots, the building is pretty typical of an older urban hotel. Floors 7, 8, and 9 have the best rooms, with great views on the water side. There's a discount on the second floor, which lacks a view, and the rates are reasonable for this market.

The Art Deco **Gold Room** restaurant is Juneau's most traditional fine-dining establishment, and among its best. The dining room combines intimacy and grandeur in a showplace of shining brass, frosted glass, and rich wood. A recent menu included scallops in pomegranate butter sauce and macadamia nut halibut, as well as lamb, duck, and veal selections. Most entrees are more than $30.

127 N. Franklin St., Juneau, AK 99801. www.westmarkhotels.com. ☏ **800/544-0970** or 907/586-2660. Fax 907/586-8315. 196 units. High season $149–$249 double; low season $109–$189 double. Extra person $20. AE, DC, DISC, MC, V. **Amenities:** 2 restaurants; bar; fitness room; room service. *In room:* TV, hair dryer, kitchenettes (in some), Wi-Fi.

Frontier Suites Airport Hotel ★ 🍴   A rambling group of four-story buildings among spruce trees provide a good option for those who want to stay in a standard room in the Mendenhall Valley, near the airport. Rooms are large, all have full kitchens, and the rates are low compared to comparable hotels in Juneau. Units are decorated with Alaska art and bedspreads and kept up-to-date, and there are a variety of options to match your needs. A courtesy van serves the airport and ferry terminal and a 5-mile radius, which will get you to basic shopping, but to visit the town's attractions, you will need a car. Pizza, pasta, and burger restaurants are on-site, as well as outdoor recreation areas, including a playground and basketball court.

9400 Glacier Hwy., Juneau, AK 99801. www.frontiersuites.com. © **800/544-2250** or 907/790-6600. Fax 907/790-6612. 104 units. Summer $159–$179 per room; winter $129 per room. Extra person no charge. AE, DISC, MC, V. **Amenities:** 3 restaurants; courtesy van; exercise room; room service. *In room:* TV, hair dryer, Internet, full kitchen.

INEXPENSIVE

The Driftwood Lodge 🦴   This downtown motel, next door to the State Museum, is popular with families, and houses legislators and aides in the winter in its apartment-like kitchenette suites. Although the building can't hide its cinder-block construction and old-fashioned motel exterior, small bathrooms, or lack of elevators, the rooms are comfortable and well maintained. The management has held prices low while making improvements, so for a rate that won't get you in the door at most Juneau hotels ($135), you can put four people in a two-bedroom suite with a full kitchen. Don't expect luxury, just a basic, clean motel room for a good price. The round-the-clock courtesy van saves big money to the airport or ferry, and the rental bikes will cover your transportation needs downtown.

435 Willoughby Ave., Juneau, AK 99801. www.driftwoodalaska.com. © **800/544-2239** or 907/586-2280. Fax 907/586-1034. 63 units. High season $95–$110 double, $120–$135 suite; low season $68 double, $98 suite. Extra person $10. AE, DC, DISC, MC, V. **Amenities:** Courtesy van; bike rental. *In room:* TV, Wi-Fi.

A HOSTEL

Juneau International Hostel 🎒   The historic yellow house among the downtown sights is a showplace of custom cabinetry and big, light common rooms. It's a volunteer-operated nonprofit with the mission of uniting people; guests pay little but are expected to pitch in with chores. Men and women sleep in a number of small separate dorm rooms, and there is one private room for families with children, which is in high demand. Office hours are from 7:30 to 9am and 5 to 11pm in the summer, 8 to 9am and 5 to 10:30pm in the winter, with lockout during the day. Wi-Fi and local calls are free. Reservations must be prepaid by mail or phone for a 5-night maximum stay, although you can stay up to 7 days if there's room. Credit cards (Visa and MasterCard) are accepted only to book reservations by phone and carry a $2 fee; otherwise, it's cash only. Alcohol, drugs, and pets are not allowed, and shoes are removed at the door.

614 Harris St., Juneau, AK 99801. www.juneauhostel.net. © **907/586-9559.** 47 beds. $10 per adult; $5 children ages 6–17 with parent, free 5 and under. Cash only. Closed intermittently Nov–Apr; check website. **Amenities:** Wi-Fi; lockers.

CAMPING

Juneau has two exceptional Forest Service campgrounds open from mid-May to mid-September. For information, call the Juneau Ranger District (www.fs.fed.us/r10/tongass; © **907/586-8800**); for reservations, see "Reserving a Cabin or Campsite," p. 96. The **Mendenhall Glacier Campground,** overlooking the lake and glacier and next to the Mendenhall River, is the best-built public campground in the state, with granite-block construction. The bathrooms have showers and flush toilets, and there is a half-mile disabled-accessible nature trail. The 69 sites are huge and broadly separated; nine have full RV hookups, and another nine have electricity and water. Tents and RVs are segregated. To get there, turn north on Montana Creek Road from Mendenhall Loop Road. Tent sites are $10, RV sites $26 and $28. The 11-site **Auke Village Campground,** 1¼ miles north of the ferry dock, is in an extraordinary place, with sites among large trees along an ocean beach, looking out on the islands of Auke Bay. The campground, reconstructed in 2006, has vault toilets and running water. Sites are $10 per night.

    Spruce Meadow RV Park, 10200 Mendenhall Loop Rd. (www.juneaurv. com; ✆ **907/789-1990**), has the good qualities of a public campground, with wooded and open sites in a forested area near the glacier. It's on the city bus line, making transit easy after parking your rig. The park offers extras such as cable and free Wi-Fi. Full hookups are $32 for up to two adults and children 12 and under, $2 per extra adult, tenting $20. Reserve ahead.

Where to Eat

Juneau has a number of excellent restaurants. Besides those detailed below, see two superb choices above, at the Gold Room, in the Baranof Hotel, on p. 175, and Zen, in the Goldbelt Hotel Juneau, p. 174.

    For breakfast or lunch, try the **Sandpiper Cafe,** near the State Museum at 429 Willoughby Ave. (✆ **907/586-3150**), with an immaculate dining room recalling a sun-faded beach-front eatery. Breakfast is terrific and reasonably priced. The short lunch menu includes tasty comfort foods and sandwiches, or get breakfast all day. A hamburger is $12. It's open daily 6am to 2pm.

    Pizzeria Roma, on the waterfront across the hall from the Hangar at 2 Marine Way (✆ **907/463-5020**), produces some of the best pizza and calzones in town in a small dining room. Hours are daily 11am to 10pm in summer.

The Hangar ★ GRILL   Situated in a converted airplane hangar on a wooden pier with large windows, this bar and grill has great views and a fun atmosphere; even off-season, it's packed. It's a fine place to drink beer (with 24 brews on tap), listen to live music, or play at one of the three pool tables. Service is quick and professional. What's surprising is that the food is usually good, too (although we've had disappointing dishes). The seared ahi sashimi appetizer, raw inside, has a pleasant texture and taste, and the jambalaya, a huge portion for $13, is spicy but balanced. The fish chowder is very thick and has a pleasing slightly smoky flavor. Although the menu's steaks and such range up to $30, plenty of choices are less than $15.

2 Marine Way. ✆ **907/586-5018.** www.hangaronthewharf.com. Reservations recommended. Main courses $13–$30. AE, MC, V. Daily 11am–10pm.

Island Pub ★ PIZZA   Across the bridge from Juneau, this is where local people go for a fun night out. The specialty is pizza with creative ingredients. The delicious scent of the brick oven hangs in the air. The dining room, dating from the 1930s, is historic by Alaskan standards and comes by its pub ambience honestly. It looks out on the Gastineau Channel through picture windows; at times, customers watch killer whales from the bar (they have the photos to prove it). The pub is easy to find. Drive across the bridge to Douglas, turn left, and, after entering the town, turn left on E Street.

1102 2nd St., Douglas. ✆ **907/364-1595.** www.theislandpub.com. Main courses $10–$12; pizza $13–$19. AE, DC, DISC, MC, V. Daily 11:30am–10pm. Bar open later.

Tarantino's ★ ITALIAN   This traditional family restaurant, a downtown corner, is good for a filling, familiar meal and quick service. The atmosphere is up-to-date and casual in the dining room, decorated in warm tones with lots of booths, but still a couple of steps up from a basic pizzeria. The sausage lasagna is very generous and nicely presented for a reasonable price, like all the main courses—for lunch, it was $11 with bread and soup or a salad.

140 Seward St. © **907/523-0344.** Lunch $9–$15; dinner $12–$25. AE, MC, V. Mon–Fri 11am–9pm; Sat noon–9pm.

Twisted Fish Co. Alaskan Grill ★★ SEAFOOD   Overlooking the water at the cruise-ship dock, in the same building as Taku Smokeries, this spot has a magnificent dining room with views of the Gastineau Channel. The quality and range of the food bring locals to a tourist zone they would otherwise avoid: items such as salmon on a cedar plank or in pastry, halibut or salmon tacos, and also little pizzas, burgers, and terrific desserts. The service is fast and attentive, but the dining room makes you want to stay long after you are done eating.

550 S. Franklin St. © **907/463-5033.** www.twistedfish.hangaronthewharf.com. Reservations recommended. Lunch $7–$15; dinner main courses $18–$30. AE, DISC, MC, V. Summer daily 11am–10pm. Closed Oct–Apr.

Zyphyr Restaurant ★★★ MEDITERRANEAN   The dining room, once an old-fashioned grocery store, was remodeled with restraint and a magnificent sense of style, using its wooden floors, very high ceilings, and huge storefront windows to create the illusion of elegance passed down for generations rather than only since late 2006. Tables robed in linen of dark rust are set so far apart that diners feel they are alone, and on the winter evening we first ate here, the darkness outside contributed to the velvety intimacy. The service—fast, courteous, but with character—lives up to the setting. Dishes are from the traditional fine-dining palette of colors: calamari, pasta puttanesca, or *osso bucco,* for example. Each meal

quick bites **IN JUNEAU**

The **Silverbow Bakery,** 120 2nd St. (© **907/586-4146;** www.silverbowinn. com), is a happening spot for bagels, hearty sandwiches, and espresso drinks. It's open long hours every day. The **Rainbow Foods** natural food grocery, an organic hangout in a former church at the corner of Franklin and 4th streets (© **907/586-6476;** www.rainbow-foods. org), is the best picnic-packing place downtown, making sandwiches and salads at the deli and with a buffet and salad bar. It's also a good place to network with a socially conscious crowd and is a Wi-Fi hot spot.

Hot Bite, at the Auke Bay boat harbor, is a local secret, serving charcoal-broiled hamburgers and halibut burgers and great milkshakes from a run-down little house. Take out or sit at one of six indoor tables.

Downtown Juneau's young, professional population supports several good coffeehouses. **Valentine's Coffee House and Pizzeria,** 111 Seward St. (© **907/463-5144**), serves light, hot meals in an authentic old-fashioned storefront. **Heritage Coffee Co. and Café,** 174 S. Franklin St. (© **907/586-1087;** www.heritage coffee.com) and 216 2nd St. (© **907/586-1752**), has two trendy, comfortable coffeehouses good for watching people. The 2nd Street location has wireless Internet and terminals. They also roast famous coffee.

we've had was memorable and flawless. On our most recent visit, the day boat scallops, seared with a soft-cooked egg and romesco sauce, were wonderfully flavored and textured. The generous portion of tender duck was perfectly complemented by a dusky sauce. Desserts are excellent, too. Save this place, one of Alaska's best restaurants, for a special romantic meal or a treat at the end of the day.

200 Seward St. ✆ **907/780-2221.** Reservations recommended. Main courses $15–$36. AE, MC, V. Summer Tues–Sun 5–9:30pm; winter Tues–Sat 5–9:30pm.

Nightlife

Alaska Travel Adventures has offered its **Gold Creek Salmon Bake** (✆ **800/ 323-5757** or 907/789-0052) for more than 30 years. It's touristy, yes, but fun, with marshmallow roasting, music, and other entertainment—great for families (I'd avoid it in the rain, however.) The cost is $42 for adults, $28 for children. They come and get you and return you to your hotel.

For more substantial performances, try to catch a show by Juneau's **Perseverance Theatre,** Alaska's largest professional theater. The winter season, starting in September and lasting until early June, includes Alaska's best cutting-edge drama, including serious homegrown work. Paula Vogel was here when she wrote *How I Learned to Drive,* which later won the Pulitzer Prize. Summer offerings are limited to youth theater and workshops. To find out what's playing, contact the theater's office at 914 3rd St., Douglas (✆ **907/364-2421**), or check the website at www.perseverancetheatre.org.

A political scandal or two put a damper on some of the infamous legislative partying that once occurred in Juneau, far away from home districts, but good places to go out drinking and dancing still exist. The **Red Dog Saloon,** 278 S. Franklin St., is the town's most famous bar, with a sawdust-strewn floor, a slightly contrived but nonetheless infectious frontier atmosphere, and walls covered with Alaska memorabilia. Locals hang across the street, at the **Alaskan Bar,** 167 S. Franklin, which occupies an authentic gold-rush hotel with a two-story Victorian barroom. Boisterous parties and music go on there all year. The **Hangar,** listed above under "Where to Eat," is the place for beer drinkers. They have a big-screen TV and live music Friday and Saturday nights, as well as pool and darts.

GLACIER BAY NATIONAL PARK

It is hard to imagine, but when the first European explorers sailed past Glacier Bay in the late 1700s, they missed it. All they saw was a huge wall of ice. Even when John Muir "discovered" the bay a century later, it was barely a fraction of the size it is now over a century later.

Long before "global warming" became a headline, the glaciers of Glacier Bay began a rapid retreat, which has created a 65-mile fjord of spectacular beauty in just more than 200 years. As you enter the bay, you begin to go back in time and watch as the forests near the mouth shrink back until you reach a landscape that was buried under ice until a short time ago; it's only now beginning to sprout vegetation and life. The land itself is literally "rebounding," rising approximately 1½ inches a year as it sheds of the weight of the glaciers.

Make no mistake, Glacier Bay is still dominated by the numerous large glaciers that cascade down from the 15,000-foot-high peaks of the Coast Range, but now the bay itself is one of Alaska's most-coveted visitor destinations.

Grand Pacific Glacier.

President Calvin Coolidge created the national monument in 1925, and it became a national park as part of the 1980 ANILCA process. The Connecticut-size park has a only a few short roads in Gustavus near its mouth, and it limits the number of cruise ships and other boats to protect the wildlife and the fragile ecosystem. Even that action has been politically contentious, as the Alaskan Congressional Delegation has promoted more ships and the environmental community has fought for fewer ships. Currently, the National Park Service appears to be charting a course between the two extremes.

The most spectacular summer "residents" of Glacier Bay are the whales, mostly humpbacks and killer whales, which are what most visitors are interested in seeing. But early scientific evidence is indicating that the ships in the narrow fjord are affecting the whale populations, making them less likely to be seen. On some visits, cruise passengers will just have to content themselves with the spectacular glaciers and the sheer mountains rising from the shore.

Of course, sea kayaking inside the bay remains the best way to see the park and increase your chance of a close—but not too close—encounter with whales or other wildlife.

Essentials

GETTING THERE

Most visitors get to the park on cruise ships that pass through the bay without landing, so those readers can skip the material below. Others begin their visit to

A breaching humpback whale in Glacier Bay.

Glacier Bay National Park

the park at the headquarters area at Bartlett Cove, but once there, you're only at the edge of a park with no roads. To go onward into the park, you need some kind of boat. That's covered below under "Activities at the Park."

BY AIR   Gustavus, covered in the next section of this chapter, is the gateway to Glacier Bay National Park, lying 10 miles by road from the Bartlett Cove headquarters. The only practical way to Gustavus is by air. Getting from the Gustavus airstrip to Bartlett Cove is easy. Vans meet planes, charging $15 adults, $8 children 8 and under (both including tax), and carry passengers to Bartlett Cove. It's free if you're traveling with a package tour; also, most of the inns and lodges in Gustavus offer free transfers to the park. **TLC Taxi** (✆ **907/697-2239**) also offers rides from the airstrip to the park or to Gustavus.

BY WATER   A summer passenger ferry, the fast catamaran *Fairweather Express II,* is operated by the park concessionaire, Glacier Bay Lodge and Tours (✆ **888/BAY-TOUR** [229-8687]; www.visitglacierbay.com), connecting Juneau's Auke Bay harbor directly to Bartlett Cove. It currently runs just once a week. The boat starts from Bartlett Cove Friday at 4pm, leaves from Auke Bay Sunday at 7:30pm, and arrives again at Bartlett Cove at 10:30pm. The fare is $75 one-way for adults, half price for children 3 to 12. New this year is weekly ferry service to Gustavus. For schedule and details, call **Alaska Marine Highway System** (✆ **800/642-0066**; www.ferryalaska.com).

VISITOR INFORMATION

Contact **Glacier Bay National Park and Preserve** at P.O. Box 140, Gustavus, AK 99826 ((*C*) **907/697-2230;** www.nps.gov/glba). The Park Service interprets the park mainly by placing well-prepared rangers onboard most cruise and tour vessels entering the bay. The park also maintains a modest visitor center, with displays of the park on the second floor of the lodge at wooded Bartlett Cove. Pick up the park map and handy guide, the *Fairweather*. Nearby are the park's offices, a free campground, a backcountry office, a few short hiking trails, a dock, sea-kayak rental, and other park facilities. During the summer, rangers lead a daily nature walk and present an evening program.

Activities at the Park

HIKING AT BARTLETT COVE There are three short hiking trails through the rainforest of Sitka spruce and western hemlock at Bartlett Cove. Each weaves through the cool, damp quiet created by these huge trees and the moss on the forest floor. Some wet spots are often crossed by boardwalks with railings. A map is included in the *Fairweather* visitor guide.

The **Forest Loop** is an easy trail about 1 mile long, beginning at the lodge and passing through the woods and past some park buildings to the cove's pebble beach. The **Bartlett River Trail** is a 4-mile round-trip leading to the Bartlett River Estuary, a good bird-watching spot, especially during migrations. The **Bartlett Lake Trail** branches off the Bartlett River Trail after about .25 mile for a 3.8-mile one-way forest hike to the lake.

BOAT TOURS Bartlett Cove is nowhere near the park's highlights. Most independent travelers take a day boat to see the vast majority of Glacier Bay. The boat is operated by a park concessionaire called **Glacier Bay Lodge and Tours,** a joint venture of ARAMARK and Huna Totem, with offices at 241 N. C St., Anchorage, AK 99501 ((*C*) **888/229-8687** or 907/264-4600; fax 907/258-3668; www.visitglacierbay.com), or, locally, in the summer only, at P.O. Box 179, Gustavus, AK 99826 ((*C*) **907/697-4000;** fax 907/697-4001). The boat leaves from the dock in Bartlett Cove at 7:30am and returns at 3:30pm, sailing to the fjords' very head and the Grand Pacific Glacier. There's a snack bar, and a simple lunch is provided. Bring binoculars, good rain gear, and layers of warm clothing. The fare is $185 for adults, half-price for children 3 to 12, lunch included.

Bartlett Cove.

CHARTERING A BOAT Local family operators based in Gustavus take visitors up the bay in comfort, with the spontaneity and intimacy of boating with friends. If you have a group, you can have a boat and guide to yourself. Mike Nigro, a former backcountry ranger and longtime resident, takes groups of four to six for $435 per person per day, two-person minimum, on a 42-foot yacht, the *Kahsteen*. His **Gustavus Marine Charters** can be reached at (✆ **907/697-2233** or www.gustavusmarinecharters.com.

KAYAKING IN THE PARK   You won't forget seeing a breaching humpback whale from a sea kayak, sitting just inches off the water. It happens around here. When we breathlessly told our innkeepers about the experience, they smiled politely. They hear the same descriptions all the time. Inexperienced paddlers should choose a guided trip. **Glacier Bay Sea Kayaks,** based in Gustavus (✆ **907/697-2257;** www.glacierbayseakayaks.com), offers half-day and all-day paddles in Bartlett Cove good for beginners. Although the trips go nowhere near the glaciers, the paddlers stand a good chance of see-ing whales, sometimes quite close up. Any fit person can enjoy it. A half-day costs $95, full day $150, including a lunch. The same folks rent kayaks for day trips in the cove. These self-guided outings begin with a briefing, and novices are welcome. The cost is $40 half-day, $50 full day. Experienced kayakers ready for an overnight in the wilderness up the bay can rent equip-ment, too, and get dropped near the glaciers for $231 round-trip. Before starting off on an overnight, you also will have to attend a Park Service brief-ing and get a backcountry permit from the headquarters. The company operates May 1 to September 15.

   Alaska Discovery (✆ **800/586-1911;** www.alaskadiscovery.com) offers 5-day guided expeditions in Glacier Bay. Although we wouldn't rec-ommend this to someone who hasn't tried kayaking before (what if you hate it?), those who do will find this the most intimate and authentic way to experience this wilderness. A 5-day trip, with 4 days of kayaking, 3 days of camping, and 1 day at an inn, costs around $2,095 from Gustavus. An 8-day trip is $3,250.

FLIGHTSEEING   One spectacular way to get into the park is by flightseeing. Gustavus-based **Air Excursions** (✆ **907/697-2375;** www.airexcursions. com) offers air tours in float or wheeled planes. Other operators fly scenic excursions from various nearby towns, including Haines and Skagway (cov-ered later in this chapter). You'll see the incredible rivers of ice that flow down into the bay, and you may even see wildlife. What you give up is the sense of scale from ground level.

Where to Stay, Camp & Eat

Glacier Bay Lodge ★   This is the only place to stay in the park. The wood-paneled bedrooms are kept in good shape—the concessionaire put in new mat-tresses in 2009—but they're aged and frankly drab, without much art or decoration. The buildings are set in the soothing quiet of large rainforest trees, and 12 units that rent for a $25 premium have water views, but essentially, guests just get a comfortable bed in a special place for their money. Meanwhile, in Gus-tavus, 10 miles down the road, you'll find some of the most attractive accommo-dations in Alaska.

   The **restaurant** has huge windows looking onto Bartlett Cove and offers standard breakfast fare, chowder, sandwiches, seafood, steaks, and pasta. The restaurant serves breakfast from 6 to 9:30am, lunch 11:30am to 2pm, and dinner 5:30 to 10pm.

The lodge also provides public showers and laundry facilities for the free Park Service **campground,** about ¼ mile away. The campground lacks running water but has a warming hut, firewood, and bear-resistant food caches. You have to cook in a fire ring in the intertidal zone and observe other bear-avoidance rules the rangers will explain. Get a camping permit at the ranger station when you arrive; the campground is almost never full.

Bartlett Cove (P.O. Box 179), Gustavus, AK 99826. www.visitglacierbay.com. ☎ **888/229-8687** or 907/697-4000. Fax 907/258-3668 or 697-4001. 48 units. $199–$224 double. Extra person $20. AE, DC, DISC, MC, V. Closed mid-Sept to late May. **Amenities:** Restaurant; bike and fishing gear rental.

GUSTAVUS: COUNTRY INNS & QUIET

This tiny village at the mouth of Glacier Bay may not be the Shangri-La it was a couple of decades ago, but it remains a remarkable little community on the edge of the one of Alaska's great wonders.

While you no longer have to bring a sleeping bag—there are several top-notch lodges and inns—it can still seem like you've found an undiscovered slice of Alaska, depending on when you visit.

A town of log cabins and wood-frame buildings, it is well maintained (certainly, compared to some other Southeast communities) and doesn't have that rain-drenched, ready-to-dissolve-back-into-the-muskeg look. It has one of the few truly sandy beaches in the region and numerous hiking, biking, and walking opportunities.

A home in Gustavus.

The town looks like the country. Houses, cabins, and a few businesses are spread far apart along gravel roads. Services are limited. On Dock Road, the Bear Track Mercantile sells necessities. Gustavus also has a gas station and a liquor store. Bring whatever else you will want with you, and reserve all accommodations in advance. The local government, founded in 2004, imposes a 2% sales tax on goods and a 4% tax on accommodations.

However, its isolation from the mainstream of Alaska comes at a cost that is just that—cost. It is not cheap to get to Gustavus, nor is it cheap to stay here, and most of the excursions you can take out of the town in the park are on the expensive side.

Essentials

GETTING THERE   It's currently possible to take a passenger ferry, the *Fairweather Express II,* only 2 evenings a week in summer from Juneau's Auke Bay to Bartlett Cove, 10 miles by road from Gustavus (p. 181). The primary mode of transportation to Gustavus is flying. During the midsummer, **Alaska Airlines** (✆ **800/252-7522;** www.alaskaair.com) flies a jet once a day from Juneau to Gustavus and back in the early evening. An advance fare is about $200 round-trip.

For more frequent service by prop from Juneau to Gustavus, at roughly the same fare as Alaska Airlines, use Gustavus-based **Air Excursions** (✆ **907/697-2375;** www.airexcursions.com), which flies numerous scheduled flights a day, as well as charters and flightseeing excursions; or **Wings of Alaska** (✆ **907/789-0790** reservations, or 697-2201 in Gustavus; www.ichoosewings.com).

VISITOR INFORMATION   The traditional way to plan a trip to Gustavus is to contact a lodge and, once you're comfortable with them, allow your hosts to advise you and book your activities. You can look up information from the **Gustavus Visitor Association** at www.gustavusak.com. A local travel agency, **Alaska's Glacier Bay Travel** (✆ **907/697-2475;** www.glacierbaytravel.com), run by the same folks as TLC Taxi (see below), can also help with choices and reservations. Be certain to reserve a place to stay before showing up in Gustavus.

GETTING AROUND   There are just a few roads. The main one starts at the airport and runs about 10 miles to **Bartlett Cove,** the Glacier Bay National Park base of operations. **Dock Road** branches off to the left, at the gas station, and leads to the ocean dock and sandy beach. There's a map and list of businesses posted near the gas station, and most businesses will give you one to take along for exploration by bicycle. Many inns and B&Bs have courtesy vans and free bicycles; ask about transportation when you reserve. **TLC Taxi** (✆ **907/697-2239**) offers transportation between the airport and Bartlett Cove, and points in between, with flat fees depending on the destination. Reserve ahead. A van can accommodate groups, gear, and kayaks. **Bud's Rent a Car** is at ✆ **907/697-2403.**

Gustavus: Country Inns & Quiet

Exploring Gustavus

Everything to do in Gustavus involves the outdoors. We've listed the activities here in the order of importance.

WHALE-WATCHING & FISHING Whales keep their own schedule, but you're certain to see them on a whale-watching excursion here, where the swirling current of Icy Strait creates such a rich feeding ground that humpbacks come back every summer without fail. The big tour boat in the national park (see the previous section) frequently sees whales, but Icy Strait, outside the park, is even more prolific. Currently, there are two operators. Since arrangements change annually, it's wise to call ahead or get advice from your lodge or B&B host.

Cross Sound Express (℃ 888/698-2726 or 907/321-2302; taz. gustavus.com) takes two viewing trips a day all summer and has never failed to find whales. To get an idea, see the amazing orca photos on their website. Their vessel, the *TAZ*, takes up to 23 passengers and can also do kayak drop-offs and other marine transportation. The cost is $120 per person, $60 children 4 to 6, 3 and younger free. The park concessionaire, **Glacier Bay Lodge and Tours** (℃ 888/229-8687 or 907/264-4600; www.visitglacier bay.com), offers a whale-watching dinner cruise on Monday, Thursday, and Saturday at 5:30pm. The cost is $138 adults, $69 ages 2 to 12.

FISHING Gustavus has superb charter-boat fishing for halibut and salmon (if salmon are running). The waters are protected and seasickness less likely than many places. Your inn host in Gustavus can make the arrangements. A boat typically charters for $300 to $350 per person for a full day, plus the cost of having your fish professionally packed and shipped home to you. Half-days are rarely available because the boats are fully booked. If you do a fishing charter and the others onboard agree, you can take some of the time for whale-watching.

SEA KAYAKING Gustavus-based **Spirit Walker Expeditions** (℃ 800/KAY-AKER [529-2537] or 907/697-2266; www.seakayakalaska.com) has a good reputation locally. They lead guided day trips to the whale-watching grounds and overnight expeditions as long as a week.

HIKING & BICYCLING There are few cars in Gustavus, but most inns provide bikes. The roads are fun to explore, and the sandy beaches, accessed from the town dock, are great for a walk and a picnic, to watch eagles and other birds and wildlife. You can go many miles for a run or long walk, but we saw little reason to go far before stopping to play and picnic on a broad sand beach undisturbed by any other human footprint.

GOLF A unique and spectacular course in Gustavus lies on the shore of Icy Strait. The 9-hole, par-36 **Mt. Fairweather Golf Course** (℃ 907/697-2214) was built and is mowed and groomed by Morgan DeBoer on his family's land. The fee for 9 holes is $15, and club and cart rental are available. Reservations are unnecessary, and you may have the course to yourself.

Where to Stay

Gustavus contains some of Alaska's best remote accommodations, more than we have room to describe here. Most accommodations are "Gustavus style," which means they charge a daily per-person price for rooms, breakfast and dinner served family style, brown-bag lunches, bicycles, and some other outdoor equipment and transfers. They also book and charge for fishing, sea kayaking, hiking, and Glacier Bay tours. It's expensive, but it's a carefree way to visit. Another set of accommodations charges less but leaves you on your own for lunch and dinner. Before choosing the less costly, a la carte approach, consider your dining options, which are covered below. Except as noted, rooms in Gustavus don't have phones. Some of the inns do not have licenses to serve alcohol; if that's a consideration, be sure to ask before you book your stay. There's a liquor store with limited hours, or you can bring your own.

Besides the lodgings described in full, we can also recommend **Homestead Bed & Breakfast,** near the center of Gustavus at 17 Faraway Rd. (www. homesteadbedbreakfast.com; ℂ **907/697-2777**), where a family opens two bedrooms and a comfortable common room to guests hoping to visit on a relative budget. A full breakfast is included in the summer rate of $135 double, as well as bikes, satellite TV, and Wi-Fi, and the Homeshore Cafe or Gustavus Inn (both below) are nearby for other meals.

Annie Mae Lodge ★   This rustic, post-and-beam lodge in the woods, near the Good River, provides a more flexible way to stay in Gustavus, with relatively reasonable rates and a good place to eat dinner—but you don't have to eat at the lodge. Although kept fresh and bright, the atmosphere is of a cozy, old-fashioned place, with antiques and reproductions, local art, and quilts. Rooms are on the small side but are nicely decorated. The lodge books activities, loans bikes, and takes care of transfers. The lodging rate includes breakfast—either continental or cooked to order—while dinner consists of a pair of entree choices, a starter, and dessert for $35 per diner. One choice is always local seafood, the other an entree such as prime rib or baked chicken. Reports on the food are consistently excellent. We emphasize the point because this is a good place to come if you are staying elsewhere and need a place to eat breakfast or dinner. Breakfast is served 6 to 9am; dinner is at a single sitting, at 6:30pm, and reservations are required.

2 Grandma's Farm Rd. (P.O. Box 55), Gustavus, AK 99826. www.anniemae.com. ℂ **800/478-2346** or 907/697-2346. Fax 907/697-2211. 11 units, 9 with private bathroom. High season $185–$200 double; low season $125 double. Extra person 13 and older $50. AE, DISC, MC, V. **Amenities:** Bike loan; courtesy van. *In room:* Wi-Fi.

Blue Heron Bed and Breakfast at Glacier Bay ★   Stay here if your budget doesn't allow a pricey all-inclusive package, and you'll still get many of the same comforts in fresh, bright rooms with features such as Wi-Fi, DVD players, comforters, and superior linens. The hosts, longtime residents, are enthusiastic about their guests and serve large gourmet breakfasts. If you rent one of the cottages, you can cook your own evening meal; the rooms have access to microwaves and refrigerators in the sunroom dining area, and a country store and deli are a few minutes' walk away. Guests can use the B&B's barbecue grill and its warm parkas for the glacier boat tours. The location is among the wildflowers and marshland near the Gustavus waterfront.

Off Dock Rd. (P.O. Box 77), Gustavus, AK 99826. www.blueheronbnb.net. ℂ **907/697-2337.** Fax 907/697-2293. 2 units, 2 cottages. $145 double; $185 double cottage. Extra adult $80. Discounts for children. Rates include full breakfast. No credit cards. Closed Oct–April. **Amenities:** Free bike loan; courtesy van; Internet access. *In room:* TV/DVD, free movie loan, hair dryer, Wi-Fi.

Glacier Bay's Bear Track Inn ★★★   Six miles from Gustavus, this extraordinary log building faces its own field of wildflowers, which, if you walk half a mile across it, leads to the shore. You look out on this scene from a lobby with a huge fireplace, a ceiling 28 feet high, and a wall of windows. The immense logs of the walls and the isolation give the place the feeling of a wilderness lodge, but the rooms are as good as those of any upscale hotel and have the advantage of large dormer windows with sweeping views. Objectively, it's the best place in Gustavus and one of the best remote lodges in Alaska, but which place you prefer depends on your taste. We also like the funky, quaint atmosphere of the rest of the town, which is absent at the more perfect Bear Track. Another difference compared to other lodges and inns: Meals here are cooked to order from a menu. Those not staying here can buy dinner, too. The inn serves beer and wine.

255 Rink Rd. (P.O. Box 255), Gustavus, AK 99826. www.beartrackinn.com. © **888/697-2284** or 907/697-3017. Fax 907/697-2284. 14 units. $575 per person, double occupancy; discounts for additional nights. Rates include round-trip air from Juneau, transfers, and all meals. DISC, MC, V. Closed Oct–Apr. **Amenities:** Restaurant; free bike loan; courtesy van; concierge; room service. *In room:* Hair dryer.

Gustavus Inn at Glacier Bay ★★★   This is the original and still our favorite of the Gustavus full-service inns. By objective standards of modern luxury, imitators have surpassed the old homestead farmhouse, but no one could duplicate the extraordinary hospitality of the Lesh family, honed over 40 years of running the inn. Dave and JoAnn know how to make guests feel immediately a part of the place. The site is unsurpassed, too, standing at the center of the community amid blowing grass and with a huge vegetable garden that provides much of the wonderful food, which is in the foreground of views from the newly expanded dining room and deck. Dave, the chef, has published a cookbook, and his ginger sablefish is now widely copied; in 2010, he won a major culinary award. He serves beer and wine with the sushi appetizers and big platters of food. Before going, talk over what you want to do with JoAnn or Dave, and let them book everything.

1 Gustavus Rd. (P.O. Box 60), Gustavus, AK 99826. www.gustavusinn.com. © **800/649-5220** or 907/697-2254. Fax 907/697-2255. 13 units. $215 per person per night. Half price for children 12 and under. Rates include all meals. AE, MC, V. Closed Sept 16–May 15. **Amenities:** Restaurant; bike loan; courtesy van; fishing rods (bring your own tackle). *In room:* Wi-Fi.

Where to Eat

Even if you don't stay at one of the full-service inns, we recommend taking at least some of your meals there. Annie Mae Lodge offers breakfast and dinner to nonguests. The food at Gustavus Inn at Glacier Bay is famous (we still try to copy some of the flavors prepared by Dave Lesh). Make reservations; you can't just show up and eat. The other choice for fine dining is the Glacier Bay Lodge, which serves three meals a day—but it's 10 miles away at the park's Bartlett Cove headquarters. Otherwise, the dining choices in Gustavus are very few and fairly basic.

The **Homeshore Cafe,** at Gustavus's central intersection on Wilson Road (© **907/697-2822**), serves meals all year in a dining room with about 40 seats next door to an art gallery. The menu includes pizza, calzones, sandwiches, salads, and the like, and beer and wine; a large pizza is $20 to $29, sandwiches $10. Summer hours are Tuesday through Saturday 11:30am to 2pm and 5 to 8pm; winter Tuesday through Friday 11:30am to 1:30pm and 4:30 to 6:30pm, staying open Friday until 7:30pm. The cafe accepts Visa and MasterCard.

HAINES: EAGLES & THE UNEXPECTED

Traditionally, Alaskans have used Haines as a weigh station. Going north, it was the last stop for vehicular visitors and residents who were planning to drive north via the Haines Highway, which connected with the Yukon Territory and eventually northern Alaska. It was a popular connection for people catching the Marine Highway for points south, and unless the ferry schedule required it, few people tended to spend much time in Haines.

Haines has always been a historic and interesting little community along the Chilkat River and is home of the Southeast Alaska State Fair; that alone shows that it's an odd little mix of Southeast frontier town and farming community. Driving along its narrow streets, it's not unusual to see horses and more than few residents (who grow their own vegetables) take advantage of the mild weather and the good glacier and river soil.

The town is a center of Native arts, with the Alaska Indian Arts Native Cultural Center. The 1904 former military base, Fort William H. Seward, lends it a dignified, parade-ground air.

And, yes, there are the bald eagles. It's almost impossible to talk about Haines without mentioning that it has more bald eagles than just about anywhere on Earth. In the winter especially, they gather along the river banks, several to each tree. Year-round, it's just about impossible to look skyward and not see several circling.

Like many small Alaskan towns, Haines is of two minds about the tourist industry. It loves visitors, but it really doesn't want too many of them (the occasional cruise-ship visits have been controversial).

Essentials

GETTING THERE   The **Alaska Marine Highway System** (© **800/642-0066** or 907/766-2111; www.ferryalaska.com) is how most people get to Haines,

Fort Seward.

and the cruise on the Lynn Canal fjord from Juneau or Skagway is among the most beautiful in the Inside Passage. The ferry takes almost 5 hours from Juneau. The Juneau-Haines fare is $37. The trip from Skagway takes an hour, and the fare is $31. The dock is 5 miles north of town.

At press time, no taxi service was operating in town, so ask about getting a ride when you reserve your lodgings. Both of the hotels in town offer courtesy shuttles.

You may be able to take a fast private boat to or from Skagway, landing in town so you don't need a ride out to the ferry dock. **Haines-Skagway Fast Ferry** (𝄞 **888/766-2103** or 907/766-2100; www.hainesskagwayfast ferry.com) charges $35 one-way, $68 round-trip. It runs daily during the summer and carries passengers only, not vehicles.

If you're driving, the **Haines Highway** leads 155 miles to Haines Junction, Yukon Territory, an intersection with the Alaska Highway. (You must pass through Canadian Customs—see "The Alaska Highway," in chapter 9, for information.) The road runs along the Chilkat River and the bald eagle preserve, then climbs into spectacular alpine terrain. Anchorage is 760 driving miles from Haines, and Fairbanks is 644.

Several air services offer scheduled prop service, air taxis, and flight-seeing tours to surrounding communities from Haines. **Wings of Alaska** (𝄞 **907/789-0790** reservations, or 766-2030 in Haines; www.ichoose wings.com) has plenty of flights, charging $218 round-trip from Juneau.

You can also fly scheduled or air-taxi service with **Air Excursions** (𝄞 **907/766-3800;** www.airexcursions.com).

VISITOR INFORMATION   The small but well-staffed and -stocked **Haines Convention and Visitors Bureau Visitor Information Center,** 2nd Avenue near Willard (P.O. Box 530), Haines, AK 99827 (𝄞 **800/458-3579** or 907/766-2234; www.haines.ak.us), is operated by the local government, which also sends out a vacation-planning packet. It's open summer Monday through Friday from 8am to 5pm, Saturday and Sunday from 8am to noon; in winter, hours are Monday through Friday from 8am to 5pm.

ORIENTATION   Haines sits on the narrow Chilkat Peninsula near the north end of the Southeast Alaska Panhandle. Highways run north and east on either side of the peninsula; the one on the east side goes to the ferry dock, 5 miles out, and ends after 11 miles at **Chilkoot Lake.** The other is the **Haines Highway,** which leads to the Canadian border, the Alaska Highway, and the rest of the world. The town has two parts: the sparsely built downtown grid and, a short walk to the west down Front Street or 2nd Avenue, the Fort William Seward area.

GETTING AROUND   Bikes are available from **Sockeye Cycle,** just uphill from the Port Chilkoot Dock on Portage Street in the Fort William Seward area (𝄞 **877/292-4154** or 907/766-2869; www.cyclealaska.com), for $14 for 2 hours or $35 for 8 hours.

Rent cars at the Captain's Choice Motel or Hotel Hälsingland (see "Where to Stay," later).

ATTRACTIONS

Alaska Indian Arts
  Cultural Center **15**
American Bald Eagle Foundation
  Natural History Museum **9**
Fort William H. Seward National
  Historic Site **12**
Hammer Museum
  & Cultural Center **7**

HOTELS

Captain's Choice Motel **3**
The Guardhouse Boarding
  House **10**
Hotel Halsingland **11**
The Riverhouse **14**
The Summer Inn B&B **2**

RESTAURANTS

The Bamboo Room **4**
Chilkat Restaurant and Bakery **1**
Commander's Room **11**
Fireweed Restaurant **13**
The Lighthouse **6**
Mosey's Cantina **16**
Mountain Market & Café **8**

[FastFACTS] HAINES

Bank **First National Bank of Alaska,** which has an ATM, is at Main Street and 2nd Avenue.

Hospital The **Haines Medical Clinic** (✆ **907/766-6300**) is on 1st Avenue, near the visitor center.

Internet Access The gorgeous **Haines Borough Library,** 111 3rd Ave. S. (✆ **907/766-2545;** www.haineslibrary.org), has public terminals and laptops.

Police Reach city police in nonemergencies at ✆ **907/766-2121.** Outside city limits, call the **Alaska State Troopers** at ✆ **907/766-2552.**

Post Office At 55 Haines Hwy., just west of Fort Seward.

Taxes The local sales tax is 5.5%. Tax on accommodations totals 9.5%.

SPECIAL EVENTS The local microbrewery, **Haines Brewing Co.** (✆ **907/766-3823**), situated at the fairgrounds, hosts a beer festival over Memorial Day weekend and offers samples and informal tours all summer. The 160-mile **Kluane Chilkat International Bike Relay** (www.kcibr.org) is held the third Saturday in June, heading steeply up and down the Haines Highway from Haines Junction, with more than 1,000 entrants riding solo or in teams of two, four, or eight.

The **Southeast Alaska State Fair** (© 907/766-2476; www.seak fair.org) is the biggest event of the summer, held for 4 days the last full weekend in July; it's a regional small-town get-together, with a logging show, a parade, a children's carnival, hobbyist exhibits, music on various stages, and other entertainment. Buildings constructed for the filming of the movie *White Fang* in 1990 were donated to the fair and form the nucleus of a retail area.

The **Alaska Bald Eagle Festival** (© 907/766-3094; www.bald eaglefestival.org) offers photography seminars and wildlife presentations to mark the annual eagle congregation. Held over 5 days in mid-November.

Exploring Haines

Haines is Alaska's center of odd or unusual museums and attractions, each somehow reflecting the character and contributions of local personalities.

You can't miss the **Fort William H. Seward National Historic Site,** a collection of large, white, wood-frame buildings around sloping parade grounds overlooking the magnificent Lynn Canal fjord. (Get the informative *History Walking Tour* brochure of the National Historic Site from the Haines Convention and Visitors Bureau to learn about each building.) The fort led a peaceful life, for a military installation. By the time the U.S. Army built it, in 1904, the Klondike gold rush was over, and there's no evidence it ever deterred any attack on this little peninsula at the north end of the Inside Passage. It was deactivated at the end of World War II, when it was used for training.

In 1947, a group of World War II veterans from the Lower 48 bought the fort as surplus, with the notion of forming a planned community. That idea didn't quite work out, but one of the new families from Outside helped spark a Chilkat Tlingits cultural renaissance in the 1950s. The Heinmillers, who still own a majority of the shares in the fort, formed a youth group that evolved into the Chilkat Dancers. A pair of elders led the group in construction of a Tlingits tribal house on the parade grounds. The **Alaska Indian Arts Cultural Center** (© 907/766-2160) grew from the same movement. Lee Heinmiller, a member of the family's second

Southeast Alaska State Fair.

generation, still manages the arts center, where you can see totem carving and silversmithing practiced. It's open from 9am to 5pm Monday through Friday. The center occupies the old fort hospital on the south side of the parade grounds. Check out the coffee shops, small galleries, and smoked salmon shop while walking around the area.

In the downtown area, the **Sheldon Museum and Cultural Center,** 11 Main St. (✆ **907/766-2366;** www.sheldonmuseum.org), contains an upstairs gallery of well-presented Tlingits art and cultural artifacts; downstairs is a collection on the pioneer history of the town. There's a uniquely personal feel to the Tlingits objects, some of which are displayed with pictures of the artisans who made them

American Bald Eagle Foundation Natural History Museum.

and the history of their relationship with the Sheldons, for whom the museum is named. The museum also has a new gallery hosting traveling exhibits and contemporary work by local artists. It's open in summer Monday through Friday 10am to 5pm, Saturday and Sunday 1 to 4pm; in winter, it's open Monday through Saturday from 1 to 4pm. Admission is $5 for adults, free for children 11 and under.

The entirely unique **American Bald Eagle Foundation Natural History Museum,** at 2nd Avenue and Haines Highway (✆ **907/766-3094;** www.baldeagles.org), is essentially a huge, hair-raising diorama of more than 200 eagles and other mounts of Alaska wildlife. A falconer is on the staff, and the museum has a falcon for presentations and a resident bald eagle and owl. Admission is $5 adults, $2.50 ages 9 to 12, free 8 and under; children need to be with an adult. It's open summer Monday through Friday from 10am to 6pm, Saturday and Sunday from noon to 4pm; call for the time of live bird presentations and for any off-season visit.

You'll recognize the **Hammer Museum,** 108 Main St., across from the bank (✆ **907/766-2374;** www.hammermuseum.org), by the 19-foot-long hammer out front. Longshoreman Dave Pahl created his collection of hammers over a couple of decades of building a homestead and added to it using the Internet. He found the prize of his collection, an 800-year-old Tlingits war hammer, while digging up the foundation of the museum itself. More than 1,800 hammers from all over the world, old and new, exotic and ordinary, fill the four rooms (Pahl has another 4,000 in storage). It's open summer Monday through Friday 10am to 5pm, closed off season. Admission is $3 adults, free for children 12 and under.

The **Kroschel Films Wildlife and Education Center,** at Mile 1.8 Mosquito Lake Rd. (✆ **907/767-5464;** www.kroschelfilms.com), is a wild animal park containing a dozen Alaskan species, including wolverines, lynx, a grizzly bear, wolves, and a snowy owl. The large enclosures are good for photography. Filmmaker Steve Kroschel and his teenage son, Garrett, show the animals off with infectious enthusiasm on a 2-hour tour. It's a funky, unscripted, and very Alaskan experience among the mountains 30 minutes outside Haines. Call

5

SOUTHEAST ALASKA

Haines: Eagles & the Unexpected

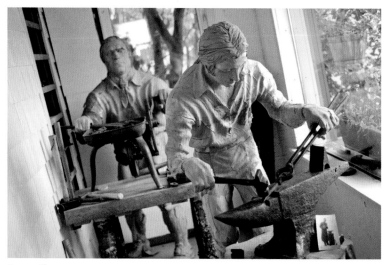

Hammer Museum.

ahead to set it up; you can't just drop in. If you don't have your own wheels, you may be able to join a cruise-ship group for transportation. Otherwise, you'll drive 28 miles out the Haines Highway, then turn right up Mosquito Lake Road. Kroschel charges independent travelers $50 for the tour, half price for kids 5 to 17, 4 and under free.

Getting Outside

GEARING UP   A fraternity of wilderness guides with few equals operates in Haines, and you can make contact with many of them through **Alaska Backcountry Outfitter,** 111 2nd Ave. (© **907/766-2876**; www.alaska naturetours.net), which books outings to ski, climb, kayak, raft, or fly, as well as the company's own Alaska Nature Tours, described below. The shop carries gear and clothing for birding, camping, climbing, hiking, skiing, snowboarding, pedaling, skateboarding, and paddling. Bike rental is covered above, under "Getting Around." Two other sporting gear shops are in town, with fishing gear as well as camping supplies and other equipment: **Outfitter Sporting Goods,** Mile 0, Haines Highway; and **Alaska Sports Shop,** 430 Main St.

EAGLE VIEWING   Haines is probably the best place on Earth to see bald eagles. The **Chilkat Bald Eagle Preserve** protects 48,000 acres of river bottom

Two bald eagles.

along the Chilkat River. From October to mid-December, peaking around Thanksgiving, up to 3,000 eagles gather in the cottonwood trees on a small section of the river, a phenomenon known as the Fall Congregation. (A healthy 200–400 are resident the rest of the year.) The eagles come for easy winter food: A very late salmon run spawns here into December in a 5-mile stretch of open water known as the Council Grounds. The best places to see them are pullouts, paths, and viewing areas along the Haines Highway from miles 18 to 21. Don't walk on the flats, as that disturbs the eagles. The preserve is managed by **Alaska State Parks** (www.alaskastateparks.org, click on "Individual Parks"). Contact the local ranger at © **907/766-2292;** the headquarters is at 400 Willoughby, 3rd Floor, Juneau, AK 99801.

Local guides offer trips on the river by raft, bicycle, or bus. Most tours happen in the summer, when the eagles are fewer but visitors more numerous. **Chilkat Guides,** based at mile 1, Haines Highway along Sawmill Road (© **888/292-7789** or 907/766-2491; www.raftalaska.com), does a rafting trip several times a day during the summer down the Chilkat to watch the eagles. The water is gentle—if it's too low, there's a chance you'll be asked to get out and push—and you'll see lots of eagles, mostly at a distance. The 3½-hour trip, with a snack, costs $89 for adults, $62 for children ages 7 to 12.

Serious bird-watchers, photographers, and others who want an in-depth tour should join **Alaska Nature Tours** (© **907/766-2876;** www.alaska naturetours.net), whose naturalists lead 3-hour wildlife-viewing tours by bus year-round for $85. The company also offers longer tours, including guided hikes, for $85 to $130, and cross-country skiing in and around the preserve. **Sockeye Cycle,** directly below, visits the eagle preserve on tours, too.

BIKING   The area is quite conducive to biking. **Sockeye Cycle,** 24 Portage St., near the dock (© **877/292-4154** or 907/766-2869; www.cyclealaska.com), leads a variety of guided trips—a couple of hours, half- or full-day, or even a 10-day trek along gold rush routes. A 3-hour ride costs $90 and could include various sites around town. Or you can rent your own bicycle for $35 a day.

FISHING   There are several charter operators in Haines for halibut and salmon fishing, and guided freshwater fishing for silver or sockeye salmon, Dolly Varden, and cutthroat trout. The **Haines Convention and Visitors Bureau,** 2nd Street near Willard (P.O. Box 530), Haines, AK 99827 (© **800/458-3579** or 907/766-2234; www.haines.ak.us), can help you find a guide or fishing lodge through the links on their website or the list of operators they keep at the office. For self-guided fishing advice and weekly summer updates of what's running, contact the local office of the Alaska Department of Fish and Game (© **907/766-2625;** www.alaska.gov/adfg, click on "Sport Fish," then the Southeast region on the state map).

FLIGHTSEEING   This is one of Alaska's best places to go flightseeing. The Inside Passage is beautiful, and one mountain away is Glacier Bay National Park; the ice field and the glaciers spilling through to the sea are a sight you won't forget. It's possible to land on an immense glacial ice field and see the sun slicing between the craggy peaks. **Alaska Mountain Flying and Travel,** 132 2nd Ave. (© **800/954-8747** or 907/766-3007; www.glacierbayflight seeing.com), offers these flights—or, as owner Paul Swanstrom says, adventures. He is known for his glacier and beach landings, and offers commentary to make flights fully guided experiences. Prices range from $159 to $299 per person, and reservations are recommended. Other flight services offer these tours, too; ask at the visitor center.

HIKING There are several good trails near Haines, ranging from an easy beach walk to a 10-mile, 3,650-foot climb of **Mount Ripinsky,** north of town (one route starts at the top of Young Rd.). Get the *Haines Is for Hikers* trail guide from the visitors' bureau. The easiest for families is the 2-mile **Battery Point Trail,** which goes along a beach decorated with wild iris. The trail starts at the end of Beach Road, which leads southeast from the Port Chilkoot cruise-ship dock. **Mount Riley** is south of town, with three trail routes to a 1,760-foot summit that features great views and feels much higher than it is; get the trail guide or ask directions to one of the trail heads. **Seduction Point Trail** is 7 miles long, starting at Chilkat State Park at the end of Mud Bay Road, south of town, and leading through forest and along beaches to the end of the Chilkat Peninsula, with great views of Rainbow Glacier. Since you'll walk the beach, check the tides; they'll give you a tide table at the visitors bureau. For a guided hike, rock climbing, or even a multi-day glacier trek, check with Alaska Mountain Guides, directly below. Their mountaineering programs cost $125 per day for 2 people minimum.

SEA KAYAKING **Alaska Mountain Guides** (✆ **800/766-3396** or 907/766-3366; www.alaskamountainguides.com) offers instruction, short guided trips, longer expeditions, and rentals ($50 a day for a single). A half-day guided paddle is $85, including a snack; a full day, including lunch, is $125.

Where to Stay

Lodging prices are reasonable in Haines, and choices include many friendly little places with lots of charm. Among them, the **River House** (www.riverhouse haines.com; ✆ **907/766-3849**), in a spectacular spot at the mouth of the Chilkat, a mile from town, is a rental cottage that can be rented in whole or in two individual units.

Captain's Choice Motel Haines lacks a chain hotel with the familiar, standard rooms we've all spent many nights in. This motel is the closest thing, with trim, red-roofed buildings in the central part of town overlooking the sea with a big sun deck. The rooms contain all the anticipated amenities, but are dated and somewhat dark, and we found fabrics and carpet in need of replacement on our last visit. The motel is friendly and homey, with a small resident dog in the lobby, and a full bar, the Captain's Lunge, which serves finger food.

108 2nd St. N. at Dalton St. (P.O. Box 392), Haines, AK 99827. www.capchoice.com. ✆ **800/478-2345** or 907/766-3111. Fax 907/766-3332. 39 units. High season $145 double; low season $116 double; year-round $160–$190 suite. Extra person $5. Rates include continental breakfast. AE, DC, DISC, MC, V. **Amenities:** Courtesy van; room service. *In room:* TV, fridge, hair dryer, microwave oven, Wi-Fi ($6.95/day).

The Guardhouse Boardinghouse 🖤 Situated on the edge of Fort Seward nearest downtown, a block from the waterfront, this B&B offers inexpensive central lodgings in an atmosphere that's like being house guests of a friendly couple. Phyllis Sage and Joanne Waterman, lifelong Alaskans, and their omnipresent spaniel and Newfoundland, share light-filled living quarters as common rooms, including the computer, a six-person Jacuzzi hot tub, and the deck out back with a barbecue and great views. Rooms have attractive decor and lots of Alaskan art.

Haines: Eagles & the Unexpected

SOUTHEAST ALASKA

One has a kitchenette and large bathroom; the least expensive room has a private bathroom that is not attached to the room. Despite the name "boardinghouse," only a continental breakfast is served.

15 Seward Dr. (P.O. Box 853), Haines, AK 99827. www.alaskaguardhouse.com. ✆ **866/290-7445** or 907/766-2566. 3 units. $105–$135 double; lower off season. Extra person 12 or older $15. MC, V. Rates include continental breakfast. **Amenities:** Jacuzzi; computer w/Internet. *In room:* TV, hair dryer, Wi-Fi.

Hotel Hälsingland ★ ✦   This grandly rambling hotel has always been the most interesting place in town to stay. The group of buildings, designated a National Historic Landmark, served as the Commanding Officer's Quarters for Fort William Seward during both World Wars. You can almost hear well-shined boots on the wood floors, echoing off high ceilings and old-fashioned woodwork. Today it's well kept, but rooms vary widely, so it's a good idea to take a look before checking in. Some share bathrooms, and some of those with private bathrooms have only shower stalls, while others have claw-foot tubs. The hotel also books tours, offers Avis car rental, and has an RV park out back.

The **Commander's Room** restaurant, open for dinner only, is among the best places to eat in town, for either fine dining or bar fare. The short dinner menu includes seafood in Continental styles and prices for main courses in the $22-to-$25 range. While it's the town's most formal dining room, it's still a friendly, low-key place. The full bar has craft brews on tap and a menu of burgers, appetizers, salads, and such, also very good, between $12 and $16. Try the sweet-potato fries.

Fort William Seward parade grounds (P.O. Box 1649), Haines, AK 99827. www.hotelhalsingland. com. ✆ **800/542-6363** or 907/766-2000. Fax 907/766-2060. 50 units, 45 with private bathroom. $79 double without bathroom; $99–$129 double with private bathroom. AE, DC, DISC, MC, V. Closed Oct–Apr. **Amenities:** Restaurant; bar; free ferry dock or airport transfers. *In room:* TV, Wi-Fi.

The Summer Inn Bed & Breakfast   This lovely old clapboard house downtown has a big porch and a living room decorated in whites and pale, lacy fabrics, like Grandma's house. The five rooms are cozy but small and share three bathrooms among them (bathrooms were immaculate when we visited). The house was built by a reputed former member of Soapy Smith's gang in 1912 (see the Skagway section below for more on Soapy), and the great big claw-foot tub is said to be the first in the history of Haines's upstairs bathtubs. No smoking or drinking is allowed.

117 2nd Ave. (P.O. Box 1198), Haines, AK 99827. www.summerinnbnb.com. ✆/fax **907/766-2970.** 5 units, none with private bathroom. High season $120 double, $130 suite; low season $110 double, $120 suite. Extra adult $20, child $15. Rates include full breakfast. MC, V.

Where to Eat

Haines has a few consistently good restaurants—which is a few more than most other Alaska towns this size—and you can also eat well during the summer at the Hotel Hälsingland (see "Where to Stay," above).

There are lots of places for a casual meal as well. The best for a hot breakfast is **Chilkat Restaurant and Bakery,** on 5th Avenue, a block north of Main Street (✆ **907/766-3653**). It's a friendly place with cute country decor serving hearty American food and a variety of Thai specials for lunch. Terrific lunches are found at the **Mountain Market & Café,** a natural food store and cafe at 3rd Avenue and the Haines Highway (© **907/766-3340**). A primary town hangout and the best espresso stop, it serves hearty and reasonably priced sandwiches, tortilla wraps, soups, and many fresh-baked goods. Pick up a picnic, or stop by for coffee, roasted in-house, or breakfast. The liquor store carries organic wine in its broad selection.

The Bamboo Room ★ DINER   The building started as a French restaurant during the gold-rush era and then became a brothel and speak-easy before the Tengs family got it in 1953. In the current generation, the food has taken center stage from the bar, although there's live music on the bar side in the summer. The diner serves breakfast, burgers, wraps, salads, pasta, and lots of seafood. A wide variety of food and prices should suit everyone, including a good children's menu. The halibut and chips is celebrated.

2nd Ave. near Main St. © **907/766-2860.** www.bamboopioneer.net. Lunch $8–$16; dinner $10–$35. AE, DISC, DC, MC, V. Summer daily 6am–10pm; winter daily 6am–2pm.

Fireweed Restaurant ★ PIZZA   A historic building in Fort Seward was remodeled into the most attractive dining room in Haines using salvaged wood from other old buildings: natural tones, handcrafted wood, and local art and photography create a soft setting. With only seven tables, the place can get a bit crowded and noisy, but the popularity attests to the quality of the casual food. The menu includes pasta dishes, hero sandwiches, and nonbeef burgers (instead portobello mushroom, chicken, buffalo, or halibut). The calzone and pizza are exceptional. Get a large pie with a few ingredients of your choice for $25.

Historic bldg. #37, Blacksmith Rd. © **907/766-3838.** Lunch $8–$14; dinner $11–$20. MC, V. Summer Tues–Sat 4:30–10pm; Apr and Sept Tues–Sat 4:30–9pm. Closed Oct–Mar.

The Lighthouse SEAFOOD   Dine here for seafood or a steak in a light, stylish dining room with a spectacular water view (don't let the saloon exterior scare you away). The local seafood is simply prepared, fusing Alaskan and South Pacific cuisine. Try the Alaskan sablefish with coconut wasabi sauce. The restaurant is open year-round and serves a lunch of burgers and sandwiches, as well as a few entrees. Service is quick and professional.

Main and Front sts. © **907/766-2442.** Lunch $8–$20; dinner $15–$30. AE, DC, DISC, MC, V. High season daily 8am–10pm; low season daily 11:30am–9pm.

Mosey's Cantina ★ 🕮 MEXICAN/SOUTHWEST   A couple gave up river guiding on the Grand Canyon for Alaskan floats, then settled in Haines and

---

A Quick Side Trip to Juneau from Haines or Skagway

Without changing your lodgings, you can travel from Skagway or Haines for a tour of Juneau's highlights and a sightseeing day cruise of the Lynn Canal. **Alaska Fjordlines'** high-speed catamaran (© **800/320-0146** or **907/766-3395;** www.alaskafjordlines.com) carries passengers for half a day in Juneau, with wildlife sightings on the way. The fare is $155 adults, $125 ages 2 to 12, under 2 free, and includes a narrated bus tour of Juneau and Mendenhall Glacier, with time for shopping and dining downtown. The whole excursion is about 12 hours.

Haines: Eagles & the Unexpected

SOUTHEAST ALASKA

began serving the cuisine they brought with them, which is re-energized with annual chili-buying trips to New Mexico. The food is authentic and well prepared. For lunch, the green chili burrito is huge and delicious, for $9; for dinner, the enchiladas chicken mole hits a perfect mix of spice and sweetness, for $19. At lunch, you order at the counter, while a server comes to the table in the evening. The atmosphere, in a gray house with a big porch, is fun, bright, and loud. As the dining room is small and the restaurant popular, calling ahead is a good idea. It's walking distance from downtown, just south of Fort Seward off Tower Road.

1 Soap Suds Alley. ℂ **907/766-2320.** Reservations accepted. Lunch $6–$16; dinner $9–$22. MC, V. Daily 11:30am–2:30pm and 5:30–8:30pm. Closed Oct–Feb.

SKAGWAY: AFTER THE GOLD RUSH

Prior to the Goldrush, Skagway—and its sister city, the now–ghost town of Dyea—were barely more than a gleam in the eye of the area's first white resident, Capt. William Moore, who claimed a 160-acre homestead at the mouth of the Skagway River in 1887. Believing the area was the best route to the potential inland gold fields, he built a log cabin, a sawmill, and a wharf. But when the gold seekers came in 1897 and 1898, the town expanded so rapidly that Captain Moore's original layout and plan was disregarded, and he was essentially driven off most of his own land, primarily by a local land surveyor, Frank Reid, who would later figure prominently in Skagway's most infamous moment.

In the rush years of 1897 and 1898, an estimated (there was literally no local government to count them) 80,000 people passed through Skagway. The semi-permanent population in those years was estimated at 15,000 to 20,000. It was a Wild West boomtown in every sense of the word.

For the prospectors who arrived in town with little savvy, there were myriad ways for the local criminal element to relieve them of money they had brought with them. The most famous of these local "characters" was Jefferson Randolph "Soapy" Smith, the most famous scoundrel in Alaskan history. Smith ruled the town with a small army of toughs and con artists. There are a million stories about Smith, most of them probably not true, but he did set up a telegraph office to help the gold rushers wire money home, long before Skagway was even connected to a telegraph line. Most of Smith's scams were probably more pedestrian, but there is no question that he controlled Skagway and separated hundreds of Argonauts from their money.

Klondike Gold Rush National Historic District.

The Slow Season

Skagway is a seasonal community. After September and before May, almost none of the commercial tourist attractions are open, and hardly any lodgings or restaurants. Many residents close their businesses and leave in the fall. This section focuses on what you can do in the summer, and you can assume that most of what is described is not available in the winter.

Finally, in July 1898, the other residents of Skagway had had enough. A vigilante committee led by Frank Reid confronted Smith and several gang members. A shootout ensued, and Smith was killed instantly. Reid was also mortally wounded and lingered 4 days before dying. Both men are buried in the Gold Rush Cemetery just outside of town.

For Skagway, the boom was generally over by 1900, but another boom was on the horizon; it would take most of the rest of the century before it arrived in gold rush–type numbers. Even before the end of the gold rush, some visitors were already arriving, not to seek gold, but to seek the seekers, so to speak. On one day in 1903, more than 300 visitors arrived on two ships just to "see" the famous Skagway. Today more than 900,000 people visit Skagway each year on cruise ships. In contrast, the current year-round population is around 900, with twice as many people living in the community during the summer. The downtown area has been largely preserved in its gold rush finery, and many of the visitors ride the White Pass and Yukon Railway up into the mountains to the Canadian border and back.

Essentials

GETTING THERE   The **Alaska Marine Highway System** (✆ **800/642-0066** or 907/983-2941; www.ferryalaska.com) connects Skagway daily with Haines and Juneau. The fare is $31 from Haines, $50 from Juneau. If you're headed to Haines without a vehicle, consider the private **Haines–Skagway Fast Ferry** (p. 190). Haines is 15 miles away by boat, but more than 350 miles by road.

Since 1978, **Klondike Hwy. 2** has traced the route of the stampeders through the White Pass into Canada, a parallel route to the Chilkoot Trail. The road runs 99 miles, then meets the Alaska Highway a dozen miles southeast of the Yukon capital of Whitehorse. The border is at the top of the pass, 14 miles from Skagway. (Information on requirements to cross the border is in chapter 9 under "The Alaska Highway," p. 443.) This is one of the most spectacular drives anywhere in Alaska, with views basically equivalent to those from the White Pass and Yukon Route railway (but a lot cheaper). The road is a well-maintained 2-lane highway with wide shoulders. Do it in clear weather, if possible, as in cloudy weather, all you'll see is whiteout.

Car rentals in Skagway are available from **Avis,** in the Westmark Hotel at 3rd and Spring streets (✆ **800/230-4898** or 907/983-2247; www.avis.com).

Riding the ferry to Skagway and then heading inland **in a rented RV** is an attractive option. Expect to pay around $150 to $250 a day, depending upon vehicle size, plus many required extras (it's not a cheap option).

ATTRACTIONS
Corrington Museum of
  Alaska History **6**
Mascot Saloon **13**
Mollie Walsh Park **8**
Moore House **7**
National Park Service Visitor
  Center **14**
Skagway Museum &
  Archives **9**
The White Pass & Yukon
  Route Depot **15**

HOTELS
At the White House **2**
The Historic Skagway Inn **5**
Mile Zero B&B **1**
Sgt. Preston's Lodge **4**
Skagway Home Hostel **3**

RESTAURANTS
Glacial Smoothies &
  Espresso **10**
Skagway Fish Company **16**
Starfire **12**
The Stowaway Café **17**
Sweet Tooth Café **11**

Skagway

Alaska Motorhome Rentals (✆ **800/323-5757;** www.bestofalaska
travel.com) rents RVs one-way to Anchorage with a drop-off fee of $795 to
$995, plus the cost of the rental, mileage, and gas. The same company,
under a different name, also offers structured RV tours from Skagway as
add-ons to cruise vacations; that's covered in chapter 11 under "Getting
There & Getting Around."

Traveling **by bus** between Skagway and Anchorage or Fairbanks is not
a practical option for most visitors. It's a marginal business to be in, and
operators change annually. At best, the journey takes a couple of days. If
taking the bus is your goal, contact the Skagway Convention and Visitors
Bureau (below) for the latest advice. They can help you figure out how to
get to Whitehorse (summer only) by tour bus or on the White Pass and
Yukon Route railway by train and bus (p. 205), and there to catch another
bus to Alaska. Do plan all the details ahead, as otherwise you could be
stranded for days.

Several air taxi operators serve Skagway. A round-trip from Juneau
costs $236 on **Wings of Alaska** (✆ **907/789-0790** reservations, or 983-
2442 in Skagway; www.ichoosewings.com).

VISITOR INFORMATION   Located in the restored railroad depot, the **National
Park Service Visitor Center,** 2nd Avenue and Broadway (P.O. Box 517),

Capt. William Moore Bridge on the Klondike Highway.

Skagway, AK 99840 (© **907/983-2921;** www.nps.gov/klgo), is the focal point for activities in Skagway. Rangers answer questions, give talks, show films, and, five times a day, lead an excellent guided walking tour. The building houses a small museum that lays the groundwork for the rest of what you'll see. The Park Service's programs are free. The visitor center is open early May through late September daily from 8am to 6pm; the rest of the year, the museum is open Monday through Friday from 8am to 5pm.

The **Skagway Convention and Visitors Bureau Center,** 245 Broadway (P.O. Box 1029), Skagway, AK 99840 (© **907/983-2854;** www. skagway.com), occupies the historic Arctic Brotherhood Hall, the building with the driftwood facade. The website contains links to lodgings and activities, or you can request the same information on paper (order at © 888/762-1898). Stop in especially for the handy and informative *Skag-way Walking Tour Map* of historic sites. The center is open summer daily 8am to 6pm but closes at 5pm on weekends; winter Monday through Friday from 8am to 5pm.

GETTING AROUND   Skagway is laid out on a simple grid, with streets branching off from Broadway. The main sights can be reached on foot. For places you can't walk, try the **Dyea Dave Shuttle** (© 907/612-0290), which operates like a taxi. Skagway also has a bus, called **SMART** (© **907/983-2743**), which runs a circuit around town for $2 a ride, or out of town to sites such as the Klondike Gold Dredge for $5 with an all-day pass. It leaves on the hour from City Hall and 7th Avenue and Spring Street. A bike is fun and practical transportation in Skagway. **Sockeye Cycle,** on 5th Avenue off Broadway (© **877/292-4154** or 907/983-2851; www.cyclealaska.com), rents good mountain bikes for $14 for 2 hours and leads guided day trips (see "Getting Outside," below).

[Fast FACTS] SKAGWAY

Bank **Wells Fargo,** at Broadway and 6th Avenue, has an ATM.

Hospital The **Dahl Medical Clinic,** staffed by advanced nurse practitioners, can be reached at © **907/983-2255** during business hours. It is located at on 14th Avenue between State Street and Broadway.

Internet Access Free at the Skagway Public Library, 769 State St. (© **907/983-2665**).

Police For nonemergency business, call © **907/983-2232.** The station is located on State Street, just south of 1st Avenue.

Post Office On Broadway, between 6th and 7th avenues.

Taxes Sales tax is 5%. The bed tax totals 8%.

SPECIAL EVENTS Skagway's July 4th Parade and Celebration, organized by the chamber of commerce and featuring lots of small-town events, has been a big deal since Soapy Smith led the parade in 1898. The **Klondike Road Relay,** a 110-mile overnight footrace over the pass, brings hundreds of runners in teams of 10 from all over the world in mid-September. Contact the visitor center for information on any of these events.

Exploring Skagway

You can see most of Skagway on foot, and everything by bike. Many companies also offer car, van, or bus tours, too. No one goes to greater lengths to give visitors a unique experience than the **Skagway Street Car Company** (© 907/983-2908; www.skagwaystreetcar.com), which uses antique touring vehicles and costumed guides performing "theater without walls." The amusing, historical 2-hour streetcar tour, based on a tour originally given to President Harding in 1923, is $42 for adults and $21 for children 12 and under. Book the tour at least 2 weeks in advance, as they're frequently sold out.

TOURING THE HISTORIC PARK

The main thing to do in Skagway is to see the old buildings and historic gold-rush places. Do it with the *Skagway Walking Tour Map,* or join a fascinating National Park Service guided walking tour (see "Visitor Information," above).

Start with a visit to the **museum** at the National Park Service Visitor Center in the building next door. It helps put everything else in context. Of greatest interest is a collection of food and gear similar to the ton of supplies each prospector was required to carry over the pass in order to gain entry into Canada, a requirement that prevented famine among the stampeders but made the job of getting to Dawson City an epic struggle.

While they prepared to go over the pass, gold-rush greenhorns spent their time in Skagway drinking and getting fleeced in the many gambling dens and brothels. Law didn't mean much in the town's heyday with the lack of civil authority. It's hard to picture at times, because everything looks so orderly now, but the Park Service has tried. For example, the **Mascot Saloon,** at Broadway and 3rd Avenue, has mannequins bellying up to the bar. It's open daily from 8am to 6pm; admission is free.

The Park Service walking tour ends at the **Moore House,** near 5th Avenue and Spring Street, open from 10am to 5pm during the summer. Ten years before the gold rush happened, Capt. William Moore brilliantly predicted it and

5

SOUTHEAST ALASKA

Skagway: After the Gold Rush

The Mascot Saloon.

homesteaded the land that would become Skagway. A block east, on 6th Avenue, is **Mollie Walsh Park,** with a good children's play area, public restrooms, and phones. A sign tells the sad story of one of Skagway's first respectable women, a lady who chose to marry the wrong man among two suitors and was killed by him in a drunken rage. The other suitor—who'd previously killed another rival for her affections—commissioned the bust of Walsh that stands at the park.

The **Gold Rush Cemetery** is 1½ miles from town, up State Street. Used until 1908, it's small and overgrown with spruce trees, but some of the charm and mystery of the place is lost because of the number of visitors and the shiny new paint and maintenance of the wooden markers. The graves of Soapy Smith and Frank Reid are the big attractions, but don't miss the short walk up to Reid Falls. About 10 miles northwest of Skagway is the ghost town of **Dyea,** where stampeders started climbing the Chilkoot Trail. It's a lovely coastal drive or bike ride: From Skagway, go 2 miles up Klondike Hwy. 2 and then turn left, continuing 8 miles on gravel road. Little remains in Dyea other than boards, broken dock pilings, a single false front, and miscellaneous iron debris. On a sunny day, however, the protected historical site is the perfect place for a picnic, among beach grasses, fields of wild iris, and the occasional reminder that a city once stood here. The National Park Service leads an interesting guided history and nature walk here daily in summer at 10am and 2pm; check at the visitor center. (See "Getting Outside," below, for more on going to Dyea.)

The little-visited **Slide Cemetery,** in the woods near Dyea, is the last resting place of many of nearly 100 who died in an avalanche on the Chilkoot Trail on Palm Sunday, April 3, 1898. No one knows how many are here, exactly who died, or how accurate the wooden markers are. In 1960, when the state reopened the Chilkoot Trail, the cemetery had been completely overgrown and the markers were replaced. The mystery makes it an even more ghostly place, and the sense of anonymous, hopeless hardship and death it conveys is as authentic a gold-rush souvenir as anything in Skagway.

MUSEUMS & ATTRACTIONS

Jewell Gardens ★   Early Skagway promoters planted big, showy gardens to impress the tourists and named the town "Garden City of Alaska." Jim and Charlotte Jewell revived this tradition using grounds originally planted by gold-rush stampeder Henry Clark, and maintain some of his original 1898 plantings, including fruit trees and a 4-foot-tall rhubarb. Besides the organic show garden, with a boardwalk and model train, the Jewells also produce food here and offer visitors lessons on composting and growing in cold conditions. Artists demonstrate their work in a glass-blowing studio, and their whimsical creations decorate the gardens. Stop in the conservatory for English tea or a meal. The restaurant, called Poppies at Jewell Gardens, serves some of the best lunches in town, including smoked salmon quiche, homemade soups, and the garden's produce. A full lunch is $12. The garden is at the far end of the town from the waterfront; take the SMART bus. Cruise-ship tours are heaviest Tuesday through Thursday.

Mile 1.5 Klondike Hwy. ✆ **907/983-2111.** www.jewellgardens.com. $12 adults, $6 ages 12 and under. Early May to late Sept daily 9am–5pm. Restaurant 11am–3pm.

Klondike Gold Fields Tour Gold mining never happened in Skagway—it was only a transit point—but more gold-rush tourists come here than anywhere else, so promoters brought a dredge to where the people are. The 1937 rig, weighing 350 tons, dug up and sorted gravel to remove gold first in Idaho, then near Dawson City, and finally near the border on the Top of the World Highway. Visitors take a tour, see a movie on the northern lights, and can dine in a brewery restaurant on-site.

Mile 2.2 Klondike Hwy. ✆ **907/983-3175.** www.klondikegolddredge.com. $45 adults, $35 ages 11 and under. Summer Sun–Fri 8:30am–4:30pm; full tours 9:30am and 1:30pm.

Skagway Museum and Archives ★ The museum contains a fine collection of gold-rush artifacts and other items reflecting Skagway's colorful history. The building is the town's most impressive and one of the state's most dignified architectural landmarks, with crisp granite walls and a high-pitched roof standing among tall shade trees on the edge of town. It began life as a short-lived gold rush–era college and later became a federal courthouse and jail. The city hall and museum have occupied the building since 1961, except for a brief hiatus for renovations.

7th and Spring sts. ✆ **907/983-2420.** Admission $2 adults, $1 students, free for children 12 and under. Summer Mon–Fri 9am–5pm, Sat 10am–5pm, Sun 10am–4pm; winter hours vary—call ahead.

The White Pass and Yukon Route ★★ A narrow-gauge railroad line that originally ran to Whitehorse, the White Pass was completed after only 2 years in 1900. It's an engineering marvel and a fun way to see spectacular, historic scenery from a train inching up steep tracks that were chipped out of the side of the mountains. Some of the cars are historic as well—originals more than 100 years old. The railroad "recommends" you don't get out of your seat, but it's a long ride on a slow train, and most people get up and socialize; however, you cannot move from car to car while the train is moving. The trick is to go in clear weather; when the pass is socked in, all you see is white clouds. Tickets are expensive, however, and you have to reserve ahead. Take the

Glass flowers at the Jewell Gardens.

gamble: Cancellation carries only a $10-per-person penalty, and you can change dates for no charge. Also, try to go on a weekend, when fewer cruise ships are in town taking up all the seats; weekend trains can be booked as little as a week ahead, while midweek excursions can book up months ahead. The summit excursion—which travels 20 miles with an elevation gain of 2,865 feet, then turns back—takes about 3 hours and costs $112 for adults. All fares are half price for ages 3 to 12 (except for Chilkoot Pass hiker's fares; see "Backpacking," below).

For a longer journey, trains travel to Carcross, Yukon, with a stop for a hot meal at Lake Bennett and a return trip by bus. That costs $239. But the biggest treat for a train lover is a steam-powered trip. Friday and Monday afternoons, steam trains go over the pass to Fraser Meadows, 6 miles beyond the pass, and return; the fare is $155. In either case, bring your passport, as the train will go into Canada. Other choices are available, too; check the website.

These days, the line operates only as a tourist attraction May through September.

2nd Ave. depot, Skagway. *C* **800/343-7373** or 907/983-2217. www.wpyr.com. For the entire schedule and fares, see the website.

Getting Outside

The **Mountain Shop,** 355 4th Ave. (*C* **907/983-2544**), rents and sells the equipment you need for backpacking or other outdoor activities in Skagway. The owner organizes guided dayhikes, backpacking trips, and kayaking trips under the name **Packer Expeditions,** 9th Avenue and State Street (*C* **907/983-3005;** www.packerexpeditions.com). **Alaska Mountain Guides,** on 4th between Main and Broadway (*C* **907/983-3365;** www.alaskamountainguides.com), offers rock climbing in Skagway for $160 per day and 5-day Chilkoot Pass hikes for $890 per person.

BACKPACKING   The National Park Service and Parks Canada jointly manage the famous **Chilkoot Pass Trail,** publishing a trail guide and offering information at their offices in Skagway and Whitehorse. Some 20,000 stampeders used the trail to get from Dyea, 9 miles from Skagway, to Lake Bennett, 33 miles away, where they would build and launch boats bound for Dawson City. Today about 3,000 people a year make the challenging hike, taking 3 to 5 days. The Chilkoot is not so much a wilderness trail as an outdoor museum, but don't underestimate its difficulty, as so many did during the gold rush.

To control the numbers, **Parks Canada,** 205–300 Main St., Whitehorse, Yukon Y1A 2B5, Canada (*C* **800/661-0486** or 867/667-3910; fax 867/393-6701; www.pc.gc.ca/chilkoot), allows only 50 hikers with permits per day to cross the summit. You should reserve ahead. To buy permits, call with a Visa, American Express, or MasterCard; give the date you plan to start; and specify the campsites you will use each night. Permits are C$51 for adults, C$25 ages 16 and under, plus a C$12 per-person reservation fee. You pick up the permit at the Trail Centre in Skagway; that's also where 8 of the 50 daily permits are held for walk-ins, to be distributed along with any no-shows. The reservation fee is nonrefundable, and the permit fee is refundable only until a month before the hike.

Once over the pass, you're on Lake Bennett, on the rail line 8 miles short of the road. You can walk to the road (stay safely off the tracks), or get back to Skagway on the White Pass and Yukon Route railway (p. 205) at

Miners making their way up Chilkoot Pass during the gold rush of 1897 to 1899.

2pm Monday, Tuesday, and Friday. The one-way fare to Fraser, B.C., is $50, and the scenic 3-hour ride to Skagway is $95. The railroad requires tickets be purchased in advance, as well as meals at Lake Bennett, if you eat there. You will also need a passport to get back into the United States.

BIKING **Sockeye Cycle,** on 5th Avenue off Broadway (✆ **877/292-4154** or 907/983-2851; www.cyclealaska.com), leads bike tours, including one that takes clients to the top of the White Pass in a van and lets them coast down on bikes; the 2½-hour trip is $79. Going up on White Pass and the Yukon Route railroad and riding back down brings the price to $179. Riders must be at least 12 years old. The company also leads a 3-hour tour of the quiet ghost-town site of Dyea for $79, going over in a van. Or ride to Dyea from Skagway on your own over the hilly, 10-mile coastal road, a very pleasant, scenic route.

FLIGHTSEEING Skagway, like Haines, is a good place to choose for a flightseeing trip, as Glacier Bay National Park is just to the west. Flightseeing operators offer flights from Skagway, too. **Temsco Helicopters** (✆ **866/ 683-2900** or 907/983-2900; www.temscoair.com) takes 80-minute tours near Skagway, with half that time spent on a glacier (not in Glacier Bay); those flights cost $289. A 90-minute helicopter and dog-sled tour, including an hour at a dog camp on Denver Glacier, is $479.

HIKING A *Skagway Trail Map* is available from the visitor center, listing 10 hikes around Skagway. An easy evening walk starts at the footbridge at the west end of the airport parking lot, crossing the Skagway River to **Yakutania Point Park,** where pine trees grow from cracks in the rounded granite of the shoreline. Across the park is a shortcut, taking a couple of miles off the trip to Dyea and to the **Skyline Trail and A.B. Mountain,** a strenuous climb to a 5,000-foot summit with great views. On the southeast side of town, across the railroad tracks, a network of trails heads up from Spring Street between 3rd and 4th avenues to a series of mountain lakes, the closest of which is **Lower Dewey Lake,** less than a mile up the trail.

Where to Stay

The accommodations in Skagway are within close walking distance of the historic district, except as noted.

At the White House ★ 🎁 The Tronrud family essentially rebuilt a burned 1902 gable-roofed inn, which has dormer and bow windows and two porticos with small Doric columns. They made the rooms comfortable and modern, all with private bathrooms, while retaining the authentic gold-rush style of the original owner, Lee Guthrie, a successful gambler and saloon owner of the early years. The inn has hardwood floors and fine woodwork. Bedrooms vary in size, but all have quilts and other nice touches, including ceiling fans.

Corner of 8th and Main sts. (P.O. Box 41), Skagway, AK 99840-0041. www.atthewhitehouse.com. *✆* **907/983-9000.** Fax 907/983-9010. 10 units. High season $135–155 double; low season $85 double. Discounts for multiple days. Extra person $10. Rates include continental breakfast. AE, DISC, MC, V. *In room:* TV, fridge, Wi-Fi.

Chilkoot Trail Outpost ★ These beautifully crafted log cabins contain comfortable, modern lodgings with carpeted floors and log interior walls, some in the form of two-room suites, with many amenities but no phones. The hiker's suite consists of two rooms in a duplex with bunk beds that rent for $145 double, including breakfast. The location, in Dyea near the Chilkoot Trail and Taiya River, puts you in quiet, natural surroundings away from the carnival atmosphere created by the crush of tourists in Skagway proper. In good weather, the hosts have a nightly campfire and provide supplies for s'mores. You can barbecue in a screened gazebo, or buy a dinner of steak or local seafood in a remarkable log building with a vaulted ceiling for $25. There's a full bar, too. The included breakfast consists of a buffet with various choices, including one hot selection.

Mile 7, Dyea Rd. (P.O. Box 286), Skagway, AK 99840. www.chilkoottrailoutpost.com. *✆* **907/983-3799.** Fax 907/983-3599. 11 units. $145 double in duplex; $175 double-occupancy cabin. Extra adult $25, extra child 2–11 years $13. MC, V. Rates include full breakfast. Closed off season. **Amenities:** Bike loan. *In room:* TV/VCR, fridge, hair dryer, microwave, no phone, Wi-Fi.

The Historic Skagway Inn ★ An 1897 building that served as a gold-rush brothel was moved to this site in 1902 and added onto until the 1950s. The inn's decoration, a mixture of Victorian and Wild West, uses wallpaper and period antiques to create homey, pleasant accommodations, and the place is loaded with character, each room named after a prostitute who may have once worked there. But prostitutes lived in small rooms, and the bathrooms created from converted closets are tiny. Also consider **At the White House,** above, which does the historic thing well for lower rates. A full breakfast is included in the rate, served in the dining room of **Olivia's,** an on-site restaurant offering gourmet dinners. It draws for produce on the inn's own large and luxuriant garden, which is also open for tours.

7th Ave. and Broadway (P.O. Box 500), Skagway, AK 99840. www.skagwayinn.com. *✆* **888/SKAGWAY** (752-4929) or 907/983-2289. 10 units. High season $119 double without bathroom,

Skagway: After the Gold Rush

SOUTHEAST ALASKA

$189 double with bathroom, $199 suite; low season $99 double, $149 suite. Extra person 16 and over $30. AE, DISC, MC, V. Rates include full breakfast. **Amenities:** Courtesy van; Internet access. *In room:* Hair dryer, Wi-Fi.

Mile Zero Bed & Breakfast ★   This building was designed to be a B&B, and it shows in details such as the soundproofing and the back doors to every room—guests can access the common rooms through one door or go outside through French doors leading to the porch. The design makes the B&B similar to a motel in its privacy and convenience, but it also has comfortable common rooms with leather furniture, where guests were enjoying wine and cheese with the outgoing hostess when we visited. Rooms, all with private bathroom, have satellite TV and iPod docks. There are barbecue facilities on-site. The inn is a few blocks from the historic area.

9th Ave. and Main St. (P.O. Box 165), Skagway, AK 99840. www.mile-zero.com. © **907/983-3045.** Fax 907/983-3046. 6 units. High season $135 double; low season $75 double. Extra person $25. Rates include continental breakfast. MC, V. **Amenities:** Internet station. *In room:* TV, Wi-Fi ($5 fee).

Sgt. Preston's Lodge ★   Four buildings sit on a landscaped lawn just steps off Broadway, Skagway's main historic street, at 6th Avenue and State Street. U.S., Canada, and Alaska flags fly out front, underlining the theme, along with the trim tan, red, and green paint scheme of the tidy image of the Royal Canadian Mounted Police. Once inside, you will find typical modern motel rooms, the best choice in town for those who simply want a comfortable place to sleep for a reasonable rate. Ten rooms have only shower stalls—no tubs. The lobby, fixed up in 2010, has a computer station and shelves of books.

370 6th Ave. (P.O. Box 538), Skagway, AK 99840. www.sgtprestonslodge.com. © **866/983-2521** or 907/983-2521. Fax 907/983-3500. 38 units. High season $90–$125 double; low season $90 double. Extra person age 12 and over $10. AE, DISC, MC, V. **Amenities:** Courtesy car; Internet. *In room:* TV.

A HOSTEL & CAMPING

The primitive **National Park Service Dyea Campground** has 22 well-separated sites along a river at the ghost town site 9 miles from Skagway. The campground has pit toilets and no water. RVs more than 27 feet are not allowed. The fee is $10. The **Pullen Creek RV Park** (www.pullencreekrv.com; © **800/936-3731** or 907/983-2768) is near the small-boat harbor, with coin-operated showers. RV sites with power, water, and dump station use are $38, car camping sites are $30, tenting with no vehicle $25.

Skagway Home Hostel   For more than 20 years, Frank Wasmer has opened his historic home to hostellers, sharing his meals, refrigerator, bathrooms, laundry machines, and hospitality side by side with guests. The atmosphere is like off-campus shared housing at college, except the house is nicer and better kept. Bunks are in separate male, female, or coed dorms. To reserve, use the website, as they don't return long-distance calls. In winter, reservations are required, as Frank might not be there. He accepts MasterCard and Visa for reservations, but you have to pay cash for your bunk. Summer registration hours are from 5:30 to 10:30pm. No pets, alcohol, or smoking.

3rd Ave. near Main St. (P.O. Box 231), Skagway, AK 99840. www.skagwayhostel.com. © **907/983-2131.** 3 dorms. $15–$20 per bunk. Cash only. **Amenities:** Computer with Internet; shared kitchen; TV.

Where to Eat

Restaurants go out of business and open up faster in Skagway's entirely seasonal economy than anywhere else we know. It's not unusual for a third of the restaurants to be new each year. Asking around for a current recommendation may pay off.

Restaurants that stay open year-round tend to be better for two reasons: They can keep their staff, and they have to be good or they wouldn't make it through the winter in a town with fewer than 1,000 residents. The **Sweet Tooth Café,** a diner at 315 Broadway (**Ⓒ 907/983-2405**), has good food and service year-round, open for breakfast and lunch. **Glacial Smoothies and Espresso,** 336 3rd Ave., off State Street (**Ⓒ 907/983-3223**), has built a year-round clientele serving good coffee, bagels, and wraps. It's a fun little place for a light meal where the kids can play Monopoly or Hungry Hippos while you sip.

A seasonal place good for a quick seafood lunch or dinner and a beer is **Skagway Fish Company,** on the boat harbor at 210 Congress Way (**Ⓒ 907/983-3474**), with a casual, noisy dining room and a water view. You should also consider Olivia's (at the Historic Skagway Inn) and Poppies at Jewell Gardens, both mentioned above, and Skagway Brewing Company, below.

Starfire ★ THAI   The specialty here is spicy Thai cuisine—stir-fries, curries, soups, and salads. The pad Thai came in a large portion with a cabbage salad and was cooked and seasoned just right. You can also choose from French dishes and local seafood cooked in basic Alaskan styles. The small, 11-table dining room is the restaurant's most memorable aspect, with dark hues and art that create an intimate and relatively upscale experience despite the paper napkins and tight quarters. You can also eat on the patio in good weather. Service is helpful and speedy, and the menu is clearly presented to help those not used to the food order intelligently.

4th Ave. btw. Spring St. and Broadway. Ⓒ **907/983-3663.** Reservations recommended. Lunch or dinner $14–$19. MC, V. Summer Mon–Fri 11am–10pm; Sat–Sun 4–10pm. Closed winter.

The Stowaway Cafe ★★ SEAFOOD   Housed in a bright blue building overlooking the boat harbor, a 5-minute walk from the historic sites, this little restaurant has for several years turned out many of Skagway's best meals. Grilled and blackened salmon and halibut anchor the menu, but you can also get either fish with various creative preparations—salmon with a wasabi panko crust or with a green-apple chipotle sauce, or even grilled halibut with Jamaican jerk spice and a cranberry chutney garnish. They also have beer and wine.

End of Congress Way near the small boat harbor. Ⓒ **907/983-3463.** Reservations recommended. Lunch $8–$15; dinner $16–$29. V. Summer daily 10am–10pm. Closed winter.

Nightlife

Incredibly, the **_Days of '98 Show_** has been playing since 1927 in the Fraternal Order of Eagles Hall No. 25, at 6th Avenue and Broadway (**Ⓒ 907/983-2545**). The tradition carries on each summer with actors imported from all over the United States, doing at least two shows a day (10:30am and 2:30pm) during the summer, and sometimes as many as four. If you can catch an evening show, you can check out an hour of mock gambling at a casino run by the actors before the curtain. The actual performances, which last 1 hour, include singing, cancan dancing, a reading of Robert Service's humorous period poetry, and the story of the shooting of Soapy Smith. All shows are $22, and evening showtimes vary depending upon the cruise-ship schedules. Children 12 and under are charged half price.

The **Red Onion Saloon,** at 2nd Avenue and Broadway, plays up its gold-rush history, with costumed waitresses wearing corsets. It was a brothel originally—what wasn't in this town?—and mock madams offer a brief but fun and interesting "brothel museum" upstairs. The tour costs $5. The saloon often has live acoustic music. It closes in winter.

The **Skagway Brewing Company,** at 7th Avenue and Broadway, is a brew-pub serving many beers made on-site, as well as a long menu of sandwiches, soup, and bar food. The simple food is quite good: pasta, burgers, salads, and hand-cut fries. Happy hour is popular here: in an attractive barroom with high tables and pub chairs, with a well-stocked bar and popular local beer.

6

ANCHORAGE & ENVIRONS

When picking up first-time visitors at the airport, Anchorage folk like to park on top of the parking garage. Those who come by car or cruise have already seen much spectacular scenery. But fliers who've spent the last 4 or more hours in a passenger jet will not have caught more than a glimpse from their seats.

When they finally step onto the open roof of the building, a visible shock hits. The panorama stretches nearly 360 degrees. Forests and skyscrapers are in plain sight. The jagged peaks of the Chugach Mountains loom like a wall. Mount McKinley itself may be in view. Some realize how far they are from home and gulp, but most sense the adventure on all sides and tingle. "Is this real?" asked one guest from New York. Assured that it was, she beamed and fairly yelped with glee, "Alright! I know I'm in Alaska now!"

The state's largest city, Anchorage is accused crushingly of being just like a city Outside, not really part of Alaska at all. It's true that the closer you get to Anchorage, the more the human development reminds you of the outskirts of Anytown, USA, with fast-food franchises, occasional traffic jams, and big-box retail development. You often hear the joke, "Anchorage isn't Alaska, but you can see it from there," and writers piously warn visitors to land in Anchorage but move on as soon as possible, as if it's catching.

But the Alaskans who choose to live here—and that's nearly half of the state's population—are generally energetic people who relish the great outdoors as much as they do the luxuries and culture of a manageable metropolis. Anyone in Anchorage with a few hundred dollars for a floatplane trip can be on a lake or river with the bears and salmon in a matter of minutes, in wilderness deeper than any you could find in the Lower 48. **Chugach State Park** is largely within the

FACING PAGE: Bikers taking in the view of downtown Anchorage; ABOVE: Floatplanes at Lake Hood Seaplane Base, the world's busiest, in Anchorage.

A fisherman drags away his catch after a day on Ship Creek.

city limits, but it's the size of Rocky Mountain National Park and has similar alpine terrain, with the critical difference that most of it is virtually never visited. Yet you can be climbing those mountains after a half-hour drive from your downtown hotel. **Chugach National Forest,** the nation's second largest, is less than an hour down the road. In downtown's **Ship Creek,** people catch 40-pound salmon from under a freeway bridge. Within the city's urban neighborhoods, you can bike dozens of miles along the coast or through wooded greenbelts, or ski one of the nation's best Nordic skiing parks.

Anchorage Yesterday & Today

Anchorage isn't old enough to have a sharp identity as a city. It started as a tent camp for workers mobilized to build the Alaska Railroad in 1915, and a few houses and businesses went up to serve the federal employees who were building and later running the railroad. The remote, sleepy town was enlivened by a couple of large World War II military bases, but one writer in the 1940s thought it still looked like the whole town had been "hacked out of the wilderness."

People started to take Anchorage seriously in 1957, when oil was discovered south on the Kenai Peninsula's Swanson River. Oil fueled Anchorage's growth: Fortunes came fast and development was haphazard. There was an explosion of residential subdivisions, for instance, but no smaller neighborhood shopping areas within walking distance. Visitors found a city full of life but void of charm.

In the last 30 years, however, Anchorage has started outgrow its gawky adolescence. It's still young, prosperous, and vibrant—and exhausting when the summer sun refuses to set—and now also has some excellent restaurants, a fine museum, a zoo, art, theater, and music.

People still complain that Anchorage isn't really Alaska, yet the great wilderness around the city remains intertwined with its streets. Along with a quarter-million people, Anchorage is full of moose—so many they're considered pests and wintertime hazards. The urban area is home to an estimated 350 black bears and 55 brown or grizzly bears. Wildlife of all kinds infiltrates a system of parks, greenbelts, and bike trails that brings the woods into almost every neighborhood.

Anchorage stands on broad, flat sediment between the Chugach Mountains and the silt-laden waters of upper Cook Inlet. At water's edge, mud flats not yet made into land stretch far offshore when the tide is at its low point, as much as 38 vertical feet below high water. There's a **downtown area** of about 8 by 20 blocks, near Ship Creek where it all started, but most of the city lies on long commercial strips. Like many urban centers built since the arrival of the automobile, the layout is not particularly conducive to any other form of transportation. But the roads go only so far. Just beyond, the wilds beckon. You'll find ways to that wilderness, and the urban pleasures by its side, throughout this chapter.

Anchorage

(Inset map: Alaska, with Anchorage and Juneau marked)

Knik Arm

mud flats

Westchester Lagoon

see downtown Anchorage map

Tony Knowles Coastal Trail

Earthquake Park

C. Smith Mem. Park

Sitka Street Park

Chester Cr.

MERRILL FIELD

E 3rd Ave.
E 5th Ave.
E 6th Ave.
W 15th Ave.
E 15th Ave.
W Fireweed Ln.
E Fireweed Ln.
W Northern Lights Blvd.
E Northern Lights Blvd.
W Benson Blvd.
E Benson
W 36th Ave.
E 36th Ave.
E Tudor Rd.
W Int'l Airport Rd.

L Hood

Spenard Lake

Wisconsin St.

Hood Cr.

Spenard Blvd.

Minnesota Dr.

Arctic Blvd.

C St.

E. Gambels St.

Ingra St.

Old Seward Hwy.

New Seward Hwy.

Lake Otis Pkwy.

TED STEVENS ANCHORAGE INTERNATIONAL AIRPORT

Connors Lake Park

Connors L.

Dowling Rd.

DeLong Park

DeLong L.

Sand L.

Jewel Lake Rd.

Raspberry Rd.

Taku L.

Campbell Cr.

Emerald Hills Park

Jewel L.

E Dimond Blvd.

W Dimond Blvd.

Campbell Lake

Minnesota Dr.

C St.

New Seward Hwy.

Old Seward Hwy.

| 0 | | 1 mi |
| 0 | | 1 km |

ATTRACTIONS
Alaska Aviation Heritage Museum 1
Alaska Botanical Garden 10
Alaska Museum of Natural History 26
Alaska Native Heritage Center 25
Alaska Wild Berry Products 14
The Alaska Zoo 11

HOTELS
Alaska Backpackers Inn 27
Courtyard by Marriott 7
Dimond Center Hotel 15
Elderberry B&B 9

Holiday Inn Express 4
Lake Hood Inn 5
Lakeshore Motor Inn 3
Millennium Alaskan Hotel 6
Motel 6 23
Residence Inn by Marriott 17
Spenard Hostel International 2

RESTAURANTS
Arctic Roadrunner 21, 13
Bear Tooth Theatrepub & Grill 23

The Golden Corral 16
The Greek Corner 19
Harley's Old Thyme Café 12
Kaladi Brothers Coffee 24
Kincaid Grill 8
The Moose's Tooth Pub and Pizzeria 18
New Sagaya's City Market 20
Spenard Roadhouse 22

ESSENTIALS
Getting There

BY PLANE   You'll probably get to Anchorage at the start of your trip by air, as the city receives by far the most flights linking Alaska to the rest of the world, on many airlines. The **Ted Stevens Anchorage International Airport** is a major hub. Seattle has the most frequent flights connecting to Anchorage, with numerous domestic carriers flying nonstop all day. (See "Getting There & Getting Around," in chapter 11, for more details.) Within Alaska, most flights route through here, even for communities that are much closer to each other than they are to Anchorage. **Alaska Airlines** (© 800/252-7522; www.alaskaair.com) is the dominant carrier for Alaska destinations and the only jet operator to most Alaska cities.

Various commuter carriers link Anchorage to rural destinations not served by jet, offering a convenient, time-saving alternative to driving to communities such as Homer, Kenai, or Valdez. Given the extraordinary taxes and fees imposed on rental cars at the Anchorage airport, you may also save money by flying to these towns and renting there. **Era Alaska** (© 800/866-8394 or 907/266-8394; www.flyera.com) is the state's largest prop carrier, serving more than 100 destinations from the Gulf of Alaska to the Arctic. Tickets can be booked through Alaska Airlines on some code-share routings.

Unless your hotel has a courtesy van or you rent a car, a taxi is probably the best way to get downtown from the airport. A **taxi ride** downtown from the airport runs $18 to $20. Try **Alaska Yellow Cab** (© 907/222-2222). Shuttle vans serve the airport, with arrangements changing frequently. Ask at the visitor information desk in the baggage claim area. The **People Mover** city bus connects the airport and the downtown transit center hourly. Take Spenard Route 7A (every other Rte. 7 bus on weekdays). For finding schedules and other details on using the People Mover, see "Getting Around," below.

BY CAR   There's only one road to the rest of the world: the Glenn Highway. It leads through the Mat-Su Valley area and Glennallen to Tok, where it meets the Alaska Highway, 330 miles from Anchorage. Thirty miles out of Anchorage, the Glenn meets the Parks Highway, which leads to Denali National Park and Fairbanks. The only other road out of town, the Seward Highway, leads south to the Kenai Peninsula. See "Alaska's Highways a la Carte" (p. 406), in chapter 9, for a review of all the roads. For more on driving to Alaska, see chapter 11.

BY BUS   **Alaska/Yukon Trails** (© 800/770-7275; www.alaskashuttle.com), a van and minibus service, runs between Anchorage and Fairbanks, with a stop at Denali National Park and Talkeetna. From Fairbanks, they run tours to Dawson City and Whitehorse. In Anchorage they stop at the airport, hostels, and downtown. A one-way ticket to Denali costs $75 and to Fairbanks $99. Various other van and bus services offer transportation to and from Seward, Homer, Talkeetna, Denali National Park, Fairbanks, and other points; options are listed in the sections on each of those places.

BY RV   A recreational vehicle is a popular way to explore the region. Renting an RV in Anchorage for a tour is covered below under "Getting Around."

Driving an RV to Alaska is covered in chapter 11. It's also possible to come to Alaska with your own RV without making the time-consuming return trip by shipping your RV back from Anchorage to Tacoma, Washington, and flying to meet it (since southbound ships are relatively empty, you get a special rate). Contact **Totem Ocean Trailer Express** (☎ **800/234-8683** in Anchorage, or 800/426-0074 in the Lower 48; www.totemocean.com).

In addition, some firms offer one-way rentals beginning or ending in Anchorage. **Alaska Motorhome Rentals** (☎ **800/323-5757**; www. bestofalaskatravel.com) offers several city pairs, allowing visitors to drive one-way from Seattle, to rent after riding the ferry partway, or to rent between Anchorage and Fairbanks. Sample rates: Skagway to Anchorage carries a drop-off fee of $795 to $995, plus the cost of the rental, $209 to $249 a day in the high season, plus mileage (or pay $35 a day for unlimited mileage), gas (budget generously), and tax. Check the website for discounts. The same company has another operation, **Alaska Highway Cruises** (☎ **800/323-5757**), that provides packages to cruise one-way, tour Alaska in an RV, and fly home. For more on that option and on one-way rentals from the balance of the Lower 48, see chapter 11.

BY RAIL   The **Alaska Railroad** (☎ **800/544-0552** or 907/265-2494; www. alaskarailroad.com) connects Anchorage with Seward and Whittier to the south and Fairbanks, Denali National Park, and Talkeetna to the north. It's a fun way to travel, with commentary in the summer, good food, and clean, comfortable cars. However, the train is priced as a tourism excursion and costs more than ordinary transportation. Most trains run only in the summer, but a snowy 12-hour odyssey to Fairbanks runs once a week all winter. The summer fare to Fairbanks is $210 one-way; the winter fare is $159 one-way, $127 for Alaska residents. See chapter 8 on Denali National Park and sections on other destinations for fares and service details.

Orientation

Many visitors never make it beyond the **downtown** area, the old-fashioned grid of streets at the northwest corner of town where the high-rise hotels and gift shops are located. Street numbers and letters work on a simple pattern, and navigation is easy. Beyond downtown, most of Anchorage is oriented to commercial strips, and you'll need a map to find your way. It's easy to orient yourself, because you can always see the huge Chugach Mountains on the east side of the Anchorage bowl. Some parts of greater Anchorage are in distinct communities outside the bowl, including **Eagle River** and **Eklutna,** within half an hour on the Glenn Highway to the northeast, and **Girdwood** and **Portage,** on the Seward Highway, 45 minutes to the south. The suburban **Matanuska and Susitna valleys** (known as Mat-Su) lie an hour north of the city on the Glenn and Parks highways.

Getting Around

BY RENTAL CAR   Driving is the most practical way for most independent travelers to tour the main part of Alaska, and the location of Anchorage at the hub of transportation networks makes it the handiest place to start. Having a car vastly improves a visit to Anchorage, as the city is spread out and public transportation and taxi service are far less practical. Most major car-rental

Downtown Anchorage.

companies operate in Anchorage, largely from the car-rental facility next to the main terminal at the airport. A compact car for $50 a day, with unlimited mileage, is a bargain. Taxes and airport fees add as much as 40% to the rental price. You can cut that approximately in half by renting off-site. One agency with a downtown location is **Avis,** at 5th Avenue and B Street (✆ **800/230-4898** or 907/277-4567; www.avis.com). If you're not interested in driving around Anchorage, you may also be able to save time and money by flying on to your next destination, such as Kenai or Fairbanks, and renting the car there. Use a website to comparison-shop with taxes and fees included. In any case, reserve ahead, as cars can sell out in summer.

BY RENTAL RV   Several large RV-rental agencies operate in Anchorage (see "Getting There," above). High-season rates for a midsize unit are around $1,610 to $1,820 a week, plus the large amount of fuel RVs use and taxes; a truck camper (the kind of unit that is on a pickup truck) rents for close to

---

Car Wheels on Gravel Roads

Contracts for most car-rental agencies do not allow vehicles on gravel roads, and none of the name-brand companies' agreements does. Pavement will get you to all the major places tourists go, but some magnificent back roads are unpaved, such as the Denali Highway or McCarthy Road (covered in chapter 9). Violating the rental contract places you at risk of paying out of pocket for repairs and the rental agency's lost business if the car is damaged. In Anchorage, **High Country Car and Truck Rental** (✆ **888/685-1155** or 907/562-8078; www.highcountryanchorage.com) does rent for use on gravel highways (although not the Dalton Hwy.). They rent one-way to Seward and Whittier, too, for the convenience of cruise or train passengers. I've also located a couple of agencies in Fairbanks that offer the service (p. 419).

$200 a day. **ABC Motorhome Rentals,** 3875 Old International Airport Rd. (*©* **800/421-7456** or 907/279-2000; www.abcmotorhome.com), charges no mileage fee. See chapter 11 for more on this option.

BY BUS   In a city as spread out as Anchorage, city buses will always be a slower and less convenient choice than cabs or rental cars, but the **People Mover** system (*©* **907/343-6543;** www.peoplemover.org) is well run and perfectly practical for destinations that are served by direct routes from downtown. A new website (http://bustracker.muni.org/InfoPoint) uses a map to track the exact location of each bus and the actual time it will arrive at any stop, making the system easy to use for a novice. Bus fares all over town are $1.75 for adults; $1 for ages 5 to 18; 50¢ for those 60 and older, those with disabilities, or those with a valid Medicare card; free ages 4 and under. The transit center bus depot is at 6th Avenue and G Street. Buses generally come every half-hour, hourly on weekends; you will need to go online and figure out your route and timing in advance.

BY BIKE   The network of bike trails is a great way to see the best side of Anchorage, but not a practical means of point-to-point transportation for most people. The **Tony Knowles Coastal Trail** starts right downtown (see "Getting Outside," later in this chapter). Good street bikes are usually for rent near Elderberry Park downtown, at the start of the Coastal Trail, from **Pablo's Bike Rental,** a booth in the parking lot near the corner of 5th and L (*©* **907/250-2871;** www.pablobicyclerentals.com). Rates are $12 for 3 hours, $30 for a day. A bike-rental shop with a wide choice of equipment is in the blue 4th Avenue Marketplace at 4th and C: **Downtown Bicycle Rental** (*©* **907/279-5293;** www.alaska-bike-rentals.com). Rates start at $16 for 3 hours, $4 each additional hour, max $32 per day. The shop also carries tandems, kids' bikes, and trailers, and clip in shoes and pedals for advanced cyclists. The shop also offers a hikers' shuttle to the Glen Alps parking lot, the trail head for Flattop Mountain (p. 253).

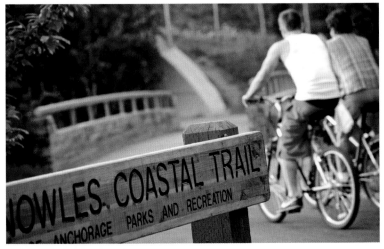

Biking the Tony Knowles Coastal Trail.

Alaska Public Lands Information Center.

Visitor Information

The **Anchorage Convention & Visitors Bureau,** 524 W. 4th Ave., Anchorage, AK 99501-2212 (✆ **907/276-4118;** fax 907/278-5559; www.anchorage.net), offers information on the city and the entire state at its centers and extensive website (the site even has a feature to allow visitors to ask questions of staffers by e-mail). The main location is the **Log Cabin Visitor Information Center,** downtown at 4th Avenue and F Street (✆ **907/274-3531;** open daily June–Aug 7:30am–7pm, May and Sept 8am–6pm, Oct–Apr 9am–4pm). If it's crowded, go to the storefront office right behind it. You'll also find visitor information desks at the airport: one tucked under the main escalators on the baggage claim level of the domestic terminal and in the international terminal.

The **Alaska Public Lands Information Center,** located at 605 W. 4th Ave. (across the intersection from the log cabin at 4th and F), Ste. 105, Anchorage, AK 99501 (✆ **866/869-6887** or 907/644-3661; www.alaskacenters.gov; open daily 9am–5pm in summer, Mon–Fri 10am–5pm in winter), can help anyone planning to spend time outdoors anywhere in Alaska. Exhibits in the grand room with high ceilings—the building was a 1930s post office and federal courthouse—orient visitors to Alaska's geography and outdoor activities and make an excellent starting point for your trip. The center is well worth passing through the federal security checkpoint at the entrance. Free walking tours are at 11am and 2:30pm daily.

Special Events

For more events, and online calendars, see "The Performing Arts," p. 261.

The **Anchorage Folk Festival** (✆ **907/529-7383;** www.anchoragefolk festival.org), January 19 to January 29, 2012, imports musicians and shows off local talent in free concerts, workshops, and jam sessions, as well as four guest musician dances that raise money for the festival. Check the website for times and venues.

The **Anchorage Fur Rendezvous Festival** (© **907/274-1177;** www.
furrondy.net), February 24 through March 4, 2012, is a winter celebration started
in 1935 and recently rejuvenated with creative, youthful events such as the exciting and funny Running of the Reindeer, an event like the Pamplona Running of
the Bulls, but far safer for all involved, since reindeer are notably gentle animals.
The Native Arts Market, the biggest and best in the state, should not be missed,
and there are many community events as well: a parade, fireworks, a carnival,
craft fairs, snowshoe softball, dog-sled rides, and so on. The Rondy's traditional
centerpiece (global warming permitting) is the speedy **World Champion Sled
Dog Race,** a 3-day sprint event of about 25 miles per heat. In addition, the last
weekend of the festival coincides with the start of the **Iditarod Trail Sled Dog
Race** (© **907/376-5155;** www.iditarod.com). The Iditarod, long Alaska's biggest winter event, brings in a flood of visitors who link seeing the race with winter
sports and festivals in Anchorage. On the weekend of the start, the streets of
Anchorage fill with foreign languages, as European visitors come in dispropor-
tionate numbers. The Iditarod begins from Anchorage the first Saturday in
March (in 2012, Mar 3) and then proceeds in trucks to the restart the next day
in the Mat-Su Valley for the 1,000-mile run to Nome (see the section on Nome
in chapter 10 for more details).

The **Anchorage Market & Festival** is a big street fair and farmer's market
held every weekend from mid-May through mid-September at 3rd Avenue and E
Street (© **907/272-5634;** www.anchoragemarkets.com).

The **Alaska State Fair** (© **907/745-4827;** www.alaskastatefair.org),
which culminates a 12-day run on Labor Day each year, is the biggest event in
the area. It takes place in Palmer, 40 miles north of Anchorage on the Glenn
Highway. It's a locally oriented state fair, with rides, booths, exhibits, contests,
fireworks, and live music. Much of which you would expect, but for the vegetables. The good soil and long days in the Matanuska Valley around Palmer boost
their growth to massive size, the stuff of childhood nightmares. Cabbages are the

Dog-sledding during the Fur Rendezvous Festival.

size of bean-bag chairs. A mere beach-ball-size cabbage would be laughed off the stage. And it's not just the 125-pound cabbages. Imagine a 19-pound carrot, 35-pound broccoli, 43-pound beet, 63-pound celery, or 76-pound rutabaga (all records from the fair, among others you can check out on the website). The flower gardens are amazing, too, although not in the same way. Note that on the weekends, the fair ties up traffic between Palmer and Anchorage, so it's wise to go early or midweek, if possible. The Alaska Railroad runs a passenger car between the Anchorage Depot and a terminal at the fairgrounds on certain days.

The **Carrs/Safeway Great Alaska Shootout basketball tournament** (© **907/786-1293;** www.goseawolves.com), hosted by the University of Alaska Anchorage, brings college men's and women's teams from all over the nation to the Sullivan Arena over Thanksgiving weekend and the preceding week.

The **Anchorage International Film Festival** (www.anchoragefilmfestival. org) has grown in a decade into a major event, with as many as a dozen screenings for 2 weeks starting in early December. The films come from every corner of the world and include the obscure and bizarre, as well as the profound.

[FastFACTS] ANCHORAGE

Banks   A bank is rarely far away, and all grocery stores and gas stations also have **ATMs.**

Hospitals   **Alaska Regional Hospital** is at 2801 DeBarr Rd. (© **907/ 276-1131;** www.alaska regional.com), and **Providence Alaska Medical Center** is at 3200 Providence Dr. (© **907/562-2211;** www.providence. org).

Internet Access   Downtown, get online at **Kaladi Brothers Coffee,** with Wi-Fi and public terminals, at 6th Avenue and G Street, in the base of the Alaska Center for the Performing Arts. It's also a comfortable and popular coffee hangout.

Police   The **Anchorage Police Department** has main offices at 4501 Elmore Rd., south of Tudor

Road; for a nonemergency, call © **907/786-8500.** For nonemergency police business outside the city, call the **Alaska State Troopers,** 5700 E. Tudor Rd. (© **907/269-5511**).

Post Office   Downtown, it's downstairs in the 4th Avenue Marketplace at D Street.

Taxes   There's no **sales tax** in Anchorage. The **bed tax** is 12%.

WHERE TO STAY

A decent hotel room under $150 a night is almost unknown in Anchorage in midsummer. To visit economically, choose a B&B or small inn. Those listed in the following section are judged to have character and reasonable prices. There are hundreds more, many of them just as good.

Dozens of B&Bs are listed on a website maintained by the cooperative **Anchorage Alaska Bed and Breakfast Association** (www.anchorage-bnb. com). You can search by area of town or preferred amenities, or browse alphabetically. Links go directly to the B&Bs' own sites. Many have online availability calendars. Without a computer, call the association's hot line (© **888/584-5147** or 907/272-5909), which is answered by hosts at member properties to offer referrals to places that meet callers' requirements.

Downtown Anchorage

HOTELS

Anchorage Downtown Marriott **26**
Anchorage Grand Hotel **9**
Anchorage International Hostel-Downtown **25**
Clarion Suites **20**
Copper Whale Inn **1**
Days Inn **17**
G Street House **27**
Hawthorn Suites **29**
Hilton Anchorage **10**
Historic Anchorage Hotel **12**
Hotel Captain Cook **3**
The Oscar Gill House B&B **31**
Sheraton Anchorage **18**
Susitna Place **30**
The Voyager Hotel **4**
Wildflower Inn **28**

RESTAURANTS

Club Paris **14**
The Crow's Nest **3**
Crush **15**
Dianne's Restaurant **21**
Fletcher's **3**
Glacier Brewhouse **23**
Kaladi Brothers **22**
Kumagoro **11**
The Marz Brothers Café **8**
The Muffin Man **5**
The Pantry **3**
Sacks Café **7**
Side Street Espresso **6**
Snow City Café **2**
Whale's Tail **3**

ATTRACTIONS

Alaska Experience Theatre **13**
Alaska State Troopers Museum **16**
Anchorage Museum **19**
4th Avenue Market Place **13**
Oomingmak Musk Ox Cooperative **24**

Downtown

VERY EXPENSIVE

Besides the Hotel Captain Cook, described in full below, three other high-rise hotels downtown offer a similar level of service without as much character or quite as many amenities. **Hilton Anchorage,** 500 W. 3rd Ave. (www.hilton.com; ✆ **800/HILTONS** [445-8667] or 907/272-7411), is a large conference hotel right at the center of downtown activities. The **Sheraton Anchorage,** 401 E. 6th Ave. (www.sheratonanchorage.com; ✆ **800/478-8700** or 907/276-8700), is comparable to the Hilton, but in a slightly less attractive area a few blocks away. The **Anchorage Downtown Marriott,** 820 W. 7th Ave. (www.marriott.com; ✆ **888/228-9290** or 907/279-8000), has a nice pool and fabulous views from rooms with wall-size picture windows.

Hotel Captain Cook ★★★   This is Alaska's great, grand hotel, where royalty and rock stars stay. Former Gov. Wally Hickel built the first of the three towers after the 1964 earthquake, and now the hotel fills a city block and anchors the downtown skyline. Inside, the earth tones and dark-wood decor contribute to a fully realized (maybe a little excessive) nautical theme, with art memorializing Cook's voyages and enough teak to build a square-rigger. The regularly renewed rooms are decorated in a rich, sumptuous style using exquisite fabrics, unique pieces of custom-built furniture, and lots of varnished trim. Rooms are comfortable in size, but not as large as those in modern upscale chains, and all have a choice only of a king-size or two twin beds. Lots of custom tile, mirrors, and granite make up for the relatively small size of the bathrooms. There are great views from all sides, and you don't pay more to be on a higher floor. The pool, spa, and fitness facilities in the below-ground lower lobby are among the best in town.

Sophisticated food and superb service justify the high prices at the **Crow's Nest ★★★**, the city's most traditional fine-dining restaurant, on the hotel's top floor. Most tables have stupendous views, and high-backed booths lend intimacy for a romantic dinner. The cuisine draws on many influences without being trendy and looks wonderful on the plate. Main courses range from $29 to $55. The wine list is voluminous, with just a few bottles under $40. **Fletcher's,** off the lobby, is an English pub serving good Italian-style pizza, pasta, and seafood. The **Pantry** is an above-average hotel cafe, with interesting entrees in moderate serving sizes. The **Whale's Tail** is a restaurant and lounge with overstuffed chairs and big TVs. It's a good place for a drink without feeling like you're in a bar.

939 W. 5th Ave., Anchorage, AK 99510-2280. www.captaincook.com. ✆ **800/843-1950** or 907/276-6000. Fax 907/343-2298. 547 units. High season $255–$265 double, $270–$1,500 suite; low season $155–$165 double, $170–$1,500 suite. Extra person $20. AE, DISC, MC, V. **Amenities:** 4 restaurants; 3 bars; concierge; separate men's and women's health clubs w/racquetball, Jacuzzi, steam room, and sauna; massage; indoor pool; room service; concierge-level rooms. *In room:* TV, fridge, hair dryer, Wi-Fi.

EXPENSIVE

Here are a few chain-hotel options downtown for those who prefer national brands: **Days Inn,** 321 E. 5th Ave. (www.daysinnalaska.com; ✆ **800/DAYS-INN** [329-7466] or 907/276-7226), which has a courtesy van to the airport and rail depot; **Quality Suites,** 325 W. 8th Ave. (www.choicehotels.com; ✆ **888/389-6575** or 907/274-1000), an all-suite building across from the Federal Building, with a small pool; and **Clarion Suites,** 1110 W. 8th Ave. (www.choicehotels.com;

(✆ **800/527-1133** or 907/222-5005), with similar facilities as the Quality Suites, plus a Benihana Restaurant on-site. The **Rodeway Inn Voyager Hotel,** 501 K St. (www.rodewayinn.com; ✆ **800/247-9070** or 907/277-9501), was an excellent small hotel favored by business travelers before a recent sale and surprising rebranding with a budget chain. At press time, it was still a fine boutique hotel in a great location.

Anchorage Grand Hotel ★★ This all-suite hotel has a rare combination of advantages: a superb central location, solid rooms, fully equipped kitchens in every unit full of housewares and with dishwashers and automatic ice makers, generous amenities, and rates competitive for this area of town. The hotel lacks much of a lobby, as the main entrance and handicap entrance lead directly into a stairway or hallway; that's because it is a reincarnation of an old concrete apartment building. But the rooms and tiled bathrooms are quite large, decorated in a trim, subdued style with fine cabinetry, and immaculate. Despite the full kitchens, we've never noticed odors in the many rooms we've checked, which is remarkable. Also despite the kitchen, they serve a free continental breakfast in the morning (and deliver the newspaper). Every unit has a bedroom and a queen-size sofa sleeper in the living room. Ask for a room on the quiet street side if you might be disturbed by railroad noise from the station facing the back of the building (although those rooms have better views).

505 W. 2nd Ave., Anchorage, AK 99501. www.anchoragegrand.com. ✆ **888/800-0640** or 907/929-8888. Fax 907/929-8899. 31 units. Summer $199 double; winter $99 double. Extra person 14 and over $20. Rates include continental breakfast. AE, DISC, MC, V. *In room:* TV, hair dryer, kitchen, Wi-Fi.

Copper Whale Inn ★★ A pair of clapboard houses overlook the water and Elderberry Park right on the Coastal Trail downtown, with attractive rooms of various shapes and sizes, all redone in 2006 and 2008 in fashionable tans and browns and comfortable new beds, huge nature photographs and Alaskan art, and granite countertops in the bathrooms and common areas. The small upstairs rooms in the main building have wonderful views and funny angles; two of those share a bathroom. Lower-level rooms open onto a patio. The rooms in the newer building, nearer the water, have high ceilings on the upper level and are larger, although none is very large. The staff is more than hospitable, creating the homey feeling of a country inn right in the urban core. They serve a large continental breakfast in the common area, which is comfortable for relaxing but not well suited for meals.

440 L St., Anchorage, AK 99501. www.copperwhale.com. ✆ **866/258-7999** or 907/258-7999. Fax 907/258-6213. 14 units, 12 with private bathroom. High season $185 double with shared bathroom, $220 double with private bathroom; low season $85 double with shared bathroom, $110 double with private bathroom. Extra person $20. Rates include continental breakfast. AE, DISC, MC, V. **Amenities:** Bike rental; guest computer; concierge; access to health club. *In room:* TV, hair dryer, Wi-Fi.

The Historic Anchorage Hotel ★★ This inn at the center of the tourist area is among the city's oldest businesses. The existing concrete building dates to 1936, in the small scale of the time, with little triangular turrets adorning the top. The historic theme carries through the building, with furniture in Queen Anne–style, brocade, and the familiar warm patterns once favored by hotels. The walls are decorated by Alaska landscapes. Rooms are average in size and equipped in modern fashion. None have views, and those on the street side can suffer from noise, which is addressed with white noise machines. The friendliness of the staff adds to the intimate feeling of being in a small building just steps from the sights and best restaurants. Breakfast is served in the attractively appointed lounge.

330 E St., Anchorage, AK 99501. www.historicanchoragehotel.com. © **800/544-0988** or 907/272-4553. Fax 907/277-4483. 26 units. High season $189–$209 double, $239–$259 suite; low season $89–$159 double, $159–$189 suite. Extra person 13 and older $10. AE, DC, DISC, MC, V. **Amenities:** Fish-freezing facility; Internet access. *In room:* TV, fridge, hair dryer, Wi-Fi.

INEXPENSIVE

Hotel rooms reliably meeting most readers' standards are not available downtown for a price that most travelers would call "inexpensive," but there are several small inns or B&Bs where you can save money and may also have a warmer, more rewarding visit.

Besides those described in full, the **Downtown Guest House,** 1238 G St. (www.downtownguesthouse.com; © **907/279-2359**), is a two-bedroom apartment, beautifully decorated and with many amenities, for $150 double in the summer. The owner is one of Alaska's most noted photographers.

Earth Bed & Breakfast ★   This house just outside the downtown core has developed a following among international visitors, mountain climbers, and other outdoor adventurers of the hardier type. The warmth of the hosts, who also make a business of arranging Alaska trips, contributes to a cheerful communal feel. Guests socialize in the backyard, with a rock garden, fire pit, and fish pond, and many have left items for the Memory Wall there—climbing gear, fishing waders, Tibetan prayer flags, and so on. The five bedrooms, named after Alaska's five highest peaks, are comfortable and quite clean, but basic; all share bathrooms. Guests eat a deluxe self-serve continental breakfast in the large and immaculate common rooms.

1001 W. 12th Ave., Anchorage, AK 99501. www.earthbb.com. © **907/279-9907.** Fax 907/279-9862. 5 units, all with shared bathroom. High season $115–$130 double; low season $70–$80 double. Extra person $25. Rates include continental breakfast. AE, MC, V. **Amenities:** Bike rental; fish-freezing facility. *In room:* No phone, Wi-Fi.

The Oscar Gill House Bed & Breakfast ★★   On the Delaney Park strip, just a few blocks from downtown, this is truly the oldest house in Anchorage—it was built in 1913, in Knik, before Anchorage was founded, and moved here on a barge a few years later. Oscar Gill was an early civic leader. The house was to be torn down in 1982 but was moved to storage by a historic preservation group; Mark and Susan Lutz saved it in 1993, transferring it to its present location and, with their own labor, restoring it authentically as a cozy bed-and-breakfast. Now it's on the National Register of Historic Places. Appropriate antiques sit on plank floors in rooms sized in those more modest times. With the period decoration, it's like visiting your grandmother's house when it was brand new. The outgoing Lutzes create a warm, social setting. Book early, as they fill; you can check availability and select a room on their website.

1344 W. 10th Ave., Anchorage, AK 99501. www.oscargill.com. ©/fax **907/279-1344.** 3 units, 1 with private bathroom. High season $115 double with shared bathroom, $135 double with private bathroom; low season $75 double with shared bathroom, $95 double with private bathroom.

Extra person $25 (except infants). Rates include full breakfast. AE, MC, V. **Amenities:** Babysitting by arrangement. *In room:* Hair dryer, Wi-Fi.

Susitna Place ★★ 🔌 Just a few blocks from the downtown core, where a narrow residential street reaches a quiet end, a nondescript door under a carport leads into a rambling house of rooms ranging from comfortable and inexpensive to grand. It turns out the street side is really the back of the house, which sits at the top of a high bluff facing an unobstructed view of Cook Inlet and Mount Susitna beyond, a view so unlike most urban vistas, it's easy to forget you are right in town. A large, gracious common room and breakfast area and an adjoining balcony command this extraordinary view. The suite is quite luxurious, but the four rooms that share two bathrooms are the rarer find: Cozy and very clean, sharing this prime location, they allow travelers to save money without compromise.

727 N St., Anchorage, AK 99501. www.susitnaplace.com. © **907/274-3344.** Fax 907/272-4141. 9 units, 5 with private bathroom. High season $105–$110 double with shared bathroom, $135–$140 with private bathroom, $165–$195 suite; low season $65–$70 double with shared bathroom, $80–$85 double with private bathroom, $95–$115 suite. Extra person $15. Rates include continental breakfast. AE, DISC, MC, V. **Amenities:** Free covered parking. *In room:* TV w/HBO, Wi-Fi.

Wildflower Inn ★ 🔌 The clapboard house behind a picket fence is across from the community's favorite gourmet grocery and casual eatery, New Sagaya's City Market. The B&B offers attractive, well-equipped two-bedroom suites for only $139 double, with full bathrooms with tubs. They're decorated in mission style. The enthusiastically friendly hosts keep the place immaculate, warm, and cozy and serve a fancy hot breakfast from 7 to 9:30am. The walk downtown is a little longer than the other choices in the area, an easy half-mile. The bus stops right in front of the house. The same folks also rent apartment-like units off-site for very reasonable prices.

1239 I St., Anchorage, AK 99501. www.alaska-wildflower-inn.com. © **877/693-1239** or 907/274-1239. Fax 907/222-3061. 3 units. High season $129–$139 suite; low season $79 suite. Extra person 7 and older $15. Rates include full breakfast. MC, V. **Amenities:** Computer/Internet access. *In room:* TV/VCR, hair dryer, Wi-Fi.

HOSTELS

Choose from two hostels downtown and another nearer the airport (described in the next section). **Anchorage International Hostel—Downtown,** 700 H St. (www.anchoragehostel.org; © **907/276-3635**), occupies a centrally located concrete building with an urban feel, with a coin-op laundry, kitchen, and free Wi-Fi. Dorm rooms are small, with just a few bunks each, totaling 82 beds. A bunk is $25, a private room $65. Dorms close between 10am and 2pm daily. The curfew is midnight and checkout is 10am. A much homier hostel that lies in a slightly seedy area just east of the downtown core, although still walkable, is **Alaska Backpackers Inn,** 327 Eagle St. (www.alaskabackpackers.com; © **907/277-2770**), which opened in 2007. The atmosphere is friendly and vibrant in rooms with murals painted on the floors and walls; large, well-equipped gathering places; bathrooms, and a kitchen. The hostel offers Wi-Fi and four Internet terminals (for a fee) and a coin-op laundry. There is no curfew or lockout period, but only guests with key cards can enter the building and the rooms. Smoking and alcohol are not allowed. A total of 94 beds and bunks fill 37 guest rooms, renting for $25 a bunk or $60 for a private room for two.

Beyond Downtown

These lodging choices are spread across Anchorage, with its long, wide commercial strips. As do most residents, you need a car to stay here. On the other hand, by leaving downtown, you can sometimes find larger, newer rooms for less cost, and you avoid downtown parking problems.

VERY EXPENSIVE

Dimond Center Hotel ★★ 🎁 This hotel is unique in several ways. Owned by the Seldovia Native Association, its primary clientele is rural Alaska residents coming to the big city for shopping and entertainment. That explains the location, on the south side of town, far from downtown sites, in a huge parking near a Wal-Mart store, a large shopping mall, and a bus transit center. Strange as it sounds, however, the location makes sense for many visitors: Chugach State Park, the zoo, and the Seward Highway and its many attractions are closer than anywhere else you could stay. Since the owners built the hotel for themselves, the attention to comfort and detail are impressive. The common areas are stylish and decorated with Native art, and the rooms are grand: high ceilings, granite counters, attractive modern furniture, 42-inch flatscreen TVs, and pillow-top beds with comforters. The bathrooms are elaborate, with large shower areas and big separate soaking tubs that can connect to the bedroom by opening wooden shutters.

700 E. Dimond Blvd., Anchorage, AK 99515. www.dimondcenterhotel.com. ✆ **866/770-5002** or 907/770-5000. Fax 907/770-5001. 109 units. High season $181–$300 double; low season $99–$179 double. Extra person $25. AE, DC, DISC, MC, V. Rates include full breakfast buffet. **Amenities:** Breakfast room; bar; free airport shuttle; access to nearby health club. *In room:* TV, fridge, hair dryer, microwave, Wi-Fi.

Residence Inn By Marriott ★★ Families that can afford it should stay here, and many business travelers would find it convenient, too. All units are suites with cooking facilities, and most have full kitchens. They're big enough to provide family members with privacy and sanity breaks, but save money over renting adjoining rooms in an ordinary hotel and dining out for all meals. Room decoration is light and hotel-typical; common areas have an Alaska Native motif reflecting the Native corporation management of the hotel. The clapboard building, with a gabled roof and stone accents, stands in a parklike enclave in the Midtown commercial area, next to a high-rise office building and walking distance from a large Fred Meyer grocery and department store. The hotel offers a daily breakfast in a common area, and light evening meals with beer and wine from 6 to 7:30pm Monday through Thursday, included in the room rate. Get driving directions, as it's a little tricky to find.

1025 E. 35th Ave., Anchorage, AK 99508. www.marriott.com/ancri. ✆ **800/314-0781** or 907/563-9844. Fax 907/563-9636. 148 units. Summer $239–$299 suite; winter $169–$205 suite (rates for any number of guests in unit). AE, DC, DISC, MC, V. Rates include full breakfast. **Amenities:** Free airport transfers; fitness room; pool; spa; outdoor basketball and mini tennis courts. *In room:* TV w/pay movies, Internet, kitchenette or full kitchen, Wi-Fi.

EXPENSIVE

Lake Hood Inn ★★ 🎁 Pilot Bill Floyd built this place right next to his float-plane slip (he flies a Cessna 180) and filled it with fascinating aviation stuff: photographs, propellers, and even rows of seats from a Russian airliner. The

Rooms Near the Airport

Good, inexpensive, standard motel rooms near the airport are rare to the vanishing point, although upscale rooms and B&Bs are readily available. The prize winner in our search for reasonably priced hotel rooms is the **Lakeshore Motor Inn** (www.lakeshoremotorinn.com; © **800/770-3000** or 907/248-3485). The rate of $159 a night double, at peak season, includes continental breakfast, Wi-Fi, and use of a 24-hour courtesy van. Don't be deterred by the older concrete building: The rooms inside are clean and comfortable, if dated in their decor.

Two good chain hotels stand near the airport, with higher rates: **Courtyard by Marriott** (www.marriott.com/ANCCY; © **800/314-0782** or 907/245-0322), with many amenities and a pool, at $199 double in summer; and the **Holiday Inn Express** (www.hiexpress.com;

© **800/HOLIDAY** [465-4329] or 907/248-8848), at $199 to $229 double in the summer.

A large, full-service hotel stands lakeside near the airport, **Millennium Alaskan Hotel Anchorage** (www.millenniumhotels.com/anchorage; © **800/544-0553** or 907/243-2300). It might be a huge fishing and hunting lodge judging by the large lobby, with its warm colors and fly rods and animal mounts on display, but the rooms, on long corridors in a wooden building, are loaded with comfort and amenities. The hotel has two restaurants and offers many services. High-season rates are $239 to $339 double.

We also recommend Lake Hood Inn (p. 228), Elderberry Bed & Breakfast (p. 230), and Spenard Hostel International (below), all of which are handy to the airport.

guestbook is an aircraft log book. On the comfortable balconies, headphones are at the ready to listen to radio traffic between the tower and the aircraft you can see taxiing on the lake in front of you. Floyd invested in commercial-quality construction, and the rooms have the feel of a solid, upscale hotel room, not a family B&B; they are decorated in cool, muted shades with Berber carpets and light flooding in through big windows. The bathrooms have large shower stalls. Beds can be configured as two twins or as one king. Two front rooms have their own balconies and cost $20 more; the two back rooms have access to a shared balcony and are smaller. All four rooms are up a flight of stairs.

4702 Lake Spenard Dr., Anchorage, AK 99509. www.lakehoodinn.com. © **866/663-9322** or 907/258-9321. 4 units. $169–$189 double. Extra person 17 and older $20. Rates include continental breakfast. DISC, MC, V. **Amenities:** Fish freezer; guest kitchen. *In room:* TV/VCR, fridge, hair dryer, high-speed Internet.

INEXPENSIVE

A cluster of new hotels has recently sprung up along the C Street–A Street corridor in Midtown, about 3 miles from the airport. They share the area with several national chain restaurants, including Outback and Applebee's. The north end is within walking distance of some shopping, Loussac Library, and the Cuddy Family Park; the hotels at the south end are frankly not close to anything. The least expensive option is **Motel 6 ★**, 5000 A St., Anchorage, AK 99503 (www.motel6.com; © **800/314-0781** or 907/677-8000). Amenities are minimal; it's the only hotel on this strip without a pool, though they can provide a swimming pass to a neighboring hotel. Pets are allowed with certain restrictions, and the price is right (summer $140 double, winter $70); they accept all major credit cards. Check online for deals at the other hotels; the Fairfield Inn has had winter specials as low as $89 a night.

Elderberry Bed & Breakfast ★ ⬛   If you want to make new friends, stay at this bed-and-breakfast, where visitors mingle in the residents' living quarters like houseguests. Linda and Norm Seitz, brimming with old-time Alaskan hospitality, enjoy telling about their experiences as longtime residents. The house, across from a large housing complex, is a typical middle-class subdivision home, surrounded by flowers and, inside, immaculate and full of memorabilia. Located near the airport, it makes a good first stop on a trip—the Seitzes take pride in orienting their guests and letting them in on local secrets. The three rooms are small but charming, with floral and nautical themes. Two have bathrooms attached, and one has a private bathroom across the hall.

8340 Elderberry St., Anchorage, AK 99502. www.elderberrybb.com. *©* **907/243-6968.** 3 units. Summer $95–$115 double; winter $75 double. Extra person $15. Rates include full breakfast in summer, continental breakfast winter. MC, V. *In room:* TV/VCR, Wi-Fi.

A HOSTEL

Spenard Hostel International, 2845 W. 42nd Ave. (www.alaskahostel.org; *©* **907/248-5036**), is a friendly place near the airport, with free phones, inexpensive bike rental, storage, free Wi-Fi and pay computer kiosks, and laundry machines. It feels more like communal housing than an impersonal hostel. There are three lounges for different activities and three kitchens. The owner has installed heat exchangers in the bedrooms to keep the air fresh. You can come and go 24 hours a day. The office is open daily from 9am to 1pm and from 7 to 11pm in summer, 7 to 11pm winter. Beds are $25 by cash or check, $27 if you use a credit card (Visa or MasterCard). Tent camping is also available for $20 a night for one tenter, $15 for a second person, a dollar extra if you pay with a credit card.

CAMPING

Anchorage is a big city, and to find natural camping, one should go beyond the urban area. The two closest state park campgrounds to Anchorage are at Bird Creek, to the south of town, and Eagle River, just to the north. The **Bird Creek Campground** is a favorite. It sits next to Turnagain Arm and the salmon-filled creek. A paved pathway passes by under the large spruce trees. There are 28 sites, and the fee is $15 per night. From Anchorage, drive 25 miles south on the Seward Highway to milepost 101. The 57-site **Eagle River Campground** sits in a thickly wooded riverside spot, and it's well developed with paved roads and large sites with lots of privacy. It costs $15 a night, and sites can be reserved in advance. Book up to a year ahead at (www.lifetimeadventures.net; *©* **800/952-8624** or 907/694-7982). They also have a couple of tents with cots for rent. Take the Glenn Highway 12 miles north from Anchorage and exit at Hiland Road. Both Bird Creek and Eagle River tend to fill up, so it's wise to arrive early in the day, especially for weekends. The Municipality of Anchorage's **Centennial Park Campground** is on the edge of the city, but getting one of the 100 sites—only 6 are drive-through—can be iffy for much of the year, and reservations are not taken. The cost is $25 a night. The address is 8300 Glenn Hwy., but turn off

Muldoon Road onto Boundary Avenue just before the Glenn Highway exit; if you miss the frontage road, it's a long way to the next exit. Information is available at ✆ **907/343-6986,** but only during the spring and summer. The next closest public campgrounds to the south are at Portage Glacier (p. 267) and to the north at Eklutna Lake (p. 254).

If you seek a place to hook up your RV in town, **Anchorage Ship Creek RV Park** (www.bestofalaskatravel.com; ✆ **800/323-5757**) is nearest to downtown. The site is in an industrial area a short drive from town but a little too far to walk to the attractions. Sites with water, sewer, and power are $47 in the summer.

WHERE TO EAT
Downtown
EXPENSIVE

Club Paris ★★ STEAK   Club Paris is the essence of old Anchorage boomtown years, when the streets were dusty and an oil man needed a classy joint in which to do business. Steak, of course, is what to order, and rare really means rare. It's consistently voted the best in town. Ask for the blue cheese stuffing; the stuffed filet is worth the years it probably takes off your coronary arteries. They have a full bar.

417 W. 5th Ave. ✆ **907/277-6332.** www.clubparisrestaurant.com. Reservations recommended. Lunch $15–$30; dinner $20–$65. AE, DC, DISC, MC, V. Mon–Thurs 11:30am–2:30pm and 5–10pm; Fri–Sat 11:30am–2:30pm and 5–11pm; Sun 4–9pm.

The Marx Brothers Cafe ★★★ NEW AMERICAN   A restaurant started by three friends, back when gourmet food was an exotic hobby in Anchorage, long ago became the standard of excellence in the state. Treatments of Alaska seafood that began here as cutting-edge creative cuisine now turn up in many of the best restaurants. The cuisine is labeled "New American" for convenience, but the cooking is truly eclectic, ranging from Asian to Italian, and always turned out flawlessly. The changing menu is not long, but the wine list is the size of a dictionary, winner of many awards, and potentially intimidating. A meal is an experience that takes much of the evening. Save room for the exceptional desserts.

627 W. 3rd Ave. ✆ **907/278-2133.** www.marxcafe.com. Reservations required. Main courses $32–$36. AE, DC, MC, V. Summer Tues–Sat 5:30–10pm; winter Tues–Thurs 6–9:30pm, Fri–Sat 5:30–10pm.

Sacks Cafe ★★★ INTERNATIONAL   This stylish cafe presents terrific food with a style of service that's both crisply professional and relaxingly casual. The small dining room, designed by a top architect, is in a storefront on a downtown side street, decorated in warm Southwest colors and sharp angles. It's a showcase for the food and diners, who can sit at tables or at a tapas bar. The cuisine defies categorization but is consistently interesting and creative, often fusing Asian influences with European or regional styles, and including plenty of local seafood. Vegetarians do as well as meat eaters. For lunch, the sandwiches are unforgettable, with choices such as shrimp and avocado with herb cream cheese on sourdough. Don't miss the tomato soup with Gorgonzola. The beer

231

and wine list is extensive and reasonably priced. They serve brunch Saturday and Sunday 10am to 2:30pm.

328 G St. ✆ **907/274-4022.** www.sackscafe.com. Reservations recommended. Lunch $11–$16; dinner main courses $18–$36. AE, MC, V. Mon–Sat 11am–2:30pm; Mon–Thurs 5–9:30pm; Fri–Sat 5–10pm; Sun 10am–3pm and 5–9:30pm.

MODERATE

Crush ★★ BISTRO   Situated in the city's small upscale shopping area, across from Nordstrom, this elegant, spare dining room occupies an appealing space in a small brick building with a curved facade. The bistro presents itself as a wine bar that also serves food, and nearly 40 choices are available by the glass, and many more by the bottle. But the cooking is terrific, too, and there's no reason to stay away even if wine holds no interest. Besides specials, the dinner menu largely consists of inexpensive shareable plates. For lunch, all selections are $10: wonderful salads or sandwiches, which are served with soup or a salad. Come here for a low-stress, reasonably priced meal created by an award-winning chef.

343 W. 6th Ave. ✆ **907/865-9198.** www.crushak.com. Lunch $10; dinner $8–$19. AE, DC, MC, V. Mon–Thurs 11:30am–10pm; Fri–Sat 11:30am–midnight.

Glacier Brewhouse ★★ BREWPUB   An eclectic and changing menu is served in a large dining room with lodge decor, where the pleasant scent of the wood-fired grill hangs in the air. It's a lively and popular place to see others and be seen. A glass wall shows off the brewing equipment, which produces eight or more hearty beers, and also turns out spent grain for bread that's then set out on the tables with olive oil. An advantage for travelers is the wide price range—a pizza with feta cheese, sun-dried tomato pesto, and roasted garlic is $11; crab legs are $37. The food and service are usually quite good. Choose this place for a boisterous meal with quick, casual service that will get you out in time to do something else with the evening. Do reserve ahead, however, as waits can be long. Also, the noise level in the former car dealership building precludes quiet conversation.

737 W. 5th Ave. ✆ **907/274-BREW** [2739]. www.glacierbrewhouse.com. Reservations recommended. Lunch $8–$15; dinner $9–$34. AE, DC, DISC, MC, V. High season daily 11am–11pm; low season Mon 10am–9:30pm, Tues–Thurs 11am–10pm, Fri–Sat 11am–11pm, Sun noon–9:30pm.

Kumagoro ★★ JAPANESE   Anchorage has several good, authentic Japanese restaurants, but this one, right on the main tourist street downtown, has the most convenient location. Among our favorite lunches anywhere is their lunch box ($16), a large sampler of many dishes, including sushi, sashimi, and other tasty things, always a little different, that we can't always identify. The dining room is pleasantly low key, with tables in rows, so you may have the opportunity to meet those seated next to you. The restaurant serves beer and wine.

533 W. 4th Ave. ✆ **907/272-9905.** Lunch $8–$16; dinner main courses $16–$42. AE, DC, DISC, MC, V. Summer daily 11am–10:30pm; winter daily 11am–10pm.

Snow Goose Restaurant ★★ GRILL   This brewpub stands atop the downtown bluff overlooking the Port of Anchorage, with a more sedate downstairs dining room and a big, festive bar room upstairs with huge windows and a sunny deck, where you can also get the full menu. The atmosphere is somehow more authentic than the other downtown brewpub—just a little looser, younger, and less contrived. The beer is good (from the Sleeping Lady Brewing Company), of course, but the food has also been remarkable on recent visits, with many specials, bold seasoning, and expert cooking. Not what you expect in a rollicking bar. You can get something fancy—seafood and such—but most meals are burgers, pizza, and the like, under $15. An on-site theater hosts a variety of performances, including touring musicians.

717 W. 3rd Ave. ✆ **907/277-7727.** www.alaskabeers.com. All items $11–$34. AE, DISC, MC, V. High season Sun–Thurs 11:30am–11pm, Fri–Sat 11:30am–midnight; low season Mon–Thurs 11:30am–10pm, Fri–Sat 11:30am–11:30pm, closed Sun.

INEXPENSIVE

Dianne's Restaurant 🍴 CAFE   This sandwich shop is our first choice for a quick, healthy, inexpensive lunch downtown. Located off the lobby of a tall glass building, Dianne's cafeteria line fills with well-dressed office workers seeking the hearty freshly baked bread, soups, sandwiches, and specials. The atmosphere is bright and casual, and you don't waste your day eating. On a sunny day, choose a table in the courtyard. The restaurant does not have a liquor license.

550 W. 7th Ave., Ste. 110. ✆ **907/279-7243.** www.diannesrestaurant.com. Main courses $4.75–$11. AE, DISC, MC, V. Mon–Fri 7am–4pm.

Snow City Cafe ★ CAFE   This is the happening spot downtown for breakfast or lunch. What started as a smaller, granola-crowd place grew on the basis of hearty, tasty food and a friendly young waitstaff into a large, busy restaurant with lots of energy and a diverse clientele. It's especially popular in the morning, when you'll rarely do better than the salmon cakes and eggs, omelets, or five kinds of eggs Benedict. Breakfast is served all day. Lunch includes comfort food such as mac and cheese or meatloaf, but also unusual sandwiches, such as roast beef and blue cheese or grilled veggie and chèvre panini. The dining room is light and colorful, with a clean feel, and tables out in the open amid lots of movement. The restaurant offers free Wi-Fi. As it's busy, consider calling 45 minutes ahead to get on the wait list. Small monthly art shows begin with artist receptions every first Friday, a pattern shared with all the downtown galleries. They serve beer and wine.

1034 W. 4th Ave. ✆ **907/272-CITY** (2489). www.snowcitycafe.com. Breakfast and lunch $8–$13. AE, DISC, MC, V. Daily 7am–4pm (espresso counter only after 3pm on weekdays).

Beyond Downtown

EXPENSIVE

Jens' Restaurant ★★★ INTERNATIONAL   Chef Jens Hansen is truly gifted. His restaurant is for the kind of diner who loves exciting food, surprises, and beautiful plates of new tastes and textures; the meals are about the food, sharing bites, and saying "Wow" and "How did he do that?" The cuisine is highly eclectic but not experimental, because these dishes work far more often than any experimentalist has a right to expect. There's often only one item on the changing menu that isn't unusual or challenging: the superb pepper steak. Like everything, even that dish has a sauce, and it is complex and memorable. The wine list is exceptional but manageable and reasonably priced, and you can sip your selection while dining inexpensively on appetizers in a pleasant bar area; try the incredible spinach ravioli with Gorgonzola, for example. Desserts are sublime. The dining room is uncluttered and decorated with modern art. Service is highly professional, with each formally attired waiter assigned to just a few tables, and they earn their keep as well by helping diners learn about food and wine they have probably never tried.

701 W. 36th Ave. ✆ **907/561-5367.** www.jensrestaurant.com. Reservations recommended. Lunch $13–$38; dinner main courses $18–$43. AE, DC, DISC, MC, V. Mon–Fri 11:30am–2pm; Tues–Sat 6–10pm; wine bar serves appetizers starting at 4pm. Closed Jan.

Kincaid Grill ★★★ NEW AMERICAN   This exquisite establishment excels in everything it offers, from Alaskan seafood and rack of lamb to smoked duck and chocolate bourbon souffle with malmsey. There's a hint of Cajun or Asian influences in many of the offerings; they serve gumbo and andouille. The filet mignon can be cut with a spoon, even when rare. On a February day, they managed to fly in fresh king salmon for the chef's special. The decor is modern and simple. They don't serve hard liquor, and the selection of beers, while good, is limited. The wine list is extensive, however. Few bottles go for less than $40, but on the other hand, nothing on the menu costs more than that. On a fine summer evening, you can dine outdoors with a sweeping view of the Chugach Mountains lit by the midnight sun. The occasional rumble of jet engines at the airport, 5 minutes away, will remind you that, alas, you have a plane to catch.

6700 Jewel Lake Rd. ✆ **907/243-0507.** www.kincaidgrill.com. Reservations recommended. Entrees $28–$38. AE, MC, V. Tues–Sat 5pm.

MODERATE

Bear Tooth Grill ★★ 🍴 SOUTHWESTERN   Food of this quality rarely comes for prices this low. Dishes such as the soy-grilled halibut are sophisticated and nicely done but take up only a small part of a menu that includes Mexican choices, sandwiches, and other selections inexpensive enough to make the restaurant fit for an after-work impulse—many main courses are less than $14. The partners who own the restaurant started in business by making beer and then opened a pizzeria to sell the beer (see the Moose's Tooth, below); next they opened a theater-pub (see "Anchorage Nightlife," later); the grill, in the same building, was the final addition. Rather than wait for a table in the grill, you can eat tacos, wraps, or pizza at tables in the movie theater lobby, a loud, free-flowing setting perfect for kids and open for lunch Monday to Friday at 11am and serving the full menu until the late-night closing. The separate grill is calmer, best for couples and parties of four or less. It can be easier to get a table at lunch; at peak

Coffeehouses

There are coffeehouses all over the city to get a cup of java and a pastry, and to meet people and engage in conversation. A favorite is **Side Street Espresso,** on G Street between 4th and 5th, a gathering place for artists, activists, and anyone who wants to trade ideas, sometimes with live acoustic music in the evening. **Cafe del Mundo,** at Northern Lights and Denali Midtown, gathers an older crowd of businesspeople, yuppies, stay-at-home parents, and those looking for a comfortable meeting spot. **Kaladi Brothers** has several locations with Internet access, including the classy space in the back corner of the Alaska Center for the Performing Arts downtown, at 6th Avenue and G Street. Their location on Northern Lights Boulevard between Spenard and Minnesota is extremely popular, in the same shopping center with essential stops such as Title Wave used book store and REI sporting goods store.

evening times, waiting is assured. Besides the beer, they have a full bar serving many margaritas and 20 wines by the glass.

1230 W. 27th Ave. ☎ **907/276-4200.** Reservations not accepted. All items $6–$20. AE, DC, DISC, MC, V. Mon–Fri 11am–11:30pm; Sat–Sun 10 am–11:30pm.

The Golden Corral ★ BUFFET   The Anchorage outpost of this national chain has a particularly big spread of all-you-can-eat popular food plus a grill for burgers and, for dinner or breakfast, steaks. Its clientele is diverse; you'll hear Spanish, Tagalog, Somali, Samoan, Korean, and other languages reflective of the Alaskan melting pot. Asked why he favored the place, a Native Alaskan answered, "Everyone is treated the same." Discounts for children make it suitable for extended family gatherings. Lunch is a particular bargain; in a town where a good cob salad can alone cost $11, here you can build your own with endless add-ons such as shrimp, steak, and chicken for $2 less before moving on to the hot dishes. On a recent day, catfish was among the entrees, along with a taco bar, pizza, sliders, and several kinds of barbecue and Chinese dishes. The desserts tend toward starchy, but the selection is large. There are no alcoholic beverages sold, and soft drinks are usually extra.

4520 Union Square Dr. ☎ **907/563-9000.** Breakfast $11; lunch $9; dinner Mon–Thurs $14, Fri–Sun $15. Senior discounts. AE, DISC, MC, V. Mon–Thurs 10:45am–9pm; Fri–Sat 7:30am–9:30pm; Sun 7:30am–9pm.

The Greek Corner ★ GREEK/ITALIAN   When you need a relaxed place for a family meal, this place should be at the top of your list. The dining room is sunny, spacious, and informal, one reason people feel comfortable bringing the kids here. The service is sincere and, when the place isn't too busy, it can feel as if you've been adopted by the waitstaff. Food comes fast. The lamb chops are tender and seasoned and cooked just right, and come with perfectly prepared asparagus and baby potatoes. A dozen authentic traditional Greek dishes are on the menu, mostly priced around $15, or you can order from a list of old Italian favorites such as spaghetti or lasagna. They serve pizza, too, and reasonably priced lunches—a gyro with soup or a salad is $9.

201 E. Northern Lights Blvd. ☎ **907/276-2820.** Lunch $5.50–$10; dinner main courses $10–$20. MC, V. Mon–Fri 11am–10pm; Sat noon–10pm; Sun 4–10pm.

Spenard Roadhouse ★ AMERICAN   Anchorage has grown up enough to have a restaurant that celebrates the kitschy frontier culture of the 1970s with loving irony, displaying old license plates on the wall and offering TV dinners as specials. But the owners, a team who started two of the city's coolest restaurants individually (Sacks and Snow City Cafe), know the younger clientele who have made this part of Spenard newly hip don't just want chocolate milk and macaroni and cheese on the menu, so they serve a broad range of choices, including a sumptuous blackened ahi tuna with yellow Thai curry, rice noodles, and pineapple salsa, as well as steaks, chops, sandwiches, pizza, and lots of small plates to share. The full bar makes good strong drinks and specializes in small-batch and single-barrel bourbons. It's a fun, social place to eat.

1049 W. Northern Lights Blvd. ℂ **907/770-7623.** www.spenardroadhouse.com. Lunch and dinner $9–$23. AE, DISC, MC, V. Mon–Fri 11am–11pm; Sat–Sun 9am–11pm.

INEXPENSIVE

Harley's Old Thyme Café ★ 🍴 AMERICAN   Far from the tourist strips, Harley's boasts of home-style cooking "like your mom tried to make." Open for breakfast and lunch, it's popular with construction workers and electrical linemen. Texas-style brisket is the big seller, but you'll also hear regulars order fried pickles and pig fingers or a reindeer philly sandwich. Harley's puts culinary attitude into old favorites. The chili has no beans, and one delicious variation features bits of meat scraped off the grill. The Harley Bennie swaps out chicken-fried pork for Canadian bacon and sausage gravy for hollandaise. Tex-Mex offerings include chorizo and scrambled eggs. Their cultured milkshakes have a hint of cheesecake, and homesick Hawaiians ask for the Loco Moco, two eggs, gravy, and a hamburger patty atop a pile of white rice. You pick your own sides from a long list that includes coleslaw, mashed potatoes, mac and cheese, black-eyed peas, cornbread stuffing, and gravy (you can get gravy with just about anything if you ask nicely). There are a variety of good burgers and po' boys. Domestic beers and mimosas are available, and service is always affable.

7550 Old Seward Hwy. ℂ **907/349-8878.** $8.90–$15. MC, V. Tues–Sat 7am–3pm; Sun 8am–3pm.

The Moose's Tooth Pub and Pizzeria ★★ ☺ PIZZA   The best pizza and beer in Anchorage undoubtedly come from this fun and friendly place. The microbrewery came first, but the pizza really is the greater accomplishment. It has a soft, light crust like Italian pizza but the oomph of American pizza. They offer many ingenious toppings, but not just to dump on—the combinations really work. The pesto supreme is our favorite, with sun-dried tomatoes, Kalamata olives, feta, and artichoke hearts. The ambience is youthful, casual, and loud; the high energy means kids aren't out of place. The dining room, although handsomely built, still looks from top to bottom like a college-town pizzeria. The only drawback is the restaurant's popularity, which can make for long waits at peak times. Also, the menu has few choices for anyone in your party who doesn't want pizza.

3300 Old Seward Hwy. ℂ **907/258-2537.** www.moosestooth.net. Large pizza $13–$25. AE, DC, DISC, MC, V. Summer Sun 11am–midnight, Mon–Thurs 10:30am–midnight, Fri 10:30am–1am, Sat 11am–1am; winter Sun 11am–11pm, Mon–Thurs 10:30am–11pm, Fri 10:30am–midnight, Sat 11am–11pm.

WHAT TO SEE & DO

This section starts with a self-guided walking tour through downtown Anchorage, followed by details on the downtown museums and then attractions that are farther afield. If you want to walk with a guide, the Alaska Public Land's Information Center (p. 220) offers free ranger-led walking tours at 11am and 2:30pm. Or tour the town by bus. **Gray Line of Alaska's** Anchorage Highlights Tour (© **800/544-2206;** www. graylineofalaska.com) takes 3½ hours to visit downtown and the Ship Creek area, the Anchorage Museum, and the Alaska Native Heritage Center. The tour costs $54 for adults, half price for children 12 and under, including admission to the center.

Roaming Helpers

Security Ambassadors, employees of a business improvement district, patrol the downtown area on bikes and on foot. Stop one to ask a question or report a problem, or call © **907/279-5650** (www.anchorage downtown.org).

WALKING TOUR: DOWNTOWN ANCHORAGE

START & FINISH:	**4th Avenue and F Street.**
TIME:	**2 hours (use the shortcuts noted for a briefer tour).**

Start at the **Log Cabin Visitor Information Center** at 4th Avenue and F Street. Outside is a sign that shows the distance to various cities and a 5,114-pound jade boulder put on display by Stewart's Photo Shop, an Anchorage institution that is just across the street.

Walk east, toward the mountains, to:

1 Old City Hall (1936)

The building is on the right of 4th Avenue as you approach E Street. The lobby contains a fun and illuminating free display on city history, including dioramas of the early streetscape, old photographs, and the fire bell and fire pole that once were used in this building.

Crossing E Street, notice on the left side of 4th Avenue that all the buildings are modern—everything on that side from E Street east for several blocks collapsed in the 1964 earthquake. The street split in half, lengthwise, with the left side ending up a dozen feet lower than the right. That land was later reinforced with a gravel buttress by the U.S. Army Corps of Engineers, and the slope below forever set aside as open space because of the earthquake risk. This stretch of 4th

The busy streets of Downtown Anchorage.

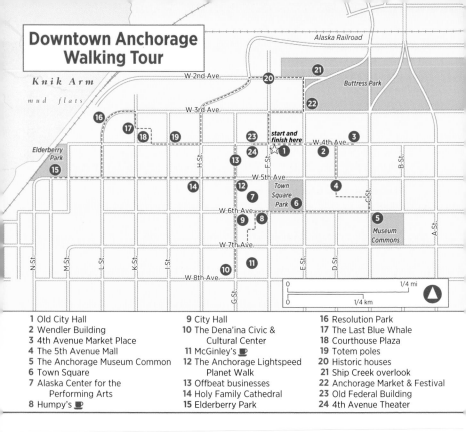

Downtown Anchorage Walking Tour

Knik Arm

mud flats

Alaska Railroad

W. 2nd Ave.

Buttress Park

W. 3rd Ave.

Elderberry Park

start and finish here

W. 4th Ave.

Town Square Park

W. 5th Ave.

W. 6th Ave.

W. 7th Ave.

W. 8th Ave.

Museum Commons

1 Old City Hall	9 City Hall	16 Resolution Park
2 Wendler Building	10 The Dena'ina Civic &	17 The Last Blue Whale
3 4th Avenue Market Place	Cultural Center	18 Courthouse Plaza
4 The 5th Avenue Mall	11 McGinley's	19 Totem poles
5 The Anchorage Museum Common	12 The Anchorage Lightspeed	20 Historic houses
6 Town Square	Planet Walk	21 Ship Creek overlook
7 Alaska Center for the	13 Offbeat businesses	22 Anchorage Market & Festival
Performing Arts	14 Holy Family Cathedral	23 Old Federal Building
8 Humpy's	15 Elderberry Park	24 4th Avenue Theater

Avenue is where the **Iditarod Trail Sled Dog Race** and the **Anchorage Fur Rendezvous World Championship Sled Dog Race** start each year in March and February, respectively.

Continue walking east. At 4th Avenue and D Street is the:

2 Wendler Building (1915)

The Club 25 is among the oldest buildings in Anchorage. The bronze statue of the dog commemorates the sled-dog races that start here. Across D Street is a mural that depicts a map of coastal Alaska and British Columbia, with the Iditarod Trail faintly marked.

Map mural across D Street.

Cross 4th Avenue to the north side to see:

3 4th Avenue Market Place

On the north side of 4th, a shopping center was converted into a Native arts and crafts mall and entertainment center, bringing together Alaska Native businesses in the heart of downtown. The Two Spirits Gallery presents carvers and artists working on-site every day. In recent years, other Native craftsmen have sold their creations on the covered sidewalk outside. Interesting graphics about the 1964 earthquake and other historical topics are posted in the eastern end of the building, and there's an exhibit of art by the late Fred Machetanz, known for mastering Arctic winter light. The new Alaska Veterans Museum recently opened on the site. If you want to take the time, the Alaska Experience Theater is housed here, too: It presents large-format films on Alaska scenery and the aurora, and has an interactive earthquake exhibit. Admission for the films is $10, for the interactive exhibit $6. Call ℂ **907/272-9076** for showtimes.

The Rusty Harpoon (p. 260) is a good craft and gift shop in the yellow building next door.

Cross back to the south side of 4th and retrace your steps to D Street, taking it south 1 block and crossing 5th Avenue to enter:

4 The 5th Avenue Mall

This grand, four-story shopping center is Alaska's fanciest mall, with Nordstrom and JCPenney as its anchor stores. A large, airy food court is on the top floor. Take a look, or walk straight through to the doors on the opposite side. (Just a block east are the Anchorage Museum at Rasmuson Center and the Alaska State Troopers Museum, described later in this chapter.)

Cyrano's Off-Center Playhouse.

239

Traverse the mall lengthwise to the doors past Sullivan's, exiting onto C Street. Turn right and walk a half-block to the corner, and cross both C and 6th Avenue to:

5 The Anchorage Museum Common

You'll be staring at "Habitat," a 24-foot-tall steel statue of a squatting human form, the first large permanent installation in North America by famed British sculptor Antony Gormley. It anchors a full city block transformed from a police station and jail into a gracious outdoor space of flowers, trees, and lawn when the Anchorage Museum was expanded. The mirrored facade of the museum itself reflects the city skyline. The bus stop next to "Habitat" won architectural awards for its simulation of caribou in migration.

Return back along 6th Avenue, following the 5th Avenue Mall for 2 blocks, and cross E Street to:

6 Town Square

Another full block of open space in the downtown, this park showcases cement terraces and water features. In the winter, skating and ice sculptures are found here. In the summer, it calls to skateboarders and sometimes musicians. On the east side of the square, behind you, the huge whale mural was painted freehand by Wyland in 1994. He painted similar whale murals in cities all along the West Coast. The building on the northeast corner of the square is one of the city's oldest and was saved from demolition when the park was created; it contains a charming gift and candy shop with a bakery and coffee shop in the back.

Town Square.

On the west side of the square is the massive, highly decorated, dominating:

7 Alaska Center for the Performing Arts

The center was completed in 1988 amid controversy about its design, among other things—it's either clever and bold or garish and busy. You decide. The lobby is usually open, and whatever your opinion of the decor, a look inside will spark a discussion. Alaskans have gotten used to it and now think of the building mostly as a focal point of our cultural life. The location is the former site Anchorage High School and was previously occupied by two earlier performance venues. The first burned down in the 1950s. Parts of the second, named after painter Sydney Laurence, were incorporated into the new facility. Some say Laurence's ghost still haunts

Russell mural at Humpy's.

the place. Check the box office for current performances in the three theaters and rehearsal hall, Alaska's premier performance venues (and see "The Performing Arts," later in this chapter).

8 Humpy's

From the performing arts center, cross 6th Avenue at the F Street light and turn right (west) to **Humpy's** (© **907/276-2337;** www.humpys.com), a popular tavern on the south side of 6th with a huge selection of microbrews, live music, and good casual meals.

The square green office building next door to Humpy's is:

9 City Hall

Turn left through the pedestrian walkway between Humpy's and City Hall. A large mural showing a timeline of the history of Anchorage faces the parking lot. A more fanciful mural, by Duke Russell, is on the wall in Humpy's outdoor seating area on the near side of the parking lot.

Cross the parking lot to 7th, where you face:

10 The Dena'ina Civic & Convention Center

The center's name honors the indigenous people of the area, as the Alaska Federation of Natives acknowledged to huge applause at the first meeting ever held here, in the fall of 2008. The airy lobby facing 7th and the corridors on either side contain several spectacular pieces of public art, and the views from the top-floor windows and the deck on the southeast corner are well worth a ride up the escalator.

Cross 7th and G to the opposite corner to find:

11 McGinley's 🍺

Though you've walked only half a block from the last tavern, the Irish pub at the corner of 7th and G Street, **McGinley's** (📞 **907/279-1782**), provides an excellent excuse for another pint, if only because of the identity of its owner: Anchorage's mayor, Dan Sullivan, elected in 2009, whose father, George Sullivan, was also mayor, from 1967 to 1981.

From 7th and G, walk north past McGinley's, cross 6th Avenue, and proceed north to 5th Avenue. In the plaza on the southeast corner of 5th and G, note an enormous, 3-ton model of the sun, at the start of:

12 The Anchorage Lightspeed Planet Walk

The sun you see here is just the beginning of a scale model of the solar system in which you walk at the speed of light. The inner planets are along 5th Avenue toward the water, where you will be going in a moment. Earth is about 8 minutes' walk away, at 5th and K (it takes light 8 min. to get from the sun to Earth). The walk continues down the Tony Knowles Coastal Trail and all the way to Pluto, in the parking lot at Kincaid Park, 5½ hours away, although you can go warp speed on a bike. High school student Eli Menaker designed the walk, which the Anchorage Rotary Club completed in 2005. Since then, the scale-model planets and their informative signs have been little molested by vandals, although several are off in the coastal trails' quiet woodlands. This first site, in the plaza, also has an interactive video kiosk. Learn more about the project at www.anchorageplanetwalk.org.

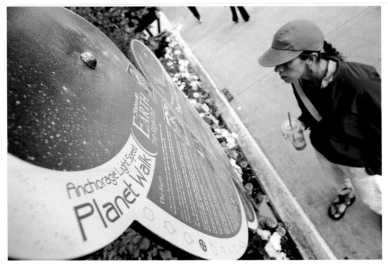

Anchorage Lightspeed Planet Walk.

Before following more of the planet walk, take a detour 1 block farther on G Street, between 5th and 4th avenues, where you'll find some of the downtown's best:

13 Offbeat businesses

First comes **Aurora Fine Arts,** an attractively cluttered arts and crafts shop with plenty to see. Next are: **Darwin's Theory,** a friendly, old-fashioned bar with character that shows up in an Indigo Girls song ("Cut It Out" from the 1997 album *Shaming of the Sun*); **Suzi's Woollies** (www.suziswoollies. net), a Celtic shop carrying imported sweaters, jewelry, and scarves, and

with live Irish music most Saturday afternoons and the first Friday of the month; and **Side Street Espresso,** where you can get into a lively discussion on art or politics and make contact with thinking people—or at least with individuals firmly convinced of their opinions.

Side Street Espresso.

Shortcut: You can cut an hour off the tour here by continuing north on G Street to 4th, then turning right and walking 1 block to the starting point at F Street.

Backtrack to 5th and G, then proceed west (away from the mountains) on 5th. Crossing H Street, you'll see the:

14 Holy Family Cathedral

This concrete Art Deco church is the seat of the Roman Catholic archbishop. The interior is unremarkable, but there's some historical interest, in that both Pope John Paul II and Thomas Merton prayed here. An outdoor meditation area with benches and statuary is west of the building.

Keep going toward the water, crossing L Street and going down the hill to:

15 Elderberry Park

Besides good playground equipment, the park offers the easiest access point to the **Tony Knowles Coastal Trail** (see "Walking & Biking," later). The trail tunnels under the Alaska Railroad tracks from the bottom of the park, where you can see the muddy shores of Cook Inlet up close, and perhaps spy some waterfowl.

Now hike back up the hill to L Street and turn left. At 3rd Avenue is:

16 Resolution Park

The bronze Captain Cook Monument stands on a large wooden deck, but he's gazing out on Cook Inlet, which he explored in 1778 aboard *HMS Resolution*. Cook didn't personally come as far as the future site of Anchorage, instead sending a boat with his ship's master, William Bligh (later Capt. Bligh of *Mutiny on the Bounty* fame). Failing to find a shortcut to the Northwest Passage here, Cook considered his 2 weeks in the inlet a waste of time, grousing in his journal, "Nothing but a trifling point in geography has been determined," and left it unnamed. Ironically, the British Admiralty chose this body of water to honor Cook after he died in Hawaii months later, naming it Cook Inlet. The park's informative signs, powerful mounted binoculars, and commanding vantage point make this a rewarding stop for gazing out at the water and the mountains beyond. The waters you see are ferocious, with whirlpool currents and a tidal range of almost 40 vertical feet. The shore across the inlet, about 2 miles away, is virtually uninhabited.

Captain Cook Monument at Resolution Park.

Follow 3rd Avenue east (back toward the mountains) 1 block and turn right on K Street. On the right is:

17 The Last Blue Whale

Joseph Princiotti's huge 1973 bronze of combat between a whale and whalers in small boats shows the whale's point of view.

Cross K Street to walk through the:

18 Courthouse Plaza

The plaza frames the Nesbett State Courthouse; the sinuous shapes of the plaza's concrete walkways are supposed to suggest both the flow of people through the court system and a braided glacial river. The metal "Grizzly Bear and Cub," by Homer sculptor Mike Sirl, was installed in 2004; local and state law requires projects to construct public buildings to set aside 1% of their budget for art, and this work is one result.

Cross the plaza to 4th Avenue, cross I Street, and take a look at the two:

19 Totem poles

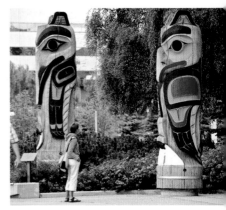

Carved of red cedar by Lee Wallace, of Ketchikan, and erected in 1997, they represent the eagle and raven moieties of the Tlingits people, intended to symbolize the balance of justice. A Tlingits creation story tells of how raven stole the moon and stars and brought them to mankind; in the raven pole here, the moon and stars are the stars of the Alaska flag. The eagle is shown trapped by a giant clam, another Tlingits legend, a warning that those who break the law will lose their freedom.

Totem poles carved by Lee Wallace.

Walk around past the courthouse on 4th Avenue and turn left onto H Street. Follow H as it crosses 3rd Avenue and becomes Christensen Drive. Descend the hill on Christensen and turn right on 2nd Avenue, toward the mountains. Look around at the:

20 Historic houses

The old wooden houses along 2nd are mostly attorneys' offices now, but once this was one of the better residential areas in town. Several houses are marked, and a kiosk at 2nd and F relates some town history. If you imagine houses like this over much of downtown, you'll know what Anchorage looked like before oil.

Bust of President Eisenhower.

Continue east on 2nd Avenue to E Street, where you will find:

21 Ship Creek Overlook

The bust commemorates Alaska's 1959 admission to the Union (in fact, Eisenhower resisted statehood for Alaska until it could be ensured for Hawaii as well). More interesting than the statue is the overlook. You can see the Alaska Railroad yards from here, and part of the port of Anchorage and the neighborhood of Government Hill across the Ship Creek river bottom. This is where the tent city of Knik Anchorage, later shortened to Anchorage, was set up in 1914.

Walk up the hill on E Street to 3rd Avenue. The extensively landscaped parking lot on the left becomes the:

22 Anchorage Market & Festival

This street fair, held every weekend from mid-May to mid-September, draws hundreds of vendors and thousands of shoppers. You can buy everything from local vegetables to handmade crafts to tourist junk. There are food booths and music, too.

Turn right on 3rd Avenue, then left on F Street. F Street Station, on the left, is a fun bar with an after-work crowd. Proceed to 4th Avenue, and you're back at the Log Cabin Visitor Information Center, but don't stop. Turn right on 4th Avenue. On the right side is the:

23 Old Federal Building

This grand, white, Depression-era structure now contains the Alaska Public Lands Information Center, with interesting displays and lots of information about the outdoors (p. 220). Don't let the security checkpoint deter you—go in and look around. At the celebration for Alaska's admission to the union in 1959, a huge 48-star flag covered the front of the building. While Anchorage watched, the Fur Rendezvous queen climbed a fire truck ladder to pin on the 49th star for Alaska. Hawaii became the 50th state later that year.

Across the street is Anchorage's most attractive historic building, the:

24 4th Avenue Theater (1947)

The theater was built by Austin "Cap" Lathrop, Alaska's first business magnate, who created it as a monument to the territory and the permanence of its new society, an old-fashioned movie palace with the bas-relief murals and a blinking Big Dipper on the ceiling. It flour-

4th Avenue Theater.

ished for decades but began losing money when one-screen downtown movie theaters became obsolete in the 1980s. Saved from destruction in 1991 and made a tourist attraction by a local businessman with a sentimental attachment to the building, the theater again closed its doors in 2006 and now faces an uncertain future.

Two Downtown Museums

Alaska State Troopers Museum   This charming little museum has more than one way into the heart. For law enforcement people, the appeal is obvious (the official name is the Fraternal Order of Alaska State Troopers Law Enforcement Museum). Others may enjoy perusing a trove of law enforcement insignia, equipment, a 1952 Hudson Hornet patrol car, and old Alaska memorabilia—even a grinning mug shot of Steve McQueen, who was picked up in 1973 spinning doughnuts in city streets in an Olds Toronado. The whole place conveys the positive spirit of pioneer Alaska.

245 W. 5th Ave. ℂ **800/770-5050** or 907/279-5050. www.alaskatroopermuseum.com. Free admission. Mon–Fri 10am–4pm; Sat noon–4pm.

Anchorage Museum at Rasmuson Center ★★★   The museum completed an expansion project in 2010 at a cost of $106 million. The design has received international accolades, and new galleries inside are extraordinary. The Smithsonian Arctic Studies Center, upstairs, contains some the world's finest treasures (600 pieces) of traditional Alaska Native Art. A science museum called the Imaginarium resides within the museum, included in the price; some

Alaska Aviation Museum.

elements are aimed at young children, but any curious adult will be enchanted and fascinated by the ingenious and well-made interactive exhibits here, spanning astronomy, with a planetarium, to marine biology, with large touch tanks of creatures. The museum's traditional attraction, the Alaska Gallery, is a popular introduction to Alaska's history and anthropology. The ground floor contains major works by Alaska's "old masters," and during the summer, the central Atrium area showcases local artists selling their work. You can spend most of a day here; plan at least 2 hours.

625 C St. ℂ **907/929-9200.** www.anchoragemuseum.org. Admission $12 adults; $9 students, seniors, military; $7 children ages 3–12. Mid-May to mid-Sept daily 9am–6pm; mid-Sept to mid-May Tues–Sat 10am–6pm, Sun noon–5pm.

Sights Beyond Downtown

Alaska Aviation Museum ★★   Alaska's late development meant it skipped a technological step: Travel and mail went straight from dog sleds and riverboats to airplanes, without the intervening development of a significant road or rail network. One day towns were separated from the outside world by perilous journeys that could last a week; the next day, people could come and go in hours. But the peril remained. In the early days, Alaska aviators crossed vast wilderness without proper maps, landmarks, weather reports, or even formal airstrips. This museum on the shore of the Lake Hood floatplane base contains five hangers of their planes, most of them beautifully restored (you can sometimes watch restoration work in progress, and they fly some of the vintage planes at an annual July 4 fundraiser). The galleries contain exhibits and artifacts from Alaska's eventful military history, films, and a flight simulator for guest use. Aviation enthusiasts shouldn't miss it, and anyone can get a strong feeling for that pioneering time. There's an aviation-themed gift store, of course. The museum's entrance faces the lake, not the road.

4721 Aircraft Dr. ℂ **907/248-5325.** www.alaskaairmuseum.org. $10 adults, $8 seniors and students, $6 children ages 5–12. Summer daily 9am–5pm; winter Wed–Sun 9am–5pm. The museum is near the international airport; driving toward the airport on International Airport Rd., turn right toward Postmark Dr., then right again on Heliport Dr., and right again on Aircraft Dr.

Alaska Botanical Garden ★ The garden is a pleasant place to walk and learn about native flora and some of the garden flowers, fruit, vegetables, and herbs that grow in this region. The plantings are in a few small clearings connected by paths on thickly wooded grounds at the edge of a large wild-land park. Gardeners will be interested in the three perennial gardens, the small rock garden, and formal herb garden. The placards on the wildflower trail will help you identify plants you see on Alaskan hikes. The Lowenfels Family Nature Trail is a 1-mile loop with a guide brochure that is pitched at an unusually thoughtful level. Along the walk is a chance to see salmon in Campbell Creek. Those without strong interest in gardening or native plants may find other attractions more deserving of limited time, however, especially considering the drive from downtown, which is 20 minutes without traffic, and possibly twice that at rush hour. The garden is open during daylight hours year-round, but the gardens are worth viewing late May to mid-September (the gift shop is open June–Aug 11am–4pm).

Campbell Airstrip Rd. (off Tudor Rd.). ✆ **907/770-3692.** www.alaskabg.org. Admission $5 per person, $10 per family. Summer daily daylight hours. Guided tours June–Aug daily 1pm. From downtown, drive out New Seward Hwy. (Gambell St.) to Tudor Rd., exit to the east (left), turn right off Tudor onto Campbell Airstrip Rd., and park at the Benny Benson School.

Alaska Museum of Natural History ★ This young museum 3 miles east of downtown focuses on paleontology, with permanent exhibits on Alaskan dinosaurs and Ice Age mammals. It's well designed to interest children. Alaska's Arctic was once warm and humid, and is now a hot spot for fossil hunters. Temporary annual exhibits have been good, too.

201 North Bragaw St. ✆ **907/274-2400.** www.alaskamuseum.org. $5 adults, $3 children ages 5–12. Summer Tues–Sat 10am–5pm, Sun noon–5pm; winter Tues–Sat 10am–5pm.

Alaska Native Heritage Center ★★★ Beautifully situated in a birch forest, this modern center is among Alaska's best Native cultural attractions. The graceful main building has a hall where storytellers, dancers, and Native athletes perform, with three 30-minute programs rotating through the day. A gallery houses educational displays and a theater showing short films. Workshops showcase artisans creating traditional crafts; they often teach crafts to visitors, too. Finally, there's a pond surrounded by six traditional Native dwellings representing each cultural group, hosted by Native Alaskans who cheerfully explain the exhibits and reconstructions to outsiders. They're not above pointing out departures from authenticity, such as the steel fire doors on a Yup'ik sod community house, required by modern safety codes. But the excellent totems and house posts at the Southeast site are by several of the best carvers in the state. A snack bar and grill serves soup, sandwiches, and other meals, and a gift shop carries both inexpensive trinkets and authentic Native art and crafts on consignment from artisans. Getting to the center requires wheels. The center offers a free shuttle from various points around town. Call for details on where and when to catch it.

From the Glenn Hwy., take the North Muldoon exit. ✆ **800/315-6608** or 907/330-8000. www.alaskanative.net. Admission $25 adults, $21 seniors and military, $17 children 7–16; Alaska residents $10 adults, $7 children. Discounts in winter, for families, or for joint admission to Anchorage Museum at Rasmuson Center. Summer daily 9am–5pm; call for winter hours.

248

The Alaska Zoo ★★ ☺ Don't expect the variety of a big-city zoo, but what the Alaska Zoo lacks in size, it makes up with a charm all its own. Anchorage residents have developed personal relationships with the animals, naming many of them. The zoo's best feature is the opportunity it affords to see familiar Alaskan animals up close. We enjoy watching the polar bears, Ahpun and Lyutyik, play and swim underwater (you can check that out on a webcam, too). Gravel paths meander through the woods past enclosures with natural flora for bears, wolves, seals and otters, muskoxen, Dall sheep, moose, caribous, and waterfowl. If you want to pass yourself off as a master wildlife photographer, crop out the Bactrian camels, snow leopards, and a few other northern creatures that don't normally live in Alaska. Two-hour naturalist tours take place every day at noon, and include some backstage stops, for $25 adults, $15 for children 12 and under. A snack bar serves basic meals, and there is a gift shop. The zoo is a 20-minute drive from downtown, without traffic; if you don't have a car, it's possible in the summer to catch the zoo's free shuttle, which picks up from several downtown locations daily (call for details).

4731 O'Malley Rd. ☎ **907/346-3242.** www.alaskazoo.org. Admission $12 adults, $9 seniors and military, $6 ages 3–17, free 2 and under. May–Aug daily 9am–6pm, till 9pm Tues and Fri Memorial Day to Labor Day; summer educational programs most Tues at 7pm, live music most Fri at 7pm. Off season open daily at 10am, closing time varies depending on the time of sunset. Drive out the New Seward Hwy. to O'Malley Rd., then turn left and go 2 miles.

Eklutna Historical Park ★ The Native village of Eklutna has a fascinating old cemetery, still in use, in which each grave is enclosed by a highly decorated spirit house the size of a large dollhouse. These little shelters excite the imagination in a way no ordinary marker would. They originally contained guns, cups, and other items the departed might need in the afterlife. There are two small Russian Orthodox churches on the site, including the **St. Nicholas Orthodox Church.** Built north of here of logs sometime before 1870, it is among the oldest buildings in the state. Tour guides offer an orientation talk before leading visitors through the site and both churches. Services in the white church, built in 1962, are Sunday morning and Thursday and Saturday evening (check the website). Wear mosquito repellent to visit the cemetery, and also take the time to see Thunderbird Falls, described below under "Hiking & Mountain-Biking."

A spirit house at Eklutna Historical Park.

About 26 miles out the Glenn Hwy. ☎ **907/688-6026.** www.eklutnahistoricalpark.org. Tours $5 adult, $2.50 ages 10–18, free 9 and under. Cemetery always open. Tours May–Sept Mon–Sat 10am–4pm. Take the Glenn Hwy. 26 miles to the Eklutna exit, then go left over the overpass.

Spectator Sports

Most big events in Anchorage happen at the **Sullivan Arena,** at 16th Avenue and Gambell Street (sometimes known as the Sully, it's named after a former Mayor Sullivan who was the current Mayor Sullivan's father). The ticket agency is Ticketmaster (**② 800/745-3000;** www.ticketmaster.com), which also sells through local Fred Meyer grocery stores.

BASEBALL   Anchorage has two semipro baseball teams—the **Anchorage Glacier Pilots** (**② 907/274-3627;** www.glacierpilots.com) and the **Anchorage Bucs** (**② 907/561-2827;** www.anchoragebucs.com)—with college athletes playing in a six-team Alaska league during June and July. Cool summer nights under the natural light at tiny Mulcahy Stadium bring the game close: the sound, smell, and rhythm. The quality may be uneven, but exceptional players grow up in this league and dozens are currently in the majors. Famed alumni include Mark McGwire, Rick Aguilera, Tom Seaver, Dave Winfield, Barry Bonds, Wally Joyner, Randy Johnson, and Jason Giambi. Check the *Anchorage Daily News* or the websites above for game times. Mulcahy is at 16th Avenue and A Street, a long walk or a short drive from downtown. Tickets are around $5. Dress warmly for evening games; a blanket is rarely out of order. A weekend day game is warmer, but then you won't get to see baseball played at night without lights.

BASKETBALL   The University of Alaska Anchorage hosts an NCAA Division I preseason basketball tournament, the **Carrs/Safeway Great Alaska Shootout** (**② 907/786-1293;** www.goseawolves.com), in late November. The noted men's tournament takes place at the Sullivan Arena over Thanksgiving weekend. The women's tournament is held on the 2 days prior to Thanksgiving. The Seawolves, themselves in Division II, play the regular season at the Well Fargo Sports Complex, on campus on Providence Drive.

HOCKEY   Anchorage is a hockey town. The biggest headline we've ever seen on the local newspaper is when the minor league hockey team won the national ECHL championship in the spring of 2006. The team, the **Alaska Aces** (**② 907/258-2237;** www.alaska aces.com), competes at the Sullivan Arena. The western division of the national conference, in which Alaska plays, pits the team regularly against Las Vegas, Boise, and Victoria, B.C. The season generally lasts from October to May.

Alaska Aces.

Most years, the **University of Alaska Anchorage Seawolves** (**② 907/786-1293;** www.gosea wolves.com) get plenty of attention all winter. They play NCAA Division I hockey at the Sullivan, a notoriously noisy and raucous venue for opposing teams.

GETTING OUTSIDE

Anchorage is special among cities of its size anywhere in the world for the number of places right in and near town to hike, bike, ski, and otherwise get into the wild. In town, the city's bike trails connect through greenbelts that span the noisy, asphalt urban core with soothing creek-side woods. Kincaid Park and Far North Bicentennial Park are both on the trail system within the city, and encompass thousands of acres and scores of miles of trails for Nordic skiing, hiking, and mountain-biking. The Chugach Mountains, which form the backdrop to the town, offer tundra hiking, backpacking, mountain-biking, and climbs that range from easy to technical. More trails and streams, only slightly farther afield, are covered in the "Side Trips" sections later in this chapter. Many cruises, tours, fishing charters, and sea-kayaking trips leave from nearby **Whittier,** easily managed as a day trip; see chapter 7 for details.

INFORMATION   The **Alaska Public Lands Information Center** (p. 220; © **907/644-3661;** www.alaskacenters.gov) offers guidance for all these recreation areas and more throughout Alaska. For information on the bike trails, parks, swimming, and other city recreation, contact **Anchorage Parks & Recreation** (© **907/343-4355;** www.muni.org/parks). Cross-country skiers can get information from the **Nordic Ski Association of Anchorage** (© **907/276-7609;** www.anchoragenordicski.com).

Get information specific to **Chugach State Park** from the public lands center or directly from the park's website (www.alaskastateparks.org; click on "Individual Parks"). **Chugach National Forest** can be reached at © **907/743-9500** or www.fs.fed.us/r10/chugach. The best trail guide to the entire region is John Wolfe, Jr., and Helen Nienhueser's **55 Ways to the Wilderness,** 5th edition (The Mountaineers), available in any bookstore in the area. Excellent trail maps of Chugach State Park, the national forest, and even paths in the city are widely available in sporting goods stores and at information centers.

EQUIPMENT   You can rent most anything you need for outdoor activities. For bike rentals, see "Getting Around," p. 217. Get advice, buy gear, and rent cross-country skis, snowshoes, bear-proof containers, and mountaineering equipment at **Alaska Mountaineering and Hiking,** 2633 Spenard Rd. (© **907/272-1811;** www.alaskamountaineering.com). It's a small shop where the staff takes the time to help you plan a trip. A block away, at 1200 W. Northern Lights Blvd., **REI** has a larger store (© **907/272-4565;** www.rei.com) that rents a wide range of gear, including lightweight canoes and touring kayaks with car-top carriers, camping gear, packs, tents, sleeping bags, and cross-country skis (but not bikes or ice-climbing gear). It is the best-stocked place in town to buy outdoor athletic clothing as well. A used equipment shop in the same area, **Play It Again Sports,** 2636 Spenard Rd. (© **907/278-7529**), rents skis inexpensively and has ice skates for $20 a day. **Champions Choice** is a more specialized place for skates; it's a hockey shop in the University Center Mall at Old Seward Highway and 36th Avenue (© **907/563-3503**). Skates rent for $10 a day. (For Arctic cold weather gear and where to buy it, see "What to Wear" on p. 43.)

6 Walking & Biking

6

Getting Outside

ANCHORAGE & ENVIRONS

Walking & Biking

Anchorage has an award-winning network of paved **bike trails** spanning the city along wooded greenbelts. You rarely see a building and almost always cross roads and rail lines through tunnels and over bridges, so you're never in traffic. Here are two of the best.

LANIE FLEISCHER CHESTER CREEK TRAIL ★ Starting at an intersection with the Coastal Trail at Westchester Lagoon, this trail runs about 4 miles east along the greenbelt to **Goose Lake,** where you can swim in a cool woodland pond at the end of a bike ride and perhaps buy

Westchester Lagoon.

ice cream—still, improbably enough, in the middle of the city. South from the lake, a wooded trail leads through the university campus and, with some navigation, to miles more riding. The paved bike trails, including the Fleischer, stay well back in the trees, so you rarely see a building, and tunnels and bridges span all road and railroad crossings, so you're never in traffic.

TONY KNOWLES COASTAL TRAIL ★★★ Leading 10 miles from the western end of 2nd Avenue along the shore to **Kincaid Park,** the coastal trail is among the best things about Anchorage. It's a unique pathway to the natural environment from the heart of downtown. One can ride parallel to beluga whales swimming along the trail at high tide and encounter several moose on a single ride. (Don't approach moose or bears or try to slip by; wait at a safe distance for them to go their own way.) One popular entrance is at **Elderberry Park,** at the western end of 5th Avenue. **Westchester Lagoon** (a pond) is 10 blocks south of Elderberry Park. From downtown, the lagoon is a good destination for a lovely stroll and a fine place to picnic and feed the ducks, which nest on small islands. A Frisbee golf course is on the northeast side.

Hiking & Mountain-Biking

Besides these hikes and bikes in Anchorage proper, more excellent nearby options are along Turnagain Arm and in Girdwood, covered later in this chapter.

EAGLE RIVER VALLEY ★★ The **Eagle River Nature Center,** at the end of Eagle River Road, 12 miles up Eagle River Valley from the Glenn Highway exit (© **907/694-2108;** www.ernc.org), resembles a public wilderness lodge, with hands-on nature displays about the area and daily nature walks in the summer and weekends year-round (2pm weekends, call for other times). Operated by a nonprofit concessionaire for Chugach State Park, it's open June through August daily from 10am to 5pm, May and September from 10am to 5pm except Monday, October through April Friday through Sunday from 10am to 5pm. There's a $5 parking fee.

The .75-mile **Rodak Nature Trail,** with interpretive signs, leads to viewing platforms over a beaver pond. The **Albert Loop Trail** is a 3-mile route; a geology guide from the center matches with numbered posts on the way. Both trails have good bird- and wildlife-watching. The 25-mile **Crow Pass Trail,** a portion of the historic Iditarod Trail, continues up the valley

Bears in the City

Most cities don't have this problem, but during the summer of 2008, two serious brown-bear attacks occurred in one of Anchorage's city parks—Far North Bicentennial—and one more on a suburban street. The maulings were rare events in unusual circumstances. Fear of bears shouldn't keep anyone indoors in Alaska. To be safe, stay off closed trails, avoid running or biking in thick woods or late at night, and follow the advice in chapter 11 under "Outdoors Health & Safety," p. 521. If you're really worried, the staff at the information centers listed earlier in this section can answer your questions.

into the mountains along the river. You can make a dayhike loop of 6 miles or less by returning on the **Dew Mound Trail.** Continuing, the Crow Pass Trail eventually surmounts the Chugach in alpine terrain and passes near Raven Glacier before descending into Girdwood (p. 268). There are campsites with fire rings along the way, and a mile up the trail, the center rents out a public-use cabin for $65 a night. A yurt on the Crow Pass Trail and another on the Albert Loop rent for the same price. Reserve well ahead for weekends. Availability is shown on the website.

FAR NORTH BICENTENNIAL PARK/CAMPBELL TRACT ★   A rectangle totaling 4,730 acres of city park and Bureau of Land Management land brings wilderness into the city on the east side of town, a habitat for bears, moose, and spawning salmon. People use it for dog mushing and skiing in winter, and for exceptional mountain-biking and dayhiking in summer. The Alaska Botanical Garden (p. 248) and the Hilltop Ski Area (p. 259) are both within the park's boundaries. A good place to start a hike or ride through the woods is the **Campbell Creek Science Center** (© 907/267-1247; www.blm. gov/ak/sciencecenter), an educational facility operated by the BLM. Staff are often on hand to answer questions, and you can consult books and maps and look at an aquarium of native fish. To get to the science center from downtown, take Gambell Street (it becomes New Seward Hwy.) south to Dowling Road, go east (toward the mountains), turn right on Lake Otis Road, turn left on 68th Avenue, and follow 68th to its end, then left at the BLM Campbell Tract entrance sign. When the center is closed, you can park outside the gates and use another trail head. (Find a trail map on the website by clicking "Campbell Tract home page.")

Far North Bicentennial Park/Campbell Tract.

FLATTOP MOUNTAIN & THE GLEN ALPS TRAILHEAD ★★★   There are many ways to reach the alpine tundra, intoxicating fresh air, and cinematic views in the Chugach Mountains behind Anchorage, but the easiest and best-developed portal is the Chugach State Park Glen Alps Trailhead. Even those who aren't up to hiking should go for the drive and a walk on a short, paved loop with incredible views and interpretive signs. If you are ready for a hike, you can start at the trail head for trips of up to several days, following the network of trails or taking off across dry, alpine tundra by yourself, but usually within mobile phone range. Camping is permitted anywhere off the trails.

Flattop Mountain is the most popular hike from Glen Alps and a great family climb, if a bit crowded on weekends. It's a steep afternoon hike, easy for fit adults and doable by school-age children. There's a bit of a scramble at the top, easiest if you stick to the painted markers on the rocks. Dress warmly and don't go in the rain, when slick rocks at the top could cause a fall.

For a longer or less steep hike or a mountain-biking trip, follow the broad gravel trail that leads up the valley from the Glen Alps Trailhead to several other great routes. Trails lead all the way over the mountains to Indian or Bird Creek, on Turnagain Arm, up some of the mountains along the way or to round alpine lakes in high, rocky valleys. You're always above the tree line, so you don't need to follow a trail if you have a good map. This is wonderful backpacking country.

To get to the trail head, take New Seward Highway to O'Malley Road, head east toward the mountains, then turn right on Hillside Drive and left onto Upper Huffman Road. Finally, turn right on the narrow, twisting Toilsome Hill Drive. Don't forget to bring cash or a check for the self-service day-use fee of $5 (not required if you are going only to the overlook and park in the designated spaces). When enough people sign up, a shuttle runs to Glen Alps May through October daily at 1pm, returning at 4:30pm, from Downtown Bicycle Rental at the 4th Avenue Market Place downtown (p. 219). Evening shuttles also sometimes run. The round-trip fare is $22 adults, $15 kids under 12. Call ✆ **907/279-3334** to sign up (www.hike-anchorage-alaska.com).

KINCAID PARK ★★   Covered in more detail below, Kincaid Park is an idyllic summer setting for mountain-biking and dayhikes. A former Nike missile site, its decommissioned bunkers now house recreational facilities and storage. Moose sightings are a common daily occurrence on wide dirt trails that snake for about 40 miles through the birch and white spruce of the park's hilly 1,500 acres of boreal forest, often with views of the sea and mountains beyond, including McKinley. Bears may also make an appearance. Trails open to bikes around June 1, or as soon as they dry, and a mountain-bike race series runs through the summer. Even on the busiest summer day, however, there is plenty of room for relaxed, solitary rambling or cycling. Within the park, wooded Little Campbell Lake is a picturesque spot for family canoeing, swimming, and fishing for stocked trout; there is no lifeguard. There's also an 18-hole Frisbee golf course. *Note:* The park gates are locked at 10pm, so get your car out before then or park in one of the lots outside the gates.

THUNDERBIRD FALLS & EKLUTNA LAKE ★★   The hike to Thunderbird Falls is an easy 1-mile forest walk with a good reward at the end. You can see the falls without the steep final descent to their foot. Take the Glenn Highway north to the Thunderbird Falls exit, 25 miles from Anchorage. Continuing 10 miles

Thunderbird Falls.

up the Eklutna Lake Road, you come to an appealing state parks campground ($10 a night, $5 day-use fee) and the glacial lake for canoeing, hiking, and exceptional mountain-biking. The Lakeside Trail leads 14 miles to Eklutna Glacier; you can camp on the way, stay at the state park's Yuditna Creek Cabin at 3 miles, or stay in the communal Serenity Falls hut at 13 miles. Advance reservations are required for the cabin or hut. See "State Parks Cabin Reservations," p. 283. For the hut, you can reserve in person only at the public information center, 550 W. 7th Ave., Ste. 1260, Monday to Friday 10am to 5pm. Rental bikes, kayaks, and other equipment, and guided kayak and bike tours, are offered by **Lifetime Adventures,** with a booth at the trail head of the Lakeside Trail (✆ **907/746-4644;** www.lifetimeadventures.net), open 10am to 6pm daily in the summer. For $75, you can kayak 8 miles to the other end of the lake and pick up a bike there to ride back; reserve 24 hours ahead for that.

All-Terrain-Vehicle Riding

Within 30 minutes of Anchorage, guides take small groups on a little-known trail through the forest of big spruce trees near Bird Creek, south of the city, leading to a hike down to a waterfall where spawning salmon and occasionally bears can be seen. The 3-hour tours with **Alaska ATV Adventures** (✆ **907/694-4294;** www.alaskaatvadventures.com) are $165 for drivers, or $120 for a passenger on the back of a machine.

Bird-Watching

The Anchorage bowl contains varied bird habitat that is easily accessed and close at hand: lakes, streams, marshes, seashore, woodlands, and mountains. Visiting birders can see species they don't encounter at home (Pacific loons, Hudsonian godwits, boreal chickadees) and familiar birds in breeding plumage unique to these northern latitudes (a red-necked grebe that actually does have a red neck, for example). Local birders have recorded more than 225 species in the city. You will need the help of a rental car or at least a bike. Potter Marsh is a superb freshwater birding area (see later in this chapter). Salt marshes and mud flats lie along much of the Tony Knowles Coastal Trail (see above). Right downtown, Ship Creek provides a river habitat. Glen Alps, described above, is the place to go for alpine birding. You can join field trips, network with local birders, and purchase a $10 birding map of the city through the **Anchorage Audubon Society** (www.anchorageaudubon.org).

A terrific booklet, *Anchorage Wildlife Viewing Hot Spots,* published by the Alaska Department of Fish and Game, is sold at the Alaska Public Lands

Information Center. It has more places to go than we can include here, detailed directions, and helpful information. Learn more about wildlife viewing around Alaska at www.wildlifeviewing.alaska.gov.

Fishing

There are hatchery salmon in several of Anchorage's streams, and stocked trout, salmon, or char in 28 lakes, so you need not leave town to catch a fish. The **Alaska Department of Fish and Game,** 333 Raspberry Rd., Anchorage, AK 99518-1599 (© **907/267-2218;** www.sf.adfg.state.ak.us), publishes informative booklets on the Web and on paper, and an online fishing report updated weekly in season. There's also a recorded information line (© **907/267-2503**) with what's hot and lots of other advice. See chapter 11 for general guidance and license information, and information for planning a fishing vacation, and see chapter 7 for the famous fishing opportunities on the Kenai Peninsula.

ROADSIDE FISHING   Although the setting (under a highway bridge in an industrial area) might not be the wilderness experience you've dreamed about, the 25- to 40-pound king salmon you pull from **Ship Creek** may make up for it. From downtown, just walk down the hill to the railroad yard. You'll probably need your own gear, as rental shacks are not currently operating. Fishing for kings is best in June and for silvers in late July, August, and September. Fish on the rising tide, when the fish come into the creek. Fishing near the end of the rising tide will mean crossing less mud, but one successful angler we know insists it's the start of the tide that's best. Either way, you'll need rubber boots, preferably neoprene chest waders, for the muddy banks, but don't go too far out, as the mud flats are dangerous and several times every summer the fire department has to rescue stuck fishermen.

    Campbell Creek, a more natural urban stream, is stocked with silver salmon that make good fishing in August and September, and rainbow trout and Dolly Varden char are in the creek year-round. The creek runs along a greenbelt across the city through residential and industrial neighborhoods; the adjacent bike trail is a good access route. You can join the trail on Dimond Boulevard east of Jewel Lake Road, or where C Street crosses the creek just north of Dimond, among other places; or ask for directions and tips at the Public Lands Information Center.

    Bird Creek, 25 miles south of Anchorage on the Seward Highway (see "Side Trips to Turnagain Arm & Portage Glacier," later in this chapter), is known for hot silver salmon fishing in the late summer and fall. Pinks run from late June to early August during even-numbered years. Other creeks along the Arm have similar but smaller runs.

FLY-IN FISHING ★★★   Serious anglers will use Anchorage as a base from which to fly to a remote lake or river with more fish and fewer people. Such a flight can be an unforgettable experience for those who are less than enthusiastic about fishing, too. The plane lifts off from Anchorage's Lake Hood floatplane base and within 30 minutes smoothly lands on a lake or river. You climb out and watch as the plane lifts off and disappears, leaving behind the kind of silence unique to true wilderness. It's on these trips that avid anglers are made—or spoiled. We've heard people complain of how sore their arms got from pulling in too many salmon.

Several companies offer fly-in trips; the best-established is **Rust's Flying Service** (ⓒ **800/544-2299** or 907/243-1595; www.flyrusts.com). It's a family-owned company with a strong safety ethic. They can take you out guided or on your own, for the day or for a longer stay in a cabin or lodge. If you fly to a lake, they'll provide a boat. They can't make fish appear if none are running, but they will try to take you to the hot spots. You can bring your own gear, or they can provide it. Prices for an unguided day trip start at around $295 per person, with a two-person minimum; guided, $495. Pickup from most hotels is included, but not fishing licenses.

Other Summer Activities

FLIGHTSEEING/BEAR VIEWING   Small planes are the blood cells of Alaska's circulatory system, and Anchorage its heart. There are several busy airports in Anchorage, and Lake Hood is the world's busiest floatplane base. If you'll be traveling to Talkeetna, Denali National Park, Juneau, Glacier Bay National Park, or Ketchikan, you may want to save your flightseeing splurge for those extraordinary places, which are closer to famous attractions. Likewise, for bear-viewing flights, Katmai National Park, Kodiak, Juneau, and Wrangell may be closer to the action. (All those places are covered in this book with the details for flights; check the table of contents or index.) On the other hand, plenty of spectacular territory is near Anchorage, and if time is short, you can see bears or Denali in an afternoon. We recommend Rust's Flying Service (see "Fly-In Fishing," directly above), a reliable operator that has designed a menu of choices around visitors' most common interests. They can take you on a floatplane ride for as little as $100. A flight to see Mount McKinley is $375 and takes 3 hours. An all-day bear-viewing tour from Anchorage is $595 to $785 per person. The exact destination—Lake Clark or Katmai national parks, or somewhere else—depends on where bears are active when you are traveling.

RAFTING   There are several white-water rivers within a 90-minute drive of Anchorage. **Nova Raft and Adventure Tours** (ⓒ **800/746-5753** or 907/745-5753; http://novalaska.com) has more than 30 years of experience offering trips all over the state, and five different half-day floats near Anchorage. Various rafting trips are available, ranging from the relatively easygoing Matanuska and Kings rivers, north of town, to the class IV and V white water of Sixmile Creek, which begins with a required instructional swim and includes fun optional swims, a 90-minute drive south of the city. White-water rafting always entails risk, but Nova's schedule allows you to calibrate how wild you want to get. Call to reserve and let them

Rafting at Sixmile Creek.

guide you as to what float fits you best. The company also offers add-ons for self-paddling, helicopter flightseeing, or glacier hiking. The half-day trips range in price from $60 to $139. Children 5 to 11 can go on the calmer Glacier Run float for $40. Other trips are suitable only for older children and adults. You'll need your own transportation to the river and may need to bring your own lunch. **Chugach Outdoor Center** (© **866/277-RAFT** [7238] or 907/277-RAFT [7238]; www.chugachoutdoorcenter.com) also offers several rafting options south of Anchorage. The company has two daily choices on Sixmile Creek, and trips in nearby Turnagain Pass that allow your party to split up, with some doing the crazy Sixmile white water and others having a leisurely float in the pass. They also raft Seward's Resurrection River.

SEA KAYAKING   Except at Eklutna Lake (see above), kayaking day trips from Anchorage go through Whittier, on Prince William Sound (see chapter 7 for complete details).

SWIMMING   Few visitors from warmer climes will be interested in chilly lake swimming in Anchorage (the best spot is Goose Lake, off Northern Lights Blvd. east of Lake Otis Pkwy.). If you have children and need to burn off some energy, however, you won't find a better spot than an indoor water park called **H$_2$Oasis** (© **888/H2OASIS** [426-2747] or 907/522-4420; www.h2oasiswaterpark.com), near the intersection of O'Malley Road and the New Seward Highway. A big wave pool and a 500-foot "watercoaster" are the top attractions. Adults should bring earplugs, as the noise level is high, and a full wallet, as admission is $24 for ages 13 and older, $19 ages 3 to 12, free ages 2 and under.

Winter Activities

The best downhill skiing and snowmobile tours are covered in the Girdwood section, p. 268.

SKIING   **Kincaid Park** is one of the best **cross-country skiing** areas in the country, with the first World Cup–certified trails in the U.S. National Championships and Olympic trials were held here in 2010. About 65km of trails are geared to every ability level, but mostly intermediate and expert. Besides the superb trails, it's a beautiful place to ski, through rolling hills of open birch and spruce, with views of the mountains and ocean. Most trails are expertly groomed for skating and classical techniques, with two loops reserved for classical only. Sixteen kilometers are lighted, an important feature on short winter days. According to some familiar with the park, one old gravel pit at the end of the airport runway dips lower than the high tide level, which would make it the only place in the world where you can ski below sea level. The **Kincaid Park Outdoor Center** (© **907/343-6397**) is open daily from noon to 9pm, shorter hours on holidays. The gate closes at 10pm, so park at one of the lots outside it if you will be skiing later. Skiing usually lasts well into March and sometimes into April. Big races come in late February and early March (see "Alaska Calendar of Events," in chapter 2). **Far North Bicentennial Park** also has some excellent trails—32km total, 7km lighted—and a slightly longer season because of a hillside location. Start at Hilltop Ski Area. Many other parks and the bike trails have lengthy skiing routes, too, some lighted, including **Russian Jack Park,** in

Skiing at Mount Alyeska.

the middle of the city. See "Equipment," on p. 251, for information on where to rent skis. For current trail conditions, check www.anchorage nordicski.com and www.crosscountryalaska.org/trails.

Anchorage has several **downhill ski areas.** The best, **Mount Alyeska,** in Girdwood, is described on p. 270. **Hilltop Ski Area,** in Bicentennial Park in town, is a great place to learn to ski, with one long beginner slope, at 7015 Abbott Rd. (*©* **907/346-2167;** www.hilltopskiarea.org). One-day lift tickets are $24 to $30, $16 for those ages 7 and younger, and ski package rentals about the same price.

Anchorage is also a great starting point for **backcountry skiing.** Non-experts should go with a guide (you can find one through Mount Alyeska Resort). Experts can get ideas from some of the folks mentioned under "Equipment," p. 251. The key safety consideration is, of course, avalanche awareness and preparation. We've described that on p. 521, but if you are turning to this book to learn how, you are not ready to go without a guide. An avalanche hot line is available for the Chugach National Forest near Anchorage (*©* **907/754-2369**); for much more information, including updated avalanche forecasts, maps, and educational material, check www.cnfaic.org.

SHOPPING

Some of the most interesting shops are mentioned earlier, in the walking tour of downtown, where most galleries and gift shops are located.

NATIVE ARTS & CRAFTS   Many downtown shops in Anchorage carry Alaska Native arts and crafts. Before making major purchases, know what you're buying (see "Native Art: Finding the Real Thing," in chapter 2). Don't miss the **4th Avenue Market Place** if you have any interest in Native Art. The mall at 4th between C and D streets contains several shops, including a Native-owned nonprofit, and stages demonstrations and performances during the summer (p. 239). Right next door, in a bright yellow building, the **Rusty Harpoon,** 411 W. 4th Ave., has authentic Native items, Alaskan jewelry, less expensive crafts, and reliable, longtime proprietors who only buy direct from Native artists they know. Locals shop here.

The **Alaska Native Arts Foundation Gallery,** at 6th Ave. and E St. (www.alaskanativearts.org), is a nonprofit promoting the best work of indigenous artists, in both traditional and contemporary forms. The gallery hosts shows dedicated to individual modern artists in a light, open space; the front area features a mix of well-made traditional crafts, including dolls, clothing, and jewelry. The website is well worth a visit and has an online shop.

Oomingmak Musk Ox Producers' Co-operative.

Nowhere else will you find another business like the **Oomingmak Musk Ox Producers' Co-operative** (📞 888/360-9665 outside Alaska, or 907/272-9225; www.qiviut.com), located in the house with the muskox on the side at 6th Avenue and H Street. Owned by 250 Alaska Native women living in villages across the state, the co-op sells scarves and other items they knit of *qiviut* (*ki-vee-ute*), the light, warm, silky underhair of the muskox, which is collected from shedding animals. Each village has its own knitting pattern. They're expensive—adult caps are $130 to $180—but the quality is extraordinary. The website contains the women's fascinating correspondence and links to a few of the rural knitters' own pages. When we bought a piece a few years ago, one of the knitters sent a thank-you card. As an aside, if you are driving north from Anchorage, you may also want to stop at the **Musk Ox Farm** (📞 907/745-4151; www.muskoxfarm.org), just north of Palmer on the Glenn Highway, where you can see the strange-looking creatures close up (summer daily 10am–6pm; admission $8 adults, $7 seniors, and $6 ages 5–12). Muskoxen also are at the Alaska Zoo (covered earlier in this chapter) and are easy to see in the wild near Nome (see "Nome: Arctic Frontier Town," in chapter 10).

Anchorage also has several small shops and local secret places to find authentic Native artwork. **Boreal Traditions,** in the lobby of the Hotel Captain Cook, at 5th Avenue and I Street, is perhaps the best source for museum-quality artwork by modern Alaskan artists working in traditional Native mediums. At the **Anchorage Museum at Rasmuson Center,** at 6th and C streets (p. 246), check out the large, light-filled gift shop for a beautifully displayed array of excellent Alaska Native art, both expensive pieces and affordable smaller items.

If you can get beyond the downtown area, you can shop at among the best places for Native crafts in Alaska, the **Hospital Auxiliary Craft Shop** in the Alaska Native Medical Center, off Tudor east of Bragaw (© **907/729-1122**), where everything is made by the indigenous people eligible to use the hospital (who come from all over the state) and where the staff are all volunteers. Proceeds go to the artists and to provide support for patients and a scholarship fund. The work you find here is all authentic and entirely traditional, and it's possible to stumble on artistic masterpieces. The shop is open Monday through Friday from 10am to 2pm and the first and third Saturday of each month from 11am to 2pm. They don't accept credit cards. There's exceptional Native art to see on the walls of the hospital, too; take the elevator to the top floor, then walk down the stairs.

FURS   If you're in the market for a fur, Anchorage has a wide selection and no sales tax. **David Green Master Furrier,** 130 W. 4th Ave. (www.davidgreen furs.com), is an Anchorage institution. Others are nearby.

GIFTS   There are lots of places to buy both mass-produced and inexpensive handmade crafts other than Alaska Native items. If you will be in town on a weekend during the summer, be sure to visit the **Anchorage Market and Festival** street fair, in the parking lot at 3rd Avenue and E Street, with food, music, and hundreds of miscellaneous crafts booths. You won't have any trouble finding gift shops downtown, but an excursion to **Alaska Wild Berry Products,** 5225 Juneau St., well off the beaten path, should not be missed. They have what must be the town's biggest selection of tourist T-shirts and souvenir items, but also wonderful candies, jams, salmon, and sausage gift packs. "The world's largest chocolate fountain" is only one of the attractions. An adjacent theme village offers shows, espresso, and the chance to have your picture taken with a reindeer.

FINE ART   Downtown has several galleries, including those mentioned under "Native Arts & Crafts," above, and others in the 4th Avenue Market Place. Openings are coordinated to happen on the first Friday of each month, allowing for an evening of free party hopping and art shopping. The **International Gallery of Contemporary Art,** 427 D St. (www.igcaalaska.org), is a nonprofit space dedicated to artists. Come here for an in-depth look at work by some of the state's most adventurous artists. Since it's run on contributions by volunteers, hours are short and changeable; currently Tuesday through Sunday noon to 4pm, closed Monday. They're also open for first Friday, 5:30 to 7:30pm.

   Artique, 314 G St., is Anchorage's oldest gallery and has a large selection. Half of the gallery is given over to big oils and other impressive originals; the other half is chock-full of prints, less-expensive ceramics, and some mass-produced stuff. At 5th and G, **Aurora Fine Arts** carries pottery, prints, and gifts. Directly across G is a gallery showing only glass sculpture.

ANCHORAGE NIGHTLIFE
The Performing Arts

WHAT'S PLAYING   The primary arts season begins in the fall and ends in the spring, but in the summer you can catch traveling performers, music festivals, and live music at the nightclubs and coffeehouses. To find out what's happening, check Friday's edition of the *Anchorage Daily News,* which has a section called "Play" that includes reviews and listings information. The website (www.play.adn.com) includes an exhaustive events calendar. The free weekly *Anchorage Press,* given away in racks all over town, also offers extensive event coverage aimed at a younger audience. See "Special Events," p. 220, for some major happenings.

BUYING TICKETS   **Ticketmaster** (✆ **800/745-3000;** www.ticketmaster.com) handles the Sullivan Arena and the convention centers, and sells tickets at Fred Meyer grocery stores. The Alaska Center for Performing Arts, 631 W. 6th Ave. (www.myalaskacenter.com), operates its own ticket agency, **CenterTix** (✆ **907/263-ARTS** [2787] or www.centertix.net), and also sells tickets for many of the smaller venues and less mainstream artists. The call center and box office in the center are open Monday through Friday 9am to 5pm, Saturday noon to 5pm, and evenings before events.

Nightclubs & Bars

We've mentioned some fun downtown bars in the walking tour, including Humpy's, Darwin's Theory, and F Street Station. The hippest downtown club is **Bernie's Bungalow Lounge,** 626 D St. (✆ **907/276-8808**), which grew from a little bungalow into a large, artsy playground with a backyard patio enclosed by a hedge. **Tap Root Café** (✆ **907/272-1341**), recently relocated to 3300 Spenard Rd., offers exceptional local blues, folk, and jazz performers nightly, along with a gourmet bar menu and a plethora of local craft beers. **Blues Central/Chef's Inn,** 825 W. Northern Lights Blvd. (✆ **907/272-1341**), has live music virtually every night. Major blues names and up-and-coming national performers come through on a regular basis. Shows start at 9:30pm. They're also known for their beef, especially the French dip.

The most famous bar in Anchorage, with the slogan, "We cheat the other guy and pass the savings on to you," is the huge **Chilkoot Charlie's,** at Spenard Road and Fireweed Lane (✆ **907/272-1010;** www.koots.com). It has two stages, three dance floors, and 10 bars on different themes, including a historic old dive from the Seward Highway called the Bird House, carefully copied, woppy-jawed angles and all, after the original burned down. The place is huge and full of entertainment, like an adult Disneyland, but we find it claustrophobic when crowded, with its low ceilings and confusing layout. It's open every day of the year from 10:30am until after 2am. If you do go there late, avoid conflict and use caution when leaving, as it can be a wild crowd.

The Movies

A movie at the **Bear Tooth TheatrePub,** 1230 W. 27th Ave. (✆ **907/276-4200;** www.beartooththeatre.net), is a chance to sit back with a big glass of craft brewed beer and a plate of nachos or a full dinner—it feels a lot like watching at home except for the big screen and the other people around you. The films tend to be second-run Hollywood output, but Monday is art-house night, and film festivals and special events come through. They also put on regular concerts; check the website. Even bad movies sell out, and there's often a crush. Unless you reserve and pay extra for a booth (a few days ahead for weekend shows), you must arrive quite early to find parking, get your ticket and seat, order your food and beer, and finish waiting in various lines before the movie starts. The staff brings the meal to you in the theater. Eating here without taking in a movie is covered under Bear Tooth Grill on p. 234.

There are several multiplexes in Anchorage playing all the current Hollywood output; check the sources at the beginning of this section for listings and reviews. **Century 16,** 301 E. 36th Ave. (✆ **907/770-2602;** www.cinemark.com), is an attractive, modern multiplex a reasonable cab ride from downtown. On the edge of town, **Regal Cinemas Tikahtnu Stadium 16 and IMAX,** 1102 N. Muldoon Rd. (✆ **907/338-6252**), is the favorite venue for local movie fans.

SIDE TRIPS TO TURNAGAIN ARM & PORTAGE GLACIER

One of the world's great drives starts in Anchorage and leads roughly 50 miles south on the Seward Highway to Portage Glacier. It's the trip, not the destination, that makes it worthwhile. The two-lane highway along Turnagain Arm, chipped from the foot of the rocky Chugach Mountains, provides a platform to see a magnificent, ever-changing, mostly untouched landscape full of wildlife. There are a lot of interesting pullouts all the way along the road. It will take at least half a day round-trip, and there's plenty to do for an all-day excursion. Use your headlights for safety even in daylight, and be patient if you get stuck behind a summertime line of cars—if you pass, you'll just come up behind another line ahead. If traffic is stopped, it usually means someone has spotted belugas or Dall sheep near the road. Mileage markers count down from Anchorage. Continue with this highway log on to the Kenai Peninsula and Seward in chapter 7, starting at p. 284. Car rental is covered in "Getting Around," earlier in this chapter. Bus tours follow the route and visit Portage Glacier. **Gray Line of Alaska** (✆ **800/544-2206** or 907/277-5581; www.graylineofalaska.com) offers a 7-hour trip that includes a stop in Girdwood and a boat ride on Portage Lake for $79 adults, $39 children 12 and under, twice daily in summer.

You can also see this awe-inspiring scenery—and more—from a train, although, of course, without stopping along the Arm for hikes or wildlife viewing.

Turnagain Arm.

The **Alaska Railroad** (📞 800/544-0552 or 907/265-2494; www.alaskarailroad.com) operates summer trains to Whittier and Seward that trace Turnagain Arm on the way (you can book the train and a Prince William Sound day boat with one call). Definitely also consider the railroad's day tour to the glaciated interior of the Kenai Peninsula, beyond Turnagain Arm where no road extends. That unique tour, called the "Glacier Discovery Train to Grandview," begins in Anchorage, Girdwood, Whittier, or Portage; if starting from Anchorage, the return from Portage is by bus. The tour costs $110 adults from Anchorage or Girdwood, $85 from Portage or Whittier, and roughly half price for children. There are several choices of what to do during your day in the backcountry: Take a hike led by a forest ranger at Spencer Glacier, go white-water rafting, or even use the whistle-stop service for your own, self-guided hike or expedition. The railroad and Forest Service are working on ambitious plans for a backcountry network of trails, campsites, public cabins, and rail stations, which will take a number of years to complete but parts of which are already usable.

An old snow-blowing locomotive at Potter Section House.

POTTER MARSH (Mile 117)   Heading south from Anchorage, the Seward Highway descends a bluff to cross a broad marsh formed by water impounded behind the tracks of the Alaska Railroad. The marsh has a boardwalk from which you can watch a huge variety of birds. Salad-green grasses grow from sparkling green water.

POTTER SECTION HOUSE (Mile 115)   Located at the south end of Potter Marsh, the section house was an early maintenance station for the Alaska Railroad. Today it contains the offices of Chugach State Park, open during normal business hours, and, outside, a few old train cars and interpretive displays. Just across the road is the trail head for the **Turnagain Arm Trail.** It's a mostly level path running down the arm well above the highway, with great views breaking now and then through the trees. Hike as far as you like and then backtrack to your car; or, if you can arrange a one-way walk with a ride back from the other end, continue 4 miles to the McHugh Creek picnic area and trail head, or 9 miles to Windy Corner.

MCHUGH CREEK (Mile 111)   Four miles south of Potter is an inviting and memorable state park picnic area, perched on terraced rock above the ocean and bisected by a series of crashing rapids and waterfalls. A daily parking fee is $5. Above the picnic area starts a challenging dayhike with a 3,000-foot elevation gain to Rabbit Lake, which sits in a tundra mountain bowl, or to the top of 4,301-foot McHugh Peak. You don't have to climb all the way;

TIDAL wave

Tides in Turnagain Arm rise and fall over a greater range than anywhere else in the United States, with a difference between an extreme high and low of more than 41 feet. When the tide is rising, the water can grow deeper by as much as 7 feet an hour, or a foot of water every 8½ minutes. If your foot gets stuck in the mud, it takes less than an hour to drown. (Yes, that has really happened.) Amazing as that speed is, the tide here can go even faster. A breathtaking wall of water up to 6 feet tall called a bore tide can roar up Turnagain Arm twice a day. To see the ocean do such a thing is so unfamiliar it looks almost like science fiction, as the wide arc of foam rushes ahead of a noticeably deeper sea.

You can (theoretically) predict the bore tide. Get a tide-table book, or look up the tide change on the Web (start at http://tidesandcurrents.noaa.gov and pull down "Products"). Note the size of the tidal range for the day you are visiting: The bore tide will be most noticeable during periods of large tides. (The magnitude of tides varies on the lunar cycle.) Find the time of low tide in Anchorage. Now add the following intervals to the time of the Anchorage low for a prediction of when the bore tide will pass each of these spots on the highway:

- Beluga Point (Mile 110): 1 hour, 15 minutes
- Bird Point (Mile 96): 2 hours, 15 minutes
- Twentymile River (Mile 80): 4 hours

The best viewing is Beluga Point to Bird Point; at the latter wayside, a set of signs explains the tides, and tide tables are posted to predict the tidal bore.

there are spectacular views within an hour of the road. The trail branches from the Turnagain Arm Trail: Hike west (back toward Anchorage) to where it heads uphill.

On the highway, you will find that. from this point onward. most of the stops are on the right or ocean side of the road: Plan your stops on the outbound trip, not on the return. when you would have to make left turns across traffic.

BELUGA POINT (Mile 110)   The state highway department probably didn't need to put up scenic overlook signs on this pullout, 1½ miles south of McHugh Creek—you would have figured it out on your own. The terrain is simply awesome, as the highway traces the edge of Turnagain Arm, below the towering cliffs of the Chugach Mountains. If the tide and salmon runs are right, you may see beluga whales, which chase the fish toward freshwater. Sometimes they overextend and strand themselves by the dozens in the receding tide, farther along, but they usually aren't harmed. The pullout has spotting scopes to improve the viewing. The farther right-hand pullouts over the next few miles have interpretive signs about the 1895 gold rush in this area and other topics.

WINDY POINT (Mile 106)   Be on the lookout on the mountain side of the road for Dall sheep picking their way along the cliffs. It's a unique spot, for the sheep get much closer to people here than is usual in the wild; apparently, they believe they're safe. Windy Point is the prime spot, but you also have a good chance of seeing sheep virtually anywhere along this stretch of road. If cars are stopped, that's probably why; get well off the road and pay attention to traffic, which will still be passing at high speeds.

You may also see windsurfers in the gray, silty waters of the Arm. They're crazy. The water is a mixture of glacial runoff and the near-freezing ocean. Besides, the movement of water that creates the huge tides causes riverlike currents, with standing waves like rapids.

Looking for Dall sheep at Windy Point.

INDIAN VALLEY (Mile 104)   Up the road by the Turnagain House restaurant is the **Indian Valley** trail head, a gold rush–era trail that ultimately leads 24 miles to the other side of the mountains. The path, while often muddy, rises less steeply than other trails along the Arm.

BIRD RIDGE TRAIL (Mile 102)   This is a lung-busting climb of 3,000 vertical feet in a little more than a mile. It starts with an easy, accessible trail, then rises steeply to views that start at impressive and get more amazing as you climb. With the southern exposure, it's dry early in the year. Parking is $5.

BIRD CREEK (Mile 101)   The excellent state campground on the right side of the highway, over the water, is described on p. 230, and the productive salmon fishing in the creek is described on p. 256. If you stop, use the lot on the left side of the road before you reach the creek. The parking fee is $5. There are also a short trail, interpretive signs, an overlook, and a platform that makes fishing easier for people with disabilities. Pink salmon run from late June to mid-August, silver salmon mostly in August. A scenic bike trail starts here and runs 10 miles to Girdwood, much of it on an older highway alignment.

Bird Point.

BIRD POINT (Mile 96) The remarkable wayside here is not to be missed. A paved pathway rises up to a bedrock outcropping with a simply wonderful view—all the severity of the Turnagain Arm, but framed by the soft green of a freshwater wetland with a beaver lodge. Take a look at the fascinating interpretive signs on many subjects. A $5 day-use fee is charged for each vehicle at a self-service kiosk.

TURNOFF TO GIRDWOOD (Mile 90) The attractions of Girdwood, covered below, are worth a visit, but the shopping center here at the intersection is not chief among them. Stop for a simple meal or a restroom break (the convenience store has large public restrooms), or to fill your gas tank for the last time for many miles.

OLD PORTAGE (Mile 80) All along the flats at the head of Turnagain Arm are large marshes full of what looks like standing driftwood. These are trees killed by saltwater that flowed in when the 1964 quake lowered the land as much as 10 feet. On the right, ¾ mile past the Twentymile River and across from the rail depot, a few ruins of the abandoned town of Portage are still visible, more than 45 years after the great earthquake.

ALASKA WILDLIFE CONSERVATION CENTER (Mile 79) The non-profit center, developed with visitors in mind, gives homes to injured and orphaned deer, moose, owls, elk, bison, muskox, bear, fox, and caribous (✆ **907/783-2025;** www.alaskawildlife.org). Visitors drive through the 200-acre compound to see the animals in fenced enclosures as large as 110 acres—you can often get a close look at the animals,

Alaska Wildlife Conservation Center.

but the larger enclosures give them natural vegetation and the ability to get away from view if they want to. There's no need to visit both here and the Alaska Zoo (p. 249). The zoo has more kinds of animals and it's a fun place to stroll, but the cages there are much smaller and often seem constricting. Here the animals' settings are more natural and perhaps more humane, but viewing is car based. A big log gift shop and outdoor snack bar are at the end of the tour. Admission is $10 for adults; $7.50 for military, seniors, and children 4 to 12, with a maximum of $30 per vehicle. Summer hours are daily 8am to 8pm (last vehicle in at 7:30pm); off-season hours vary but in the spring and fall are at least daily 10am to 5pm.

PORTAGE GLACIER (Take the 5½-mile spur road at Mile 78) The named attraction has receded out of sight of the visitor center. (The glacier you *can* see is Burns.) When the center was built in 1985, it was predicted that Portage Glacier would keep floating on its 800-foot-deep lake until 2020. Instead, it withdrew to the far edge of the lake in 1995. Today the exhibits in the lakeside **Begich–Boggs Visitor Center** focus on the Chugach National Forest as a whole rather than just the glacier, and they're worth an hour to become oriented to the area's nature, history, and lifestyles. Children and adults find much to hold their interest here. Admission is $5 adults, free age 15 and younger. It is open from the end of May through September daily from 9am to 6pm. To see Portage Glacier itself, take the road toward Whittier that branches to the left just before the visitor center, and stop at a pullout beyond the first (toll-free) tunnel; or take the boat mentioned below.

Several short trails start near the center or along the spur road from the Seward Highway. Check at the center for ranger-led nature walks. The Moraine Trail is an easy, paved quarter-mile. Another trail leads less than a mile to Byron Glacier, in case you're interested in getting up close to some ice. Always dress warmly, as cold winds are the rule in this funnel-like valley.

A **day boat** operated by **Gray Line of Alaska** (© **800/478-6388,** 907/277-5581 for reservations, or 783-2983 at the lake; www.graylineofalaska.com) traverses the lake to within a few hundred yards of Portage Glacier on hour-long tours, ice conditions permitting. It costs $29 adults, $15 ages 12 and under, and goes five times daily in summer, every 90 minutes starting at 10:30am. If this is your only chance to see a glacier in Alaska, it's a good choice, but if your itinerary includes any of the great glaciers in Prince William Sound, Kenai Fjords National Park, or the like, you won't be as impressed by Portage. Sandwiches and other simple meals are sold at a cafeteria near the visitor center called the **Portage Glacier Lodge** (© **907/783-3117**). There are no lodgings in Portage, but two **Forest Service campgrounds** are on the road to the visitor center, with 72 sites between them (more details are in the Chugach National Forest section in chapter 7). At the Williwaw Campground, there's also a place to watch red salmon spawning in mid-August, but no fishing.

SIDE TRIPS TO GIRDWOOD & MOUNT ALYESKA

Girdwood, 37 miles south of Anchorage, is proof that a charming little town can coexist with a major ski resort, as long as the resort goes undiscovered by the world's skiers. Girdwood still has a sleepy, offbeat character. Retired hippies, ski bums, and a few old-timers live in the houses and cabins among the big spruce trees in the valley below the Mount Alyeska lifts. They all expected a development explosion to follow the construction of an international resort here a number of years ago, but it never happened. That may not have been good news for the Japanese investors who finally sold the resort in 2006, but it is for skiers and other visitors who discover this paradise. They find varied, generally uncrowded skiing through long winters, superb accommodations, and an authentically funky community.

The primary summer attractions are the hiking trails, the tram to the top of Mount Alyeska, and the Crow Creek Mine, described below. In winter, and as late as June, it's skiing. Half the mountain's skiing is above the tree line, with stunning views of the Chugach Mountains and glistening Turnagain Arm below. Olympian Tommy Moe trained here, the Alpine national championships have raced down these slopes many times, most recently in 2009. For advanced skiers, Alyeska is a fairly large mountain—major areas of very steep, challenging terrain are open for their use, and helicopter and Sno-Cat skiing make the opportunities almost limitless. But the developed mountain doesn't have the size of the famous

Ski Conditions

The rainforest of Girdwood and the dry Anchorage bowl often have different weather, despite being within the same municipality. Before heading down the road for a day of skiing, check out the conditions. Call ☎ **907/SKI-SNOW** (754-7669) for snow, weather, and visibility conditions, or check that information online at www.alyeskaresort.com. For visibility from below, check out the cam at www.chairfive.com.

resorts in the Rockies, and intermediate skiers find themselves skiing the same runs repeatedly during a day.

ESSENTIALS   A **rental car** is the most practical means for getting to Girdwood. If you will only ski, however, you may be able to take a shuttle; call the resort before you come. The **Girdwood Chamber of Commerce** maintains a website at **www.girdwoodalaska.com**. For more guidance, check the Anchorage visitor information listed earlier in this chapter.

Exploring Girdwood

Crow Creek Mine ★   This mine, opened in 1896, is still operated mostly as an attraction for visitors by the pioneering Toohey family. They use the paths and eight small original buildings to show off the frontier lifestyle and teach about gold mining. Rabbits and ducks wander around, and weddings are held in the pleasant compound. A bag of dirt, guaranteed to have some gold in it, is provided for gold panning, and you can dig and pan to get more if you have the patience for it. Crow Creek Road, off the Alyeska Highway, is only partly paved and can be quite rough and muddy in the spring. Camping is $5 a night, with flush toilets.

Crow Creek Rd. (off the Alyeska Hwy.; PO Box 113), Girdwood, AK 99587. ☎ **907/278-8060.** www.crowcreekmine.com. $5 adults, free for children. Gold panning $15 adults, $10 seniors and active military, $5 children 7 and under (includes admission). May 15–Sept 15 daily 9am–6pm, off season by reservation.

Mount Alyeska Tram ★   The tram isn't cheap, but it's worth it for anyone who otherwise might not make it to high alpine tundra during an Alaska trip. (In winter, ride on your lift ticket; in summer, ride free with a meal at the Seven Glaciers Restaurant at the top, p. 272.) The tram takes 7 minutes in summer to get to the 2,300-foot level, where it stops at a station containing both the Seven Glaciers and an attractive but pricey cafeteria, the Glacier Express. Whether or not you eat here, the tram presents an opportunity for everyone, no matter how young, old, or infirm, to experience

Mount Alyeska Tram.

the pure light, limitless views, and crystalline quiet of an Alaskan mountaintop. Take the opportunity to walk around and enjoy it. Dress very warmly.

At the Hotel Alyeska (see below). $18 adults, $15 ages 60 and older, $15 ages 8–17, $9 ages 4–7, free 3 and younger. Summer daily 9am–9pm; winter, when lifts operate (call to check as hours vary).

Activities

In Whittier (p. 291), south of Girdwood and on the Prince William Sound side of the mountains, you can go ocean fishing or sea kayaking, or take a glacier and wildlife cruise. See "Turnagain Arm and Portage" (p. 263) for information on sightseeing along Turnagain Arm, hiking and other summer activities, and how to take the train into the mountainous backcountry for hiking or white-water rafting.

SKIING   Mount Alyeska, at 3,939 feet, has 1,400 acres of skiing, beginning from a base elevation of only 250 feet and rising 2,500 feet. The normal season is from late November through April, and it's an exceptional year when there isn't plenty of snow all winter (although the warming climate has brought some late starting ski seasons). Recently the resort has experimented with skiing into June on the upper mountain, so don't rule out a day on the slopes if you come in May. Snow lasts a long time with average snowfall of 721 inches, or 61 feet. Because it's near the water, the weather is rarely very cold. Light is more of an issue, with short days in midwinter. There are 27 lighted trails covering 2,000 vertical feet on Thursday, Friday, and Saturday evenings from mid-December to late March, but the best Alaska skiing is when the days get longer and warmer in the spring.

Alyeska has nine lifts, including the tram. Two chairs serve beginners, with a vertical drop of around 300 feet. The other 89% of the mountain is geared to intermediate to expert skiers. The biggest drawback for less experienced skiers is a lack of runs in the low-intermediate ability range. After graduating from the primary beginners' lift, chair 3, skiers must jump to significantly more challenging slopes, which explains the long lines in busy periods on chair 3. More confident skiers like the mountain best. Most of it is steep, and the expert slopes are extensive and extreme. The vertical drops from the north face of the slope are claimed as the longest double black diamond runs in North America, if not the world. Helicopter and Sno-Cat skiing goes right from the resort's hotel as well.

An all-day lift ticket costs $60 for adults, $45 for ages 13 to 18 or 60 to 69, $30 for ages 6 to 12, $5 for accompanied children age 5 and under, and $15 for skiers age 70 and older. Private and group instruction is available, and you can save a lot by buying your lessons, lift ticket, and equipment rental at the same time. A basic rental package costs $35 a day for adults, $27 for ages 13 to 18, $20 for ages 6 to 12 or 60 and over; high-performance and demo packages (at the hotel rental location only) are $45 to $75. There are groomed **cross-country trails** as well, which are pleasant but either flat or, if you go up the Sno-Cat trail, very steep. You can rent at the hotel, but the best Nordic skiing is in Anchorage.

The resort's utilitarian **day lodge** is a large, noisy building with snack and rental counters, located at the front of the mountain. The relatively cozy **Sitzmark Bar and Grill** nearby has long been a more comfortable place for a meal (burgers are around $10). The Hotel Alyeska (p. 272) is on the other side of the mountain, connected to the front by the tram to the top and beginner-level chair 7 (you can ski right from the door). It makes a quieter and more genteel starting point for day-trippers as well as guests, with the same equipment rental prices as the day lodge, plus higher-priced demo rentals. There are several dining choices here and at the top of the tram (see "Where to Stay," below).

HIKING   There are a couple of great Chugach National Forest trails starting in Girdwood. Among the best trails in the region for a family hike is the **Winner Creek Trail,** which begins behind the Hotel Alyeska and leads to a roaring gorge where Winner Creek and Glacier Creek meet; a hand-operated tram crosses the water. The trail is essentially level and a good length for an afternoon: The round-trip to the gorge is about 4.5 miles.

The **Crow Pass Trail** is more ambitious. The route rises into the mountains and continues all the way over to Eagle River, after a 26-mile hike that can take a couple of days. But with less expenditure of time, you can make a strenuous dayhike of it going just up to the pass, where you can see the glaciers, wildflower meadows, and old mining equipment. The Forest Service's A-frame Crow Pass public-use cabin makes an excellent destination for an overnight from Girdwood; it lies on a lake at 3,500 feet of elevation, half a mile from the pass. The trail head is up Crow Creek Road, off the Alyeska Highway. For more information on the national forest and cabin reservations, see "Chugach National Forest: Do-It-Yourself Wilderness," in chapter 7.

Winner Creek Trail.

SNOWMOBILING   Glacier City Snowmobile Tours (✆ **877/783-5566** or 907/783-5566; www.snowtours.net) operates out of the Great Alaskan Tourist Trap gift shop in the shopping center on the Seward Highway. Guides suit up clients—most of whom have never been on a snowmobile—and drive them to a promising site, determined according to snow conditions. At best, the winter tours make it all the way to Spencer Glacier. Groups are no larger than six, and the attitude is casual: After a brief introduction, you are driving your own machine, using your own judgment. A 5½-hour outing is $250 per person.

Where to Stay

Besides the resort hotel, there are plenty of condos and B&Bs in town. **Alyeska Accommodations,** 203 Olympic Mountain Loop (www.alyeskaaccommodations. com; ✆ **888/783-2001** or 907/783-2000), offers rooms, condos, cabins, and luxurious houses.

Hidden Creek Bed & Breakfast (www.hiddencreekbb.com; ✆ **907/783-5557**) is a beautiful craftsman-style inn built among huge spruce and hemlock trees by a pair of outgoing corporate dropouts, Ron and Michelle Tenny, who came to Alaska on vacation and fell in love with Girdwood. Their warmth and hospitality are exceptional. Each of the three well-equipped rooms is large, stylish, and finely crafted in its own way, and Michelle, a culinary school graduate, creates elaborate full breakfasts. Summer rates are $175 to $225, winter $145 to $195.

Hotel Alyeska ★★★   This hotel is among Alaska's best. The beauty of the building alone separates it from the competition, as does its location in an unspoiled mountain valley among huge spruce trees. Studded with dormers and turrets, it impresses on first sight. Inside, sumptuous cherrywood and rich colors unite the welcoming common rooms and elegant guest rooms. Although not large, rooms have every convenience. The saltwater swimming pool is magnificent, with a cathedral ceiling and windows by the whirlpool overlooking the mountain. A full-service spa offers all the latest pampering. A few days spent here skiing, swimming, and relaxing make the rest of life seem too drab. Now for the bad news. On weekends and school holidays in the winter, the hotel is overrun by partying families from Anchorage who overtax the facilities and destroy the peaceful ambience. Children run wild, the pool becomes impossibly crowded, and service deteriorates. Avoid these times for a skiing vacation.

Six dining options vie for attention. The Seven Glaciers, 2,300 feet above the lobby by tram on Mount Alyeska, serves wonderful, sophisticated food in a sumptuous dining room floating above the clouds. Service is warm, professional, and slow, so plan to spend your entire evening. The restaurant opens only on the weekends in the winter. A mountaintop cafeteria is right next door (great views, limited choices). At the base level, choices include a teppanyaki and sushi place, a hotel cafe, a bar and grill, and a casual cafe.

1000 Arlberg Ave. (PO Box 249), Girdwood, AK 99587. www.alyeskaresort.com. ✆ **800/880-3880** or 907/754-1111. Fax 907/754-2200. 304 units. Summer and Christmas $275–$360 double; $400–$1,500 suite. Winter $145–$240 double; $300–$1,500 suite. Extra adult $25. Children stay free in parent's room. AE, DC, MC, V. **Amenities:** 6 restaurants; 2 bars; babysitting; bike rental; children's programs; concierge; health club; massage; indoor pool; room service; spa; Wi-Fi. *In room:* TV w/pay movies, fridge, hair dryer, Internet.

Where to Eat

Also see directly above for restaurant options at the Hotel Alyeska.

Chair 5 Restaurant ★ ☺ AMERICAN   This is where Girdwood locals meet their friends and take their families for dinner, and it's also one of our favorites after skiing or on a drive to the Kenai Peninsula. The casual feeling is enhanced by the relaxed, sunlit bar at the front of the restaurant, often occupied by pony-tailed guys sipping microbrews and sharing a game of pool. The dining rooms are small and quiet, but the nicely funky atmosphere continues throughout. A lengthy menu offers choices pleasing to each family member, including pizza, burgers, fresh fish, steaks, and even game. The food and service are consistently good.

5 Lindblad Ave., in the New Girdwood Town Sq. ✆ **907/783-2500.** www.chairfive.com. Lunch $9–$13; dinner $18–$28; large pizza $16–$23. AE, DC, DISC, MC, V. Daily 11am–11pm (bar until 2am).

Double Musky Inn ★★★ CAJUN   The ski-bum-casual atmosphere and rambling, cluttered dining room among the trees match the wonderful Cajun and New Orleans food in a way that couldn't have been contrived—it's at once too improbable and too authentic. Service is as relaxed and friendly as at a greasy spoon. Food takes a long time to arrive, but when it does, every dish is flawless. The gumbo is a work of art, and the steaks are famous (really famous—Food Network chose this as one of the 10 best restaurants in America). The Double Musky isn't to everyone's taste, however; your senses can feel raw after the noise, highly spiced food, and crowds, and parking can be difficult. Loud groups will enjoy it more than couples, and families don't really fit. Since the restaurant doesn't take reservations, here's an important tip: Grab seats in the bar and dive into your meal there with appetizers and drinks rather than simply waiting.

Mile 3, Crow Creek Rd., Girdwood. ✆ **907/783-2822.** Reservations not accepted. www.double muskyinn.com. Main courses $18–$37. AE, DC, DISC, MC, V. Tues–Thurs 5–10pm; Fri–Sun 4:30–10pm. Closed Nov.

SIDE TRIP TO THE MATANUSKA & SUSITNA VALLEYS

On a longer visit, you may want to spend a day or two in the suburbs to the north, known as the Mat-Su Valley. Reached by the Glenn Highway about 40 miles from Anchorage, Mat-Su is a bedroom community for the city superimposed on a former frontier farming region. Folks commute an hour or more each way to live out here, gaining space to run snow machines and all-terrain vehicles, and for lower-priced land. In the well-populated central valley, fields have turned into commercial sprawl, with little to interest a visitor. But beyond the suburban blight, vast wild lands of unspoiled mountains, glaciers, and rivers remain relatively close at hand.

If you're driving anywhere north from Anchorage, especially toward Denali National Park or Fairbanks, you'll pass through this area. You can learn more about visitor attractions, lodging, and the area's greatest strength—its hiking, fishing, and skiing—from the **Mat-Su Visitors Center,** 7744 E. Visitors View Court, Palmer, AK 99645 (✆ **907/746-5000;** www.alaskavisit.com). The center

Mat-Su Valley.

is open mid-May to mid-September, 8:30am to 6:30pm. It's easy to find: Take the Parks Highway north from the interchange with the Glenn Highway; the center is on the right, in front of the Mat-Su Regional Medical Center.

Through Hatcher Pass

If you're headed north to Denali National Park or Fairbanks, the winding road through Hatcher Pass to Willow makes a glorious alpine detour around the least attractive part of your drive. Note, however, that past the mine and skiing area, the road is unpaved, open only in summer, and not suitable for large RVs. From the Parks Highway, just after it branches from the Glenn Highway, exit to the right on Trunk Road and keep going north when you reach Palmer–Fishhook Road, which becomes Hatcher Pass Road. From the Glenn Highway near Palmer, take Palmer–Fishhook just north of town.

Even if you're not headed north, a trip to Hatcher Pass combines one of the area's most beautiful drives, access to great hiking and Nordic skiing, and interesting old buildings to look at. The **Independence Mine State Historical Park** ★★ (© **907/745-2827** or 745-3975; www.alaskastateparks.org, click on "Individual Parks," then "Matanuska and Susitna Valleys") takes in the remains of a hard-rock gold mine that operated from 1938 to 1951. Some buildings have been restored, including an assay office that's a museum and the manager's house that's a welcoming visitor center, while a big old mill, towering on the hillside, sags and leans as a picturesque ruin. A visit is interesting even if you don't go inside, using the interpretive panels and map on a self-guided tour. The paved trails are easily navigable by anyone, and the rugged, half-mile Mill Trail leads up to that building's ruins. The setting, in a bowl of rock and alpine tundra, is spectacular. The day-use fee is $5 per vehicle. The visitor center is open from 10am to 7pm daily in the summer, closed off season.

Leave some time for a summer ramble in the heather if you visit the mine. In the winter, the Nordic or telemark skiing is exceptional, with a few kilometers of groomed trail and miles of open country to explore. (See the Hatcher Pass Lodge, below, for more details.) There are four hiking trails and two mountain-biking routes in the area—ask at the visitor center. The **Gold Cord Lake Trail** is less than a mile. The **Reed Lakes Trail** is spectacular for its mountain scenery and waterfalls with challenging terrain; one boulder field is known as "knee-cap valley." Starting from the Archangel Road, it gains 3,000 feet over 4.5 miles to Upper Reed Lake. Another challenging hike is the **Gold Mint Trail,** which starts across the road from the Motherlode Lodge on Hatcher Pass Road and leads 8 miles to the Mint Valley.

The park maintains two campgrounds along Hatcher Pass Road, charging a $10 fee. Backcountry camping is allowed without a permit, but fires are prohibited outside of campground fire rings.

On the Parks Highway

The **Museum of Alaska Transportation and Industry ★**, off the Parks Highway at mile 47 on Museum Drive, west of Wasilla (📞 **907/376-1211;** www. museumofalaska.org), is a paradise for gearheads and tinkerers. The volunteers have gathered every conceivable machine and conveyance—14 airplanes, 13 fire trucks, 7 locomotives, and 2 steam cranes, for example—and fixed up to running order as many as they can. It's open May 1 to September 30 daily 10am to 5pm, winter Tuesday 10am to 2pm. Admission is $8 for adults; $5 for students, seniors, and military with military ID; $18 for families.

Independence Mine State Historical Park.

Where to Stay & Eat

See the accommodations described below for some good places to eat in the Valley. In addition, there are unlimited fast-food spots and roadhouse burger places. One place of note is **Vagabond Blues,** in Palmer at 642 S. Alaska St. (www. vagblues.com; © **907/745-2233**), a coffeehouse and cafe offering sandwiches, wraps, baked goods, homemade bread and soup, and music. The food is great and the music is exceptional: A steady stream of national folk and alternative acoustic acts that come to Anchorage also make a pilgrimage to this small-town venue; check the website for dates. The coffeehouse is open Monday through Saturday 6am to 8pm, Sunday 8am to 6pm.

Two good, down-home places to eat—popular with the locals—can also allow you to escape franchise food. On the Parks Highway in Wasilla, the **Windbreak Cafe** (www.windbreakalaska.com; © **907/376-4484**) serves good diner food in a price range of $5 to $30, and is open in summer Sunday through Thursday 6am to 11pm, Friday and Saturday 6am to midnight; off season it opens half an hour later and closes an hour earlier. In Palmer, on the Glenn Highway, the **Noisy Goose Cafe** (© **907/746-4600**) is also a friendly rural eatery full of locals. It's open daily 6am to 10pm, closing an hour earlier off season. The price range is $6 to $26.

HATCHER PASS

Hatcher Pass Lodge ★ 🎁   A charming family presides at this tiny mountain lodge 3,000 feet high in a treeless alpine bowl near Independence Mine State Historic Park. Out on the open snowfield in winter, or the heather in summer, the nine cabins and A-frame lodge seem far more remote than they really are, just 90 minutes from Anchorage. There is a phone in the main lodge for emergencies but no TV. The cabins are nicely set up but basic, with chemical toilets and drinking water from an urn. Guests go to the main lodge for showers, meals, and drinks;

Hatcher Pass Lodge.

the family produces surprisingly good meals there. Stay in summer for a taste of the real Alaska with doorstep access to wonderful alpine hiking.

PO Box 763, Palmer, AK 99645. www.hatcherpasslodge.com. © **907/745-5897.** 9 cabins, 3 lodge rooms. $150 cabin for 2; lodge rooms $95 double. Extra person $15. AE, DISC, MC, V. **Amenities:** Restaurant; bar; sauna.

WASILLA

Best Western Lake Lucille Inn ★   This attractive hotel in Wasilla sits on the same lake as former governor Palin's house. It offers the best standard rooms in the valley. They're large and well appointed, and those facing the lake have balconies and a grand, peaceful view. Flightseeing trips and self-guided canoeing go from the dock below the lawn. You'll have to take meals off-site, which will most likely require a drive.

1300 W. Lake Lucille Dr., Wasilla, AK 99654. www.bestwesternlakelucilleinn.com. © **800/528-1234** or 907/373-1776. Fax 907/376-6199. 54 units. High season $189–$224 double, $299 suite; low season $99 double, $175 suite. Extra person $20. Rates include continental breakfast. AE, DC, DISC, MC, V. **Amenities:** Exercise room; Jacuzzi; sauna. *In room:* TV, fridge, hair dryer, Wi-Fi.

PALMER

Colony Inn ★ ✴   This classic country inn occupies a restored teacher's dormitory from the New Deal Colony Project, right in the middle of Palmer. The rooms are attractively old-fashioned, although a little worn in spots, with rockers and comforters but also Jacuzzi bathtubs in most rooms. A large sitting room and a dining room downstairs are decorated with historical photographs that help tell the building's story. Meals are served here at the **Inn Cafe** (© **907/746-6118**): lunch Monday through Friday and a popular Sunday brunch. Guests check in at the comparatively downscale Valley Hotel, which has a cafe open around the clock, at 606 S. Alaska St. (© **907/746-3330**), as there often is no innkeeper on-site to let you in or help with problems.

325 E. Elmwood, Palmer, AK 99645. © **907/745-3330.** Fax 907/746-3330. 12 units. $100–$120 double; $180 suite. AE, DISC, MC, V. **Amenities:** Restaurant. *In room:* TV/VCR, fridge, Wi-Fi.

THE KENAI PENINSULA & PRINCE WILLIAM SOUND

Geography endowed this one stretch of coast with several of the world's great natural places. On the east, near Cordova, the **Copper River**'s immense, entirely unspoiled delta is one of the largest contiguous wetlands in the Western Hemisphere, where flocks of rare, graceful waterfowl congregate on shallow ponds surrounded by miles of waving grass. **Prince William Sound** is a vast protected sea of wooded mountains and mammoth glaciers, a place where you can camp among the otters and eagles on tiny islands out of contact with the rest of civilization. **Kenai Fjords National Park** takes in bays off the open ocean where the mountains soar a mile straight up from the water. Boaters here spot humpback, gray, and orca whales; otters, seals, and sea lions; and colonies of puffins and other seabirds. The **Kenai River** harbors the world's biggest salmon, on the western side of the peninsula. On its southern tip, **Kachemak Bay** is like a miniature Prince William Sound, but with people and tiny towns with lodges, art galleries on pilings, and some of Alaska's best restaurants.

The region is exceptionally accessible, by Alaska standards. The Kenai (*Keen-eye*) Peninsula, in particular, is easy to get to without the expense and exhausting travel that can make much of the state difficult. Most of what you're looking for lies along a few hundred miles of blacktop, within reach of a rental car and perhaps a tour-boat ticket: glaciers, whales, legendary sportfishing, spectacular hiking trails, interesting little fishing towns, moose, bears, and high mountains.

Anchorage residents go to the peninsula for the weekend to fish, hike, dig clams, paddle kayaks, and so on, and certain places can get crowded. There's a special phrase for what happens when the red salmon are running in July on the Kenai and Russian rivers: *combat fishing*. At hot times in certain places, anglers stand elbow to elbow on the bank, each casting into his or her own yard-wide slice of river, and still catch plenty of hefty salmon. The peninsula also exerts a powerful magnetic force on RVs. During the summer, the fishing rivers, creeks, and beaches on the west side of the peninsula and the end of Homer Spit can become sheet-metal cities of hundreds of Winnebagos and Airstreams parked side by side.

Yet the decision is yours as to whether you spend time in the company of tourists. If the roadside fishing is hairy, hiking a little farther down the bank usually means you can be by yourself. Being alone is easy. You can paddle among

FACING PAGE: **Hiker overlooking Portage Lake.**

otters in Resurrection Bay; tramp over the heather in Turnagain Pass; and hike, bike, or ski one of the many maintained trails in Chugach National Forest. When you're ready to come back to the comforts of civilization, you'll find that some of the state's best restaurants and most interesting lodgings are here, too.

EXPLORING THE KENAI PENINSULA & PRINCE WILLIAM SOUND

The Towns

Kenai, on Cook Inlet on the west side of the Kenai Peninsula, is the largest town in the region. Ten miles up the Kenai River, **Soldotna** is Kenai's twin. Together they form a unit with almost half of the Kenai Peninsula's population of 53,000. They're also the least interesting of the peninsula's towns. **Homer,** at the southern end of the peninsula, has wonderful art and character and lots of ways to get out on the water. **Seward,** on the east side, is smaller and quieter, a charming gateway to Kenai Fjords National Park.

There are three towns on Prince William Sound. **Valdez** is an oil town at the southern terminus of the trans-Alaska pipeline where tankers are loaded. **Cordova** is more attractive, a historic community on the eastern side of the Sound, with outdoor activities close at hand. **Whittier** is a grim former military outpost, but a convenient gateway to the protected fjords and glaciers of the western Sound.

Getting There & Getting Around

BY CAR Highways connect all the region's major towns, except Cordova, which is reached only by air or water. Like all of Alaska's main highways, these are paved two-lane roads. The Seward Highway runs south from Anchorage to the Kenai Peninsula. That route is described below. A road built in a railway tunnel connects Whittier, on Prince William Sound, to the Seward Highway. The Glenn and Richardson highways reach from Anchorage to Valdez through Alaska's Interior. Stops along that route are described in chapter 9, and all of Alaska's highways are summarized on p. 406.

BY FERRY The ferry system connects Whittier with Valdez and Cordova via the fast ferry *Chenega.* Driving from Anchorage to Whittier, taking the ferry to Valdez, and then driving back to Anchorage (or north to Fairbanks) makes a great loop (see chapter 3). The ferry *Tustumena* (the *"Tusty"*) connects Homer to Kodiak Island and the Aleutian Archipelago (covered in chapter 10) and also runs from Homer to Seldovia. The schedule is not convenient for Seldovia, however; for that trip, it's easier to take one of the private passenger ferries that serve the towns and remote sites around Kachemak Bay from Homer. A U.S. Fish and Wildlife Service ranger offers programs on the *Tusty.* For more on the ferry system, see "Exploring Southeast Alaska," in chapter 5; call *©* **800/642-0066;** or visit www.ferryalaska.com.

BY AIR Commuter aircraft connect Anchorage to Kenai, Homer, Valdez, and Cordova. You can also fly between Anchorage and Cordova on an Alaska Airlines jet daily in each direction (the northbound originates in Seattle).

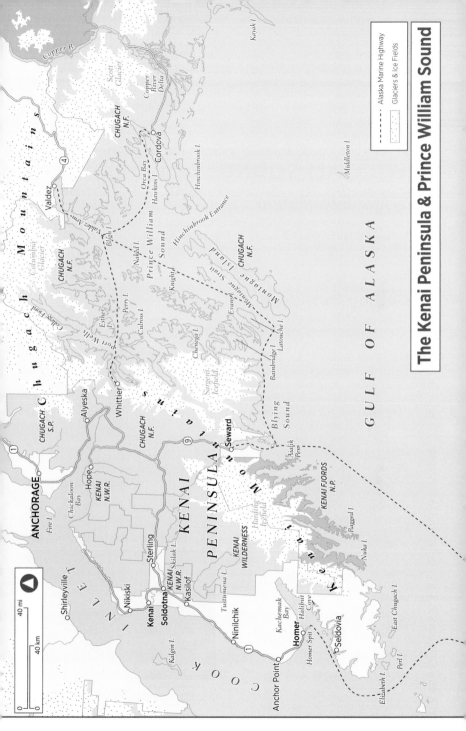

The Kenai Peninsula & Prince William Sound

Alaska Marine Highway
Glaciers & Ice Fields

GULF OF ALASKA

Chugach Mountains

Copper R.

Scott Glacier

Copper River Delta

CHUGACH N.F.

Cordova

Orca Bay

Hawkins I.

Hinchinbrook I.

Valdez

Valdez Arm

Bligh I.

Naked I.

Columbia Glacier

CHUGACH N.F.

Prince William Sound

Hinchinbrook Entrance

Knight I.

Montague Island

Montague Strait

CHUGACH N.F.

Evans I.

Latouche I.

Bainbridge I.

Blying Sound

College Fjord

Port Wells

Esther I.

Perry I.

Culross I.

Chenega I.

Sargent Icefield

Middleton I.

CHUGACH S.P.

Alyeska

Whittier

Chugach N.F.

Sound

ANCHORAGE

Chickaloon Bay

Fire I.

Hope

KENAI N.W.R.

Sterling

Seward

Aialik Pen.

KENAI FJORDS N.P.

KENAI PENINSULA

Mountains

Harding Icefield

KENAI WILDERNESS

Kenai Fjords

Ragged I.

Nuka I.

Shirleyville

Nikiski

Kenai

Soldotna

Kasilof

Skilak L.

KENAI N.W.R.

Tustumena L.

COOK INLET

Kalgin I.

Ninilchik

Kachemak Bay

Halibut Cove

Homer

Homer Spit

Seldovia

East Chugach I.

Anchor Point

Perl I.

Elizabeth I.

Nuka I.

40 mi

40 km

Scheduled and air-taxi services use these towns as bases for the villages, carrying passengers, mail, and cargo, and flying to remote lodges and cabins for fishing or other outdoor activities. Valdez, Cordova, and Anchorage operators serve Prince William Sound. Kenai and Anchorage companies cover Cook Inlet and remote public lands such as Lake Clark National Park. Homer is the base for villages around Kachemak Bay and lower Cook Inlet bear-viewing sites.

BY TRAIN The **Alaska Railroad** (© **800/544-0552** or 907/265-2494; www. alaskarailroad.com) runs from Anchorage south to Seward or Whittier and back daily in the summer.

Visitor Information

For information on the peninsula, contact the **Kenai Peninsula Tourism Marketing Council,** 35571 Kenai Spur Hwy., Soldotna, AK 99669 (© **800/535-3624** or 907/262-5229; www.kenaipeninsula.org), which distributes a vacation planner (order through the website). The staff will answer inquiries during normal business hours.

Getting Outside

The towns of the region are like beads strung along the laces of the highways; everything else is wilderness. You can find all the activities and isolation you seek here, yet the presence of the towns means that comfort is closer at hand than in other parts of Alaska.

Chugach National Forest takes in all of Prince William Sound and most of the eastern Kenai Peninsula. At 5.3 million acres, it's more than double the size of Yellowstone National Park. Anywhere else but Alaska, it would be a national park, and one of the largest and most spectacular, with some of the best sea kayaking, hiking, backpacking, wildlife-watching, and scenery anywhere. General information, camping, and ideas on remote areas in the Chugach are covered in "Chugach National Forest: Do-It-Yourself Wilderness" (p. 285); details about national forest areas near towns are in the relevant town sections.

Kenai Fjords National Park protects the outer edge and ice cap of the Kenai Peninsula's southern side. The park is incomparable in its remoteness, stark beauty, and abundance of marine wildlife. Access is through Seward.

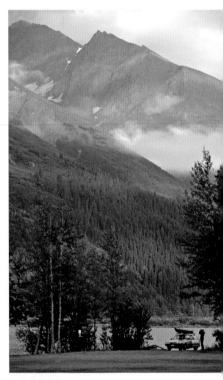

Portage Lake.

Alaska's state parks rent remote public cabins similar to the famous Forest Service cabins (see "Chugach National Forest: Do-It-Yourself Wilderness," p. 285), but they're usually newer, larger, and easier to get to. Most are in Southcentral Alaska—in this chapter, they're mentioned near Homer, Seward, and Valdez. Like the Forest Service cabins, it takes a hike, boat ride, or air taxi to get to the state cabins, and you need equipment such as a cookstove and sleeping bags, but once there, you can experience the real Alaska all by yourself.

Some cabins book up the minute they become available, and since Alaska residents get a jump on the reservation system, visitors are unlikely to reserve the most popular cabins at peak times. But if you can be flexible about where and when you travel, you can probably find a cabin. Alaska residents can reserve 7 months ahead, nonresidents 6 months ahead. Reservations do not open on weekends or holidays, only at 10am Alaska time on the following business day. Once a date opens on the system, it stays open until someone takes it.

The easiest way to reserve is via the online system with a MasterCard or Visa. You can also reserve in person, by mail, or by fax (you can ask questions by phone, but not apply). The staff is friendly and will guide you around the system, and help you find a cabin where you can get a permit, even if it's not your first choice. The main information and reservations desk is the **Department of Natural Resources Public Information Center—Anchorage,** 550 W. 7th Ave., Ste. 1260, Anchorage, AK 99501-3557 (© **907/269-8400,** or 269-8411 TDD; fax 907/269-8901; www.alaskastateparks.org; open Mon–Fri 10am–5pm). The website is the best source of information about the cabins, with a picture and description of each and a real-time availability calendar. Cabins rent for $25 to $75 a night, with fees highest for popular cabins at peak periods.

On the peninsula's western side, **Kenai National Wildlife Refuge** (p. 323) has Alaska's most accessible wilderness lake and river canoeing as well as extraordinary fishing, with access from roads near Soldotna ("Kenai, Soldotna & Sterling: Giant Salmon," p. 315).

Kachemak Bay State Park offers good sea-kayaking waters and wilderness hiking not connected to any road. The **Alaska Maritime National Wildlife Refuge** protects the wildlife habitat of remote islands and seashores around the state. Both are covered in "Homer & Kachemak Bay: Cosmic Hamlet by the Sea," later in this chapter.

VISITOR INFORMATION The best place to get outdoor information about the region is the **Alaska Public Lands Information Center,** 605 W. 4th Ave., Ste. 105, Anchorage, AK 99501 (© **866/869-6887** or 907/644-3661; www.alaskacenters.gov). You can talk with rangers who have spent time in the places you'll be visiting, and there are exhibits on the wildlife and outdoor opportunities in the region—even maps showing where to find various species of fish. Land agencies provide information on the whole state, and the bookstore is well stocked with maps, field guides, and such. Summer hours are daily from 9am to 5pm, winter Monday through Friday from 10am to 5pm. Visitor centers for particular areas are covered in the appropriate sections.

7

THE KENAI PENINSULA & PRINCE WILLIAM SOUND

Exploring the Kenai Peninsula & Prince William Sound

THE SEWARD HIGHWAY: A ROAD GUIDE

The Kenai Peninsula's lifeline is the road from Anchorage, a 127-mile drive to Seward on a good two-lane highway, mostly through public land without development or services. Hwy. 1, commonly known as the Seward Highway, is more than scenic—it's really a wonderful attraction in itself, designated a National Scenic Byway and an All-American Road. Excellent campgrounds and hiking trails are all along the way in the Chugach National Forest; see "Chugach National Forest: Do-It-Yourself Wilderness," below.

The mileposts start in Seward. Here we count backward, since you'll likely start from Anchorage.

MILE 127–79   The highway begins at the south end of Anchorage, the only way out of town in that direction, and runs along Turnagain Arm to the Portage Glacier (see "Side Trips to Turnagain Arm & Portage Glacier," in chapter 6).

MILE 79–75   Beyond the Portage Glacier turnoff, the road traverses the salt marshes to the south side of the Arm. These wetlands are good bird-watching grounds. The area was inundated in the 1964 earthquake, when the entire region shifted, lowering this area 12 feet and raising areas to the east as much as 38 feet. Everything moved laterally, too, up to 60 feet. People who were here tell of their surprise when the tide came far higher than they had seen it before in the days after the quake, until they realized that the land itself had sunk. Large parts of Homer, Hope, and Seldovia disappeared under the waves at high tide. Seward, Whittier, Valdez, and Kodiak were swept by destructive tsunami waves.

MILE 75–68   The highway steeply climbs through the spruce forest to the fresh, towering alpine terrain of the 1,000-foot-elevation **Turnagain Pass.** The vistas are stupendous year-round. At mile 68, if you feel the urge to walk among the meadow and tundra, park at the pullout with the toilets on the right side at the pass summit and follow the path, or amble off into the wildflowers (assuming the ground is dry). In winter and spring, this is a backcountry skiing and snowmobiling paradise. Skiers go on the left (east) side of the road and snowmobilers on the right. Always check with the Chugach National Forest (see "Chugach National Forest: Do-It-Yourself Wilderness," below) for avalanche conditions first. Avalanches have taken lives here more than once.

MILE 68–57   The pass forms a divide; crossing it, Granite Creek flows down toward the south. The road follows, falling back below the tree line of stunted spruce and then popping back up into sweeping views. Arcing to the northwest after the Granite Creek Campground, the highway follows another north-flowing river, Sixmile Creek. At mile 57, the Hope Highway divides off to the north and west along Sixmile Creek, while the Seward Highway continues south.

MILE 57–46   The Seward Highway climbs steeply from the Hope Highway intersection, up the canyon of Canyon Creek, before leveling out above the tree line at about 1,400 feet elevation. At mile 46, Upper Summit Lake lies smooth and reflective in a steep alpine valley. On the far side is Tenderfoot Creek Campground (p. 290), a calming spot warmed by sun off the water. On the near side, **Summit Lake Lodge** (© **907/244-2031;** www.summit lakelodge.com) is a traditional log roadhouse that's been updated to house a modern restaurant. Meals can take some time, so eat here if you're not in a rush. If you don't want dinner, you can enjoy ice cream from the counter in the log gift shop while you stroll near the lake. The lodge rents six motel rooms ($125 double) with private bathrooms, but without TVs or phones.

MILE 46–37   The highway continues through similar mountain terrain before descending into the trees again and branching at **Tern Lake.** This is a stirringly beautiful spot year-round, and a good place to get out and taste the fresh mountain air and watch for moose, waterfowl, and other birds. A 13-site picnic area is to the right at the intersection.

MILE 36   Look on the right to turn for the luxurious **Inn at Tern Lake** (✆ **907/288-3667;** www.ternlakeinn.com), a lodge surrounded by mountains and hiking opportunities with four airy, well-made rooms overlooking a pond. The inn has many amenities, including an on-site fishing guide, Chugach Backcountry Fishing. This is a place to spend a few days of quiet, as you'd be too sorry to leave if you stopped only overnight. Summer rates are $175 to $200 double, winter $100.

MILE 32   **Moose Creek** has a viewing platform to watch thousands of spawning salmon, in season; half a mile on, the Trail Lake Fish Hatchery sits on the edge of Upper Trail Lake. This is the first of a string of sparkling mountain lakes that the road will follow for the next 15 miles.

MILE 18–0   Down among the big spruces of the coastal forest, the highway comes to **Seward.**

CHUGACH NATIONAL FOREST: DO-IT-YOURSELF WILDERNESS

I've lived near the Chugach National Forest all my life, but it wasn't until well into adulthood that I had seen all its parts and appreciated its vastness and variety. Still, I doubt I'll ever really know this seemingly infinite land. **Prince William Sound,** just one of the Chugach's three parts, has 3,500 miles of shoreline among its folded islands and deeply penetrating fjords and passages. The **Copper River Delta** is another world entirely. Unlike the musty secrets of the Sound's obscure passages, the delta opens to the sky like a heavenly plain of wind and light, its waving green colors splashed by the airiest brushstrokes. It's a huge area: Driving across the delta and back from Cordova takes most of a day. The western part of the national forest, on the **Kenai Peninsula,** is largely alpine. It's got remote, unclimbed peaks, but also many miles of family hiking trails, accessible fishing streams, and superb campgrounds.

The Chugach is managed primarily for recreation and conservation. President Theodore Roosevelt created it in 1907. The next historic moment for the national forest came with the 1989 *Exxon Valdez* oil spill, which evolved into a story of conservation politics, when environmentalists demanded Exxon pay to stop large-scale logging on private lands that threatened to further damage in the Sound. Logging had never occurred on national forest lands in the Sound. Ultimately, Exxon was forced to pay $1 billion to a recovery fund, half of which government trustees spent to buy back timber rights in the Sound and beyond, protecting the trees. Here and elsewhere in the spill region, the newly purchased protected lands include 1,419 miles of coastline and almost as much land as is in all of Yosemite National Park.

Essentials

GETTING THERE & GETTING AROUND   There are many ways to the Chugach National Forest. For Prince William Sound, use Whittier, Valdez, or Cordova as gateways; for the Copper River Delta, go through Cordova. Trails and campgrounds on the Kenai Peninsula generally meet the Seward or Sterling highways, or spur roads from the highways. The individual town listings later in this chapter provide details on how to get there and into that part of the national forest.

VISITOR INFORMATION   The most central place for information on the national forest is the Alaska Public Lands Information Center in Anchorage (p. 220). You can download a 16-page guide to the forest at www.alaskageographic. org (click on "Trip Planning"). For general forest inquiries, you can also contact the **forest headquarters,** 3301 C St., Ste. 300, Anchorage, AK 99503 (✆ **907/743-9500;** www.fs.usda.gov/chugach). The national forest also has three ranger district offices, where you can get up-to-date local information and personal advice: **Glacier Ranger District,** 145 Forest Station Rd., near the Seward Highway off Alyeska Road, in Girdwood (✆ **907/783-3242**); **Seward Ranger District,** 334 4th Ave. (at Jefferson St.), in Seward (✆ **907/224-3374**); and **Cordova Ranger District,** 612 2nd St. (at Browning St.), in Cordova (✆ **907/424-7661**). You can't reserve campground sites and remote cabins through these local offices—for that, you must use the national system listed below under "Where to Stay"—but you can call them with questions.

Getting Outside

HIKING, MOUNTAIN-BIKING & BACKPACKING

Alaska's best long trails lead through the mountain passes of Chugach National Forest, including historic gold-rush trails and portions of the original Iditarod trail (the race doesn't use these southern portions). The Forest Service maintains **public cabins** on many of these trails and in other remote spots reachable only with a boat or small plane. If the nights you need are available, you can use the cabins instead of a tent on a backpacking trip. Or make a cabin your destination and spend a few days there hiking or fishing. I've covered trails near Cordova under "Cordova: Hidden Treasure," later in this chapter, and some shorter hikes are mentioned below with the campgrounds under "Where to Stay." In addition, the superb Winner Creek Trail and Crow Pass Trail, from Girdwood, are described on p. 271. Two excellent trail guides cover the peninsula: **55 *Ways to the Wilderness,*** by Helen Nienhueser and John Wolfe (5th edition, The Mountaineers), with detailed coverage in readable prose; and ***Kenai Trails*** (✆ **866/257-2757;** www.alaskageographic.org), with a detailed topographic map along with each trail description. **Trails Illustrated** publishes excellent plastic recreation maps of the region (✆ **800/962-1643;** www.natgeomaps.com).

CARTER LAKE TRAIL   An excellent dayhike starts from mile 33 of the Seward Highway, a few miles east of Tern Lake (p. 285), rising about 1,000 feet over 2 miles to alpine views and Carter Lake, which is stocked with rainbow trout.

JOHNSON PASS TRAIL   The 23-mile trail climbs to a pair of lakes above the tree line at the 1,450-foot Johnson Creek Summit, tracing impressively narrow mountain valleys. The route, part of the Iditarod National Historic Trail, leads from near the Trail Lake Fish Hatchery, at mile 32 of the

Seward Highway, to near the Granite Creek Campground, on the highway at mile 63. Plan to do the trail as an overnight and have transportation ready at each end.

LOST LAKE TRAIL & PRIMROSE TRAIL   With fields of alpine wildflowers and small lakes, these connected trails offer one of the most beautiful hikes in the area. Snow lasts until late in the season at the top. The upper, northern trail head is at the 10-site Primrose Campground, on vast Kenai Lake, 17 miles from Seward off the Seward Highway on Primrose Road. The trail rises through hemlock past a waterfall about 2 miles up (look for the spur to the right when you hear water), past an old mining cabin, and then through ever-smaller trees and above the tree line. A Forest Service cabin is on a 2-mile spur about 11 miles along the 16-mile route. Strong hikers can do the whole trail in a long day, but it makes more sense to hike in and out on the upper end, or to spend the night along the way. The lower, Lost Lake trail head is in a subdivision near Seward; ask for directions at one of the visitor centers.

RESURRECTION PASS TRAIL   This gold-rush trail begins 4 miles above the town of Hope and runs over the top of the Kenai Peninsula to Cooper Landing (see "Cooper Landing: Road Meets River," later in this chapter). It's a beautiful, remote, yet well-used trail for hiking, mountain-biking, Nordic skiing, or snowshoeing; it rises through forest, crosses the alpine pass, and then descends again to a highway trail head where you'll need to have transportation waiting. The 39-mile trail has eight public-use cabins, available for $35 to $45 a night. (See "Where to Stay," below, for reservation information.) The cabins are well spaced to cover the trail in an easy 5 days; cabins on lakes have boats for fishing. Cabins book up well ahead winter and summer, but there are lots of good camping spots, too. The **Devil's Pass and Summit Lake trails** cut off from the Resurrection to the Seward Highway south of Summit Lake, shortening the route. The difficulty of doing the

Resurrection Pass Trail.

whole trail, by any of the entrances, is that you need either two cars or someone willing to drive you back to your starting point.

RUSSIAN LAKES TRAIL This trail begins in Cooper Landing (see "Cooper Landing: Road Meets River," later in this chapter), near the end of the Resurrection Pass Trail, and leads to three remote cabins and a series of lakes. There's excellent fishing and wildlife viewing (bears are common). It's less than 3 miles, with little elevation gain, to Lower Russian Lake and the cabin there, or you can make a backpacking trip over the entire 21 miles.

FISHING

The national forest contains some of the most famous, and crowded, fishing banks in Alaska, including the **Russian River,** near Cooper Landing, with its incredible run of red salmon in July and good fishing lasting into September. The easiest access is at the Russian River Campground, just west of the village. There are plenty of other roadside salmon streams and remote fishing rivers and lakes in the national forest where you can lose sight of other anglers. Some remote lakes have Forest Service cabins for rent on their shores, with rowboats. The Forest Service publishes information on these opportunities. See chapter 11 for other information sources.

SEA KAYAKING & BOATING

A variety of Prince William Sound tour boats are listed in the Whittier, Valdez, and Cordova sections of this chapter. Whittier offers the greatest number of boats and the most impressive scenery, with big glaciers that come right to the water. It's also possible to rent your own boat there.

All three communities also have operators offering sea-kayak rentals and guided outings of various lengths. The best sea kayaking is near Cordova or east of Whittier. The long fjords reached from Whittier feature calving glaciers, narrow passages, and Forest Service cabins, but to get out there, you need a boat ride first—the waters right around Whittier aren't as interesting—and that is expensive. The local sea-kayaking operators can help you arrange drop-off service. Cordova has more interesting waters near town, so you can paddle from the boat harbor. Those who haven't done much sea kayaking should consider a guided day trip rather than an overnight.

Where to Stay

CABIN & CAMPSITE RESERVATIONS

Some campsites in the Chugach can be reserved in advance, and public-use cabins are available only by reservation. The **National Recreation Reservation Service** works well, but it is operated from upstate New York, so reservation agents are not the best people to ask for information about which remote cabin or campground is right for you. Instead, use the Chugach National Forest website (www.fs.usda.gov/chugach) and follow up with questions with the ranger stations (p. 286). The easiest way to reserve a cabin or campsite is online at **www.recreation.gov**, because the availability calendars allow you to shop for open days at various places. To reserve by phone, call ✆ **877/444-6777** or 518/885-3639. The phone lines are open March through October daily 10am to midnight Eastern time, November through February 10am to 10pm. The system accepts payment by debit or credit card: American Express, Discover, MasterCard, or Visa. All reservations open 180 days ahead on a first-come, first-served basis.

Chugach National Forest: Do-It-Yourself Wilderness

THE KENAI PENINSULA & PRINCE WILLIAM SOUND

REMOTE CABINS

Chugach National Forest maintains more than 40 remote recreation cabins for rent to the public. This is simple shelter: Cabins don't have electricity or plumbing; you bring your own sleeping bags, cooking equipment, and other gear; and the cabin is only as clean as the last user left it. But no other room you can rent has a better location or greater privacy. Some cabins are along hiking and skiing trails, others on shores where boats and kayaks can pull up, and others on remote fishing lakes accessible only by floatplane. You can stay up to a week in most, with a summer limit of 3 days in the Resurrection Trail cabins.

The Forest Service produces descriptions of each cabin online or in printed form. You will also need a trail guide and detailed map (see "Getting Outside," above). Some cabins rent for $35 a night, most for $45 a night. Typically, the price of the cabin itself is not your major expense: You'll need a way to get there, either by plane, by boat, or by having a vehicle to drive to a trail head and then hiking. If you're flying, contact flight services in the nearest town (listed in the sections later in this chapter) to find out the cost before you book the cabin. Flight time is several hundred dollars an hour. You can rent the camping equipment you'll need at the businesses listed in the Anchorage chapter on p. 251, but you should talk to a ranger first to get details about access and what to take. And start planning early. For summer dates, many cabins book up the second they become available on the reservation system, 6 months prior. This is not an exaggeration. Reservation details are above.

CAMPGROUNDS

Forest Service campgrounds mostly have pit toilets and water from hand pumps, and roads usually are not paved. But some of these places are truly spectacular. I've listed them in order of distance from Anchorage, counting in reverse direction on the Seward Highway mileposts. For information on campgrounds below mile 60, call the Seward Ranger District; for the others, call the Glacier Ranger District, in Girdwood (see p. 286 for phone numbers). Sites in a few of the following campgrounds, as noted, take reservations through the national system explained above. RVs and cars can access and park at all of the campgrounds.

Williwaw & Black Bear   These two campgrounds are next to each other near Portage Glacier, along a creek where you can watch spawning red salmon in mid-August (no fishing is allowed). Williwaw is one of the more developed campgrounds in the national forest, with paved roads and pumped water, and is intended primarily for RVs.

Mile 4, Portage Glacier Rd. (turn at mile 78.9 Seward Hwy.). Williwaw: 59 sites. Reservations accepted with additional fee. $12 single site per night; $18 double site per night. Black Bear: 12 sites. $10 per night.

Bertha Creek   This one's in the high country.

Mile 65.5, Seward Hwy. 12 sites. $14 per night.

Granite Creek   Near the Johnson Pass trail head.

Mile 63, Seward Hwy. 19 sites. $14 per night.

Porcupine   This campground near the gold-rush village of Hope is among the most beautiful in Chugach. The widely separated sites are on a mountainside overlooking Turnagain Arm, five with sweeping ocean views. Thick trees make for privacy, but also mosquitoes. Bring repellent. Two good dayhikes leave from the campground: The level 5-mile trail to **Gull Rock** is a good family ramble, and with some effort, you can scramble down to remote beaches along the way, where we've enjoyed a picnic. The **Hope Point Trail** is a stiff climb that rises 3,600 feet to expansive views.

At the end of the Hope Hwy. 24 sites. $14 per night.

Tenderfoot Creek   This pleasant campground lies across Summit Lake from the Seward Highway as it passes through a narrow mountain valley above the tree line. Campsites look out on the water from a peaceful, sunny hillside. The nearby Summit Lake Lodge, described on p. 284, offers meals and is the only business on the Seward Highway for many a mile.

Mile 46, Seward Hwy. 27 sites. $10 per night.

Ptarmigan Creek & Trail River   Near the tiny towns of Moose Pass and Crown Point, the Ptarmigan Creek campground is at the start of the trail to Ptarmigan Lake, 4 miles away with only 500 feet in elevation gain—a good place for a picnic or fishing for Dolly Varden char and rainbow trout. Trail River campground is a mile away and on the other side of the highway.

Mile 23, Seward Hwy. 16 and 91 sites, respectively. Reservations accepted, with additional fee. Ptarmigan Creek $14 per night. Trail River $10 for both single and double sites per night.

Primrose   Another favorite, this lovely campground lies on the edge of Kenai Lake and at the base of the Primrose Trail to Lost Lake, one of the area's most beautiful (see "Getting Outside," above). This campground is the closest to Seward that has a sense of natural isolation.

Mile 17, Seward Hwy. 10 sites. $10 per night.

Russian River   This large, well-developed campground mainly serves fishermen pursuing red salmon on the river. When the fishing is good, the campground can be full and noisy. Overnight parking is $6. Reserve ahead.

Mile 52, Sterling Hwy., just west of Cooper Landing. Reservations accepted, with additional fee. 80 sites. 3-day limit. Flush toilets. $18 single site per night; $28 double site per night.

Cooper Creek   The campground has two halves bisected by the highway right in Cooper Landing. Ten sites are on the Kenai River; the balance are across the road and somewhat better screened and separated.

Mile 50.7, Sterling Hwy. Reservations accepted. 26 sites. $18 single site per night; $28 double site per night.

Quartz Creek   Thickly wooded sites stand well separated a bit off the highway, many right on Kenai Lake and others with good mountain views. There is a boat ramp in the campground and a lodge nearby.

Quartz Creek Rd., at mile 45 Sterling Hwy. 45 sites. Reservations accepted. Flush toilets, boat launch. $18 single site per night; $28 double site per night.

Crescent Creek   This campground is quieter and more secluded than others near Cooper Landing, at the Crescent Lake trail head. The 6.5-mile trail leads to the Crescent Lake Forest Service Cabin, where renters have a boat for grayling fishing.

Mile 3 Quartz Creek Rd., at mile 45 Sterling Hwy. 9 sites. $10 single site per night; $28 double site per night.

WHITTIER: DOCK ON THE SOUND

Whittier is Anchorage's portal to Prince William Sound. Although Anchorage itself is on Upper Cook Inlet, that muddy, fast-moving water is little used for recreational boating. Whittier, on the other hand, stands on the edge of a long fjord in the northwest corner of the Sound, whose clear waters are full of salmon, orcas, and otters, and bounded by rocky shores, rainforests, and glaciers. The only land access to Whittier is a railway tunnel that has been paved for cars, making it North America's longest highway tunnel—and one of the most inconvenient to use. The tunnel has only one lane to be shared by traffic and trains in both directions, and the tunnel often must be aired out, so vehicles have to wait, sometimes for an hour or more.

Whittier certainly has major advantages for visitors seeking to get out on the water. The ocean is calmer here than on excursions to Kenai Fjords National Park, so seasickness is rare, and the glaciers are even more numerous. Prince William Sound boats also see otters and sometimes whales; Kenai Fjords tours, on the other hand, more often see whales and see more birds. Sea kayakers also have great places to go from Whittier. Almost all of Prince William Sound is in Chugach National Forest, with its public-use cabins in lovely, remote spots on the shores (see the previous section). I do recommend going to Whittier for all this—and the cute and unusual businesses along the harbor add to the experience if you have some extra time, and you can find a good, simple meal there.

There's little reason to go to Whittier other than the Sound, unless you're on a quest to find the oddest towns in America. Most of the roughly 180 townspeople live in a single 14-story concrete building with dark, narrow hallways. The grocery store is on the first floor and the medical clinic on the third. The rest of the people live in one other building. The **Begich Towers,** as the dominant structure is called, was built during the 1940s, when Whittier's strategic location on the Alaska Railroad and at the head of a deep Prince William Sound fjord

Whittier's boat harbor.

Be Prepared

Whittier lacks a bank, large stores, or downtown businesses. Bring what you need. But if you forget something, a little harbor store is amazingly well stocked.

made it a key port in the defense of Alaska. Today, with its barren gravel ground and ramshackle warehouses and boat sheds, the town maintains a stark military-industrial character. The pass above the town is a funnel for frequent whipping winds, it always seems to rain, and the glaciers above the town keep it cool even in summer (although it's glorious in the sun).

Essentials

GETTING THERE   By Car: Take the Seward Highway to the Portage Glacier Road, at mile 78.9 (48 miles from Anchorage). The road through the 2¾-mile-long World War II rail tunnel to Whittier is only one lane and also accommodates trains, so you'll have to wait your turn. Get the schedule on the tunnel's website (www.tunnel.alaska.gov), through its phone recording (🕾 **877/611-2586** or 907/566-2244), or by tuning to 1610AM in Portage or 530AM in Whittier. Checking the schedule may help you avoid a wait of an hour or more if you miss an opening, but you can also wait if you arrive just on time at peak hours when there can be too many vehicles to get through in one open period. Typically, the crowding comes in the summer around 6 to 7pm Friday to Sunday. In summer, the first opening from Whittier is at 5:30am and the last to Whittier is at 11:15pm. The tunnel closes at night. Winter hours are shorter and changeable, so check ahead. The toll is $12 for cars; $20 for RVs, cars with trailers, or large vans. It is charged only going toward Whittier. Special permits are required for huge vehicles (over 14 ft. high or 10 ft. wide). Parking in Whittier is $10 a day.

By Train: If you take a day trip on the Sound from Anchorage (or Girdwood)—the way most people use Whittier—you can leave the car behind and take the train. The large tour operators will book it for you when you buy your boat ticket. The **Alaska Railroad** (🕾 **800/544-0552** or 907/265-2494; www.alaskarailroad.com) runs a daily train timed to match the schedules of Prince William Sound tour boats. Unless you have planned an activity or tour on the water, however, you'll find the 6-hour stay in Whittier is too long to just hang around. The round-trip fare is $80, one-way $65, half price ages 2 to 11.

By Bus: Boat tour operators have buses that can save time and money over the train. Reserve when you buy your boat cruise ticket.

By Ferry: Ferries of the **Alaska Marine Highway System** (🕾 **800/ 642-0066;** www.ferryalaska.com) connect Whittier, Valdez, and Cordova. The fast ferry *Chenega* crosses 110 miles of Prince William Sound in 3 hours. Passenger areas are enclosed, quiet, and smooth—hardly like being on a boat at all. The fare from Whittier to Valdez or Cordova is $89 for an adult, half price ages 6 through 11, free 5 and under. A 15-foot car costs $105 to take along. The Whittier-to-Valdez run creates the opportunity for a wonderful loop tour of a couple of days or more: Drive Anchorage to Whittier, take the ferry to Valdez, and then return to Anchorage via the Glenn Highway or continue up the Richardson Highway to Fairbanks and drive back to Anchorage on the Parks Highway. See chapter 3 for a complete loop itinerary.

Whittier is the main port connecting Southeast and Southcentral Alaska via the oceangoing ferry *Kennicott*. The ship's route runs from Prince Rupert, B.C., to Juneau, across the Gulf of Alaska to Whittier, around the Kenai Peninsula to Homer, and out to Kodiak. The loop takes 2 weeks. The fare for the 2-day voyage between Whittier and Juneau is $221 for adults, $508 for a 15-foot vehicle, and roughly $200 to $350 for a cabin. See "Exploring Southeast Alaska," in chapter 5, for more about the system. A Chugach National Forest ranger interprets the scenery on the Prince William Sound ferry in the summer.

VISITOR INFORMATION   There is no visitor center, but you can contact the **Whittier Chamber of Commerce** (© **907/677-9448;** www.whittieralaska chamber.org), which includes a business directory with links on its website.

The people at the Harbormaster's office are helpful and maintain public toilets and showers; it's the two-story building at the harbor (© **907/472-2327,** ext. 6; www.whittieralaska.gov).

SPECIAL EVENTS   Whittier holds a summer-long halibut derby and a silver salmon derby from July 1 through September. The town also has an old-fashioned Fourth of July celebration, beginning with fireworks at midnight on July 3. Contact the Chamber of Commerce, above, for information on any of the events.

Getting Out on the Sound

Whittier is the entrance to western Prince William Sound, at the end of one of many long, deep fjords where marine mammals and eagles are common. Glaciers at the heads of many of the fjords dump ice in the water for the tour boats that cruise from Whittier.

LARGE TOUR BOATS

Several companies with offices in Anchorage offer day-trip tours to the Sound's western glaciers. Besides having spectacular scenery, the water is calm, making seasickness unlikely—for the queasy, this is a better choice than Kenai Fjords National Park. Each operator times departures to coordinate with the daily Alaska Railroad train from Anchorage, described above, which means they have up to 6 hours for the trip, depending on the speed of the boats, the pacing of the tours, and the route. Between the train and boat fare, expect to spend around $250 per person for this day's outing, leaving Anchorage at 10am and returning at 9:30pm. You can save $30 a person and up to 3 hours by taking a bus the tour boat arranges instead of the train. If you have two or more people, you can save by renting a car and driving. You will be able to buy meals onboard or one will be provided.

Major Marine Tours   This company operates a smaller, 149-passenger vessel at a slower pace than Phillips—they hit a mere 10 glaciers but spend more time waiting for them to calve. Another important feature: The tour is narrated by a Chugach National Forest ranger, not the company. The route goes up Blackstone Bay, not to College Fjord. The salmon and prime rib buffet is $19 for adults, $9 for children. It's quite good. Time on the water is 5 hours. Check on prices, as they are expected to change.

© **800/764-7300** or 907/274-7300. www.majormarine.com. $107 adults, $53 children ages 11 and under.

Phillips Cruises and Tours   The 26-glacier cruise travels the Sound on a fast three-deck catamaran, allowing it to cover many miles of scenery and count the glaciers in College Fjord as they go, more territory than the competitors reach. The tour also now includes narrow Esther Passage and a visit to a sea lion haul-out. The boat ride is 5 hours, so if you use their bus, you cut the total time from Anchorage to under 8½ hours. The boat has a snack bar and bar, and a hot lunch is provided with the fare.

ⓒ **800/544-0529** or 907/276-8023. www.26glaciers.com. $139 adults, $79 children 11 and under; fees $17 per passenger.

Prince William Sound Glacier Cruises   The emphasis of this Native-owned firm is on the indigenous culture and natural history of the Sound, while also showing off the area's glaciers and wildlife. Cruises last 4 or 6 hours. The shorter cruises go to Blackstone Bay only, where crew members gather plankton for guests to observe through microscopes; the 6-hour trip travels to the more impressive Surprise Glacier and includes Esther Passage and a stop at a salmon hatchery. Interpretation is by captain and crew, and a meal of crab cakes is included in the price.

ⓒ **877/777-4054** or 907/277-2131. www.princewilliamsound.com. $114 4-hr. cruise, $144 6-hr. cruise; ages 2–11 half price.

SMALL-BOAT TOURS

Instead of getting on a giant tour boat with a crowd of people, you can go on a small boat with a local whom you'll get to know as they show off favorite places and land on beaches to picnic and walk. If you see a whale or other point of interest, you stay as long or as short a time as you like. You give up the comfort of a large vessel, you pay more, and most small boats have a four-person minimum.

Lazy Otter Charters   A family runs three sturdy aluminum boats built for these waters, specializing in personal tours, water transportation, and kayaker drop-offs. They operate with a minimum of four passengers; by paying the four-person minimum, you can have a boat to yourself. For larger groups, their *Qayaq Spirit* carries up to 30 passengers for kayaking or sightseeing cruises. Bring your own food.

On the Whittier waterfront (P.O. Box 747), Whittier, AK 99693. ⓒ **800/587-6887** or 907/694-6887. www.lazyottercharters.com. 4-5-hr. cruise $185 per person; 8-9-hr. cruise $235 per person.

Sound Eco Adventures   Beloved Gerry Sanger is a retired wildlife biologist who spent years researching the waterfowl and ecology of Prince William Sound.

The Sound by Yacht

The *Discovery* is a classic old wooden vessel, and accommodations are nautical and yachtlike, not as fancy even as a small cruise ship. But it's comfortable, groups are only about a dozen per trip, and the owner and skipper knows the Sound well, taking passengers to its most intimate and beautiful spots—places such as that cove that hardly anyone knows about. It's like a first-class wilderness lodge afloat. A 7-day itinerary, including 5 nights aboard and 2 nights at a B&B in Anchorage, starts at $3,900 per person, double occupancy. Contact Discovery Voyages (ⓒ 800/324-7602; www.discoveryvoyages.com).

A few times a week, he carries up to six passengers on whale, wildlife, and glacier sightseeing and photography tours from his speedy 30-foot aluminum boat. Fares include snacks; bring your own lunch.

P.O. Box 707, Whittier, AK 99693. ✆ **888/471-2312** or 907/472-2312. www.soundecoadventure. com. 8-hr. glacier and wildlife tour $194; 5-hr. sightseeing tour $154.

FISHING

About 30 charter fishing boats operate out of Whittier, the closest saltwater fishing to Anchorage, mostly targeting halibut and occasionally salmon. Contact the Whittier Chamber of Commerce or Harbormaster (see "Visitor Information," above) for a list of operators. **MJ's Bread N Butter Charters** (✆ **888/472-2396** or 907/472-2396; www.breadnbuttercharters.com) has a long reputation. They charge $285 per person for a day of halibut fishing.

You can rent your own boat, for fishing, exploring, or even sleeping, from **Whittier Boat Rentals** (✆ **907/232-2783;** www.alaska-boat-rentals.com). They carry quality equipment, including boats suitable for an extended trip. Full-day rentals range from $550 to $950; they rent rods and shrimp pots as well. Or book a guided charter, with a choice of vessels with experienced skippers, from **Whittier Marine Charters** (✆ **907/440-9510;** www.fishwhittier.com).

SEA KAYAKING

Whittier is a popular starting point for kayak trips to beautiful and protected western Prince William Sound. Day trips for beginners paddle along the shore near Whittier, often visiting a bird colony, or take a boat 5 miles from the harbor to Shotgun Cove and paddle back. Longer multiday trips go by boat to waters where you can visit glaciated fjords and paddle narrow passages. **Alaska Sea Kayakers** (✆ **877/472-2534** or 907/472-2534; www.alaskaseakayakers.com) offers 3- and 5-hour day trips, for $79 to $220; paddles at Blackstone Glacier that begin and end with a charter boat ride, for $330; and extended trips. Guides are well trained, and occasional weekend instructional clinics are offered (check the website for times). Offices are at each end of Whittier Harbor. **Prince William Sound Kayak Center** (✆ **877/472-2452** or 907/472-2452; www.pwskayak center.com) offers guided half-day trips starting at $80, as well as full days and other options, and rents kayaks. They've been in business since 1981.

Most self-guided kayakers charter a boat to drop them off among the islands beyond the long, deep fjord in which Whittier is located. There are six Forest Service cabins in this idyllic area (reserve 6 months ahead). Flat sites suitable for a tent are not plentiful on these rocky shores, so do some research with the Forest Service or Alaska Public Lands Information Center in Anchorage before you go (the tent platforms at Surprise Cove State Marine Park make an excellent remote base camp). For information and cabin reservations, see "Chugach National Forest: Do-It-Yourself Wilderness," earlier in this chapter.

Where to Stay & Eat

Most meals served in Whittier are for people grabbing a sandwich or fish and chips while waiting for a boat or otherwise passing through. Several such restaurants are in the triangle at the east end of the harbor.

June's Whittier Condo Suites ★ These units are on the top two floors of the Begich Towers, the concrete building that dominates Whittier. A small elevator leads to rooms with breathtaking views and hummingbirds feeding at the high-rise windows. You are essentially renting an equipped apartment for the night; you check in at apartment 1506. All units have full kitchens, and some have big living rooms that are the equivalent of a nice family home. Housekeeping is first rate. The friendly hostess, June Miller, and her husband, Ken, have been in business here almost 20 years.

P.O. Box 715, Whittier, AK 99693. www.whittiersuitesonline.com. © **888/472-6001** or 907/472-6001. Fax 907/472-6000. 12 units. $155–$445 double. Extra adult $10. AE, MC, V. **Amenities:** Harbor shuttle. *In room:* TV/DVD, Internet, kitchen.

SEWARD: GATEWAY TO RESURRECTION BAY & KENAI FJORDS

Located by the broad fjord of Resurrection Bay, Seward's main reason to exist has always been its ocean dock. The agreeable little town started life as a place to fish and to get off boats arriving in Alaska, then continued as a place for Alaskans and visitors to get *on* boats and see the bay and Kenai Fjords National Park. With the growth of the cruise industry, Seward again is a place to get off the boat. Many cruises that cross the Gulf of Alaska start or end here, with their passengers taking a bus to or from the airport in Anchorage. The few cruise passengers who spend any time in town find a mountainside grid of streets lined with old wood-frame houses and traditional businesses operating in historic store fronts. The community has a lot of pride, and wonderful murals appear on the side of many buildings.

Seward's history is among the oldest in Alaska. The Russian conquistador Alexander Baranof stopped here in 1793, named it Resurrection Bay, and built a ship, which later sank, perhaps because Baranof's workers didn't have proper materials. Gold prospectors blazed trails from here to finds on Turnagain Arm starting in 1891, and in 1907 the army linked those trails with others all the way to Nome, finishing the Iditarod Trail. Today that route is discontinuous south of Anchorage, but you can follow it through Seward and hike a portion of it on the Johnson Pass Trail north of town. More relevant for current visitors and the local economy, the federal government took over a failed railroad-building effort in 1915, finishing the line to Fairbanks in 1923. The train ride to Anchorage, daily during the summer, is still supremely beautiful.

Seward's in-town highlight is the Alaska SeaLife Center, a research aquarium that's open to the public. Combined with Seward's excellent ocean fishing, the national park, the wonderful hiking trails, and the unique and attractive town itself, the center helps make Seward well worth a 2-day visit.

Essentials

GETTING THERE   By Car: See "The Seward Highway: A Road Guide," earlier in this chapter, for making the spectacular 127-mile drive down from Anchorage. All major car-rental agencies are in Anchorage.

By Bus: The **Seward Bus Line** (© **888/420-7788** or 907/224-3608 in Seward, 907/563-0800 in Anchorage) makes a round-trip from Seward to Anchorage daily, year-round (except Sun Oct–Apr); the fare is $50 one-way, $95 round-trip. They'll pick up and drop off passengers anywhere en route and, for an extra $5, take you to the airport.

Fresh Water Lagoon

Harbor

Cruise Ship & State Ferry Dock

R e s u r r e c t i o n

B a y

0 1/4 mi
0 1/4 km

Seward Hwy.
4th Ave.

D St.
C St.
B St.
A St.
Monroe St.
Mt. Marathon Trail

1st Ave.
2nd Ave.
3rd Ave.
4th Ave.
5th Ave.
6th Ave.
Madison St.
Jefferson St.
Adams St.
Washington St.
Railway Ave.
Ballaine Blvd.

Anchorage
Seward
Juneau

ATTRACTIONS
Alaska SeaLife Center **16**
Iditarod Trailhead **14**
Seward Museum **8**
St. Peter's Episcopal Church **10**

HOTELS
Ballaine House B&B **6**
The Breeze Inn **2**
Harborview Inn **5**
Holiday Inn Express Seward **1**
Best Western Edgewater **13**
Moby Dick Hostel **7**
Murphy's Motel **4**
Van Gilder Hotel **9**

RESTAURANTS
Apollo Restaurant **11**
Christo's Palace **15**
Ranting Raven **12**
Ray's Waterfront **3**

The **Park Connection Motorcoach Service** (℗ **800/266-8625** or 907/245-0200; www.alaskatravel.com/bus-lines) connects Seward with Anchorage, Talkeetna, and Denali National Park twice daily in summer in each direction with big, comfortable coaches. The fare is $55 between Seward and Anchorage, $145 between Seward and Denali, half off under age 12. Passengers going to Anchorage get a free pass to the Anchorage Museum at Rasmuson Center.

By Train: The Coastal Classic route between Anchorage and Seward is one of miraculous beauty. The **Alaska Railroad** (℗ **800/544-0552** or 907/265-2494; www.alaska railroad.com) offers passenger service from Anchorage and back daily in summer. The route is even prettier than the highway, passing close by glaciers and following a ledge

Coastal Classic train route.

Mount Marathon Race.

halfway up the narrow, vertical Placer River gorge, where it ducks into tunnels and pops out at bends in the river. The landscape looks as it did when the first person beheld it. The fare for basic service is $75 one-way, $119 round-trip; children ages 2 to 11 half price. Gold Star Service on double-decker cars with white tablecloth dining is $130 adults one-way, $219 round-trip. The railroad also offers packages with lodging and activities in Seward. Don't try to do it in 1 day from Anchorage—the 16-hour marathon is too much. A rental car will almost always be cheaper for the day than the train, but here's a fluke of pricing and taxation that could save money: Rental-car taxes are so high in Anchorage that, depending on how long you keep your car, you may find it makes financial sense to take the train to Seward, rent a car from there from the local office of **Hertz** (𝐶 **800/654-3131;** www.rentacaralaska.com), and return the car in Anchorage.

GETTING AROUND   You can easily cover downtown Seward on foot, but a little help is handy to get back and forth from the boat harbor. If it's not raining, a bike may be the best way. **Seward Bike Shop** (𝐶 **907/224-2448**), in a railcar near the depot at the harbor, rents high-performance mountain bikes and models good for just getting around town, plus accessory equipment. A cruiser is $12 half-day, $19 full day; a mountain bike is $18 and $30. For a cab, try **Alaska Mike's Taxi** (𝐶 **907/224-6453**) and **PJ's Taxi** (𝐶 **907/224-5555**).

VISITOR INFORMATION   The **Seward Chamber of Commerce,** P.O. Box 749, Seward, AK 99664 (𝐶 **907/224-8051;** www.seward.com), has a visitor center, on the right side of the Seward Highway as you enter town, that's open year-round (summer daily 8am–6pm; winter Mon–Fri 9am–5pm). The chamber can give business information and last-minute help in finding a room.

SPECIAL EVENTS   The **Fourth of July** is the biggest day of the year in Seward, when the whole town explodes with visitors, primarily from Anchorage. Besides the parade and many small-town festivities, the main attraction is the 3¼-mile **Mount Marathon Race,** run every year since it started as a bar bet in 1915. The racers go from the middle of town straight up rocky

Mount Marathon to its 3,022-foot peak, then tumble down again, arriving muddy and bloody at the finish line in town. Strong binoculars allow you to see the whole thing from town, including the pratfalls of the runners on their way down.

The huge **Silver Salmon Derby** starts the second Saturday of August, although excellent fishing continues into the fall, including the peak of the silver run. The chamber of commerce visitor centers can provide tickets and rules.

[FastFACTS] SEWARD

Bank   **Wells Fargo** is at 908 3rd Ave., with an ATM.

Hospital   **Providence Seward Medical Center** is at 417 1st Ave. (✆ **907/ 224-5205**).

Internet Access   Free at the **Seward Public Library,** 5th and Adams.

Police   For nonemergency situations, call the **Seward Police Department** (✆ **907/224-3338**) or, outside the city limits,

the **Alaska State Troopers** (✆ **907/224-3346**).

Post Office   At 5th Avenue and Madison Street.

Taxes   **Sales tax** is 7%. The **room tax** totals 11%.

Getting Outside

Here I've described things to do out of Seward other than visiting the national park, which includes the fjords and Exit Glacier. See "Kenai Fjords National Park," later in this chapter, for that information. Fishing and other marine activities are the main event in Seward.

DOG MUSHING & GLACIER FLIGHTS

When Mitch Seavey won the Iditarod Trail Sled Dog Race in 2004, many agreed it couldn't have happened to a nicer guy. He had made a lot of friends over the years offering rides with his dogs. **IdidaRide** (✆ **800/478-3139** or 907/224-8607; www.ididaride.com) is a family business, including the four boys (one is a Junior Iditarod champ), making use of their kennel on Old Exit Glacier Road off Herman Leirer Road. They offer summer rides in Seward and in winter in Sterling (near Soldotna). The summer ride uses a wheeled sled and a full, 12-dog team—not the real thing (no snow), but you get a feel for the dogs' power and intelligence. The 90-minute tour costs $59 for adults, $29 for children 11 and under. Husky puppies are available for cuddling, too.

Those willing to spend much more should consider mushing on snow at the height of summer by joining a helicopter tour to Godwin Glacier from the Seward Airport with **Godwin Glacier Dog Sled Tours** (✆ **888/989-8239** or 907/224-8239; www.alaskadogsled.com). A chopper lands at a camp of 100 dogs, where guests take a ride in the dog sled or even drive it themselves. The company also offers overnight camping on the ice. For the mushing program, they charge $450 adults, $420 children 12 and under; the overnight is $520 per person; or just fly up to the glacier for $300.

FISHING

Seward is renowned for its saltwater silver salmon fishing. The silvers start show-ing up in the bay in mid-July and last through September. You can catch the fish from shore, from Lowell Point south of town, or even near the boat harbor, but your chances of success are far greater from a boat. I prefer small, six-passenger boats because you can get to know the skipper better and can learn more about fishing. If your party has the whole boat, you can control where it goes, perhaps adding whale-watching or sightseeing to the day. Larger boats add more comfort and stability in the waves. The going rate for a guided charter, with everything provided, is around $199 per person, or $299 to go for salmon and halibut on the same day. Andrew Mezirow, a marine biologist and maritime instructor, operates two boats, including a 12-passenger vessel and a six-passenger boat custom-built for fishing salmon in Resurrection Bay year-round. Besides day fishing, he takes guests on multiday fishing expeditions to extremely remote and beautiful places. His business is **Crackerjack Sportfishing Charters** (☏ **800/566-3192** or 907/224-2606; www.crackerjackcharters.com). The office is on the boardwalk at the top of the harbor ramps.

There are many other fishing charter companies, mostly booked through central charter agencies, which make life simpler for visitors. The **Fish House** is the largest charter-fishing agency in Seward, located at the Small Boat Harbor. The store also sells and rents ocean-fishing and spin-casting gear, and carries some fly-fishing supplies. For charters, reserve ahead at P.O. Box 1209, Seward, AK 99664 (☏ **800/257-7760** or 907/224-3674; www.thefishhouse.net). If you want a small boat, ask to be put on a "six pack," as vessels licensed for six or fewer passengers are known.

HIKING

There are several excellent hiking trails near Seward. You can get a complete list and directions at the Kenai Fjords National Park Information Center (p. 308).

The **Mount Marathon Trail** is a tough hike to the top of a 3,022-foot mountain in less than 4 miles. The route of the famous Mount Marathon foot-race is the most strenuous choice, basically straight up from the end of Jefferson Street; the hikers' route starts at the corner of 1st Avenue and Monroe Street. Either trail rises steeply to the top of the rocky pinnacle and its incredible views. Allow all day, unless you're a racer; in that case, allow just under 45 minutes.

The **Caines Head State Recreation Area** (www.alaskastateparks.org, click on "Individual Parks") has a 7-mile coastal trail south of town. Parts of the trail are accessible only at low tide, so it's best done as an overnight or with some-one picking you up or dropping you off in a boat beyond the beach portion—the Miller's Landing water taxi offers this service (p. 301). The trail has gorgeous views, rocky shores, and a fascinating destination at the end—a towering prom-ontory with the concrete remains of Fort McGilvray, a World War II defensive emplacement. Take flashlights to poke around in the spooky, pitch-dark under-ground corridors and rooms, and imagine what each was used for (going in with-out lights is foolhardy). Three campsites are at Tonsina Point, about 2 miles in, and a state park public-use cabin is 2 miles farther (see "Where to Stay," below and "State Parks Cabin Reservations," p. 283). At North Beach, 4½ miles from the trail head, are two camping shelters, a ranger station, and the trails to the fort and South Beach. For an easy 2-mile hike to Fort McGilvray, start with a boat ride to North Beach. The main trail head is south of town on Lowell Point Road;

pull off in the lot right after the sewage plant, then cross the road through the gate and follow the dirt road until it becomes the trail. The Kenai Fjords National Park Information Center has tide conditions and advice.

SEA KAYAKING & WATER TAXI

Sunny Cove Sea Kayaking (© 800/770-9119 for reservations, or 907/224-4426; www.sunnycove.com) has earned a good reputation for guided kayaking in Resurrection Bay and beyond. Their day trips suitable for beginners are offered as part of the Kenai Fjords Tours trips to its Fox Island lodge. For a more ambitious day trip, and for multiday trips, they venture into the fjords (see the Kenai Fjords National Park section, later in this chapter). If you're on a budget, take one of Sunny Cove's tours from Seward. They launch from Lowell Point, following the shore toward Caines Head State Recreation Area, where you can see sea otters, seabirds, intertidal creatures, and the salmon in Tonsina Creek. Three-hour paddles are $65; 8-hour trips are $130. A trip to Fox Island is more expensive but comes with a fjords boat tour and salmon bake.

Another highly regarded sea-kayaking firm in Seward, **Kayak Adventures Worldwide** (© 907/224-3960; www.kayakak.com) offers a wide selection of day trips and expeditions; packages involving other activities, such as glacier hiking; and water taxi drop-off for clients. Owners Wendy and Dave Doughty have a strong education and environment ethic, and they make a point of serving families—they even have a couple of three-seat kayaks so kids can ride in the middle. Their guide training program is impressive. The couple's B&B, Bear Paw Lodge, is listed below; their storefront office downtown is at 328 3rd Ave.

Miller's Landing, at Lowell Point, 3 miles south of town (© 866/541-5739 or 907/224-5739; www.millerslandingak.com), is the primary water taxi operator in Seward, charging flat rates to take travelers to remote beaches and public cabins around the bay or to the national park—great for sea kayakers or those who want to get off on their own or for a one-way day hike to Caines Head (p. 300). Per person rates are $38 one-way, $48 round-trip to Caines Head; $275 round-trip to the Park Service cabin in Aialik Bay. The company rents kayaks ($55 double, $45 single per day) and skiffs, too ($110 for 4 hr.), and offers many other services (fishing charters, camping, cabins, and even potluck dinners).

Exploring the Town

Besides the Alaska SeaLife Center (see below), most of Seward's in-town attractions are of the modest, small-town variety. The **Iditarod Trailhead,** on the water just east of the SeaLife Center, is where pioneers entered Alaska. The broken concrete and twisted metal you see on the beach walking north are the last ruins of the Seward waterfront, which was destroyed by a tsunami wave in the 1964 earthquake. Sometimes you can see sea otters swimming just offshore. During silver salmon season, in August and September, it's possible to catch fish by casting from shore here, although your chances are far better from a boat (see "Fishing," above).

Seward Museum, at 3rd and Jefferson (© 907/224-3902), is a charming grandma's attic of a place, with clippings, memorabilia, and curiosities recalling the history of the town and of the Iditarod Trail, painter Rockwell Kent, and the ways of the past. Admission is $2 for adults, 50¢ under age 18. It's open during the summer daily from 10am to 5pm, in winter usually weekends noon to 4pm (call ahead). Evening slide programs take place during the summer months.

The steep-roofed **St. Peter's Episcopal Church** (☎ **907/224-3975**; www.stpeters-seward.org) is a sweet little chapel under the mountains at 2nd Avenue and Adams Street finished in 1906, within a few years of the town's founding. Behind the altar is a mural painted in 1925 by Dutch artist Jan Van Emple showing the Resurrection as if it had happened at Resurrection Bay. The apostles are depicted as real Alaska Natives and pioneers who were living in town at the time, in their contemporary dress.

St. Peter's Episcopal Church.

To get into the church, attend a Sunday morning service at 8 or 11am, or ask for the key at the Seward Museum or the Softly Silk shop at 416 4th Ave. (☎ **907/224-6088**).

Alaska SeaLife Center ★★★ The center's role as an important research institution makes it an especially vibrant and fascinating aquarium to see creatures from Alaska waters. You may have seen puffins diving into the water from a tour boat; here you can see what they look like flying *under* the water. Seabirds, harbor seals, octopus, and sea lions reside in three spectacular exhibits viewed from above or below—you can get within a few feet of the birds without glass. There are smaller tanks with fish, crab, and other creatures; a touch tank where you can handle starfish and other tide-pool animals; and exhibits on current ocean changes and hot research issues. A remarkable exhibit traces the life cycle of salmon; the staff hatches salmon eggs on a schedule, so fish at each stage of development will always be present in their realistic habitats. I don't want to oversell the place, however: The center is not as large as a big-city aquarium, and you'll likely spend no more than a couple of hours unless you sign up for one of the lectures or special behind-the-scenes programs for adults and children that happen all day.

301 Railway Ave. (P.O. Box 1329), Seward, AK 99664. ☎ **888/378-2525** or 907/224-6300. www.alaskasealife.org. $20 adults, $15 students (12–17 or with ID), $10 children 4–11, free for children 3 and under. May 14–Sept 14 Mon–Thurs 9am–6:30pm, Fri–Sun 8am–6:30pm; Sept 15–May 13 daily 10am–5pm. Hours may change; call or check website.

Where to Stay

Alaska's Point of View Reservation Service (www.alaskasview.com; ☎ **907/224-2323**) is a Seward lodging- and tour-booking agency. The website has a handy search function for B&Bs, cabins, hotel rooms, and all other lodgings. You can get a list of B&Bs from the chamber of commerce visitor center (p. 298).

Seward has several hotels beyond those I can list here; in fact, I'm not aware of a bad hotel in Seward. The **Holiday Inn Express Seward Harbor** (www.hiexpress.com/sewardak; ☎ **800/HOLIDAY** [465-4329] or 907/224-2550) stands right on the small boat harbor wall, with its ramp down to the floats, and is only steps from the railroad depot. The hotel has a charter-booking office and a tiny pool. The well-equipped rooms have red carpets but otherwise are typical of a national chain. Summer rates are $219 to $269 double, with the lower-priced units facing the parking lot instead of the harbor. Breakfast and Wi-Fi are included in the price.

Equally attractive to the Holiday Inn is the downtown **Best Western Hotel Edgewater,** 200 5th Ave. (www.hoteledgewater.com; ℂ **888/793-6800**). The unique building near the SeaLife Center looks across streets to the ocean on two sides. Rooms vary in shape and size and are decorated in bold colors. All were renovated in 2008 with pillow-top mattresses, flatscreen TVs, and other amenities. Summer rates are $199 to $289 double, including continental breakfast and Wi-Fi.

Save over either of those choices at **Murphy's Alaskan Inn** (www.murphys motel.com; ℂ **800/686-8191** or 907/224-8090), near the boat harbor, which has attractive, well-equipped rooms with views in a newer building and good budget rooms remodeled in 2009 in an older building. Summer rates are $129 to $169 double, winter $59 to $79, including Wi-Fi.

Ballaine House Bed and Breakfast ⚜ This 1905 house near downtown is a classic B&B, with wooden floors, a large living room, and tall, double-hung windows. It's on the National Register of Historic Places and the town walking tour. It's a social place with service that is accommodating and fun, and the hostess offers raincoats, binoculars, and other gear for outings; cooks breakfast to order; and even does laundry. The B&B can also book your activities and boats in Seward and some other towns, giving you the booking commission, which can save as much as 20%. The rooms are not large, suitable for only one or two people, and all bathrooms are shared. The B&B does not take children 7 and under.

437 3rd Ave. (P.O. Box 2051), Seward, AK 99664-2051. www.superpage.com/ballaine. ℂ **907/224-2362.** 5 units, none with private bathroom. $65–$85 double. Rates include full breakfast cooked to order. No credit cards. No children 7 and under. *In room:* TV/DVD, Wi-Fi.

Bear Paw Lodge 👫 An environmentally oriented couple running Kayak Adventures Worldwide (see above) open their remarkable log house in a forest outside of town to visitors with the same warmth and energy that has made their paddling business a success (and kayak customers get a discount, too). The lodge has four rooms: a big master bedroom under the eaves and three simpler but very comfortable rooms with shared bathroom. Guests use all common rooms, including cooking any meals in the large kitchen and using the broadband-connected computer, and there's a big hot tub on the deck. Check in at the kayak shop downtown at 328 3rd Ave.; you need a car and directions to get to the house, 4½ miles out of town.

P.O. Box 2249, Seward, AK 99664. www.sewardbearpawlodge.com. ℂ **907/224-3960.** Fax 907/224-2255. 4 units, 1 with private bathroom. $125 double with shared bathroom; $185 double with private bathroom. Extra person $15. Rate includes self-serve continental breakfast. **Amenities:** Hot tub; Internet access; TV/DVD in common room; grill. *In room:* Wi-Fi.

The Breeze Inn ★ Located at the busy boat harbor, this three-story hotel completed a large expansion in 2008 that added many spacious rooms, all with good amenities and a polished feel. The original wing is a bargain; it features older motel rooms, but they're clean and well maintained. The setup lets visitors choose the level of luxury they want and the price they want to pay, and the property is consistently well run. The location is the most convenient in town for a fishing charter or Kenai Fjords boat trip, which means the building occupies a busy harbor parking lot near the highway and isn't landscaped. A courtesy van helps guests get around town.

1306 Seward Hwy. (P.O. Box 2147), Seward, AK 99664-2147. www.breezeinn.com. ☏ **888/224-5237** or 907/224-5237. Fax 907/224-7024. 100 units. Summer $139–$279 double; winter $49–$119 double. Extra person $10. AE, DC, DISC, MC, V. **Amenities:** Restaurant; bar; courtesy van. *In room:* A/C, TV, fridge, hair dryer, Wi-Fi.

Harborview Inn 🍴   This inn offers rooms with lots of light and Mission-style furniture for reasonable rates by Seward's expensive standards; older rooms in an annex are not as appealing. The location, midway between the Small Boat Harbor and downtown, puts both within long walking distance. A variety of suites or off-site apartment units offer savings for families and large groups.

804 3rd Ave. (P.O. Box 1584), Seward, AK 99664. www.sewardhotel.com. ☏ **888/324-3217** or 907/224-3217. Fax 907/224-3218. 35 units, 4 apts. High season $149 double, $169–$299 apt.; low season $79 double, $99–$249 apt. Extra person $10. AE, DISC, MC, V. *In room:* TV, hair dryer, Wi-Fi. Closed Oct to mid-May.

Seward Windsong Lodge ★★   This hotel is the only one near Kenai Fjords National Park with a national park atmosphere. The big lobby, with its high ceiling, huge wood beams, fireplace, and cedar shingles, could be at Yellowstone. The location is out of town, among spruce trees on the broad valley of the Resurrection River, and the collection of buildings goes on and on. Rooms are in separate lodges with entry from exterior porches. They have a crisp feel, all with two queen-size beds and rustic-style furniture and good amenities, including large flatscreen TVs. Family suites are available with separate TVs in the kids' room. Staff members drive a schedule shuttle van to town and the railroad depot, and offer a daily trip to Exit Glacier.

The restaurant, the **Resurrection Roadhouse,** has lots of natural light, pale wood, and an exhaustive selection of Alaska craft brews on tap. The menu includes fish, venison, and ribs smoked in-house, as well as hand-thrown gourmet pizzas. Main courses for dinner range from $9 to $24. The restaurant and lodge close mid-September to mid-May.

Mile .5, Exit Glacier Rd., also known as Herman Leirer Rd. (P.O. Box 1889), Seward AK 99664. www.sewardwindsong.com. ☏ **888/959-9590** or 907/777-2800 in Anchorage, or 907/224-7116 in Seward. 180 units. High season $249–$299 double; low season $149–$199 double. Extra person 12 and over $15. AE, DISC, MC, V. Closed Oct–Apr. **Amenities:** Restaurant; courtesy van; Wi-Fi and Internet station in lobby. *In room:* TV/DVD.

Van Gilder Hotel ★   This 1916 building on the National Register of Historic Places was restored with authentic period details and decorated in a Victorian style that complements the woodwork and stained glass. The bedrooms are small, and some of the bathrooms that were added are tiny, all but one with shower stalls, not tubs, but that's all easy to forgive in a place that feels very cozy and very real. A community kitchen on the main floor allows guests to stop for a free hot drink at any time, or even cook their own meals. The hotel is a good value, yet it would be the first choice of many visitors who want to experience an authentic part of this interesting town. The location is right downtown.

308 Adams St. (P.O. Box 609), Seward, AK 99664. www.vangilderhotel.com. ☏ **800/478-0400** or 907/224-3079. Fax 907/224-3689. 23 units. High season $119 double with shared bathroom, $159–$179 with private bathroom, $219 suite; low season $59 double with shared bathroom, $69–$89 with private bathroom, $159 suite. Extra person $10. AE, DISC, MC, V. *In room:* TV, Wi-Fi.

A HOSTEL, CAMPING & CABINS

A friendly, multilingual family that lives in a remote area in the winter runs the **Moby Dick Hostel** in summer. It's at 432 3rd Ave., PO Box 624 (www.mobydickhostel.com; © **907/224-7072**). They charge $20 for a bunk, $64 for private hostel rooms, and $75 to $80 for kitchenette rooms. The bright colored hostel has Wi-Fi and is centrally located downtown. There is no lock-out or curfew, and the office is open 9 to 11am and 5 to 10pm.

The best campgrounds near Seward are those in Chugach National Forest, described under "Chugach National Forest: Do-It-Yourself Wilderness," earlier in this chapter, especially Primrose Campground on Kenai Lake (p. 290). The only campground in Kenai Fjords National Park is near Seward, the **Exit Glacier Campground,** at mile 8.5 of Herman Leirer Road (also known as Exit Glacier Rd.). The campground is on willow-covered gravel ground that plants haven't yet reclaimed from the retreating ice. Sites are far apart and almost completely private but lack any amenities—no picnic tables, fire grates, or anything. Use the food lockers and central cooking to keep bears away. Snow lingers into early June; later in the summer, the campground often fills by early evening. There is no fee for the 12 sites, and reservations are not taken. It's open for tents only and has pit toilets and hand-pump water.

In the town of Seward itself, the seaside **Waterfront Park** on Ballaine Boulevard is good for RV camping—units stand side by side like townhouses facing the ocean—but the tent sites are too noisy and exposed for my liking. Seward has tried to crack down on drinking and rowdiness in its campgrounds with partial success. The fee is $10 for tents, $15 for dry RV sites, $30 for RV sites with electricity and water; showers are $2. It's operated by the city parks and recreation department (www.cityofseward.net/parksrec; © **907/224-4055**). A quieter town campground is **Forest Acres Park,** among the spruce trees at Hemlock and Sealion Boulevard, just off Seward Highway near the Army Recreation Center. Fees are the same. Neither campground accepts reservations. RVs are welcome at Forest Acres, but there are no hookups.

The Alaska Division of Parks maintains two cabins for rent in the **Caines Head State Recreation Area,** south of town, and two in **Thumb Cove State Marine Park,** across the bay from Caines Head (see "State Parks Cabin Reservations," under "Exploring the Kenai Peninsula & Prince William Sound," earlier in this chapter). These cabins are in high demand and difficult to reserve, but there are good areas for camping in both parks. It's possible to hike to the Caines Head cabins (see "Hiking," earlier), but to get to Thumb Cove, you need a boat. Water taxi service is offered by Miller's Landing (p. 301). The Thumb Cove cabins lie in an impossibly steep bowl of mountains, a grand and lovely setting that, along with the excellent salmon fishing nearby, explains their popularity. Camping is permitted along the same beach without a permit, with plenty of space and an outhouse for campers' use.

Cabins in Chugach National Forest and Kenai Fjords National Park are mentioned in those sections.

Where to Eat

There are various places at the harbor to grab a sandwich or other quick meal on the way out to sea; they change too frequently for me to include them here. Downtown, the **Ranting Raven,** 228 4th Ave. (© **907/224-2228**), is a great little gift and coffee shop serving homemade pastries and light lunches, open

April through Christmas. Art shows open on the first Friday of the month through the visitor season, and the shop carries locally crafted jewelry.

For dessert, Seward also has a delightful old-fashioned confectioner, **Sweet Darlings,** 209 4th Ave. (✆ **907/224-3011;** www.sweetdarlings.com), with lots of candy, fudge, taffy, gelato, and such treats, in one of the downtown's historic storefronts.

Apollo Restaurant ☺ MEDITERRANEAN/SEAFOOD   Seward families come here for a menu that includes anything they might want: Greek and southern Italian cuisine, steaks, seafood, pizza, and much more. They'll even cook your own day's catch. The service is fast, skilled, and flexible, great for families with children. The dining room, with many booths, takes the Greek theme as far as it will go—I especially enjoyed the miniature Doric columns. They serve beer and wine.

229 4th Ave. ✆ **907/224-3092.** www.apollorestaurantak.com. Main courses $10–$24. AE, MC, V. Daily 11am–11pm.

Christo's Palace ★ SEAFOOD/ITALIAN/MEXICAN   I was skeptical of a restaurant with faux 1890s decor and Formica tables serving a family friendly menu of pizza, pasta, tacos, burgers, subs, fried fish, steaks, and much finer dining, including rack of lamb and stuffed halibut. Who could do so many things well? But I became a believer. First, the service was too friendly and efficient for me to keep up my guard. Next, the children's menu met their needs exactly, and my teen said the pizza was first rate. Finally, the seafood platter was prepared just right, consisting of fried salmon, halibut, shrimp, and scallops. Everything was served so quickly, the children didn't have time to squirm.

133 4th Ave. ✆ **907/224-5255.** www.christospalace.com. Lunch and dinner main courses $9–$38. AE, DC, DISC, MC, V. Daily 11am–11pm.

Ray's Waterfront ★★ STEAK/SEAFOOD   The lively, noisy dining room looks out from big windows across the small-boat harbor, with tables on terraces so everyone can see. The atmosphere is fun and the consistently good food is just right after a day on the water. Unlike many popular waterfront restaurants, Ray's has stayed up with the times, keeping the food interesting while keeping the traditional seafood choices many diners will be looking forward to (such as the famous plank salmon). On my last visit, the seafood chowder was tasty and so thick with goodies, the spoon almost stood up in the cup. The jambalaya was beautiful, not too spicy, and loaded with shrimp. Most important, they don't overcook the fresh local fish—and that's really all you can ask. Service is excellent when the restaurant isn't overrun with guests on holiday weekends. They have a full bar.

1316 4th Ave., at the small-boat harbor. ✆ **907/224-5606.** www.rayswaterfrontak.com. Dinner reservations recommended. Lunch $9–$17; dinner main courses $19–$35. AE, DISC, MC, V. 18% gratuity added for parties of 6 or more. Daily 11am–11pm. Closed Oct to mid-Apr.

KENAI FJORDS NATIONAL PARK

Kenai Fjords is all about remote rocks, mountains, and ice that meet the ocean, and the animals that live there. The park comprises 670,000 acres of the south coast and interior landmass of the Kenai Peninsula. The shore is exposed to the Gulf of Alaska, whose wild, recurrent storms beat against the mountainous shore unbuffered by any landmass from the vast expanse of the Pacific to the south. Wildlife thrives, but humans have never made a mark.

LEFT: **A group of sea lions;** TOP: **A mountain goat.**

The park's history has barely started. The fjords became a park only in 1980. In 1976, when the National Park Service explored more than 650 miles of coastline, including the park area, they didn't find a single human being. The same was true when geologists came in 1909. British explorer Capt. James Cook made the first maps of the fjords area in 1778, but saw no one and didn't land. We don't know much about Native Americans who lived in the fjords. Scientists have found some areas where people lived, or at least had camps, but no one knows exactly who they were or what they were doing here. Anthropologists call these people Unegkurmiut and believe they were Alutiiq, Eskimos who lived on the Pacific coast, closely related to the people of Prince William Sound and Kodiak Island.

The Natives probably never ventured inland over the impossibly rugged interior of the Kenai Peninsula, leaving its heart to be discovered in 1968, when the first mountain climbers crossed the Harding Ice Field, which covers most of the national park. **Exit Glacier** and all the glaciers of Kenai Fjords flow from this Ice Age leftover, which may be a mile thick. The ice field lies in a high bowl of mountains that jut straight out of the ocean to heights of 3,000 to 5,000 feet. When moisture-laden ocean clouds hit those mountains, they drop lots of rain and snow—up on the ice field 40 to 80 feet of snow fall each winter, with a water equivalent of 17 feet. Summer weather isn't warm enough to melt the snow at that elevation, so it packs down ever deeper until it turns into the hard, heavy ice of glaciers and flows downward to the sea.

The area's history got an ugly start in 1989, when the tanker *Exxon Valdez* crashed into a rock about 150 miles northeast of the park in Prince William Sound and spilled at least 11 million gallons of oil. Exxon did a poor job of catching the oil before it spread, and by the end of the summer, the sticky, brownish-black muck had soiled beaches in the western Sound, across the fjords, and all the way to Kodiak Island and the Alaska Peninsula. More than 1,000 miles of shoreline were oiled to some degree, 30 miles in the park. Thousands of sea otters and hundreds of thousands of seabirds were killed in the Sound and on the islands near the fjords. Nature scrubbed the oil off the rocks again, and you will see no evidence of it in the park today, although government scientists say hidden damage remains in some areas affected by the spill.

Most of the park is remote and difficult to reach. A large vessel, such as a tour boat operating out of Seward, is the only practical way for most people to see the marine portion of the park. That's not cheap or quick, and there are better destinations for people subject to seasickness. The inland portion is accessible only at Exit Glacier, near Seward.

Essentials

GETTING THERE   Seward is the threshold to the park. Exit Glacier is 13 miles from the town by road; the Kenai Fjords National Park Information Center is at the Seward Small-Boat Harbor; and the tour boats that visit the park leave from Seward.

Some visitors try to see the park in a day, coming from Anchorage by train or road, touring the park by boat, then returning that evening. I do not recommend this. To really get to the park, you need to be on an all-day boat trip—most half-day trips barely leave Resurrection Bay and hardly see the park proper. More important, a lot of visitors riding the train back to Anchorage after a 16-hour marathon to Kenai Fjords are so tired they can't keep their eyes open for the extraordinary scenery passing by. A better plan is to spend at least 1 night in Seward and take in the full Kenai Fjords boat trip and Exit Glacier.

VISITOR INFORMATION   At the **Kenai Fjords National Park Information Center,** Seward Small Boat Harbor (P.O. Box 1727), Seward, AK 99664 (© **907/224-7500;** www.nps.gov/kefj), you will find rangers to answer questions about the park and provide information on the all-important tour boats, and a small but handy bookstore. Call or drop by here for advice on public-use cabins for rent in the fjords, guidance on a sea-kayaking expedition there, or information on hikes and trail conditions. They're open late May through early September daily 8:30am to 7pm, the balance of May and September 9am to 5pm. The center is closed October through April.

ACCOMMODATIONS & CAMPING   There are no roads into the main part of the park. The vast majority of visitors base themselves in Seward and tour the park on a day boat. My recommendations for Seward lodgings are earlier in this chapter, including the description of the **Exit Glacier Campground,** the only campground in the park. But there are options for staying in the fjords themselves. Like most wilderness travel, these choices are either rugged or expensive.

Kenai Fjords Glacier Lodge, in Aialik Bay (© **800/334-8730** or 907/783-2928; www.kenaiglacier.com), which opened in 2009, is the only lodging in the park and is reachable only by boat. The lodge was built to take advantage of an incredible location, in a lagoon with views of Pedersen Glacier. Guests join nature walks or kayak with guides in this coveted area, rich in wildlife and amazing scenery. Accommodations are in 16 cabins with private bathrooms, with meals and common areas in a central lodge. The rate of $650 per person ($575 for children 7–11) for a 2-night session includes meals and guiding.

Otherwise, staying in the heart of the park means camping, either on a guided sea-kayaking trip (see below) or sea kayaking on your own, if you have the expertise for such a journey. A free Park Service map shows the location of food lockers and hanging cables to keep your stuff away from bears in the kayaking waters of Aialik Bay and Northwestern Fjord. The Park Service gives voluntary permits to record your itinerary and an emergency contact phone number in case you don't return. The park will send a packet of information, which you can request through the website. They also rent out two **public-use cabins** in the fjords, reachable only by boat or floatplane. Contact the Alaska Public Lands Information Center in Anchorage (p. 220) for a $50-a-day cabin permit, open for reservations starting January 2 each year.

Seeing the Park

SIGHTSEEING & WILDLIFE CRUISES

Kenai Fjords is essentially a marine park. On a boat tour, you'll see its mountains, glaciers, and wildlife, including sea otters and sea lions, and, depending on the season, conditions, and luck, humpback whales, orcas, mountain goats, and black bears. Gray whales come in the early spring, and huge fin whales show sometimes, too, but are hard to see. Bird-watchers may see bald eagles; puffins (both tufted and horned); murrelets (marbled, ancient, and Kittlitz's); cormorants (red faced, pelagic, and double-crested); murres (common and thick billed); auklets (rhinoceros and parakeet); and various other sea ducks, alcids, and gulls.

The farther you go into the park, the more you'll see. If you really want to see Kenai Fjords National Park and glaciers that drop ice into the water, the boat has to go at least into Aialik Bay to Holgate Glacier or Aialik Glacier. Northwestern Glacier is even deeper in the park. Half-day Resurrection Bay cruises offer plenty of impressive scenery but pass only one large glacier, and that at a distance. They have less chance of seeing whales and see fewer species of birds. The longest trips into the heart of the park encounter the greatest variety and number of birds and animals. If you're lucky with the weather, you can make it to the exposed Chiswell Islands, which have some of the greatest bird colonies in Alaska, supporting more than 50,000 seabirds of 18 species. I've seen clouds of puffins swarm here. The day-long trips also allow you more time to linger and really see the behavior of the wildlife. Whatever your choice, binoculars are a necessity, but if you didn't bring your own, you can often rent them onboard.

Resurrection Bay.

It's Not Easy Being Green

A critical factor in choosing your boat tour is your susceptibility to **seasickness.** To reach the heart of the park, vessels must venture into the unprotected waters of the North Pacific. Large, rolling waves are inevitable on the passage from Resurrection Bay to the fjords themselves, although once you're in the fjords, the water is calm. On a rough day, most boats will turn back for the comfort of the passengers and change the full-day trip into a Resurrection Bay cruise, refunding the difference in fare. Of course, they'd rather not do that, and the decision often isn't made until the vessel is out there and some people are sick. If you get seasick easily, my advice is to stick to the Resurrection Bay cruise or take a boat tour in protected Prince William Sound, where the water is always smooth, from Whittier or Valdez. Detailed advice for seasickness is on p. 524.

Prices are around $170 to go to Northwestern Glacier in Northwestern Fjord off Harris Bay, a 10- to 12-hour trip; $140 to $160 to go to Holgate or Aialik Glacier in Aialik Bay, which takes 6 to 8 hours (the most common destinations); and $60 to $90 for a 3- to 5-hour Resurrection Bay tour, which doesn't go to the national park at all. Children's prices are around half off. If publicity material from a tour operator is vague or confusing, ask exactly where the boat goes or get a map of the route. Bear Glacier, within Resurrection Bay, is unimpressive, because boats can't get close to it. You have to go at least to Aialik Bay for a noteworthy glacier encounter.

The season begins in April with tours to see the gray whale migration, mostly within Resurrection Bay. That's done by mid-May, when the regular schedule of tours begins, which lasts into September. Fares with each operator differ little, although you can sometimes get early season or Web specials; instead, shop for the destination, length of trip, food service, interpretation, and size or intimacy of the boat. Consider the seating arrangement. How many passengers will be onboard? Is lunch provided, and what does it consist of? Another important point of comparison is whether you have a ranger doing the commentary or the captain—some of these captains don't know when to shut up, and they can give inaccurate information.

Try to schedule loosely so that if the weather is bad on the day you choose for your boat trip, you can wait and go the next day. If the weather's bad, you'll be uncomfortable and the animals and birds won't be as evident, or the boat may not go out of Resurrection Bay. If you pay upfront to hold a reservation on a boat—probably a good idea in the busy season—find out the company's refund and rescheduling policy.

Most operators offer packages with the Alaska Railroad and the SeaLife Center, or even with a local hotel, which may save money, but make sure you have enough time to do everything you want to do in Seward. All have offices at the Small Boat Harbor in Seward. Here are some of the best.

Kenai Fjords Tours   This is the dominant tour operator, with the most daily sailings and choices of destination. The main part of the operation uses 90- to 150-passenger vessels, many of which have forward-facing seats, like an airplane's, and large wraparound decks where you can get outside at any time. They're professionally staffed. The whole operation runs remarkably smoothly, and the crew is extremely attentive. When the ships are crowded, however, the experience becomes more impersonal. Onboard, the captain primarily narrates, with other employees sometimes helping. With a great variety of tour options, Kenai Fjords has one of the area's least expensive choices, a dinner cruise in Resurrection Bay that costs $59. Meals are included in the price of all tours. The same company owns **Mariah Tours,** which operates more intimate 16-passenger vessels. Their trips are more spontaneous and go all the way to Northwestern Fjord every day, weather permitting; the downside is that the smaller boats move more in the waves.

Most of the large Kenai Fjords vessels call on a day lodge the company owns on Fox Island, in Resurrection Bay, for lunch and Park Service ranger talks. The lodge sits on a long cobble beach near Sunny Cove, where painter Rockwell Kent lived in seclusion with his son in 1918 and 1919 and produced the art that made him famous. It is an inspiring spot. The lodge itself stands on a narrow strip of land between the beach and a pond, which visitors overlook from large wooden decks. Lunch is grilled Alaska salmon and prime rib, with an option of adding king crab. Some passengers spend the night here at the company's Kenai Fjords Wilderness Lodge on all-inclusive packages; for this kind of experience, the price of $379 per person for a 1-night package, including all meals, boat transportation from Seward, and a national park tour, is quite reasonable. You can also plan a sea-kayaking paddle from the island as part of your day trip or on an overnight. The price is $80 to $100 per person as an add-on for overnighters, or $89 to $169, including a Resurrection Bay tour boat ride, for day-trippers.

At the Seward Small Boat Harbor. ✆ **800/478-8068,** 907/224-8068 in Seward, or 907/276-6249 in Anchorage. www.KenaiFjords.com.

Major Marine Tours   This company pioneered first-class onboard dining and commentary by park rangers, who go on every trip—a strong selling point, since it ensures accurate and thoughtful narration. The company has both slower single-hull boats and speedy catamarans that either go to Holgate Glacier or tour Resurrection Bay around Seward. They serve a buffet of salmon and prime rib onboard for $19 per person, $9 for children. The food is surprisingly good. I also like their table-seating arrangement with forward-facing seats. Your seat is assigned, so there's no need to rush aboard or try to stake out your spot.

411 W. 4th Ave., Anchorage. ✆ **800/764-7300** or 907/274-7300, or 907/224-8030 in Seward. www.majormarine.com.

SEA KAYAKING

The fjords are calm yet rugged, intricate, and full of wildlife and soaring vistas. It's hard to imagine a better place for a sea-kayaking expedition. They also are extremely remote and very rainy, so a trip there is a poor choice for your first outing. **Sunny Cove Sea Kayaking** (p. 301) offers a kayaking day trip to Aialik Bay. They take guests out on a small charter boat for a wildlife tour, then you launch and paddle in front of the glacier while the boat stands by. The price for the day trip is $399—expensive, but it is the best of the best. To get more of a feel for the place, spend a couple of days. Sunny Cove's overnight glacier trip costs $699; a 3-day, 2-night journey in Northwestern Fjord is $1,249. Experienced cold-water paddlers can rent kayaks and explore Aialik Bay on their own, using the Park Service cabins for shelter (see above under "Accommodations & Camping"). Miller's Landing (p. 301) rents kayaks and offers water taxi drop-offs.

EXIT GLACIER

When I visited Italy, I got to the point where I thought I'd scream if I saw another painting of the Madonna. If your trip to Alaska is long, you may start to feel the

Exit Glacier.

same way about glaciers. But, although relatively small, Exit Glacier really is unique, and my family still enjoys it even as jaded lifelong Alaskans. (And I've probably seen even more glaciers than Madonnas.)

You can walk close to Exit Glacier, see its brittle texture, and feel the cold, dense spires of looming ice. Cold air breathes down on you like air from an open freezer door. Approaching the glacier, you can see the pattern of vegetation reclaiming the land that the melting ice has uncovered, a process well explained by interpretive signs and a nature trail. A National Park Service nature center adds to the comfort and educational content of a visit. You can easily spend a couple of hours on a casual visit to the glacier (longer if you do a hike). *A safety note:* Big chunks fall off the glacier ever more frequently as Alaska's climate warms. Stay behind the signs, or you stand a good chance of being crushed.

The easiest way to get to the glacier is to drive. The clearly marked 9-mile road splits from the Seward Highway about 3¾ miles north of town. In winter, the road is closed to vehicles. If you don't have a car, a shuttle may be available; check with the park information center (p. 308) to see who is currently offering service. Entrance to the park is currently free.

Following the road along the broad bed of the wandering Resurrection River, you'll see in reverse order the succession of vegetation, from mature Sitka spruce and cottonwood trees down to smaller alders and shrubs. It takes time for nature to replace the soil on sterile ground left behind by a receding glacier. As you get closer, watch for signs with dates starting a couple of centuries in the past; they mark the retreat of the glacier through time.

The Exit Glacier Nature Center is open Memorial Day weekend through Labor Day daily 9am to 8pm, sporadically in May, and September daily 9am to 5pm. Ranger-led nature walks start daily at 10am, 2pm, and 4pm on the short trail to the glacier. It's easy to find your way to the glacier and back on a variety of short trails.

One of the glacier's striking features is a high berm of gravel that fits around its leading edge like a necklace. This is a moraine, the glacier's refuse pile. The glacier gouges out the mountains with its immense, moving weight as new ice flows down from the ice field above and melts here. It carries along the rock and gravel torn from the mountain like a conveyor belt. This moraine is where the conveyor belt ends and the melting ice leaves the debris behind in a big pile. Probably without knowing it, you've seen hundreds of moraines all over North America, where the glaciers of the last Ice Age piled debris into hills, but this moraine helps you understand how they work.

An all-day hike, 8 miles round-trip, climbs along the right side of the glacier to the Harding Icefield. It's a challenging walk with a 3,000-foot elevation gain, but it's the easiest access I'm aware of to visit an ice field on foot. The upper trail isn't free of snow until late June or early July. The ice field itself is cold and dangerous, and there's an emergency shelter maintained by the Park Service. Don't trek out on the ice unless you have glacier-climbing experience. The Park Service leads hikes up the trail Saturdays in July and August, leaving at 9am from the nature center.

The Resurrection River Trail, in Chugach National Forest, begins from the road just short of the last bridge into the Exit Glacier area. It's a pleasant dayhike, with lots of wildflowers in the fall, or the start of a long hike deep into the mountains.

COOPER LANDING: ROAD MEETS RIVER

The little roadside community of Cooper Landing, in a wooded mountain valley along Kenai Lake and the Kenai River, begins about 8 miles west of Tern Lake, where the Sterling Highway splits from the Seward Highway, and continues sporadically along the highway for about 7 miles. (The Sterling runs generally west until Soldotna, where it heads south again.) The frothing upper **Kenai River** is the community's lifeline, each summer bringing the salmon that draw visitors who

fill hotels, restaurants, and the date books of fishing guides. The **Russian River** meets the Kenai at the western edge of the community, where a mad fishing frenzy for the July red salmon season occurs. A ferry takes anglers across the river from the highway. For information on how to fish the Kenai, see "Fishing" in "Kenai, Soldotna & Sterling: Giant Salmon," later in this chapter.

If you're not an angler, there's not much here—a couple of operators do rafting trips, and some trails start here. Cooper Landing is the starting or ending point for backpacking trips in the Chugach National Forest, described under "Chugach National Forest: Do-It-Yourself Wilderness," earlier in this chapter. Look there also for descriptions of several campgrounds for tents or RVs.

Cooper Landing has a post office, service stations, and small stores selling fishing gear and essentials, but it's not a real center of commerce. For banking or anything else not directly related to catching a salmon, you'll have to drive to Sterling, 30 miles away to the west, or Soldotna, 14 miles beyond that.

Fishermen clean their bounty at Kenai River.

Fishing Lodges

The three lodges below can take care of everything, so you can set up your fishing and other activities with a single phone call. Also consider the **Inn at Tern Lake,** just 8 miles east on the Sterling Highway (p. 285). The inn has its own fishing guide, Corey Hetrick, a son of the owners, going by the name **Chugach Backountry Fishing** (© 907/362-1224; www.chugachbackcountryfishing. com), who offers drift fishing on the Kenai and specializes in hike-in fishing to more remote streams.

If you want a simple room or cabin that is clean, comfortable, and inexpensive, try the **Hutch Bed and Breakfast,** Mile 48.5, Sterling Highway (© 907/595-1270; www.arctic.net/~hutch). In nice weather, you can sit at the fire pit and watch the rabbits hop by. The B&B has Wi-Fi and a covered picnic pavilion with a couple of grills.

Kenai Princess Wilderness Lodge ★★   Contrary to its name, this lodge is not in the wilderness, but it is one of the best accommodations in the region. Each room in the red-roofed buildings feels like a remote cabin, with balconies overlooking the wooded valley, woodstoves stocked with firewood, and many unique details; yet they're luxurious hotel rooms at a resort with a fine restaurant. Bathrooms are surprisingly small in all the rooms. The lodge books guided fishing, horseback riding, tours, and other activities, and there are hiking trails nearby. An attractive 35-space RV park with full hookups is on-site, with access to the facilities.

The Eagle's Crest restaurant has a varied and sophisticated menu, with good use of Alaskan seafood, professional service, and a light dining room that follows the hotel's generally rustic theme. Dinner main courses are $20 to $30; the lunch menu has the expected items, plus choices such as calamari and some unusual salads, generally under $10. Even if you have no reason to stay in Cooper Landing, consider stopping for a meal here that will be several steps up from highway fare and enjoy the relaxing ambience of the lodge.

Up Bean Creek Rd. to Frontier Circle, above Cooper Landing (P.O. Box 676, Cooper Landing, AK 99572). © **800/426-0500** or 907/595-1425. Fax 907/595-1424. www.princesslodges.com. 86 units. High season $179–$289 double; low season $129–$219 double. RV sites $35. AE, DC, DISC, MC, V. Closed mid-Sept to mid-May. **Amenities:** Restaurant; bar; exercise room; Jacuzzi. *In room:* TV.

Kenai River Sportfishing Lodge/Kenai Riverside Lodge ★★   The compound lies between the highway and the river, but down among the trees, it feels like a remote lodge. I'd call the cabins faux rustic—I've never seen real Bush cabins with smooth walls, wainscoting, bright rag rugs, and private bathrooms—but they feel like the real thing, with no TVs or phones. The comfortable but not-too-grand central lodge building fits in, too. In the evening, guests can sit by a fire on a deck at riverside or cook in a woodsy sauna. Location is the fundamental advantage: Kenai River fishing frontage. Whitewater rafting rides and fishing floats leave from its riverfront. The lodge also possesses coveted guide permits for the hot fishing river section that runs through the Kenai National Wildlife Refuge.

Everything is covered by one price: transportation from Anchorage, meals in the central lodge building, guided salmon fishing or fly-fishing for rainbow trout in drift or power boats, and, on longer visits, halibut fishing (done from boats in saltwater). You pay for your own booze, fishing license, and tips. The company customizes fishing trips of 2 to 7 days, including nonfishing activities such as river rafting, Kenai Fjords sightseeing, or Alaska Railroad tours. Or come as part

> ## Floating or Fishing the Kenai River
>
> The Kenai is more famous for fishing than for rafting, but the area is beautiful and the Kenai Canyon, below Cooper Landing and above Skilak Lake, has frothy water between vertical canyon walls. **Alaska Wildland Adventures,** at the Kenai Riverside Lodge (✆ **800/478-4100** or 907/783-2928), is the most established operator and has a great reputation. They offer a 7-hour float through the canyon for $140 adults, $99 children, and a placid 2-hour float down the upper Kenai for $54 adults, $34 children. Their guided fishing is $275 for a full day, including lunch and gear. **Alaska Rivers Co.,** Mile 50, Cooper Landing (✆ **907/595-1226;** www.alaskariverscompany.com), has more than 25 years of experience. They offer scenic rafting three times daily ($49, children half price), daily canyon floats ($142), and guided fishing ($110 half-day, $205 all day). They rent cabins, too.

of a "safari" package that includes outdoor activities and sites, such as the Alaska Wildland Adventures safari that's described in chapter 11 on p. 518.

Alaska Wildland Adventures, Mile 50.1 Sterling Hwy. (P.O. Box 389, Girdwood, AK 99587-0389). ✆ **800/478-4100** or 907/783-2928. www.alaskasportfish.com. 16 cabins. 3-day, 4-night inclusive package $2,150. MC, V. **Amenities:** Restaurant (family style); sauna; river equipment included.

A Wilderness Lodge

Kenai Backcountry Lodge ★★   On the far side of Skilak Lake from the Sterling Highway, reached by boat, this lodge is not about fishing—it's about being in a beautiful place, hiking to tree line, lake kayaking, and enjoying quiet in an environmentally sustainable place. The tent cabins and log cabins are hidden in the woods on the lakeshore, connected by gravel paths, and the feeling is authentically wild and remote, but there are flush toilets and hot showers in the shower house and the food offered in the central lodge is terrific. You can stay as part of one of their package trips or come for the lodge alone. Log cabins are $50 more than tent cabins; a cabin with its own bathroom is $100 more.

Alaska Wildland Adventures, Skilak Lake (P.O. Box 389, Girdwood, AK 99587-0389). ✆ **800/334-8730** or 907/783-2928. Fax 907/783-2130. www.alaskawildland.com. 10 cabins. $1,306 adult, 2-night stay, double occupancy. Rates include all meals and guiding. DISC, MC, V. Closed Sept–May. **Amenities:** Restaurant (family style); boating and other outdoor equipment. *In room:* No phone.

KENAI, SOLDOTNA & STERLING: GIANT SALMON

These quintessential western U.S. towns, dominated by shopping malls and fast-food franchises facing broad highways, have a single claim to fame, but it's a pretty good claim: The largest sport-caught king salmon in the world, almost 100 pounds, came from the Kenai River. The Kenai's kings run so large, there's a different trophy class for the river—everywhere else in the state, the Alaska Department of Fish and Game will certify a 50-pounder as a trophy, but on the Kenai, it has to be at least 75 pounds. That's because kings in the 60-pound class—with enough wild muscle to fight ferociously for hours—are just too common here. Anglers prepared to pay for a charter will be in their element on the river when the fish are running hot. Catching a big king is not easy or quick, however, and success rates vary greatly year-to-year and week-to-week.

Those not interested in fishing will find, at most, a day's sightseeing in these towns. Instead, use the towns as a base for the outdoors. Kenai has a strangely beautiful ocean beach and the Kenai River mouth, with exceptional bird-watching during migrations. Beyond the towns, you'll find a wealth of outdoor activities, primarily in the lake-dotted **Kenai National Wildlife Refuge,** which has its headquarters in Soldotna. The refuge is covered in the next section.

Kenai came into being with the arrival of the Russians at the mouth of the Kenai River more than 200 years ago, but it came into its own only with the discovery of oil on the peninsula in 1957. Today its economy relies on oil, commercial fishing, and, to a smaller extent, tourism. Soldotna, a smaller, newer, and less attractive town, is the borough seat and the primary destination for anglers. Sterling is just a wide place in the road—incredibly wide, as a matter of fact (no one can quite explain why such a small town needs such a big road).

Essentials

GETTING THERE   From Anchorage, the drive on the Seward and Sterling highways to Soldotna is 147 miles. Allow 3 hours, without stops: In summer, traffic will slow you down; in winter, speeds are limited by ice and the fear of hitting moose. Kenai is 11 miles from Soldotna on the Kenai Spur Highway, the first major right as you enter Soldotna from the north on the Sterling Highway.

A backpacker van called the **Stage Line** (✆ **907/235-2252;** www.thestageline.net) connects Anchorage, Homer, Seward, and points between. In summer they run to Homer daily from Anchorage and Seward, less frequently in winter. The fare from Anchorage to Soldotna is $66 one-way, $120 round-trip. The pickup point in Soldotna is the Chamber of Commerce Visitors Center. The Anchorage ticket office is at 412 W. 53rd Ave. (✆ **907/868-3914**).

Kenai receives very frequent flights from Anchorage from **Era Alaska** (✆ **800/866-8394;** www.flyera.com).

GETTING AROUND   The area is so spread out that walking most places really isn't practical, and there's no public transportation. Everyone drives. Several major car-rental companies operate at the Kenai airport: **Hertz, Avis, Budget,** and **Payless.** If you plan only to fish, however, you may not need a car, instead getting rides from your guide, your host, or a taxicab. Ask about transportation options when you reserve your rooms. There are several cab companies; try **Alaska Cab** (✆ **907/283-6000** in Kenai, or 907/262-1555 in Soldotna).

VISITOR INFORMATION   The **Soldotna Visitor Information Center,** 44790 Sterling Hwy., Soldotna, AK 99669 (✆ **907/262-9814** or 262-1337; www.visitsoldotna.com), is located on the south side of town; drive through the commercial strip and turn right after the Kenai River Bridge. It's open daily in summer from 9am to 7pm, in winter Monday to Friday from 9am to 5pm. Besides the usual brochures and free maps, they offer help with lodging, camping, charters, and other services. Anglers should stop in to see the world-record 97-pound king salmon and a 20-pound rainbow trout. Stroll behind the center to the river walk to get close to the water and a handy site for streamside fishing.

In Kenai, the **Kenai Visitors and Cultural Center,** 11471 Kenai Spur Hwy., Kenai, AK 99611 (✆ **907/283-1991;** www.visitkenai.com), contains a set of museum galleries. A history and culture exhibit includes first-edition journals of Capt. James Cook, who explored Cook Inlet in 1778, and the "King of Snags," an immense conglomeration of lost fishing lures, rods, and sticks pulled from the river bottom. Large temporary art exhibitions are mounted, too. To get there, follow the Spur Highway past Main Street and look for the large, landscaped building on your left. In summer, admission to the museum is $5, free for students through high school; off season, admission is free. The center is open in summer Monday to Friday from 9am to 7pm, Saturday and Sunday from 10am to 6pm; and off-season Monday to Friday from 9am to 5pm and Saturday 11am to 4pm.

SPECIAL EVENTS Kenai Visitors and Cultural Center (see above) hosts invitational art shows each summer. Works usually cross mediums and include contemporary art and traditional Alaska Native work.

In Soldotna, the **Peninsula Winter Games and Tustumena 200 Sled Dog Race** (✆ 907/262-9814), an Iditarod qualifier, are held in late January. **Progress Days** (✆ 907/262-9814), in late July, offers a parade, rodeo, car shows, and other festival events commemorating the completion of a gas pipeline in 1960.

In Ninilchik, the **Kenai Peninsula State Fair** (✆ 907/567-3670; www.kenaipeninsulafair.com), south at mile 136 on the Sterling Highway, is the third weekend in August (August 18–20, 2012), with rodeo, music, crafts, games, agricultural and craft exhibits, and other country attractions, plus a few kids' rides. One-day admission is $8 adults, $6 ages 6 to 12 and seniors.

[Fast FACTS] KENAI & SOLDOTNA

Banks You will find banks on the Kenai Spur Highway in the middle of town, and in Soldotna on the Sterling Highway commercial strip.

Hospital **Central Peninsula General** is in Soldotna at 250 Hospital Place (✆ **907/262-4404**); from the Sterling Highway, take Binkley Street to Marydale Avenue.

Internet Access Connect to the Web for free at the **Kenai public library,** 163 Main St. Loop (✆ **907/283-4378**), or at the **Soldotna public library,** 235 Binkley St. (✆ **907/262-4227**).

Police For nonemergencies in Kenai, call the Kenai Police Department (✆ **907/283-7879**); in

Soldotna, call the Soldotna Police Department (✆ **907/262-4455**); outside city limits, call the Alaska State Troopers (✆ **907/262-4453**).

Taxes There's a 6% **sales tax** in Kenai and Soldotna, and 2% outside city limits.

Fishing

Fishing the Kenai River is the whole point of coming to the area for most visitors. Check at the Soldotna Visitor Information Center (p. 316) for information and regulation booklets, which you must read and understand before fishing.

Regulations are also available at sporting goods stores, or contact the **Alaska Department of Fish and Game,** 43961 Kalifornsky Beach Rd., Ste. B, Soldotna, AK 99669 (© **907/262-9368** or 262-2737, for a recorded fishing report; www.alaska.gov/adfg). Serious anglers shouldn't miss that website, which includes daily sonar counts of salmon in the river and information on biology and fishing techniques. Licenses are for sale on the site and in virtually any sporting goods store. Also read "A Salmon Primer" and "Fishing" in chapter 11. There are more than two dozen public access points over Kenai River's 80 miles. A **guide brochure** with a map is available from the state **Division of Parks,** P.O. Box 1247, Soldotna, AK 99669-1247 (© **907/262-5581;** www.alaskastateparks. org), or you can pick up a copy at one of the visitor centers.

KINGS King salmon, the monsters of the river, come in two runs. The early run comes from mid-May to the end of June, peaking in mid-June. On average less plentiful and smaller, in the 20- to 40-pound range, the run did also produce the sport-caught world's record (97 lb., 4 oz.). The second run comes during the month of July and includes more of the massive fish. Most people fish kings from a boat, fishing certain holes. Boats hold stationary or back slowly down the river, or fishermen drift down river. Your chances from the bank are low; on average, with or without a boat, it takes 29 hours of fishing time to land a king (you'll likely get at least a dozen strikes for every fish that makes it into the boat). With a guide, the average time to land a fish is cut in half, but that still means that if you fish for only 1 day, chances are good that you'll get skunked. A boat of three anglers on a half-day guided charter has roughly a 50% chance of landing a king among them.

A guided charter averages $150 to $170 for a 6½-hour day trip, $250 to $265 full day. There are dozens of guides. Contact the visitor center in Kenai or Soldotna (p. 308 or 316) to get in touch with a guide; also, many hotels and lodges make their own. It's possible to rent a boat, but this is advisable only if you are experienced in boats and stay out of the hazardous, faster flowing parts of the river. The **Sports Den,** 44176 Sterling Hwy. in Soldotna (© **907/262-7491;** www.alaskasportsden.com), is one charter operator, with river and ocean trips for salmon or halibut, fly-in fishing and hunting, and they also offer lodging packages with large units.

REDS The area really goes crazy when the red (or sockeye) salmon join the kings in the river, from mid-July to early August. Reds are plankton eaters; some say they won't strike a lure, some say they do. In some popular fishing areas, regulations allow only the use of flies; check the regulations or contact Fish and Game for details. The best approach is to fish from the bank with coho or streamer flies with small weights 18 to 36 inches from the fly. Flip the rig upstream, allowing the fly to drift down with the current, near the bank. This can be done with a bait, spinning, or fly rod, as you aren't really casting: just pull out 15 feet of line, flip upstream, let the fly drift by in front of you, and repeat. While waiting for a strike, debate whether the fish really attack the flies or get caught when they instinctively move their mouths in an eating motion, which they do in quick-moving water.

SILVERS Silvers first arrive in late July, peaking during August, but continuing to be in the river through September and even in October. They're easiest to catch anchored in a boat, but you can also do well from shore. Lures work well, such as spinners, spoons, and plugs, as does sinking bait such as salmon eggs.

OTHER SPECIES Trophy-size rainbow trout and Dolly Varden char are hooked in the river, catch-and-release only. Anglers using light tackle may also enjoy catching pink salmon, which are plentiful in the Kenai during even-numbered years, arriving in late July and lasting until mid-September. Use spinning gear and lures. Most Alaskans turn up their noses at this easy-to-catch 4-pound fish; just smile and keep hauling them in. Fresh, bright pinks taste great over a campfire.

Exploring the Towns

Kenai's historic sites, beach walking, and bird-watching can occupy you for part of a day. Start at the visitor and cultural center mentioned above and get a copy of the *Old Town Kenai Walking Map;* follow the numbered markers. Not many of the simple, weathered buildings remain from Kenai's life before oil, but those that do are interesting and lie only a few blocks down Main Street from the center, along the Cook Inlet and Kenai River bluff.

Holy Assumption of the Virgin Mary Russian Orthodox Church.

The **Holy Assumption of the Virgin Mary Russian Orthodox Church** is the area's most significant building. The parish was founded in 1845, and the present church was built in 1895. It's a quaint, onion-domed church, brightly kept but with old icons. A donation is requested. Several nearby buildings are interesting for their interlocking log construction and weathered exteriors. A charming cafe called Veronica's occupies one of these strange and fascinating little structures (p. 322).

The bluff nearby overlooks the broad, sandy ocean beach. A dirt path runs down from Alaska Avenue between the apartment building and the houses that contain professional offices (please don't park near here, as an excess of tourists' cars has caused a problem for the apartment building). To drive down, return to the Kenai Spur Highway, turn to the northwest (left), then turn left on South Spruce Street. There's a big parking lot with a $10 fee, which seems strange on the deserted beach unless you arrive during dip-netting season, the last few weeks in July (the only time the fee is actually charged). If you come then, you'll see a fish gold rush. Alaska residents are permitted to fish from this beach by scooping up passing red salmon with long-handled dip-nets. It's a time for filling freezers and smokers for the winter. That's also when you can see white beluga whales chasing salmon upriver, sometimes in great numbers. If you just want to watch, the viewpoint from the top of the bluff at Erik Hansen Scout Park, at Cook and Mission avenues, is a prime spot. However, the beach also is a lovely place for a walk. It's easy to imagine the Russians' first arrival. On a calm day, the beach sand, the mud flats, and the Inlet's gray glacial water seem to meld together into one vast shimmering plain. The water is far too cold and the currents too swift for swimming.

The mouth of the river and the wetlands of its delta make for fine **bird-watching,** especially during spring and fall migrations. One of the best places to get to the tidal Kenai River Flats is along Bridge Access Road, which branches from the Spur Highway, where one sometimes also sees caribou and moose. The state of Alaska has developed viewing areas at each end of the bridge.

A family looking for something to do while one parent is off fishing may enjoy the magnificent **North Peninsula Recreation Area Nikiski Pool** (℧ **907/776-8472**), 10 miles north of Kenai on the Kenai Spur Road. The facility occupies a large dome and has a 136-foot water slide, mushroom fountains of water, and a raised hot tub from which parents can watch their children play in the pool below. The water slide is open Tuesday through Sunday from 1 to 5pm and from 6 to 9pm in the summer (lap swimming opens those days at 7am); the winter hours are complicated, so call for details. Pool admission is $4, or $7 to use the slide and pool. Weekends can be crowded.

Where to Stay

Rates at many hotels are on seasonal schedules with three, four, or even more levels linked to the salmon runs. I've listed the highest and lowest. One unique lodging choice, worth an exploratory visit if you don't stay, is the **Historic Kenai Landing** (www.kenailanding.com; ℧ **907/335-2500**), where a complex of cannery buildings dating from 1912 has been remodeled into simple rooms, a restaurant, and shops. The inexpensive but rather spartan lodgings appeal most to single-minded fishermen, but the restaurant is well equipped and has live music, and the buildings on a long river dock are interesting and atmospheric. This scenic spot is out of the way, on the opposite side of the river mouth from Kenai: After crossing the bridge, turn right on Kalifornsky Beach Road and right again on Cannery Road.

Aspen Hotel Soldotna ★★ The area's best hotel rooms are here, in a rectangular building just back from the highway strip in Soldotna, a stone's throw from fishing on the river bank. The building isn't old, and the management constantly renews it, putting in new carpet, paint, and fabrics in 2009. The rooms have high ceilings and a solid feeling of quality, and the improvements give them a clean but soothing feel. High-end amenities and professional service contribute to an up-to-date corporate style unique in Soldotna. Family suites have bunk beds, privacy between parents and kids, and PlayStation video games. Suites with cooking facilities are available, too. A rebuild of the pool in 2009 made it like new as well.

326 Binkley Circle, Soldotna, AK 99669. www.aspenhotelsak.com. ℧ **888/308-7848** or 907/260-7736. Fax 907/260-7786. 63 units. High season $169–$179 double, $199 suite; low season $99 double, $119 suite. $10 each additional person 19 and over. Rates include continental breakfast. AE, DC, DISC, MC, V. **Amenities:** Exercise room; pool; whirlpool. *In room:* TV/DVD, fridge, hair dryer, microwave, Wi-Fi.

Great Alaska Adventure Lodge ★★ For anglers, it's the location that counts, and for that, this lodge is hard to top, with about ¼ mile of river frontage where the Moose and Kenai rivers converge, a hot fishing spot since time immemorial, as an ancient Native site attests. In the evening, the lodge keeps a guide and campfire on the beach so that you can cast in the midnight sun. Lodge rooms overlooking the river are spacious and have gas fireplaces and private bathrooms. Unfortunately, the site suffers from vehicle noise from the adjacent Sterling Highway. The lodge offers a wide variety of guided fishing activities, including fly

THE KENAI PENINSULA & PRINCE WILLIAM SOUND   Kenai, Soldotna & Sterling: Giant Salmon fishing and halibut outings. For guests interested in seeing wildlife, the lodge offers trips to its own backcountry tent camps, including one across Cook Inlet with good brown bear viewing. The lodge's website details the many tours and wilderness safaris on offer, as well as rates, which are too extensive to itemize here.

Moose River, 33881 Sterling Hwy., Sterling, AK 99672 (in winter, P.O. Box 2670, Poulsbo, WA 98370). www.greatalaska.com. ✆ **800/544-2261** or 907/262-4515. Fax 907/262-8797 in summer, or 360/697-7850 in winter. 25 units. Rates $295–$550 for a day trip without lodging; packages of 2–10 days $1,195–$5,495. Rates include all meals, guide service, and pickup in Anchorage. AE, MC, V. Closed Oct to mid-May.

Harborside Cottages Bed and Breakfast ★   On a grassy compound at the top of the bluff over the mouth of the Kenai River in Old Town, these little white cottages make the most of a perfect site. The view and quiet can keep you in a peaceful reverie all day. Inside, the cottages are clean and trim, each with its own light country decoration. They have either king-size beds or pairs of twin beds. There are no tubs, just shower stalls. Outside is a patio with a picnic table and gas barbecue.

13 Riverview Dr. (P.O. Box 942), Kenai, AK 99611. www.harborsidecottages.com. ✆ **888/283-6162** or 907/283-6162. 5 cottages. High season $185 double; low season $150 double. AE, DISC, MC, V. Closed winter. *In room:* TV, fridge, Wi-Fi.

Log Cabin Inn ★ 🦫   A beaver sometimes resides in a pond in front of this huge log building on the south side of the Kenai River, across from Kenai. The inn offers comfortable rooms with pleasant views and private bathrooms for bargain rates. The central great room is reminiscent of a big wilderness lodge, with a towering ceiling and lots of rough-hewn wood in every direction. Hosts Teresa and Keith Moyer and their five children share the house with guests. The accommodations vary, including large, charming rooms under the eves, cute but smaller units in a half basement, and outdoorsy cabins with refrigerators and microwaves. Teresa serves a full breakfast at the time of individual guests' choosing.

49860 Eider Dr., Kenai, AK 99611. http://alaskalogcabininn.com. ✆ **907/283-3653.** 7 units, 3 cabins. High season $125–$130 double, $135 cabin for 2; low season $89–$99 double, cabins not available. Rates include full breakfast. AE, MC, V. **Amenities:** Hot tub. *In room:* Wi-Fi.

CAMPING

Soldotna's appealing **Centennial Park Campground** extends along a long section of the Kenai River bluff among thick spruce and birch trees with ramps down to fishing spots on the river, next door to the visitor center and close to stores. Turn right on Kalifornsky Beach Road just after the bridge on the Sterling Highway. Camping fees are $17 a night and day use is $6, payable at a staffed entrance booth (plus tax). The park is open May 1 to October 1. A dump station is usable for an $11 fee. **Swiftwater Park** is a similar city-operated riverside campground near a Fred Meyer grocery store and Taco Bell as you enter town from the north. For a quieter, oceanfront public campground, see Captain Cook State Recreation Area (below).

RV parks are scattered about. **Beluga Lookout Lodge and RV Park,** 929 Mission Ave. (www.belugalookout.com; ✆ **907/283-5999**), has the best location. It's in Kenai's Old Town, at bluff's edge over Cook Inlet at the mouth of the Kenai River. Full hookups are $35 to $60 a night. They offer bike rentals and charters for salmon and halibut fishing, and bear- or beluga-watching.

Where to Eat

Franchise fast-food and burger-steak-seafood places dominate in Kenai and Soldotna. Among the most popular restaurants without a name brand is **Sal's Klondike Diner,** 44619 Sterling Hwy. (✆ **907/262-2220**), a classic Western highway diner, with big portions, fast service, cheap prices, and nothing fancy that doesn't have to be. It's open 24 hours a day all year long under a movie-style false front.

At the other end of the cultural spectrum, **Veronica's Old Town Cafe,** 602 Pederson Way (✆ **907/283-2725**), is in a weathered old Russian building of interlocking logs in Kenai's historic area, with a tiny dining room whose low ceiling, bare wood, and cockeyed angles could not be contrived. The coffeehouse cuisine includes sandwiches, wraps, soup, and a specialty, quiche on a polenta crust. It's open in summer Monday through Thursday 9am to 6pm, Friday and Saturday till 9:30pm, with live music; in winter the hours Monday through Thursday are 10am to 3pm, while the weekends remain the same.

Charlotte's Bakery, Café & Espresso ★ 🎁 CAFE   Some of the very best sandwiches I've ever tasted came from this little strip mall restaurant in Kenai. They're anchored by rich-textured bread and enlivened by unique combinations—for example, a sub with olive tapenade, or a turkey sandwich with cranberry cream cheese. The salads, soup, and chili are memorable, too, and the desserts amazing—all baked in-house. The dining experience is a delight, with service by women who seem to know all their customers and work efficiently in a bright, clean room with cheerful, feminine decor.

115 S. Willow, Kenai. ✆ **907/283-2777.** All items $5–$12. MC, V. High season Mon–Fri 7am–4pm, Sat 8am–3pm; low season Mon–Fri 7am–3pm, Sat 8am–3pm.

Mykel's ★★★ SEAFOOD   This is a traditional fine-dining restaurant for a date or an especially relaxing evening, located in the Soldotna Inn, near the intersection of the Sterling and Kenai Spur highways. The cuisine is exceptional and the service professional and more than friendly. Nothing else in the area even plays in the same league, and Mykel's is only a half step below Alaska's best. The dinner menu contains many familiar beef and chicken dishes done just right. In addition, the restaurant offers various ways of having local seafood in creative ways. Servings are large, even for the exceptional desserts, so don't order extra courses. The full bar serves 18 wines by the glass and six local microbrews. At lunchtime, there are lots of salads to choose from besides the expected sandwiches.

35041 Kenai Spur Hwy., Soldotna. ✆ **907/262-4305.** www.mykels.com. Reservations recommended. Lunch $9–$18; dinner $15–$35. AE, DISC, V. High season daily 11am–10pm; low season Tues–Thurs and Sun 11am–9pm, Fri–Sat 11am–10pm, closed Mon.

Paradisos ★ GREEK   The restaurant is a fine example of an old-fashioned type that was once common: a place that's fancy enough to take Grandma for Sunday dinner, but also has a lengthy menu with choices for each member of the family and a relaxed atmosphere where children fit in. I suppose chains have taken over in this category elsewhere—Olive Garden, Applebee's, and such. In business here since 1971, Paradisos has the formula right: big portions of familiar food, reasonable prices, and speedy, friendly service. The owner's specialty is Greek cuisine, but they also turn out Italian and Mexican food, pizza, steaks, crab, and the like.

Main St. and Kenai Spur Hwy. in Kenai. ✆ **907/283-2222.** Lunch $8–$18; dinner $8–$38. AE, DC, DISC, MC, V. Summer daily 11am–11pm; winter daily 11am–10pm.

Suzie's Cafe DINER   If you are traveling the Sterling Highway and want a pleasant and filling lunch or dinner, you'll do no better than this local favorite on the east side of the road in the town of Sterling itself. Cheerful, efficient servers bring big plates of comfort food and hearty sandwiches. The dining room, heavily decorated in burly country style, has eight tables and a small lunch counter, and no room for waiting. They offer meals to go.

Mile 87.2 Sterling Hwy., Sterling. 📞 **907/260-5751.** All items $7–$25. MC, V. Summer daily 11:30am–9pm. Closed mid-Sept to May.

KENAI NATIONAL WILDLIFE REFUGE

Floating through the Kenai National Wildlife Refuge in a canoe narrows the world into a circle of green water, spruce, and birch. You can paddle and hike for days without encountering more than a few other people, your only expense the cost of your canoe and the vehicle that carried you to the trail head. Out there with my older son, I once noticed that, other than his voice, the only sounds I had heard in 2 days were the gurgling of the water and the wind shushing in the birch leaves. You rely on yourself, but your greatest tests are not overly taxing. Trail a line behind the canoe, and when you catch a rainbow trout, land it and make a fire to cook it. Jump into the clear, frigid water to rinse off after a warm day. Float slowly, watching eagles circle the treetops and puffy clouds drift like ships past your little world.

Most of the western half of the Kenai Peninsula lies within the 2 million acres of the refuge—it's almost as large as Yellowstone National Park—and much of that land is impossibly remote and truly dedicated to the wildlife. The Kenai River flows through part of the refuge, but the refuge is just a name to the anglers who pursue its salmon. (Information about fishing and rafting the river is above, on p. 317 and 315, respectively.) Canoeists will be more interested in the lowlands on the west side, west of the Sterling Highway and north of Kenai and Soldotna. The lakes there are as numerous as the speckles on a trout's back, or at least that's how they appear from the air. From the ground, the region is a maze of lakes connected by trails—more than 70 lakes you can reach on canoe routes stretching more than 150 miles. It's the easiest way to real Alaska wilderness.

A moose in the Kenai National Wildlife Refuge.

Essentials

GETTING THERE   The refuge surrounds much of the land from Cooper Landing at the north to Homer at the south and Cook Inlet to the west. The Sterling Highway and roads that branch from it are the main ways to the lakes, trails, and rivers, and there is no practical way there without a vehicle.

VISITOR INFORMATION   Stop in at the **Kenai National Wildlife Refuge Visitor Center,** Ski Hill Road (P.O. Box 2139), Soldotna, AK 99669 (© **907/262-7021;** http://kenai.fws.gov), for guidance before plunging into the wilderness. The U.S. Fish and Wildlife Service, which manages the refuge, exhibits natural history displays here, shows a film each hour in the afternoon in the summer, and maintains a 3-mile nature trail. The staff offers advice and sells books and maps that you'll need for a successful backcountry trip. To find the center, turn left just south of the Kenai River Bridge, taking a right turn in front of the building-supply store uphill on the unpaved road. It's open April to September Monday to Friday from 8am to 5pm, Saturday and Sunday from 9am to 5pm; October to March Monday to Friday from 8am to 4:30pm, Saturday from 10am to 5pm. The website also contains detailed trip-planning information for the canoe routes.

Getting Outside

CANOEING

Once known as the Kenai National Moose Range, the refuge's brushy wetlands are paradise for moose, rich in their favorite foods of willow and birch shoots and pond weeds. Moose like to dine while wading. Waterfowl and other birds, beavers, muskrats, and other aquatic animals are common on the lakes. People also must be partly aquatic to explore the lakes, paddling canoes across their surfaces, pushing through lily pad passages between lakes, and frequently hiking in rubber boots between lakes while carrying the canoe and camping gear.

There are two main canoe routes, both reached from Swanson River and Swan Lake roads, north of the Sterling Highway from the town of Sterling. The **Swan Lake Canoe Route** is a 60-mile network of 30 connected lakes. It meets Swan Lake Road twice, allowing a loop of several days, but most people go in a lake or two and find a campsite to relax and from which to base explorations. If you're more ambitious, an adventure can be had by penetrating many lakes deep into the wilderness, visiting remote lakes you'll have to yourself. It's possible to canoe a couple of days through to the Moose River and ride its current 17 miles over a long day back to the Sterling Highway.

Getting anywhere requires frequent portages of a quarter-mile or so, and more ambitious routes have mile-long portages. You can skip all the portaging, however, by floating 2 days down the **Swanson River** to its mouth, at the Captain Cook State Recreation Area (see below), joining the river at a landing at mile 17.5 of Swanson River Road. The water is slow and easy all the way.

The most challenging of the routes is the **Swanson River Canoe Route,** which connects to the river's headwaters through a series of lakes and longer portages. The route covers 80 miles, including 40 lakes and the river float. Both routes have many dozens of remote campsites—just lakeside areas of cleared ground with fire rings—and most of the portages are well marked and maintained with wooden planking over the wet areas.

You can rent canoes and everything else you need for a wilderness trip on the refuge canoe routes near the intersection of Swanson River Road and the Sterling Highway in Sterling, where the Finch family operates **Alaska Canoe & Campground** (© **907/262-2331;** www.alaskacanoetrips.com). Lightweight canoes rent for $53 for 24 hours. A shuttle service carries canoeists from one entrance to another. They give valuable expert advice, and they rent a lot of other outdoor stuff: kayaks, mountain bikes, rafts, and so on. Call ahead to check on equipment and to reserve. Their campground is fully equipped, too, a good base where you can return for showers and laundry, and they rent a couple of large cabins with full kitchens and TVs, for $150 a night double, plus $10 for each additional person; the cabins sleep eight.

The Finches no longer offer guided trips because they don't think guides are really needed for anyone who knows how to paddle a canoe and use common sense in the wilderness. If you want a guide, they can give you a referral.

If you go on your own, look for *The Kenai Canoe Trails,* by Daniel L. Quick (Northlite Publishing). The book can be hard to find but is available to order from **Alaska Geographic** (© **866/257-2757;** www.alaskageographic. org). This extraordinary guide contains superdetailed maps and directions, and advice on how to plan your trip and fish and camp on your way.

I haven't provided detailed driving instructions for the canoe routes because you'll need detailed maps to go at all. **Trails Illustrated** produces a good map of the whole area, printed on plastic (p. 286). A serviceable free map is distributed by the visitor center. There's much more to do in the refuge too, including several upland hiking trails. The visitor center provides guidance and maps.

Camping

For car camping in a wild, oceanfront setting, remote from the region's fishing mayhem, try the **Captain Cook State Recreation Area.** The lovely and underused 3,460-acre area faces Cook Inlet 25 miles north of Kenai on the North Kenai Road at the mouth of the Swanson River. There are lots of attractive sites among large birches, trails, beach walking, a canoe landing at the end of the Swanson River Canoe Route, and lake swimming. The state parks camping fee is $10.

There are many campgrounds within the refuge, too, some of them lovely, quiet spots on the edge of uninhabited lakes, such as the small **Rainbow Lake** and **Dolly Varden Lake campgrounds,** on Swanson River Road near the start of the canoe routes; and the **Watson Lake** and **Kelly-Peterson Lake campgrounds,** on the Sterling Highway between Sterling and Cooper Landing. Get a complete listing from the visitor center. Only two campgrounds have fees: **Hidden Lake** and **Upper Skilak Lake.**

HOMER & KACHEMAK BAY: COSMIC HAMLET BY THE SEA

Homer's leading mystic, the late Brother Asaiah Bates, always maintained that a confluence of metaphysical forces causes a focus of powerful creative energy on this little seaside town. It's hard to argue. Homer is full of creative people: artists, eccentrics, and those who simply contribute to a quirky community in a beautiful place. Indeed, Brother Asaiah may have been the quintessential Homeroid, although perhaps an extreme example, with his gray ponytail, extraordinary openness and generosity, and flowery rhetoric about "the cosmic wheel of life." Homer is full of outspoken, unusual, and even odd individualists—people who make living in the town almost an act of belief. I can say this because I'm a part-time Homeroid.

The geography of Homer—physical as well as metaphysical—has gathered certain people here the way currents gather driftwood on the town's pebble beaches. Homer is at the end of the road; the nation's paved highway system comes to an abrupt conclusion at the tip of the Homer Spit, almost 5 miles out in the middle of Kachemak Bay, and believers of one kind or another have washed up here for decades. There were the "barefooters," a communal group that eschewed shoes, even in the Alaska winter (Brother Asaiah came with them in the early 1950s). There are the Russian Old Believers, who organize their strictly traditional communities around their objection to Russian Orthodox church reforms made by Peter the Great. There are the former hippies who became successful commercial fishermen after flocking here in the late 1960s to camp as "spit rats" on the Homer Spit beach. And there are even the current migrants—artists and retired people, fundamentalist preachers and New Age healers, wealthy North Slope oil workers and land-poor settlers with no visible means of support—all people who live here simply because they choose to.

The choice is understandable. Homer lies on the north side of Kachemak Bay, a branch of lower Cook Inlet of extraordinary biological productivity. The halibut fishing especially is exceptional. The town has a breathtaking setting on Homer Spit and on a wildflower-covered bench high above the bay. The outdoors, especially on the water and across the bay, contains wonderful opportunities. And the arts community has developed into an attraction of its own. There are exceptional galleries, and the Pratt Museum has a fine reputation.

You'll be disappointed, however, if you expect a charming fishing village. Poor community planning has created a town that doesn't live up to its setting—indeed, highway sprawl is in the process of ruining some of it. Homer Spit in summer is a traffic-choked jumble of cheap tourist development and RVs.

Homer began to take its modern form after two events: In the 1950s, the Sterling Highway connected it to the rest of the world, and in 1964, the Good Friday earthquake sank the spit, narrowing a much larger piece of land with a small forest into the tendril that now barely stands above the water. If not for constant reinforcement by the federal government, the spit long since would have become an island, and Homer would hardly exist. As long as it survives, however, the town makes the most of that unique finger into the sea. Whether or not it is a cosmic focal point, it certainly is an exceptional launching point to one of the nation's great marine recreation areas.

Essentials

GETTING THERE   **By Car:** Homer is about 235 miles, roughly 4½ hours, from Anchorage by car, if you don't stop at any of the interesting or beautiful places along the way. It's a scenic drive. If you take a rental car, drive it both ways, as the drop-off fees from Anchorage to Homer are high.

By Bus: If you can't drive or can't afford to fly, the **Stage Line** (© **907/235-2252;** www.thestageline.net) is a backpacker van that runs from Homer to Anchorage and Seward and back daily during the summer, less frequently the rest of the year. The Anchorage-to-Homer fare is $78 one-way, $144 round-trip. Tickets are for sale at 1213 Ocean Dr. in Homer. In Anchorage, the ticket office is at 412 W. 53rd Ave. (© **907/868-3914**).

By Air: Era Alaska (© **800/866-8394;** www.flyera.com) serves Homer from Anchorage several times a day. Small air-taxi operators use Homer as a hub for outlying villages and the outdoors.

By Ferry: The **Alaska Marine Highway System** (© **800/642-0066;** www.ferryalaska.com) connects Homer to Seldovia, Kodiak, and points west along the Alaska Peninsula and Aleutian Archipelago. The run

Homer

Fairview Ave.

East Rd.

Svedlund St.

Lake St.

Pioneer Ave.

Bartlett St.

Main St.

Heath St.

Sterling Hwy.

Olsen Ln.

Lake St.

Beluga Lake

Lake Shore Dr.

Ocean Dr.

Homer Spit Rd.

Ocean Dr. Loop

to Homer Spit

Anchorage
Homer — Juneau

Homer Spit

Homer Spit Rd.

same scale as main map

Kachemak Bay

| 0 | 1/2 mi |
| 0 | 1/2 km |

ATTRACTIONS	HOTELS	RESTAURANTS
Art Shop Gallery **5**	Driftwood Inn **9**	Boardwalk Fish & Chips **17**
Bunnell Street Gallery **10**	Homer Hostel **2**	Café Cups **6**
Fireweed Gallery **13**	Land's End Resort **18**	Chart Room **18**
Islands and Oceans	Ocean Shores Motel **1**	Cosmic Kitchen **14**
Visitor Center **11**	Old Town B&B **10**	Duncan House Diner **7**
Pratt Museum **4**	Pioneer Inn **3**	Fat Olive's **8**
Ptarmigan Arts **12**	The Sea Lion Cove **16**	Fresh Sourdough Express
Sea Lion Gallery **16**		Bakery & Cafe **15**

to Kodiak takes 10 hours and costs $74 for an adult walk-on passenger (children 6–11 half off). It's a long but memorable trip.

VISITOR INFORMATION The **Homer Chamber of Commerce Visitor Information Center,** 201 Sterling Hwy. (P.O. Box 541), Homer, AK 99603 (✆ **907/235-7740;** www.homeralaska.org), is on the right as you enter town. In summer, staff is on hand Monday through Friday from 9am to 7pm, Saturday and Sunday 10am to 6pm. Besides answering questions and handing out brochures on local businesses and public lands, they sell tickets for the halibut derby (p. 329). Winter hours are Monday through Friday from 9am to 5pm.

The **Islands and Ocean Visitor Center,** 95 Sterling Hwy., Homer, AK 99603 (✆ **907/235-6961;** www. islandsandocean.org), is more than a visitor center. It's one of Homer's best attractions—a sort of museum of the outdoors for the Alaska Maritime National Wildlife Refuge and the Kachemak Bay Research Reserve, the cosponsoring organizations. Everyone coming to Homer should see the building,

Islands and Ocean Visitor Center.

an architectural gem that perfectly reflects the rocky shores that the refuge and reserve take in, and to experience exhibits, some added in 2010, that use technology, interactive fun, and a sense of theater to re-create remote places in thought and feel. Films show frequently. The center is also the best place to stop for information if you plan to go outdoors anywhere in the area. An easy nature trail descends to the slough below the center. Admission is free. The center is open summer daily 9am to 6pm; check the website or call for winter hours.

The refuge itself consists of islands off Alaska from the Arctic to near British Columbia that include some of the world's most prolific bird and marine mammal habitat. The U.S. Fish and Wildlife Service manages these lands for the benefit of the animals, and people rarely set foot on their shores, but rangers in Homer offer daily programs and walks during peak summer season three times a day, at 11am, 1pm, and 3pm. Call for times and topics. The ranger's birding walks and guided tide pool treks could be a highlight of your trip. Birders can also call the **Kachemak Bay Bird Alert Information Line** (✆ 907/235-7337) to find out about recent sightings and upcoming birding events, and to leave news of their own observations, in season.

The **Kachemak Bay State Park District Office,** mile 168.5 on the Sterling Highway, 4 miles from town (✆ **907/235-7024;** www.alaskastate parks.org), staffs rangers that can help answer questions about planning a trip to the trails and beaches across Kachemak Bay from Homer and give advice on renting remote cabins (although you make the reservation through the Anchorage office—see "State Parks Cabin Reservations," p. 283). Depending on staffing, the office should be open Monday through Friday from 9am to 5pm.

GETTING AROUND   The best way to get to and around Homer is by car. If you didn't bring one, you can rent a car at the airport from **Hertz** (✆ **800/654-3131** or 907/235-0734; www.hertz.com) or one of three local firms. Taxis are available from **Kostas Taxi Service** (✆ **907/399-8008**) or **Kachecab Taxi** (✆ **907/235-1950**).

For strong riders, a bike is a good way around town. You have to dodge traffic in places downtown, but a paved trail parallels the road for the 5 miles of the spit and another runs 5 miles east of town. Some excellent mountain-biking routes are mentioned below. **Homer Saw and Cycle,**

1532 Ocean Dr. (☏ **907/235-8406**), rents mountain bikes, street bikes, kids' bikes, and tag-a-longs. Bike rentals start at $25 a day and come with helmets and locks. The shop keeps track of trail conditions and is a good source of advice. It is open Monday to Friday from 9am to 5:30pm, Saturday from 11am to 5pm. It's wise to reserve bikes a day or two ahead, especially if an outing depends on one.

SPECIAL EVENTS   Unless otherwise noted, the **Homer Chamber of Commerce** (☏ **907/235-7740;** www.homeralaska.org) is the best source of information for all these community happenings and for others listed on the events page of its website. **Homer's Winter Carnival,** in early February, the weekend after the Super Bowl, is a big community event, a small-town celebration with a beer-making contest, a parade, a Mardi Gras celebration, auto racing on the ice of Beluga Lake, and more.

The **Winter King Tournament** is a 1-day fishing competition on the third Saturday of March, for the largest king salmon caught by a fleet of sportfishing boats trolling for the fish in their winter ocean habitat. The purse exceeds $100,000 in cash and merchandise. The **Jackpot Halibut Derby** (www.homerhalibutderby.com), which runs from May through September, has a top prize that has reached over $50,000 for the biggest fish of the season, and smaller monthly prizes and tagged fish prizes. Grand prize fish are usually 300 pounds or more. Of course, you must buy your $10 ticket before you fish.

The **Kachemak Shorebird Festival,** in early May, includes guided bird-watching hikes and boat excur-

Boat at the Kachemak Bay Seafest and Wooden Boat Festival.

sions, natural history workshops, art shows and performances, and other events. It's organized by Alaska Maritime National Wildlife Refuge and the Homer Chamber of Commerce to mark the return of the annual migration.

Concert on the Lawn, in late July, sponsored by KBBI public radio (☏ **907/235-7721**), is a 2-day outdoor music, craft, and food festival that brings together the whole town.

[FastFACTS] HOMER

Banks   Three banks with ATMs, including **Wells Fargo** (which has a lovely mural inside), are on the Sterling Highway near Heath Street.

Hospital   **South Peninsula Hospital** is at the top of Bartlett Street, off Pioneer Avenue (☏ **907/ 235-8101**).

Internet Access   **Tech Connect Computer Sales and Services,** 432 E. Pioneer Ave. (☏ **907/235-5248**), offers broadband access for $5 an hour on their computers or Wi-Fi on yours. Other Wi-Fi hotspots are not hard to find; the visitor center can give you a list.

Police   For nonemergencies within the city limits, call the **Homer Police Department** (℃ **907/235-3150**); outside the city, phone the **Alaska State Troopers** (℃ **907/235-8239**). The police station is on Heath Street at Pioneer Avenue, right behind the Fire Department.

Post Office   Sterling Highway at Heath Street.

Taxes   **Sales tax** in Homer is 7.5%. Outside the city, you pay 3%.

Exploring the Town

The best activities are on the beaches, in the hilltop meadows, and on Kachemak Bay. The best man-made attractions all somehow relate to that setting. The art inspired by Homer's environment shows in more than a dozen galleries and studios in town, not including those across the bay in Halibut Cove (p. 336). New shows open all over town on the first Friday of the month, when restaurants hold special evenings and the entire community comes out for an evening of gallery hopping.

A widely distributed brochure lists most of the galleries in town, with a map. (Find it online at www.fireweedgallery.com/cs4.pdf.) Most are close together on Pioneer Avenue. You'll generally find photography, prints, pottery, fabric, woodwork, and other crafts, since these are small businesses owned by local people trying to make a living. But there is some expensive fine art, too.

Among my favorite galleries are **Ptarmigan Arts,** 471 E. Pioneer Ave. (℃ **907/235-5345;** www.ptarmigan arts.com), an artists' co-op showing a cross section of what the area offers; the **Fireweed Gallery** (℃ **907/235-3411;** www.fireweedgallery.com), next door to Ptarmigan, with true fine art in an elegant, airy space; and the large and well-stocked **Art Shop Gallery,** 202 W. Pioneer Ave. (℃ **800/478-7076** or 907/235-7076; www.artshop gallery.com), in a two-story, octagonal building that hosts major shows in the summer.

Fireweed Gallery.

There are galleries on Homer Spit, too, among all the ticky-tacky gift shops, food stands, and fishing charters offices. My favorite there is Gary Lyon's **Sea Lion Gallery,** on the Central Charters Boardwalk at 4241 Homer Spit Rd. (℃ **907/235-3400;** www.sealiongallery.com). Lyon's work captures Alaska wildlife in spectacular detail but also transforms his subjects with a distinctively dreamy vision. His gallery is a tiny jewel box of valuable works.

Bunnell Street Arts Center ★★   This nonprofit gallery/performance and studio space, located in a perfect space in an old hardware store near Bishops Beach at the lower end of Main Street, is my favorite in Alaska. Unlike most other Alaska galleries, which double as tourist gift shops, Bunnell was made by and for artists, and the experience is noncommercial and often challenging. You may be tempted to become a member of the nonprofit corporation that runs it, for membership comes with a one-of-a-kind plate made by one of the artists. The arts center also mounts invitational or juried art shows from beyond the community and puts on performance art and art workshops, concerts, poetry readings, and films.

106 W. Bunnell Ave. (✆ **907/235-2662.** www.bunnellstreetgallery.org. Suggested donation $2. Summer daily 10am–6pm; winter Mon–Fri 10am–5pm, Sat noon–5pm.

Norman Lowell Studio & Gallery ★ 🎁 Lowell built this huge gallery on his homestead to show his life's work. The immense oils of Alaska landscapes, which are not for sale, hang in a building that counts as one of Alaska's larger art museums. Although Lowell's work is traditionally representational, many paintings carry raw emotions capable of reaching the most cynical viewer. Admission is free, and Lowell and his wife, Libby, usually host guests who walk through. Their old-time Alaskan hospitality is a delight. A large gift shop sells nothing but Lowell's work; paintings range from $750 to $30,000, and prints start at $100 (no credit cards). Wander the grounds to see a real wilderness homestead. The Lowells are trying to sell, so stop at this unique place while you still can.

Norman Lowell Dr. (✆ **907/235-7344.** Free admission. Mon–Sat 9am–5pm; Sun 1–5pm. Closed mid-Sept to May 1. Turn from Sterling Hwy. at mile 160.9 (4½ miles from Anchor Point, about 12 miles from Homer).

Pratt Museum ★★ Homer's award-winning museum is as good as any you'll find in a town of this size. The Pratt displays art and explains local history and science. It helped pioneer technology that allows viewing of wildlife through live remote-control cameras without disturbing the animals. Visitors at the museum can watch puffins and other birds on Gull Island and operate the camera's controls. Another remote camera focuses on the brown bears of Katmai National Park. There is a saltwater aquarium housing local marine life, and if you're curious about all the fishing boats down in the harbor, you can find out about the different types of gear, as well as the fish they catch. In the small botanical garden outside, you can learn to identify all the local wildflowers, and a forest trail

Pratt Museum.

teaches about the area's ecology. There's much more to see, too, including a good gift shop.

3779 Bartlett St. (at Pioneer Ave.). 📞 **907/235-8635.** www.prattmuseum.org. Admission $8 adults, $6 seniors, $4 children ages 6-18, $25 family rate. High season daily 10am–6pm; low season Tues–Sun noon–5pm. Closed Jan.

Getting Outside

The best **map of the Kachemak Bay area** is produced by Alaska Road and Recreation Maps and is available all over town.

ON THE HOMER SIDE OF KACHEMAK BAY

EXPLORING TIDE POOLS   Exploring Kachemak Bay's tide pools is the best way to really get to know the sea and meet the strange and wonderful animals that live in it, and it doesn't cost anything but the price of a pair of rubber boots. First, check a tide book, available for free in virtually any local store, or ask a local to check one for you. You'll do best on a low tide of −1 or lower, meaning that low water will be at least 1 foot below the normal low, some 25 feet below the high. Extralow tides expose more of the lower intertidal zone that contains the most interesting creatures. At a −5 tide, you could find octopus and other oddities. The lower the tide, the more time you'll have to look. But keep track of the time: The tide comes in faster than you imagine, and you could get stranded.

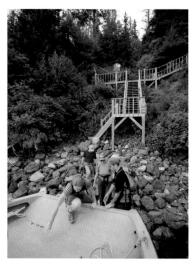

The best place to go tide pooling right in town is reached from Bishops Beach Park, near the lower end of Main Street. Walk west on the beach toward the opening of the bay to Cook Inlet. It's at least a half-hour brisk walk to the Coal Point area, where the sand and boulders end. This is

Kachemak Bay.

where you'll find pools of water left behind by the receding tide, many full of life. Explore patiently and gently—look at the animals and touch them, but always put them back as they were and try not to crush them underfoot. Marine invertebrate identification keys and many other field guides are sold at the Islands and Ocean Visitor Center, earlier under "Visitor Information," where rangers happily give advice. They also offer ranger-guided tide-pool beach walks. If you want to keep going beyond Coal Point, there's usually a raft of sea otters offshore about 3 miles down the beach. Just continue walking, keeping your eyes on the water. As always with watching wildlife, binoculars will improve the experience.

HIKING & NATURE WALKS   The **Wynn Nature Center,** operated by the non-profit **Center for Alaskan Coastal Studies** (© **907/235-6667;** www. akcoastalstudies.org), offers a chance to learn about the ecology of the area and see its birds and wildflowers on an easy walk or hike while taking in sweeping ocean views. The center encompasses 140 acres of spruce forest and wildflower meadow off Skyline Drive, with an 800-foot boardwalk accessible to people with disabilities. The center has done a fine job of adding an educational component without diminishing it—including a log cabin where you can meet a host and ask questions. The center is open daily from 10am to 5pm mid-June through Labor Day, with guided walks twice a day. You can also hike on your own with a printed guide. Fees for adults are $7, seniors $6, 17 and younger $5. Call about interesting daily programs as well.

More ambitious hikes explore more of the bench of land above Homer or the mountains across the bay at Kachemak Bay State Park (see below). The 7-mile **Homestead Trail** is an old wagon road used by Homer's early settlers. A map and guide produced by the Kachemak Heritage Land Trust is available at the visitor center.

HORSEBACK RIDING   Ranchers have worked around Kachemak Bay for decades. Drive east of town on East End Road to see pastures overlooking spectacular marine and mountain views. Go beyond the road, and you're in some of Alaska's most beautiful untamed country. Mark Marette guides trail rides to the head of Kachemak Bay, leading every group himself, as he has since 1986. Guests used to typical, boring tourist horseback riding come back thrilled at how adventurous their ride has been. Mark's a real working cowboy in the old style (he recently apologized to me for being out of touch with a note that said, "I'm off the road system calving out my cows"). His business is called **Trails End Horse Adventures** (© **907/235-6393**), 11 miles out East End. He charges $25 per hour, or $85 for a 4-hour trip. He takes all ages and raw beginners.

MOUNTAIN-BIKING OR DRIVING   Several gravel roads around Homer make for exquisite drives or bike rides. Mountain-bikers can use the Homestead Trail, too (it is described above under "Hiking & Nature Walks"). A lovely drive leads out **East End Road,** through seaside pastures, a forest, and the village of Fritz Creek, then follows the bluff line through meadows toward the head of the bay. When the road gets too rough, explore onward on a mountain bike. **Skyline Drive** has extraordinary views of high canyons and Kachemak Bay; drive up East Hill Road just east of Homer. **Homer Saw and Cycle,** the bike shop listed earlier, under "Getting Around," can give you many more ideas. The great mountain-biking across the bay is described below.

ON & ACROSS KACHEMAK BAY

Along the south side of the Kachemak Bay, glaciers, fjords, and little wooded islands are arrayed like a smorgasbord before Homer. A quick boat ride puts you there for sea kayaking, mountain-biking on unconnected dirt roads, hiking in the mountains, or eating sushi in a top-flight restaurant on pilings. Or gallery hopping, resting at a remote lodge, studying at a nature center, or walking the streets of a forgotten fishing village. The far side of the bay has no road link to import the mundane, mass-produced world, but it does have people, and they make the landscape even richer and more enchanting than it would be alone. And underneath the water, there's a wealth of halibut and salmon.

TRANSPORTATION ACROSS THE WATER   Many water taxis operate from Homer to wilderness cabins, kayaking waters, hiking trails, and mountain-biking roads accessible from the Jakolof Bay Dock, Seldovia, Halibut Cove, Kachemak Bay State Park, and other remote points. Rates vary little; it's around $75 per person to get to Kachemak Bay State Park, plus a $4 park fee, for example. **Mako's Water Taxi** (🕿 **907/235-9055;** www.makoswatertaxi. com) has experience and a good reputation. Mako Haggerty also rents sea kayaks and drops them off; with his advice, you can plan a one-way paddle, with the water taxi providing a lift at each end. Karl Stoltzfus's **Bay Excursions Water Taxi and Tours** (🕿 **907/235-7525;** www.bayexcursions. com) offers transportation across the bay but also specializes in small-group tours—he takes no more than 12 at a time—for serious bird-watching or, on other days, to encounter sea otters as well as see the bird rookeries. Stoltzfus rents kayaks, too. Contact other water-taxi operators, and make other outdoors booking arrangements, through **Inlet Charters Across Alaska Adventures** (🕿 **800/770-6126;** www.halibutcharters.com).

KACHEMAK BAY STATE PARK   The park comprises much of the land across the water that makes all those views from Homer so spectacular. For around $75, you can be dropped off there after breakfast, walk the beach, hike in the woods, climb the mountains, and meet your boat in time to be back in Homer for dinner. Enough people are doing it now that some water taxis offer scheduled service to the most popular trail head. If you want to be on your own, there are plenty of lesser-used trails as well.

The park's main office is at the ranger station listed on p. 328. Its center is the summer-only **ranger station** in Halibut Cove Lagoon, where there's a dock and mooring buoys for public use, three public rental cabins over the water, a campsite, and excellent king salmon fishing in mid-June.

The park has about 80 miles of trails, many linking at the ranger station; a free trail guide is available there, but you're well advised to get a good map before you leave Homer. The trails generally start at tidewater amid a lush, mossy forest and rise into the craggy mountains—up sharp peaks or, if you don't want to climb that much, over the hills to the next secluded beach. The most popular is the **Saddle Trail,** which rises through forest from a staircase at the east side of Halibut Cove over a low ridge to the icy lake in front of Grewink Glacier. It's an easy hike of around 3 miles total. If you want to be away from other hikers, however, discuss choices with a ranger or your water taxi provider, as there are plenty of quieter trails; since some trails are not adequately maintained, local advice is critical.

All hikers should prepare with proper shoes and clothing and bring mosquito repellent. Review bear-avoidance skills (see "Outdoors Health & Safety," in chapter 11). Mobile phones work over much of the bay.

Besides the three cabins at Halibut Cove Lagoon, you can hike to two more public rental cabins less than 3 miles from the lagoon's dock. The park's fifth cabin is on Tutka Bay, off the Halibut Cove trail network. Cabins rent for $65 a night peak season and $50 nonpeak, and can be reserved 6 months in advance (see "State Parks Cabin Reservations," p. 283). Seven remote yurts with woodstoves and sleeping platforms are for rent from a concessionaire, **Alaska Yurt Rentals** (© **907/235-0132;** www.alaskan yurtrentals.com), also for $75, and may be easier to reserve. You use can any of these places as a base for self-guided sea kayaking, and most are at trail heads.

SELDOVIA This historic fishing village is like Homer without all the cars and people: just a lot of quiet, the lovely ocean waters, and some nice places to stay. It belongs in this outdoor section because there's nothing at all to do there other than bike, paddle, or fish (you can do nothing there very well, too). Seldovia comes alive a couple of days a year: for Independence Day celebrations, which include a parade and small-town games and activities, and for a community festival for Memorial Day.

The trip across Kachemak Bay to Seldovia is one of the best parts of going there. For most people, the **Rainbow Tours** (© **907/235-7272;** www.rainbowtours.net) daily round-trips are the practical alternative. They offer shuttle service from Homer Harbor that allows a long day there and a narrated natural history tour with a 3-hour stop in the village. You don't need to stay overnight in Seldovia to get a feel for the town and take a bike ride, a kayak tour, or just walk around the town. Round-trip fares to Seldovia, with or without the nature tour, are $45 adults, $40 seniors, $35 children 12 and under; going one-way is $30 for everyone. A passenger ferry began operating in 2010 using a large, fast catamaran and offering service three times a day. The **Seldovia Bay Ferry** (© **877/703-3779;** www.seldoviabayferry. com) also offers nature tours on some runs.

Go sea kayaking in Seldovia with **Kayak'atak** (© **907/234-7425;** www.alaska.net/~kayaks). The couple leading the tours, longtime Seldovia residents, take pride in showing off the wildlife and beauty of this area. They charge $120 for a 5-hour tour, including lunch, or $80 for a 3-hour tour, without lunch. They also rent kayaks and offer overnight trips. For a less taxing look at Seldovia Bay, take their evening skiff tour for $35 per person (with two to four passengers).

King salmon are stocked in Seldovia Slough, which passes right through the town. The run peaks in mid-June, and you can fish from shore. Seldovia also has an edge for halibut anglers, because you start out an hour closer to the **halibut** grounds than in Homer, potentially giving you more time to actually fish. The best source of town information is its extraordinary website, **www.seldovia.com**.

JAKOLOF BAY A state-maintained dock opens an area of gentle shorelines and abandoned roads to visitors who seek the wilderness without paying to stay at a wilderness lodge. West of Kachemak Bay State Park and east of Seldovia, the lands have roads, but the roads aren't connected to anything and are

A DAY TRIP TO halibut cove

The artists' colony of Halibut Cove sits on either side of a narrow, peaceful channel between a small island and the mainland; the water in this channel is the road. Board-walks connect the buildings, and stairs reach down to the water from houses perched on pilings over the shore. The post office floats on a dock. Visitors arrive each after-noon to walk the boardwalks, visit the galleries, and eat at the restaurant, the **Saltry** (© **907/399-2683;** www.halibut-cove-alaska.com/saltry.htm), which also manages transportation to the cove. The Saltry's deck is a place to sip microbrews and eat fresh baked bread, mussels, sushi, and locally grown salads, followed by fresh fish grilled over charcoal.

The Saltry's classic wooden boat **Danny J** leaves Homer daily in the summer at noon, brings back day-trippers, takes guests to the Saltry Restaurant at 5pm, and brings back the diners later in the evening. The noon trip includes bird-watching at Gull Island. Seating is mostly outdoors. You also take the *Danny J* if you're spending the night in Halibut Cove. The noon trip is $50 for adults, $45 seniors, $30 children; the dinner trip is $30 for everyone, and you must have a dinner reservation at the Saltry, usually made at least a few days ahead. On the noon trip only, they sometimes take more passen-gers than the *Danny J* can carry, putting the overflow aboard the steel *Storm Bird* (same reservations and fares apply).

On the afternoon trip, you can bring lunch or eat at the Saltry and then explore the **boardwalk** that runs from the restaurant along Ismailof Island past the galleries, boat shops, and houses. There's also a barnyard, perched on a patch of ground along the boardwalk, where kids,

who already will be in heaven, can look at horses. The summer-only **Halibut Cove's Experience Fine Art Gallery** (© **907/ 296-2215**) is the first building past the farm on the boardwalk, on pilings above the water. The airy room contains works by Halibut Cove artists only.

Exceptionally appealing overnight accommodations at Halibut Cove are covered under "Lodgings Across the Bay," p. 342.

used as much by mountain-bikers as by anyone else. You can take a water taxi straight to the Jakolof dock. Lodgings are nearby at **Across the Bay Tent and Breakfast,** p. 342. The waters of Jakolof, Little Jakolof, Kasitsna, and Little Tutka bays, and the tiny Herring Islands, are appealing and pro-tected for sea kayaking. Supreme mountain-biking trails lead along the shore and right across the peninsula through forest and meadows for berry picking. The Red Mountain and Rocky River roads are prime routes, differ-ent each year depending on wash-outs and intermittent maintenance—that's part of the adventure. A maintained 10-mile road west leads to the charming village of Seldovia, described above.

GULL ISLAND   This rock across the bay from Homer Spit is a busy bird colony in the summer. It's easy to get to and boats can edge close, as the water is deep all around. You may see tufted and horned puffins, black-legged kitti-wakes, common murres, red-faced and pelagic cormorants, pigeon guille-mots, and glaucous-winged gulls. Tour boats to Halibut Cove or Seldovia may cruise by the island, and if you are taking a water taxi to Halibut Cove Lagoon, ask for a look on your way.

ACTIVITIES

FISHING   Homer is known for **halibut,** and the harbor is full of charter boats that take you out for the day for around $275 per person in the high season. Every day, a few people catch fish that are larger than they are, and halibut more than 50 pounds are common. Using gear and lines that look strong enough to pick up the boat, you jig the bait (chunks of herring or cod) up and down on the bottom. Halibut aren't wily or acrobatic, and fighting one can be like pulling up a sunken Buick. Regulations allow anglers to keep two halibut per day in this region, as opposed to one in Southeast Alaska, but those rules could change; if keeping fish is important to you, check before you go. You can download the Alaska Department of Fish and Game regula-tion booklet from www.alaska.gov/adfg. Getting out to where the fish are plentiful requires an early start and a long ride to unprotected waters. Peo-ple who get seasick easily shouldn't go, as the boat wallows on the waves during fishing. One good full-day operator is **Silver Fox Charters** (© **800/478-8792** or 907/235-8792; www.silverfoxcharters.com).

Half-day charters have less chance of getting way out to the biggest fish but cost a lot less. **Rainbow Tours** (© **907/235-7272;** www.rainbow tours.net) operates a big boat for the shorter outings, charging $105 adult, $95 senior, and $85 12 and under. This choice makes good sense if you are not a fishing fanatic or are taking kids, as full day halibut fishing is exhaust-ing and can be tedious. Other halibut charter boats can be booked through **Inlet Charters Across Alaska Adventures** (© **800/770-6126;** www.halibutcharters.com), with many years' experience setting up fishing trips and other activities.

Salmon use Cook Inlet year-round, and anglers pursue kings with trolling gear even in winter, though most fishing occurs in spring and sum-mer. The town has a Winter King Salmon Tournament in March (see "Spe-cial Events," p. 329). The most popular spot to fish from shore is the small inlet on Homer Spit called the Nick Dudiak Fishing Lagoon, which is stocked with king and silver salmon. Kings return to the lagoon from late May to the end of June. Silvers arrive in mid- to late July, peaking in early August. These salmon have nowhere to spawn, so all must be caught. At the end of the runs, Fish and Game may allow snagging, which is something like mugging salmon and can be a lot of fun, if not something to brag about. For saltwater salmon fishing in a more natural setting, head across the bay to Halibut Cove Lagoon (see Kachemak Bay State Park, above) or Seldovia. The closest road-accessible streamside fishing is 10 miles up the Sterling Highway. The Anchor River is a lovely fishing stream with steelhead and rainbow trout (both catch-and-release only), salmon, and Dolly Varden char. Popular fishing streams cross the Sterling Highway farther north toward and Soldotna. The **Alaska Department of Fish and Game** maintains a fishing hot line at © **907/235-6930.** They're located at 3298 Douglas Place (© **907/235-8191**).

NATURE TOURS The nonprofit **Center for Alaskan Coastal Studies** (© **907/235-6667**; www.akcoastalstudies.org) is dedicated to educating the public about the shore, with harbor walks and day guided tours across Kachemak Bay. The Creatures of the Dock walking tour takes an hour to check out the life living underneath; it costs $5 per person and runs June through August daily at 1pm and 4pm from the center's yurt on the spit. But I strongly recommend their all-day trip. Visitors ride a boat across Kachemak Bay to join daily explorations from a field station in the Peterson Bay and China Poot Bay area, across the water from Homer. At low tide, guides lead guests on a fascinating tide-pool walk. The field station also has access to lovely woodlands where nature walks cover forest ecology and geology and visit an archaeological site. Saltwater tanks at the station contain creatures from the intertidal zone and microscopes to inspect your finds. You can add on guided sea kayaking or a reasonably priced overnight stay in a yurt so you're there ready for an early morning low tide. Reserve by calling the center at the number above. The all-day tour is $120 adults, $80 ages 11 and under, and operates daily Memorial Day to Labor Day. Pack your own lunch, and bring both footwear suitable for hiking and potentially wet beach walks and warm clothing for the boat ride.

SEA KAYAKING Silence fell as the boat pulled away from the beach, leaving us behind with the kayaks and our guide. For the rest of the day my son and I absorbed the water-reflected sunlight and glided past fancifully shaped rocks and resident sea otters around Yukon Island. We explored beaches, picnicked, raced, and discovered tiny bays too small for any other craft. At the end of the day, we had a new friend in our quietly cheerful guide, Alison O'Hara, and discovered that she'd imperceptibly taught us a lot about sea kayaking. O'Hara runs **True North Kayak Adventures** (© **907/235-0708;** www.truenorthkayak.com). Her 8-hour beginner day trips cost $150, including lunch and passage across the bay. The firm also offers an all-day trip combining a glacier hike with sea kayaking, for $199, and more challenging overnight and multiday trips to remote waters in the area. A $375 package includes the day tour, a night in the attractive Hesketh Island Cabins, and a second day of hiking.

Rick and Dorle Harness offer another kind of special kayaking day trip, or overnight, from their place in Little Tutka Bay. After boating across Kachemak Bay from Homer, guests join kayaking, bird-watching, and foraging expeditions, gathering kelp, roots, beach greens, and other wild foods to add to halibut and salmon for a special meal. Rick himself guides every trip, as he has for more than 20 years. They also offer a couple of cabins for overnight stays. The business is called **Seaside Adventure Ecotours** (© **907/235-6672;** www.seasideadventure.com). A day trip costs $150 per person.

Experienced paddlers can explore Kachemak Bay's protected waters, tiny islands, and remote settlements on their own. Take a water taxi across and explore at will, camping or staying in cabins over much of the bay. Check with Kachemak Bay State Park for guidance. **Mako's Water Taxi** (© **907/235-9055;** www.makoswatertaxi.com) offers rides and rents and delivers kayaks. True North Kayak (see above) also rents to experienced paddlers and rents camping gear. For kayaks, expect to pay $65 a day for a double, $45 single.

Homer & Kachemak Bay: Cosmic Hamlet by the Sea

THE KENAI PENINSULA & PRINCE WILLIAM SOUND

GETTING YOUR FISH HOME

An angler can easily come back from a halibut charter with 60 pounds of fish that, when cleaned, will yield 30 pounds of filets. A serving is around half a pound of halibut. Eat as much fresh as you can, as it will never be better, but be prepared for how you will deal with the rest of your bounty, which, if bought in a grocery store, would cost as much as $500 (it's illegal to sell sport-caught fish). If it is properly and quickly frozen, it will retain much of its quality well into the winter; if not, you waste this superb food. If you're lucky enough to catch that much salmon, the problem is even more immediate, as salmon is more sensitive to proper handling. Most fishing towns have a sport processor that can vacuum-pack and flash-freeze your catch for $1 to $1.25 a pound. You can get it home conveniently as checked baggage; depending on your airline baggage fees, that may or may not be a cost-effective option. The processor can provide sturdy fish boxes and cold packs. If you aren't leaving right away, processors may hold the fish, and many hotels have freezer facilities. If you have to ship it, use an overnight service and make sure someone is there to put it in the freezer on the other end. Above all, keep the fish *hard frozen;* thawing and refreezing diminishes the quality off any fish and can turn salmon into mush. Consider having some of your salmon smoked, if possible, making it a ready-to-eat delicacy very welcome as a homecoming gift. Halibut can be smoked, too, but because of its low fat content and delicate flavor and texture, it doesn't come out as well as salmon. See p. 39 and 40 for more tips on handling and cooking Alaskan fish.

In Homer, **Coal Point Trading Co.,** 4306 Homer Spit (© **907/235-3877;** www.welovefish.com), will process and pack your catch as ordered. Ask your charter captain, who will come and get the fish directly from the boat.

Where to Stay

Homer has many good B&Bs. The Homer Chamber of Commerce (www.homer alaska.org) has links to many of them, as well as an updated availability calendar that shows rooms at many B&Bs and lodges.

In addition to the places I've listed in detail, the **Sea Lion Cove,** above the Sea Lion Gallery on Homer Spit (www.sealiongallery.com/cove; © **907/235-3400** in summer, or 235-8767 in winter), has two spacious units with limited cooking facilities, private phones, Wi-Fi, and a deck right over the beach where you can hear the waves roll in at night. They rent for $135 and $145 a night.

Up the hill on the other side of town, **A Memorable Experience Bed and Breakfast** (www.amemorableexperience.com; © **800/720-9275,** ext. 7374, or 907/235-7374) offers huge rooms and a large cottage with spectacular views and an expansive garden setting. The owners also run the Fresh Sourdough Express restaurant (p. 344). Prices range from $145 to $200 per night.

You'll find good, simple lodgings and excellent value downtown at the **Pioneer Inn,** 244 W. Pioneer Ave. (www.pioneerinnhomerak.com; © **800/782-9655** or 907/235-5670). Big, apartment-style units start at $119 in summer with up to four people in a room. Rooms with two twins or a queen-size bed start at $99 in summer. A house that sleeps up to nine goes for $275 a night.

Driftwood Inn ★★ 🍴   This is a rare find, a hotel appropriate for either a budget-minded backpacker or a well-off family seeking lovely beachfront lodgings. The original part of the inn is a historic building a block from Bishops Beach and across from the Bunnell Gallery. It resembles a lodge or B&B, with its large fireplace of beach rock, the hot coffeepot and inexpensive self-serve breakfast in the lobby, and a friendly attitude. Next door, the upscale rooms are in newer buildings, with spectacular views and fresh, charming seaside decor. A cottage that sleeps eight has its own deck and lawn over the beach. The original building has rooms like Pullman compartments in size and configuration—besides being inexpensive, they're cute and clean and have some real style. Nine of those units share two bathrooms. In the old building, the upstairs walls are thin, so there's a no-noise policy during evening hours. The lodge also has an appealing 22-site RV park and a fenced playground, a fish-cleaning station and freezing facility, and year-round fishing charters. Smoking is not allowed.

135 W. Bunnell Ave., Homer, AK 99603. www.thedriftwoodinn.com. © **800/478-8019** or ©/fax 907/235-8019. 33 units, 24 with private bathroom. High season $95–$245 double; low season $59–$125 double. RV sites $44–$75, full hookups. Extra person $10. MC, V. *In room:* TV.

Land's End Resort ★★★   Traditionally *the* place to stay in Homer, Land's End would be popular no matter what it was like inside because of its location at the tip of Homer Spit, the best spot in Homer and possibly the best spot for a hotel in all of Alaska. It's near the boat harbor, and you can fish right from the beach in front. Buildings sprawl along the low beach crest linked by long corridors, a mismatched collection that resulted from the successive additions over many decades expanding a quaint old nautical hangout into the well-appointed and even luxurious hotel that exists now. The local family that owns the hotel has kept much of the charm while maintaining high standards and making constant improvements. Rooms range widely in size and configuration, from cozy and relatively inexpensive little nautical compartments to giant two-story suites with lofts. The best are a series of privately owned townhouse condos next door; for groups or for couples on extended visits, these are the best accommodations in the region, with stylish furniture, lots of space and light, and a beachfront location second to none. The condos rent for $325 to $450 a night, with a 2-night minimum stay in the summer.

The **Chart Room Restaurant** makes good use of its wonderful location, looking out over the beach and bay from big windows. There's a casual, relaxing atmosphere in the long, wood-trimmed dining room. The deck outside has glass windbreaks, making it a warm, satisfying place to sit over coffee on a sunny day. You can watch otters, eagles, and fishing boats while you eat. The selection of main courses, priced $16 to $38, is fairly typical of a seaside fine-dining restaurant, and the food is good, if not memorable. The appetizer menu, however, is much more extensive and interesting, and the portions are generally large enough to make a full meal.

4786 Homer Spit Rd., Homer, AK 99603. www.lands-end-resort.com. © **800/478-0400** or 907/235-0400. Fax 907/235-0420. 95 units. High season $149–$259 double; low season $85–$145 double. Extra person $10. AE, DC, DISC, MC, V. **Amenities:** Restaurant; bar; exercise room; outdoor Jacuzzi; indoor lap pool; sauna; spa. *In room:* TV/DVD, Wi-Fi.

Ocean Shores Motel ★   Buildings have a commanding view of Kachemak Bay, with a path leading down to Bishops Beach. The location is right off the Sterling Highway as you enter town, within walking distance of downtown

Homer. Rooms are fresh and bright, most with private balconies, refrigerators, and microwaves; four have full kitchens. The less expensive rooms lack the views and are older, but are still modern and have cute touches. The place is decorated with photographs and art collected over a family's five generations in Alaska. Smoking is not allowed.

451 Sterling Hwy., Homer, AK 99603. www.oceanshoresalaska.com. 𝄞 **800/770-7775** or 907/235-7775. Fax 907/235-8639. 38 units. High season $129–$189 double; low season $79–$109 double. Extra person $5. AE, DISC, MC, V. *In room:* TV, fridge, microwave, Wi-Fi.

Old Town Bed and Breakfast ★ 🎁 These rooms combine the artiness of the excellent Bunnell Street Arts Center downstairs (see "Exploring the Town," earlier in this chapter) and the funky, historic feel of the old trading post/hardware store that the building used to house. The wood floors undulate with age and settling, their imperfections picked out by light from tall, double-hung windows that look out at Bishops Beach. The antiques, handmade quilts, and spectacular oil paintings in the bedrooms fit in as if they have always been there, yet the rooms are comfortable, fresh, and clean. The B&B has no TVs or in-room phones. The rates include a hot breakfast at 8am in the parlor and afternoon tea. This place is not a good choice for people who have any trouble with stairs.

106–D W. Bunnell, Homer, AK 99603. www.oldtownbedandbreakfast.com. 𝄞 **907/235-7558.** 3 units, 1 with private bathroom. High season $95 double with shared bathroom, $115 double with private bathroom; low season $60 double with shared bathroom, $85 double with private bathroom. Extra person $15. Rates include full breakfast. MC, V.

CAMPING & HOSTELS

The most popular place to camp in Homer is out on the spit, amid the sand and pebbles. It can be windy and crowded, but waking up on a bright, pebbled beach makes up for much. The city charges $8 for tents, $15 for RVs, payable at the Camp Fee Office (𝄞 **907/235-1583,** summer only) in a small log cabin on the spit across the road from the fishing hole (RVers should read the next paragraph for another option on the spit). The city also operates the more protected Hornaday Campground near the hospital: From Pioneer Avenue, take Bartlett Street uphill; turn left on Fairview and right on Campground Road. Both camping areas are managed by **Homer Public Works** (www.cityofhomer-ak.gov/recreation; 𝄞 **907/235-3170**).

If RV hookups are a priority, you can stay on the Homer Spit—for a price. **Heritage RV Park** is on the spit right next to the fishing hole (www. alaska heritagervpark.com; 𝄞 **800/380-7787** or 907/226-4500) and has all the usual amenities. Sites with full hookups, including Wi-Fi, telephone with voicemail, and satellite TV, rent for $78 a night. There are plenty of places to go off the spit and get RV hookups more affordably, including the Driftwood Inn, above, and **Oceanview RV Park,** 455 Sterling Hwy. (www.oceanview-rv.com; 𝄞 **907/235-3951**), with 100 spaces near downtown overlooking the water and a trail to the beach. Rates are $37 to $45 a night for full hookups at peak season, including cable TV ($25 for tent camping). Campers also get halibut charter discounts.

Find conveniently located hostel rooms at **Homer Hostel,** 304 W. Pioneer Ave. (www.homerhostel.com; 𝄞 **907/235-1463**), charging $25 a night for beds in dorms with four to six bunks each, or $65 double for private rooms (tax included). It's a nice old house with a shared full kitchen, but common areas are small. They also rent bikes and have a grill on the porch guests can use.

LODGINGS ACROSS THE BAY

These places to stay all are based across Kachemak Bay from Homer, each in its own remote cove, bay, or village, and each in its own market niche, from family lodgings to luxurious accommodations. If you want to stay at a wilderness lodge, you can't just show up and get a room. Besides getting to the lodge by boat, you also need to reserve a place well in advance, although there's always a chance of something being open if you call a day or two ahead. I regret I can't include more that are also deserving—and there are many—which you can find listed with links at www.homeralaska.org. Here are some standouts to consider: The **Otter Cove Resort** (www.ottercoveresort.com; C **800/426-6212** or 907/235-6212), overlooking Eldridge Passage from attractive, affordable cabins and a shower house, and nearby hiking and sea kayaking; **A Stillpoint In Halibut Cove,** home of the Center for Creative Renewal (www.stillpointlodge.com; C **907/296-2283**), an all-inclusive remote lodge experience, with hiking and kayaking guides, massage, and home-grown organic food, offering retreats and workshops for groups as well as visits for individuals—all in a building that's an astonishing work of art itself, full of exquisite stone, dramatic spaces, and even an indoor creek and waterfall; and, in Seldovia, **Alaska Dancing Eagles Cabin Rental** (www.dancingeagles.com; C **907/234-7627** in summer, or 360-6363 in winter) a picturesque house and cabin on the town's historic boardwalk overlooking calm water and, usually, a sea otter.

Across the Bay Tent and Breakfast ★

Tony and Mary Jane Lastufka created this unique place, a spot where you don't have to be rich to stay in a backwoods paradise, beachcombing by day and feasting on Tony's grilled seafood in the evening. Guests have a choice of large canvas tents on wooden platforms or new cabins, all standing off by themselves on a steep hillside among towering spruce trees. There's a central house for relaxation, evening games, or conversation; an organic garden to produce the food; two outhouses with stained-glass windows; and a bathhouse with plumbing. The beachfront faces placid Kasitsna Bay—where water taxis drop off visitors and where guided sea-kayaking excursions depart. Up the stairs to the road, mountain bikes are for rent to explore the area's network of abandoned logging roads or to pedal to Seldovia. The tents or cabins have beds, but you sleep in your own sleeping bag. You can save further by cooking your own meals. Check the website for workshops you may want to join.

On Kasitsna Bay (P.O. Box 81), Seldovia, AK 99663. www.tentandbreakfastalaska.com. C **907/235-3633.** (Winter P.O. Box 112054, Anchorage, AK 99511; C 907/345-2571.) 6 tents. $75 per person with breakfast; $110 per person with all meals. Half price for children 6–11, free for children 5 and under. MC, V. Closed mid-Sept to Memorial Day.

Kachemak Bay Wilderness Lodge ★★★

I can think of no more idyllic way to become acquainted with Alaska's marine wilderness than by staying at this intimate lodge, run for nearly 40 years by hospitable and generous Michael and Diane McBride. The site, on China Poot Bay, is uniquely perfect: on an isthmus, arrayed among big trees, beach grass, and interesting topography, a peaceful and lovely setting with excellent tide pooling, kayaking, and good hiking trails nearby. Environmentally conscious guides, who have included noted experts on the science and history of the area, lead just a few guests at a time for sea kayaking, hiking, wildlife-watching, and learning about nature; guests set the agenda, and everything is included. The man-made part of the lodge is extraordinary, too. Instead of trying to pack glossy luxuries into their cabins and main lodge, the

McBrides have retained the rough texture of a remote Alaskan camp while subtly enhancing it: One cabin has linoleum floors and well-used furniture, but also fine rugs, a hidden Ethernet connection, and a wine list. Meals are legendary, and guests can spend the evenings in yoga classes, the private sauna, or the hot tub, or view a natural history slide show. Add on a visit the remote Loonsong Mountain Camp, where Mike and Diane personally guide and cook for just two couples or one family of four at a time in a lodge on its own mountain lake reached by floatplane.

China Poot Bay (P.O. Box 956), Homer, AK 99603. www.alaskawildernesslodge.com. 🕾 **907/235-8910.** 5 cabins. $1,750 per person for a 2-night stay, $2,400 3-night, $3,750 5-night; children half price; children 6 and younger free. Rates all-inclusive, including boat transportation from Homer. Boating, kayaking, and all guiding included. 2-, 3- or 5-night package only. V. Closed Sept 15–May 25. **Amenities:** Hot tub; sauna.

Quiet Place Lodge ★★★ A series of beautifully finished cabins and lodge buildings perch on the edge of the narrow waterway that is the main street of the artists' colony of Halibut Cove (p. 336), putting a few guests in the heart of this fascinating community in complete, relaxed comfort. You can walk down to the floating dock and get aboard your own hand-built wooden row boat or sea kayak to explore the village or paddle across the water for a spot of sushi at the Saltry Restaurant. Packages include all meals, guided fishing, and sea kayaking. The owners' openness and authentic hospitality are among the lodge's best assets.

Halibut Cove. www.quietplace.com. 🕾 **907/296-2212** summer, or 235-1800 winter. 3 cabins. All meals and limited guiding included. 3-day minimum package, $2,175 per person. MC, V. Closed Sept–May. **Amenities:** Guided fishing; sauna; rowboats; sea kayaks.

Where to Eat

Besides those places listed here, consider the **Chart Room** at Land's End, described under "Where to Stay," above, and the special across-the-bay option at the **Saltry** (p. 336).

Our current favorite in Homer for a quick, casual meal is **Cosmic Kitchen** (🕾 **907/235-6355;** www.cosmickitchenalaska.com), a cheerful place on Pioneer Avenue producing Mexican lunches and breakfasts, especially large burritos stuffed with fresh, high-quality ingredients along with rice and other side items. An enormous meal comes in at under $9. Limited indoor seating is supplemented by a pleasant deck out front, but during peak hours, the place can be jammed and taking away your meal may be advisable. A second location near the boat harbor on Homer Spit is open May to September.

For fresh local halibut and cod, salmon, burgers, chicken, and milkshakes in an attractive beachfront dining room, try **Boardwalk Fish and Chips** (🕾 907/235-7749), on the boardwalk across from the harbormaster's office on the spit. It's relaxed fast food, but the place is clean and grown-up and serves 10 beers on tap.

Duncan House Diner, downtown at 125 E. Pioneer Ave. (🕾 **907/235-5344**), is a nice, traditional place for a casual meal in a friendly atmosphere. You can eat at a counter or in booths. It is open for breakfast and lunch daily.

Café Cups ★★★ SEAFOOD The facade of the yellow house on Pioneer Avenue is unmistakable, with its elaborate bas-relief sculpture. The small dining room is a work of art, too, a masterpiece of wood, light, and space. Jennifer Olsen seats guests, and her husband, David, is the chef. As the owners, they've combined a love for good food with practicality in a small town. The menu comes in two parts. The regular daily menu is mostly mainstream—aimed at local diners looking for something familiar—but they also have an extensive daily menu of verbally described specials, usually including many interesting choices based on local seafood. Do not make a choice before considering these, which are the heart of the experience. David has a terrific sense of the texture of food—the lamb chops were a sensual delight, crisply seared on the outside, tender and juicy inside, on rich mashed potatoes. Portions are large. They serve beer and wine.

162 W. Pioneer Ave. ℂ **907/235-8330.** Reservations recommended. Main courses $18–$30. MC, V. Tues–Sat 4:30–10pm.

Fat Olives ★★ MEDITERRANEAN   Built with great style in a former school bus garage on the Sterling Highway near the visitor center, the restaurant is a wonder of warm Mediterranean colors, shiny metal, and primitive art—not the sort of place you expect to find in a small town in Alaska. The cuisine brings further surprises: bold flavors and textures, a little Tuscany, and plenty of Homer, too, including lots of local seafood. The centerpiece is a wood-fired Italian brick oven that produces pizza, grilled sandwiches, steaks, and much else. They serve local beers on tap and 30 wines by the glass. Although the restaurant is not oriented to children, my kids love it because of the big pieces of pizza available by the slice (which means adults can eat here inexpensively, too). Note that, at peak hours, it can take a long time to get a table, and they don't take reservations.

276 Olson Lane. ℂ **907/235-8488.** Reservations not accepted. Lunch $7–$12; dinner main courses $16–$26. MC, V. Daily 11am–9pm.

Fresh Sourdough Express Bakery and Restaurant ★ ☺ CAFE   Ebullient Donna and Kevin Maltz's organic eatery is quintessential Homer, starting with its motto: "Food for people and the planet." But there's no New Age dogma here. The Sourdough Express is fun and tasty, even as it grinds its own grain and recycles everything in sight. An inexpensive lunch menu includes many vegetarian choices, as well as hearty sandwiches. The evening menu includes many specials, elaborate dishes, including huge portions of local seafood with rich sauces, and, perhaps more remarkably, simple, solid choices, too, for those who don't want to spend a lot. All-you-can-eat crab is served from 3 to 8pm. Families will enjoy the relaxed atmosphere, and the big sandbox and an old van out front where kids can play while you wait for your meal. Stop by on the way to the harbor for a brown bag lunch you will need for a charter fishing trip. Don't miss dessert from the made-from-scratch bakery.

1316 Ocean Dr. ℂ **907/235-7571.** www.freshsourdoughexpress.com. Breakfast $6–$12; lunch $6.50–$15; dinner main courses $10–$25. DISC, MC, V. High season daily 8am–8:30pm; low season daily 8am–3pm.

The Homestead ★★★ SEAFOOD   The ambience is that of an old-fashioned Alaska roadhouse, in a large log building decorated with contemporary art and lots of summer light. The food is terrific, often sophisticated in preparation, and relies largely on fresh Alaskan fish. What I like best is when this perfect seafood is prepared in a way that emphasizes its qualities in flavor and texture without drawing attention away from the fish itself, and that's what I anticipate without disappointment every time I eat here. The portions are generous, and if you want a big piece of rare prime rib, go no further. After a day outdoors, it's a warm, exuberant place for dinner, but with polished edges: white table linens, usually with intimate, professional service. The owners work hard to bring new flavors and wines to the Homer community in the off season, and even offer wine classes. The wine list is well selected and arranged—not intimidating; plenty of bottles are in the $21-to-$34 range. They also have a full bar with local wine, mead, and beer on tap.

Mile 8.2, East End Rd. (✆ **907/235-8723.** www.homesteadrestaurant.net. Reservations recommended. Main courses $21–$39. AE, MC, V. June–Aug daily 5–10pm; Mar–May and Sept–Dec Wed–Sat 5–9pm. Closed Jan–Feb.

Homer Nightlife

The **Pier One Theatre** (✆ 907/235-7333; www.pieronetheatre.org) is a strong community theater group housed in a small red building on the spit, between the fishing hole and the small-boat harbor. Instead of the ubiquitous gold rush melodrama and Robert Service readings, Pier One often presents serious drama, musicals, and comedy—not just schlock. They also produce dance, classical music, and youth theater events during the summer. There's generally something playing Thursday through Sunday nights in the visitor season. Check the *Homer News* or the website for current listings. They strongly recommend making reservations by phone; a reservation can be changed or canceled, if necessary. Tickets may also be available at the door.

The landmark **Salty Dawg Saloon** is a small log cabin on the spit with a lighthouse on top. It's the place to swap fish stories after a day on the water. Wherever you go to hoist a beer, order a draft from the **Homer Brewing Company** (Red Knot Ale is my favorite).

VALDEZ

Big events have shaped Valdez (val-*deez*). The deepwater port, at the head of a long, dramatic fjord, first developed with the 1898 Klondike gold rush and an ill-fated attempt to establish an alternative route to the gold fields from here. Later the port and the Richardson Highway, which connected Valdez to the rest of the state, served a key role in supplying materials during World War II. On Good Friday, March 27, 1964, all of that was erased when North America's greatest recorded earthquake occurred under Miners Lake, west of town off a northern fjord of Prince William Sound. It set off an underwater landslide that caused a huge wave to sweep over the waterfront and kill 32 people. The U.S. Army Corps of Engineers moved the town, rebuilding a drab replacement in a safer location that slowly filled with nondescript modern buildings.

The construction of the trans-Alaska pipeline, completed in 1977, brought a new economic boom to Valdez and enduring economic prosperity as tankers came to fill with the oil. Then on March 24, 1989, on Good Friday 25 years after the earthquake, the tanker *Exxon Valdez,* on its way south, hit the clearly marked Bligh Reef, causing an oil spill ranked largest ever in North America until it was surpassed in 2010 by the BP spill in the Gulf of Mexico. The spill cleanup added another economic boom. More than 20 years later, most wildlife populations have recovered and visible signs of the spill are difficult to find, but the spill's impact remains indelible and the marine ecosystem has changed.

Today Valdez is a middle-American town, driven by industry but turning to the vast resources of Prince William Sound for outdoor recreation. Despite a spectacular setting and pleasant waterfront, it isn't the sort of historic or charming fishing village that justifies a trip all by itself. A day is enough to tour the small museums and take a hike or a river float. Instead, come for the setting—the wildlife, fishing, kayaking, and sightseeing in the Sound, and the spectacular drive down the Richardson Highway.

Because Valdez lies at the end of a funnel of steep mountains that catches moisture off the ocean, the weather tends to be overcast and rainy in summer and extremely snowy in winter.

Essentials

GETTING THERE By Car: The **Richardson Highway** (see "Richardson Highway & Copper Center," in chapter 9) dramatically crosses Thompson Pass and descends into the narrow valley where Valdez lies. Try to do the trip in daylight, in clear weather, and stop at the Worthington Glacier. This is the only road to Valdez. The drive from Anchorage is 6 hours without stops.

By Ferry: The **Alaska Marine Highway System** (✆ **800/642-0066** or 907/835-4436; www.ferryalaska.com) connects Valdez, Whittier, and Cordova by ferry. One time-tested way to see the Sound is to put your vehicle on the ferry in Whittier for the run to Valdez, then drive north on the Richardson Highway. The fast ferry *Chenega*

Richardson Highway.

cuts travel time from Anchorage to Valdez to less than driving: about 90 minutes by car from Anchorage to Whittier and less than 4 hours by ferry from Whittier to Valdez. Fare is $89 for an adult, half price ages 6 through 11, free 5 and under. A 15-foot car costs $105 to take along.

By Air: Era Alaska (✆ **800/866-8394;** www.flyera.com) flies between Anchorage and Valdez.

GETTING AROUND The main part of the town and boat harbor are compact enough to walk, but you will need wheels for the airport, the attractions on Dayville Road, most of the hiking trails, and the two B&Bs I mention below. Rental cars are available at the airport from **Valdez-U-Drive** (✆ **907/835-4402;** www.valdezudrive.com). Taxis are available from **Valdez Yellow Cab** (✆ **907/835-2500**).

VISITOR INFORMATION The Valdez Convention and Visitors Bureau maintains a **Visitor Information Center** at 104 Chenega St., at the corner of Egan Drive (P.O. Box 1603), Valdez, AK 99686 (✆ **907/835-4636;** www.valdez alaska.org). Pick up the free town map and useful *Vacation Planner*. They're open in summer daily 8am to 7pm and winter Monday through Friday 8am to 5pm.

Valdez

ATTRACTIONS
Maxine & Jesse Whitney Museum **3**
Remembering Old Valdez
    Museum Annex **2**
The Valdez Museum &
    Historical Archive **4**

HOTELS
Best Western Valdez Harbor Inn **5**
Blueberry Mary's B&B **1**
Mountain Sky Hotel & Suites **6**
Totem Inn **7**
Wild Roses by the Sea B&B Retreat **1**

RESTAURANTS
Fu Kung Chinese Restaurant **8**
The Harbor Cafe **9**
Totem Inn **7**

Valdez Bay

SPECIAL EVENTS   Valdez is famous for extreme skiing and snowboarding, mostly done by helicopter, and celebrated by the **Tailgate Alaska** festival at the end of March and beginning of April. The town has three **summer fishing derbies:** The **Halibut Derby** runs all summer, the **Silver Salmon Derby** is late July to early September, and the **Women's Silver Salmon Derby** is the second Saturday in August. Derby tickets are available all over town. The convention and visitors bureau is the best source of information on any of those events.

The **Fireweed Bicycle Race Across Alaska** (www.fireweed400. com) covers big mileage on the Glenn and Richardson highways between Sheep Mountain and Valdez, with 50-, 100-, 200-, and 400-mile events, usually the second weekend in July. Finish line festivities in Valdez include a kids' bike rodeo.

The **Last Frontier Theater Conference** (② **907/ 834-1614;** www.pwscc.edu) brings playwrights, directors, and actors from all over the U.S. for seminars and performances. Performances are staged every night over the 7-day event, and workshops and readings last all day. Those interested in literature and theater will find it worth arranging a trip around the event, usually in June, but check for changes to dates.

Last Frontier Theater Conference.

Valdez Gold Rush Days includes 5 days of community events, such as a parade and fish fry, at the end of July or beginning of August. Contact the visitor center for information.

[FastFACTS] VALDEZ

Banks   Two banks are on Egan Drive, both with ATMs.

Hospital   **Providence Valdez Medical Center** (📞 **907/835-2249**) is at 911 Meals Ave.

Internet Access   The comfortable **Valdez**

Consortium Library (📞 **907/835-4632**), at 260 Fairbanks St., has computers and free Wi-Fi, with tables where you can plug in a laptop.

Police   For nonemergencies, phone the **Valdez Police Department**

(📞 **907/835-4560**) at 212 Chenega Ave.

Post Office   Galena Drive and Tatitlek Street, 1 block back from Egan Drive.

Taxes   Valdez has no sales tax but does charge a 6% **room tax.**

Getting Outside

The best things to do in Valdez relate to Prince William Sound, so I've put those options first, in order of their interest to most readers.

SIGHTSEEING & WILDLIFE TOURS

For most visitors, a daylong ride on a tour boat into the Sound is likely to be the most memorable part of a visit to Valdez. The main tour-boat company in town is **Stan Stephens Glacier and Wildlife Cruises** (📞 **866/867-1297** or 907/ 835-4731; www.stanstephenscruises.com). The office is on the dock at the end

Touring Prince William Sound by boat.

of the small boat harbor near the Best Western Valdez Harbor Inn. Stephens has been showing off the Sound and defending it from pollution for decades. After passing through the long fjord of Port Valdez, boats enter an ice-choked bay in front of **Columbia Glacier** on a 6-hour tour that often encounters birds, seals, sea otters, sea lions, and sometimes whales, for $115 adults. A light lunch is served. Going on to Meares Glacier, farther west, adds 3 hours to the round-trip but brings you to a glacier that you can get a better look at and that may drop ice into the water. That cruise is $150 and includes a hot lunch and a snack. Prices are half for children 2 to 12 on either trip.

SEA KAYAKING & SAILING

Right around Valdez, short sea-kayaking day trips to see wildlife on the Duck Flats may be just what you want for a first try at the sport, but that area is hardly wilderness, as it's also reached by road and is within sight of the oil facilities. Day trips to Shoup Glacier get you into more of the beautiful, remote country that makes Prince William Sound so exceptional. **Pangaea Adventures** (✆ **800/ 660-9637** or 907/835-8442; www.alaskasummer.com) offers guided sea kayaking from Valdez or rentals for experienced paddlers, for whom the Sound is a paradise. Their Shoup Glacier trip combines amazing scenery, lunch on the beach near the ice, and satisfying paddling that's a bit more challenging than the very easy outings usually offered to visitors. They also operate multiday guided camping trips deeper into the Sound, or, for those who prefer a bed, lodge, and "mother ship" expedition, wherein clients paddle by day and stay onboard or in a lodge at night. Pangaea offers many other services as well: water-taxi and kayak drop-off, ice climbing and glacier hiking, river rafting, and even trips that combine these activities in the Sound and Wrangell–St. Elias National Park. Check out the website.

    Raven Charters, Slip C-25, Valdez Boat Harbor (✆ **907/835-5863;** www. alaska.net/~ravenchr), is run by a family that shares its home on a substantial 50-foot ketch with clients to sail and explore the Sound. The wind tends to be light and changeable, but a sailboat makes a comfortable base for discovering interesting, isolated places. All-inclusive prices for the whole boat start at $1,050 per day for up to four passengers, or $850 for a day charter, with discounts for longer trips.

FISHING & BOATING

The ocean waters around Valdez are rich in salmon and halibut. It's possible to fish for salmon from shore. Popular spots include Dayville Road west of the fish hatchery, the city dock near the ferry dock in town, or even the harbor floats. Except at the hatchery, you're hoping a fish swims by your lure or bait at the right moment: There isn't a freshwater destination to concentrate the fish. Chances and the fishing experience are improved if you get out on the water. Many small fishing charter boats are available in the boat harbor, or you can rent your own boat and gear; book either through **Fish Central** (✆ **888/835-5002** or 907/835-5002; www.fishcentral.net). They can also take care of processing and freezing your catch for shipment.

HIKING & MOUNTAIN-BIKING

Valdez has a broad selection of good dayhikes and an overnight. The visitor center can advise you on choices beyond those I list here. In addition, you can join guided hiking and glacier activities, including ice climbing, with Pangaea Adventures (see "Sea Kayaking & Sailing," above).

The easiest hike is a pleasant forest and shore walk to **Dock Point,** starting at the east side of the boat harbor, at the end of North Harbor Drive. It's a peaceful, natural walk close to town, with boardwalks and overlooks and berries along the way in season.

For a longer hike and perhaps an overnight, the **Shoup Glacier Trail** runs 12 miles west from town along the shore of Port Valdez to a lagoon in front of the glacier's face. The going is generally flat, and there are many places to get down to the beach, with wild iris and many other flowers. Cool yourself in a waterfall. Camping is unrestricted, but be sure to bring mosquito repellent and review bear avoidance techniques (see "Outdoors Health & Safety," p. 521). If you plan to go all the way, consider reserving one of the three state parks cabins near the glacier (see

Bridal Veil Falls.

"State Parks Cabin Reservations," in "Exploring the Kenai Peninsula & Prince William Sound," earlier in this chapter). Or you can get a lift one-way from a water taxi, such as the service offered by Pangaea Adventures. The trail starts at the end of West Egan Drive.

The **Solomon Gulch Trail** starts across from the fish hatchery on Dayville Road (see below) and goes steeply up to Solomon Lake, where locals swim. Be prepared for bears. Trails off **Mineral Creek Road,** above town off Hanagita Street, are great for walking, mountain-biking, or berry picking, and in winter there is a fine cross-country skiing trail network. The **Valdez Goat Trail** runs from the spectacular Bridal Veil Falls at mile 13.8 of the Richardson Highway for a distance of 2.5 miles on an abandoned roadbed, past some great views.

HELI-SKIING

Valdez is a magnet for backcountry alpine and extreme skiing and snowboarding, thanks to its prodigious snow and limitless steep mountains. A bunch of guide companies offer these trips, operating by helicopter from early March to early May. One established operator is **Valdez Heli-Ski Guides** (© **907/835-4528;** www.valdezheliskiguides.com). Expect to pay around $925 for a day of around six runs, or book a package with lodgings and meals.

Exploring the Town

Maxine & Jesse Whitney Museum ★   A couple arriving after World War II spent a lifetime collecting arrowheads, Native crafts, and trophy animal mounts for a roadside museum and rock shop in Fairbanks, then donated everything to the community college in Valdez. As unpromising as that sounds as the basis for a serious museum, the curators here have turned the collection into one of the most evocative exhibits on Alaska anywhere. To do so, they bypassed the usual approach of focusing on the objects—necessitated in part because the Whitneys didn't

Maxine & Jesse Whitney Museum.

record the context of the things they collected—instead making a museum about a bygone world, with its old-time roadside rock shop and the tough but warm pioneer culture that surrounded it. Exploring that past is well worth an hour.

303 Lowe St. ⓒ **907/834-1690.** www.pwscc.edu. Free admission. May to mid-Sept daily 9am–7pm; winter Mon–Fri 9 am–noon and 1–5 pm.

The Solomon Gulch Hatchery   When the pink salmon return from late June to early August, they swarm on the hatchery in a blizzard of fish. The hatchery releases more than 200 million pinks and 2 million silvers (or coho) each year. There is no stream for the salmon to return to, so they try to get back into the hatchery, crowding together in a solid sea of fighting muscle. Seals and birds come in to feed, and you can stand onshore and watch (and smell) the spectacle. Surefire fishing is allowed up the shore on Dayville Road. A self-guided tour of the hatchery starts from the parking lot near the Solomon Creek bridge.

On Dayville Rd. on the way to the tanker terminal. ⓒ **907/835-1329.** Free self-guided tour. Summer daily 7am–10pm.

"Remembering Old Valdez" exhibit at the Valdez Museum and Historical Archive.

The Valdez Museum and Historical Archive ★★   The museum's primary exhibit is a chronological walk through the area's history from explorers' visits through the oil spill. Objects and photographs bring back some of those moments and places with emotional force, with humor, or with something like nostalgia—if that's the word to describe longing for a time before one's own birth. Despite its professionalism, the museum has friendly, small-town hospitality and shows items of small town pride, such as the shiny old fire engines in the lobby, dating back to 1886. An annex, near the ferry dock, is less polished but shouldn't be missed. It contains the "Remembering Old Valdez" exhibit, a ¹⁄₂₀-scale model of how Valdez looked at its old site, before the 1964 earthquake forced the town to move. Using photographs, records, and old-timers' memories, a dedicated worker brought that lost city back with 400 miniature buildings on tables, like model train dioramas without the trains. A well-made 37-minute film covers the earthquake's effect on Valdez. The annex is at 436 S. Hazelet Ave. Admission covers both buildings.

217 Egan Dr. ✆ **907/835-2764.** www.valdezmuseum.org. $7 adults, $6 ages 63 and over, $5 ages 14–17, free for children 13 and under. Memorial Day to Labor Day both buildings daily 9am–5pm. Low season main building Mon–Sat 1–5pm, annex by appointment.

Where to Stay

The hotels listed here are near the boat harbor and museums, so you may not need a car if you stay there. For the B&Bs, you probably will want transportation, as the walk is long.

Best Western Valdez Harbor Inn ★★   This up-to-date hotel commands the best location in town, right on the harbor near the tour boats, although a minority of rooms have good water views. The rooms are well equipped, with flatscreen TV and DVD players, and set up to make snacks. Bathrooms are tiled, and everything is clean and trim. The lobby brings in lots of light from a grassy area by the harbor entrance that's a nice spot to sit and watch boats pass by. There's a welcoming breakfast area, too. Overall, this is the town's most appealing hotel. A bar and restaurant on-site had just changed hands at this writing, too late for a review; the dining room has a wonderful harbor view, and the restaurant has traditionally been the town's main spot for fine dining, as the management promises to keep it.

100 N. Harbor Dr. (P.O. Box 468), Valdez, AK 99686. www.valdezharborinn.com. ✆ **888/222-3440** or 907/835-3434. Fax 907/835-2308. 88 units. High season $169–$199 double; low season $99–$109 double. Extra person age 12 or older $15. Rates include continental breakfast. AE, DISC, MC, V. **Amenities:** Restaurant. *In room:* TV/DVD, fridge, hair dryer, microwave, Wi-Fi.

Mountain Sky Hotel and Suites ★   Stay here for good standard rooms with few compromises. Service is good and common areas spacious. There's a small pool, and the lobby has a handy breakfast area. Rooms are decorated in burgundy, hunter green, and dark wood, with lots of extras, large TVs, and mirrors. Our family of six fit nicely in a family suite, which has a large main bedroom and a separate children's room with bunk beds and its own TV.

100 Meals Ave., Valdez, AK 99686. www.mountainskyhotel.com. ✆ **800/478-4445** or 907/835-4445. Fax 907/835-2437. 102 units. High season $179–$199 double; low season $115–$129 double. AE, DISC, DC, MC, V. **Amenities:** Exercise room; Internet station in lobby; indoor pool; spa. *In room:* TV/VCR, fridge, hair dryer, microwave, Wi-Fi.

Totem Inn ★ 🔥   Although the street view of these brown buildings suggests a dated motel, many of the rooms inside have all the qualities of a good modern hotel, including units entered from a breezeway with two queen-size beds, flatscreen TVs, and many amenities. Reasonably priced suites in a newer two-story building have full kitchens and washing machines in the unit. The cottages are on the rough side.

The restaurant, where guests check in, is Valdez's primary local hangout, a traditional, friendly small-town restaurant with a TV always turned on. Meals are plentiful, hours long, and the coffee cups never empty. Besides pleasing residents, the owners strive to bring in visitors with specials and salads a step above the good diner food.

114 E. Egan Dr. (P.O. Box 648), Valdez, AK 99686. www.toteminn.com. © **888/808-4431** or 907/835-4443. Fax 907/834-4430. 69 units. High season $149 double, $189 suite; low season $89 double, $139 suite. AE, DISC, MC, V. **Amenities:** Restaurant; bar. *In room:* TV/DVD, fridge, micro-wave, Wi-Fi.

Wild Roses by the Sea B&B Retreat ★   Light pours from bay windows that overlook the water and surrounding woods into large, elegantly appointed rooms with high ceilings, decorated with Asian and contemporary art and finished in light colors, wood floors, and Berber-style carpets. Best of all is the spacious and private Ocean View Guesthouse, a downstairs suite with a kitchen and living room. The hostess, Rose Fong, prepares elaborate breakfasts in the summer and feeds guests snacks and beverages all day. The location is half a mile from the Shoup Glacier Trail (see above) and less than a mile from a state park beach.

629 Fiddlehead Lane (P.O. Box 3396), Valdez, AK 99686. www.alaskabytheseabnb.com. © **907/835-2930.** 3 units. Summer $134–$173 double, including full breakfast; winter $79 dou-ble, including continental breakfast. Extra adult $20, child $15. MC, V. *In room:* TV, hair dryer.

CAMPING

The **Bear Paw RV Park,** 101 N. Harbor Dr. (www.bearpawrvpark.com; © **907/835-2530**), is in the middle of town, next to the boat harbor. Full hookups are $35, tent sites $25 for two. The same operators offer an adult-only campground less than 2 blocks away, at 300 Wyatt Way, charging $40 for full hookups.

The best campground in the area is the state's **Blueberry Lake Camp-ground,** 24 miles out of town on the Richardson Highway, just below Thompson Pass. The campground is above the tree line, with mountaintop views and access to limitless alpine hiking. It can be windy and cold. The small lake is stocked with trout. Twenty-four well-screened sites are $10 on a self-serve system. There are pit toilets. RVs are welcome, but there are no hookups.

Where to Eat

Besides the eateries described below, the waterfront dining room at the **Best Western Valdez Harbor Inn** (p. 352) is usually one of the town's best; it changed hands just before my deadline, so I couldn't complete a review.

Fu Kung Chinese Restaurant ★ CHINESE   This long-established family restaurant near the harbor serves some of the best meals in town; in Valdez, that's not a huge claim to fame, but this place is good. The interior is clean and pleas-ant, with a fish tank, warm colors, and plenty of room. The food is plentiful and tasty, especially the gingery bean curd with vegetables, the hot-and-sour soup, and the kung pao chicken. They feature local seafood in Chinese dishes and serve some Thai and sushi selections, too. Service is fast and attentive. In winter, they often close earlier than listed below.

207 Kobuk Dr. (1 block from the boat harbor). © **907/835-5255.** Lunch $9–$11; dinner main courses $12–$16. AE, DISC, MC, V. Daily 11am–11pm.

The Harbor Café ★★ 🏠   The restaurant seems to be trying to pass itself off as a boat harbor burger joint, with picnic tables outside a boothlike building. The first clue it is something more is the line of relatively mature diners ordering at the window. Their choices include burgers, bratwurst, and sandwiches, but also items such as the Caesar salad with blackened shrimp and scallops that I got—a masterpiece of spicy roughness offset by creamy crispness. Friends say the food is always delicious. It's the work of a Peruvian owner, who makes the meals look as well as taste wonderful. (My unique beverage also was fantastic: lemon-ginger juice mixed with a little Sprite.) In the evening and during the colder months, meals are served in a tiny dining room with just a few tables, where a recent menu listed just four entrees, all over $30—steak, salmon, crab, or halibut, the last of which had a choice of three interesting marinades and sauces.

255 N. Harbor Dr. © **907/835-4776.** Lunch $7-$15; dinner $30-$56. MC, V. High season Mon-Sat 11am-8pm; low season Tues-Sat 11am-7pm.

CORDOVA: HIDDEN TREASURE

The first time I went to Cordova, my companion and I arrived at the Mudhole Smith Airport in a small plane and happened upon an old guy with a pickup truck who offered to let us ride in back to town. The highway led out onto a broad, wetland plain—among the largest contiguous wetlands in the Western Hemisphere, as it happens. Our guide's voice, studded with profanity, boomed through the back window as he told us proudly about the diversity of the wildlife to be found out there. Then, absolutely bursting with enthusiasm, he leaned on the horn and bellowed, "Look at them f—ing swans!" We looked; trumpeters paddling in the marsh looked back. He would have invited them along to the bar, too, if he'd known how.

Every time I've been to Cordova since, I've been taken under the wings of new friends. Although they usually don't express themselves the same way that first gentleman did, they are just as enthusiastic to show off the amazing natural riches of their little kingdom. Tourists are still something of a novelty here, for Cordova isn't just off the beaten track—it's not on the track at all. There's no road to the rest of the world. Boosters call their town "Alaska's Hidden Treasure," a nickname I endorse. But that's for folks who enjoy the outdoors; if you're looking for commercial tourist attractions, you won't find them. Go to Cordova as a traveler, not a tourist, ready to create your own fun.

Cordova.

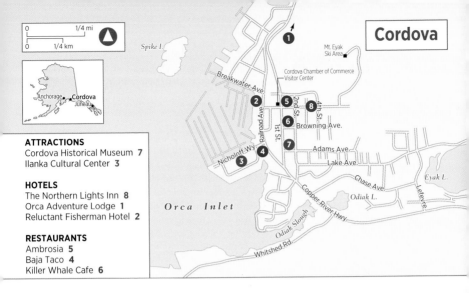

Cordova owes much of its uniqueness to a rich history and remote location. Its biggest political controversy—simmering for 70 years—concerns whether to build a road to the outside world. The town's heyday was in 1911, when the Copper River and Northwestern Railroad opened, carrying copper ore down from the mine at Kennecott; it hit a low when the mine closed in 1938. Since then, boosters have been trying to get a road built on the old rail line, north along the Copper River to Chitina (covered in chapter 9, under "Wrangell–St. Elias National Park & Kennecott"). The road builders have made it only about 50 miles out of town so far. From Cordova, the **Copper River Highway** provides access to the best bird-watching and, in my judgment, the most impressive glacier in Alaska, as well as trails and magnificent vistas and areas to see wildlife. In town, the small-boat harbor is a doorway to Prince William Sound.

Essentials

GETTING THERE   **By Ferry:** Cordova is served by ferry daily from Valdez and Whittier by the **Alaska Marine Highway System** (𝄢 **800/642-0066** or 907/424-7333 local dock; www.ferryalaska.com). It's a spectacular ride aboard the fast ferry *Chenega*. The passenger fare from Valdez is $50, from Whittier $89; children 5 to 11 pay half. Taking a vehicle under 15 feet one-way from Valdez to Cordova is $94, Whittier $105. You can also rent a car in Cordova. See "Exploring Southeast Alaska," in chapter 5, for information about the ferry system.

    By Air: Alaska Airlines (𝄢 **800/426-0333;** www.alaskaair.com) flies daily each direction, from Anchorage to the west and Yakutat, Juneau, and Seattle to the southeast, with more flights from Anchorage operated by **Era Alaska** (𝄢 **800/866-8394;** www.flyera.com).

GETTING AROUND   You can easily walk around downtown Cordova, but that's not where the most interesting sights are. To get out on the Copper River Highway, you'll need a car, a bus, or, if you're vigorous, a bike. Cars are for rent from **Chinook Auto Rentals** (𝄢 **877/424-5279** or 907/424-5279) at Northern Nights Inn (p. 361). Taxis are available from **Cordova Taxi**

(© **907/424-5151**). Water taxi and rental of bikes, kayaks, skiffs, canoes, and fishing and camping gear are available at **Cordova Coastal Outfitters,** south of the boat harbor near the Alaska Commercial grocery store (© **800/357-5145** or 907/424-7424; www.cordovacoastal.com). They also offer drop-off and pickup service on the Copper River Highway, allowing visitors to go for a canoeing or cabin trip without renting a car.

To get to remote cabins and fishing, try **Fishing & Flying** (© **907/424-3324**), operated by Gayle Ranney, a warm and authentic Alaskan bush pilot. She has a choice of planes to get where you want to go and relationships with some other great businesses, including a lighthouse that's for rent in one of the most spectacular, rugged, and out-of-the-way spots in Alaska.

VISITOR INFORMATION The **Cordova Chamber of Commerce Visitor Center** (© **907/424-7260;** www.cordovachamber.com) is at 404 1st St., north of Council Avenue (P.O. Box 99, Cordova, AK 99574). They're open Monday through Friday 9am to 5pm, with occasional Saturday hours.

The **Cordova Ranger District** of the Chugach National Forest, upstairs in the old white courthouse at 2nd Street and Browning (P.O. Box 280), Cordova, AK 99574 (© **907/424-7661;** www.fs.fed.us/r10/chugach), has displays and provides maps and guide information that's indispensable for planning outdoor activities. The staff will sit down and help you figure out what you want to do.

SPECIAL EVENTS The **Cordova Ice Worm Festival,** in late January/early February, is a winter carnival culminating in the appearance of the big ice worm—or, to be precise, ice centipede—in a parade. The **Copper River Delta Shorebird Festival,** the first weekend of May, revolves around the coming of dizzying swarms of millions of shorebirds that use the delta and beaches near the town as a migratory stopover. The whole community gets involved to host bird-watchers and put on a full schedule of educational and outdoor activities that lasts 3 days. The **Old Time Downtown 4th of July Party** includes a community salmon barbecue, games, music, dancing, parade, and pie social. **Copper River Wild! Salmon Festival,** in mid-July, has a marathon and a music festival. For details, contact the Cordova Chamber of Commerce or check their website, listed above under "Visitor Information."

[FastFACTS] CORDOVA

Banks There are two banks on 1st Street, with **ATMs.**

Hospital **Cordova Community Medical Center** and **Ilanka Community Health Center** are located together on Chase Street (© **907/424-8000**), off the Copper River Highway near the Odiak Slough.

Internet Access Find it at the **Cordova Public Library** (© **907/424-6667**) and at **Orca Book and Sound** (© **907/424-5305**), both on 1st Street.

Police For nonemergency business, call © **907/424-6100.**

Post Office At Railroad Avenue and Council.

Taxes **Sales tax** is 6%; rooms and car rentals carry an additional 6% tax.

Exploring the Town & Nearby Hiking

ATTRACTIONS   Cordova mostly is for outdoor activities (covered below), but save some time to wander around town, make discoveries, and meet people. The **Cordova Historical Museum,** 622 1st St. (☏ **907/424-6665;** www.cordovamuseum.org), mostly in one room, does a good job of presenting some valuable artifacts reflecting Cordova's eventful past, a collection of classic Alaskan art, and some odd and fascinating stuff. There's a historic lighthouse lens, a Linotype machine, the interior of a fishing boat, a parka made of bear gut, basketry, and photographs of fishing and historical scenes. The museum is open summer Monday through Saturday from 10am to 6pm, Sunday from 1 to 5pm; winter Tuesday through Friday from 10am to 5pm, Saturday from 1 to 5pm. Recommended donation is $1.

Cordova is a center for the Eyak, a small but linguistically and ethnographically distinct people, and a crossroads of other Native peoples. Make a point of stopping in at the Native Village of Eyak's **Ilanka Cultural Center,** at 110 Nicholoff Way, across from the Fishermen's Memorial at the small-boat harbor (☏ **907/424-7903;** www.ilankacenter.org). Although small, the center is new and growing, and I always experience a warm link with the Eyak people I met. The collection includes Eyak, Alutiiq, Tlingits, and Ahtna artifacts, photographs, and oral histories. There is also a fully reconstructed orca whale skeleton. A disturbing and powerful totem pole by Mike Webber, in the Native tradition of the "shame pole," reflects Cordova's still-raw anger and grief over the *Exxon Valdez* oil spill. The gallery sells art, books, and other items made in Alaska, especially by Alaska Natives. Artists sometimes offer classes and demonstrations. Hours are summer Monday through Friday 10am to 5pm; winter Tuesday through Friday 10am to 5pm. Admission is free, but donations are encouraged.

HIKING   Cordova has more good hiking trails per capita than any place I know. The Cordova Ranger Station can provide you with a free trail-guide booklet with lots of ideas and maps. There are three hikes close to town and more on the Copper River Delta, covered below in the section on the Delta, and at Hartney Bay (ask at the ranger station).

The **Tripod Mountain Trail** begins right from town and climbs 1,255 feet over less than a mile up the first mountain back from the shore, a half-day hike with views that present the Sound and Cordova like a map below you. The trail begins at the foot of the town ski lift, on 6th Street—take Browning up the hill.

Partway up Tripod Mountain, near the middle drop-off of the ski lift, a 1-mile trail links to the **Crater Lake Trail,** which eventually joins the **Power Creek Trail** on a loop of 12 miles. An easier start for that route is the Power Creek Road—drive it along the north side of Eyak Lake to the end, 7 miles from town. The creek has spawning red salmon in July and attracts a lot of bears; watch, but don't get out of your car if you come upon one. The trail follows the creek through dramatic scenery 4.3 miles to the Power Creek Forest Service cabin, with a great view (reserve through the system described on p. 283).

The Copper River Delta

The delta and its star attraction, the **Childs Glacier,** make an unforgettable day trip by car or tour bus from Cordova, but if you have a couple of days, you can do much more. The backwaters, sloughs, and ponds beg to be explored by canoe. Bird-watchers will especially enjoy paddling here and visiting the boardwalks and blinds set up by the Forest Service. You can raft the rivers. There are excellent hiking trails and mountain-biking routes branching from the road, and Forest Service cabins to stay in. And the river itself has many miles of deserted sandy beaches for long walks or sand castles on a sunny day.

The delta seems to go on forever, a vast patchwork of marsh, pond, small hills of trees, and the huge, implacable gray river itself. The glacial silt it carries away—some 2 million tons a day—has built this 700,000-acre wetland. A well-maintained gravel road leads across it, all in Chugach National Forest, and the rangers have done a good job of providing ways and places to enjoy and learn about the area. The road itself is the old bed of the Copper River and Northwestern Railroad. It leads 48 miles to the **Million Dollar Bridge.** Built by Michael Heney,

Million Dollar Bridge.

a magician of a 19th-century railroad builder who also constructed the White Pass and Yukon Route in Skagway, the 200-mile Copper River line was an engineering triumph that brought the mind-boggling wealth of the Kennecott Copper Corporation to ships in Cordova (read more about the mine in "Wrangell–St. Elias National Park & Kennecott," in chapter 9). The bridge over the Copper River was built in a race against time between two surging glaciers in 30-foot-deep, fast-flowing glacial water, during winter. It stood for 50 years, until the 1964 earthquake knocked down one end of one of the spans, driving it into the riverbed. In 2004, your highway dollars repaired that span, and once again you can drive to the other side, where an unmaintained road soon peters out into a rough trail.

GETTING THERE

BY CAR   Driving gives you the most freedom. The **Copper River Highway** is gravel, but it's wide and level. If you've brought a rental car and your contract does not allow driving on gravel, I recommend parking in Cordova and renting a car there for the drive on the Copper River Highway. The Northern Nights Inn (p. 361) offers rentals. Beyond the Million Dollar Bridge, the road becomes a rough four-wheel-drive track, and if you get stuck, you'll be there for a long time. Check at the Forest Service Cordova Ranger Station for the latest news about the road and pick up their road guide.

BY BIKE   Mountain-biking the highway is the adventurous way to travel, camping or staying in a Forest Service cabin on the way. The drawbacks are the distances, the delta's strong winds, and a lot of road dust. Of course, you don't have to ride all the way to see lots of birds and wildlife, and there are good mountain-biking routes on the delta away from the road. The 3-mile **Saddlebag Glacier Trail,** at mile 25 of the Copper River Highway, leads to a vista of a glacial lake surrounded by rocky peaks. Bikes are for rent from Cordova Coastal Outfitters (see "Out on Prince William Sound," below) for $18 a day.

ALONG THE ROAD

Keep your eyes scanning the wetlands and mountains around you as you drive out the road. The **wildlife** you may see along the way includes black and brown bears, wolves, coyote, moose, and mountain goats. The entire world population of dusky Canada geese nests on the delta, and you're likely to see eagles and trumpeter swans without really looking. The ranger station provides a wildlife-viewing guide, and there are several places to stop along the way designed for bird-watching. The first is a platform with interpretive signs as you leave town, an introduction to the delta; this stretch of the road is fine for bird-watching.

Don't skip the **Alaganik Slough Boardwalk.** Take the 3¼-mile spur road to the right 17 miles out the Copper River Highway; it's marked. The sky here is big and certain, while the land is ambivalent—it doesn't know if it wants to be waving grass of green and gold or shallow, shimmering ponds and tendrils of water. The road leads to the start of the 1,000-foot boardwalk with a blind and to a riverside path. Water reflects the sun and the colors of the marsh. We were speechless one evening at sunset, even in the complete absence of birds. Often in the summer, you can see breeding trumpeter swans, ducks, and grebes, and in the spring and fall, migrating waterfowl and shorebirds make appearances. The path is on the left just before you arrive at the boardwalk and picnic area; the 1-mile Fisherman's Trail is a meandering route among water and brush.

You can stop at any of the bridges crossing the Copper River for a romp in the sand. The river beaches of fine sand extend practically forever.

The highway ends with the area's best attraction, the advancing **Childs Glacier.** This is the most amazing glacier I've ever seen, and no one seems to know about it outside Cordova. The advancing wall of ice, 300 feet tall, comes right down to the quarter-mile-wide river, battling the flowing water for control of the land here. The glacier tries to divert the river, while the river tries to cut the glacier like a knife, eroding the base and bringing down huge ice chunks. As you sit on the opposite bank, the glacier on the opposite side is too large to see—it completely fills your field of vision, creating an eerie and hypnotic sense of scale. On a warm summer day, you can feel the glacier's thunder as the ice shifts and see pieces fall off. A chunk the size of a car barely registers, but when an office build-ing–size hunk falls, there's a roar

The Alaganik Slough Boardwalk.

and gray breakers radiate out across the river. Falling glacier pieces have made waves large enough to uproot trees here, not to mention hurl a few fish around—at the Forest Service viewing and picnic area across the river, salmon have been found high up in the trees and boulders in odd places. Several years ago, such a wave injured some visitors, and now the Forest Service warns that anyone who can't run fast should stay in the observation tower. A path leads less than a mile to the **Million Dollar Bridge,** or drive by on your way out.

The Forest Service maintains a camping and picnic area at the glacier, with RV and tent sites, restrooms, and sheltered tables. RV sites are $25, walk-in tent sites $10, at a self-pay station. Three hand-pump wells produce drinking water.

ACTIVITIES

CANOEING The delta's canoe routes are little used, leading to remote places where birds and aquatic animals rule. You can launch on Alaganik Slough at a picnic area at mile 22 on the Copper River Highway, paddling placid waters into stunningly beautiful marsh lands, perhaps headed for the Tiedeman Forest Service Cabin for a few days. Taking the "Wrong Way" route that starts a couple of miles up the road, you can float several miles of challenging water down to McKinley Lake, stay at the Forest Service cabin, then float downstream again to the slough launch, back at the road. It's ideal overnight, or you could do it in a day or, as we did, spend an extra day and night at the cabin. The couple that runs **Cordova Coastal Outfitters** (see below, under "Out on Prince William Sound") rents canoes for $50 a day (additional days discounted 15%), offers drop-off, and will help you decide what route to take. You can ride out on one of their bicycles and pick up the canoe already at the launch site. They rent camping gear, too. Make sure to get their advice on current conditions before setting out on the water.

FISHING Anglers can fish the delta's lakes and streams for all species of Pacific salmon except kings (which you can fish in saltwater), as well as Dolly Varden char and rainbow and cutthroat trout. The Cordova Ranger Station can offer guidance, or contact the Cordova office of the **Alaska Department of Fish and Game** (© **907/424-3212;** www.alaska.gov/adfg). See "Fishing," in chapter 11, for general guidance.

HIKING The Forest Service maintains several trails on the delta. The **Alaganik Slough Boardwalk** and **Saddlebag Glacier Trail** are mentioned on p. 359 and 359. The Copper River beaches make for sublime off-trail hikes.

The **Haystack Trail,** starting on the right just past the 19-mile marker on the highway, climbs through mossy rainforest from the delta's floor onto an odd little hill. The glaciers that once covered the delta spared this bedrock outcropping. The trail is steep in places but only three-quarters of a mile in length, and it leads to an overlook.

The **McKinley Lake Trail,** at mile 21.6 on the highway, leads 2.5 miles through rainforest vegetation to a lake bearing trout, and a little farther to the overgrown ruins of a gold mine. You can also get there by canoe (see above). There are two Forest Service cabins on the trail, the small McKinley Trail Cabin, near the highway, and the McKinley Lake Cabin, beautifully situated among big trees above the lake. Each costs $35 a night and can be reserved through the national system described on p. 288.

Out on Prince William Sound

The waters of Prince William Sound around Cordova, although lacking the tide-water glaciers found in the western Sound, are protected and rich in marine life. Sea otters don't receive a second glance from locals, congregating in rafts of many dozens or even hundreds. Sea lions can be found predictably, too, and orcas and humpback whales are not unusual. Bird-watchers can expect harlequin ducks and many other marine birds.

Cordova Coastal Outfitters is a good place to start for any outdoor activi-ties (✆ **800/357-5145** or 907/424-7424; www.cordovacoastal.com). Andy Craig and Seawan Gehlbach know the equipment, the skills, and the area, and they convey that knowledge with casual enthusiasm. Their office is south of the boat harbor, between the Alaska Commercial grocery store and Baja Taco. They guide sea kayaking, rent kayaks, and offer water taxi drop-off for kayakers. The **guided sea-kayaking trip** for beginners lasts 4 hours and costs $75, $60 ages 12 and under, concentrating on wildlife sightings; a 7-hour guided trip is $115, $100 ages 12 and under, including lunch. An advantage of planning your kayak-ing here is that there is plenty to see near the harbor and not much boat traffic. If your group isn't up to kayaking, consider renting a motorboat. You won't believe the sense of freedom you feel clearing the harbor breakwater to explore Orca Inlet and the bays of Hawkins Island, on the far side. Boats rent for $150 to $225 a day; fishing gear is extra.

A few vessels are available for fishing charters or day trips to see whales and other wildlife. The chamber of commerce (p. 356) has links to charter operators on its website, or call them for a referral.

Where to Stay

The Northern Nights Inn ★ 🌶 Families will enjoy this big apartment-style room. Cordova is so safe, the kids were able to walk out the front door and explore on their own—they couldn't believe it. Each room has been lovingly reno-vated, with antiques, reproductions, and quilts. They're generally spacious, some have views, and all are loaded with amenities—an almost unreal value. All but one has a full kitchen, and cereal is provided for breakfast. The inn is Becky Cha-pek and Bill Myers's historic 1906 house, a couple of blocks above the town's main street. Becky loves to talk and share her enthusiasm for Cordova, and you couldn't start with a better person for figuring out what you want to do. She also rents older-model vehicles that are okay to drive on the Copper River Highway out to Childs Glacier.

500 3rd St. (P.O. Box 1564), Cordova, AK 99547. www.northernnightsinn.com. ✆ **907/424-5356.** Fax 907/424-3291. 5 units. $85–$110 double. Extra adult $20. Children 15 and under stay free in parent's room. AE, DISC, MC, V. **Amenities:** Babysitting. *In room:* TV/VCR, fridge, hair dryer, microwave, Wi-Fi.

Orca Adventure Lodge ★ A picturesque old cannery north of town was renovated into simple guest rooms with private bathrooms (no phones or TVs, however) while retaining the exterior and muscular ambience that made it attrac-tive in the first place. But it's the location and the things you can do here that make the place: on a gravel beach with a dock where sea kayaks, fishing boats, and floatplanes pick up guests, and where thousands of pink salmon spawn in a small creek. In the late winter, helicopters land on the grounds to carry guests to ski in the vast and trackless Chugach Mountains. Guests can use the place as a hotel, paying the regular nightly rates listed below, or come with a package, which includes all meals and outdoor equipment, such as kayaks, bikes, and fishing poles (guiding is extra), for $155 per person per day.

2500 Orca Rd. (P.O. Box 2105), Cordova, AK 99574. www.orcaadventurelodge.com. ℂ **866/424-ORCA** (6722) or 907/424-7249. 40 units. Summer $155 double, $190 suite; winter check for rates. **Amenities:** Restaurant.

Reluctant Fisherman Inn ★★   This is where most visitors will stay, the town's main hotel. A commercial fishing family with three generations of history in Cordova bought the failed business and poured money and effort into reviving the place, a process that continues as needed improvements spread room to room. The sale of Greg Meyer and Sylvia Lange's fishing assets became a new roof, a sun deck over the harbor, and much else. Their children help staff the desk and make the hotel friendly and homey. The location certainly justifies the effort, with its riveting view at the heart of the town. Despite the age of the building, the rooms have the amenities of a good midrange hotel. The hotel's restaurant serves good evening meals. A continental breakfast is provided to guests in the lobby.

407 Railroad Ave. (P.O. Box 150), Cordova, AK 99574. www.reluctantfisherman.com. ℂ **907/424-3272.** Fax 907/424-7465. 40 units. High season $130–$150 double, $160–$330 suite; low season $95–$115 double, $160 suite. Extra adult in room $10. Children free to age 18. Rates include continental breakfast. AE, MC, V. **Amenities:** Restaurant; bar; airport shuttle ($10). *In room:* TV w/HBO, Wi-Fi.

CAMPING

A Forest Service campground is located well out of town, at Childs Glacier (p. 359).

Where to Eat

Some of Cordova's best meals—breakfast, lunch, and dinner—come from **Baja Taco** (ℂ **907/424-5599**), near the south end of the boat harbor. The kitchen and espresso machine are in an old bus, with a window for ordering, and there are comfortable indoor and outdoor seating areas for diners, with free Wi-Fi. The salmon tacos are exceptional, and all the meals are tasty and generous. The restaurant serves wine and both Alaskan and Mexican beer. It's open April through September.

   Ambrosia, 410 1st St. (ℂ **907/424-7175**), is a solid standby, a well-run family restaurant in a light storefront with an extensive menu, including pizza. It's the kind of place that stays in business in a small town: The food is reliable, the portions large, and the service friendly and helpful. My children became addicted to the gooey fettuccine Alfredo with chicken. The restaurant serves beer and wine. Prices range from $10 to $21. Hours are daily 4pm to 10pm.

   The primary small-town eat-and-meet place is the vegetarian-friendly **Killer Whale Cafe** (ℂ **907/424-7733**), on 1st Street. All-day breakfast includes a selection of omelets and other ways of having eggs, and for lunch there are sandwiches in the $8-to-$11 range, including salmon and halibut, burgers, and the like. Besides the expected, the cafe serves salmon cakes, biscuits and gravy, smoothies, milkshakes, and espresso. Hours are daily 6:30am to 3pm.

THE DENALI NATIONAL PARK REGION

8

D enali (Den-*al*-ee) stands alone among the national parks: It gives regular people easy access to real wilderness, with sweeping tundra vistas, abundant wildlife, and North America's tallest mountain. Other wilderness areas in Alaska may have equally inspiring scenery and even more animals, but Denali is unique because of its accessibility to visitors—and because that accessibility hasn't spoiled the natural experience, as it has at so many other parks.

The Denali experience spreads beyond the park. After all, the park boundary is an artificial line—the wildlife and the scenery of the Alaska Range don't observe its significance. To the east, the **Denali Highway** runs through the same extraordinary terrain, with opportunities for hiking over the tundra and canoeing on the lakes managed by the Bureau of Land Management. To the south, **Denali State Park** and the town of **Talkeetna** provide another vantage on Mount McKinley, with the advantage of salmon fishing in the rivers. The construction of comfortable new lodges and a variety of good outdoor guides have helped make Talkeetna a popular alternative gateway to Denali. Even though it's 150 miles from the park entrance by car, Talkeetna is physically closer to the mountain than is the park headquarters.

TOURS At Denali, you can see the heart of the park for little more than it would cost for you to visit Yellowstone. And when you get there, it's a pristine natural environment where truly wild animals live in a nearly complete ecosystem without much human interference. A single National Park Service decision makes this possible: The only road through the park is closed to the public. This means that to get into the park, you must ride a **bus** over a dusty gravel road hour after hour, but it also means that the animals are still there to watch and their behavior remains essentially normal. From the window of the bus, you're likely to see grizzly bears doing what they would be doing even if you weren't there. It may be the only $30 safari in the world.

RELAXATION What's even more unique is that you can get off the bus pretty much whenever you want to, walk across the tundra, out of sight of the road, and be

PREVIOUS PAGE: **A caribou in Denali National Park.** ABOVE: **Boarding the park bus.**

alone in this wilderness. Unfortunately, many Denali visitors never take the opportunity, which normally would cost a lot of money or require a lot of muscle and outdoor skill. Being alone under the big sky makes many people nervous. But that's the essence of Alaska—learning, deep down, how big creation is and how small you are, one more mammal on the tundra under the broad sky. At Denali, you can experience that wonder, and then, when you're ready to return to civilization, you can just walk to the road and catch the next bus—they come every half-hour.

PLANNING A VISIT TO THE PARK

Orientation

Denali National Park and Preserve is rock- and ice-robed in tundra and stands of stunted black spruce, a huge slice of the Alaska Range that stands like a pivot in the center of Alaska. It encompasses 6 million acres, a roughly triangular polygon about 20% larger than Massachusetts. The only park entrance is 237 miles north of Anchorage and 120 miles south of Fairbanks on the paved George Parks Highway or the Alaska Railroad. Although **Mount McKinley** is visible from as far away as Anchorage, you can't see it at all from the park entrance (where you will find the railroad depot and all the services accessible by private vehicle) because it's on the far side of the park. A mile north of the park entrance on the Parks Highway, along a cliff-sided canyon of the Nenana River, is **Glitter Gulch,** the local term for the seasonal roadside strip that's home to hotels and restaurants; it's also called **Nenana Canyon,** and local boosters want to stamp out the name "Glitter Gulch," but I keep using it because it is the common name (and descriptive, too). Other services are at **Carlo Creek,** 13 miles south on the Parks Highway; at another roadside development 7 miles south of the park entrance; and in the year-round town of **Healy,** 12 miles north of the park entrance. From the park entrance, a road accessible only by shuttle bus leads west 89 miles through the park, past a series of campgrounds and a visitor center, and ends at the **Kantishna district,** a patch of park-surrounded private land with wilderness lodges.

When to Go & How Far Ahead to Plan

Crowding is relative. Once you're out in the park, Denali is never crowded. The bottleneck created by the shuttle- and tour-bus system, which prevents vehicles from entering the heart of the park, protects it from overuse. What makes the July to mid-August season difficult is getting through that bottleneck from the crowded park entrance into the wilderness. At that time, travelers who just show up at the visitor center without any reservations might have to spend a day or two outside the park before they can get a desirable shuttle-bus seat, a campground site, or a backcountry permit.

The flow of visitors varies greatly from year to year. During past busy years, you needed to make **reservations** by March for a July visit; other years, such as during the recent economic downturn, a few weeks of advance planning has been enough. To be on the safe side, get your shuttle tickets and campsites as soon as you know the dates of your visit. Lodgings also get tight in July but are not as critical to the success of your visit. Reserve a room as far ahead as you can, but don't worry about getting stuck in a dive if you don't get your first choice, as there are few really bad places to stay near the park.

Summer residents come to the park beginning in early May, when snow remains; they migrate south again in mid- to late September, when winter is closing in. In the off season, fewer than 200 residents stay in the area, and sled dog–driving rangers patrol the backcountry. The shuttle-bus system doesn't begin operation until the last week of May; going any earlier is inadvisable, and even early June can be iffy. The visitor season gets into high gear in mid-June and starts to wind down in mid-August. There are several weeks of relative quiet, reduced hotel prices, and easy reservations at the end of the season, a wonderful time to go to Denali. The weather gets nippy at night, and there can be surprise snowfalls, but rain is less likely, and the trees and tundra turn wonderful colors. By early September, visitors are few. By mid-September, the shuttle buses stop operating and private cars can drive on the park road for a few days—the Park Service holds a lottery in July to determine who will get that treat.

Another way to avoid the crowds is to book a stay in a **wilderness lodge.** Lodges in Kantishna, listed under "Denali Wilderness Lodges" (p. 395), have the right to carry clients to their businesses over the park road in buses and vans, avoiding the bottleneck. A fly-in (Skyline Lodge) is on p. 396.

Sample Itineraries

The more you're willing to rough it, the closer you can get to the real Denali. There are no hotels inside the park.

THE HOTEL STAY ITINERARY

Drive to the park or take the train. If arriving by train, choose accommodations near the park—shuttles and courtesy vans can get you around—or rent a car for use while in the area. Visit the exhibits at the Denali Visitor Center, attend a ranger talk, see the *Cabin Nite* dinner-theater show, or go on a short nature walk around the park hotel in the evening. Get to bed early, and the next morning take a shuttle bus by 7am into the park to see the terrain and animals, and possibly to get a view of the mountain. By late morning, you'll be at a point with a commanding view of McKinley (in good weather). Now ride partway back toward the entrance before getting off the bus at a place of your choosing for a walk and to eat the bag lunch you've brought along with you (pack out all trash, of course), or take one of the National Park Service guided walks. After enjoying the wilderness for a few hours, head back on the bus, finishing a long day back at the hotel. The next day, try an educational program at the Murie Science and Learning Center or take a rafting ride, a flightseeing trip, or another activity near the park entrance before driving onward or reboarding the train.

THE FAMILY CAMPING ITINERARY

Arrive at the park entrance by car with your camping gear and food for a couple of nights. (You can rent the camping gear and car in Anchorage or Fairbanks.) Camp that evening at the Riley Creek Campground near the visitor center. Enjoy the evening ranger program, see the exhibits at the visitor center, take a nature walk, or go straight to a campsite farther within the park (either way, you'll need to reserve well ahead). The next day, catch a shuttle bus to get deeper into the park for sightseeing and hiking. If you have another day after that within the park, you can do more hikes and have the cushion of a weather day. Add a rafting excursion at the park entrance before driving on, if you like, and possibly a night in a hotel with a soft bed and your very own bathroom.

Denali National Park

HOTELS

Camp Denali/North Face Lodge **1**
Cedar Hotel at Denali Grizzly Bear Resort **19**
Denali Backcountry Lodge **1**
Denali Bluffs Hotel **13**
Denali Cabins **21**
Denali Crow's Nest Cabins **11**
Denali Dome Home B&B **19**
Denali Grizzly Bear Resort **20**
Denali Mountain Morning Hostel and Lodge **23**
Denali Outdoor Center Otto Lake
    Campground & Cabins **17**
Denali Princess Lodge **9**
Denali Salmon Bake Cabins **12**
Denali Touch of Wilderness B&B Inn **15**
Earthsong Lodge **14**
Igloo Campground **3**
Kantishna Roadhouse **1**
McKinley Chalet Resort **7**
McKinley Creekside Cabins **25**
McKinley RV and Campground **18**
Motel Nord Haven **16**
Riley Creek Campground **10**
Sanctuary River Campground **5**
Savage River Campground **6**
Skyline Lodge **1**
Teklanika River Campground **4**
Wonder Lake Campground **2**

RESTAURANTS

Black Diamond Grill **17**
Courtyard Cafe **7**
Denali Salmon Bake **12**
King Salmon Restaurant **9**
Lynx Creek Pizza **8**
McKinley Creekside Cafe **25**
Nenana View Bar and Grill **7**
The Overlook Bar and Grill **11**
The Perch/Panorama Pizza Pub **24**
229 Parks Restaurant & Tavern **22**

THE DENALI HIGHWAY: THE drivable DENALI

From Cantwell, 27 miles south of the Denali National Park entrance, the Denali Highway leads 133 miles east to another tiny village, Paxson, on the Richardson Highway. The little-known road is a lesson in how labels influence people. It runs due east from the Denali National Park border, a natural extension of the park over the Alaska Range, with scenery that's equal to and in some ways more impressive than the park's. Yet without the national park name, the terrain along the Denali Highway is comparatively little used.

The Bureau of Land Management (BLM) controls the land along the Denali Highway, and it's pretty much open for any recreational activity. Much of the highway passes through high, alpine terrain, with views that extend infinitely and good chances of seeing caribou, moose, and black and grizzly bears. At **Maclaren Pass,** at 4,086 feet, you stand in high Alaska Range terrain of tundra and rock, with views of Maclaren Glacier. The land invites you to walk at least a little way out across it. The **Tangle Lakes** are perfect canoeing waters, where you can see an extraordinary variety of waterfowl, including trumpeter swans, sandhill cranes, and loons. **Tangle River Inn,** at mile 20 (☎ **907/822-3970;** www.tangleriverinn.com), rents canoes for $5 an hour or $35 a day.

Simply **driving** the road is an experience. If you're traveling to Denali National Park from Anchorage or Fairbanks, consider making a return trip via the Denali Highway and Richardson Highway. But check out road conditions first. The road is gravel and sometimes in poor condition. Consult the Alaska Department of Transportation's **road condition hot line** (☎ **511;** http://511.alaska.gov). When the road is good, you can cover its length in less than 4 hours. Agencies that rent cars and

THE BACKCOUNTRY CAMPING ITINERARY

Arrive by train, bus, or car with your backpack, camping gear, and food for at least several days' hiking. Go immediately to the Backcountry Information Center to orient yourself to the backcountry permit process, buy the information you need for your trek (see "Denali on Foot: Dayhiking & Backpacking," later in this chapter), and choose the unit area that looks most promising. Backcountry permits cannot be reserved in advance; you can apply for them in person only at the center 2 days in advance, and they go fast. If you're lucky, permits will be left for the day after you arrive; more likely, you'll need to camp for a night nearby and arrive at the Backcountry Information Center by the 9am opening (in high season) to get your permit for the following day. Now you've got another day to wait; if you've reserved a shuttle-bus seat, you can get a preview of the park and see some wildlife. The next morning, you can start your backcountry hike, taking the camper bus to your unit and then traveling for up to 2 weeks in a huge area of wilderness reserved almost exclusively for your use.

THE KANTISHNA WILDERNESS LODGE ITINERARY

For those who can afford it, this may be the best way to see Denali. The lodge will drive you through the park, and you'll immediately be away from the crowds in remote territory. The lodges all have activities and guides to get you out into the wilderness.

RVs for use on these gravel highways are listed under "Equipped for the Backroads," p. 419, and "Car Wheels on Gravel Roads," p. 218. Most companies don't allow their vehicles on the Denali. For the adventurous, **biking** the road is one of the best ways to see it. Trails and remote roads from the highway offer some exceptional mountain-biking and hiking routes, especially in the Tangle Lakes National Register Archaeological District.

Lodgings on the highway are limited to a few small roadhouses. At mile 42, the friendly **Maclaren River Lodge** (www.maclarenlodge.com; (*) **907/822-5444**)

makes a welcome break with good basic food from the grill and boat tours on the river. Check the cabins before deciding on a night's stay; although inexpensive and clean, they are definitely no-frills. One reportedly has a ghost. The BLM maintains **campgrounds** at Brushkana Creek and Tangle Lakes, and you can camp anywhere you want outside a campground.

For more details, get the BLM's *Denali Highway Points of Interest* road guide and its *Trail Map and Information Guide to the Tangle Lakes Archaeological District.* They're available at the Alaska Public Lands Information Centers in Fairbanks, Anchorage, or Tok, or directly from the BLM's Glennallen Field Office (p. 450), where rangers can give advice on a Denali Highway trip. The agency also has a website devoted to the highway at www.blm.gov/ak/gdo/denali.html (or just Google it at "BLM Alaska Denali Highway").

THE TALKEETNA OPTION

Drive or take the train only as far as Talkeetna, about 110 miles north of Anchorage, and board a flightseeing plane from there to the park, perhaps landing on a glacier on Mount McKinley. You'll stand a better chance of seeing the mountain than anyone else, since the weather tends to be better on the south side and you can fly above most clouds. You'll also save yourself hours of driving to the park and the bus ride into the park, and you'll have the pleasure of staying in a town with some character, unlike the park entrance area. If you want the on-the-ground wildlife-viewing opportunities that can be had only in the park, you can fly from Talkeetna for the day, for a price. (See "Talkeetna: Back Door to Denali," later in this chapter, for more information.)

PARK ESSENTIALS
Visitor Information

Getting the information you need to plan your visit is especially important at Denali because of the need for advance reservations.

The most important resource for setting up a trip is the concessionaire: **Doyon/ARAMARK Joint Venture,** 2445 W. Dunlap Ave., Phoenix, AZ 85021 ((*) **800/622-7275** or 907/272-7275; fax 907/258-3668; www.reservedenali.com). The concession is operated by a joint venture of ARAMARK, which manages visitor services at many parks around the country, and the Doyon Native Corporation of Interior Alaska. They handle the reservations system for the campgrounds and shuttle buses, as well as several hotels, bus tours, a rafting operation, and a dinner theater. The best place to make in-person contact with the concessionaire is at the reservation and ticketing desks in the **Wilderness Access Center,** on the Denali Park Road, half a mile from the park entrance. The access center is open from mid-May to mid-September daily from 5am to 7pm (reservation desks don't open until 7am); it's closed October through April. Since there's no park entrance station, this center is also a good stop for the park map, a copy of the *Alpenglow* park newspaper, and other handouts. A small store offers a limited selection of conveniences and camping supplies.

The **National Park Service** can be reached at P.O. Box 9, Denali National Park, AK 99755 (© **907/683-2294;** www.nps.gov/dena). Make contact in person at the **Denali Visitor Center,** near the railroad depot at mile 1.5 of the park road on the right side. It's open summer daily 8am to 6pm. Find more on park service educational facilities under "Learning About the Park," p. 383.

Besides the centers at the park and the website, you can get park information on the way there at the interagency **Alaska Public Lands Information Centers** in Anchorage (chapter 6) and Fairbanks and Tok (chapter 9). The park's nonprofit publishing arm is the **Alaska Geographic,** Denali Branch, P.O. Box 230, Denali National Park, AK 99755 (© **907/683-1272** summer, or 683-1258 off season; www.alaskageographic.org). They operate the shops in the park visitor centers, and you can use their website to order books, maps, and the *Alpenglow* before coming.

The Reservations System

Here's the system for reserving shuttle-bus tickets and sites at the developed campgrounds. This section may look long, but paying attention to the details of the reservations system greatly improves your chances of a good visit to the park. (The backcountry permit system is covered under "Denali on Foot: Dayhiking & Backpacking," p. 380.)

FOR ADVANCE RESERVATIONS

Sixty-five percent of shuttle-bus seats and all campground sites (except Sanctuary and Igloo) are offered for booking by Internet, telephone, fax, or mail; the balance is held back for walk-ins up to 2 days before the trip. Use the Doyon/ARAMARK Joint Venture contact information above under "Visitor Information."

Reservations online, or by phone, fax, or mail, open for the whole summer on December 1 of the preceding year. Phone lines are answered daily from 7am to 5pm Mountain Standard Time (that's 2 hr. later than Alaska Standard Time, where the hours would be 5am–3pm, and 2 hr. earlier than Eastern Standard Time, where they would be 9am–7pm). Using the Internet (www.reservedenali. com) allows you to reserve any time. You will need a Visa, MasterCard, American Express, or Discover Card. You can pay by check if you're reserving by phone, mail, or fax; payment is due within 10 days. But this option is not available within 30 days of the date you are arriving. If using mail or fax, you will need to go online or call anyway to get a form.

A **confirmation** will be sent out within 2 days of making the reservation. Take it to the reservation desk at the Riley Creek Mercantile. If closed, go to the Wilderness Access Center. Campers check in at the Riley Creek Mercantile, near the Riley Creek Campground. Exchange the confirmation for a camping permit and bus ticket. The Wilderness Access Center closes at 7pm, and the Riley Creek Mercantile closes at 11pm most of the summer. If you'll be later, call ☏ **907/683-9274** to avoid losing your site or shuttle seat.

FOR WALK-INS

Walk-in reservations begin 2 days out, offering the 35% of shuttle-bus seats that are held back for those visitors and any leftover car-camping sites (usually none), and all sites at Sanctuary and Igloo campgrounds. Desirable shuttle reservations may be snapped up early in the day, so you may not get a good reservation for the day of your arrival or even the day after, only the next day after that. That's why it's so critical to reserve in advance.

On the other hand, don't despair if you arrive without reservations, as the flow of visitors rises and falls unpredictably. It's perfectly possible that you'll walk into the visitor center and get a good shuttle seat on the same day.

Fees

Park entrance fees are $20 per vehicle (up to eight passengers) or $10 per person, good for 7 days. There is no entrance station to collect the fee, but it is automatically added to your bill when you make shuttle or campground reservations. If you have one of the national passes for seniors, those with disabilities, or frequent park users (the America the Beautiful—National Park and Federal Recreational Lands Pass), you can get a refund when you get to the park. Entrance fees are in place year-round and are collected at the Murie Science and Learning Center during winter months.

Campground fees are $16 to $28 per night for car or RV camping, $14 for the backpackers' campground at Riley Creek Campground, and $9 at Sanctuary Campground and Igloo Campground. A reservation fee of $5 is charged for the first night of stays in campgrounds other than Riley Creek and Savage River. (See "Where to Stay," later in the chapter, for more particulars.) **Bus fees** are listed in the chart "Denali Park Road Bus Facts," under "Denali by Shuttle Bus." A $5 fee is charged for canceling or changing a campsite or bus ticket, except for free children's tickets. You can cancel until 11pm the day before arrival for campground reservations or 24 hours before departure for shuttle tickets. Tundra Wilderness Tour reservations can be canceled only 7 days or more in advance.

Getting There

BY TRAIN

The **Alaska Railroad** (☏ **800/544-0552** or 907/265-2494; www.alaskarailroad. com) pioneered tourism to the park before the George Parks Highway was built in 1972. In summer, trains leave both Anchorage and Fairbanks daily at 8:15am, arriving at the park from Anchorage at 3:45pm and from Fairbanks at 12:15pm, crossing and going on to the opposite city for arrival at 8pm in each. The basic fare from Anchorage to Denali is $146 one-way for adults, from Fairbanks $64, half price for children ages 2 to 11, free 1 and under. First-class Gold Star seats are $85 more per leg. Descriptions of the different classes of service are below under "Train Choices." The train also stops in Wasilla and Talkeetna; see the website for details. The full train runs only from mid-May to mid-September, with somewhat lower fares in the first and last few weeks of the season. During

Alaska Railroad executives know that their fares are high for a simple ride to Denali. As one told me, "We're selling entertainment," and that's how you should judge your choices. So, to review the entertainment: All the cars are luxurious, and some are grand and highly memorable; the rail line follows a historic, unspoiled route through beautiful countryside; there's a good chance of seeing moose and caribous; and the food is good. There are disadvantages, too. The train is very expensive. You can rent a small car for a week for the same price as one Anchorage round-trip on the train. It's slow, adding 3 hours to a trip from Anchorage to the park, and when it's late, it can be very late. And once you arrive, you have to rely on shuttles and courtesy vans to get around outside the park.

After you decide to ride the train, you have to choose which part of the train. One set of Alaska Railroad locomotives pulls the Alaska Railroad cars and other sets of cars with full glass domes owned by cruise lines, two of which have seats for independent travelers (although 90% or more are filled with their older cruise-ship customers). The two cruise lines are both owned by the same company. **Princess Cruises and Tours** (© 800/426-0500; www.princess lodges.com) has tall, all-dome cars with table seating upstairs and dining rooms downstairs; there's plenty of head room and large balconies at the ends of the cars on the lower deck, where you can ride outdoors. **Gray Line of Alaska,** a part of Holland America (© 888/452-1737; www.graylinealaska.com), has newer cars that are even better than Princess's. They're huge and comfortable, with all seats facing forward upstairs—an advantage over table seating—and dining rooms below that are large enough so only two seatings are needed for each meal. (All meals are served at assigned seatings in the cruise-line cars.)

The **Alaska Railroad** offers two classes of service. The basic service is in traditional railroad cars. They're clean and have big windows and forward-facing seats. Passengers stroll around and dine when and how they please rather than at assigned seatings. Old-fashioned Vista Dome cars provide a limited but adequate number of shared dome seats. By paying another $85, you can upgrade to Gold Star service, with your own full-dome seat for the entire trip on custom-built double-decker cars like the cruise lines', with a sumptuous white-tablecloth dining room downstairs (eat when you like). These are my favorite cars on the train. They're decorated with original fine art and are very luxurious, but you still know you're on a train, not a cruise ship, and you're not treated as a herd animal. Also, the cars have large outdoor vestibules on the upper deck. The views and open air there are incredible.

All passenger seats are assigned on all the cars. You can't walk from one company's cars to another, but you can walk between cars in your own train section. Fares on all three options are similarly high, but they're more advantageously priced as part of lodging and tour packages, which you can buy from the railroad or the cruise lines.

the winter, the Alaska Railroad runs a single passenger car from Anchorage to Fairbanks and back once a week—a truly spectacular, truly Alaskan experience.

BY CAR

Renting a car and driving from Anchorage or Fairbanks is far cheaper and far faster than taking the train. It's easy to average 65 mph on a good two-lane highway, making the drive about 4½ hours from Anchorage and 2½ hours from Fairbanks. (The train averages 40 mph and takes 7½ hr. to get from Anchorage to Denali.) Many of the views along the **Parks Highway** are equal to the views on the train, but large stretches, especially in the Matanuska and Susitna valleys, near Anchorage, have been spoiled by ugly roadside development (which you don't see from the train). A long but spectacular detour around the mess leads through **Hatcher Pass** on a mountainous gravel road open only in the summer (see "Through Hatcher Pass," under "Side Trip to the Matanuska & Susitna Valleys," in chapter 6). Farther north from Anchorage, the Parks Highway passes through **Denali State Park.** If the weather's clear, you can see Mount McKinley from the pullouts there. The state park also contains several campgrounds, public-use cabins, hiking trails, and a veterans' memorial. Byers Lake is a nice stop with a good campground and with canoe and kayak rental from **Denali Southside River Guides** (© **907/733-RAFT** [7238]; www.denaliriverguides. com)—the company also offers guided river rafting, kayaking, and fly-fishing. The park has a visitor contact station at the memorial, at mile 147. For information, contact the **Mat-Su Area Park Headquarters** (© **907/746-5000;** www. alaskastateparks.org). From Fairbanks, the drive is pleasant but rarely spectacular. Allow an hour to stop in the quaint riverside town of Nenana, where you can see an old railroad depot museum (p. 411).

BY BUS

Several van and bus services inexpensively connect Anchorage and Fairbanks to Denali. Most will carry bikes and other gear for an additional fee. The **Park Connection Motorcoach Service** (© **800/266-8625;** www.alaskacoach. com) runs big, comfortable coaches to Denali from Anchorage and Seward, with two buses daily in each direction. The Anchorage fare is $90, Seward $145. Children 11 and under ride for half price; those 4 and under need a car seat. **Alaska/ Yukon Trails** (© **800/770-7275;** www.alaskashuttle.com) also offers daily service from Anchorage and Fairbanks, with stops at any other point on the way. The one-way fare is $75 from Anchorage, $55 from Fairbanks.

BY AIR

McKinley Flight Tours, also known as Talkeetna Aero Services (© **888/733-2899** or 907/683-2899; www.talkeetna-aero.com), offers the only scheduled air service to Denali from its base in Talkeetna, or from Anchorage (summer only). Flights are 1-day packages that include flightseeing on the way, a bus tour at the park, a box lunch, and ground transfers. It's the only way to "do" Denali in a day. The package from Anchorage is $595, from Talkeetna $495; they need at least four passengers.

Getting Around

If you take the train or bus, you'll find that most accommodations have arrangements to get you around, although this becomes less convenient as you get farther from the park entrance. Ask how courtesy transportation works when you book your room. There are cabs available, too, but they are an expensive option. If you must rely on cabs, get a firm quote when you call. Try **Denali Taxi/ Shuttle** (🕾 **907/227-0936** or 683-4765 www.denalitransportation.com. A few cars are for rent at the park from **Keys to Denali,** operated out of Denali Dome Home Bed and Breakfast in Healy (🕾 **800/683-1239** or 907/683-1239; www. denalidomehome.com).

If you drive to the park, you'll still need to take the shuttle bus, described below, to get into its heart, except under certain circumstances. You can drive past mile 14 on the park road only if you have a 3-night camping permit at Teklanika Campground, 29 miles in; then your vehicle must remain parked at the campground for the entire 3 days. The rules loosen at the end of the season, when winners of a drawing can drive the road for a few days in late September (check with the Park Service for lottery details). After the permit driving is over, the road is open to anyone as far as mile 30 until the snow flies; then it's maintained only as far as the headquarters, 3 miles from the entrance.

Bicycles have unlimited access to the park road, but you must still pay the park entrance fee (see "Activities Within the Park," later in this chapter).

[FastFACTS] DENALI NATIONAL PARK

Bank The region's only bank, **First National Bank Alaska,** is in Healy, 12 miles north of the park. A couple of ATMs are in the Glitter Gulch (Nenana Canyon) area, including one at the Lynx Creek Store and Deli.

Emergencies For emergencies, dialing 🕾 **911** will work inside the park, but be sure to tell the operator you are within Denali National Park. However, cellphone coverage reaches only along the highway, and there are no telephones except at the developed areas. Bus drivers on the park road are equipped with radios.

Gear Rental Denali Mountain Works (🕾 **907/ 683-1542;** www.akrivers. com), a clothing and

outfitting shop, rents binoculars, sleeping bags, tents, backpacks, and stoves. It is right across from the McKinley Chalet Resort. Bikes are for rent at **Denali Outdoor Center** (🕾 **888/303-1925** or 907/ 683-1925; www.denali outdoorcenter.com); see p. 384.

Hospital The seasonal **Canyon Clinic at Denali** (🕾 **907/683-4433**) is among the big hotels near the park entrance. It is open daily 9am to 6pm, with help on call 24 hours. In Healy, 12 miles north of the park entrance, the year-round **Community Interior Health Center** (🕾 **907/683-2211**) is open Monday through Friday

9am to 5pm. Neither clinic has a full-fledged doctor.

Police Alaska State Troopers (🕾 **907/683- 2232** or 768-2202) have a post in Healy, 12 miles north of the park, and in Cantwell, 28 miles south.

Post Office The post office is just within the park entrance, before the Riley Creek Campground. The bulletin board has news of local events.

Stores You should do major shopping before leaving Anchorage or Fairbanks, but there are handy stores at Denali. **Riley Creek Mercantile** (🕾 **907/ 683-9246**) is at the Riley Creek Campground, near the park entrance. It's open daily from 7am to

11pm in the summer. Besides convenience groceries, they have firewood, some basic camping supplies, RV supplies, a dump station, fax and copy service, binoculars rentals, showers, and laundry. On the highway, near the Denali Salmon Bake, the **Canyon Market and Sled Dog Liquor** is open 24 hours a day during the visitor season, is well stocked and reasonably priced, and has a deli with good sandwiches.

Taxes   The local **room tax** is 7%. There is no sales tax.

DENALI BY SHUTTLE BUS

Your visit to Denali will likely revolve around a ride on the shuttle bus into the park to see the wildlife and to stop for a walk in the wilderness. Some planning will make it a more successful trip.

Choosing Your Destination

You can buy shuttle tickets to the Toklat (*Toe*-klat) River, 53 miles into the park; Eielson Visitor Center, at around 66 miles; Wonder Lake, at 85 miles; or Kantishna, at 89 miles (see "Denali Park Road Bus Facts," below, for fares). On any day trip, you have to go both ways, so you're in for a long ride. If you don't get off the bus along the way, the round-trip takes 5 hours to Toklat, nearly 8 hours to Eielson, 11 hours to Wonder Lake, and 12 hours to Kantishna. You must bring your own water and food.

In choosing your destination, you need to balance your stamina, your desire to save time for a dayhike, and your desire to see wildlife. There are no firm rules about where wildlife shows up, but my own observations are that in the early morning, you can often see moose on the first part of the road; in midsummer, brown (grizzly) bears seem to appear most in the higher country, beyond Toklat, which also is the best area for caribous; and in the fall berry season, the grizzlies show up all along the drive.

A gray wolf.

Bus Concerns & Complaints

The Denali concessionaire uses only school bus–type vehicles for shuttles on the park road, which are not as comfortable as highway motorcoaches and do not have bathrooms onboard. Safety concerns permit only these tough, lightweight buses to operate on the narrow, gravel park road. Some of the Tundra Wilderness Tour buses—unlike the shuttles and camper buses—are tricked out with higher-backed cloth seats and video monitors that allow the driver to zoom in on wildlife, but the basic bus is essentially the same. (They sell DVDs of the onboard video after the ride for $40.) The road itself can be an issue, too. I've heard from visitors complaining of white knuckles. The buses act a bit like mountain goats on the heights of Polychrome Pass and near Eielson Visitor Center as the road climbs without guardrails. If you're afraid of heights, you might not like it.

The best views of Mount McKinley show up beginning around Highway Pass at the east side of the causeway at about mile 58, beyond Toklat (where the mountain cannot be seen at all). The mountain is most likely to be visible in the morning, as clouds often pile up during the day. Going all the way to Wonder Lake provides more amazing views, including the land-covered Muldrow Glacier and many classic images of Mount McKinley. There's really no reason to go as far as Kantishna unless you are headed to a lodge there (see "Denali Wilderness Lodges," later in this chapter). In general, I think Eielson Visitor Center is the best destination for most people, offering them the chance to see the mountain and some wildlife while leaving them time to get out and walk. (I've included ideas on where to hike later.)

You won't be able to time your trip for good weather, as you need to book ahead. But don't despair if it rains—the sun may be out at the other end of the park. The best weather for wildlife sightings is cool, overcast skies without rain.

View from Polychrome Pass.

Eielson Visitor Center.

One trick of the system that allows visitors to wait for sun is to stay at Teklanika Campground. If you drive to a campsite there, agreeing to stay for a minimum of 3 nights, you're eligible to buy a special shuttle ticket that's good for rides deeper into the park the entire time you're staying at the campground ($32 for adults, half price for children ages 15–17, free for children 14 and under). Wherever you stay, you can buy a three-trip pass for the price of a two-trip pass.

Denali can be a challenge for families. Young children will go nuts on an 8-hour bus ride and often can't pick out the wildlife—this isn't a zoo, and most animals blend in with their surroundings. Older children also have a hard time keeping their patience on these trips, as do many adults. The only solution is to get off the bus and turn your trip into a romp in the heather. When you've had a chance to revive, catch the next bus. Besides, just because you buy a ticket to Wonder Lake doesn't mean that you have to go that far. Keep in mind, too, that if your child normally needs a car seat, you must bring the seat along on the bus.

The park has alternatives to the shuttle bus, with commentary, more comfortable seats, and other amenities. Doyon/ARAMARK Joint Venture operates two narrated bus tours, booked mostly as part of package tours. The **Denali Natural History Tour** provides just a taste of the park, going 17 miles down the park road, but also includes a cultural component, with a film, a history talk at a cabin, and a presentation by an Alaska Native, which could include singing, storytelling, or information about living off the land. The **Tundra Wilderness Tour** goes to Toklat when the mountain is hidden by clouds, and 8 miles farther, across Highway Pass to Stony Hill, when it is visible. Programmed commentary provides background on what you are seeing. Food is provided, but you can't get off the bus along the way (that's the fatal flaw, in my opinion). Three narrated tours go all the way to Kantishna, a 13-hour, 190-mile round-trip to the far end of the park road. One is operated by the park's concessionaire and the other two by lodges that have the right to use the road because of where their land is located. The park's concessionaire-operated **Kantishna Experience** picks up a ranger at Wonder Lake to provide commentary and to lead a hike and a visit to a historic cabin in Kantishna. The tour costs $159, half price for children 14 and under, including lunch and snacks. The private operations, **Kantishna Wilderness Trails** (© **800/230-7275** or 907/683-1475; www.seedenali.com) and **Denali Backcountry Adventure** (© **888/560-2489** or 907/683-2643), run similar tours, but with bus drivers doing the commentary and with different activities at the far end: gold panning (with either) and a sled-dog demonstration (with Kantishna), or a hike (with Denali Backcountry). In any event, it's a marathon and you can't get off the bus along the way. They charge $149 to $169, with no discount for children. But I wouldn't take a child on a 13-hour bus ride and expect to remain sane.

Getting Ready

Reserve your shuttle ticket for as early as you can stand to get up in the morning. This strategy will give you more time for dayhikes and enhance your chances of seeing the mountain and wildlife. Many animals are more active in the morning, especially on hot days. During peak season, the first bus leaves the visitor center at 5:30am and then one leaves roughly every 15 to 30 minutes in the morning. A few buses leave in the afternoon, mostly to pick up stragglers on the way back, returning late under the midnight sun.

By taking an early bus, you have more time to get off along the way for a hike, walking back to the road and getting the next bus that comes along with a spare seat. Time it right, and you could have more than 8 hours for hiking plus a tour of most of the park road before returning on a late bus. (To be on the safe side, don't push it to the very last bus.) The sun won't set until after 11pm May through July, and it will be light all night. If you need to get back to the park entrance at a certain time, leave yourself plenty of time, because, after getting off your westbound bus, you can't reserve seats going back the other way, and you may have to wait an hour for a bus with room to take you.

Before you leave for the Wilderness Access Center to get on your shuttle bus, you'll need a packed lunch and plenty of water. You should wear sturdy walking shoes and layers of warm and lighter clothing with rain gear packed, you should have binoculars or a spotting scope at the ready, and you should have insect repellent. You may also want a copy of Kris Capps's worthwhile booklet ***Denali Road Guide,*** sold at the Denali Visitor Center bookstore and published by Alaska Geographic (see "Visitor Information," earlier in this chapter). It provides a milepost commentary you can follow as you ride. Alaska Geographic also publishes guides to Denali birds, mammals, geology, and trails. If you'll be doing any extensive dayhiking, you may also want to bring a detailed topographic map printed on waterproof plastic (published by Trails Illustrated and sold from the visitor center or by ordering from Alaska Geographic), as well as a compass; if you're just going to walk a short distance off the road, you won't need such preparations.

On Your Way

There are no reserved seats on the bus, but if you arrive early, you can find a place on the left side, which has the best views on the way out. Bus riders often see

---

Shuttle-Bus Etiquette

It's common courtesy on the shuttle bus to yell out when you see wildlife so others can see it, too. The driver will stop and everyone will rush to your side of the bus. After you've had a look, give someone else a chance to look or get a picture. Be quiet and don't stick yourself, your camera, or anything else out of the bus. You will scare away the animals or worse, help habituate them to humans.

DENALI PARK ROAD BUS FACTS

Note: WAC is Wilderness Access Center. All prices rounded to nearest dollar.

BUS	PURPOSE	ROUTE	FREQUENCY	FARE
Riley Creek Loop	Links facilities within park entrance area	Visitor facilities, learning center, Riley Creek Campground, rail depot	Continuous loop	Free
Savage River Shuttle	Public transport to hiking and picnicking near the Savage River, which can also be reached by car	From visitor center to Savage River Day Use Area, about 14 miles into the park	Peak season every hour 9am–9pm	Free
Camper Shuttle (Green Bus)	Access to campgrounds and back-packing beyond the park entrance	From the WAC to Wonder Lake Campground, 85 miles into the park	Several times a day	$32 adults, half price ages 15–17, free 14 and younger
Shuttle bus (or just "the shuttle"; Green Bus)	General access to the park and wildlife viewing; limited commentary, depending on the driver; no food or water	From the visitor center as far as Kantishna, 91 miles away through the park	Every 30 minutes to Fish Creek/Eielson, every hour to Wonder Lake, 4 times daily to Kantishna	$25 to Toklat, $32 to Eielson, $43 to Wonder Lake, $47 to Kantishna; half price ages 15–17, free 14 and younger
Natural History Tour (Tan Bus)	5-hour guided bus tour at the edge of the park	From the WAC 17 miles into the park	Three times daily	$64 adults, half price ages 14 and younger
Tundra Wilderness Tour (Tan Bus)	7- to 8-hour guided bus tour with lunch provided; passengers may not get off en route	From the WAC to the Toklat River or Stony Hill, 53–61 miles into the park	Twice daily	$108 adults, half price ages 14 and younger
Kantishna Experience	13-hour guided tour and hike to the end of the road	From the WAC to Kantishna	One daily	$159 adults, half price ages 14 and younger

THE ALASKA-OHIO name game, NEXT GENERATION

In 1896, Prospector William Dickey named the mountain Mount McKinley in honor of Republican candidate William McKinley, who won the White House and was later assassinated. Alaskans have long believed this name to be irrelevant, since Natives bestowed various names that mainly translate to "The Great One"

or "The High One." In 1975, the state of Alaska petitioned the U.S. Geographic Names Board to change the name back to "Denali" just as the name of the national park was changed in 1980. But a single congressman from Ohio blocked that change, and the battle has continued in Congress for the past 4 decades.

grizzly bears, caribou, Dall sheep, moose, and occasionally wolves, but, as one driver said, the animals aren't union workers, and it's possible that you won't see any at all. Of course, you have to stay on the bus when animals are present.

The shuttle-bus drivers often offer commentary about the sights on the road, but they aren't required to do so. Some do a great job and some don't say much. The tour-bus drivers do a formal presentation, but you can't get off the bus on the way.

DENALI ON FOOT: DAYHIKING & BACKPACKING
Dayhiking in the Backcountry

One of the unique aspects of Denali is the lack of developed trails—you really can take off in any direction. The Park Service long resisted building any trails, but finally gave in and recognized some trails visitors had created, including those at the Eielson Visitor Center and the 2-mile path that leads from the Wonder Lake Campground to the McKinley River Bar, which extends far to the east and west. You can drive or take a free shuttle to the Savage River Day Use Area, at mile 14, which has a 1-mile loop trail and longer, informal routes for great alpine tundra hiking. Kris Capps's **Denali Walks** (Alaska Geographic) is a handy Denali hiking guide covering all the trails in the park. No permit is needed for dayhiking.

The broad, hard-gravel flats of the **braided riverbeds,** such as the McKinley, Toklat, Teklanika, and Savage, are among the best routes for hiking in the park. **Stony Creek,** leading up a gorge to the north from the road at mile 60, is an excellent walk into the mountains. You can also hike on the tundra, of which there are two varieties: The **wet tundra** lies on top of permanently frozen ground called permafrost; it's mushy, at best, like hiking on foam rubber laid over bowling balls. At worst, it's a swamp. **Dry tundra** clothes the mountainsides and generally makes for firmer footing and easier walking. The brush and stunted forest of the region are virtually impenetrable.

The major risks of hiking here relate to the weather and rivers. It can get cold and wet in midsummer, and if you're not prepared with warm, waterproof clothing, you could suffer the spiraling chill of hypothermia. The rivers are

Stony Creek.

dangerous because of their fast flow and icy-cold water. Experienced back-country trekkers plan their routes to avoid crossing sizable rivers. See the notes on handling river crossings, managing hypothermia, and getting lost in the "Outdoors Health & Safety" section in chapter 11. Bears, which people worry most about, are far less likely to become hazards, but do follow the tips on avoiding them that are found in chapter 11 and are widely distributed at the park.

For a first foray beyond the trails, consider joining one of the Park Service guided hikes. One or two daily **Discovery Hikes** take off from the park road. One follows a route well inside the park, and the other goes nearer to the entrance end of the park. A ranger takes only 11 hikers, leading them into wilderness while teaching them about the nature of the places they visit. Plan a 5- to 11-hour day, including the shuttle ride; actual hiking time is about 4 hours. The hikes generally are not too strenuous for families with school-age children, although it is wise to inquire how steep it will be if you have any doubts. They cost no more than the price of an Eielson shuttle ticket. You need to wear hiking shoes or boots and bring food, water, and rain gear. Reserve a place in advance, as hikes fill up in July, and you'll need to know when and where to catch the special bus. Rangers lead other walks, too, although the lineup can change each year. A recent offering was the Alpine Hike, a strenuous 2-hour climb that goes 900 feet up Thoroughfare Mountain from the Eielson Visitor Center, at mile 66 of the park road. Check with any visitor center for the current offerings.

Dayhiking in the Park Entrance Area

There are several trails at the park entrance, weaving through the boreal forest around small lakes. Only one strenuous trail leads from the entrance area, but it is a gem. The steep and spectacular hike to the **Mount Healy overlook** is a 5-mile round-trip. The trail breaks through the tree line to slopes of tundra and rock outcroppings, where you can see just how small the pocket of human infestation at the park entrance area is: The Alaska Range and its foothills extend far into the distance. If you continue on an all-day hike right to the top of Mount Healy, you can see McKinley on a clear day. Several interpretive trails offer the chance to learn, stroll, or even get somewhere. A bike and pedestrian trail connects the entrance area, near the Riley Creek Mercantile, to Glitter Gulch, allowing pedestrians to get back and forth without walking on the road. The McKinley Station, Morino, and Spruce Forest trails teach about nature and history.

Backpacking

Imagine backpacking over your own area of wilderness, without trails, limits, or the chance of seeing other people. There's no need to retrace your route to get back: Anywhere you meet the 91-mile Denali Park Road, you can catch a bus back to the world of people. Any experienced backpacker should consider a back-country trek at Denali.

Yes, it can be challenging. Hiking on the tundra, broken-rock mountain-sides, and braided rivers is tiring, and it's easy to fall or turn an ankle. You must be prepared for river crossings and cold weather, know how to find your way with a map and compass, and know how to avoid attracting bears. But if you've done a backpacking trip in a less challenging area, you surely can manage it here, so long as you prepare and don't underestimate the additional time you'll need in trail-less terrain. Nor do you need to trek far—you can camp just a few miles off the road and still be in a place that looks like no one has ever been there before.

You must be flexible about where you're going and be prepared for any kind of terrain because you can't choose the backcountry unit you will explore until you arrive at the Backcountry Information Center, adjacent to the Wilderness Access Center, and find out what's available. This information, and a map of the units, is posted on a board at the center. Groups of four or more may have a hard time finding a place to hike, but there's almost always *somewhere* to go. You can reserve permits only 2 days in advance, and you're unlikely to get one for the day you arrive, but you can reserve permits for continuation of your trip for up to 14 days at the same time. The first night of a trip is the hard one to get—for one thing, you can reserve only units that are contiguous to the park road for the first night—but after that, each night gets progressively easier. A couple of rangers are there to help you through the process.

Buy the ***Denali National Park and Preserve* topographical map,** published by Trails Illustrated, available from Alaska Geographic, listed earlier in this chapter under "Visitor Information." Printed on plastic, the map includes the boundaries of the 43 backcountry units and much other valuable information. Also, you'll want a copy of the ***Backcountry Companion*** (Alaska Geographic), which describes conditions and routes in each area. You'll find it at the visitor center, or you can glance at a well-thumbed copy kept at the backcountry desk.

The alpine units from the Toklat River to Eielson Visitor Center are the most popular. That's where you get broad views and can walk across heathery dry

Backpacking Kesugi Ridge in Denali National Park.

tundra in any direction. But to travel far, even there, you may have to climb over rugged, rocky terrain, and the tundra can be deceptively difficult to walk on—it's soft and hides ankle-turning holes. The wooded units are the least popular, since bushwhacking through overgrown country is anything but fun. The best routes for making time here (and anywhere in the Alaska Bush) are along the braided river valleys and streambeds. Be ready to walk in water. You'll have to take the **camper bus** ($31 adults) to get to your backcountry unit.

Before venturing into the backcountry, everyone is required to watch an **orientation film** covering safety and environmental issues, including how not to attract bears. I've spoken to competent backpackers who considered abandoning their trip because of the severity of the warnings they received about bears. That's unfortunate because sensible people taking normal precautions don't need to worry. The Park Service provides bear-resistant food containers in which you are required to carry all your food. For bear self-defense, you can carry a pepper spray, such as Counter Assault. Bear safety is covered in chapter 11 under "Outdoors Health & Safety."

Before you decide to go backpacking at Denali, however, you may want to broaden your thinking—if you're up to a cross-country hike without a trail, there are tens of millions of acres in Alaska available for backpacking that don't require a permit. Check with the Alaska Public Lands Information Center in Anchorage or Fairbanks for ideas about road-accessible dry tundra and other suitable areas on the Denali Highway (see "The Denali Highway: The Drivable Denali," earlier in this chapter), and on the Dalton Highway and in Wrangell–St. Elias National Park (see chapter 9). I've listed some great trail hikes in chapter 7, under Chugach National Forest, and in chapter 9, in the sections on Chena Hot Springs Road and the Steese Highway.

ACTIVITIES WITHIN THE PARK
Learning About the Park

Everyone wants to get into the heart of the park to see the wildlife and mountains as soon as possible, but time is well spent as well in the front country, learning about Denali.

The 14,000-square-foot **Denali Visitor Center** introduces the park and its connections to the rest of the world in a building that takes stock of its surroundings. The structure is environmentally advanced, using solar power for electricity and clever design to save solar warmth. Inside, life-size models of cranes overhead lead to an enormous mural, 60×28 feet in size, showing the landscape types found at the park. The carpet simulates a flowing river of gray and brown, making a path to an exhibit area with re-creations of Denali wildlife, including a full-scale moose stepping through deep snow. You will also find exhibits on the Athabascan people, mining, tourism, and scientific research. On the upper floor, a large topographic model of the park demonstrates the arbitrary nature of its boundaries, and another exhibit shows the six-continent routes of migratory birds found at Denali. Drawers open to reveal discoveries: a cross-section of Earth, or of different kinds of trees. An award-winning orientation film, *Heartbeats of Denali,* lasts 18 minutes. The photography is impressive and the narration says much with few words. Summer hours are daily 8am to 6pm; the center is closed in the winter.

The **Murie Science and Learning Center** (*✆* **866/683-1269** or 907/ 683-1269; www.murieslc.org) supports research and offers science programs

Denali Visitor Center.

about the park. It is located about a mile in along the park road on the right side. The lobby houses changing science exhibits. A variety of organizations participate in programming, with evening lectures, morning walk-in science presentations, a speaker series, youth camps, and natural history field seminars for adults and for families with older or younger children. Three-day courses are around $320 per person. Check topics and register well in advance on the website. The center is open summer daily 9:30am to 5pm, winter daily 9am to 4pm.

Mountain-Biking

A bicycle provides special freedom in the park. Bicyclists can ride past the checkpoint where cars have to turn back, at mile 14 on the park road. Riding is gritty, however, as buses come frequently and kick up a lot of dust. Bikes are not permitted off-road. Park campgrounds have bike stands and, with enough prior planning, you can set up a trip riding from one to the next. The longest stretch on the park road between campgrounds is 52 miles. With a reservation, you can take a bike on the camper bus so you can ride one-way. The shuttle system lacks much capacity for bikes, however, as only two can fit on each camper bus, although the park is gradually installing racks on the buses. Given this shortage, it can be hard for cyclists to find room on buses returning to the park entrance; instead, get a reserved spot on an outbound bus and bike back. Until more racks are added, groups larger than two must split up onto different buses. Pick up a copy of the bicycle rules from the Backcountry Information Center before you start. **Denali Outdoor Center** (✆ **888/303-1925** or 907/683-1925; www.denalioutdoorcenter.com) rents front-suspension bikes for $40 for 24 hours, $25 for 6 hours, with discounts for longer rentals. The center has an office in Glitter Gulch, and its headquarters are near Healy, at Otto Lake Road.

Sled-Dog Demonstrations

In the winter, rangers patrol the park by dog sled, as they have for decades. In the summer, to keep the dogs active and amuse the tourists, they run a sled on wheels around the kennel, and a ranger gives a talk, normally at 10am, 2pm, and 4pm. Although it's no substitute for seeing dogs run on snow, you can get a sense of their speed and enthusiasm from the show. It can be the highlight of the trip for youngsters. There's no parking at the kennels, near the headquarters at mile 3.4 on the park road, so take a free bus that leaves the Denali Visitor Center 40 minutes before each show. Times are listed in the *Alpenglow* park newspaper.

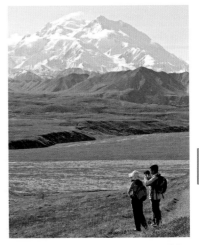

Backpackers taking in the view of Mount McKinley.

Fishing

Fishing is poor at Denali. There are grayling in some rivers, but the water is too cold and silty for most fish. Those who don't care if they catch anything, however, do enjoy fishing in this wonderful scenery. You don't need a fishing license within park boundaries, but you do have to throw back everything you catch. Bring your own gear.

For a better chance of catching something—and an opportunity to learn about fly-fishing, too—go to a private lake outside the park with guide Rick McMahan of **Denali Fly Fishing Guides** (ⓒ **907/768-1127;** www.denali fishing.com). He picks up clients at their hotels and takes them lake or stream fishing, on the bank or wading, mostly for Arctic grayling but also rainbow trout. The per-person cost is $175 for a half-day, $325 for a full day, lunch included. He also provides jet boat trips to wilderness streams for $275.

Climbing Mount McKinley

Because of its altitude and weather, Mount McKinley is among the world's most challenging climbs. Summer temperatures at the high camp average –20° to –40°F (–29° to –40°C). If you're looking here for advice, you're certainly not up to an unguided climb. A guided climb is a challenging and expensive endeavor requiring months of conditioning and most of a month on the mountain. Get names of authorized guides from the Park Service's **Talkeetna Ranger Station,** P.O. Box 588, Talkeetna, AK 99676 (ⓒ **907/733-2231**). The climbing season lasts from late April or early May until the snow gets too soft, in late June or early July. Climbers fly from Talkeetna to a 7,200-foot base camp on Kahiltna Glacier. About 1,200 climbers attempt the mountain annually in about 300 parties; about half typically make it to the top each year, and usually a few die trying.

ATTRACTIONS & ACTIVITIES OUTSIDE THE PARK

Flightseeing

A good, close look at McKinley is best accomplished by air. Frequently, you can see McKinley from above the clouds when you can't see it from the ground. Best of all, Talkeetna operators that fly mountaineers also land visitors on the mountain, a unique and unforgettable experience (see "Talkeetna: Back Door to Denali," p. 396). Regardless of how close you approach the mountain, a flight shows how incredibly rugged the Alaska Range is.

Small planes and helicopters fly from the park airstrip, from private heliports and airstrips along the Parks Highway, and from the Healy airstrip. **Denali Air** (© **907/683-2261**; www.denaliair.com) has an office in the Nenana Canyon area and operates flights at mile 229.5 of the Parks Highway. An hour-long flight going within a mile of the mountain costs $350 for adults, $175 for children ages 2 to 12. **Fly Denali** (© **888/733-7768** or 907/683-2359; www.fly denali.com), flying out of Healy, is the only operator offering mountain landings from the park area at this writing (others do so from Talkeetna). **Era Helicopters** (© **800/843-1947** or 907/683-2574; www.eraflightseeing.com) has 50-minute flights for $335, including van pickup from hotels in the area. Their heli-hikes land for a 4-hour walk on a mountain ridgeline, the difficulty tailored to the customers' abilities, for $465. A 2-hour outing that includes a 20-minute glacier landing costs $435.

Rafting

Rafting on the Nenana River, bordering the park along the Parks Highway, is fun and popular. Several commercial guides float two stretches of the river: an upper portion, where the water is smoother and the guides explain passing scenery; and the lower portion, where the river roars through the rock-walled Nenana Canyon and rafts take on huge splashes of silty, glacial water through class III and IV rapids. Guides take children as young as 5 on the slow trip (although I wouldn't let my kid go at that age); the youngest accepted for the fast portion is age 10. White-water

Rafting on the Nenana River.

rafting carries risks you shouldn't discount. Each session takes 2 to 2½ hours, including safety briefings, suiting up, and riding to and from the put-in and take-out points. Prices vary from $82 to $112 for adults, with discounted rates for children (from $10 less to half off). **Denali Outdoor Center** (© **888/303-1925** or 907/683-1925; www.denalioutdoorcenter.com) is a professional operation, offering rafting trips and instruction in river techniques. The firm also offers self-paddled inflatable kayaks, popular with those who want to take an active hand in their float. Its main office is at Otto Lake Road, at mile 247; and the company also has an office right in Glitter Gulch. Plan a shower afterward—the silt in the river water will stick to your skin and hair.

All-Terrain Vehicle Rides

Most Alaskans who venture into the Alaska Range backcountry (outside the park) do so on snow machines or, in the summer and fall, on ATVs. Their purpose is usually hunting or trapping, but these balloon-tire buggies are handy just for seeing a lot of country as well. They're easy to drive. **Denali ATV Adventures** (© **907/683-4288**; www.denaliatv.com) offers rides on one- or two-person machines north of the park, in the Otto Lake area and on the Stampede Trail, for scenery and wildlife viewing. Commentary is delivered through radio headsets inside riders' helmets. A 2½-hour tour, including instruction, costs $95 as a driver, $65 as a passenger; a 4-hour trip is $175 and $100. The firm has an office in Glitter Gulch and headquarters north of the Denali entrance at Mile 238.6, Parks Highway.

A Kennel Tour

Like the free dog-sled demonstration at the park, former Iditarod champion Jeff King shows off his dogs at his **Husky Homestead Tour** (*(C)* **907/683-2904;** www.huskyhomestead.com). What makes his tour hugely popular, however, is the program telling about living and raising a family on a homestead in this remote area. Admission is $49 for adults, $29 children 3 to 12; not recommended for children 2 and under.

WHERE TO STAY
Park Service Campgrounds

I've explained how to make camping reservations under "The Reservations System," p. 370. Camping fees are listed here, but reservation fees and entrance fees may be added when you pay. Only Riley Creek Campground is open after September (water is off in winter). The rest reopen when the snow is gone in May, except Wonder Lake, which opens in June. I have noted where RVs are permitted in the description of each campground. The maximum-size sites are for 40-foot units, and there are not many of those. There are no RV hookups at any campground in the park.

CAR-ACCESSIBLE CAMPGROUNDS

Riley Creek   This large campground right across the road from the visitor center is best for those who want to be in the middle of things. It's near the Riley Creek Mercantile, with its showers, laundry, Wi-Fi, and sewage dump station. The free front-country shuttle connects the campground with other facilities. Reservations are relatively easy to get. Sites are wooded with small birch and spruce, and they're adequately separated, but this isn't exactly wilderness camping. Twenty-seven walk-in sites are available only for tent users without vehicles and can be reserved only 2 days ahead, in person.

Near the visitor center. 147 sites; RVs or tents. $22–$28 vehicle sites; $14 walk-in sites. Campfires allowed; flush toilets.

Keeping Clean at Denali

The only showers within the park are at **Riley Creek Mercantile,** the store near the Riley Creek Campground, which also has laundry machines and other services. You pay by the shower, so there's no coin-operated timer to feed. You can also wash your clothes and shower at **Miners Market and Deli/McKinley RV and Campground** in Healy, covered below under "Commercial Campgrounds." The larger park campgrounds have the typical cold-water bathrooms found in the national parks, while others have vault toilets.

Savage River   On the taiga—the thin spruce forest and tundra—this is a wonderful campground with unforgettable views. Campers can wander from their sites on some of the park's best hikes. This is the only campground you can readily drive to that's away from the activity at the park entrance. There is no telephone.

On Denali Park Rd., 13 miles from entrance. 33 sites; RVs and cars or tents. $22–$28 per site. Campfires allowed; flush toilets.

Teklanika River   This campground lies beyond the checkpoint on the park road. To hold down traffic, the Park Service requires campers to keep their vehicles in place for at least 3 nights. Sites are among the small trees of the boreal forest. The big advantage of staying here is that you begin the morning much closer to the heart of the park, cutting the time you have to spend on the bus. You can buy one bus ticket for the regular price and use it for your entire 3-night stay. That makes Teklanika a good base to really explore different areas of the park in varying kinds of weather.

On Denali Park Rd., 29 miles from entrance; access by camper bus, or drive in with a minimum 3-night stay. 53 sites; RVs only, no tents. $20 per site. Campfires allowed; flush toilets.

BUS-ACCESSIBLE CAMPGROUNDS

To use these campgrounds, you'll need a camper ticket on the shuttle bus, which costs $32 for adults, half price for children ages 15 to 17, free for ages 14 and under. There are no businesses and no phones beyond the park entrance area; you must bring in everything you need. Wildlife management concerns sometimes close these campgrounds unexpectedly.

Sanctuary River & Igloo   These two small, primitive campgrounds offer a backcountry experience away from cars. You can't reserve sites in advance; permits are available only in person at the visitor center when you arrive.

On Denali Park Rd., Sanctuary River Mile 23, Igloo Mile 34. 7 sites each; tents only. $9 per site. No campfires; stoves permitted; chemical toilets.

Wonder Lake   It takes almost 6 hours to get here on the bus, but this campground by placid Wonder Lake, at the foot of Mount McKinley, puts you in the most beautiful and coveted area of the park. Set among a patch of spruce trees on the mountain side of the lake, the sites can be tough to get to, especially those with views of McKinley. The secret is to stay more than 1 day. When campers with a coveted site leave in the morning, grab it. A central area with bear-resistant food storage lockers has tables covered by an awning where campers prepare food and meet each other; choose a site away from this area and the noise and foot traffic there. The mosquitoes at Wonder Lake can be horrendous.

On Denali Park Rd., 85 miles from entrance. 28 sites; tents only. $20 per site. No campfires; stoves permitted; flush toilets.

Commercial Campgrounds

There are several commercial campgrounds in the general vicinity of the park entrance, although none in walking distance. **Denali Outdoor Center Otto Lake Campground and Cabins** (www.denalioutdoorcenter.com; ✆ **888/303-1925** or 907/683-1925) will appeal most to those looking for a quiet park setting. Located at .5 Mile, Otto Lake Road (turn west at mile 247 of the Parks Hwy., 10 miles north of the park entrance), the campground has 30 sites, half on the shore of Otto Lake, half on a ridge above the lake with excellent mountain views. On the downside, it can be very windy. Nightly camping rates are $8 per adult, $4 per child. There are no RV hookups. Three basic log cabins sit at lakefront, renting for $92 in the high season, $78 in spring and fall ($10 each additional adult, free children 12 and younger). Showers are extra. The Denali Outdoor Center also guides rafting outings, described above.

Denali Grizzly Bear Cabins and Campground (www.denaligrizzlybear. com; ☎ **866/583-2696** or 907/683-2696) is about 6 miles south of the park entrance at mile 231.1 of the Parks Highway. Some sites sit on an exposed hillside, while others are among small trees. Small cabins and tent cabins dot the property as well; they range from $65 without a bathroom to $260 for a unit with a full bathroom and kitchen. There are coin-operated showers. Tent sites are $24 for up to four people, with electrical and water hookups $12 more. (The hotel on the property is described on p. 392.)

A campground with birch trees and attractive sites is 10 miles north of the park, next to the highway in Healy. **Miners Market and Deli/McKinley RV and Campground,** at mile 248.5 on the Parks Highway (www.mckinleyrv.com; ☎ **800/478-2562** or 907/683-2379), also has a gas station, a token-operated laundry, hot showers, and a free hourly shuttle to the park. Basic tent sites are $10, full hookups $32.

Hotels

Patterns of land ownership and the uncontrolled development around Denali have led to a hodgepodge of roadside hotels, cabins, lodges, campgrounds, and restaurants in pockets arrayed along more than 20 miles of the Parks Highway. There are rooms of good quality in each of the pockets, but the going rates vary widely. The most expensive rooms, and the first booked, are in the immediate vicinity of the park entrance. Better bargains are in pockets south of the park, with prices getting lower the farther you go. Both these areas are entirely seasonal. Good deals are had in **Healy,** too, 12 miles north of the park, where you can find a hotel room for less than a comparable room near the park entrance. A few links to B&Bs are on Healy's **Denali Chamber of Commerce** website (www.denalichamber.com, click on "Directory"). If you don't have a car, Healy is not convenient; in that case, stay nearer the park entrance. The other choices are wilderness lodges in the **Kantishna** area (see "Denali Wilderness Lodges," p. 395); or **Talkeetna,** the back door to the park (see "Talkeetna: Back Door to Denali," p. 396). Despite their high prices, rooms can be hard to find at peak season (although not during the economic recession), and it's wise to book ahead.

NEAR THE PARK

This area, known formally as Nenana Canyon or more commonly as "Glitter Gulch," extends about a mile north of the park entrance on the Parks Highway. Large, luxurious hotels dominate. Owned by the Princess and Holland American cruise lines, each hotel has superb rooms and public areas that were rebuilt in grand style within the last few years. Objectively the best lodgings in the area, I give them brief mention mainly because they serve escorted-tour passengers nearly to the exclusion of other guests. The giants are **Denali Princess Lodge,** Mile 238.5, Parks Highway (www.princesslodges.com; ☎ **800/426-0500** reservations, or 907/683-2282 local), and the **McKinley Chalet Resort,** Mile 239.1, Parks Highway (www.denaliparkresorts.com; ☎ **800/276-7234** reservations, or 907/683-8200 local). Rack rates are high at each of these places, but you usually don't have to pay them. You can stay for much less if you arrive on one of the days when the flow of cruise-ship passengers is down, or early or late in the season, or if you book one of the owners' packages. Good deals are to be had as well on packages with the Alaska Railroad.

At one time, the canyon contained a variety of smaller, locally owned hotels catering to independent travelers, but the extraordinary value of the property and ever-growing flow of cruise-ship passengers has led to consolidation of lodgings, campgrounds, shops, restaurants, and other businesses into the hands of the two main cruise lines (which are, in reality, only two arms of the same corporation, Carnival), and ARAMARK, the park concessionaire, which operates under the name Denali Park Resorts outside park boundaries.

All the hotels in this area are open only during the tourist season, roughly from May 15 to September 15.

Denali Bluffs Hotel ★   A series of 12 buildings on a steep mountainside looks down on the Nenana Canyon area from above the highway. The light, tastefully decorated rooms have two double beds and good amenities, and those on the upper floor have vaulted ceilings and balconies with great views. The courtesy van will take you anywhere in the area. The same company manages the hotel and the 169-room **Grande Denali Lodge,** which perches impossibly high above the Nenana Canyon and charges more for the view. Use caution and observe the mirrors at the switchbacks on the gravel road up from the highway. The information below is for Denali Bluffs, but the toll-free number and website are good for either.

Mile 238.4, Parks Hwy. www.denalialaska.com. ℭ **907/683-8500.** 112 units. High season $256–$291 double. Extra person age 12 and older $20. AE, DISC, MC, V. *In room:* TV.

Denali Crow's Nest Log Cabins ★   Perched in five tiers on the side of Sugarloaf Mountain looking down on Horseshoe Lake and the other, larger hotels, the cabins are roomy and comfortable, especially those on the 100 and 200 level. A log cabin and the warmth of the Crofoot family seem more Alaskan than the modern, standard rooms that have filled the canyon, and the rates are not out of line for the area. You spend a lot of time climbing stairs, however, and the rooms have shower enclosures, not tubs. Smoking is not allowed. The restaurant, the **Overlook Bar and Grill,** is recommended separately under "Where to Eat," below.

Mile 238.5, Parks Hwy. (P.O. Box 70), Denali National Park, AK 99755. www.denalicrowsnest.com. ℭ **888/917-8130** or 907/683-2723. Fax 907/683-2323. 39 cabins. $189 double. Extra person 12 and older $20. MC, V. **Amenities:** Restaurant; bar; courtesy shuttle to park and activities; outdoor hot tub. *In room:* TV, Wi-Fi.

Denali Salmon Bake Cabins 🔥   For those looking to save money while staying near the park entrance, and satisfied with basic shelter, these cabins may be the solution. They're behind the salmon bake that has become the area's hip cultural center, and guests get into the entertainment there without cover charge (see "Where to Eat," below). The highway and busy restaurant are nearby, but the cabins, shielded by trees, are surprisingly well hidden. The least expensive units are tent cabins. Four others with private bathrooms are a bit larger. All are clean but rustic, a step up from camping.

Mile 238.5, Parks Hwy. (P.O. Box 107), Denali National Park, AK 99755. www.denaliparksalmon bake.com. ℭ **907/683-2733.** Fax 907/683-2259. 12 cabins, 4 with private bathroom. $69 double with shared bathroom; $145 double with private bathroom. AE, DC, DISC, MC, V. **Amenities:** Courtesy shuttle. *In room:* No phone, Wi-Fi.

IN HEALY

Healy is 10 miles north of the park entrance, but a world away. It's a year-round community with an economy based partly on a coal mine. It sits in a large, windy valley with a few patches of stunted trees and big, open spaces of tundra. There are hotels and B&Bs with rooms well below the cost of those near the park, and most businesses stay open in the winter, when the rest of the region shuts down tight. They say the water tastes better, too. On the downside, you need a car to stay in Healy.

Besides the lodgings listed below, **Denali Dome Home** (www.denalidome home.com; ✆ **800/683-1239** or 907/683-1239) is a huge house in a geodesic dome on 5 acres, run year-round by a family for 20 years. The seven rooms are $170 to $190 double in summer and have many amenities, including a cooked-to-order breakfast. Use the same contact information for their **Keys to Denali** car rental.

Denali Touch of Wilderness Bed and Breakfast Inn ★   This special inn has won a place in the hearts of residents of this remote region, who congregate for retreats, quilting, wedding rehearsals, and the like. Visitors will find immaculate rooms decorated in a Victorian country theme. The common areas create a warm feeling—large sitting rooms with expansive views on the nearby Alaska Range, and a kitchen guests can use. The location is about 3 miles out in the country on Stampede Road. The hosts serve generous breakfasts from 7 to 10am.
Mile 2.9, Stampede Rd. (P.O. Box 397), Healy, AK 99743. www.touchofwildernessbb.com. ✆ **800/683-2459** or 907/683-2459. 9 units. High season $189–198 double, 2-night minimum stay suggested; low season $125–$135 double. Extra person $20. AE, DISC, MC, V. Rates include full breakfast. **Amenities:** Guest computer. *In room:* Hair dryer, Wi-Fi.

Earthsong Lodge ★★ 🐾   These solid-log buildings on the windy open tundra, with sweeping views of the Alaska Range, are well off the beaten path, 17 miles north of Denali National Park and 4 miles down the Stampede Trail Road, but it's worth the trip to stay in an authentically Alaskan lodge. One- and two-bedroom cabins have quilts on the beds and other cozy features. The lodge common rooms include a library and living room, and a coffeehouse, Henry's, serves breakfast and dinner and packs sack lunches. In winter, the lodge is the dog-sledding concessionaire for Denali National Park, and in summer you can tour the kennel.
Stampede Trail Rd., off the Parks Hwy. at mile 251 (P.O. Box 89), Healy, AK 99743. www.earthsong lodge.com. ✆ **907/683-2863.** Fax 907/683-2868. 12 cabins. Summer $155–$195 double. Extra person 18 and over $10, ages 12–17 $5, 11 and under free. MC, V. **Amenities:** Restaurant (coffeehouse). *In room:* Hair dryer, Wi-Fi.

Motel Nord Haven ★★   This fresh little gray hotel with a red roof has large, immaculate rooms, each with one or two queen-size beds. They're equal to the best standard rooms in the Denali Park area and a lot less expensive. Bill and Patsy Nordmark offer all kinds of extras, even free newspapers and a sitting room with a collection of Alaska books. The rooms, decorated with Alaska art and oak trim, all have interior entrances and have been smoke-free since their construction. Up to four people can stay in the rooms with two beds for the price of a double. There are three kitchenette units. The Nordmarks pack sack lunches for $10.
Mile 249.5, Parks Hwy. (P.O. Box 458), Healy, AK 99743. www.motelnordhaven.com. ✆ **800/683-4501** or 907/683-4500. Fax 907/683-4503. 28 units. Summer $135–$165; spring/fall $90–$115; winter $75–$90. Summer rate includes continental breakfast. AE, DISC, MC, V. **Amenities:** Free hot drinks; guest computer. *In room:* TV, Wi-Fi.

SOUTH OF THE PARK

Lodgings south of the park are in widely separated pockets of private land concentrated 7 and 14 miles down the highway. (Anything south of that is covered with Talkeetna, under "Talkeetna: Back Door to Denali," p. 396.) I've listed a few in detail below, but you may also want to try **Denali Cabins,** Mile 229, Parks Hwy. (www.denali-cabins.com; ℂ **877/233-6254** or 907/376-1992).

Cedar Hotel at Denali Grizzly Bear Resort ★   Four buildings over the Nenana River contain comfortable, modern rooms with the highway mostly out of view. You can hear the water from your bed or emerge on a small deck to enjoy the view (and the company of other guests, who are an arm's length away). Rooms are decorated in the Alaska rustic motif with lots of cedar. The adjoining campground (Denali Grizzly Bear; p. 389) has the same owner.

Mile 231.1, Parks Hwy. (P.O. Box 7), Denali National Park, AK 99755. www.denaligrizzlybear.com. ℂ **866/583-2696** or 907/683-2696. 105 rooms. High season $192 double; low season $162 double. Extra person $10. DISC, MC, V. **Amenities:** Internet access. *In room:* TV, hair dryer, no phone, Wi-Fi.

Denali Mountain Morning Hostel and Lodge ⚜   The hostel offers cozy, clean accommodations, and a common room and shared kitchen, contained in an octagonal log building, wall tents, and cabins. Sleeping arrangements are in private units or hostel bunks, which are in gender-separated or coed dorms. All guest use the bathhouse. A free shuttle runs to the park's Wilderness Access Center four times a day, and linens are included in the price. The hostel is in the Carlo Creek area, where there are a couple of good casual restaurants.

Mile 224.1, Parks Hwy. (P.O. Box 208), Denali National Park, AK 99755. www.hostelalaska.com. ℂ **907/683-7503.** 17 units (housed in 6 dorms and 8 private cabins). $32 per bunk; $80 double private room; $75–$95 double cabin. Extra person age 5 or older $15, free 4 and under. 2-night minimum in private rooms and cabins. MC, V. **Amenities:** Courtesy shuttle to park entrance; Internet access; shared kitchen; shared phone. *In room:* Wi-Fi.

McKinley Creekside Cabins ★   These cozy cabins are right by the highway and the pleasant cafe of the same name (covered below), but you would never know it, thanks to how they are situated in the woods on the banks of Carlo Creek. The cabins' rustic decoration, in subdued tones, includes log bedposts made by a local craftsman. They have decks and nice private bathrooms, and some have refrigerators and microwaves. Family units sleep up to six. There are communal spots for visiting around barbecues, horseshoes, and fire pits, some at the creek's edge.

Mile 224, Parks Hwy. (P.O. Box 89), Denali National Park, AK 99755. www.mckinleycabins.com. ℂ **888/5-DENALI** (533-6254) or 907/683-2277. 30 units (housed in 6 rooms, 24 cabins). High season $139–$199 unit for 2–4; special rates May and September. DISC, MC, V. Closed Oct–Apr. **Amenities:** Restaurant; barbecue. *In room:* Wi-Fi, no phone.

WHERE TO EAT

Since Denali is entirely seasonal, it lacks the range of inexpensive family restaurants that develop in year-round communities. While you may find reasonably priced food in Healy, to the north, or Carlo Creek, to the south, near the park most meals are overpriced by 25% to 50% due to the short season and captive audience. Unless otherwise stated, all restaurants listed are open only during the visitor season.

Near the Park Entrance

You'll have no trouble finding an espresso at Denali. The large hotels in the canyon each have fine-dining and casual restaurants. There are plenty of spots for a low-key meal or takeout. The **Courtyard Cafe** at the McKinley Chalet Resort serves a buffet and has a children's menu. **Lynx Creek Pizza** is something of a tradition but inconsistent from year to year. **Alaska Fish & Chip Co.** serves the seafood of the name and more exotic choices, too. Order at the counter and then find a table.

Denali Park Salmon Bake ★ 📖 GRILL   Amid the more corporate places where the casual park atmosphere is relatively contrived, at "The Bake" you'll find a rollicking local hot spot that becomes a center of the community each summer. You can't miss the homemade highway frontage as you enter Glitter Gulch. The extremely casual staff is friendly, led by owners who in 2008 won the Alaska small-business-of-the-year award. The restaurant is also the area's cultural focus, with live music acts coming through regularly during the summer. The food goes well beyond the $20 grilled salmon entree, also including crab cakes, pulled pork sandwiches, Tex-Mex selections, and even trendier cuisine such as Parmesan- and Asiago-crusted halibut. It's all good, and priced in a broad range appropriate for many budgets. They'll also pick you up and drive you back to your hotel. The cabins are described under "Hotels," above.

Mile 238.5, Parks Hwy. ☎ **907/683-2733.** www.denaliparksalmonbake.com. All items $8–$37. AE, DC, DISC, MC, V. Daily 7am–midnight.

King Salmon Restaurant ★★ SEAFOOD   This is a terrific place for a special night of dining out right near the park. The waiting area has a cozy fireplace, and the dining room perches on the edge of the Nenana Canyon, where you can watch rafters float by during your meal. The food and service are up to Princess Tours' excellent standards—steak and salmon, the usual choices for Alaska tourists—expertly prepared. For something a bit more casual, try the Basecamp Bistro next door.

In the Denali Princess Lodge, Mile 238.5, Parks Hwy. ☎ **907/683-2282.** Reservations recommended. Dinner main courses $20–$40. AE, DC, DISC, MC, V. Daily 6–11am, 11:30am–3pm, and 4:30–10pm. Basecamp Bistro daily 3–10pm.

Nenana View Bar & Grill ★ GRILL   This is an attractive restaurant in the McKinley Chalet Resort with a fireplace at one end of the dining room and outdoor seating overlooking the river at the other. They serve delicious pizza and great fire-grilled steaks.

Mile 238.9, Parks Hwy., in McKinley Chalet Resort. ☎ **907/683-8200.** All items $12–$35. AE, DISC, MC, V. May–Sept daily 11am–2:30pm and 5–11pm. Bar until 1am.

The Overlook Bar & Grill ★ GRILL   This fun, noisy place has the feel of a classic bar and grill, with a vaulted ceiling of rough-cut lumber and a spectacular view of the Nenana Canyon. There are two dining rooms, one with the bar and another, behind a glass partition, which is quieter and has tablecloths. A huge variety of craft beers is available, with 24 on tap. The food is always good, and at times I've gotten excellent fare here. Call ☎ **907/683-2723** for courtesy transportation from all area hotels.

Mile 238.5, Parks Hwy., up the hill above the Denali Canyon area. ☎ **907/683-2641.** Main courses $9–$15 lunch, $11–$44 dinner. MC, V. Daily 11am–11pm. Bar until 1am.

Within Driving Distance

These restaurants are as much as 13 miles from the park entrance, so you will need a car.

Black Diamond Grill ★★ GRILL   A unique 9-hole golf course lies amid the mountains and rolling taiga north of the park at a center of activities, including all-terrain vehicle tours, GPS treasure hunts, minigolf, and covered wagon rides with delicious full-service camp-style meals. The restaurant produces excellent food from a menu mostly influenced by Northern Italian cookery, with lots of Alaskan seafood. For lunch, sandwich choices include a pesto chicken hoagie for $7.50, and for dinner there is halibut in parchment with fresh rosemary and garlic for $20. The dining room is light and cheery, with pine furniture and flowers on the tables.

Mile 247, Parks Hwy. (take the highway north 10 miles, then turn left at Otto Lake Rd.). ⏱ **907/683-4653.** www.blackdiamondgolf.com. Lunch $7.50–$9; dinner $14–$24. AE, DISC, MC, V. Daily 7am–11pm.

McKinley Creekside Cafe ★ ☺ STEAK/SEAFOOD/SANDWICHES   This friendly spot in the Carlo Creek area, south of the park, is a favorite of the locals. You can dine on steak or baked salmon with brown sugar, apples, and toasted almonds for around $20, or order a burger for around $9. The food is consistently good, including breakfast, and craft brews and wine are served. There is a playground outside and a kids' menu. They also pack substantial sack lunches for the park shuttle-bus ride.

Mile 224, Parks Hwy. ⏱ **888/533-6254** or 907/683-2277. www.mckinleycabins.com. Lunch $6–$10; dinner $8–$21. DISC, MC, V. Daily 6am–10pm.

The Perch/Panorama Pizza Pub ★ STEAK/PIZZA   Two restaurants share this spot. The Perch gets its name from its location, atop an odd, knoblike hill. It's a friendly, family-run place serving a straightforward steak and Alaskan seafood menu—they don't try anything fancy, just good ingredients done right. The home-baked bread is noteworthy. The dining room is light, with well-spaced tables and big picture windows on three sides. Down on the highway level, the Panorama Pizza Pub is a hot spot for pizza and music and also includes a bakery/deli that packs lunches in cloth tote bags for the park bus. You can often hear local musicians playing here in the evening.

Mile 224, Parks Hwy., 13 miles south of the park. The Perch: ⏱ **888/322-2523** or 907/683-2523. www.denaliperchresort.com. Dinner main courses $14–$40. MC, V. Daily 6–9am and 5–10pm. Panorama Pizza Pub: ⏱ **907/683-2623.** Pizza $13–$32. MC, V. Daily 11am–11pm.

229 Parks Restaurant and Tavern ★★★ INTERNATIONAL   The name of the restaurant, which is the best in the area, comes from the milepost, which puts it in a quiet area about 8 miles south of the park entrance in a beautiful post-and-beam building. The owners, Laura and Land Cole, live here year-round. Laura is a professionally trained chef and veteran of Alaska's best dining rooms. Whenever possible, she uses organic ingredients and local produce—eggs are naturally nested by free-range chickens. The menu changes daily and has included main-course items such as tenderloin filet, lemon pasta with asparagus, venison chops, and, of course, salmon. A sweet-potato soup with king crab meat was fabulous. The appetizer list is long and interesting, including spring rolls second to none. Breakfast is coffeehouse fare, such as quiche, granola, and fruit.

Locals keep the place busy even on winter weekends, but they close at 1pm on winter Sundays so everyone can go play hockey on Deneki Lakes.

Mile 229, Parks Hwy. ☎ **907/683-2567.** www.229parks.com. Reservations accepted. Dinner $18–$33. MC, V. Summer Tues–Sun 7–11am and 5–10pm; winter Fri–Sat 9am–9pm, Sun 9am–1pm (call ahead, because hours can vary in winter).

DENALI NIGHTLIFE

Locals and young people go to the **Denali Park Salmon Bake** in the evening to hear the live music and dance there (see "Where to Eat," above). National touring bands stop in on their way from Anchorage to Fairbanks. A shuttle will come get you. The area also has many other restaurants with bars, many of which I've described.

The main tourist-oriented evening event is the concessionaire's **Cabin Nite Dinner Theater,** at the McKinley Chalet Resort (☎ **800/276-7234** or 907/683-8200), a professionally produced musical revue about a gold rush–era woman who ran a roadhouse in Kantishna. You can buy the $63 tickets (half price ages 2–12) virtually anywhere in the area. The actors, singing throughout the evening, stay in character to serve big platters of food to diners sitting at long tables, doing a good job of building a rowdy, happy atmosphere for adults and kids. Shows happen nightly at 5:30 and 8:30pm.

Princess Cruises and Tours puts on its own evening show, *The Music of Denali,* at the Denali Princess Lodge. The musical performance lasts an hour, the entire dinner 2 hours. Tickets are for sale at the hotel's tour desk (☎ **800/426-0500** or 907/683-2282) for $55 (half price ages 6–12).

DENALI WILDERNESS LODGES

Staying in a wilderness lodge makes for a completely different experience of Denali, and that's why I've segregated these choices here. These lodges are self-contained vacations, and if you choose to stay, you don't need to worry about the shuttle bus or the other issues of escaping the "front-country." The lodges also are expensive and require a significant commitment of time. It doesn't make sense to spend fewer than 3 days, and some lodges require longer minimum stays.

All lodges within Denali National Park are in the Kantishna district, on private land where gold miners staked claims before the park was created. The lodge operators who later obtained this land gained something more valuable than gold: the opportunity to bring visitors to the far end of the park from the entrance, as near as a vehicle can get to Mount McKinley, without using the park's shuttle system. Hosts drive visitors to Kantishna in their own buses or vans over the 91-mile park road. These lodges are open only in summer. More wilderness lodges in the wider region are described in chapter 11. Besides the three lodges I have room to describe here in detail, I also recommend **Denali Backcountry Lodge** (www.denalilodge.com; ☎ **877/233-6254** or 907/376-1992).

Camp Denali/North Face Lodge ★★★ In the cabins of Camp Denali, a pioneering eco-tourism establishment, you can wake to the white monolith of Mount McKinley filling your window. Also uniquely, the naturalist guides here have the right to use the park road free of the shuttle system for hiking and field trips to observe wildlife, botany, and birding, all included in the substantial price. During some sessions, nationally respected academics and other experts join the programs. All arrivals and departures are on fixed session dates of 3, 4, or 7 nights. Energy comes from the sun and the lodge's own hydro power: The whole place is about as ecofriendly as you can get. Each of the Camp Denali cabins has its own outhouse, and all share a central bathhouse and lodge common rooms. If your own flush toilet is a priority, North Face Lodge has smallish traditional rooms with private bathrooms, but without McKinley views from every unit. Each lodge has its own dining room for family-style meals.

Kantishna area (P.O. Box 67), Denali National Park, AK 99755. www.campdenali.com. ☎ **907/683-2290.** Fax 907/683-1568. 33 units (18 cabins), none with private bathroom at Camp Denali; 15 units with bathroom at North Face Lodge. $515 per adult per night; $389 per child per night. Sessions of 3, 4, or 7 nights only. Rates include all meals, guided activities, and transportation from park entrance. No credit cards. *In room:* No phone.

Kantishna Roadhouse ★★ This property along Moose Creek in the old Kantishna Mining District trades on both the mining history and outdoor opportunities of the area. Some rooms are large and luxurious, while others are in smaller single cabins with lofts. The log central lodge has an attractive and busy lobby—it's got more of a hotel feel and might be more attractive to an older, less active set or to families than the other lodges in the Kantishna District. It also has a bar. Rates include guided hikes, fishing, interpretive programs, biking, gold panning, and a daily sled-dog demonstration. ***Note:*** They charge a baggage fee of $50 for each piece beyond one checked and one carry-on piece on the bus to the lodge.

Kantishna District, Denali National Park (Mailing address: 1 Doyon Place, Ste. 300, Fairbanks, AK 99701). www.seedenali.com. ☎ **800/942-7420** or 907/683-1475. Fax 907/683-1449. 32 units. $435 per person double plus 8% tax; Extra person $330. Rates include all meals, guided activities, and transportation from park entrance. Minimum stay 2 nights. AE, DISC, MC, V. **Amenities:** Bar; mountain bikes; sauna.

Skyline Lodge ★ 🗲 Run by pilot Greg LaHaie, owner of Kantishna Air Taxi, the lodge offers a unique alternative in Denali's backcountry: a place you don't have to be a millionaire to afford. With room for only 10 guests and a self-serve philosophy, it's far simpler and more casual than the full-service lodges in Kantishna, and costs less than a fourth as much. Also, there's no minimum stay, and you can fly there with Greg. It costs $40 a day to join the family style lunch and dinner (breakfast is already included in the price). Rooms are in cabins and sleep up to four, each with a double or queen-size bed and a loft. Large windows overlook Moose Creek. The kitchen, TV, and other amenities are in the central lodge building. The most important amenity, however, is that you are in the heart of Denali's backcountry.

Kantishna District (P.O. Box 46), Denali National Park, AK 99755. www.katair.com. ☎ **907/683-1223.** Fax 907/683-1223. Oct–May: 303/449-1146. 4 units, none with private bathroom. $235 for 1 to 2 people; $283 for 3 people; $335 for 4 people. Rates include continental breakfast. DISC, MC, V. **Amenities:** Courtesy shuttle; free mountain bikes; sauna.

TALKEETNA: BACK DOOR TO DENALI

Talkeetna, a historic and funky little town with a sense of humor but not much happening, slept soundly from its decline around World War I until about 15 years ago. Now there are paved streets (both of them), a fancy National Park Service building, a larger railroad depot, and two large luxury lodges. It seems that while Talkeetna slumbered in a time capsule, an explosion of visitors was happening at Denali National Park. Now, not entirely voluntarily, Talkeetna has been enveloped in that boom.

As a threshold to the park, Talkeetna has significant pros and cons that you should take into account. On the positive side, it's closer to Anchorage; the development is much more interesting and authentic than that at the park entrance; there's lots to do outdoors; and Mount McKinley is seen more frequently, because of both geography and weather. On the negative

Talkeetna.

side, a big minus: You can't get into the park from here without a long drive or an expensive flight. That may mean you miss the dramatic scenery, easy backcountry access, and unique wildlife viewing on the park road.

The town dates from the gold rush and has many charming log and clapboard buildings. With 16 sites of historic note, the entire downtown area has been listed on the National Register of Historic Places. You can spend a couple of hours looking at the museum and meeting people in the 2-block main street, then go out on the Talkeetna or Susitna rivers for rafting, a jet-boat ride, or fishing, or take a flightseeing trip to the national park.

Essentials

GETTING THERE   Talkeetna lies on a 14-mile spur road that branches from the Parks Highway 99 miles north of Anchorage and 138 miles south of the park entrance. The **Alaska Railroad** (✆ 800/544-0552; www.alaskarailroad. com) serves Talkeetna daily on its runs to Denali National Park during the summer and weekly in the winter. (See "Park Essentials," earlier in this chapter, for additional details.) The summer fare from Anchorage to Talkeetna is $89 one-way for adults, half price for children ages 2 to 11, for basic service.

It's possible to stay in Talkeetna but do the Denali National Park shuttle-bus ride and other park activities by flying there for the day. **McKinley Flight Services,** also known as Talkeetna Aero Services (✆ 888/733-2899 or 907/733-2899; www.talkeetnaaero.com), offers daily round-trips for this purpose during the summer, with a flightseeing tour circling Mount McKinley en route. They charge $495 as a package with ground transfers, a bus tour, and a box lunch.

VISITOR INFORMATION   Built to serve people aiming to climb Mount McKinley, the **Denali National Park Talkeetna Ranger Station,** at 1st and B streets (P.O. Box 588), Talkeetna, AK 99676 (✆ 907/733-2231; www.nps. gov/dena), makes a fascinating stop for anyone curious about mountaineering. Inside the handsome structure, a large sitting room contains a river-rock fireplace, climbing books, and pictures of the mountain—it's like an old-fashioned explorers' club. Fascinating records open for inspection cover the history of McKinley climbs. Rangers are on hand to answer questions, too.

It's open May through Labor Day daily from 8am to 5:30pm, winter Monday through Friday from 8am to 4:30pm.

The **Talkeetna/Denali Visitor Center,** located in a tiny cabin at the intersection of the Parks Highway and Talkeetna Spur Road and on Main Street (P.O. Box 688), Talkeetna, AK 99676 ((℗ **800/660-2688** or 907/733-2641; www.talkeetnadenali.com), is a commercial center belonging to a local flight service and providing brochures, information, and advice while earning commissions from bookings. It's the handiest commercial information stop in the region. The center is open daily from 8am to 8pm in summer, and they respond to inquiries year-round with free trip-planning help.

[Fast FACTS] TALKEETNA

Bank A local credit union is near the Parks Highway on the Talkeetna Spur Road. There is no bank in the town center, but several businesses have ATMs, including Nagley's General Store.

Hospital **Sunshine Community Health Center,** on the Talkeetna Spur Road near the town

(℗ **907/733-2273;** www.sunshineclinic.org).

Internet Access Free for up to 30 minutes at the **Talkeetna Public Library** (℗ **907/733-2359**), at Mile 13.5 of the Talkeetna Spur Road, just across the tracks.

Police For nonemergencies, call the **Alaska State Troopers** at

℗ **907/733-2256.** The station is near the Parks Highway on the Talkeetna Spur Road.

Post Office In the town center, near the intersection of Talkeetna Spur Road and Main Street.

Taxes There is no **sales tax. Room tax** in the area is 5%.

SPECIAL EVENTS The **Mountain Mother Contest,** held over the second weekend in July, is a fundraiser for the Talkeetna Historical Society (℗ **907/733-2487;** www.talkeetnahistoricalsociety.org). It is open only to mothers, who race to demonstrate their bush skills, including splitting wood and diapering a baby.

Exploring the Town

Talkeetna is famous for its laid-back atmosphere and outdoors, not for "attractions," but there are several places to stop in to get the sense of the place. One is the ranger station mentioned below in this section under "Visitor Information." If you come in May or June, you're sure to meet many international mountain climbers; you'll have no difficulty picking them out (see "Climbing Mount McKinley," p. 385). Along Main Street are shops where artists and craftspeople often can be found at work. For your walk, pick up a copy of the "Talkeetna Historic District Walking Tour" brochure from the museum (in the next paragraph) for a map and informative explanation of the town's story, including details such as the site of its first bathtub, which arrived in 1923.

The **Talkeetna Historical Society Museum,** in five buildings on the Village Airstrip a half-block south of Main Street (℗ **907/733-2487;** www.talkeetnahistoricalsociety.org), is well worth a stop. The first building contains artifacts and displays on local mining history, including engaging photographs and biographies of individual characters. The second is an old railroad depot, relocated here and furnished with period decor. The third holds climbing displays and a huge scale model of Mount McKinley and the nearby mountains (don't miss it if you will fly over the mountain). The fourth is a 1916 trapper's cabin and the fifth a 1924 cabin, both with period artifacts. The museum is a handy information stop. It is open daily in summer from 10am to 6pm, generally closed in winter. Admission is $3, free for children 16 and under.

I've found the most affecting site in town to be the **Mount McKinley Climbers' Memorial** at the town cemetery, near the airstrip on the east side of the railroad tracks. Besides a memorial of granite plaques for lost mountaineers, there is a garden of monuments to many individual climbers, some in Japanese.

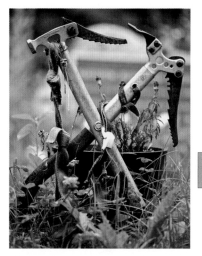

Mount McKinley Climbers' Memorial.

The bodies of at least 36 climbers who died on the mountain have never been recovered. The propellers in the cemetery mark the graves of bush pilots.

Getting Outside

FLIGHTSEEING

There is no more dramatic or memorable experience available to the typical tourist in Alaska than to fly with one of the glacier pilots who support Mount McKinley climbs. Climbers typically begin with a flight from here to the 7,200-foot level of the Kahiltna Glacier. These immense mountains grow ever larger as you fly toward them until, like a tiny insect, you fly among their miles-tall folds, watching the climbers toiling on the ice below you. I was simply speechless.

Several operators with long experience offer the flights. The least expensive excursions cost around $195 and approach McKinley's south face, flying over the Ruth and Tokositna glaciers. If at all possible—and if the weather is good—buy an extended tour that circles the mountain and flies over its craggy heights, for $240 to $385 per person. Best of all, arrange a landing on the mountain itself, just as the climbers do. The Don Sheldon Amphitheater on the Ruth Glacier is a stunning spot high on McKinley; only after you stand there do you realize the incredible scale of what you have seen from above. These landings are treated as add-ons to the tours mentioned above, for an additional price of $75 to $85 per person, plus the $10 park entrance fee.

Should you reserve ahead or wait to see the weather? It used to be you could reliably walk in and grab a seat, but the popularity of these flights now makes reservations advisable. That's the best way to get a guaranteed price, too; otherwise, prices sometimes depend on the number of passengers aboard the plane. If you do decide on the walk-in approach, make your appearance early in the morning.

A number of air taxi companies offer these flights, all operating out of the Talkeetna airport, including these three that I can wholeheartedly recommend: **Talkeetna Air Taxi** (✆ **800/533-2219** or 907/733-2218; www.talkeetnaair. com), **K-2 Aviation** (✆ **800/764-2291** or 907/733-2291; www.flyk2.com), and

Talkeetna: Back Door to Denali

A skier loads up.

McKinley Flight Services, also known as Talkeetna Aero Services (✆ 888/733-2899 or 907/733-2899; www.talkeetnaaero.com).

JET BOAT TOURS

Talkeetna is at the confluence of the Talkeetna and Big Susitna rivers. **Mahay's Riverboat Service** (✆ 800/736-2210 or 907/733-2223; www.mahaysriverboat.com) covers these fast-moving waters of glacier silt on speedy, comfortable jet boats. Tours that leave several times a day from a dock near the Talkeetna River public boat launch range from 2 to 5 hours, priced at $65 to $155 per person. Owner Steve Mahay is legendary, the only person ever to shoot Devil's Canyon in a jet boat.

RAFTING

Talkeetna River Guides, on Main Street (✆ 800/353-2677; www.talkeetnariverguides.com), offers a 2-hour wildlife river-rafting tour, without white water, over 9 miles of the Talkeetna three times a day for $79 adults, $59 children 10 and under. They also offer longer rafting expeditions, including overnights that include fishing.

Where to Stay & Eat

There are good restaurants at each of the lodgings listed here. One other place stands out, **Café Michele,** in a quaint little house at the corner of Talkeetna Spur Road and 2nd Street (✆ 907/733-5300). It's a classy little bistro, serving sandwiches on homemade focaccia bread from a lunch menu ranging from $12 to $16, and dinner entrees such as ginger-soy salmon or pesto cream seafood pasta in the range of $23 to $39, including vegetarian dishes. Save room for dessert, as the baking is exceptional—Michele even bakes the area's wedding cakes. The cafe is open summer only, daily 11am to 3pm and 5:30 to 10pm.

At mile 11 of the spur road, **Flying Squirrel Bakery Cafe** (www.flyingsquirrelcafe.com; ✆ 907/733-NUTS) serves wholesome and tasty baked goods, sells soup for lunch, and has pizza nights. It's easy to find a burger, pizza, or sandwich on Main Street.

A public campground for tents only is at the end of Main Street and costs $10. A larger campground with more privacy and sites for RVs, but no hookups, is at the boat launch (cross the railroad tracks to the airport, then turn left) and charges $13 a night.

Mt. McKinley Princess Lodge ★★ ✦   Princess Cruises built the main lodge building to take advantage of a striking view of the mountain, only 42 miles away as the crow flies. The property isn't near any town—100 miles south of the park entrance and about 45 road miles from Talkeetna—but, like a resort, they offer everything you need on-site and a full set of activities, including a short network of trails. If you want a ride to Talkeetna, the lodge provides shuttle service. The design and decoration are an inspired modernization of the classic national park style. There are several dining choices, including a steak and seafood place, a cafe, and a bar and grill.

Mile 133.1, Parks Hwy., Denali State Park, AK 99683. www.princesslodges.com. ℂ **800/426-0500** or 907/733-2900. Fax 907/733-2922. 460 units. Summer $199 double; spring and fall $149 double. AE, DC, DISC, MC, V. Closed mid-Sept to mid-May. **Amenities:** 4 restaurants; bar; shuttle to Talkeetna. *In room:* TV, hair dryer.

Swiss Alaska Inn 🏠   This is the essence of Talkeetna: a family business in the same hands for decades where guests are made to feel like old friends among the real old friends often found sipping coffee with the proprietor in the small restaurant. They serve good, familiar American meals, plus a few German dishes. Most of the rooms are decorated in light colors and, although small, are clean, comfortable, and reasonably priced. The larger rooms in the newer building are quite preferable. The TVs don't pick up anything but have DVD players, and there is a video shop across the street.

F St., near the boat launch (P.O. Box 565), Talkeetna, AK 99676. www.swissalaska.com. ℂ **907/733-2424.** Fax 907/733-2425. 20 units. $130 double. Extra person 12 and over $15. AE, DISC, MC, V. **Amenities:** Restaurant; bar; courtesy car (to railroad station); Wi-Fi in restaurant. *In room:* TV/DVD (no broadcast reception), hair dryer.

Talkeetna Alaskan Lodge ★★   The Cook Inlet Region Native corporation spared no expense building this magnificent hotel of big timbers and river rock 2 miles from Talkeetna, but it's not a gaudy showplace. Trim of regionally harvested birch finishes rooms and hallways in understated geometric designs, hung with Native art. Because the hotel sits atop a high river bluff, views from common rooms and many guest rooms take in a broad-canvas masterpiece of the Alaska Range, with McKinley towering in the center. Rooms in the main building are somewhat larger and have either one king- or two queen-size beds, and the hallways connect to several sumptuous lobbies with reading areas. As much as I like the hotel, however, the rates are high; those listed here are for standard units without the mountain view. Fine meals are served in front of big windows with the magnificent view in the Foraker Room, which has an award-winning wine list; the casual Basecamp Bistro also has the view.

Mile 12.5, Talkeetna Spur Rd. (mailing address: P.O. Box 727, Talkeetna, AK 99676). www.talkeetnalodge.com. ℂ **888/959-9590** or 907/265-4501 reservations; 733-9500 at lodge. Fax 907/733-9545. 212 units. Summer $279–$309 double; off season $189–$209 double. Extra person 11 and over $15. AE, DISC, MC, V. Closed Oct–Apr. **Amenities:** 2 restaurants (dining room; bistro); bar; courtesy shuttle; fitness center. *In room:* TV, hair dryer, Wi-Fi.

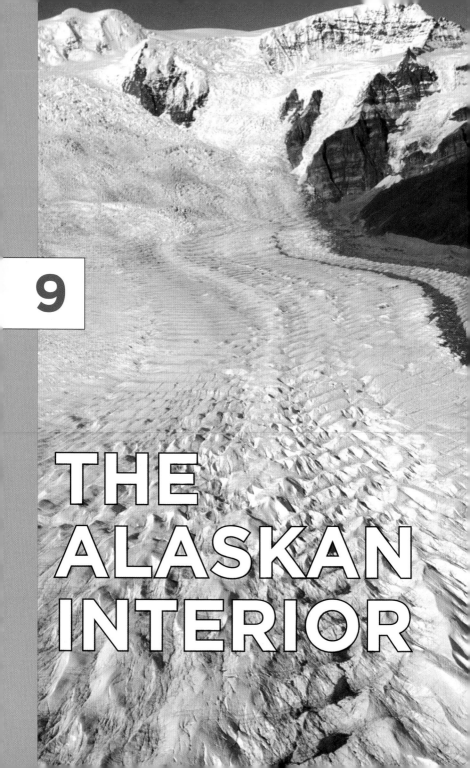

9

THE ALASKAN INTERIOR

nterior Alaska is so large—it basically includes everything that's not on the coasts or in the Arctic—you can spend a week of hard driving and not explore it all. Or you can spend all summer floating the rivers and still have years of floating left to do before you see all the riverbanks. It's something like what the great mass of America's Midwest once must have been, perhaps a century and a half ago, when the great flatlands had been explored but not completely civilized and Huckleberry Finn could float downriver into a wilderness of adventures. During an Interior summer, nature combines its immensity with a rare sense of gentleness, patiently awaiting the next thunderstorm.

Winter is another matter. Without the regulating influence of the ocean—the same reason summers are hot—winter temperatures can often drop to –30°F or –40°F (–34°C or –40°C), and during exceptional cold snaps, even lower. Now the Earth is wobbling over in the other direction, away from the sun. The long, black nights can make Fairbanks, the region's dominant city, feel more like an outpost on a barren planet, far off in outer space. That's when the northern lights come, spewing swirls of color across the dome of the sky and *crackling* with electricity. Neighbors wake each other and, rising from bed to put on their warmest parkas and insulated boots, stand in the street, gazing straight up. Visitors lucky enough to come at such times may be watching from a steaming hot-spring tub. During the short days, they can bundle up and watch sled-dog racing or race across the wilderness themselves on snowmobiles.

Fairbanks stands second in Alaska in population, with 94,000 in the greater area, but the Interior otherwise is without any settlements large enough to be called cities. Instead, it's defined by roads, both paved and gravel, which are strands of civilization through sparsely settled, often swampy land. Before the roads, development occurred only on the rivers, which still serve as thoroughfares for the Athabascan villages of the region. In the summer, villagers travel by boat. In the winter, the frozen rivers become highways for snowmobiles and sled-dog teams. White homesteaders and gold miners live in the woods, too. Gold rush history is written on the land in piles of old gravel tailings and abandoned equipment, as well as in prettier tourist attractions and historic sites. Gold mining goes on today in small one-man operations and huge industrial works employing hundreds, but today the economy is based more on military and other government spending, the oil industry, and, of course, tourism. You'll find warm rural hospitality and great vistas on these highways, and, perhaps, a sense of slow-river laziness Huck Finn would have recognized.

FACING PAGE: **Root Glacier.**

EXPLORING THE INTERIOR

More than anywhere else in Alaska, the Interior is the place where having your own car provides you with the freedom to find the out-of-the-way places that give the region its character. Trains and buses run between Fairbanks and Anchorage, but that approach will show you only the larger, tourist-oriented destinations.

If you have the time and money, you may enjoy driving one of the remote gravel highways, or just poking along on the paved highways between the larger towns, ready to stop and investigate the roadhouses and meet the people who live out in the middle of nowhere. You'll find them mostly friendly and often downright odd—*colorful*, to use the polite term. As I drove an abandoned highway a few years ago, I saw a hand-lettered sign advertising coffee. It wasn't your typical espresso stand, just a log cabin dozens of miles from the nearest building. A squinting high-plains drifter stepped out of the cabin, wearing a cowboy hat on his head and a huge revolver on his hip, and asked, "Yeah?" The coffee came from a percolator warming on the woodstove, and the proprietor and I struck up a good conversation in his dark little dwelling. He was living the life of the old-time frontier.

FAIRBANKS: ALASKA HEARTLAND

Fairbanks is Alaska's second-largest city, with a population of about 46,000 in the city and 94,000 in the surrounding area, but it has never learned to put on airs. It sprawls, broad and flat, along big highways and the Chena. It's a friendly, easygoing town, but one where people still take gold and their independence seriously. They're still prospecting and mining around here, fighting off environmental regulation and maintaining a traditional Alaskan attitude that "it's us against the world." Fairbanks is the birthplace of strange political movements, including the secessionist Alaskan Independence Party. It's an adamant, loopy, affable place; it doesn't seem to mind being a little bizarre or residing far from the center of things. And that makes it an intensely Alaskan city, for those are the qualities Alaskans most cherish in their myth of themselves.

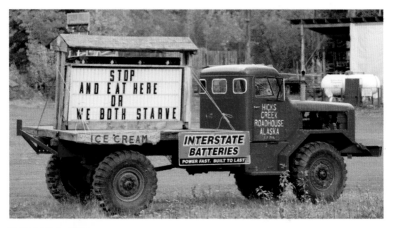

Hick's Creek Roadhouse.

Fairbanks can strike a visitor a couple of ways, depending on what you expect and what you like. Fairbanks can come across as a provincial outpost, a touristy cross between Kansas and Siberia. Driving one of the franchise-choked commercial strips, you can wonder why you went out of your way to come here. Or you can relax and take Fairbanks on its own terms, as a fun, unpretentious town that never lost its sense of being on the frontier.

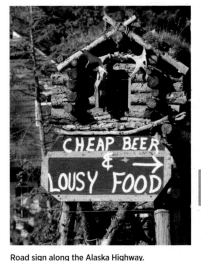

There's plenty for families to do in Fairbanks, much of it at least a little corny and requiring drives to widespread sites at the university, on the Chena River, in the gold mining area north of town, and at Pioneer Park. (You *must* have wheels in Fairbanks.) There are good opportunities for hiking and mountain-biking, and great opportunities for canoeing and slow river-float trips.

Essentials

Road sign along the Alaska Highway.

GETTING THERE

BY CAR OR RV Fairbanks is a transportation hub. The Richardson Highway heads east 100 miles to Delta Junction, the endpoint of the Alaska Highway, then south to Glennallen and Valdez. The Parks Highway heads due south from Fairbanks to Denali National Park, 120 miles away, and Anchorage, 360 miles south.

Rollin' on the River

Floating any of the thousands of miles of the Interior's rivers opens great swaths of wilderness. Beginners should take a guided trip before venturing out on their own. (See the lists of operators in chapter 11.) To plan your own trip, start with the **Alaska Public Lands Information Center** in Fairbanks (p. 408), Tok (p. 446), or Anchorage (p. 220). Among the most accessible and historic rivers are the Chena, Chatanika, and Yukon (see the sections on Fairbanks and Chena Hot Springs Rd. and the boxes on the Steese Hwy. and Dawson City in this chapter).

Of course, not every mile of back road is scenic, nor are all the stops interesting. Driving a car through Alaska takes a long time, including many hours spent in dull, brushy forest, and calls for a high tolerance for greasy hamburgers and a willingness to occasionally relieve yourself in the bushes. In this often-frozen land, paved highway sections can develop frost heaves—backbreaking dips and humps caused by the freeze and thaw of the road base and ground underneath. The gravel roads generate clouds of dust and quickly fatigue drivers, and windshields and headlights often succumb to their flying rocks. For tips on renting a vehicle to drive on gravel roads, see "Equipped for the Backroads," on p. 419.

ALASKA'S highways A LA CARTE

You won't need a detailed highway map of Alaska, because Alaska doesn't have detailed highways. A triangle of paved two-lane highways connects Tok, Fairbanks, and Anchorage. From this triangle, a few routes reach to discrete destinations, and gravel roads penetrate the periphery of the Bush. Beyond a few miles of freeway around Fairbanks and Anchorage, highways all are narrow strips of asphalt or gravel through the wilderness. (See "The Roster of Rural Roads," on p. 430, for a rundown of Alaska's unpaved and minor highways.) Always fill your tank before leaving town, as gas stations are far apart. A centralized report on road conditions and construction is operated by the Alaska Department of Transportation (✆ 511; http://511.alaska.gov). To help readers figure driving times, I have included my estimate of reasonable average speeds on each road (without stopping). These are based purely on my experience and assume dry, daylight conditions in summer.

ALASKA HIGHWAY
Route 2 from the border to Delta Junction
Average speed (Alaska section): 55–65 mph

Running nearly 1,400 miles from Dawson Creek, British Columbia, to Delta Junction, Alaska, a couple of hours east of Fairbanks on the Richardson Highway, this World War II road today is paved and generally easy driving. Two tiny towns lie on the Alaska portion of the road, Delta Junction and Tok. The prettiest part is on the Canadian side, in the Kluane Lake area (p. 454).

GLENN HIGHWAY
Route 1 from Anchorage to Tok
Average speed: 55–65 mph, except 45 mph on Matanuska Glacier section

From the Alaska Highway, this is how you get to Southcentral Alaska, including Anchorage, 330 miles southwest of Tok. The northern section, from Tok to Glennallen (sometimes called the "Tok Cut-Off"), borders Wrangell–St. Elias National Park, with broad tundra and taiga broken by high, craggy peaks. Glennallen to Anchorage is even more

spectacular, as the road passes through high alpine terrain and then close by the Matanuska Glacier, where it winds through a deep canyon valley carved by the glacier's river. See p. 450 for more information.

PARKS HIGHWAY
Route 3 from near Anchorage to Fairbanks
Average speed: 60–65 mph

The George Parks Highway goes straight from Anchorage to Fairbanks, 360 miles north, providing access on the way to Denali National Park. The best parts are the vistas of Mount McKinley from south of the park and the alpine terrain on either side of distant peaks of southern Wrangell–St. Elias National Park. North of Glennallen, the road climbs into the Alaska Range, snaking along the shores of long alpine lakes. The road descends again to the forested area around Delta Junction and meets the Alaska Highway before arriving in Fairbanks. See p. 452 for more on the highway.

SEWARD HIGHWAY

Route 1 from Anchorage to Tern Lake, Route 9 from Tern Lake to Seward
Average speed: 45–60 mph, depending on traffic

The highway leaves Anchorage on the 127-mile drive to Seward following the rocky edge of mountain peaks above a surging ocean fjord. Abundant wildlife and unfolding views often slow cars. Later, the road climbs through high mountain passes above the tree line, tracing sparkling alpine lakes. Alaska's best trail hikes are here. The section from Anchorage 50 miles south to Portage Glacier is covered in chapter 6; the remainder, to Seward, in chapter 7.

STERLING HIGHWAY

Route 1 from Tern Lake to Homer
Average speed: 50–60 mph, except 45 mph near Cooper Landing

Leading 142 miles from the Seward Highway to the tip of the Kenai Peninsula, the highway has some scenic ocean views on its southern section, but is mostly a way to get to the Kenai River, the Kenai National Wildlife Refuge, Kachemak Bay, and the towns of Cooper Landing, Soldotna, Kenai, and Homer.

Broad Pass, where the road crosses the Alaska Range and the park entrance. However, the Parks Highway is mostly a transportation route, less scenic than the Richardson or Glenn highways. From the northern (Fairbanks) end, the highway passes Nenana (p. 411), then Denali and Talkeetna (chapter 8), and finally the towns of the Matanuska and Susitna valleys (chapter 6).

RICHARDSON HIGHWAY

Route 4 from Valdez to Delta Junction, Route 2 from Delta Junction to Fairbanks
Average speed: 50–60 mph, except 45 mph in Thompson Pass section

The state's first highway, leading 364 miles from Valdez to Fairbanks, lost much of its traffic to the Parks Highway, which saves more than 90 miles between Anchorage and Fairbanks, and to the Glenn Highway, which saves about 120 miles from Glennallen to Tok. But it's still the most beautiful paved drive in the Interior. From the south, the road begins with a magnificent climb through Keystone Canyon and steep Thompson Pass, just out of Valdez (see chapter 7), then passes the huge,

BY VAN OR BUS   Alaska/Yukon Trails (📞 800/770-7275; www.alaskashuttle. com) offers daily service, summer only, to and from Denali National Park and Anchorage (one-way fares are $55 and $99, respectively). In Fairbanks, the van stops at Billie's Backpackers and GoNorth hostels (p. 428 and 419), among other places, and will pick up at the airport or your hotel for an added fee. The shuttle also runs as a tour to Dawson City and Whitehorse, Yukon. On most routes, they pick up and drop off along the way, but not in Canada.

BY TRAIN   The **Alaska Railroad** (📞 800/544-0552; www.alaskarailroad. com) links Fairbanks with Denali National Park and Anchorage, with tour commentary provided along the way. The high-season one-way fare is $64 to Denali and $210 to Anchorage (nearly twice the cost of flying between the cities); first-class, Gold Star service is $149 and $320, respectively.

BY AIR   Alaska Airlines (📞 800/252-7522; www.alaskaair.com) connects Fairbanks to Anchorage. Fares vary, and sometimes there are bargains. A bargain round-trip fare can be just under $300. The airport is a hub for various small carriers to Alaska's Interior and Arctic communities. A cab downtown from the airport is $18 to $20 with **Yellow Cab** (📞 907/455-5555). **Airlink Shuttle and Tours** (📞 907/452-3337) charges $3.50, with a three-person minimum and $1 fee per bag, for a ride from the airport to anywhere in town.

VISITOR INFORMATION   The **Morris Thompson Cultural and Visitors Center,** downtown at the corner of Wendell and Dunkel streets, houses the **Fairbanks Convention and Visitors Bureau** (📞 800/327-5774 or 907/ 456-5774; fax 907/459-3787; www.explorefairbanks.com) and the **Alaska Public Lands Information Center** (📞 907/459-3730; www.alaska centers.gov), as well as a nonprofit **Alaska Geographic** book and gift store (📞 907/459-3710; www.alaskageographic.org), and cultural and educational programs. The center has information kiosks in the main lobby, as well as a video nook featuring films about the area and Alaska. The visitor bureau's staff and volunteers answer questions and provide useful maps, driving tour pamphlets, and walking tour audio players, and can help you find a room with their daily vacancy listing (weekly in winter). The building has free Wi-Fi, and several computers are set up for free e-mail access or to look up travel information. Visitor bureau hours are May to mid-September daily 8am to 9pm; the rest of the year the bureau is open daily 8am to 5pm, with shorter hours on holidays. The organization also has information desks at the airport and train depot, staffed summer only, and at Pioneer Park, closed entirely off season.

The **Alaska Public Lands Information Center** (📞 907/459-3730; www.alaskacenters.gov) staffs an information counter at the Morris Thompson Center, as well as tables where you can spread out maps and computers to gather trip-planning information. This is an indispensable stop for anyone planning to spend time in the outdoors. The staff is remarkably knowledgeable and can tell you about trips and activities based on first-hand experience. The counter operates in summer daily 9am to 6pm, in winter Monday to Saturday 9am to 5pm.

The Morris Thompson Center as a whole also is worth visiting, with impressive exhibits, naturalist programs, a theater that features daily free films, and summertime classes, workshops, and demonstrations teaching

Fairbanks

Creamer's Field

College Rd.

Danby St.

Johansen Expwy.

Aurora Dr.

Hanson Rd.

College Mack Blvd.

College Rd.

Yukon Dr.

Noatak Dr.

UNIVERSITY OF ALASKA FAIRBANKS

Farmers Loop Rd.

Geist Rd.

Fairbanks St.

Alaska Railroad

Chena Pump Rd.

Chena Ridge Rd.

Phillips Field Rd.

Peger Rd.

Chena R.

1st Ave.

10th Ave.

Hilton Ave.

Wilbur St.

Cowles St.

Illinois St.

Steese Expwy.

Ringstad Park

see downtown Fairbanks map

University Ave.

Boat St.

19th Ave.

Airport Wy.

Noyes Slough

Chena R. S.R.S.

Holden Rd.

Davis Rd.

Chena Small Tracts Rd.

Discovery Dr.

Broadmoor Ave.

Western Ave.

Ravenwood Ave.

Dale Rd.

Hoselton Rd.

Chena R.

FAIRBANKS INTERNATIONAL AIRPORT

Airport Wy.

0   1/2 km
0   1/2 mi

Fairbanks
Anchorage   • Juneau

ATTRACTIONS
Fountainhead Antique Auto Museum **18**
Georgeson Botanical Garden **1**
Large Animal Research Station **3**
Pioneer Park **17**
Riverboat Discovery **5**
UA Museum of the North **2**

HOTELS
Billie's Backpackers Hostel **16**
Fairbanks Princess Riverside Lodge **6**
Golden North Motel **9**
GoNorth Alaska Hostel **11**
Minnie Street B&B Inn **19**
Pike's Waterfront Lodge **7**
River's Edge Resort Cottages **8**
Sophie Station **10**
Wedgewood Resort **18**

RESTAURANTS
The Bakery **20**
Bun on the Run **12**
College Coffeehouse **13**
College Town Pizzeria **14**
Hot Licks Homemade Ice Cream **15**
Pike's Landing **7**
The Pump House Restaurant & Saloon **4**

409

about Athabascan culture put on by local Native organizations. Parking is free and plentiful.

GETTING AROUND Fairbanks is designed around the car, and that's the practical way to get around. Without one, sticking only to downtown, you will leave with a low opinion of the place. The city is too spread out to use taxis much. **Avis, Hertz, Dollar, Budget, Payless, Alamo,** and **National** are located at the airport. If you plan on driving any of the region's unpaved highways, see "Equipped for the Backroads," p. 419, as the brand-name rental-car agencies do not allow it.

The Fairbanks North Star Borough's **MACS bus system** (✆ **907/459-1002;** www.co.fairbanks.ak.us/transportation) links the university, downtown, the nearby North Pole community, shopping areas, and some hotels. Service is every 30 minutes at best, worse Saturday, and nonexistent Sunday. Pick up timetables at the visitor center or online. Almost all buses connect at the transit park downtown, at 5th Avenue and Cushman Street. The fare is $1.50 for adults; 75¢ for seniors, children, teens, and people with disabilities; free for children 4 and under.

Fairbanks's car-oriented layout does not lend itself to using bikes as the primary means of transportation, but there are great mountain-biking opportunities (see "Getting Outside," later in this chapter).

[FastFACTS] FAIRBANKS

Banks   Fairbanks has numerous banks with **ATMs** in the downtown area and along the commercial strips. **Key Bank** is at 100 Cushman.

Business Services & Internet Access   **FedEx Copy Center** is at 418 3rd St. (✆ **907/456-7348**). You can check e-mail for free at the **Morris**

Thompson Cultural and Visitors Center at 101 Dunkel St. (see "Visitor Information," above) and at numerous coffee shops.

Hospital   **Fairbanks Memorial** is at 1650 Cowles St. (✆ **907/452-8181**).

Police   For nonemergency police business, call the **Alaska State Troopers**

(✆ **907/451-5100**) or, within city limits, the **Fairbanks Police Department** (✆ **907/459-6500**).

Post Office   At 315 Barnette St.

Taxes   Fairbanks has no sales tax. North Pole charges 4%, with a cap of $8 in tax on any one purchase. **Room tax** is 8%.

SPECIAL EVENTS   A recording of current local happenings can be reached at ✆ **907/456-INFO** (4636), maintained by the Fairbanks Convention and Visitors Bureau, which also posts an events calendar at **www.explore fairbanks.com.**

The **Yukon Quest International Sled Dog Race** (✆ **907/452-7954;** www.yukonquest.com) starts February 4, 2012, in Fairbanks, and ends 10 to 14 days later in Whitehorse, Yukon (in odd-numbered years, the direction is reversed). Many mushers say this rugged 1,000-mile race is even tougher than the Iditarod.

The **Nenana Ice Classic** (✆ **907/832-5446;** www.nenanaaice classic.com) is a sweepstakes held annually since 1917 based on who can

If you are driving south from Fairbanks toward Denali National Park or Anchorage, plan a short stop in the town of Nenana, about 60 miles along your way. It's a town out of a Mark Twain novel, a sleepy, dusty riverside barge stop left over from the past. Here President Warren Harding drove the golden spike on the Alaska Railroad in 1923; a monument with a depiction of the spike is on display outside the memory-stirring old depot museum, although the train hasn't stopped regularly in decades. On the waterfront, riverboats are still loaded with cargo for villages down the Tanana and Yukon rivers. That's also where you can see the Alfred Starr Nenana Cultural Center, with a little museum and Native crafts shop, including some crafts by locals. The oldest building in town is the picturesque 1905 log cabin church on Front Street.

guess closest to the exact minute when the ice will go out on the Tanana River. The classic starts with Tripod Days, the first weekend in March, when they set up the so-called four-legged tripod; when it moves 100 feet, it trips a clock, determining the winner. Thanks to the game, this is one of the most carefully kept climate measurements in the north; scientists have used it to demonstrate long-term warming of the weather. The Tripod Days celebration includes dance performances, dog mushing, and other activities.

Also in March, the **World Ice Art Championships** (📞 907/451-8250; www.icealaska.com) bring carvers from all over the world to sculpt immense, clear chunks cut from a Fairbanks pond. Among ice carvers, Fairbanks ice is famous for its clarity and the great size of the chunks. Some

spectacular ice sculptures stand as tall as two-story buildings. It's long been worth planning a visit around, but recent organizational problems put the future of the championships in doubt. Check for the latest, as many details are unknown at this writing.

The **North American Sled Dog Championships** (📞 907/457-MUSH [6874]; www.sleddog.org) are the oldest running, taking place over 2 weekends in mid-March. Sprint mushers from all over the world compete with teams of as many as 24 dogs, streaking away from the starting line on 2nd Avenue or the Chena River.

Lots of events happen around the **summer solstice,** usually June 21. The **Midnight Sun Run** (📞 907/452-6046; www.midnightsunrun.us) is a 10K race and walk, with winners chosen for both their times and their funny costumes. The race is run on a Saturday near the solstice. It starts at

A sculpture at the World Ice Art Championships.

Church of the Immaculate Conception.

10pm on the university campus and ends at Pioneer Park.

The **Midnight Sun Baseball Game,** hosted by the semipro Alaska Goldpanners of Fairbanks (© **907/451-0095;** www.goldpanners.com), begins at 10:30pm on June 21. The game, which began with a pair of pick-up teams in 1906, is played with no artificial lights. The 'Panners have hosted since 1960.

Also in June, the free **Fairbanks Summer Folk Fest** (www.fairbanks folkfest.org) fills a Pioneer Park lawn with music, food, and art booths; live music starts at 1pm and lasts late into the night.

The **Fairbanks Summer Arts Festival,** held the last 2 weeks in July on the University of Alaska Fairbanks campus (© **907/474-8869;** www. fsaf.org), brings artists of international reputation for performance and teaching. Classes are for all levels in music, dance, ice skating, visual arts, healing arts, literary arts, and other subject areas.

The **Tanana Valley State Fair** (© **907/452-3750;** www.tananavalley statefair.com), in early August, shows off the area's agricultural production, arts and crafts, businesses, and entertainment, and includes rides and competitive exhibits.

In late August, Friends of Creamer's Field (© **907/452-5162**) hosts an annual **Sandhill Crane Festival,** with nature walks, lectures, and other activities, mostly at Creamer's Field.

Exploring the Town
STROLLING AROUND DOWNTOWN

Exploring downtown won't take more than an hour or two, but there are a few interesting spots in addition to the ice museum and community museums covered below. Start with the exhibits at the **Morris Thompson Cultural and Visitors Center** at 101 Dunkel St. The visitors bureau there lends audio players with spoken tours for the other sights.

A graceful footbridge spans the river. On the other side, peek into the lobby of the **Doyon Native corporation offices** to see Native cultural displays from all over Alaska, the traditional Athabascan tool collection, and the colorful modern art hanging from the walls and ceiling. Downriver, toward Cushman Street, is the town's most interesting building, the Roman Catholic **Church of the Immaculate Conception.** The white clapboard structure, built in 1904, has ornate gold-rush decoration inside, rare for its authenticity, including a pressed-tin ceiling and stained-glass windows—an appealing, if incongruous, mix of gold-rush and sacred decor.

Crossing back on the Cushman Street Bridge, you'll see on the left a large log cabin with a sod roof, the **headquarters of the Yukon Quest Sled Dog Race,** where you can get race souvenirs and see displays of equipment that teach about the race and dog mushing. Next door, the **Golden Heart Park** is a waterfront plaza with a fountain and a bronze statue of a Native family, where community events often occur. Farther downriver, at 1st Avenue between Kellum and Bonnifield streets, **St. Matthew's Episcopal Church** is an old log church with a working rope-pull bell. It was founded by missionary and dog-sled explorer Hudson Stuck in 1904, who organized the first successful climb of Mount McKinley. The original church burned; the present structure dates from 1948.

SPECIALTY MUSEUMS

Fairbanks has a lot of museums for a town its size, including those at the University of Alaska, at Pioneer Park, and at the commercial tourist attractions, all described below. Here are three unique museums to visit; the first two are within walking distance downtown.

At 500 2nd Ave., the **Fairbanks Ice Museum ★** (*C* **907/451-8222**) aims to show summer visitors a bit of Fairbanks ice carving. A big-screen, high-tech slide show plays hourly, explaining the annual World Ice Art Championships (see "Special Events," above), and four expansive freezers with large picture windows contain ice sculptures with an ice artist usually at work. Admission is $12 for adults, $11 for seniors and military, $6 for children ages 6 to 12, $2 for ages 5 and under. It's open from 10am to 8pm daily from May to September.

The **Fairbanks Community Museum ★**, in the old city hall at 410 Cushman St. (*C* **907/457-3669**), is well worth a stop for the charming historical exhibits and the sense of local pride it contains. A series of cramped galleries

⊙ SEEING THE AURORA BOREALIS

One fall evening, I left the house of friends in Fairbanks to the sight of a swirling green glow that filled the dark sky. I knocked on the door and brought them out to see, only to have my friends laugh in my face. They informed me, with mock contempt for my Anchorage home, that in Fairbanks they don't even bother to bend their necks back for northern lights as dim as these. It's true—a bright aurora borealis is routine in Fairbanks. Some of the world's top experts on the phenomenon work here, at the **University of Alaska Geophysical Institute** (their aurora predictions, in season, and extensive background on the aurora are posted at www.gi.alaska.edu). Hours-long displays can be incredibly spectacular and moving.

Most visitors never see these wild strands of bright colors whipping across the sky, because when most visitors come, the sky is never dark. Alaskans rarely see the stars from late May to early August, and to see the aurora well, you need an especially dark night sky. To improve your chances, plan your trip in the fall or winter. An early September trip offers brilliant fall foliage, dark night skies, and the remnants of summer weather. In midwinter, the sky is dark all night and most of the day. Many hotels near Fairbanks cater to travelers coming to see the aurora in winter, as well as visitors who come for such winter sports as dog mushing and snowmobiling; the best for that kind of trip is Chena Hot Springs Resort (p. 435).

offers up old photographs, maps, newspapers, and other bric-a-brac, as well as skillfully created explanatory exhibits focusing on the 1967 flood and the area's gold-mining history and development. An exhibit of whimsical photographs shows how modern-day Fairbanksans entertain themselves in the winter. Volunteers run the museum, open Tuesday through Saturday from 10am to 6pm, with reduced hours in the off season. Admission is free, but donations are accepted. It is usually closed during April.

Beyond downtown, the **Fountainhead Antique Auto Museum** (© **907/450-2100;** www.fountainheadmuseum.com) is on the grounds of Wedgewood Resort (p. 425), with more than 50 historically significant American cars predating World War II, many of them involved in Alaska history. Interesting displays show how Alaskans modified their vehicles for different tasks, such as cutting firewood, powering a boat, traveling on snow, and riding railroad tracks. Admission is $8 for adults, $5 ages 3 to 12, free 2 and under. It's open mid-May to mid-September Sunday to Thursday 11am to 10pm, Friday and Saturday 11am to 6 pm; in winter, open only Sunday noon to 6pm.

PIONEER PARK ★★

Built for the Alaska purchase centennial in 1967, **Pioneer Park** (formerly **Alaskaland**) is the boiled-down essence of Fairbanks on grounds at the intersection of Airport Way and Peger Road (© **907/459-1087;** www.co.fairbanks.ak.us/ pioneerpark). It's called a theme park, but don't expect Disneyland or anything like it. Instead, Pioneer Park is a city park with a theme. It's relaxing and low key, entrancing for young children, and interesting for adults if you can give in to the charm of the place. Admission to the park is free, and the tours and activities are generally inexpensive. The park is open year-round, but the attractions operate only Memorial Day weekend to Labor Day, daily from noon to 8pm. Pick up a map and schedule when you arrive; here I've listed the highlights, but there is more to see. Depending on the pace you like to keep and the age level of your group, you can spend anything from a couple of hours to most of a day here.

The **SS Nenana ★★** is the park's centerpiece. Commissioned by the federally owned Alaska Railroad in 1933, the large sternwheeler plied the Yukon and Tanana rivers until 1952. In 1967, the *Nenana* came to what was then Alaskaland but was unmaintained and had nearly collapsed from rot when it was saved by a community restoration effort, completed in 1992. Another restoration had closed the upper-deck tours in 2010, but those areas should be reopened as work is completed. During the work, self-guided entry is open to the ground-floor cargo deck, with its engaging set of dioramas showing all the riverside towns and villages where the boat called, modeled as they looked in its heyday.

Much of Fairbanks's history has been moved to Pioneer Park. A village of log cabins contains shops and restaurants, each marked with its original location and place in town history. **Judge Wickersham's house,** built around 1904, is kept as a museum, decorated

The paddle wheeler *Nenana* at Pioneer Park.

appropriately according to the period of the town's founding. The house is less than grand—it may remind you of your grandmother's—but it's worth a stop to strike up a conversation with the historical society volunteers who keep it open. **President Warren Harding's railcar,** from which he stepped to drive the golden spike on the Alaska Railroad, sits near the park entrance. The **Pioneer Air Museum** (✆ **907/451-0037**) is housed in a geodesic dome toward the back of the park. Besides the aircraft, there are displays and artifacts of the crashes of Alaska's aviation pioneers. Admission is $2 for adults, free for children 12 and under with a parent, $5 for families.

A different kind of attraction shows off Fairbanks winter in summer. **40 Below Fairbanks,** at Cabin no. 3, just down from the Palace Saloon (✆ **907/347-5451**), puts visitors in an 8×10-foot room at a temperature at least −40°F (−40°C), a chill seen at least once most winters here. While in the freezer, you can use a rock-solid banana to pound a nail and toss a cup of hot water into the air to watch it explode into steam. Admission is $6.

Other park attractions include an illustrated gold-rush show, kayak and bike rentals, a dance hall, an art gallery, and Alaska Native and gold-rush museums. If you have children, you certainly won't escape Pioneer Park without a ride on the **Crooked Creek and Whiskey Island Railroad** that circles the park twice, with a tour guide pointing out the sights; rides cost $2 for adults, $1 for children and seniors. Kids will also enjoy the large **playground,** with equipment for toddlers and older children, where lots of local families come to play, and the two 18-hole miniature golf courses. The only carnival ride is a nice old **merry-go-round,** which costs $1.

Tour groups generally come to Pioneer Park in the evening from mid-May to mid-September for the combined **Alaska Salmon Bake,** at the mining valley area, and the **Golden Heart Revue,** at the Palace Theatre (✆ **800/354-7274** or 907/452-7274; www.akvisit.com). Cost for all-you-can-eat prime rib and fish (halibut, cod, or salmon) is $31, $15 ages 3 to 12, or $6 for child's hot dog plate. Beer and wine are available. The seating area is pleasant, with indoor or outdoor dining. The revue, nightly at 8:15pm from mid-May to mid-September, covers the amusing story of the founding of Fairbanks with comedy and song in a nightclub setting; admission is $18 for adults.

UNIVERSITY OF ALASKA FAIRBANKS

The state university's main campus contains several interesting attractions and makes a point of serving tourists. The campus is on the west side of town; major entrances are via Thompson Drive off Geist Road and at the intersection of University Avenue and College Road. A widely distributed brochure lists tours, hours, and fees. A free 2-hour **walking tour** meets at Signers' Hall Monday through Friday at 10 am, June through August (except for 2 days around July 4). Call ✆ **907/474-7500** or check www.uaf.edu/visituaf for more information. Several campus attractions are listed below, and more are on the website, where you'll also find a campus map. The university's trail system is covered later in this chapter under "Winter Activities."

UA Museum of the North ★★★   This magnificent on-campus museum of science and art is the most intellectually engaging I've ever visited. Instead of categorizing the content by discipline, curators have thematically combined art, science, anthropology, and natural history to tell Alaska's story and to raise questions in viewers' minds—not only answer them. The building is a swooping combination of grand, graceful shapes, recalling moving icebergs or perhaps the northern lights. The natural history collection is Alaska's best and most scholarly, with information presented at advanced as well as elementary levels, and memorable items such as Blue Babe, the mummified steppe bison; a 5,400-pound copper nugget; and the state's largest public display of gold. The mixed cultural and scientific objects are linked by region of Alaska, creating a rich mental map of the state in one room. In a towering newer gallery, the thematic presentation is based more on concepts and issues. This is where you'll find the hypnotic sound-and-light installation called "The Place Where You Go to Listen," which *The New Yorker* said confirmed Fairbanks composer John Luther Adams as "one of the most original musical thinkers of the new century." For extra fees, carry an audio tour ($4) or take in a film ($5).

An exhibit at the UA Museum of the North.

907 Yukon Dr. ℂ **907/474-7505.** www.uaf.edu/museum. Admission $10 adults, $9 ages 60 and older, $5 ages 7–17, free ages 6 and under. Summer daily 9am–9pm; winter Mon–Sat 9am–5pm, closed Sun.

Georgeson Botanical Garden ★ I really enjoy the mix of science and contemplation I find at this relaxed working garden. Plots are laid out to compare seeds and cultivation techniques, usually well posted with explanatory information on the experiment; but at the same time, the flowers and vegetables are spectacular and there are peaceful memorials and places to picnic. You don't need a tour to enjoy the garden. Nearby, the barn of the university's experimental farm is open for visitors, and reindeer can be viewed in a neighboring paddock. A children's garden is slowly being created and includes a fun maze in the form of a five-petal flower.

117 W. Tanana Dr. ℂ **907/474-7222.** http://georgesonbg.org. Admission $3. Under 6 is free. Summer daily 9am–8pm, store 9am–5pm.

Large Animal Research Station ★ The university studies captive muskoxen, reindeer, and caribous here on a property often called the "muskox farm." Tours are given daily in the high season, with naturalists bringing animals into an amphitheater for close-up viewing. At any time, on a walk along the fence from the parking lot on Yankovich Road, you can see the animals behaving naturally in the large pastures. Best times are the cool morning or evening hours, and binoculars help. A small gift shop specializes in qiviut, the soft underwool of the muskox.

Yankovich Rd. ℂ **907/474-7207.** http://lars.iab.uaf.edu. Tours $10 adults, $9 seniors, $6 students, free ages 6 and under. Tours Memorial Day through Labor Day daily each hour 10am–4pm. Call ℂ 907/474-5724 to check on tour times and changes. Drive north from campus, turn left on Ballaine Rd., left again on Yankovich.

COMMERCIAL TOURIST ATTRACTIONS

Three major for-profit attractions around Fairbanks owned by the Binkley family pack in visitors by the hundreds of thousands, most of them on group tours. These places are educational and fun, as I've described below, but prices for all are high.

The Riverboat *Discovery* ★★
The *Discovery* belongs to the pioneering Binkley family, which has been in the riverboat business since the Klondike gold rush and has run this attraction since 1950. The *Discovery* is a real sternwheeler, a 156-foot steel vessel carrying up to 900 passengers on as many as three trips a day. There's nothing intimate or spontaneous about the 3½-hour ride, which mostly carries package-tour passengers off fleets of

Riverboat *Discovery*.

buses, but it's a diverting outing that doesn't feel cheap or phony. After loading at a landing with shops off Dale Road, near the airport, the boat cruises down the Chena to Tanana past demonstrations on shore—among others, a bush plane taking off and landing, fish cutting at a Native fish camp, and a musher's dog yard. Finally, the vessel pulls up at the bank for an hour-long tour of a mock Athabascan village.

1975 Discovery Dr. ℂ **866/479-6673** or 907/479-6673. www.riverboatdiscovery.com. Tours $55 adults, $38 ages 3–12, free ages 2 and under. Sailings mid-May to mid-Sept daily at 8:45am and 2pm.

The El Dorado Gold Mine ★ A train such as you would find at an amusement park carries visitors though an impressively staged educational tour, including a trip through a tunnel in the permafrost. This is like a land version of the riverboat tour that's operated by the same family. But the gold miners who act as hosts are the real attraction here. Visitors gather around a sluice to hear the amusing and authentic Dexter and Lynette (also known as Yukon Yonda) Clark and watch a swoosh of water and gold-bearing gravel rush by. You pan the resulting pay dirt, and everyone goes home with enough gold dust to fill a plastic locket—typically $5 to $35 worth. Drive out to the mine after making reservations, or take a $5 shuttle.

Off the Elliott Hwy., 9 miles north of town. ℂ **866/479-6673** or 907/479-6673. www.eldorado goldmine.com. Tours $35 adults, $23 ages 3–12, free ages 2 and under. Tours mid-May to mid-Sept daily; call for times.

Gold Dredge No. 8 ★ This is the area's most authentic gold-mining attraction. The centerpiece is a 1927 gold dredge, similar to machines in Dawson City and Nome, standing five stories tall on a barge in a pond it created. When it operated, huge scoops would dig from one end, the mechanism inside would digest the gold from the gravel, and then it would dump the tailings out the back—in this way, the pond and the dredge it supports crept 4½ miles across the frozen ground north of Fairbanks. Many sterile areas you see in this area were created by these earth-eaters, because little grows on their leavings for decades afterward. Visits are self-guided, allowing you to walk through the dredge and examine museums housed in relocated gold camp buildings, showing the harsh, colorless life lived by the miners. Lunch is included in admission, and after eating, most guests spend 45 minutes to an hour looking around, although you can stay as long as you like. Because of the orientation to the meal, times to visit are narrow and you must reserve ahead.

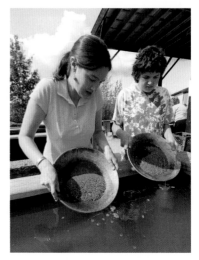

Panning for gold at Gold Dredge No. 8.

1755 Old Steese Hwy. ℂ **907/457-6058.** www.golddredgeno8.com. Admission $21 tour only, $25 tour with gold panning, $35 with lunch of stew. Call to reserve, as lunch times vary. Open mid-May to mid-Sept. To get there, go north on the Steese Expwy. from town, turn left on Goldstream Rd., turn left again on the Old Steese Hwy.

Getting Outside

In this section, I've described the outdoor opportunities local to Fairbanks, but some other choices are barely farther afield: See "Chena Hot Springs Road" (p. 433) and the feature later in this chapter, "Steese Highway: Into the Wild." Get guidance at the **Alaska Public Lands Information Center,** in the Morris Thompson Center at 101 Dunkel St. (ℂ **907/459-3730;** www.alaskacenters. gov). The staff will advise you on outings, provide maps, and answer questions. Three publications you can buy at the **Alaska Geographic** bookstore (ℂ **907/ 459-3710;** www.alaskageographic.org) could also help greatly. The *Fairbanks Area Wildlife Watching Guide* is a booklet that contains thorough descriptions of the best places to go and tips for success. *Outside in the Interior,* by Kyle Joly (University of Alaska Press), describes more than 50 routes for a variety of activities and includes detailed maps of each. The *Fairbanks Area Hiking and Birding Guide,* a map of hiking trails and birding locations in the area, is produced by the local chapter of the Audubon Society. All are for sale in local bookstores as well.

GEARING UP

You can rent most of what you need for outdoor explorations around Fairbanks and along the region's extraordinary rural highways from a set of local businesses that have grown up around the needs of adventurers. Some of the outdoor opportunities I describe require a drive on unpaved roads, including portions of the Steese Highway. Two businesses that rent vehicles you can take on these roads are listed in the feature "Equipped for the Backroads," p. 419. For ski rentals, see the appropriate sections below.

    Alaska Outdoor Rentals & Guides, owned by the knowledgeable Larry Katkin, is located on the riverbank at Pioneer Park (ℂ **907/457-2453;** www. akbike.com or www.2paddle1.com). The company rents canoes, kayaks, and bikes, and offers pickup or drop-off for paddlers in town or far afield. For an easy in-town paddle—say, from the park to the Pump House Restaurant and Saloon—you pay $37 for the canoe half-day, $52 full day, and $19 for the pickup. To go beyond the road system, Larry carries foldable canoes that will fit in a bush plane. He also offers lessons. This is a good place to start a mountain-biking outing, too. Bikes rent start for $19 for 3 hours, $27 for a day.

GoNorth Alaska Adventure Travel Center, 3500 Davis Rd. (✆ **855/236-7271** or 907/479-7271; www.gonorth-alaska.com), rents canoes, rafts, bikes, and camping gear, and offers a shuttle for canoeists and hikers. The firm also runs a tent-camp hostel and campground, and can arrange self-guided outdoor trips.

The **Outdoor Adventures Program** at the University of Alaska Fairbanks's Wood Student Center (✆ **907/474-6027;** www.uaf.edu/outdoor) rents a variety of outdoor equipment, including expedition-quality tents, backpacks, sleeping bags, and camp stoves.

CHENA LAKE RECREATION AREA   This is a wonderful and unique place for a family camping trip. A birch-rimmed lake created for a flood-control project has been developed by the local government to provide lots of recreational possibilities: flat walking and bike trails; a swimming beach; fishing; a place to rent a variety of nonmotorized boats; a self-guided 2.5-mile nature trail; a playground; big lawns; volleyball courts; and the terrific campground, with 80 camping sites, from pull-throughs for RVs to tent sites on a little island you can reach only by boat. In the winter, it's a popular area for cross-country skiing, ice fishing, dog mushing, and snowmobiling. Use of the area in summer requires a $4 fee per vehicle. Tent sites are $10 per night, and RV sites are $12. Drive about 15 miles east of Fairbanks on the Richardson Highway and take the exit for Dawson Road. Turn left on Dawson, go under the overpass, then turn right on Mistletoe Drive. When you reach Laurance Road, turn left. Signs are posted along the way. For information, contact Fairbanks North Star Borough Chena Lake Recreation Area (✆ **907/488-1655;** www.chenalakes.com). Follow the same directions to the **Moose Creek Dam Salmon Watch,** driving along the dike past the recreation

Equipped for the Backroads

Exploring Alaska's gravel highways—camping and fishing along the way, perhaps launching a canoe in a remote lake—can be tough for visitors to arrange because of the policies of most car-rental agencies, which don't allow clients to drive off pavement. An exception is **Arctic Outfitters** (✆ **907/474-3530;** www.arctic-outfitters.com), which rents the Ford Escape. The vehicles are equipped with CB radios, maintenance kits, and two full-size spare tires. Drivers must be at least 30 years old and have their own insurance. One-day rental rates exceed $200, with discounts for additional days, and mileage charges start after 250 miles. **GoNorth Car and Camper Rental,** 3713 South Lathrop St. (✆ **866/236-7271** or 907/479-7271; www.gonorth-alaska.com), rents SUVs, vans, and trucks, and also campers on four-wheel-drive pickups and motor homes. All are allowed on gravel roads, but for the motor homes, there's an extra fee. See "Car Wheels on Gravel Roads," p. 218, for an Anchorage firm.

Canoeing the Chena River.

area. This picnic and viewing site was built by the U.S. Army Corps of Engineers atop the flood-control project so that people could watch spawning salmon in crystal-clear water from late June to the end of July. Use of the salmon watch is free, so tell the recreation-area gatehouse you are going there.

CREAMER'S FIELD This 2,000-acre migratory waterfowl refuge right in Fairbanks is a former dairy farm that was saved from development in 1966 by a community fund drive. In the spring and fall, the pastures are a prime stopover point for Canada geese, pintails, golden plovers, and large flocks of sandhill cranes. Fewer birds are present during midsummer. The **Friends of Creamers Field** (1300 College Rd.; ✆ **907/452-5162;** www.creamers field.org) operates a small visitor center (✆ **907/459-7307**) in the old farmhouse, with displays on birds, wildlife, and history, open mid-May through mid-September daily from 10am to 5pm, off season Saturdays noon to 4pm. They offer guided nature walks in summer Monday through Friday at 10am and Wednesday at 7pm. You don't need a guide to explore more than 5 miles of trails through the forest, field, and wetland. The Boreal Forest Trail nature walk is interpreted by signs and an excellent booklet you can pick up at the visitor center or from a kiosk at the trail head. The **Alaska Bird Observatory** (✆ **907/451-7159;** www.alaskabird.org) conducts research and educational programs on the Creamer's Field refuge, including bird walks and bird banding that visitors can observe (call for times). Admission is free and the observatory is open Monday to Wednesday 9am to 9pm, Thursday to Saturday 9am to 5pm, and Sunday 9am to 1pm.

SUMMER ACTIVITIES

BIKING & HIKING Traffic goes fast in Fairbanks, and the separated bike trails are few, but strong cyclists can get by. Mountain-biking is good on many dirt roads and byways within and beyond Fairbanks and on the ski trails at Birch Hill Recreation Area and the University of Alaska Fairbanks (see "Winter Activities," below). The ski trails are also good for easy summer hikes, or go farther afield for more ambitious trail hikes off Chena Hot Springs Road (in the next section of this chapter) or the Steese Highway (p. 436). Inquire about all the options or other ideas at the Alaska Public Lands Information Center.

CANOEING The rivers in and around Fairbanks are best seen by floating slowly along in a canoe. Paddling is as popular as hiking around here. See "Gearing Up," p. 418, for businesses that rent canoes and provide drop-off and pickup service along the area's waterways.

The Chena River is slow and meandering as it flows through Fairbanks, and several restaurants on the bank cater to boaters. Farther upriver, the canoeing passes wilder shores, and near the headwaters becomes more challenging (see "Chena Hot Springs Road," later in this chapter). For beginners, try the wilderness section from the Chena Lake Recreation Area downstream (see "Chena Lake Recreation Area," above). It's 12 to 16 hours from there all the way into town, or you can take out at one of the roads crossing the river along the way. The **U.S. Army Corp of Engineers** (*©* **907/488-2748**) produces the *Chena River Float Guide,* with put-in and take-out points and float times, available at the Alaska Public Lands Information Center (see "Visitor Information," earlier).

For something a bit more challenging but still manageable for most paddlers with some experience, the clear, class I water of the Chatanika River is perfect for day trips or relaxed expeditions of a week or more, if you know how to handle river hazards such as sweepers and snags that show up on any Alaska stream. Alaska State Parks produces a brochure covering the float from the Upper Chatanika River Campground, at mile 39 of the Steese Highway, to a boat launch on the Elliott Highway (get it at the Alaska Public Lands Information Center, p. 408). Low water and logjams requiring portages can slow down the trip so that it takes a long day; in better conditions, expert canoeists can do it in a few hours.

FISHING Salmon season here is brief, and the fish this far inland have turned spawning colors and have softer, less palatable flesh compared to coastal salmon. Most fishing is in the streams for Arctic grayling, northern pike, and burbot, and in stocked lakes for rainbow trout, Arctic char, and silver salmon. You can fish in the Chena as it flows through town, although getting out of town and hiking away from a road yields better results. Fly-in fishing will further increase your chances and add sheefish and Dolly Varden char to your list, but you can find better salmon fishing to go along with the freshwater fish in Anchorage or another coastal community. The Alaska Public Lands Information Center (p. 408) offers guidance, or contact the **Alaska Department of Fish and Game,** at Creamer's Field, 1300 College Rd., Fairbanks, AK 99701 (*©* **907/459-7207,** sportfish information recording *©* 907/459-7385; www.alaska.gov/adfg).

WINTER ACTIVITIES

Fairbanks has real Jack London winters. The visitor bureau guarantees it. For the growing number of visitors who want to experience real cold, see the aurora borealis, and ride a dog sled, Fairbanks is the place. Chena Hot Springs Resort (p. 435) and A Taste of Alaska Lodge (p. 425) are the best destinations for winter immersion, but you can also have a good time in town, especially in March, when the days lighten up, the temperatures are moderate, and the town gets busy with dog mushing and the ice-carving contest (see "Special Events," earlier in this chapter).

The **Birch Hill Recreation Area,** off the Steese Expressway just north of town, has about 25km of good cross-country ski trails, most groomed for classical or skate skiing, and two warm-up buildings in which to change clothes. Several loops of a few kilometers each offer advanced skiing on the steep southern side of the hill; loops of up to 10km provide more level but still challenging terrain to the north. Some trails are lighted. The **University of Alaska Fairbanks** offers a trail network of roughly the same length, two-thirds of it groomed for skate technique. The university trails pass through lovely lands and are better suited for beginners. One trail head is at the west end of campus, near the satellite dishes at the top of Tanana Loop. Another is off Farmers Loop Road at Ballaine Lake. Find current information, including events, trail conditions, and maps, from the website of **Nordic Ski Club of Fairbanks** (www.nsc fairbanks.org).You can rent skis, poles, and boots—skating and classic—from a couple of different stores in town. **Beaver Sports** is near the university at 3480 College Rd. (© **907/479-2494;** www.beaversports.com). Nearer to Birch Hill, **Play It Again Sports,** 160 Old Steese Hwy. (© **907/ 457-7427;** www.playitagainsports.com), also has children's sizes.

DOG MUSHING The long winters and vast wild lands make the Fairbanks area a center of dog sledding, for both racers and recreationists, and there are plenty of people willing to take you for a lift, which is really an experience not to be missed. **Sun Dog Express Dog Sled Tours** (© **907/479-6983;** www.mosquitonet.com/~sleddog) has a good reputation, and charges at little as $15 for a quick spin, with day camps to learn mushing yourself, and summer mushing demonstrations. Or try **Paws for Adventure** (© **907/378-3630;** www.pawsforadventure.com), which offers 30-minute rides for $60, or an hour for $90, as well as trips up to a week long.

During the summer, learn about mushing by taking a wonderfully intimate tour with Mary Shields, the first woman to finish the Iditarod. Rather than a tour, a visit to Mary's home on the outskirts of Fairbanks feels more like a chat with a fascinating new friend. You'll meet and pet Mary's dogs, talk about dog mushing, and hear tales of her extraordinary experiences as a musher. The tour, called **Alaskan Tails of the Trails** (© **907/455-6469;** www.mary shields.com), happens every evening in the summer. It costs $35 and lasts 2 hours ($25 for children age 11 and under). Call for reservations, as she keeps groups small.

Dog mushing.

DOWNHILL SKIING Fairbanks has two community-size downhill skiing areas, including the relatively large **Moose Mountain Ski**

Great Alaskan Bowl Company.

Resort (© **907/479-4732,** snow report 459-8132; www.shredthemoose. com), with 1,300 vertical feet of skiing. Instead of freezing on a lift, you ride up the hill and socialize in heated buses.

Shopping

Fairbanks has a few good shops downtown. The **Arctic Travelers Gift Shop,** at 201 Cushman St. (© **907/456-7080;** www.arctictravelersgiftshop.com), specializes in Native art and crafts, carrying both valuable art and affordable but authentically Alaskan gifts. The staff is knowledgeable about what they sell. Right next door, at 215 Cushman, **If Only . . . a fine store** (© **907/457-6659;** www.ifonlyalaska.com) is a charming gift and stationery shop with items to hold locals' as well as visitors' interest—not just tourist stuff.

Near the airport, at 4630 Old Airport Way, the **Great Alaskan Bowl Company** (© **800/770-4222** or 907/474-9663; www.woodbowl.com) makes and sells bowls of native birch—salad bowls, of course, but also bowls for many other purposes. Some of these bowls are simply amazing. They can carve up to seven nested bowls from one piece of wood and even laser-engrave a photo inside one. The workshop also produces cutting boards of birch, bird feeders, serving utensils, and a variety of other items. Through a glass wall looking into the shop, you can see workers cutting the bowls from raw logs. It's hard to depart without buying a bowl. The shop is open daily all year.

Where to Stay

Going the bed-and-breakfast route is a good choice in Fairbanks. At the B&Bs I've listed below, you can save money over a hotel and get a private room just as good while staying in a unique place with interesting people. The **Fairbanks Association of Bed and Breakfasts** lists about 10 more on its website at **www. ptialaska.net/~fabb.** The visitor bureau also provides B&B information and up-to-date vacancy data in person at the Morris Thompson center (p. 408), or by calling © **907/459-3785.**

EXPENSIVE

There are many hotels here in the expensive category, so I have included one for each taste. The enormous **Fairbanks Princess Riverside Lodge (**www.princess lodges.com; © **800/426-0500** or 907/455-4477; fax 907/455-4476) also merits a mention as a luxurious and well-run hotel in a pleasant setting near the airport (it's quite similar to Pike's Waterfront). However, in summer, the Princess usually books fully with the owner's cruise-line clients. Rooms are most often available Friday, Saturday, and Sunday. The **Marriott Fairbanks Springhill Suites** (www.marriott.com; $\textcircled{C}$ **800/314-0858** or 907/451-6552; fax 907/451-6553) offers spacious rooms in a prime spot in the center of town, and has Lavelle's Bistro (mentioned later) and one of the few hotel pools in town.

Pike's Waterfront Lodge ★★ When Pike's appeared on the Chena River next to the Pike's Landing restaurant (see later), it initially looked like a big rectangle the size and shape of innumerable chain hotels along interstates, but the local owner kept adding features until it became utterly unique, including a greenhouse, an ice cream parlor with an airplane sticking out of it, an extraordinary wildlife art collection, and 28 cabins. Now he's received recognition for going green, with solar panels, low-power TVs, and special cleaning products, paper towels, and carpet. Rooms, while not large, are well equipped, and many look out on the river. The location is a stone's throw from the airport. The place can fill on certain days in the summer with package tour guests—at this writing, Monday through Wednesday—but usually has room the rest of the week. Summer only, a steak-and-seafood restaurant operates on-site.

1850 Hoselton Dr., Fairbanks, AK 99709. www.pikeslodge.com. $\textcircled{C}$ **877/774-2400** or 907/456-4500. Fax 907/456-4515. 208 units. High season $149–$225 double, $255–$465 suite; low season $69–$99 double, $89–$235 suite. Extra person age 13 and over $10. Rates include continental breakfast in winter. AE, DC, DISC, MC, V. **Amenities:** Restaurant (summer); bar; free airport transfers; exercise room; sauna; steam room. *In room:* A/C, TV, fridge, hair dryer, microwave, Wi-Fi.

River's Edge Resort Cottages ★★ ☺ An afternoon on a sunny riverbank exemplifies the best of Interior Alaska; this place is built around that knowledge. Trim little cottages stand in a grassy compound along the gentle Chena River, where guests can fish for grayling. Inside, each light, airy cottage is an excellent standard hotel room, with high ceilings and two queen-size beds. Outside, they're like a little village, where guests can sit on the patio, watch the river go by, and socialize. It's perfect for families, as the outdoor areas are safe for playing and noise inside won't bother the neighbors. A large, summer-only restaurant sits at river's edge, with dining on a deck or inside at round oak tables. Dinner entrees—steak, seafood, and down-home cooking—range up to $30; a burger is $10.

4200 Boat St., Fairbanks, AK 99709. www.riversedge.net. $\textcircled{C}$ **800/770-3343** or 907/474-0286. Fax 907/474-3665. 94 units (86 cottages, 8 suites). High season $195 double; low season $155 double. Extra person 13 and over $10. AE, DISC, MC, V. Closed Oct–Apr. Take Sportsman Way off Airport Way to Boat St. **Amenities:** Restaurant; bar; free airport transfers. *In room:* A/C, TV, hair dryer, Wi-Fi.

Sophie Station Hotel ★ This all-suite hotel, near the university and airport, is well equipped for business travelers or longer stays, with full kitchens, sitting rooms, and separate bedrooms in every suite. The decoration in the rooms is pleasantly muted. Everything is very clean, well maintained, and comfortable. Bathrooms and closets are quite large. Quality of the food and service in the hotel restaurant, called **Zach's,** is excellent. The cuisine includes Alaska seafood and familiar American dishes. Dinner main courses top out at $36.

1717 University Ave., Fairbanks, Alaska 99709. www.fountainheadhotels.com. $\textcircled{C}$ **800/528-4916** reservations, 907/479-3650, or 456-3642. Fax 907/479-7951. 148 units. High season $169–$245

Downtown Fairbanks

ATTRACTIONS
Church of the
    Immaculate Conception **6**
Fairbanks Community Museum **5**
Golden Heart Park **7**
Ice Museum **9**
Morris Thompson Cultural &
    Visitors Center **10**
St. Matthew's Episcopal Church **2**

RESTAURANTS
Gambardella's Pasta Bella **4**
Lavelle's Bistro **8**
Thai House **11**

HOTELS
All Seasons Inn **1**
Bridgewater Hotel **3**
Marriott Fairbanks
    Springhill Suites **8**
Westmark Fairbanks Hotel &
    Conference Center **12**

double; low season $89–$120 double. Extra person $10. AE, DC, DISC, MC, V. **Amenities:** Restaurant; bar; free transfers to airport and some attractions; exercise room; Internet access in lobby. *In room:* A/C, TV, hair dryer, kitchen, Wi-Fi.

A Taste of Alaska Lodge ★   Situated atop a grassy slope on 280 acres and facing Mount McKinley, the handcrafted log main building feels like a wilderness lodge but is less than half an hour from Fairbanks. The family that originally homesteaded this property still lives here and runs the lodge; a new generation recently took over. Each family member I've met is an Alaskan original. A nearby musher offers dog team rides in winter (but make sure that's available when you reserve if it's a priority). During the dark months, visitors come for exceptional aurora viewing. Each room has a door straight onto the grounds, where moose often wander. The cabins are large and especially luxurious. Breakfast is served at 8am on the dot, and guests have to remove their shoes at the door.

551 Eberhardt Rd. (turn right 5¼ miles out Chena Hot Springs Rd.), Fairbanks, AK 99712. www. atasteofalaska.com. © **907/488-7855.** Fax 907/488-3772. 8 units, 2 cabins. $185 double; $205–$235 cabin. Extra person $35. Rates include full breakfast. AE, MC, V. *In room:* TV, Wi-Fi.

Wedgewood Resort ★★   Off College Road near the Creamer's Field Refuge, this well-kept hotel sprawls across a grassy, 23-acre complex in eight large buildings. Seven of them are three-story apartment buildings converted into suites, regularly refitted, without elevators but with large living rooms, separate

Going with the Flow

Many of the large, top-quality hotels in Fairbanks—including the Princess, Westmark, Pike's Waterfront Lodge, Sophie Station, River's Edge Resort, and Wedgewood Resort—cater to enormous escorted tours, which flow through town on a rhythm set by the arrival of cruise ships hundreds of miles away. As a result, certain nights are booked up every week many months in advance, while others are wide open. Fortunately, this flow alternates on different nights for different companies, so when one hotel is full, another is empty. If you find your first choice is booked, just call one of the others. If they have rooms, ask for a discount, as they may have a lot of empty rooms.

dining areas, fully equipped kitchens, air-conditioners, two TVs, balconies, and phones with voice mail in both the living room and bedroom. Another 157 units are large, standard hotel rooms in the three-story Bear Lodge, which has its own lobby; however, those are closed mid-September to mid-May. A scheduled courtesy van runs to the airport and train depot and various tourist sites in the summer. Several attractions are on-site or nearby: a large new antique auto museum (p. 414), trails to a pond and Creamer's Field (p. 420), and the Alaska Bird Observatory research and educational center (p. 420).

212 Wedgewood Dr., Fairbanks, AK 99701. www.fountainheadhotels.com. ℂ **800/528-4916** reservations, 907/452-1442, or 456-3642. Fax 907/451-8184. 463 units. High season $170 double, $170–$245 suite for 2; low season standard double rooms not offered, $95–$120 suite for 2. Extra person in suite $10. AE, DC, DISC, MC, V. **Amenities:** 3 restaurants (summer only); bar; Internet cafe; free transfers to airport and some attractions; courtesy van; computers in each lobby. *In room:* A/C, TV, hair dryer, Wi-Fi.

Westmark Fairbanks Hotel & Conference Center ★★★   This Fairbanks landmark, the town's grand meeting place, owned by Holland America Lines, fills a city block and includes the city's tallest tower (not exactly a skyscraper, but you don't need to be very high for good views in Fairbanks). The decor in newer rooms is the city's most stylish, with a post-mod pastiche that includes fabrics and lamps from the Jetsons along with colonial woodwork; big, manly furniture; and lots of color. I like it. The rooms are packed with amenities. Downstairs, the hotel has a cafe with a dining room that's a work of art (open summer only) and a comfortable steakhouse. A complimentary breakfast is served in the winter months.

813 Noble St., Fairbanks, AK 99701. www.westmarkhotels.com. ℂ **800/544-0970** reservations, or 907/456-7722. Fax 907/451-7478. 400 units. Summer $225 double, $240–$500 suite; winter $84 double, $94–$500 suite. Extra person 19 and older $15. AE, DC, DISC, MC, V. **Amenities:** 2 restaurants; bar; fitness center. *In room:* A/C, TV, hair dryer, Wi-Fi (in most).

MODERATE

All Seasons Inn ★ ⛳   This charming and comfortable country inn on a pleasant residential street a couple of blocks from the downtown core is the creation of Mary Richards, a longtime transplant from the Southern United States who retains, along with a slight accent, the gentle hospitality and refined style she brought with her. Each cozy room has its own inspired decorative details in bold colors, and the housekeeping has always been perfect on our many visits. For visiting with Mary or other guests, a series of elegant common rooms connect downstairs, where you'll find a bar with hot drinks and a sun porch with books and games. Shoes are removed at the front door in winter.

763 7th Ave., Fairbanks, AK 99701. www.allseasonsinn.com. *(C)* **888/451-6649** or 907/451-6649. Fax 907/474-8448. 8 units. High season $179–$215 double; low season $119–$139 double. Extra person $35. Rates include full breakfast. DC, DISC, MC, V. **Amenities:** Computer center. *In room:* A/C, TV, hair dryer, Wi-Fi.

Aurora Express Bed and Breakfast ★★ ⛵ Susan Wilson's late grandmother appeared to her in a dream and told her there would be a train on a bank below her house, on the family's 15 acres high in the hills south of Fairbanks. So Wilson went out and got a train—a collection that includes a pair of 1956 Pullman sleepers, a dining car, a locomotive, a caboose, and a World War II hospital car—and her husband, Mike, brought it all up the mountain to install below the house, right in the spot indicated. Some cars are close to their original form, and Susan says older guests sometimes weep over the memories they bring back. Others were elaborately remodeled into rooms, some small, some huge, on themes related to Fairbanks history. A full breakfast is served in the dining car, which also houses the common area, TV, and phone. They're located 6½ miles out of town, so you will need your own car if you stay here. Call before coming with children, as they discourage visits by the very young.

1540 Chena Ridge Rd. (P.O. Box 80128), Fairbanks, AK 99708. www.fairbanksalaskabedand breakfast.com. *(C)* **800/221-0073** or 907/474-0949. 7 units. $145–$160 double. Rates include full breakfast. MC, V. Closed mid-Sept to mid-May. *In room:* No phone.

Bridgewater Hotel ★ 🗡 This older building in a prime downtown location near the river contains comfortable, immaculate rooms that sacrifice little of substance to places charging as much as $40 a night more. Decoration in pastels creates a feminine, boutique tone in common areas. Rooms are bright and airy, and those on the corners have exceptional views. Most have shower stalls only, not tubs. A cafe serves breakfast, and one of Fairbanks's best restaurants, Gambardella's, is just steps away. A great choice for summertime travelers who like staying in a traditional downtown hotel but don't need luxury hotel trappings. Weekends have the most vacancies and best bargains.

723 1st Ave., Fairbanks, AK 99701. www.fountainheadhotels.com. *(C)* **800/528-4916,** 907/452-6661, or 456-3642. Fax 907/452-6126. 94 units. $115–$145 double. Extra person $10. AE, DC, DISC, MC, V. Closed mid-Sept to mid-May. **Amenities:** Free transfers to airport and some attractions; Internet access. *In room:* A/C, TV, hair dryer, Wi-Fi.

Minnie Street Bed & Breakfast Inn ★★ Across the river from the downtown center, four buildings around a garden courtyard contain large, clean, brightly decorated rooms with stylish furniture and many amenities. The inn reflects the personality of its serene but exacting hosts, managing to feel both homey and polished. A full breakfast is served in a dining room with a high-vaulted ceiling and continental breakfasts in some rooms. Huge one-bedroom suites have kitchens and extra beds for one or two, and all but one have a Jacuzzi tub. Guests have access to laundry machines, paying on the honor system.

345 Minnie St., Fairbanks, AK 99701. www.minniestreetbandb.com. *(C)* **888/456-1849** or 907/456-1802. Fax 907/451-1751. 12 units, 10 with private bathroom. High season $109–$169 double, $239 suite; low season $79–$99 double, $199–$239 suite. Extra person $35. Rates include full breakfast. AE, DISC, MC, V. **Amenities:** Massage. *In room:* TV, fridge (in most), hair dryer, microwave (in most), Wi-Fi.

INEXPENSIVE

Golden North Motel 🦆   The Baer family, owners since 1971, works hard to keep up the rooms in this two-story motel, making it the best bargain in town for those seeking a basic budget room. They're always replacing something, and where carpets and furniture are worn, they're still quite clean. You have a choice of small rooms and units that combine two of the smaller rooms; although strictly functional, they're very reasonably priced and have extras you might not expect, such as available DVD players, refrigerators, and microwave ovens. The building, on a side street near the airport, is a nondescript brown rectangle brightened by flower boxes on the outdoor walkways. Family members greet guests warmly with free pastries and coffee in the small lobby.

4888 Old Airport Rd., Fairbanks, AK 99709. www.goldennorthmotel.com. 📞 **800/447-1910** or 907/479-6201. Fax 907/479-5766. 62 units. Summer $79–$99 double; winter varies, call first. Extra person 13 or older $10. Rates include continental breakfast. AE, DC, DISC, MC, V. **Amenities:** Free airport transfers. *In room:* TV, VCR/DVD (available from office), fridge and microwave in many, Wi-Fi.

HOSTELS & CAMPING

There are several hostels in Fairbanks. Among the best is the homey **Billie's Backpackers Hostel,** near the university, at 2895 Mack Blvd. (www.alaskahostel.com; 📞 **907/479-2034**). It's a charming place with a charming owner—a real home, but quirky and fun. Billie assigns bunks as people arrive, and you could luck into a private room for the same $30 a night she charges everyone. Rooms are coed, and the price includes tax, all linens, coffee and tea, the Internet, and much else. The Alaska/Yukon Trails shuttle stops out front (see "Getting There," p. 405). To find the hostel, turn south off College Road on Westwood Way and look for the first house on the left just past Mack Boulevard. I also recommend the hostel at GoNorth Alaska Adventure Travel Center, near the airport (p. 419).

Tent camping is a good way to go in Fairbanks, with its mild summers and ample public lands, but stock up on mosquito repellent. In town, **Chena River Wayside** (📞 **907/455-8881** or 452-7275) is located where University Avenue crosses the river. (The campground is also known as the Chena River State Recreation Site and should not be confused with the recreation "area" of the same name described in the next section of this chapter.) Sites are surrounded by birch and spruce, some are near the river, and there are flush toilets. Arrive early to camp close to the river instead of at one of the noisier sites nearer the road. Eleven sites have water and power hookups for RVs and cost $25 a night; another 45 drive-in sites for tent campers or RVs, without hookups, are $17; and 5 tent-only walk-in sites $10. Getting a bit out of town, there are superb public campgrounds at Chena Lake Recreation Area (see "Gearing Up," earlier in this chapter) and along Chena Hot Springs Road (p. 433).

Fairbanks has plenty of commercial RV parks, some with full service and then some. Pick up a list at the visitor center. Among the best is **River's Edge RV Park and Campground,** at a riverside bend of the Chena at 4140 Boat St., off Airport Way and Sportsman Way (www.riversedge.net; 📞 **800/770-3343** or 907/474-0286), with lots of services, including shuttles and a tour desk. Full hookups are $42 and tent camping $24. The same people operate the cottage resort and restaurant next door.

Where to Eat

DOWNTOWN

Gambardella's Pasta Bella ★★ ITALIAN   This warm, charming restaurant is right in the center of things. The chicken rustico (which sits on polenta) is tasty; they serve seafood in interesting ways; and the lasagna, made with sausage, thin noodles, and a rich, dusky tomato sauce, will improve your opinion of this abused dish. Dining rooms are narrow and segmented, so you always seem to be sitting with just a few other people, with elaborate decoration that adds to a pleasingly busy feeling. The restaurant added more space with a second-story dining room and patio while keeping the cozy ambience. Unlike the synthetic ambience of some of Fairbanks's other fine-dining places, Gambardella's feels real, a place where a family shares its cuisine. They serve beer and wine.

706 2nd Ave. (*C*) **907/456-3417.** www.gambardellas.com. Lunch $7–$13; dinner main courses $14–$28. 15% gratuity added for parties of 5 or more, or for split checks. AE, MC, V. Mon–Sat 11am–10pm; Sun 4–10pm; closes an hour earlier off season.

Lavelle's Bistro ★★★ BISTRO   In a big room of chrome, stone, and glass right downtown (at the base of the Marriott SpringHill Suites), Lavelle's has a grown-up, cosmopolitan feel that is quite welcome when you weary of the Alaskan rustic or gold rush themes of many of the area's restaurants. It also has consistently superb food, ambitious in conception and fine in execution, and expert service. The cuisine is difficult to categorize, as Southwest and Italian influences might be brought to a single dish, and Northwest, Asian, and French influences turn up variously. Dinner main courses are mostly more than $20, but you can dine economically on the ample appetizers and salads, or choose a vegetarian lasagna that, for $17, comes with soup or a salad and side dishes. The wine list is impressive, and the 3,000-bottle cellar is behind glass in the middle of the dining room.

575 1st Ave. (*C*) **907/450-0555.** www.lavellesbistro.com. Reservations recommended. Lunch $11–$16; dinner $17–$46. AE, DC, DISC, MC, V. Summer daily 11am–2pm and 4:30–10pm; winter Tues–Sat 4:30–10pm, Sun–Mon 4:30–9pm.

Thai House ★★ THAI   In a small, brightly lit dining room in the downtown area, this is a simple, family-run restaurant with authentic Thai cuisine. Every time we've dined here, the food came quickly and was deftly seasoned and cooked to a turn. You can rely on the servers, beautifully attired in national costumes, to help you order; just believe that when they say "hot," they really mean

---

Quick Treats Unique to Fairbanks

A shop that makes its own delicious natural ice cream started near the university and sells its creations in good restaurants all over Alaska. **Hot Licks Homemade Ice Cream,** at 3453 College Rd. ((*C*) **907/479-7813;** www.hotlicks. net), has all the standard flavors, plus some of their own, including blueberry and cranberry made in season with local wild berries. If you have children, their joy will be completed by a visit to the playground behind the Radio Shack next door. Right across from Hot Licks on College Road, summer only, a travel trailer in the parking lot of a sporting goods store contains a bakery called **Bun on the Run,** which turns out fantastic cinnamon rolls and other baked treats, as well as hearty sandwiches.

it. Thanks to this terrific restaurant and at least seven others, Fairbanks has gone a bit Thai crazy. This one is the most centrally located and among the best, although that debate is part of the fun.

412 5th Ave. ℭ **907/452-6123.** Lunch items $8–$10; dinner main courses $12–$15. MC, V. Mon–Sat 11am–4pm and 5–9:30pm.

WITHIN DRIVING DISTANCE

Besides the restaurants listed here, consider the salmon bake at Pioneer Park, described earlier, and the restaurant at Sophie Station Hotel (p. 424).

Fairbanks has every flavor of fast food, many of them along the commercial strip of Airport Way, and many a greasy spoon diner as well. Among the best burgers and shakes can be had at two **Brewsters** restaurants: 3578 Airport Way (ℭ **907/456-2538**) and 354 Old Steese Hwy. (ℭ **907/374-9663**).

Some of the best pizza in town comes from **College Town Pizzeria,** near the intersection of College and University roads (ℭ **907/457-2200**), an East Coast, order-at-the-counter family place. The crust is wonderful—crisp yet chewy—and they prepare it either in the American style or as Italian gourmet

THE ROSTER OF rural ROADS

Minor roads reach beyond the settled lines through Alaska into places where visitors can have real adventures. You'll find few other cars or tourists, lots of open land, friendly rural people, and limitless opportunities for solitude and discovery.

However, unpaved highways can be hazardous. Plan on driving only 40 to 45 mph on gravel highways, and be aware of the risks of bouncing off the road or damaging your vehicle with rocks. Check road conditions, construction, and weather with the Alaska Department of Transportation (ℭ **511;** http://511.alaska.gov). Bring at least one full-size spare tire and consider carrying extra gasoline in jugs. Insect repellent is an absolute necessity. Drive with your headlights on at all times, and wipe the dust off them and your taillights periodically. Keep an eye on your rearview mirror, slowing down or even stopping to allow vehicles to pass; to save your windshield from rocks, it's wise to slow down even for vehicles going the opposite direction. Also, pull off for views or pictures—don't stop on bridges or in the middle of the road, as some people do. (Further safety and packing

suggestions for rural highways are in "Driving Safety," p. 525.)

Chena Hot Springs Road A relatively civilized road into the outdoors, this paved 57-mile highway east of Fairbanks meets hiking and river routes on the way to Chena Hot Springs. See "Chena Hot Springs Road," below.

Dalton Highway (Rte. 11) Built to haul equipment to the Prudhoe Bay oil fields, about 500 miles north of Fairbanks, the supremely scenic Dalton reaches the heart of the wilderness, crossing the Brooks Range and the North Slope. Services are as much as a day's drive apart. See "The Dalton Highway," later in this chapter.

Denali Highway (Rte. 8) This 133-mile gravel road connects the midpoints of the Parks and Richardson highways, passing stunning alpine vistas high in the Alaska Range that rival those within Denali National Park. Along the pizza with pesto instead of tomato sauce and toppings such as spinach and chicken. A 16-inch combo is $25. They also serve beer and wine. The pizzeria is open from 11:30am to 9pm and closed Sundays and holidays.

The Bakery 🎁 DINER   There are an infinite number of old-fashioned coffee shops in and around Fairbanks—the kind of place where a truck driver or gold miner can find a hearty, down-home meal, a bottomless cup of coffee, and motherly waitresses who call grown men "sweetie" or "honey." This is one of the better versions. The sourdough pancakes are good, the menu is long and inexpensive, portions are huge (sometimes they require two plates), and the service is fast and friendly. Of course, you can get breakfast all day. They have no liquor license.

69 College Rd. Ⓒ **907/456-8600.** Lunch items $8–$12; dinner main courses $9–$23. MC, V. Mon–Thurs 6am–4pm; Fri–Sat 6am–7pm; Sun 7am–4pm.

Pike's Landing Riverside Dining ★ STEAK/SEAFOOD   The dining room of the fine-dining section overlooks the Chena River near the airport from a series of tiered levels, each with well-separated tables. The menu includes a nice range of simple to more ambitious selections; highlights include the appetizer of

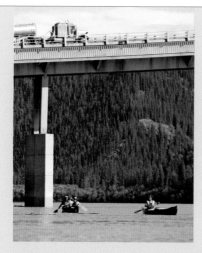

town of Chitina, where the McCarthy Road, a one-lane track, penetrates Wrangell–St. Elias National Park to the historic sites at McCarthy and Kennecott. The journey of 93 miles takes half a day (p. 455).

Steese Highway (Rte. 6)   This road, paved for the first 52 miles, climbs the rounded tundra mountains 162 miles east of Fairbanks to the Native village of Circle, on the Yukon River. It's a rare road deep into Bush Alaska (p. 436).

Taylor Highway (Rte. 5)   At times rough, narrow, and a little scary, this dirt road leads 161 miles from a junction on the Alaska Highway east of Tok to the fascinating Yukon River village of Eagle, an island in time (p. 444).

way are a rich network of trails and mountain lakes and a good chance to see caribous, bear, moose, and waterfowl (p. 368).

Edgerton Highway & McCarthy Road (Rte. 10)   Running east from the Richardson Highway south of Glennallen, the Edgerton leads to the tiny

Top of the World Highway (Yukon Rte. 9)   Connecting to the Taylor Highway and crossing the Canadian border to Dawson City, a distance of 79 miles, the road rides mountaintop to mountaintop, above the tree line nearly the entire way (p. 444).

spicy crab-stuffed mushrooms with a thick, chowderlike sauce, the salmon Caesar salad, and a lunch of halibut and chips. Portions are quite large. Sunday brunch is big and delicious. The deck is open for dining in summers from 11am to 10pm, with an inexpensive but limited bar menu offered from 2:30 to 5pm. It's a pleasant choice on a sunny day.

4438 Airport Way. ℂ **907/479-6500.** Lunch items $9–$16; dinner main courses $10–$40. AE, DC, DISC, MC, V. Mon–Sat 11am–2pm and 5–9pm; Sun 10am–2pm and 5–9pm.

The Pump House Restaurant and Saloon ★★ REGIONAL   The historic, rambling, corrugated tin building on the National Register of Historic Places is elaborately decorated and landscaped with authentic gold-rush relics. Sitting on the deck over the Chena, you can watch the riverboat paddle by or a group in canoes stop for appetizers and drinks from the full bar. For dinner, the cuisine is a cut above the area's typical steaks and seafood and includes game you may not have tried, including reindeer and elk. Dishes such as Alaskan bouillabaisse or the seafood chowder—hearty, creamy, and flavorful—make the most of the regional ingredients without trying to get too fancy. Many of the side dishes are a la carte, so although main courses are generous, it's expensive to order a large meal. Besides, you'll want to save room for one of the exceptional desserts.

Mile 1.3, Chena Pump Rd. ℂ **907/479-8452.** www.pumphouse.com. Main courses $18–$34. AE, DISC, MC, V. Summer Mon–Sat 5–11pm, Sun 10am–2pm and 5–11pm; winter Tues–Sat 5–9pm, Sun 10am–2pm and 5–9pm.

The Turtle Club ★ 🏨 STEAK/SEAFOOD   Locals pack into this squat, windowless building, with its vinyl tablecloths and stackable metal chairs, for a menu with just a few famous selections: prime rib, lobster, king crab, and prawns. These are simple, burly meals with friendly, roadhouse-style service; the menu is printed on the place mat and vegetables are an afterthought from an indifferent salad bar. But when the beef comes, you know it—the middle-size prime-rib cut is over an inch thick and covers a large plate, an insanely large portion—and the meat is tender and cooked right. The atmosphere is noisy and super casual; people laugh loud and don't worry about putting their elbows on the table or spilling a little beer. You won't run into many other tourists here, north of the city in Fox, but you do need reservations, and even with them, you often wait half an hour in the smoky bar or a narrow corridor.

10 Mile Old Steese Hwy., Fox. ℂ **907/457-9504.** www.alaskanturtle.com. Reservations recommended. Main courses $21–$37. AE, DISC, MC, V. Mon–Sat 6–10pm; Sun 5–9pm.

Fairbanks Nightlife

Fairbanks has a lot of tourist-oriented evening activities, as well as entertainment also attended by locals. Call the 24-hour event recording of what's playing currently (ℂ **907/456-INFO** [4636]), or get a copy of the *Fairbanks Daily News-Miner*. The Regal Goldstream 16-screen **multiplex** (ℂ **800/326-3264** movie listings, or 907/456-1882 office) is located at 1855 Airport Way. The evening show at the **Palace Theatre** is discussed earlier in this chapter under "Pioneer Park."

There are places to go out in the evening without having to hear about the gold rush (in other words, places locals go). Check out the "Downtown Guide" and "Events" pages of the **Downtown Association of Fairbanks** (ℂ **907/452-8671;** www.downtownfairbanks.com) for an updated list of entertainment in that part of town. In the university area, hear local and imported folk music live

at the **College Coffeehouse,** 3677 College Rd. (© **907/374-0468;** www.
collegecoffeehousefairbanks.com). The website lists upcoming acts.

Three miles southwest of town on the Parks Highway, the **Blue Loon**
(© **907/457-5666;** www.theblueloon.com) has live music, many beers on tap,
and good burgers. They even show movies. For something a bit wilder, the **Howl-
ing Dog Saloon,** out in Fox, 2160 Old Steese Hwy. (© **907/456-4695;** http://
howlingdogsaloon.alaskansavvy.com), has long been the place to cut loose in the
summer. Besides a bar, "The Dog" offers live music Wednesday to Saturday, a
cafe, and volleyball out back. It is open May to October.

CHENA HOT SPRINGS ROAD

The 57-mile paved road east from Fairbanks is an avenue to an enjoyable day trip
or a destination for up to a week's outdoor activities and hot-spring swimming. Of
all the roads radiating from Fairbanks, this short highway will be most rewarding
to outdoors people, and there is a funky and relaxing resort at the end.

The road travels through the Chena River State Recreation Area, with spectacular hikes and float trips and well-maintained riverside campgrounds, and
leads to the Chena Hot Springs, where there's a year-round resort perfect for
soaking in hot mineral springs and for use as a base for summer or winter wilderness day trips. The resort is open to people who want to rent one of the comfortable rooms or to campers and day-trippers, and it's even more popular in the
winter than in the summer (the slow seasons are spring and fall).

A pair of prospectors, the Swan brothers, discovered the hot springs in
1905, having heard that a U.S. Geological Survey crew had seen steam in a valley
of the upper Chena. Thomas Swan suffered from rheumatism; incredibly, he and
his brother poled up the Chena River from Fairbanks, found the hot springs,
built a cabin and rock-floored pool, and spent the summer soaking. He was
cured! More visitors followed, drawn by stories that whole groups of cripples
were able to dance all night after soaking in the pools—by 1915, a resort was in
operation, drawing worn-out miners and gold-rush stampeders and many others
as well. It has been in constant use ever since.

Essentials

GETTING THERE The Chena Hot Springs Road meets the Steese Expressway
about 5 miles north of downtown Fairbanks. (Information on renting a car
in Fairbanks can be found at the beginning of this chapter.) The resort offers
rides for hotel guests from anywhere in Fairbanks. Rates are $150 round-
trip for one person or $125 per person for two or more passengers on the
same reservation. Arrange for this at least 72 hours in advance.

VISITOR INFORMATION For outdoors information, check the Fairbanks **Alaska
Public Lands Information Center,** in the Morris Thompson center at
101 Dunkel St. (© **907/459-3730;** www.alaskacenters.gov). The Chena
River State Recreation Area is managed by the **Alaska Division of Parks,**
which interacts with the public through a Public Information Center (© **907/
451-2708;** www.alaskastateparks.org). The agency's trail, river, and road
guides are available at trail-head kiosks, from the public lands center, on the
website, or in the area's *Chena Trailmarker* brochure. Contact the parks
public information center with questions about the public cabins in the area
(see "State Parks Cabin Reservations," p. 283, for how to reserve).

The Chena River State Recreation Area

The recreation area takes in 254,000 acres along the river valley and over the rolling mountains of heather around it. Some of Interior Alaska's best hiking and floating are found here. As everywhere in the Interior, the mosquitoes are brutal.

ACTIVITIES

FISHING   Several of the ponds in the Chena State Recreation Area are stocked with rainbow trout, which you can keep subject to harvest limits. Signs along the road mark access points to the ponds and river. You can catch and release Arctic grayling in the Chena, but check current regulations and bait restrictions. Contact the **Alaska Department of Fish and Game,** 1300 College Rd., Fairbanks, AK 99701 (✆ **907/459-7207,** sportfish information recording 907/459-7385; www.alaska.gov/adfg).

HIKING & BACKPACKING   The best trail hikes in the Fairbanks area are in the Chena Hot Springs State Recreation Area, all of which start on the road. Backcountry camping requires no permit, and many of the trails go above the tree line, so it's a good area for backpackers to get into the wilderness. Trail descriptions are available from the information sources mentioned in the previous section.

The **Angel Rocks Trail** is a sometimes steep hike of around 4 miles round-trip to a group of large granite outcroppings, an impressive destination with good views of the valley below.

The 15-mile-loop of **Granite Tors Trail,** starting at mile 39.5 of the road, is a challenging dayhike rising through forest to rolling alpine terrain, but the towering tors on top more than reward the effort.

For a longer backpacking trip, the **Chena Dome Trail** makes a 29-mile loop, begging at mile 50.5 and ending at mile 49.1.

RIVER FLOATING   The Chena is a lovely river, growing from a clear, frothy creek near the end of the road to a lazy, brown class I river as it flows off toward Fairbanks, several days downstream. Where you choose to start depends on your expertise. Easier water is downstream from Rosehip Campground (mile 27), with the slowest of all nearer Fairbanks, but the upper portion is more popular if you are up for something a bit more challenging. The road crosses the river several times, and the state park system has developed other access points, so it's possible to plan a float that matches your time and abilities. Choose your route with the help of the river guide produced by the Alaska Division of Parks (see "Visitor Information," above). Agencies offering canoe rental and shuttle service are covered in the Fairbanks section, above under

A hiker atop a tor, a giant granite outcropping.

Taking a soak at Chena Hot Springs Resort.

"Gearing Up," p. 418. Chena Hot Springs Resort offers guided raft trips down the Chena (see below).

CAMPING & CABINS

Three beautiful campgrounds with water and pit toilets lie along the road by the Chena River, managed by the Alaska Division of Parks (see "Visitor Information," above). Although they can't be reserved ahead, the campgrounds are unlikely to be full except on a sunny holiday weekend. The **Rosehip Campground,** at mile 27, has 37 sites, well separated by spruce and birch, with six sites suitable for RVs. Some sites are right on the river, and some are set up for more private tent camping in the woods. The **Granite Tors Campground** is across from the trail head at mile 39.5; it has 24 sites, seven suitable for RVs. Some sites front on a river slough, and, as at Rosehip, float trips can start or end here. The **Red Squirrel Campground,** at mile 42.8, has 12 sites and a pleasant picnic area on the grassy edge of a small, placid pond, where swimming is permitted. Camping is $10 a night at each of these campgrounds.

There are several public-use cabins in the recreation area, three of them easily accessible to summer visitors and not hard to book a month or two ahead. (See "State Parks Cabin Reservations," p. 283, for how to get one.) These are primitive cabins; you must bring your own sleeping bags, lights, fuel, and cooking gear. The **North Fork Cabin** is at mile 47.7 of the road, the **Hunt Memorial Cabin** is at mile 42.3, and the **Chena River Cabin** faces the river at mile 32.2. You can get to all by car or canoe, and each costs $50 a night in the summer, $40 off season. Most of the other public cabins in the area primarily serve winter users and are difficult to reach when the ground thaws. However, the **Stiles Creek Cabin,** midway on a 15-mile multi-use trail, can be reached year-round. The trail meets the road at miles 31.6 and 36.4. As with other off-road cabins, the rent is $25 a night in summer, $20 off season.

The Hot Springs

Chena Hot Springs Resort ★★ Bernie Karl is a recycling entrepreneur who makes things happen. After buying the struggling Chena Hot Springs Resort, he built an outdoor, boulder-rimmed swimming pond of hot mineral water without chlorine or treatment, geothermal greenhouses that grow produce year-round for

STEESE HIGHWAY: into the wild

Driving the Steese Highway north from Fairbanks is like following a river upstream as it diminishes into its headwaters. First it's a four-lane freeway, then a two-lane highway, then the pavement gives out (at about mile 60), and eventually the gravel gives way to dirt. The road climbs over round tundra mountains, leaves behind the last tiny town, and then drifts through uninhabited woods before ending on the banks of the Yukon River at a tiny Athabascan village, Circle (named for the Arctic Circle, which it isn't on). It's a rough 162-mile drive to nowhere. But if nowhere is where you want to go, the Steese Highway may be the right adventure for you. Just don't forget the mosquito repellent.

Much of the land surrounding the Steese is controlled by the federal **Bureau of Land Management (BLM),** 1150 University Ave., Fairbanks, AK 99709 (℗ **800/437-7021** or 907/474-2200). Small- and large-scale gold mining takes place in the area, but most of the land is managed for conservation and recreation, with several campgrounds, some popular river floats, and a couple of beautiful hikes. The BLM website contains a lot of good information, but you'll need to type in this ungainly URL to get started: www.blm.gov/ak/st/en/prog/recreation.html#. In addition, the state parks department manages the **Upper Chatanika River Campground,** at mile 39, with 24 sites, pit toilets, a hand pump for water, and a $12 fee. This is the starting point for the most popular river float on the highway (covered, with others, in the Fairbanks section under "Canoeing," p. 421). Before heading out, call state parks at ℗ **907/451-2705,** as the campground hasn't been consistently open.

Without driving to the bitter end at Circle (where the only attraction is the Yukon River itself), you can make a goal of **Eagle Summit,** at mile 107, the highest place on the highway (3,624 ft.), and a good spot to be on June 21 each year, the summer solstice. Although it's still a

degree of latitude below the Arctic Circle, the sun never sets here on the longest day because of the elevation and atmospheric refraction. People come out from Fairbanks and make a celebration of it. The midnight sun is visible for about 3 days before and after the solstice, too, assuming the sky is clear. The BLM has installed a toilet and a viewing deck on a 750-foot loop trail at the trail head to the 27-mile **Pinnell Mountain National Recreation Trail.** This is a challenging 3-day hike over amazing terrain of rounded, windblown, tundra-clothed mountaintops. To hike it in the easier, more downhill direction, start at Eagle Summit and end at Twelvemile Summit, mile 85.5. Two emergency shelters along the trail provide protection from the ferocious weather that can sweep the mountains. Get the free BLM trail brochure before going or check the trail's web page at the BLM site mentioned above.

The next sensible destination is the tiny town of Central, population 96, which occupies a birch grove 128 miles along the highway. It's a real, old-fashioned gold-mining community and home of the remarkable **Circle District Museum** (℗ **907/520-1893;** www.cdhs.us), which displays old mining equipment outdoors and has a large indoor gallery on the area's history. The museum's normal hours are summer Thursday through Sunday noon to 5pm, but check on the website before going, as there's concern it won't be able to stay open with the potential loss of the only accommodations in town. That's the **Steese Roadhouse** (℗ **907/520-5800**), which, if operating, offers rooms, gas, food, and drink. A campground is open in the summer on a spur road to Circle Hot Springs, the site of a historic hotel and swimming pool that shut down years ago. To learn more about the area, check out these websites maintained by community members: www.steesehighway.org and www.bottomdollar.us.

the in-house restaurant, an innovative geothermal power plant that supplies the resort's electricity, and an ice museum that stays frozen even in the summertime.

Tours of the museum are $15 per person ($7.50 ages 6–17), but you can rent a room for the night ($600 a night gets you arctic clothing and an indoor room, just in case you change your mind in the middle of the night).

The resort also offers free tours of the power plant and greenhouses, which have attracted international attention in this age of energy shortages.

This place still has the rough edges of rural Alaska, so don't expect the standards and polish of a corporate resort. If you stay, I recommend renting the newest, most expensive rooms. Or, camp out; during summer it's a perfect option.

There's an indoor pool, several indoor and outdoor hot tubs, and the outdoor hot pond (100–110°F/38–43°C); kids are not allowed in the outdoor pond. The swimming facility is open daily 7am to midnight. Swim passes are free for guests. Otherwise, a day pass is $10 adults, $8 60 and older, $7 6 to 17, free for kids 5 and younger. Towel rental is another $5, or just bring your own.

Winter is the high season, when aurora viewing is exceptional. There's also Nordic skiing on groomed trails, Sno-Cat and snowmachine tours, dog-sled rides, and more. Many activities are guided and cost extra.

Accommodations range from simple yurts to large hotel rooms with televisions, phones, and coffeemakers. The newest rooms, in the Moose building, are very nice. Yurts do not have indoor plumbing.

The main lodge contains the restaurant and bar. Overall, this is a good place to have fun in the real Alaska, but be ready for some rough spots.

Mile 56.5, Chena Hot Springs Rd. (P.O. Box 58740), Fairbanks, AK 99711. © **907/451-8104.** Fax 907/451-8151. www.chenahotsprings.com. 80 units. $189–$249 double; $65 yurt (used mid-May to mid-Sept only). Extra person $20. AE, DC, DISC, MC, V. **Amenities:** Restaurant; bar; guided activities; hot tubs and Jacuzzis; massage; indoor and outdoor pools. *In room*: TV.

THE DALTON HIGHWAY

The original purpose of the Dalton Highway was utilitarian: to haul equipment north from Fairbanks for the trans-Alaska oil pipeline, which runs from Prudhoe Bay, on the Arctic Ocean, to Valdez, on the Pacific. But the experience of the Dalton Highway for a traveler is so far beyond the ordinary as to require a whole new frame of reference to take it all in. The road is so very long, so remote and free of traffic, and the scenery is so mind-boggling in its grandeur and repetition, that after a time it feels as if you're living in a dream. At some point, you have to swallow and say to yourself, "I guess I didn't know that much about the world after all."

Part of the wonder comes in the difficulty of the drive. This is an extreme road trip, one that dives into deep wilderness as far from help as most people ever get. In 500 miles there are only three service stations, two of which are within 4 miles of each other. The road averages only 250 vehicles a day over its entire length. Driving the Dalton is not to be taken lightly or done on a whim. You need to prepare and you need to know you want to do it, because you will be rumbling over dirt for many, many hours, breathing dust and beating the crud out of your car. If it was easy, they wouldn't have made a TV show about it (the History Channel's *Ice Road Truckers*).

The drive starts in Fairbanks (officially, you drive parts of the Steese and Elliott hwys. before the real Dalton Hwy. begins), traversing the rounded hills and low forest of that region before spanning the Yukon River on a high, wood-decked bridge. Over the miles that follow, trees grow sparser and the road crosses some spectacular alpine plateaus until, entering the Brooks Range, arctic vegetation and the mountains' rocky severity take over. Beyond towering Atigun Pass, the Arctic Slope extends 170 miles, first through sensuous tundra foothills, then over the broad, lake-dotted flatlands that extend to the Arctic Ocean. Arrival at the oil facilities can be a letdown, especially if you haven't made arrangements for the tour that is the only way to the shore. More on that below.

Wildlife shows up all along the road: moose, caribous, and grizzly bears, sportfish and songbirds. Animals far outnumber people. Two highway businesses are near the Yukon; in Coldfoot there is a truck stop; and Wiseman is 16 miles up the road from Coldfoot, where the 2000 census counted 21 people. And that's it for another 240 miles of dirt road to Prudhoe Bay. There are no ATMs, no grocery stores, no cellphone coverage, no medical facilities—civilization just isn't there. Drive carefully.

Dalton Highway Essentials

PRACTICAL TIPS   You can drive the highway yourself, staying in the few motels along the way or in a tent or motor home. From Fairbanks, take the Steese Highway north to the Elliott Highway. The total road distance from Fairbanks to the Arctic Ocean is 497 miles. Road conditions are notoriously bad on the gravel-and-dirt Dalton, but now much of it is kept in good condition, with pavement working its way steadily north. Speeds of 60 mph are possible on some parts of the road, while doing 35 mph will keep you in one piece on rougher spots; even the good sections can have nasty surprises, however, with unmarked, bone-jarring potholes. The drive takes 13 hours each way, without stops. It's dusty, shoulders are soft, and flat tires are common. In the Fairbanks section, I listed two businesses that rent vehicles you can take on the Dalton (see "Equipped for the Backroads," p. 419). Generally, rental companies don't allow their vehicles on the road.

Trans-Alaska pipeline.

Bridge over the Yukon River.

Preparing for the drive is essential. Pick up the road guide produced by the BLM and get firsthand, personal advice (see "Visitor Information," below). Read the safety advice under "The Roster of Rural Roads," p. 430. If you want to let someone else do the driving, a bus package is listed in the section of chapter 10 on Prudhoe Bay.

VISITOR INFORMATION   Getting up-to-date advice is critical before heading off on the Dalton Highway, and the best place to do that is the Fairbanks **Alaska Public Lands Information Center,** in the Morris Thompson center at 101 Dunkel St., Fairbanks, AK 99701 (✆ **907/459-3730;** www.alaskacenters.gov). Staffers there drive the road annually to stay on top of current conditions.

Much of the road runs through land managed by the **Bureau of Land Management,** 1150 University Ave., Fairbanks, AK 99709 (✆ **800/437-7021** or 907/474-2200; www.blm.gov/ak/dalton). From the informative website, you can download an invaluable ***Dalton Highway Visitor Guide,*** a 24-page booklet; or get it free at the public lands information center or from any BLM information center, or by mail by calling the number above.

Two information stops are along the highway, both open summer only. A **contact station** at the Yukon River crossing is staffed by BLM volunteers and open daily in summer from 9am to 6pm. It has no phone. The **Arctic Interagency Visitor Center** is at mile 175 on the west side of the highway in Coldfoot (✆ **907/678-5209** or 678-2014), open late May to early September from 10am to 10pm daily, subject to change. The free center is far grander than one would expect in the middle of the wilderness. It has award-winning exhibits about the north, a theater for nightly educational programs, a planning room for backcountry trips, a bookstore, and knowledgeable staff. Even if you don't have any questions, you should definitely make this stop.

On the Road

The bridge over the Yukon River at mile 56 is the only crossing of the river in Alaska, and many people drive the Dalton just to get to the **Arctic Circle** at mile 115, where you'll find a sign for pictures as well as a crude camping area. Many, many places along the highway have incredible views; among the most famous are Finger Mountain, at mile 98, which has a short interpretive nature trail; Gobbler's Knob, at mile 132, which offers the first view of the Brooks Range; and

4,739-foot Atigun Pass, at mile 245, where the road crosses the Brooks Range, winding through impossibly rugged country. The pass is the highest point on the Alaska road system, and you may find summer snow. All along the highway are opportunities to see birds and animals, including rabbits, foxes, moose, Dall sheep, bears, and caribous. Sit still if you see the skittish caribous, as they are more likely to wander closer to an unmoving vehicle. Beware of wolves, which several times attacked Dalton travelers in 2006, although that's very rare. Keep pets under control, and if a wolf approaches, yell and throw rocks at it.

The road parallels the 4-foot-wide **trans-Alaska pipeline.** The line, completed in 1977, serves America's largest and second-largest oil fields, Prudhoe Bay and Kuparuk, carrying the hot crude 900 miles from the Arctic Ocean to docks in Valdez, where tankers pick it up for shipment primarily to the West Coast. The public road ends before reaching the Prudhoe Bay complex and the Arctic Ocean. The only way through the gate is with a tour operator, and you must make arrangements at least 24 hours ahead to clear security. To do that, call the **Arctic Caribou Inn (© 907/659-2368;** www.arcticcaribouinn.com). See "Prudhoe Bay: Arctic Industry" (p. 501), for more details.

HIGHWAY SERVICES: FOOD, FUEL & LODGINGS

Among the few places offering services along the 414 miles of the Dalton, you won't find anything approaching the quality of even budget chains. The service is generally quite friendly, but except for two small B&Bs in the tiny town of Wiseman, all lodgings are in former construction camp dormitories.

Near the spectacular wooden-decked bridge over the Yukon River, at mile 56, is a decidedly unspectacular motel, restaurant, and gas station. **Yukon River Camp (© 907/474-3557),** open daily 9am to 9pm, has a gift shop, fuel (usually), and tire repair, as well as food and lodging, and is open mid-May to mid-September. Just 5 miles up the road from the river, the **Hotspot Café (© 907/451-7543),** open daily 10am to midnight, offers dining, lodging, a gift shop, gas (usually), tire repair, and Ice Road Trucker gifts. It also operates only mid-May to mid-September.

The **Coldfoot Camp** truck stop at mile 175 (www.coldfootcamp.com; **© 866/474-3400** or 907/474-3500) is the one big stopping place along the road. After the endless wilderness miles on the road, no one could stand to pass it by. The year-round camp includes several buildings on a large gravel pad. Most important are the gas pumps and the 24-hour restaurant where you pay for the fuel—a typical but friendly highway diner. Across the lot, the camp's inn is built of leftover construction camp modular units. The small rooms with low ceilings are perfectly comfortable, with private bathrooms, but far from grand. The camp also provides minor vehicle repairs, RV hookup, laundry, a post office, a gift shop, and a saloon. They offer guided rafting on the Middle Fork Koyukuk River, flight tours to the village of Anaktuvuk Pass, tours of Wiseman, and shuttles for hiking. In the winter, the camp offers dog-sled rides and aurora-viewing tours. An air taxi, **Coyote Air (© 907/479-5995** winter or 907/678-5995 summer; www.fly coyote.com), offers flightseeing of this amazing country from the air. There are other activities farther afield offered by **Northern Alaska Tour Company (© 800/474-1986** or 907/474-8600; www.northernalaska.com). Don't miss the remarkable new interagency visitor center, described above. The pleasant BLM Marion Creek Campground is 5 miles north of Coldfoot.

Wiseman, 13 miles north of Coldfoot and 3 miles off the road, is the only real town on the entire drive, and well worth a stop to see a tiny rural community about a century out of time's progress. There's not a thing commercial about it. The general store, Wiseman Trading Company, established 1910, was operating on the honor system when we stopped in. A sign read, IF YOU NEED CHANGE COME TO THE DOOR AND YELL FOR EIGHT BALL OR WALK TO THE CABIN ACROSS THE LAWN. Other residents sell furs or crafts from their homes. There's not much to do here but see how our great-grandparents lived, when food came from gardens, streams, and forests. Get advice at the interagency visitor center staff in Coldfoot. To spend the night in a homier place than the Coldfoot truck stop, stay here in Wiseman. **Boreal Lodging** (www.boreallodge.com; © **907/678-4566**) has four lodge rooms and a cabin, as well as a summer-only shop selling handmade gifts, snacks, and a few essentials. **Arctic Getaway Cabin and Breakfast** (www.arcticget away.com; © **907/678-4456**) is another good choice for lodgings in Wiseman.

After Coldfoot, the next service area is **Deadhorse,** at the end of the road another 240 miles north, with rooms, fuel, restaurants, a post office, vehicle maintenance, a general store, and an airport. See the Prudhoe Bay section in chapter 10.

Getting out of the Car

ACTIVITIES

FISHING   The streams and lakes of the Arctic are cold, poor in nutrients, and frozen much of the year; fishing is not a good reason to drive the Dalton. However, if you are taking the adventure anyway, there are fish in streams from July to mid-September and in lakes that don't freeze to the bottom. Many of the streams have Arctic grayling, but you'll want to hike farther than a quarter-mile from the road to increase your chances (off-road vehicles are not allowed). A good bet is the **Jim River area** between miles 140 and 144, where the river follows the road and fishing pressure is spread out. Most North Slope rivers have good Dolly Varden fishing in late August and early September. Many of the lakes along the road have grayling, and the deeper ones north of the Brooks Range have lake trout. Check current regulations. Contact the **Alaska Department of Fish and Game,** 1300 College Rd., Fairbanks, AK 99701 (© **907/459-7207;** www.alaska.gov/adfg); they produce a booklet called *Sportfishing Along the Dalton Highway,* which you can download from the website or get at the office, at some visitor centers, or by mail.

HIKING   The road has no established hiking trails, but most of the area is open to self-reliant hikers who know how to pick their own route. Hiking brushy or marshy Interior country isn't fun, but the dry tundra of the ridge tops and mountains creates a wonderful sense of freedom. The country opens up north of the Chandalar Shelf at mile 237. The best hiking area is the zone of dry tundra in the foothills north of the Brooks Range. But even at upper elevations, you still run into tussocks, wet ground, and stream crossings. Topographical maps and advice on hiking the Brooks Range are available at the sources listed under "Visitor Information," above. The book *Outside in the Interior* (p. 418) describes a handful of hikes along the road. Remember, this is remote wilderness; do your research, be prepared, and tell someone where you're going and when you'll be back.

Camping

The Bureau of Land Management has a few campgrounds along the road, but there seems little reason to wait to reach them, as there are any number of places to pull off the road on a spot of gravel and spend the night, often in places of stunning beauty. Just take these important precautions for safety and the environment: Get far enough off the road to avoid the fast-moving truck spewing rocks as far as 30 feet; read up on bear avoidance on p. 521; don't leave toilet paper or anything else behind (see "Keeping the Wilderness Clean," p. 513); and stay no longer than 14 days in one spot. Managers prefer if you don't park on pipeline access roads, and if you do, be sure not to block the road or security gates. I have listed the BLM's developed areas along the Dalton, which include campgrounds and spots where you can park for a while and obtain water. Unless the description mentions a formal campground, these are just gravel pads where you can park or sleep in your car. Add 83 miles to the mileposts to get the distance from Fairbanks.

MILE 60 (FIVE MILE)   Undeveloped campground with an outhouse, artesian well with potable water nearby, and free public dump station (this is the last dump station on the highway). Don't wash your vehicle here, as it will contaminate the groundwater. Camping costs $8.

MILE 98 (FINGER MOUNTAIN)   Nice views, outhouse, and wheelchair-accessible trail with interpretive signs.

MILE 115 (ARCTIC CIRCLE)   Outhouses, picnic tables, and an interpretive display; camp only in the undeveloped campground up the hill, which has an outhouse but no water.

MILE 150 (GRAYLING LAKE)   Wayside with outhouse.

MILE 175 (COLDFOOT)   A private campground with hookups is part of the truck stop described above.

MILE 180 (MARION CREEK)   A developed BLM campground with 27 campsites, 11 of them for large RVs (no hookups). The campground has a potable well and outhouses. Fee is $8 per night.

MILE 235 (FARTHEST NORTH SPRUCE TREE)   Outhouse; not an attractive camping site due to truck traffic on a steep grade.

MILE 275 (GALBRAITH LAKE)   Undeveloped campground with an outhouse and interpretive signs about 4 miles off the highway; follow the access road past the state-operated landing strip, then continue 2½ miles on an unimproved road. Filter or boil water from the nearby creek before use. The camping fee is $8.

MILE 301 (SLOPE MOUNTAIN)   Land north of this point is managed by the Alaska Department of Natural Resources, not the BLM; however, you can use the same visitor information sources mentioned above.

MILE 355 (LAST CHANCE)   Wayside with an outhouse.

MILE 414 (DEADHORSE)   The end of the road. Deadhorse has a post office, general store, hotels, RV parking sites, and other services, but no campground, and tent camping isn't safe among the bears and heavy equipment (instead, stop short of Deadhorse to camp, perhaps along the Sagavanirktok River). An operator offers tours through to the Arctic Ocean, the only way to get there (arrange in advance). See p. 501.

THE ALASKA HIGHWAY

Detailed coverage of the entire 2,400-mile drive to Alaska is beyond our scope, but chapter 11's "Getting There & Getting Around" section provides the planning basics. Here I've covered the Alaska portion of the road, the 200 miles of the Alaska Highway that run from the border with Canada to the terminus in Delta Junction. This is mostly boring driving, miles of stunted black spruce and brush, either living or burned out. It's a relief when you hit the first major town, **Tok** (rhymes with Coke), 100 miles along. But don't get your hopes up. This is the only place where I've ever walked into a visitor center and asked what there is to do in town, only to have the host hold up her fingers in the shape of a goose egg and say, "Nothing." Another 100 miles (I hope you brought plenty of music, because no radio station reaches out here), and you've made it to **Delta Junction.** There's a little more to do here, but it's still not a destination. Another 100 miles, and you're in Fairbanks.

The main sources of information for the drive are based in Tok, the first town you hit after you cross the border. It acts as a threshold for the entire state. To plan the journey ahead, contact them, and see "Exploring the Interior" at the beginning of this chapter. If you're headed to Anchorage or other points south, see the sections on the Glenn and Richardson highways later in this chapter; those roads branch from the Alaska Highway at Tok and Delta, respectively.

I've arranged this section in order from the border with Canada heading west.

Crossing the Border

Besides remembering to set your watch back an hour when crossing the border into Alaska—it's an hour earlier than in Yukon Territory—also keep in mind you are spanning an international boundary. An adult U.S. or Canadian citizen needs a **passport, passport card,** or **enhanced driver's license** to enter the country over the road or water. A child needs a passport or, if under age 16, only a birth certificate. A website explaining the requirements is at www.getyouhome.gov. See chapter 11 to learn more about passports and entry requirements for international visitors. There are no duties on products made in the United States or Canada. For duties on items that you buy that originated in other countries or on alcohol or smoking supplies see chapter 11. Products you buy in Alaska made of **wildlife** will probably require special permits to be taken out of the United States, and most marine mammal products cannot be exported (p. 526). If you are a U.S. resident, send the item home by mail without trying to take it through Canada. U.S. authorities no longer let noncitizens into the country with firearms except for permanent resident aliens or foreigners holding both a special permit from the Bureau of Alcohol, Tobacco, Firearms and Explosives and a nonresident hunting license (p. 526). It's complicated for U.S. residents to travel through Canada with **firearms** as well. Guns other than hunting rifles or shotguns generally are not allowed, and you need to fill out a form and pay a $25 fee for guns that are allowed; contact the Canadian Firearms Center (© **800/731-4000;** www.cfc-cafc.gc.ca) before you go to avoid problems. You should also register your firearms with U.S. Customs and Border Patrol (no fee) before entering Canada to ease your return to the United States. Before entering the U.S., **dogs** more than 3 months old require a rabies certificate with an expiration date; it should have the signature of a licensed veterinarian that is dated at least 30 days before

DAWSON CITY & EAGLE: detour into history

Instead of taking the Alaska Highway directly from Whitehorse, Yukon, to Tok, consider driving north on the Klondike Highway (Yukon Hwy. 2) to Dawson City, then west and south over the **Top of the World Highway** and partially unpaved **Taylor Highway** to rejoin the Alaska Highway just east of Tok. This represents 502 miles of driving, about 127 miles more than if you just stay on the Alaska Highway, and includes 43 miles of sometimes rough dirt road, but it's worth doing at least one-way to see historic Dawson City and the fabulous mountain scenery of the Top of the World Highway. Dawson was the destination of the 1898 Klondike Gold Rush; the bed of the Klondike River near here contained thick veins of gold. The town maintains the look of those days, when it was briefly the second largest city on the West Coast, after San Francisco. Many buildings, a gold dredge, and a riverboat were restored as part of the Klondike National Historic Sites, managed by **Parks Canada.** Besides the buildings and their setting, there are museums, a working not-for-profit casino, a center of indigenous culture, and other attractions, easily enough for 2 days of sightseeing. The **Klondike Visitor Association,** P.O. Box 389, Dawson City, YT, Canada Y0B 1G0; ☎ **867/993-5575;** fax 867/993-6415; www.dawsoncity.ca), offers information on local businesses, accommodations, and community events. For information on the historic sites, contact **Parks Canada** at P.O. Box 390, Dawson City, YT, Canada Y0B 1G0 (☎ **867/993-7200;** www.parkscanada.gc.ca, click on "National Historic Sites," then "Dawson Historical Complex"). For information on the **Han Nation people** here and their cultural center, call ☎ **867/993-7100** (www.trondek.com).

After passing into the United States on the Top of the World Highway (**Note:** this border crossing is open only during the day, and only during the summer), a further detour leads north on the Taylor Highway to the forgotten town of Eagle on the bank of the Yukon River (going south on the Taylor leads you back to the Alaska Hwy.). The trip to Eagle adds 66 miles each way on a

crossing the border. If in doubt about any of these issues, call before you go, as the border is a long way from anywhere: **Canadian Customs** in Whitehorse (☎ **867/667-3943**) or **U.S. Customs and Border Protection** on the highway (☎ **907/774-2252**), in Skagway (☎ **907/983-2325**), or in Anchorage (☎ **907/271-6855**).

FROM THE BORDER TO TOK

The first 65 miles after entering the United States, the road borders the Tetlin National Wildlife Refuge. These broad wetlands and low forests are a migratory stopover in April and May and in the fall for thousands of songbirds, birds of prey, and waterfowl, and the summer home of trumpeter swans and lesser sandhill cranes, among 30 resident and 96 migratory species. The refuge holds a migratory bird festival in May with activities at the refuge and in nearby Tok. Activities change each year. Caribou also show up along the road, especially in the early spring and late fall. Interpretive signs are at six points along the highway. The Fish and Wildlife Service's Tetlin Refuge Visitor Center, 8 miles past the border, winding, narrow dirt road; allow 2 hours each way. But if you have the time, the destination more than rewards the effort. Eagle is lost in time, a treasure of a gold-rush river town with many original buildings full of original artifacts from a century ago. It's entirely authentic and noncommercial, with few businesses. The **Eagle Historical Society and Museums** (✆ **907/547-2325;** www. eagleak.org) shows off the buildings and several museums of materials left behind in this eddy in the stream of history. Their 3-hour walking tour starts once a day at 9am daily, Memorial Day to Labor Day, and costs $7. Sadly, a

devastating flood in 2009 severely damaged the town and its historic customs house. Huge blocks of ice demolished many buildings and, a year later, the cafe and motel still had not reopened and were unlikely to do so. Even without a motel, you can still camp in Eagle. Call ahead for information on that and other services to the Eagle Field Office of the **Yukon–Charley Rivers National Preserve,** P.O. Box 167, Eagle, AK 99738 (✆ **907/547-2233;** www.nps.gov/yuch). That office is important as well for planning a float trip on the Yukon River from Eagle. It lies on the far side of the airstrip from the main part of town.

The funny little village of Chicken is the other stop on this drive (the old joke is that they wanted to name the town "Ptarmigan" but didn't know how to spell it). There are a couple of businesses worth a stop for gold panning, for a meal, or to shop for gifts. Chicken, too, is mixed up in the area's time warp: The town has never had phone service but has free Wi-Fi.

at mile 1,229, is open May 15 to September 15 daily from 8am to 4:30pm, longer when staffing allows. There are exhibits, a 1-mile trail, and an observation deck with a great view. The refuge also has two small lakeside campgrounds: Deadman Lake, at Mile 1,249, with 15 sites, some okay for RVs (but no drinking water); and Lakeview, at mile 1,256, with 11 (no RVs over 30 ft.). Rangers give evening campground programs in the summer at Deadman Lake. The refuge headquarters is in Tok (✆ **907/883-5312** headquarters; http://tetlin.fws.gov).

Tok

Born as a construction station on the highway, Tok's role in the world has never expanded much beyond being a stop on the road. With its location at the intersection of the Alaska Highway and the Glenn Highway to Anchorage and Prince William Sound (see the next section), the town has built an economy of gas stations, gift stores, cafes, and hotels to serve highway travelers. It brags of being the coldest community in North America, a dubious distinction made possible by both the latitude and the distance from the moderating influence of the ocean.

ESSENTIALS

GETTING THERE   You're surely passing through Tok with your own set of wheels. If you get stuck for some reason, one shuttle service or another can get you on your way. **Alaska/Yukon Trails** (✆ 800/770-7275; www.alaskashuttle. com) runs through Tok summer only between Fairbanks and Dawson City or Whitehorse.

VISITOR INFORMATION   Public land agencies jointly operate an informative visitor center to introduce highway travelers to Alaska's outdoors. The **Alaska Public Lands Information Center,** P.O. Box 359, Tok, AK 99780 (✆ 907/883-5667; www.alaskacenters.gov), is in the same building as the Alaska State Troopers on the right (north) side of the road coming from the direction of Canada on the Alaska Highway. It is open daily from 8am to 7pm in summer and Monday through Friday from 8am to 4:30pm in winter. You can make ferry reservations on the Alaska Marine Highway System here, too.

The next building over, at the intersection of the Alaska Highway and Tok Cut-Off (also known as the Glenn Hwy.), the town's **Main Street Visitor Center** is operated by the Tok Chamber of Commerce, P.O. Box 389, Tok, AK 99780 (✆ 907/883-5775; www.tokalaskainfo.com). The center provides information on Tok and anywhere else you may be bound on the highway. They're open from May 1 to September 15 daily from 8am to 7pm.

[FastFACTS] TOK

Bank   Denali State Bank has an ATM, as does the Three Bears Food Center, two doors down.

Hospital   Tok Clinic is on the Tok Cut-Off across from the fire station (✆ 907/883-5855).

Police   Contact the Alaska State Troopers (✆ 907/883-5111), next to the visitor center near the intersection of the Alaska Highway and Tok Cut-Off (Glenn Hwy.).

Post Office   At the highway junction next to the Westmark Hotel.

Taxes   There are none in the region.

AN ACTIVITY

A river guide based in Tok offers trips on various Interior rivers. **Canoe Alaska** (✆ 907/883-2628; www.canoealaska.net) specializes in white-water canoe instruction for beginners and intermediate paddlers, and leads guided canoe and raft outings and expeditions; a guided trip is around $100 a day. They also rent canoes and offer shuttle service.

WHERE TO STAY

The motels are numerous and competitive in Tok. There also are many B&Bs. Check at the visitor center. Be sure to get the 50¢ state highway and campground map from the public lands center (see above), which includes all the public campgrounds in Alaska. Three attractive state park campgrounds lie near Tok on the three highway links that radiate from the town. Each has a $15 self-service fee.

There are lots of competitive RV parks in Tok, too. One that has wooded sites suitable for tent camping as well is the **Sourdough Campground,** 1¼ miles south of town on the Glenn Highway (www.sourdoughcampground.com;

$\textcircled{c}$ **907/883-5543**). They charge $39 to $43 for full hookups, $20 dry, showers included. The campground, claiming to be "Alaska's funnest," offers some unusual free services, including a Wi-Fi hot spot, evening music shows, and a nightly pancake toss with a chance to win a free breakfast. Besides a breakfast buffet, they sell evening meals.

Snowshoe Motel & Fine Arts and Gifts ✦ The motel is behind the gift shop. The best units are the newer smoke-free rooms near the front, and all are reasonably priced. Each is divided into two sections by the bathroom, providing two separate bedrooms—great for families. They have phones. Outside walkways are decorated with flowers. The gift shop carries some authentic Native art as well as highway kitsch. It is open daily in summer, Saturdays in winter.

Across the highway from the information center (P.O. Box 559), Tok, AK 99780. $\textcircled{c}$ **800/478-4511** in Alaska, Yukon, and part of B.C.; or 907/883-4511. Fax 907/883-4517. 24 units. High season $95 double; low season $78 double. Extra person $5. MC, V. *In room:* TV, fridge, microwave.

Westmark Tok The central hotel in town is closed in the winter, as its clientele is primarily the package-tour bus trade. It's made up of several buildings connected by boardwalks. Rooms are comfortable, air-conditioned, and regularly updated. The newer section has larger rooms for the same price. The company offers significant discounts for booking on their website. The restaurant serves breakfast and dinner of Mexican and standard American fare, with dinners in the $14-to-$23 range.

Intersection of Alaska and Glenn hwys. (P.O. Box 130), Tok, AK 99780-0130. www.westmark hotels.com. $\textcircled{c}$ **800/544-0970** reservations, or 907/883-5174. Fax 907/883-5178. 92 units. $110–$130 double. AE, DC, DISC, MC, V. Closed mid-Sept to mid-May. **Amenities:** Restaurant; bar; computer access and Wi-Fi in lobby. *In room:* A/C, TV, hair dryer.

Young's Motel Good standard motel rooms occupy three one-story structures on the parking lot behind Fast Eddy's restaurant (described below), where you check in. Eighteen newer, smoke-free rooms are the top pick, but all are acceptable.

Behind Fast Eddy's Restaurant on the Alaska Hwy. (P.O. Box 482), Tok, AK 99780. $\textcircled{c}$ **907/883-4411.** Fax 907/883-5023. 43 units. High season $94 double; low season $69 double. Extra person $5. AE, DISC, MC, V. **Amenities:** Restaurant (described below); bar. *In room:* TV, Wi-Fi.

WHERE TO EAT

A reliable restaurant of many years' tenure, **Fast Eddy's** ($\textcircled{c}$ **907/883-4411**) is on the right as you enter town from the east. Begun as a typical roadside cafe, it has developed into a place where a wine list and fine-dining entrees don't seem out of place. Yet the proprietor knows that most highway travelers just want a simple, relaxing meal, and the varied menu offers anything they might have in mind. I relish the salad bar and light dishes that offer a break from the usually carnivorous greasy-spoon choices found elsewhere along the highway. The dining room is decorated in maroon, dark wood, and brass. They're open daily in summer from 6am to 11pm, in winter from 6am to 10pm. Wine and beer are available with meals.

Delta Junction

This intersection with the Richardson Highway, which runs from Valdez to Fairbanks (p. 452), is the official end of the Alaska Highway. It's an earnest little

Delta Junction.

roadside town set in a broad plain between the Delta and Tanana rivers. People make their livings from farming and tourism and by working at a trans-Alaska pipeline pump station south of town and Fort Greely, one of the bases of the national missile defense system. For visitors, there are two historic roadhouse museums, several good campgrounds, and an unpredictable chance to spy a herd of bison—but not enough to hold most for more than a few hours.

ESSENTIALS

VISITOR INFORMATION   A helpful **visitor center** run by the Delta Chamber of Commerce, P.O. Box 987, Delta Junction, AK 99737 (☏ **877/895-5068** or 907/895-5068, 895-5069 summer only; www.deltachamber.org), stands at the intersection of the Alaska and Richardson highways, in the middle of town; it's open from mid-May to mid-September.

[FastFACTS] DELTA JUNCTION

Bank   **Wells Fargo,** with an ATM, is next door to the IGA Food Cache on the Richardson Highway at the center of town; another bank with an ATM is just south of the visitor center.

Hospital   The **Family Medical Center** is at Mile

267.2 of Richardson Highway, 1½ miles north of the visitor center (☏ **907/895-4879** or 895-5100).

Police   For nonemergency calls, reach the

Alaska State Troopers at ☏ **907/895-4800.**

Post Office   On the Richardson, half a mile north of the visitor center.

Taxes   None of any kind.

EXPLORING THE AREA

Before construction of the first road to Fairbanks in 1917 (today's Richardson Hwy.), travelers to the Interior followed a trail on basically the same route by horse in summer and dog sled in winter, stopping at roadhouses that provided food and shelter a day apart or less on the 2-week trip. Two well-preserved examples of the roadhouse system survive near Delta Junction.

In 1996, the Army saved the 1905 **Sullivan Roadhouse** (☏ **907/895-4415**), which had stood abandoned since 1922 on what became an Army bombing range. Today the log building stands near the town visitor center and is open free of charge in summer Monday through Friday 9am to 5pm. Many of the Sullivan's original belongings have been set back in their original places, giving a strong feel for frontier life, but the heart of the restoration is the authentic hospitality of the local volunteers who show off the place with great pride.

The next stop on the trail beyond Sullivan's Roadhouse was 16 miles toward Fairbanks. **Rika's Roadhouse and Landing,** 8 miles northwest of Delta at mile

275 on the Richardson Highway (ⓒ **907/895-4201;** www.rikas.com/roadhouse), still makes a pleasant stop on your drive. This roadhouse lasted later than the Sullivan's because drivers had to board a ferry here to cross the Tanana River until the 1940s, and the landing was the end of the line for Tanana sternwheelers. The 1906 log building, on the National Register of Historic Places, has been altered too much by its gift shop to feel authentic, but the grassy 10-acre compound completes a vivid scene of Alaska pioneer life with surviving outbuildings, including telegraph cabins, a museum, a barn, a gorgeous vegetable garden, and livestock pens. The entire site overlooks the riverbank, and an impressive suspension bridge carries the trans-Alaska pipeline over the Tanana just beyond the park. A private operator does a good job of managing the site for the state of Alaska, including operating a restaurant that serves simple meals daily from 9am to 5pm; the grounds and museum are open daily from 8am to 8pm from May 15 to September 15.

WHERE TO STAY

Check at the visitor center for a referral to one of the many B&Bs. The cute, funny, and hospitable **Kelly's Alaska Country Inn,** at the intersection of Richardson and Alaska highways (www.kellysalaskacountryinn.com; ⓒ **907/895-4667**), has rooms for $139 double in summer, $119 winter, right in the middle of town. The 20 rooms have TVs, telephones, Wi-Fi, microwave ovens, refrigerators, and coffeemakers; most are small and ordinary, but a funky few are an in old Quonset hut and have arched wood ceilings. This is a family-run business going way, way back.

   Alaska 7 Motel, 3548 Richardson Hwy. (www.alaska7motel.com; ⓒ **907/895-4848**), is a small, low-slung building containing standard rooms with lots of amenities, including refrigerators, microwave ovens, coffeemakers, Wi-Fi, and satellite TV for $99 double.

CAMPING

Alaska State Parks maintains five campgrounds on the rivers and lakes in and around Delta Junction and a couple of public cabins. Right on the highway near town, the **Delta State Recreation Area campground** lies among large spruce and birch trees, the sites well separated, some with walk-in privacy. It is among the most attractive campgrounds on the highway. The **Quartz Lake State Recreation Area,** 11 miles northwest of town on the Richardson Highway and down a 3-mile turnoff, has more than 100 camping sites on two fishing lakes. The camping fee is $10. For information, contact the **Department of Natural Resources Public Information Center,** 3700 Airport Way, Fairbanks, AK 99709 (www.alaskastateparks.org; ⓒ **907/451-2705**).

   To park an RV, or if you're tent camping and need a shower, **Smith's Green Acres RV Park and Campground,** 1½ miles north on the Richardson Highway from the visitor center, at mile 267.9 (www.smithsgreenacres.com; ⓒ **800/895-4369** or 907/895-4369), has pull-through RV sites and tent sites among the trees. The place also has cabins, a small playground, laundry facilities, and Wi-Fi. Full hookup sites are $36, tent sites $18.

WHERE TO EAT

For a picnic or quick, simple meal on your drive, try the **IGA Food Cache** (ⓒ **907/895-4653**), on the south side of the highway in Delta. The deli counter sells fried food, subs, and ice cream, and the store also has a bakery counter and coffee stand. You can eat in as well as carry out. They're open Monday through Saturday 6:30am to 9pm, Sunday 8am to 8pm, closing an hour earlier in winter.

THE GLENN HIGHWAY

Glenn Highway.

The Glenn Highway, Alaska Route 1, leads from the Alaska Highway at Tok to Anchorage (the section from Tok to Glennallen is also called the Tok Cut-Off). It connects the most populous part of the state to the outside world, a 328-mile strip of blacktop that grows from two lanes in Tok to six or more in urban downtown Anchorage. In this section, I cover the stretch from Glennallen to Palmer. From Tok to Glennallen, the road passes through wilderness. The portion from Palmer to downtown Anchorage is all part of the greater city and encompassed in chapter 6.

Glennallen

The town may look like just a wide place in the road, but this little community near the junction of the Glenn and Richardson highways is the commercial hub for the Copper River Country, a great, thinly settled region. The two highways overlap for a few miles. At their southern split, a handy information stop, the **Copper Valley Chamber of Commerce and Visitor Center,** occupies a gray building next to the Hub gas station and store (P.O. Box 469, Glennallen, AK 99588; ℭ **907/822-5555;** www.traveltoalaska.com). Volunteers open the center May 15 to September 15 daily 9am to 7pm, or longer as staffing allows. Besides the hotel and restaurant listed below, Glennallen has two banks with ATMs, a post office, groceries, a medical center, and government offices, all centered along a strip of the Glenn Highway around mile 187, west of the visitor center.

Apart from Wrangell–St. Elias National Park, much of the outdoor recreation in the Copper River Country occurs on lands managed by the **Bureau of Land Management Glennallen Field Office,** with a log cabin office in town on the north side of the Glenn Highway at mile 186.5 (P.O. Box 147), Glennallen, AK 99588 (ℭ **907/822-3217**). The Internet address is too long to repeat; go to www.blm.gov/ak, and navigate to "Glennallen Field Office." The office is open Monday through Friday from 8am to 4:30pm. Information is also available from the public land information centers in Anchorage, Fairbanks, and Tok. This huge area, about as large as a midsize eastern U.S. state, is more accessible than most of the national park, but it's still a rough, remote land with few visitor facilities. There are several large alpine lakes, two National Wild Rivers, several hiking trails, and five campgrounds (including the state park campground just north of Glennallen), all reached on the Richardson, Glenn, and Denali highways. Guides are available for rafting and fishing in the rivers. Check at the visitor center or BLM office for a list of operators.

Standard accommodations are at the **New Caribou Hotel,** in town at mile 187 of the Glenn Highway (www.caribouhotel.com; ℭ **800/478-3302** or

907/822-3302). The rooms have the amenities of a roadside chain, but the hotel as a whole has the character of its place. They book up in the summer, so reservations are important. The summer rate is $149 double. Budget rooms are in an annex building, a former pipeline construction camp, for $79 double. Their **Caribou Restaurant** is inexpensive but nice inside, with lots of brass and booths. Choices include burgers, fish, and steak.

The Matanuska Glacier Area

From Glennallen, the highway traverses a broad tundra area where there's a good chance of seeing caribous and other wildlife from a distance. Next, the road climbs between two mountain ranges—the coastal Chugach Mountains that hold the glaciers around Prince William Sound, and the craggy old Talkeetna Mountains to the north. The road winds through steep, rocky terrain with wonderful, scary views, including a good look at the Matanuska Glacier. In the fall, when the tundra and the birches, aspens, and cottonwoods turn yellow and red, this drive is dizzying in its beauty. Plan on driving this section at no more than 45 mph.

The **Matanuska Glacier State Recreation Site** overlooks the glacier and has a 1-mile interpretive nature trail and a good, 12-site campground ($15 per site or $10 to park overnight in a paved lot). To get closer to the glacier, you have to take a rough side road and pay a fee to the people who own the land in front of it, doing business as **Glacier Park** (② 888/253-4480). The cost for the self-guided hike is $15 adults, $13 seniors, $10 students and military, $5 children 6 to 12. They also offer camping for $15 a night. Turn at mile 102. The side road is 3 miles, followed by a 15-minute walk to the glacier's face. From October to April, it's wise to call to reserve and check conditions.

Two exceptional lodges lie along the highway near the Matanuska Glacier, about 70 miles from Glennallen or 115 miles from Anchorage. In this remote area, phones are in common rooms.

Majestic Valley Wilderness Lodge ★★ ❚❚ This friendly place offers a choice of basic, inexpensive rooms and cabins and more luxurious lodge rooms, and serves excellent family style meals to guests and others who reserve in advance. Dining is in the extraordinary log lodge building with a towering ceiling and wonderful mountain views—a quintessentially Alaskan space. It's set in spectacular terrain, a quiet spot off the highway with a 20km network of well-groomed cross-country skiing trails. Anchorage families come here for fun winter or spring weekends, skiing and sledding, playing cards in the evening, and staying in the simple budget rooms. The four fancier lodge rooms with satellite TVs, granite counters, and radiant floor heating, still reasonably priced, appeal to another set. In the summer, the hiking, mostly above tree line, is exceptional, and river rafting, glacier trekking, and flightseeing are offered.

Mile 114.9, Glenn Hwy. (16162 W. Glenn Hwy., Sutton, AK 99674). ② **907/746-2930.** Fax 907/746-2931. www.majesticvalleylodge.com. 12 units, 2 cabins. $120–$165 double; $155 cabin double. Extra person age 9 and older $10; extra child ages 3–8 $5. MC, V. **Amenities:** Restaurant.

Sheep Mountain Lodge ★ On a mountainside above the road, this historic log lodge attracts many muscle-powered athletes, hosting a December dog-sled race and, in July, the huge Fireweed 400 Bicycle Race that ends in Valdez. Guests can hike and mountain-bike over spectacular trails on the tundra-covered mountains in summer and ski groomed trails in the winter. Cabins are large and nicely decorated, with high ceilings and walls of rough wood to remind you of the rural location. A few have kitchenettes. The porches have wonderful views down the mountainside. They rent a sleeping-bag bunkhouse, too, and have a guest sauna and indoor hot tub. The little cafe serves simple, healthy food in the summer.

Mile 113.5, Glenn Hwy. (17701 West Glenn Hwy., Sutton, AK 99674). ℭ **877/645-5121** or 907/745-5121. Fax 907/745-5120. www.sheepmountain.com. 11 cabins. Summer $159 double, $189 kitchenette; winter $99–$149 double. Extra person $10. Bunkhouse $60 for 4, extra person $5. MC, V. Closed 1 month each in spring and fall (call ahead). Cabins available year-round. **Amenities:** Restaurant; Jacuzzi; sauna.

Chickaloon & Sutton

Road construction projects working along the highway year by year, and planned years into the future, have imposed delays of up to an hour, slow driving, and nighttime closures. Contact ℭ 511 or check http://511.alaska.gov for the latest. The scenery is attractive, with country-style development cropping up along the road as you approach urban Alaska. Chickaloon is the base of Nova Raft and Adventure Tours, the river riding company listed in chapter 6; if you're already passing through here, you may want to arrange a float. Sutton is a little town left behind by a coal mine that once operated in these mountains. The charming little historic park there is worthy of a stop to stretch your legs.

RICHARDSON HIGHWAY & COPPER CENTER

The 364-mile drive from Fairbanks to Valdez unfolds as a grand cross section of Alaska. It begins in the broad Interior valleys at the north, rises to the tundra and lakes of the Alaska Range, descends back down to the Copper River Country, and finally climbs over the steep coastal mountains into the Prince William Sound fjord where Valdez resides. This was the first route into Alaska, but today it is little traveled and mostly free of development, an opportunity to see real wilderness by car on paved road.

Delta Junction is covered on p. 447. The intersection with the Denali Highway (see chapter 8) comes 81 miles south of there. This section has the most extraordinary scenery—broad vistas, the Delta River, amazing alpine lakes (including long Summit Lake), and many views of the trans-Alaska pipeline. About 40 miles south of Delta Junction, a family has built an extraordinary 10-room wilderness lodge with post-and-beam construction and a copper roof. The **Lodge at Black Rapids** (www.lodgeatblack rapids.com; ℭ **877/825-9413**), overlooking the Black Rapids Glacier, is a luxurious outpost in the middle of nowhere. Rates are $175 to $190 double. There are just a few other widely

The Copper Center Lodge.

scattered campgrounds and seasonal businesses on this stretch of highway. Eighty miles from Delta Junction, the spot on the map known as Paxson, the intersection with the Denali Highway has a business called the Paxson Inn. You can fill your tanks there, but I wouldn't recommend the restaurant or the rooms.

The next town on the Richardson is Glennallen, which is covered on p. 450. Fourteen miles south of Glennallen, **Copper Center** is a tiny Athabascan community on the old Richardson Highway near many major rivers, around which people here orient their lives in the summertime. To get out on the water, for fishing or just floating, contact **Alaska River Wrangellers** (✆ **888/822-3967** or 907/822-3967; www.riverwrangellers.com), based at the landing strip, a rafting firm owned by pioneers of the industry in Alaska, Nova Raft and Adventure Tours. They offer half-day floats for as little as $99, with a schedule that allows clients to choose the level of risk, adventure, and remoteness they are comfortable with, or to combine white-water rafting with salmon fishing. Those trips allow access to areas on the Tonsina River most anglers don't brave, for $299 full day.

The town's historic roadhouse, the **Copper Center Lodge** (www.copper centerlodge.com; ✆ **866/330-3245** or 907/822-3245), has long been worthy of a stop for a meal or even overnight. The history of the lodge dates from the bizarre gold-rush origins of Copper Center and Valdez, when about 4,000 stampeders to the Klondike tried a virtually impossible all-American route from Valdez over the glaciers of the Wrangell–St. Elias region. Few made it, and hundreds who died are buried in Copper Center. The original lodge was built of the stuff they left behind. The existing building dates from 1932, and the site also has a museum and quilt store. Rooms for up to four are $130 to $165, and they're open year-round.

Copper River Princess Wilderness Lodge ★★ This first-class lodge built by the Princess Cruise Line brings the comforts of the outside world to this rough and isolated corner of the planet. On clear days, the eastward views of Mounts Drum, Wrangell, and Blackburn are incredible. Princess has tried to capture the trim, red-painted look of the historic Kennecott mining district. Inside, common areas are spacious and warm, with a big slate fireplace in the lobby. Rooms are in earth tones, with faux rustic furniture and art reflecting mining history, and have king- and queen-size beds. The restaurant serves three meals a day, including sophisticated cuisine for dinner; those meals are not just in another league, but in a completely different game than anything else found on the highway. Breakfast of smoked salmon eggs Benedict was terrific, as were the salmon chowder and the evening entrees of moist cod and chicken. Dinner main courses are $15 to $39.

1 Brenwick-Craig Rd (P.O. Box 422), Copper Center, AK 99573 (turn at mile 102 Richardson Hwy.). www.princesslodges.com. ✆ **800/426-0500** or 907/822-4000. Fax 907/822-4044. 85 units. High season $139–$219 double. AE, DISC, MC, V. Closed Sept–May. **Amenities:** Restaurant; courtesy van to Gulkana airport and national park visitor center. *In room:* TV, hair dryer.

WRANGELL–ST. ELIAS NATIONAL PARK & KENNECOTT

Looking at a relief map of Alaska, you'd think the portion drained by the Copper River was so overweighted with mountains that it might topple the whole state into the Pacific. The Alaska Range, in the center of the state, has the tallest mountain, but this Gulf of Alaska region, straddling the Alaska–Yukon border, has more mass—the second- and fourth-tallest mountains in North America (Logan and St. Elias), plus 9 of the tallest 16 peaks in the United States. Four mountain ranges intersect, creating a mad jumble of terrain covering tens of millions of acres, a trackless chaos of unnamed, unconquered peaks. The Copper River and its raging tributaries slice through it all, swallowing the gray melt of innumerable glaciers that flow from the largest ice field in North America. Everything here is the largest, most rugged, most remote; words quickly fall short of the measure. But where words fail, commerce gives a little help: These mountains are so numerous and remote that one guide service makes a business of taking visitors to mountains and valleys that no one has ever explored before.

Wrangell–St. Elias National Park.

Ironically for such a wild land, the area's main attraction for visitors is its history. The richest copper deposit in the world was found here in 1900 by a group of prospectors who mistook a green mountaintop for a patch of green grass where they could feed their horses. It was a mountain of almost pure copper, with metallic nuggets the size of desks (one is at the UA Museum of the North in Fairbanks). The deposit produced trainloads of 70% pure copper. The first ore was so rich it required no processing before shipping, then came lots more copper that did need minimal processing. Much more lower-grade ore still lies underground. The Alaska Syndicate, an investment group that included J. P. Morgan and Daniel Guggenheim, built the Kennecott Copper Corporation from this wealth (its name was a misspelling of the Kennicott River and Glacier, where the copper was found—today, only the river and glacier go by the correct spelling). To get the copper out, they paid for an incredible 196-mile rail line up from Cordova (see chapter 7) and created a self-contained company town deep in the wilderness, called **Kennecott.** When the high-grade ore was gone, in 1938, they pulled the plug, leaving a ghost town of extraordinary beauty that still contains machinery and even documents they left behind.

Wrangell–St. Elias National Park and Preserve now owns Kennecott and more than 13 million acres across this region of Alaska. It's the largest national park in the United States by a long shot, six times the size of Yellowstone and about 25% larger than the entire country of Switzerland. The protected land continues across the border in Canada, in **Kluane National Park,** which is similarly massive. Most of that land is impossibly remote, but Wrangell–St. Elias has two rough gravel roads that allow access to see the mountains from a car. The main route is the abandoned roadbed of the Copper River and Northwestern Railroad leading to Kennecott and the historic sites there. It's an arduous but rewarding journey by car, requiring at least 2 days to do it right. Air taxis, river guides, and remote lodges offer other ways into the park's untouched wilderness, mostly starting from **McCarthy,** a historic village near Kennecott. There are a few trails near Kennecott, but only for day hikes. This is a country where experienced outdoors people can get away from any trace of humans for weeks on end.

The Kennecott & McCarthy Area

This historic copper area is the only part of the park most visitors see, as it's the most accessible and has the most services, interesting sites, and paths to explore. It's still not easy to get to, however—that's why it's still so appealing—and there's little point in going without adequate time. You can hit the highlights at Kennecott and McCarthy in a full day, but just getting there takes time.

The main event is the ghost town of **Kennecott,** whose red buildings gaze from a mountainside across the Kennicott Glacier in the valley below. Now owned by the Park Service, the buildings made up an isolated company town until 1938, when it abruptly shut down. Tourists coming here as late as the 1960s saw it as if frozen in time, with breakfast dishes still on the tables from the day the last train left. Most of that was looted and destroyed in the 1970s, but when I toured the company store a few years ago, old documents still remained, and the powerhouse and 14-story mill buildings still had their heavy iron and wood equipment. Besides the buildings, there are excellent hiking trails, including one that traverses the glacier. The town now has only a few year-round residents, but in summer is busy with a lodge, a couple of bed-and-breakfasts, guide services, and park rangers.

Five miles down the road, Kennecott's twin town of **McCarthy** served the miners as a place to drink, gamble, and hire prostitutes on rare days off—the company didn't allow any frivolity in Kennecott or in the bunkhouses high up on the mountain. McCarthy retains the relaxed atmosphere of its past, with businesses and residents living in false-front buildings not much changed from Wild West days. More of a year-round community, McCarthy has a restaurant, lodging, flight services, and other businesses.

Yet even this most populous part of the park is isolated and sparsely inhabited, with few services. Only about 50 people live in the greater area year-round. You will find no banking services, general stores, gas stations, clinics, police, or anything else you're used to relying on. Phones came to McCarthy and Kennecott only in the late 1990s and still are few. Cellular and Internet services exist, but not always reliably. Bring what you need.

ESSENTIALS
Getting There
BY CAR The paved **Edgerton Highway** starts 17 miles south of Copper Center on the Richardson Highway, then runs east for 33 miles to the tiny, dried-up former railroad town of **Chitina** (*chit*-na),

Kennecott.

the last reliable stop for groceries, gas, and other necessities until you return here. Do fill your tank; prudence also demands a full-size spare tire. Heading east, into the park, the **McCarthy Road** continues along the roadbed of the Copper River and Northwestern Railway. This is 60 miles of narrow dirt road, muddy in wet weather and clouded with dust when it's dry. Each year it has been improved a little, and two-wheel-drive cars can normally make it. The drive is a fun adventure, passing through tunnels of alders and crossing rivers on some of the original wooden railroad trestles; one wood-decked bridge spans a canyon more than 200 feet deep. There are virtually no services, very few buildings, and little traffic on the 3-hour drive. If you are driving a rented car, consider using the van or air options mentioned below, leaving the car in Chitina. I have listed companies that rent cars that can be driven on this unpaved road in Fairbanks (p. 419) and Anchorage (p. 218).

The road ends at a parking lot and collection of seasonal businesses on the banks of the Kennicott River. You can drive no further; several businesses offer overnight parking for $5 to $10 per night. Next, you walk across two footbridges. Late in the summer, the Kennicott Glacier releases a flood from a glacier-dammed lake, but at other times the second channel is a dry wash. Handcarts are available to move your luggage across, and on the other side you can catch a van. The place where you are staying will send one, or you can ride the **van** operated by **McCarthy–Kennicott Shuttle** (℃ 907/ 554-4411), $2 to McCarthy or $5 per person, one-way, to Kennecott. It runs every half-hour. A public telephone is near the bridge that you can use to call your lodgings.

BY VAN   **Backcountry Connection** (℃ 907/822-5292; www.kennicott shuttle.com) runs vans from Glennallen, Copper Center, Kenny Lake, and Chitina to the Kennicott River footbridge daily in summer. The van leaves Glennallen at 7am, Copper Center 7:30am, Kenny Lake 8am, and Chitina at 8:30am, arriving at the footbridge at 11am. The return trip departs from the footbridge at 4:30pm, getting back to Chitina around 6:30pm, Kenny Lake 7:30pm, Copper Center 8pm, and Glennallen 8:30pm. The same-day round-trip fare is $99, or $139 if you return on a different day; they also offer the option of flying one-way.

BY AIR   A simple way to Kennecott and McCarthy is to drive to Chitina—as far as you can go on pavement—and fly the rest of the way on one of the air taxis. Once there, get around in the vans that shuttle back and forth over 5 miles of dirt road. **Wrangell Mountain Air** (℃ 800/478-1160 or 907/ 554-4411; www.wrangellmountainair.com) offers three flights daily from Chitina to McCarthy for $247 round-trip, with a little flightseeing around the glaciers and peaks, and including ground transportation once there. You can add on lunch and activities, such as a half-day glacier hike or ghost town walking tour. This day trip option gives you enough time at Kennecott without having to spend the night there. A reputable service operating between Chitina and McCarthy on an on-demand basis is **McCarthy Air** (℃ 907/ 554-4440; www.mccarthyair.com). Flightseeing over the national park and charters to remote valleys and lakes for backcountry trips is covered below under "Getting Outside: Hiking & Backpacking."

Wednesday or Friday, it's possible to fly in a prop plane all the way from Anchorage. A couple of flight services team up to do this: You fly on one from Anchorage to Gulkana and then on the mail plane from Gulkana to

McCarthy. Check prices ahead of time. Contact **Copper Valley Air Service** (© 866/570-4200 or 907/822-4200; www.coppervalleyair.com), which handles all the booking and flies the Gulkana-to-McCarthy leg.

VISITOR INFORMATION   The main park visitor center is on the Richardson Highway near Copper Center (© **907/822-5234;** www.nps.gov/wrst). Stop in to buy maps and publications, watch a movie, or get advice from a ranger on outdoor treks. Hours are Memorial Day to Labor Day daily from 9am to 6pm; in winter, Monday through Friday from 8am to 4:30pm. You can write for information to P.O. Box 439, Copper Center, AK 99573. The Park Service is restoring buildings and offers visitor services in Kennecott itself. A former general store has become a visitor center, a good place to stop with questions for rangers, plan a backcountry trip, or join one of the daily guided activities. A ranger station for the less-visited northern area of the park lies on the Nabesna Road near its intersection with the Tok Cutoff Highway, about 80 miles north of Glennallen. That's an area for solitary roadside camping among broad views.

EXPLORING THE TOWNS

CHITINA   Chitina lost its reason to exist in 1938, when the last train ran on the Copper River line, but it lives on with 125 residents supporting themselves largely with salmon from the river, produce from their gardens, berries from the forests, and the few tourists who stop. There's a general store and a couple of gas stations (the last gas for many miles), a wayside interpretive area at the site of the old depot, a pond where you can often see trumpeter swans, and, down by the river, lazily rotating fish wheels plucking salmon from the river. The Copper River is too turbid for angling, but clear-water tributaries and stocked lakes in the area have fish.

KENNECOTT   This has got to be one of the world's greatest ghost towns, with some 40 buildings, mostly in good enough condition to be reused today—indeed,

Chitina.

until the current park service restoration project began, the community still played basketball in one structure. Some historic buildings have become lodgings, and the park service is using others. Locals still pick rhubarb and chives from the company garden. History has the same kind of immediacy here that you get from holding an old diary in your hand, quite different from the sanitized history-through-glass that you're used to at more accessible sites.

The Park Service bought most of the buildings a few years ago. On the eve of the takeover, items remained out on the ground that would be in museums in many places. If Kennecott were an ordinary industrial site, that would be interesting enough, but this place was something well out of the ordinary: an outpost beyond the edge of the world where men built a self-contained city a century ago. The hardship of the miners' lives and the ease of the managerial families' lives also present a fascinating contrast. The stabilization and restoration work continues, so the tour gets better every year.

You can take in some of the story by wandering around with a walking tour booklet available from the Park Service and reading signs, but it would be a big mistake to miss going inside the buildings—and to do that, you need to join a **guided tour** with **St. Elias Alpine Guides** (© **888/933-5427** or 907/345-9048; full listing below under "Hiking & Backpacking"). They have an office in the old Chinese laundry right in the ghost town. Tours, which happen three times daily, last 2½ hours and go into real depth on the geology and history, climbing to the perilous 14th floor of the mill building. I've never been on another tour like it: fascinating, challenging, and even exciting; I cannot recommend it strongly enough. They operate mid-May to mid-September and charge $25 per person. Consider making a day of it by adding a glacier-hiking trip with the same company. The guides will arrange a custom tour, too.

MCCARTHY   McCarthy feels authentic as soon as you walk down the dirt main street between the false fronts. There are flight service offices to arrange a trip out, a lodge, hotel, and a few other businesses. Then, a street beyond, unbroken wilderness for hundreds and perhaps thousands of miles. On a summer evening, young backpackers and locals stand on porches meeting and talking, laughing loudly, creating a small-town scene from another era. Visitors quickly mix in, as everyone seems eager to talk about the town and its history and their own peculiar wilderness lives. The people here know it's unique, and everyone hopes it doesn't change much. There are no tourist attractions in McCarthy other than a tiny museum with fun old items such as a sewing machine and typewriter, and maps, photos, and a model of a historic mine.

GETTING OUTSIDE

HIKING & BACKPACKING   There are a few trails radiating from Kennecott, for which crude maps are available from the rangers and others around town; or buy the **Trails Illustrated** topographic map, printed on plastic, for sale from some local businesses, or order ahead (see "Fast Facts: Alaska," in chapter 11). An impressive walk continues through the ghost town up the valley, paralleling the Kennicott Glacier and then its tributary, the Root Glacier. You can climb along the Root's edge to a towering ice fall, but a much better outing is to be had by joining a group to walk on the glacier itself. St. Elias Alpine Guides, listed below, accepts walk-ins for daily glacier dayhikes and other hikes and tours. A half-day on the glacier goes for $70 a person, while all-day hikes are $100 and ice-climbing lessons $125. We combined the half-day hike with the company's ghost town tour for one of the best days of Alaska tourism we've ever spent. Another fascinating hike you can do on your own leads straight up the mountain behind the Kennecott buildings to the old Bonanza Mine and bunkhouses, 3,000 feet higher on the alpine tundra.

Beyond the trails, the park is endless miles of trackless wilderness—one of Earth's last few places that really deserves that name. Fit hikers without the backcountry experience to mount their own expedition should join one of the guides who work in the area. **St. Elias Alpine Guides** (② **888/933-5427** or 907/345-9048; www.stelias guides.com) offers dayhikes, rafting, backpacking trips, and alpine ascents,

Root Glacier.

but specializes in guiding extended trips to unexplored territory. Bob Jacobs, the company's founder, stopped guiding on Mount McKinley years ago because of the crowds. At Wrangell–St. Elias, it's rare to encounter another party, and peaks remain that have never been climbed by anyone: The firm offers the chance to be one of the first.

Hiking on your own in a wilderness largely without trails is a whole new kind of experience for experienced backpackers and outdoors people who are used to more crowded parts of the planet. You feel like an explorer rather than a follower. At times, there's a fairy-tale sense of the world unfolding around you, as fresh as creation. If you're not prepared to select your own route—a task only for those already experienced in trackless, backcountry traveling—there are various established ways through the park you can follow with a topographic map. You can get a trip synopsis from the visitor center or ranger station, or download from their website (www.nps.gov/wrst). Rangers can help you choose a route to suit your party, although none is easy.

Some routes start from the roads, but a better way to go is to charter a flight into a remote valley from one of the two **air services** in McCarthy, Wrangell Mountain Air or McCarthy Air (p. 456). The planes land on gravel strips, river bars, glaciers, alpine tundra, or any other flat place the pilots know about. These companies make a business of flying out backpackers, and so have established rates for different landing sites and can help you determine a route that's right for you, as well as provide a list of supplies. Wrangell Mountain Air rents bear-proof containers and two-way radios, and McCarthy Air and the Park Service lend the containers. You can charter a flight for $200 to $600 per person, with at least two passengers. Or fly in to a lake for fishing or an alpine area for exploring from a base camp, reducing the worry about how much you pack.

Note: I wouldn't want to scare off anyone who could manage one of these trips, but people do get into trouble in the Alaska wilderness every year, and some of them don't come back. Before you head out into the backcountry, you must know how to take care of yourself where help is unavailable; this includes handling river crossings, bear avoidance, hypothermia prevention, basic first aid, and other issues. Unless you have plenty of backpacking experience in less remote areas, I don't recommend starting here.

MOUNTAIN-BIKING Anywhere else, the 60-mile road that leads to this area would be considered a mountain-biking trail. You also can make good use of bikes between McCarthy, Kennecott, and the footbridge. An old **wagon road** parallels the main road that connects the two towns, 4½ miles each way; the road itself is a one-lane dirt track. Advanced cyclists can also ride the trails around Kennecott described above under "Hiking & Backpacking." Bikes are for rent at Glacier View Campground (below).

RAFTING Many great, wild rivers drain these huge mountains, which are still being carved by enormous glaciers. The **Kennicott River,** starting at the glacier of the same name, boils with class II or III rapids for some 40 minutes starting right from the footbridge at the end of the McCarthy Road. As the area lacks roads, however, most trips must include a plane ride at least one-way, and that makes white-water rafting day trips here more expensive than outings near Copper Center, Denali, or Anchorage. At Wrangell–St. Elias, floats punch deep into the backcountry.

WHERE TO STAY & EAT

The closest standard hotel rooms are in Copper Center (in the previous section). In the Kennecott–McCarthy area itself, there are several attractive places to stay, all thick with the history the towns represent, but not ordinary American lodgings. Dining is mainly at the lodges. If you're not staying there, it is a good idea to check ahead to make sure they will be ready for you for a meal.

CAMPING & HOSTELLING There is one hike-in campground on the Kennecott–McCarthy side of the Kennicott River footbridge, on the Root Glacier trail. The park service allows camping anywhere in the park without a permit, but there are few handy spots on public land (much of the land along the roads is private), except on the Nabesna Road, which is most of a day's drive from the historic zone.

At the end of the McCarthy Road you'll find a couple of private campgrounds and a hostel. **Glacier View Campground** (www.glacierview campground.com; © **907/554-4490,** or 243-6677 off season) charges $24 a night for camping and has a cabin for rent. The owners also rent mountain bikes and offer showers. Their cafe offers barbecue for lunch and dinner and serves beer and wine. Besides the backpacker's hotel mentioned in the review of the **McCarthy Lodge** on p. 461, **Kennicott River Lodge and Hostel** (www.kennicottriverlodge.com; © **907/554-4441** summer, or 941/447-4252 winter), located at the end of the road 400 feet from the footbridge, offers bunks for $30 per person. Sheets and pillows are included; other bedding is extra. The lodge also rents rooms for two for $100 to $150 a night and cabins for $100 to $150 double, plus $25 for each additional person. They have a common kitchen, lounge, sauna, and showers.

There are several campgrounds along the Edgerton Highway and McCarthy Road on the way to the footbridge area. The most attractive is State Parks' **Liberty Falls Campground,** at mile 23 on the Edgerton Highway, which is set among big trees at the foot of a crashing waterfall. Many of the sites are walk-ins, with wooden tent platforms and lots of privacy. The self-service camping fee is $15 per vehicle; the day-use fee is $1. There are pit toilets and no running water.

Kennicott Glacier Lodge ★★ This is the largest and most comfortable accommodation in the Kennecott–McCarthy area, taking the edges off the isolation. The lodge accurately re-creates an old Kennecott building, with the same red-and-white color scheme, and stands among the historic structures of the ghost town. Guests can sip drinks on a long, flower-hung front porch overlooking the glacier, or relax on a lawn with play equipment and the same view. Rooms in the main lodge building are not large and have bathrooms down the hall (six shower rooms and eight bathrooms, all clean but small). The 10 rooms in a newer south wing are larger, with two queen-size beds and private bathrooms. All the bedrooms are remarkably clean and decorated with interesting mine artifacts and papers—telegrams, blueprints, and the like. All but eight overlook the glacier and ghost town, and those on the main floor have second entrances on the veranda.

Filling dinners are served family style at 7pm on long tables, with a fixed menu in the $35-to-$45 range, available to nonguests by prior reservation. The food is excellent and portions are generous. On various nights and visits, we've had Copper River salmon with sun-dried tomatoes and pine nuts; prime rib; and New York steak with potatoes, asparagus, and Caesar salad—all flawless. A large breakfast buffet is $18, continental breakfast $12. Lunch is by menu service, with sandwiches, salads, and specials ranging from $10 to $18. Sack lunches are available, too. There's nowhere else to eat right in Kennecott, so it makes sense to book the inclusive meal package, which is $325 double in the shared-bathroom units, $389 in the newer units; a third person is $85 with the meal package, and children ages 4 to 12 are half price.

P.O. Box 240567, Anchorage, AK 99524. www.kennicottlodge.com. (✆) **800/582-5128** or 907/258-2350; 554-4477 in season only. Fax 907/248-7975. 35 units, 10 with private bathroom. $205 double with shared bathroom, $269 double with private bathroom. Extra adult $30; extra child age 4–12 $15; free age 3 and under. AE, DISC, MC, V. Closed mid-Sept to mid-May. **Amenities:** Restaurant; courtesy van to footbridge and McCarthy.

McCarthy Lodge ★★ The lodge is the center of the relaxed village of McCarthy, 5 miles from the historically more buttoned-up Kennecott. Although you are not among the mining ruins when you stay here, you are in a real community where you can meet year-round residents and the many interesting characters who spend the summer here among historic buildings. The lodge building is a restaurant and bar. Rooms are in a building called Ma Johnson's Hotel across the street, an authentic old false-front structure that you might see in an old Western movie. The owners treasure the area's history and take great pains to preserve and decorate the old buildings appropriately. Bedrooms are small but full of period charm, with antiques, quilts, and memorabilia. They even excluded electrical outlets from the bedrooms because they wouldn't belong historically, although they'll happily bring an extension cord in from the hallway. Every two rooms share a bathroom.

The 10-table restaurant is an authentic Bush roadhouse in an unmistakably backwoods structure that was moved here from the abandoned town of Katalla in 1916. The dining room is decorated with artifacts, early photographs, and heavy drapes. Our meals were all perfectly prepared: chicken Alfredo, Cajun halibut, and, best of all, semolina-encrusted Copper River red salmon. The price range for dinner is $15 to $32. Or order from the casual and reasonably priced bar menu of pizza and the like.

P.O. Box MXY, McCarthy, AK 99588. www.mccarthylodge.com. ℂ **907/554-4402.** Fax 877/811-6172. 20 units, none with private bathroom. $169 double. MC, V. Closed mid-Sept to mid-May. **Amenities:** Restaurant; bar; courtesy van.

THE BUSH

10

The Bush compromises much of Alaska and is what visitors imagine when they think about Alaska. Still, most visitors to Alaska—and quite a few permanent residents—never go to the real "Bush," which is generally considered to be the Arctic, the Aleutians, or the vast wetlands of Western Alaska. There is limited human activity in much of these areas; once, several years ago, there was a million-acre "forest" fire in the Brooks Range, and it never came within 100 miles of any human habitation. Until you fly over the Bush or attempt to cross it on the ground, you have absolutely no idea how big—and how generally "empty"—it is. Of course, it's only "empty" of humans. It's full of the "wilderness" and all that entails.

To many, the Bush is the real Alaska, the place where people continue to live off the land as they have for millennia, the place where, if you are not careful, nature can—and will—kill you. But if the landscape and wildlife are unforgiving, the few people who live in the Bush more than make up for it. The rare visitors who make the effort to get off the beaten path are treated as welcomed—sometimes honored—guests. Most of the people who survive life in the Bush do so by banding together, and newcomers are nearly always invited to share in meals and community events.

The Natives' physical environment is extreme in every respect—the weather, the land, even the geography. There's a special feeling to walking along or upon the Arctic Ocean, the virtual edge of the Earth. The quantity and accessibility of wildlife are extreme, too, as are the solitude and the uniqueness of what you can do. Unfortunately, the prices also are extreme. Getting to a Bush hub from Anchorage costs more than getting to Anchorage from Seattle; it's usually cheaper to get to Europe from Anchorage than to the Aleutians. And once you're at the rural hub, you're not done; getting into the outdoors can cost as much as getting there in the first place. Many travelers can't afford a Bush sojourn, instead satisfying their curiosity about the state's unpopulated areas on Alaska's rural highways (covered in

PREVIOUS PAGE: **Native Eskimo girl.** ABOVE: **Iñupiaq Eskimo at sunset.**

chapter 9). Most who can afford the trip usually make the most of their time and money with brief prearranged tours or trips directly to wilderness lodges. Only a few explorers head for the Bush unguided, although there are some good places to go that way—Nome, Barrow, Kodiak, and Unalaska among them.

EXPLORING THE BUSH

Alaska's Bush is better defined by what it's like than by where it is. The most common and convenient conception says the Bush is everything beyond the road system. On a map, almost everything north and west of Fairbanks meets that definition, but many Bush villages lie elsewhere in the Interior, in Southcentral, and in Southeast Alaska. In fact, there are some Bush villages you can drive to. No simple definition works. You know a Bush community by how it feels. It's a place where the wilderness is closer than civilization, where people still live off the land and age-old traditions survive, and where you have to make a particular effort to get in or out.

 Map Pointer

To locate these towns and regions, see the "Alaska" map in the front of the book.

The Regions

THE ARCTIC   The Arctic Circle is the official boundary of the Arctic. The line, at 66° 33' north latitude, is the southern limit of the true midnight sun—south of it, at sea level, the sun rises and sets, at least a little, every day of the year. But in Alaska, people think of the Arctic as beginning at the **Brooks Range,** which is a bit north of the circle, including **Barrow** and **Prudhoe Bay.** The northwest Alaska region, which includes **Kotzebue** and, south of the Arctic Circle, **Nome,** also is Arctic in climate, culture, and

Caribous crossing a snowfield.

A brown bear mother and her cubs in Katmai National Park.

topography. The biggest geographic feature in Alaska's Arctic is the broad **North Slope,** the plain of tundra that stretches from the northern side of the Brooks Range to the Arctic Ocean. It's a swampy desert, with little rain or snowfall, frozen solid all but a few months a year.

SOUTHWEST ALASKA/ALEUTIAN ISLANDS   Stretching from the Aleutians—really a region of their own—to the Alaska Peninsula, Kodiak Island, and the southern part of the mountainous west side of Cook Inlet, this is a wild maritime region. The hub of the wet, windy **Aleutians** is **Unalaska** and its port of **Dutch Harbor. Katmai National Park** and the adjoining wild lands are the main attraction of the Alaska Peninsula, although there also are fishing lodges on the salmon-rich rivers and on the lakes to the north, including areas in **Lake Clark National Park** and **Iliamna Lake.** On the peninsula's west side, **Bristol Bay** is known for massive salmon runs, and avid anglers may be interested in its wilderness lodges, using **Dillingham** or **King Salmon** as a hub. The lakes and west side of **Cook Inlet** are accessed primarily by Kenai, Homer, and Anchorage flight services for fishermen and hunters. **Kodiak** is hardly a southwest Bush community, but it fits better in this chapter than anywhere else, and the town is a hub for villages and bear viewing on Kodiak Island.

WESTERN ALASKA   This is the land of the massive, wet **Yukon–Kuskokwim Delta,** or the Y-K Delta, as it's known. Their land never exploited by white explorers, the Yup'ik people here live in some of Alaska's most culturally traditional villages. In places, Yup'ik is still the dominant language. **Bethel** is the main hub city of the delta but holds little attraction for visitors.

Getting Around

With a few exceptions for strongly motivated travelers who might take the ferry to Kodiak and Unalaska or drive to Prudhoe Bay, getting to each town in this chapter will require flying. **Alaska Airlines (© 800/252-7522;** www.alaskaair. com) offers the only jet service to Bush hubs. Other, smaller operators serve these towns with prop aircraft. Throughout the chapter, we've listed the plane fare to various communities from Anchorage, based on flying coach and getting a significant discount for advance purchase and some restrictions. Full fares cost more. You may be able to save by including a flight leg to a Bush hub community as part of your round-trip ticket to Alaska, making Anchorage technically a stop-over on the way. With the way fuel costs and airfares are fluctuating, we hesitate to mention firm prices for plane tickets at all. Generally, getting to these towns will cost $400 to $1,000 round-trip from Anchorage. To get a current fare, use a travel agent or the Internet.

Kodiak, which barely fits in a chapter on the Bush, is the most accessible of the communities in this chapter, but it still requires either a 10-hour ferry ride from Homer or a $400 flight from Anchorage. This charming, historic town is similar to towns in Southeast Alaska or Prince William Sound, but it is also a hub for Native villages on the island and remote wilderness. **Unalaska and Dutch Harbor,** in the Aleutian Islands, is an interesting place to go way off the beaten path while staying in complete comfort. From Anchorage, a visit requires a 3-hour flight on a turboprop aircraft—fares less than $950 are rarely seen. Otherwise, only a ferry ride that lasts most of a week will get you there. **Prudhoe Bay,** an industrial complex without a real town associated with it, lies on the Arctic Ocean at the end of the 500-mile Dalton Highway and receives Alaska Airlines service. Otherwise, the places in this chapter can be reached only by plane. **Barrow,** the **Pribilof Islands, Kotzebue,** and **Kaktovik** are the most purely Native of the communities in the chapter. **Nome** has the advantages of Arctic surroundings easily accessible on gravel roads, but is more of a gold rush town than a Native village. Fares from Anchorage range from $450 to $850 for these communities.

KODIAK: WILD ISLAND

Alaska's "Emerald Isle" is largely undis-covered country for visitors. The second largest island in the United States, after Hawaii, it is larger than Rhode Island and Delaware combined, yet is home to only 13,000 people—and more than 3,000 of the magnificent Kodiak bears, the largest bears in the world.

Millions of salmon return to the hundreds of Kodiak streams, which are fed by an average of 6 feet of rain and 7 feet of snow the island gets every year. The heavy precipitation also gives the island a green covering that leads to its name and makes it look like a slightly more temperate version of Hawaii. With nearly all the residents clustered in either Kodiak city or the six Native villages on the island, most of the island is truly wilderness, a large por-tion of which is accessible from Kodiak's more than 100 miles of roads.

Bear tracks on Kodiak Island.

Kodiak is also the center of the early Russian history in Alaska, dating from the first settlement in 1784. It remained the capital of Russian America until

Alexander Baranof relocated his operations to Sitka in 1808. Much of historic Kodiak was lost when a 30-foot tidal wave surged along the waterfront after the 1964 Good Friday Earthquake, but one of the buildings that was spared was the 1808 Russian warehouse, the oldest building in Alaska, which now serves as the Baranov Museum.

Kodiak remains a major Alaskan fishing port and features the largest Coast Guard base in America. It is a working community that, thus far, has been only slightly touched by the wave of tourism that has swept over much of the rest of coastal Alaska.

There are six **Native villages** on and around the island. A flight to one of them and back on a clear day is a wonderful, low-cost way to see remote areas of the island and to get a taste of how Alaska Natives live. It's also popular to fly out to see the famous bears on a day trip, or stay at one of several **wilderness lodges** for wildlife-watching, fishing, sea kayaking, or hunting.

Essentials

GETTING THERE It's a 1-hour flight from Anchorage to Kodiak on **Alaska Airlines** (☎ 800/252-7522; www.alaskaair.com). A round-trip ticket from Anchorage costs around $400. **ERA Aviation** (☎ 800/866-8394, ext. 8386; www.flyera.com) also serves the route with prop aircraft, which may save a little money. A **cab** from A&B Taxi (☎ 907/486-4343) or Big Bear Taxi and Charters (☎ 907/942-4141) costs about $20 from the airport downtown.

The ferries *Tustumena* and *Kennicott*, of the **Alaska Marine Highway System** (☎ 800/642-0066 or 907/486-3800; www.ferryalaska.com), serve Kodiak from Homer, the closest port with a road. The run takes 10 hours, but it is truly memorable. The vessels leave land behind and thread through the strange and exposed Barren Islands, often seeing whales and porpoises on the way. The ocean can be quite rough, and when it is, lots of passengers get seasick; read and follow the advice on p. 524. A cabin is a good idea for an overnight run. Without a cabin, the adult passenger fare from Homer is $74. Fares for children 6 to 12 are half price on all ferries, free for 5 and under. The U.S. Fish and Wildlife Service staffs the ferry with a naturalist on runs to Kodiak.

VISITOR INFORMATION The **Kodiak Island Convention and Visitors Bureau,** 100 E. Marine Way, Ste. 200, Kodiak, AK 99615 (☎ 800/789-4782 or 907/486-4782; fax 907/486-6545; www.kodiak.org), occupies part of the ferry terminal at Pier 1. Hours increase in the summer, but the center is open year-round Monday through Friday from 8am to 5pm.

The **Kodiak National Wildlife Refuge Visitor Center,** 402 Center St. (☎ 888/592-6942 or 907/487-2626; www.kodiakwildliferefuge.org), is across from the ferry terminal at Mission Road. The center provides information on a 1.9-million-acre refuge, home of the famous Kodiak brown bear, that covers two-thirds of Kodiak Island. It exhibits a complete gray whale skeleton and three full-size replicas of Kodiak brown bears. Hours in summer are daily 9am to 5pm, the balance of the year Tuesday through Saturday only. There are nine remote public-use cabins around the refuge, reachable by chartered plane. Permits are $45 a night. Reserve up to 6 months ahead through www.recreation.gov.

ORIENTATION   The Kodiak Archipelago contains Kodiak, Shuyak, and Afognak islands and many other, smaller islands; the city of Kodiak is on a narrow point on the northeast side of Kodiak Island. There are five Native villages on other parts of the island and a sixth on a nearby island. The airport and the nation's largest Coast Guard base are several miles southwest of town on **Rezanof Drive,** which runs through town and comes out on the other side. The center of Kodiak is a hopeless tangle of steep, narrow streets—you need the excellent map given away by the visitor center, but it's all walkable. The ferry dock is on **Marine Way,** and most of the in-town sights are right nearby. Several paved and gravel roads, totaling 100 miles, make wonderful exploring from Kodiak to deserted shorelines, gorgeous views, pastures, recreation areas, and salmon streams. The visitor guide contains a mile-by-mile guide to each drive.

GETTING AROUND   Several companies rent cars, including **Budget** (✆ **800/ 527-0700** or 907/487-2220; www.budget.com), which has offices at the airport and downtown. **Avis** is at the Kodiak airport (✆ **800/331-1212** or 907/487-2264; www.avis.com). Airport and ferry shuttles, as well as city tours beginning at $25 per person (reservations required), are available from Kodiak Lodging and Reservations (✆ **907/539-5346;** kodiak-guides@ iserv.net).

[FastFACTS] KODIAK

Banks   Several banks downtown have ATMs, including **Key Bank** and **Wells Fargo** on the mall at the waterfront.

Hospital   **Providence Kodiak Island Medical Center** is at 1915 E. Rezanof Dr. (✆ **907/486-3281**).

Internet Access   At **A. Holmes Johnson Memorial Library,** 319 Lower Mill Bay Rd. (✆ **907/486-8686**).

Police   Contact the **Kodiak Police Department** at ✆ **907/486-8000.**

Post Office   Next to the library, at 419 Lower Mill Bay Rd.

Taxes   **Sales tax** is 6% within city limits, and the **room tax** is 5% everywhere on the island; rooms are thus taxed 11% in Kodiak city, 5% elsewhere.

SPECIAL EVENTS   **Russian Orthodox Christmas,** January 7, includes the evening **Starring Ceremony.** A choir follows a parishioner carrying a star to sing at the homes of church members. **Whale Fest Kodiak** (✆ **907/539- 2266;** www.whalefestkodiak.com), over 2 weeks in late April and early May, marks the arrival of the entire population of gray whales as they migrate, as well as the presence of killer and humpback whales near Kodiak. The festival includes whale-watching excursions, natural history events, and community activities.

The 5-day **Kodiak Crab Festival** (✆ **907/486-5557**), over Memorial Day weekend (late May), is a big event, including a parade, a king crab feed, a carnival, many fun community events, the solemn blessing of the fleet, and a memorial service for fishermen and mariners lost at sea.

On Labor Day weekend (early Sept), the **Kodiak State Fair and Rodeo** has all kinds of small-town contests, music, and family entertainment, including bull riding, barrel racing, and a horse show. Call the visitor bureau for information.

The bureau also maintains an extensive community calendar online at **www.kodiak.org**.

Exploring the Town

The highlights downtown include the **Fishermen's Memorial,** near the harbormaster's office at the head of the St. Paul Harbor, where a soberingly long list of Kodiak fishermen who have lost their lives at sea is posted on plaques. The warship set in concrete on Mission Way is the ***Kodiak Star,*** the last World War II Liberty Ship built. It came here as a fish processor after the 1964 earthquake destroyed the canneries and is still in use. Along Shelikof Avenue, overlooking St. Paul Harbor, the **Kodiak Maritime Museum** has mounted 12 attractive and interesting signs explaining the differences among different kinds of fishing boats, North Pacific commercial fishing and geography, and other nautical topics. In the same area, stop in at **Kodiak Island Brewing Co.,** 338 Shelikof St. (www.kodiakbrewery.com), where Ben Millstein brews beer that's mostly organic and offers tours. You can buy a pint to drink on-site or get some for later; local restaurants serve it, too. The "Sarah Pale" T-shirt commemorates a brew named for Alaska's former governor. Nearly next door, the **B-and-B Bar** is the oldest licensed tavern in Alaska and a real commercial fishermen's bar. Don't be put off by the rough appearance; it's a friendly place.

Most of Kodiak's visitor attractions are near the ferry terminal, including the two museums listed below and the two visitor centers, operated by the town and by the Kodiak National Wildlife Refuge. A historic church is near there, too, at Kashevarof and Mission streets: the **Holy Resurrection Russian Orthodox Church,** which was founded in 1794, although the present building dates only from 1945, when the original building burned.

The survival suit contest at the Kodiak Crab Festival.

Alutiiq Museum.

Alutiiq Museum ★ This exceptional, professional museum, governed by Natives, documents and revitalizes Kodiak's Alutiiq culture, which Russian and American settlers virtually wiped out in the 19th and early 20th centuries. Besides teaching about Alutiiq culture with permanent and temporary exhibits, the museum manages its own archaeological digs, teaches Alutiiq arts and language, and manages collections of more than 250,000 artifacts, photographs, and recordings.

215 Mission Rd., Ste. 101. ℭ **907/486-7004.** www.alutiiqmuseum.org. Admission $5 adults, free for kids 15 and under. Summer Mon–Fri 9am–5pm, Sat 10am–5pm; winter Tues–Fri 9am–5pm, Sat 10:30am–4:30pm.

The Baranov Museum ★ The museum occupies the oldest Russian building of only four standing in North America, Alaska's oldest building of any kind. Alexander Baranof, who ruled Alaska as manager of the Russian American Company, built the log structure in 1808 as a magazine and storehouse for valuable sea otter pelts—the treasure that motivated the Russians' interest here—and also served as headquarters for the invasion he led across Alaska and the Pacific Northwest coast. The museum stands across from the ferry dock in grassy Sargent Park, overlooking the water, and is packed with Russian and early Native artifacts. The gift store is exceptional, selling antique Russian items and authentic Native crafts.

101 Marine Way. ℭ **907/486-5920.** www.baranovmuseum.org. Admission $5; free for children 12 and under. Summer Mon–Sat 10am–4pm; winter Tues–Sat 10am–3pm. Closed Feb.

Getting Outside

RECREATION AREAS

Four miles north of downtown on Rezanof Drive, the **Fort Abercrombie State Historical Park** encompasses World War II ruins set on coastal cliffs amid huge trees adjacent to beaches, a swimming lake, and the remains of World War II–era gun emplacements and bunkers. A group of local World War II buffs displays war artifacts in the **Kodiak Military History Museum** (ℭ **907/486-7015;** www.kadiak.org), a former ammunition bunker at Miller Point. Open May to mid-Sept Friday to Monday 1 to 4pm. A wonderful 13-site campground sits atop the cliffs among the towering Sitka spruce trees and ruins. Camping is $15. The **Alaska Division of State Parks,** Kodiak District Office, 1400 Abercrombie Dr.,

Fort Abercrombie State Historical Park.

Kodiak, AK 99615 (☏ **907/486-6339;** fax 907/486-3320; www.alaskastate parks.org, click on "Individual Parks," then "Kodiak Islands"), maintains an office here where you can ask a question and possibly pick up a walking-tour brochure. Most summer days, a naturalist guides nature and beach walks. Or investigate the tide pools on your own, picking up an identification guide at the park's natural history bookstore.

The **Buskin River State Recreation Site,** 4 miles south of town off Rezanof Drive, near the Fish and Wildlife Service headquarters, has 15 campsites, a hiking trail, and access to fishing. Camping is $15.

OUTDOOR ACTIVITIES

BROWN BEAR VIEWING To count on seeing Kodiak's famous bears, you need to get out on a plane or boat and visit at the right time of year. The easiest way is a Kodiak-based floatplane; expect to pay around $475 per person, with a two- or three-person minimum for a guided half-day trip. Landing on the water, you don rubber boots (provided) and walk up to 30 minutes to get to where bears congregate. In early July to early August, depending on salmon runs, flights land on Frazer Lake for viewing at Frazer fish pass. A .75-mile walk on a dirt lane leads to the viewing area. The Kodiak National Wildlife Refuge (☏ **888/408-3514** or 907/487-2600; kodiak.fws.gov; see "Visitor Information," above) controls the viewing area. Flights also sometimes visit Ayakulik and Karluk rivers when fish are present. At any of these sites, binoculars and telephoto camera lenses are essential. Bears congregate only when salmon are running, so the timing of your visit is critical. From early July to mid-August, you're almost certain of seeing bears fishing in streams on Kodiak, sometimes in large numbers; at times, you can even drive to rivers where bears are feeding. Contact the refuge for more information on timing and bear activity.

When fish aren't running on Kodiak, such as in June or after mid-August, air services concentrate on flights to the east coast of the Alaska Peninsula, often in Katmai National Park, to watch bears digging clams from the tidal flats and eating grass and greens on the coastal meadows or catching fish in August. It's interesting and the flight is spectacular, but the viewing may be from a greater distance than on the streams. Generally, the flight services charge their standard bear-viewing seat rate regardless of how far they have to fly to find bears; if you charter, it may cost much more, but you will have freedom to determine where the plane goes, for added sightseeing. Several small flight services offer bear viewing, including **Sea Hawk Air** (☎ **800/770-4295** or 907/486-8282; www.seahawkair.com), **Island Air** (☎ **800/478-6196;** www.kodiakislandair.com), or **Andrew Airways** (☎ **907/487-2566;** www.andrewairways.com).

If a bear-viewing day trip is the whole reason you're going to Kodiak, compare your options. You can go directly from Anchorage (see chapter 6) or go to Katmai National Park to see bears up close (p. 476).

For additional money, you can see more of Kodiak's bears on a longer outing: A flight service can leave you at a lodge for an extended stay in bear habitat. Check the visitor center for a referral. Harry and Brigid Dodge host small groups at their rustic, solar-powered Aleut Island Lodge in Uyak Bay, taking an environmentally sensitive approach while spending the time to know the bears and their habitat. The business is called **Kodiak Treks** (☎ **907/487-2122;** www.kodiaktreks.com). Rates are $350 per person per night, double, with a 3-night minimum. Besides meals and bear viewing, the rate includes activities such as kayaking and fishing, but not the cost of getting there (about $350 per person round-trip from Kodiak).

Here are a couple of other Kodiak Island lodges with good reputations. **Munsey's Bear Camp,** in Uyak Bay (☎ **907/847-2203;** www.munseys bearcamp.com), has been in operation since 1956 and takes only six guests at a time. A 5-day stay is around $2,200 per person, plus a $350-per-person flight to get there. **Zachar Bay Lodge** (☎ **800/693-2333;** www.zachar bay.com) offers excellent bear viewing, but has an emphasis on fishing. A 2-night stay, including the flight across the island to get to the lodge, is $1,890 per person and up for longer stays.

FISHING The roads leading from Kodiak reach six good-size rivers with productive fishing for salmon and Dolly Varden char. At times, you can drive to

A young brown bear.

places with fishing pressure as light as at some fly-in locations on the mainland. Going beyond the road network puts you on some of the best and least-used fishing opportunities in Alaska. The visitor center provides a list of where to fish and the names and addresses of guides for remote fishing. You can also seek advice and regulations from the **Alaska Department of Fish and Game,** 211 Mission Rd., Kodiak, AK 99615 (© **907/486-1880;** www.alaska. gov/adfg; click on "Sport Fish," then on the Southcentral region, then on "Kodiak/Aleutians"). To fish the remote areas, you'll need to charter a plane, going for a day or staying at a remote public-use cabin or wilderness lodge.

About 65 boats are available in the boat harbors for ocean fishing. An advantage of coming to Kodiak is that it puts you near rich halibut and rock-fish grounds—you don't have to take a long boat ride for excellent fishing. Angling for silvers is good in August, and increasingly anglers troll for king salmon through the summer and fall, although success rates are hard to predict. Check with the visitor center for a referral.

HIKING & BIRD-WATCHING There are good dayhikes in Kodiak, some starting from downtown. The local Audubon Society publishes the *Kodiak Hiking & Birding Guide* that you can pick up at the visitor center. Audubon's guided hikes go to a different place every Saturday and Sunday of the summer, meeting at the visitor center parking lot at 9:30am for carpooling. The hikes range from easy walks on groomed trails to steep climbs up local mountains. In any case, you'll meet friendly locals enthusiastic about Kodiak's outdoors. Check http://kodiakaudubon for the latest hiking schedule.

SEA KAYAKING The Kodiak Archipelago, with its many folded, rocky shorelines and abundant marine life, is a perfect place for sea kayaking. Kayaks were invented by Natives here and on the Aleutian Islands to the west. For beginners, it is best to start with a day trip, and the waters around the town of Kodiak are lovely for such a paddle. Several operators can arrange an outing, although most concentrate on more ambitious trips. **Alaskan Wilderness Adventures** offers a variety of outings (© **907/487-2397;** www.kodiakswildside.com). Expect to pay $140 per person for a half-day, $220 for a full day.

Shuyak Island State Park, 54 miles north of Kodiak, is famous for sea-kayaking expeditions. The park is a honeycomb of islands and narrow passages in virgin Sitka spruce coastal forest. The Division of State Parks (see addresses under "Recreation Areas," above) distributes a free kayaking guide with route descriptions and maintains four public-use cabins, which rent for $75 a night in the summer season. These cabins can be quite hard to get in August. See "State Parks Cabin Reservations," in chapter 7.

Where to Stay

Kodiak has more than 30 B&Bs. Beyond the roads, some of Alaska's best wilderness lodges are on Kodiak Island in remote areas and near Native villages. The visitor center posts links to many B&Bs and lodges on its website at **www. kodiak.org**, or you can call Kodiak Lodging and Reservations (© **907/539-5346**) for information about a variety of short-term and long-term options.

Recently opened is the **Kodiak Island Hostel and Laundry** (www.kodiak islandhostel.com; © **907/486-0373**). Proprietor Rhonda Maker offers sparkling clean rooms with a variety of bed configurations for $30 and up per night.

A Smiling Bear Bed & Breakfast, near Fort Abercrombie (www.asmiling bear.com; © **907/481-6390**), has suites with Jacuzzis and serves gourmet breakfasts for $150 to $175 double in the high season. The couple that offers the Galley Gourmet dinner cruise (below) also operates the well-appointed **Cliff House Bed and Breakfast,** with four rooms from $125 to $150 double. It's on a quiet street with ocean views within walking distance of downtown.

Best Western Kodiak Inn ★   This is the best hotel in downtown Kodiak, with attractive rooms perched on the hill overlooking the boat harbor, right in the center of things. The wooden building is tall, full, and somewhat mazelike; the elevator goes only to the second floor. Rooms with oak vary in size and view, but all are acceptable standard units with good amenities, including pillow-top beds and high-definition TVs with DVD players. On our last visit, some rooms had been recently renewed, while others were a bit worn.

The **Chart Room** restaurant, specializing in seafood and with an interesting view of the harbors and Near Island Channel, serves three meals a day and is a good choice for a nice dinner out. The numerous entrees—steak, chops, seafood, chicken, and vegetarian—are in the $15-to-$40 range. The hall outside the restaurant and bar is almost a museum, with dozens of photographs showing the devastation of downtown by the 1964 tsunami.

236 W. Rezanof Dr., Kodiak, AK 99615. www.kodiakinn.com. ☎ **888/563-4254** or 907/486-5712. Fax 907/486-3430. 81 units. High season $170–$260 double; low season $99–$170. Extra person 18 and older $15. Rates include continental breakfast. AE, DC, DISC, MC, V. **Amenities:** Restaurant; bar; free airport transfers; outdoor Jacuzzi. *In room:* TV/DVD, fridge, hair dryer, microwave, Wi-Fi.

Comfort Inn Kodiak ★   A 50-room hotel, facing the airport parking on one side and the Buskin River on the other, offers some of the area's best standard accommodations. Rooms are up-to-date and are equipped with many amenities; suites are simply larger rooms. The location is 5 miles from Kodiak's downtown or historic sites, but that won't matter much if you rent a car. Those planning remote outdoor activities may prefer it for the close access to air services. A restaurant on-site serves lunch and dinner daily, with excellent seafood dinners in the evening in a price range of $18 to $50.

1395 Airport Way, Kodiak, AK 99615. www.choicehotels.com/hotel/ak025. ☎ **800/544-2202** or 907/487-2700. 50 units. High season $180–$260 double, $227 suite; low season $110–$150 double, $129 suite. Extra person 18 and older $15. Rates include continental breakfast. AE, DC, DISC, MC, V. **Amenities:** Restaurant; bar; exercise room. *In room:* TV, fridge, hair dryer, microwave, Wi-Fi.

Kodiak Russian River Lodge ★   This B&B, 12 miles south of town on Women's Bay, reflects Kodiak's burly fishing culture and is a perfect place for anglers. The host, Gus Gustafson, a former Bering Sea crab fisherman, often regales guests with stories of high-sea adventures. Bedrooms are around a second-floor common area in a three-story house. A huge deck with grills is on the third floor, along with another common area with TVs, a billiards table, and a small bar with local beer on tap. Alaskan art decorates the rooms and halls. The fish-cleaning and -freezing area on the ground floor has commercial-grade equipment. Gus offers free shuttle service to and from the ferry terminal downtown or the airport.

11322 S. Russian Creek Rd., Kodiak, AK 99615. www.kodiakrussianriverlodge.com. ☎ **907/487-4430.** Fax 907/487-2327. 5 units. High season $120–$165 double, $260 suite; low season $80–$130 double, $200 suite. Extra person 16 and older $15. Rates include continental breakfast. AE, MC, V. **Amenities:** Free airport and ferry transfers; fish-processing facility; guest kitchen. *In room:* TV, no phone, Wi-Fi.

Where to Eat

Besides the hotel restaurants listed above at the Best Western Kodiak Inn, Kodiak has several restaurants catering to locals. The best restaurant in town is **Mill Bay Coffee & Pastries,** 3833 Rezanof Dr. (© **907/486-4411;** www.millbaycoffee. com), near Fort Abercrombie, about 3 miles out of downtown. Award-winning, Paris-trained chef Joel Chenet produces wonderful pastries and, for lunch, brilliant combinations of local seafood and international seasonings to inexpensive sandwiches. The Kodiak sea burger is made of salmon, crab, shrimp, and cream cheese, among other ingredients, and costs $13. The comfortable, casual dining room, managed by Chenet's wife, Martine, is a local hub and has Wi-Fi.

For a special dining experience, Marty and Marion Owen serve dinner for six on their 42-foot yacht, the *Sea Breeze* (© **907/486-5079;** www.kodiak-alaska-dinner-cruises.com). The meals are usually elaborate seafood creations. The evening starts at 6pm with a 60-minute cruise among the picturesque islands near Kodiak's harbor, where guests may see puffins, sea lions, and whales. Dinner is served at anchor in a quiet lagoon, and you're back at the dock at 9:30pm. The price is $140 per person. The couple offers day-long wildlife-watching cruises, too.

Henry's Great Alaskan Restaurant, 512 Marine Way (© **907/486-8844;** www.henrysalaska.com), on the waterfront mall, is a smoke-free bar and grill where you'll meet many commercial fishermen and other locals. The menu includes daily specials, local seafood, and good halibut sandwiches, as well as steaks, pasta, and such. The smoked salmon chowder is excellent.

The **Old Power House Restaurant,** 516 E. Marine Way (© **907/481-1088**), sits on the edge of downtown with a dining room and deck overlooking the Near Island Channel. Primarily a sushi restaurant housed in a historic electric powerhouse, this eatery also excels at seafood and steaks. The salmon with miso butter should not be missed. Sushi is available a la carte, or in combinations with soup or salad from between $15 and $25.

KATMAI NATIONAL PARK

Most of the land of the Alaska Peninsula, pointing out to the Aleutian Archipelago, is federally protected as "wilderness" or "refuge," centering on Katmai National Park. The park, pronounced *"cat-*my," lies just west of Kodiak Island, across the storm-infested Shelikof Strait. Bear and salmon are the main attractions.

Brooks Camp, with a campground and lodge within Katmai, is probably the most comfortable place for foolproof bear viewing in Alaska during peak season. Bears congregate thickly at the falls on the Brooks River when red salmon try to pass up the falls at the beginning of July (more on the seasons later, under "Exploring the Park," below). At times, you can sit back on a deck and watch 900-pound brown bears walk by, going about their business of devouring the fish that contribute to their awesome size. (A brown bear is the genetic twin of the grizzly, but generally larger due to its coastal diet of salmon.)

Staying the night will require you to reserve a place in the 16-space campground the previous winter or stay in the pricey lodge, where rooms can book up more than a year ahead for the bear season. You can go for a day trip with less planning if you can stand to pay around $650 round-trip airfare from Anchorage for 2 or 3 hours at the camp (this information is covered in "Getting There," below). Bear viewing on the Katmai Coast is covered in the Kodiak section

Novarupta.

(p. 472), where flight services offer trips. If you're comparing, also look at the flights described in "Getting Around" (p. 466).

Katmai was set aside in 1918 for reasons unrelated to bears. The area had exploded into world consciousness in 1912 with the most destructive volcanic eruption to shake the Earth in 3,400 years. When Katmai's Novarupta blew, it released 10 times more energy than the Mount St. Helens eruption of 1980 and displaced twice as much matter as 1883's Krakatoa. The **Valley of Ten Thousand Smokes,** the vast wasteland created by the blast, belched steam for decades after. Today Novarupta is dormant and the steam is gone, but the area is still a barren moonscape, making a fascinating day tour or hiking trip.

Essentials

GETTING THERE   Most people fly to Katmai from Anchorage by way of the village of **King Salmon,** which lies just west of the park. **Alaska Airlines** (© 800/252-7522; www.alaskaair.com) flies to King Salmon daily in the summer, charging around $450 round-trip.

Air taxis carry visitors the last leg from King Salmon to **Brooks Camp** for a fare of around $180 round-trip. **Katmai Air,** operated by park concessionaire Katmailand (© 800/544-0551 or 907/243-5448; www.katmaiair.com), offers these flights, with round-trip airfare packages from Anchorage that save some money and simplify planning, $629 for a day trip.

As an alternative to Brooks Camp, more and more visitors are exploring the supremely rugged wilderness on the east side of the park from the beaches along **Shelikof Strait.** Air-taxi operators make drop-offs and provide bear-viewing day trips from Homer or Kodiak (see the Kodiak section of this chapter, earlier, or see the Homer section in chapter 7). In a park with more than 2,000 resident brown bears (the world's largest protected population), it's easy for pilots to find them digging clams on the tidal marshes, then land on floats for a good look.

RESERVATIONS & FEES   No entry fee or permit applies for day trips to Katmai, but once you're there, you may have to sign up for an hour on the bear-viewing platforms (see below). Camping costs $5 per person, per night with a $10 entrance fee. Campground capacity is allocated by person, not by site, and the limit of 60 people per night is far lower than the many visitors who want to stay during the bear season in July. The crowds are smaller in September, but the bears are not quite as numerous. Camping reservations become available for the entire summer as early as January 5, but the exact day changes each year; if you want a spot, check for the date and follow up the moment reservations open. To reserve, call or log on to the **National Recreation Reservation Service** (☎ **877/444-6777** or 518/885-3639; www.recreation.gov).

VISITOR INFORMATION   For advance planning, contact **Katmai National Park Headquarters** at P.O. Box 7, King Salmon, AK 99613 (☎ **907/246-3305;** www.nps.gov/katm). At Brooks Camp, the Park Service has a center where all visitors are required to attend a 20-minute orientation called "The Brooks Camp School of Bear Etiquette," designed to train visitors (not bears) and keep them out of trouble. In Anchorage, you can get information at the **Alaska Public Lands Information Center,** 4th Avenue and F Street (☎ **907/271-2737;** see the complete listing in chapter 6). The King Salmon **Visitor Center** is next door to the airport (☎ **907/246-4250**), staffed jointly by the U.S. Fish and Wildlife Service, National Park Service, and Alaska Geographic, a nonprofit book publisher. It's open 8am to 5pm daily in the high season, Monday through Saturday in winter.

GETTING AROUND   Once you've made it to Brooks Camp, a **bus** carries visitors to the Valley of Ten Thousand Smokes, 23 miles by gravel road from the camp. The park concessionaire, **Katmailand,** charges $88 per person round-trip for the all-day guided excursion, plus $8 more for lunch. A ranger leads a walk down into the valley. One-way transfers for hikers are $51.

[Fast FACTS] KATMAI & REGION

Bank   **Wells Fargo,** with an ATM, is in the King Salmon Mall adjacent to the airport on the Peninsula Highway in King Salmon.

Hospital   The **Camai Clinic,** in Naknek (☎ **907/246-6155**), is open during normal business hours; calls to the number go to emergency dispatchers after hours.

Police   In **King Salmon,** call 911 in an emergency, or call ☎ **907/246-4222;** elsewhere, call **Alaska State Troopers** at ☎ **907/246-3346** or 246-3464. There are no phones or cellular service out in the park.

Shopping   The park is remote, and other wild lands in the region are

without businesses other than remote lodges, such as Brooks Camp. King Salmon is the last stop for basic supplies or groceries. This is where you must buy fuel for a camp stove, matches, bear spray, or other needs you cannot carry on the jet from Anchorage.

Exploring the Park

Katmai's famous bear viewing occurs at **Brooks Camp,** where the bears congregate near the Brooks River to catch salmon. Viewing peaks in early July but can begin in late June and last through July, with a smaller congregation in September. The summer fish run is when you're assured of seeing bears from the elevated platforms near the Brooks River falls, half a mile from Brooks Camp, even

Bear viewing at Brooks Camp.

on a day trip. Forty to 60 bears feed here. Indeed, bears are seen all along the trail to the falls and elsewhere—the falls are just the most concentrated spot. Rangers don't guide visitors but are on hand to manage the foot traffic. The platforms allow a good view of the bears and just enough separation. The Park Service recommends that people with mobility problems avoid this trail when bears are present. Considering the expense and potential difficulty, we'd advise those with trouble getting around to choose another venue for bear viewing. Due to the popularity of the experience, there may be a 1-hour limit on the falls platform during the peak season, although the limit is lifted when the platform is below its capacity. After your turn is up, you can sign up on a waiting list to get another chance. The falls platform and trail are closed 10pm to 7am. In September, when the smaller group of bears gathers, they group near the mouth of the river, not the falls, and crowding is less of an issue. Outside of these salmon runs, there are better places to see bears, so if that's your goal, don't spend the money to come here. Bears feed all summer on clams on Katmai's Pacific coast. See "Getting There," above.

The Brooks Camp area has a small Park Service campground, visitor center, and lodge, located where the Brooks River flows into Naknek Lake. When the area was first developed for fishing in the 1950s, the camp was built in the middle of a major bear corridor, where it never would be allowed today, creating a unique opportunity to stay right in some of the most concentrated bear habitat on the globe. The most comfortable way is to stay at the **Brooks Lodge,** operated by Katmailand (✆ **800/544-0551** or 907/243-5448; www.brookslodge. com). The lodge has 16 units, with private bathrooms with shower stalls. To save money, book the lodge rooms as packages with air travel from Anchorage. The least expensive, 1-night visit is $949 per person, double occupancy, meals not included; 3 nights is $1,608. A double room without airfare is $652. Peak dates (when the bears are concentrated) book up 12 months out or earlier; for your choice, call as soon as the reservation system opens 18 months ahead, January of the year before the visit. Three buffet-style meals are served daily for guests and visitors who aren't staying in the lodge. Breakfast is $15, lunch $20, and dinner

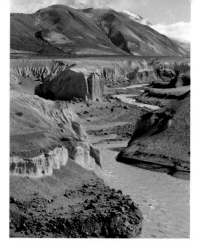
Valley of Ten Thousand Smokes.

$35. For food, they take MasterCard and Visa at the lodge. Also at Brooks Camp, there's a small store, the Park Service visitor center, and a campground. See "Reservations & Fees," above, for info on campground reservations, which should be made 6 months in advance. The rangers require special precautions to keep bears away from campers.

The rivers and lakes of Katmai lure human anglers as well as ursine ones. Katmailand operates two lodges within the park other than Brooks Lodge for remote fishing, the **Kulik** and **Grosvenor lodges.** Check their website at www.katmailand.com for fishing details.

The Park Service also has a list of dozens of fishing, hiking, and air guides. There is no central clearinghouse for remote fishing, but you can find and book a good place through an agency such as **Sport Fishing Alaska,** 9310 Shorecrest Dr., Anchorage, AK 99502 (✆ **888/552-8674** or 907/344-8674; www.alaska tripplanners.com), full review on p. 512.

Backcountry hiking in Katmai means crossing a wilderness without trails, including the hazards of river crossings. Only experienced backpackers should plan extended trips. The Park Service asks hikers to obtain a voluntary permit for backcountry travel, thereby clueing them in to your plans in case you need to be rescued. You are required to store food and items with odors in bear-resistant containers, which you can check out from the park. Anyone can walk for the day without such precautions in the desolate **Valley of Ten Thousand Smokes.** This 40-square-mile plain remains a moonscape almost a century after the titanic volcanic blast that buried it, little changed except that the famous plumes of smoke are gone and rivers have sliced through the debris in places to create narrow, white-walled canyons. Although it looks like a desert and is subject to dust storms, rain is common and temperatures rarely go higher than 65°F (18°C). Katmailand operates a tour bus from Brooks Camp, mentioned above under "Getting Around." The visitors on those tours usually stay on a short trail on the valley's rim, where a visitor center is located, but a 3-mile round-trip hike descends 800 feet to the valley floor, where you can get a better look at the ash that creates the bizarre landforms here.

UNALASKA & DUTCH HARBOR: ALEUTIAN BOOMTOWN

With the protected port of Dutch Harbor, in a ferocious ocean habitat rich in crab and bottom fish, Unalaska has grown from a tiny, forgotten Native village to a land with a greater volume of fish than any other port in the nation. The pattern of growth followed the form of the early gold rushes. There was a wild, lawless time in the 1970s when crab fishermen got rich quick and partied like Old West cowboys. Then the overfished crab stocks crashed, only to be replaced, starting

10

Unalaska & Dutch Harbor: Aleutian Boomtown

THE BUSH

in the mid-1980s, by an even bigger boom, when waters within 200 miles of the U.S. shore were rid of foreign vessels and American bottom fishing took off. Big factory ships began unloading here, and huge fish plants were built on flat ground chipped from the rock.

The process of the town's domestication had long ago taken hold when Hollywood discovered the fishery with the hit cable TV program *Deadliest Catch*. As the program shows, crabbing in these waters is dangerous and lucrative—but it's far safer, tamer, and less profitable today than in the days when fishermen died by the dozens every year or came home rich men. The legendary rough bars closed years ago. As a visitor, it can be fun to visit the docks and bars, where it's easy enough to strike up a conversation with a fisherman about his adventures and close calls.

Is a hike over the tundra and a beer with a rugged fisherman enough to justify the $1,000 plane fare? Unless you're looking for the "real," rugged Alaska, maybe not. Unalaska has less than a full day of historic sightseeing; beyond that, you need some motivation. The fishing grounds are rich in large halibut, and it is possible to find someone to take you out; likewise, the countryside offers bird-watching opportunities you likely haven't experienced before, if you go find them.

Unalaska's history is Alaska's longest. The value of a good port out in the middle of the ocean was recognized from the beginning by the Aleuts. In 1759, the Russians began trading here and brutally massacred the Aleuts to subjugate them as slaves. The Russians built a permanent settlement here in 1792, their first in Alaska. Unalaska also was a key refueling stop for steamers carrying gold rush stampeders to Nome a century ago, which brought an epidemic that killed a third of the indigenous population.

In 1940, Dutch Harbor—the seaport on Amaknak Island associated with the town and island of Unalaska—was taken over by the U.S. Navy to defend against Japanese attack. That attack came: In June 1942, Japanese planes bombed Unalaska, killing 43. The Aleut people were removed from the islands for the duration of the war and interred in inadequate housing in Southeast Alaska, where many died of disease. The military pulled out in 1947, but the remains of their defenses are interesting to explore, part of a unique unit of the national park system. Thanks to a 1971 act of Congress settling Native claims, the Aleut-owned Ounalashka Corporation owns much of the land around town. But the National Park Service protects and interprets the World War II historic sites on Native-owned land.

Essentials

GETTING THERE   Alaska Airlines (✆ **800/252-7522;** www.alaskaair.com) serves Dutch Harbor with turboprops operated by Pen Air. The use of the smaller planes allows flights to land on the nearby Alaska Peninsula and wait for the weather to clear when a squall passes over the Dutch Harbor airport. The flight from Anchorage takes 3 hours, and a ticket is $1,000 or more round-trip. You can save substantially if you combine that flight leg with your round-trip ticket to Alaska, making Dutch Harbor your final destination and Anchorage a stopover. Combining this excursion on your larger ticket also means the airline will rearrange your other flights without charge if you get stuck by weather at the Dutch Harbor airport, a common occurrence.

The **Alaska Marine Highway System** ferry *Tustumena* (✆ **800/642-0066;** www.ferryalaska.com) makes a 4-day trip from Homer to Dutch

Harbor just a handful of times a year, from April to October, stopping in Kodiak and the villages along the way. The one-way passenger fare is about $351, and a two-berth outside (with windows) cabin with shared facilities is $311 more. Travelers who have done this open-sea adventure have given us glowing reports of incomparable scenery and wonderful encounters with the people of the villages along the way, best of all if camping on the solarium deck (with duct tape to hold down the tent). Since the ship is in the open ocean, seasickness is a real concern; read the advice on p. 524. Unless you want to spend only 7 hours in Unalaska and then make the long return trip, you'll need to fly back.

VISITOR INFORMATION   The **Unalaska/Port of Dutch Harbor Convention and Visitors Bureau,** P.O. Box 545, Unalaska, AK 99685 (🕿 **877/581-2612** or 907/581-2612; www.unalaska.info), is at 5th Street and Broadway.

A visitor center for the **Aleutian WWII National Historic Area** (🕿 **907/581-9944;** www.nps.gov/aleu) occupies a war-era building at the airport but is open only short hours. The historic area encompasses World War II ruins on the island that stand on Native-owned lands. The National Park Service helped fund the improvements and interprets the history; however, to hike to the main area of ruins, on Ulatka Head, you will need to buy a permit from the Ounalashka Corporation, which you can get here or at the corporate offices (see "Exploring the Town," below). Admission to the center is $5, and it's open Thursday through Saturday 11am to 5pm.

GETTING AROUND   The main historic part of town is a tiny street grid on a narrow peninsula facing Iliuliuk Bay. The **Bridge to the Other Side** (as everyone knows it) leads to Amaknak Island, the site of the airport, the Grand Aleutian Hotel, the fishing industrial area of Dutch Harbor, and the World War II ruins on Ulatka Head. Traveling down the road in the other direction leads a little way up into the mountains, a starting point for some hikes.

Van taxis are the main way of getting around town for the hordes of fishermen, and the best way for most visitors. One company is **Blue Checker Taxi** (🕿 **907/581-2186**). You can rent a car from **BC Vehicle Rentals** (🕿 **907/581-6777**) or **North Port Car Rentals** (🕿 **907/581-3880**), both at the airport; however, there's little need for a rented vehicle other than access to remote hiking trails.

[FastFACTS] UNALASKA & DUTCH HARBOR

Bank   **Key Bank** is attached to Alaska Ship Supply and has an ATM, as does the Safeway grocery store.

Hospital   **Iliuliuk Family and Health Services**

(🕿 **907/581-1202**) is a clinic.

Internet Access   Free at the **public library** (🕿 **907/581-5060**).

Police   **Unalaska Department of Public**

Safety (🕿 **907/581-1233**) is just above the bridge on the Unalaska side.

Taxes   **Sales tax** is 3%; the total **tax on rooms** is 8%.

Holy Ascension Cathedral.

Exploring the Town

Unalaska's most significant historic site is the **Holy Ascension Cathedral.** Completed in 1896 on the site of churches that had stood since 1808, the white church with green onion-shaped domes contains 697 icons, artifacts, and artworks, a significant collection that has been continuously in use by the Aleut congregation. The congregation was founded by Father Ivan Veniaminov, who translated the Gospel into Aleut and has been canonized as St. Innocent. Besides his many other accomplishments, he recorded the environmental devastation of Russian fur hunting in this region in the 19th century. A $1.3-million restoration saved the church from collapse in 1996. It is a dignified, geometric counterpoint to the soft edge of sparkling Iliuliuk Bay and easy to find. Vespers services are Saturday at 6:30pm; Sunday services are 8:30am in the summer, 9:30am in the winter.

The professionally curated **Museum of the Aleutians,** next door to the Ounalashka Corporation on Margaret Bay on the Amaknak Island side of town (© **907/581-5150;** www.aleutians.org), contains some of the region's best artifacts, including some from North America's oldest coastal sites on Umnak and Unalaska islands. Exhibits also cover the region's 9,000-year history, including material on World War II in the Aleutians. Temporary exhibits have focused on topics ranging from fishery history to underwater photography. Admission is $5. It's open summer Tuesday through Saturday from 9am to 5pm, Sunday from noon to 5pm; in winter, it's open Tuesday through Saturday from 11am to 5pm.

There are several **World War II military ruins** around town, including some that are still in use, such as the submarine dry dock that today fixes fishing boats. Trails lead over the island to other sites included in the Aleutian World War II National Historic Area, which preserves this evidence of war on American soil and helps tell the story of the Native people who were interred by both the Japanese and Americans during the war (see "The Aleutians: The Quiet After War," below). Bunker Hill is a quick walk, off Henry Swanson Drive next to the bridge. The main area of ruins requires a climb to Ulatka Head, site of U.S. Army

THE aleutians: THE QUIET AFTER WAR

Once thousands of men died for the rocky islands of the Aleutians. What began as a Japanese military diversion became a ferocious fight for honor, one of the worst of World War II's Pacific Theater. Yet when the fighting was done, most of the islands were abandoned and left uninhabited, littered with military ruins, for half a century. In recent decades, the tragedy has been officially recognized by lonely monuments and the National Park Service visitor center in Unalaska, but it has scarcely entered national consciousness.

The Japanese attacked the islands of **Kiska** and **Attu** at the start of the Pacific war to divert the main core of the American navy away from what became the Battle of Midway. But the Americans had intercepted and decoded Japanese transmissions and weren't fooled. Meanwhile, the Japanese had sent 24 ships, including two aircraft carriers, on a fool's errand to bomb the new American naval base at Dutch Harbor and occupy islands in the western Aleutians. Those ships could have tipped the balance at Midway, among the most important battles of the war. Instead, the Japanese met stiff antiaircraft fire in 2 days of bombing at Dutch Harbor; although 43 Americans were killed, the defensive function of the base was not greatly impaired.

The Japanese then took Kiska and Attu, meeting no resistance from 10 Americans staffing a weather station or from an Aleut village whose 43 inhabitants were all—even the children—sent to a prison camp in Japan to mine clay for the duration of the war. About half the prisoners survived to return to Alaska.

The Americans had their own plan to remove the Aleuts, but the idea of depopulating all the islands had been turned down. Now, with the Japanese attack, it was swiftly put into effect. All

the Aleuts were rounded up and put on ships. Their villages were burned or trashed by weather and vandalism. With little thought given to their living conditions, the Aleuts were interred in abandoned summer camps and similarly inadequate facilities in Southeast Alaska. Shunned by the local communities and without the basic necessities of life or proper sanitation, 10% died. The U.S. Fish and Wildlife Service took Aleut hunters to hunt furs as virtual slaves, much as the Russians had done 200 years before.

The Japanese and American military fared not much better on their new real estate. Although the Aleutians quickly became irrelevant to the rest of the war, significant resources were committed to a largely futile air and sea battle in the fog and endless storms. Flying at all was difficult and extremely dangerous, and finding the enemy in the fog over vast distances close to impossible. The Americans couldn't spare a land invasion force at first and had to rely on bombing Kiska and Attu to punish the Japanese and try to deter a further advance up the chain. To that end, they built a large base at Adak, among others, so shorter-range fighter escorts could accompany the bombers. Construction in the spongy tundra was

Fort Schwatka, about an hour's hike from the airport. The fort once had more than 100 buildings. Many remain, including the best-preserved gun mounts and lookouts of all the nation's coastal defenses from the war. Besides, it's a spectacular site where you can see ships returning. You will first need a permit from the Native-owned Ounalashka Corporation (See "Hiking," below).

difficult in any case, made more so by the length of supply lines.

The Japanese high command never had any intention of advancing up the chain, but also saw no reason to abandon their new Kiska air base when it was causing the Americans to exert such effort. The Japanese concentrated on fortifying Kiska, which became a honeycomb of underground bunkers and heavy antiaircraft guns and withstood constant bombing raids by the Americans.

Finally, on May 11, 1943, almost a year after the Japanese took the islands, Americans landed on Attu and a brutal 18-day battle for the rugged island began. The Japanese were massively outnumbered but heavily dug in. Finally, with only 800 soldiers left from an original force of 2,600, the Japanese mounted a suicidal banzai attack. Only 28 were taken prisoner—the rest were killed in battle or committed suicide. The Americans lost 549, 1,148 were wounded, and 2,132 were injured by severe cold, disease, accident, mental breakdown, or other causes. In the end, it was the second-most-costly island battle in the Pacific, after Iwo Jima.

The battle for Kiska was less dramatic. The Japanese withdrew under cover of fog. After a massive bombardment of the empty island and the rallying of heavy reinforcements, the Americans landed to find that no one was there. Still, 105 American soldiers died in the landing in accidents and fire from their own forces.

After the Aleutian battle was over, American forces in Alaska declined drastically, but a new era had arrived. Military spending was the biggest economic boom the territory had ever seen, connecting it by a new road to the Lower 48 and bringing precious year-round jobs.

The end of the war was bitter for the Aleuts. Returning to villages they had departed hastily 3 years before, they found homes and subsistence gear ruined and even historic Russian Orthodox churches and icons severely damaged. Many who had survived the terrible period of internment never returned. Most of the ancient villages never revived; bureaucrats managing the evacuation wiped them off the map as a cost-saving measure, relocating residents to larger villages such as Unalaska.

Awareness of this injustice began to resurface in the 1980s, and in 1988, Congress and President Reagan formally apologized to the Aleuts and paid compensation of $12,000 to each survivor, then about half the 900 who were evacuated. That act also helped fund restoration of the five historic churches, including the beautiful church in Unalaska, and construction of one replacement.

Today the Aleuts own their islands. It's fitting that the National Park Service's Aleutian World War II National Historic Area is their guest, on their land.

To learn more, see Brian Garfield's readable *The Thousand-Mile War: World War II in Alaska and the Aleutians* (University of Alaska Press).

That's about it for sightseeing in Unalaska, unless you take a walk in the port. The activity there is interesting for the size of the vessels and harvest and the incredible investment in buildings and equipment.

Getting Outside

BIRD-WATCHING   Flip through the crisp, unused pages of your bird book to find out what you may see in the Aleutians. Several rare bird species nest in the area, and Asian birds occasionally drop in as accidentals. The whiskered auklet and red-legged kittiwake are among the birds commonly found around Unalaska that you probably haven't seen. Birding will mostly be self-guided, but there is a tour operator in town offering historic and birding excursions: **Extra Mile Tours** (✆ **907/581-6171;** www.unalaskadutch harbortour.com). A 2-hour tour is $50 per person; a ferry/cruise ship special of $75 includes stops at local visitor attractions. For an offshore tour to the island's rich seabird colonies, contact the visitor center; at this writing, no one is regularly offering such trips.

FISHING   Unalaska is famous for huge **halibut.** In 1995, a local sport fisherman caught a 395-pound halibut from an 18-foot skiff within a half-mile of town; to kill the behemoth he had to beach it and beat it over the head with a rock. The next year, Fairbanks angler Jack Tragis landed the world's record halibut here, which weighed 459 pounds. If you're having trouble imagining a fish that big, drop by City Hall, where a replica hangs stuffed in the lobby. Unfortunately, few businesses exist that regularly offer fishing charters. Before deciding on a trip to the island, contact the convention and visitor bureau for a referral; you'll have to size up the skipper yourself before booking your charter.

HIKING   The island's green heather and rounded mountains of wildflowers are inviting for a walk. You can walk pretty much in any direction. Explore the abandoned World War II defenses or make a goal of a beach or one of the small peaks around the town. There are no bears and not many bugs, but there's great berry picking in late summer and beachcombing. The weather can be a threat, however, and fox holes can trip you up. Dress warmly, with rain gear; summer high temperatures rarely exceed 60°F (16°C). As always

Red-legged kittiwake.

An eagle among wildflowers.

in remote outdoor areas, leave word of where you're going and when you'll be back.

Here are a few of the many places to hike. Several good routes lead into the hills behind the houses in the valley on Unalaska Island (that will be enough directions for a cab to get you there). Follow the Ugadaga trail or the Peace of Mind trail off of Overland Drive to lovely Beaver Inlet. Another interesting destination is reached by walking a gravel road that runs behind the Russian Orthodox Church, past the landfill: It leads to the rocky beaches of Summer Bay and Morris Cove, and the opportunity to see feral horses.

Hikers beyond have to pay a fee to the **Ounalashka Corporation** (© **907/581-1276;** www.ounalashka.com), the Native village corporation that owns much of the land around town. A 1-day hiking permit is $6 per person or $10 per family; permits for longer periods are available, too. Buy permits from the historic area visitor center (p. 482) or the corporation's office at 400 Salmon Way, the building between the Grand Aleutian Hotel and the Museum of the Aleutians on Amaknak Island. The office is open Monday through Friday 8am to 5pm. The office also sells high-quality maps of local hiking trails, although some of the longer trails are more theoretical than real.

Where to Stay & Eat

The primary place for accommodations and food for most visitors is the Grand Aleutian Hotel, described below. There are also a variety of fast-food places and locals eateries, including a multi-ethnic restaurant at the airport serving those stranded by weather delays, and a not-so-fast place called Dutch Harbor Fast Food, near the Russian Orthodox church on Iliuliuk Bay.

One place meriting greater mention is **Harborview Bar and Grill,** at the edge of the Unisea Fish Processing Campus near the Museum of the Aleutians on Amaknak Island (© **907/581-7246**). Its a very casual spot to get a halibut sandwich, salad, quesadilla, or terrific fish tacos, with quick service and a large bar, which is where you go to dance or hear open-mic musical performances in the evening; it's open daily for lunch and very late at night. All meals are $12 to $15. Within the Harborview, **Harbor Sushi** (© **907/581-7190**) had a very good chef on our last visit producing some great combinations with local seafood. It's open every evening but Wednesday, 5 to 11pm; prices are $15 to $20.

Grand Aleutian Hotel ★★ The impressively sized Grand Aleutian is just minutes away from the island's rugged fishing, hiking, and bird-watching opportunities. The rooms resemble any in a chain hotel from the '90s, when the building was constructed, with floral patterns and pastel colors. They have TVs with cable, but the Internet connections (either Wi-Fi or wired) are painfully slow and cost $10 to use. Many rooms have good water views, and the lobby is grand, with a huge stone fireplace. There's a highly civilized, if sometimes noisy, lounge—not the rip-roaring Dutch Harbor bar of lore. As you walk outside into a driving gale, it's like teleporting from a big-city hotel back to an exposed rock out in the North Pacific.

The **Chart Room** restaurant, on the second floor, allows bird-watchers to see waterfowl in the bay while dining on steak, seafood, or pasta. The menu is Unalaska's most sophisticated, by far, and is supplemented by daily specials and an extensive wine list. Dinner entrees range from $18 to $65. The **Margaret Bay Cafe,** downstairs, also has a good view, with sandwiches, lunch buffet, and some lighter fare. It is open only for breakfast and lunch.

498 Salmon Way (P.O. Box 921169), Dutch Harbor, AK 99692. www.grandaleutian.com.
✆ **866/581-3844** or 907/581-3844. Fax 907/581-7150. 120 units. $164 double; $274 suite. Extra person $20. AE, DISC, MC, V. **Amenities:** 2 restaurants; 2 bars; free airport transfers; room service. *In room:* TV, hair dryer, Internet ($10).

THE PRIBILOF ISLANDS: BIRDER'S PARADISE

The Pribilof Islands of St. Paul and St. George sit out in the middle of the Bering Sea, due north of Unalaska, teeming with marine mammals and seabirds. Some 600,000 fur seals meet at the breeding rookeries in the summer, and two million birds of more than 270 species use the rocks. Bird-watchers visit St. Paul for one of the most exotic and productive birding and wildlife-viewing opportunities anywhere. It's best during the spring migration, from mid-May to mid-June, when great numbers of birds show up, including rare Asian accidental species; the fall migration comes in September to mid-October. You can count on making rare sightings any time during the summer. Indeed, the National Audubon Society's *Field Guide to North American Birds* calls this "perhaps the most spectacular seabird colony in the world."

Visitors interested in birding and wildlife generally come on tours, which are sold as a package with airfare, lodging, meals, and guiding by expert birders provided. With the guides' help and radio communication, your chances of seeing

Fur seals.

Abandoned elevated train.

exotic species are much enhanced. Visits are offered by Native-owned **St. Paul Island Tours** (✆ 877/ 424-5637; www.stpaultour.com). Check the website for birding news and information about the island. Packages from Anchorage start at $2,029 for a 2-night visit and operate from mid-May to mid-October. Travelers can choose to ride on a bus as a group or hike on their own. Permanent blinds are in place for watching birds and seals. Count on cool, damp, windy weather.

NOME: ARCTIC FRONTIER TOWN

The locals proclaim "There's No Place Like Nome," and they're right. From the outside, it may appear to be a mismatched collection of odd-shaped buildings piled up on the Norton Sound coast, many on stilts because of the permafrost, but Nome is more than the sum of its rag-tag parts. Nome is truly a state of mind, one of the few cities in Alaska that still resembles its earliest years. As you walk its streets, you can clearly relate to the early prospectors who stormed the same beaches looking for gold dust that passed through their fingers like sand.

It's been a century since the prospectors arrived, but Nome retains that frontier character especially in the entertainment downtown "district," where bars operate nonstop and local characters can be seen leading pet reindeer down the sidewalks.

More than a collection of characters, Nome is one of the few places that visitors can access the Arctic "bush" without resorting to expensive charters. There are more than 250 miles of roads leading into and out of Nome into the wilds of the Seward Peninsula. You never know what you will find outside of Nome, wildlife such as reindeer and muskox, and even the remains of an old steam engine that appears to have just stopped in the middle of the tundra one day.

Nome is also the center of a thriving trade in Iñupiaq arts and crafts, with many artists in the villages sending their work to Nome to be sold on consignment to visitors.

Nome was once part of the Alaska Airlines circle tour involving Fairbanks and Point Barrow, but large-scale tourism has fallen off in recent years. If you want to see both frontier and Native Alaska, Nome is a great place to start.

Muskoxen.

Essentials

GETTING THERE Flying is the only way to get to Nome. **Alaska Airlines** (📞 **800/252-7522;** www.alaskaair.com) flies 90 minutes by jet direct from Anchorage or with a brief hop from Kotzebue. Prices are around $500 round-trip. Many visitors come on escorted tour packages sold by **Alaska Airlines Vacations** (📞 **866/500-5511;** www.alaskaairalaska.com); a day-trip package costs around $575; staying overnight on the package costs around $665 per person, double occupancy.

All taxis operate according to a standard price schedule you can get from the visitor center. A ride to town from the airport is generally $5. There are three companies, including **Louie's Cab** (📞 **907/443-6000**).

VISITOR INFORMATION The **Nome Convention and Visitors Bureau,** 301 Front St. (P.O. Box 240), Nome, AK 99762 (📞 **907/443-6555;** www.visit nomealaska.com), provides maps and detailed information for diverse interests. The office is open daily June, July, and August from 7am to 7pm, and the balance of the year Monday through Friday 9am to 5pm.

The **Bering Land Bridge National Preserve Headquarters,** 214 Front St. (P.O. Box 220), Nome, AK 99762 (📞 **907/443-2522;** www.nps. gov/bela), is a good source of outdoors information from the rangers who staff a desk and are responsible for a rarely visited 2.7-million-acre national park unit, which covers much of the Seward Peninsula north of the Nome road system. Rangers offer a variety of programs all year, especially during the Iditarod finish in March. Their bird tours and ranger hikes are mentioned below.

Also check the *Nome Nugget* website, at **www.nomenugget.com**, a real window into the community.

GETTING AROUND The town is a street grid along the ocean. **Front Street** follows the sea wall, **1st Avenue** is a block back, and so on. A harbor is at the north end of town, and the gold-bearing beach is to the south. You can mostly walk to see this area. Three roads branch out from Nome. We've described them below, under "Venturing Beyond Town by Road." To get out on the roads, you need to take a tour or rent a car, or bring a bike with you.

Several local car-rental agencies operate in town; the visitor center maintains a list, with rates. **Stampede Car Rental,** 302 E. Front St. (📞 **800/354-4606** or 907/443-3838; www.aurorainnnome.com), charges $100 to $175 for SUVs and vans. The same people operate the Aurora Inn (see "Where to Stay," below).

[Fast FACTS] NOME

Bank **Wells Fargo,** with an ATM, is at 250 Front St.	**Internet Access** **Nome Public Library** is at 200 Front St. (📞 **907/443-6626**).	**Post Office** At Front Street and Federal Way.
Hospital **Norton Sound Regional** is at 5th Avenue and Bering Street (📞 **907/443-3311**).	**Police** At Bering Street and 4th Avenue (📞 **907/443-5262**).	**Taxes** The **sales tax** is 5%; the tax on **rooms** totals 6%.

SPECIAL EVENTS The biggest event of the year is the **Iditarod Trail Sled Dog Race** (© 907/376-5155; www.iditarod.com), a marathon of more than 1,000 miles that ends in Nome in mid-March. Sled-dog racers, world media, and international visitors descend on the town for a few days of madness, with lots of community events planned. The activities last most of the month; contact the Nome visitor center, or download the calendar from www.visitnomealaska.com. See p. 519 for information about the exciting option of volunteering for the race; see p. 33 for information on the emotional issue of the animal rights opposition to the sport.

One of the March Iditarod events, showcasing Nome's well-developed sense of humor, is the **Bering Sea Ice Golf Classic,** where six holes are set up on the sea ice. The pressure ridges constitute a bad lie. Various similarly silly events take place all year, including the **Polar Bear Swim** that happens around June 21 as part of the **Midnight Sun Festival.** The festival celebrates the summer solstice, when Nome gets more than 22 hours of direct sunlight. A parade, handmade raft race, folk festival, bank holdup, and other events headline the festival. Winners of the raft race get a honey bucket (known in some places as a chamber pot). For information on any event, contact the **Nome Convention and Visitors Bureau** (© 907/443-6555; www.visitnomealaska.com).

Exploring the Town

Most of Nome's original buildings were wiped out by fires or by storms off Norton Sound that tore across the beach and washed away major portions of the business district. A sea wall, completed in 1951, now protects the town. Among the few historic sites that survived are the gold rush–era Board of Trade Saloon, a church, and a bust of Roald Amundsen, who landed near Nome, in Teller, after crossing the North Pole from Norway in a dirigible in 1926. Below the library, at Front Street and Lanes Way, the small **Carrie M. McLain Memorial Museum** (© 907/443-6630) contains an exhibit on the town's gold rush. The museum is free and open summer Monday through Friday 10am to 5:30pm, Saturday 10am to 5pm, and Sunday 10am to 3pm, with closures for lunch. The rest of the year, expect Tuesday through Friday noon to 5:30pm.

In good weather, you can take a pleasant walk southeast of town along the **beach.** Small-time miners may be camped there, but the gold-bearing sand extends for miles more of solitary walking. You can buy a gold pan in town and try your luck, but the sand has been sifted for nearly 100 years, so don't expect to gather any significant amount of gold. The **Swanberg Dredge** you can see from here operated until the 1950s; a large dredge north of town worked into the mid-1990s. The 38 gold dredges that once operated on the Seward Peninsula crept across the tundra, creating their own ponds to float in as they went. The **cemetery,** with white wooden crosses on top of a little hill just out of town, also is worth a look.

If you're in the market for walrus ivory carvings and other **Iñupiaq arts and crafts,** you'll find low prices and a large selection on Front Street in Nome. A legendary collection for sale is in the barroom of the historic **Board of Trade Saloon** on Front Street. The **Arctic Trading Post** is more of a traditional gift shop and also has a good ivory collection, as does **Maruskiyas of Nome. Chukotka-Alaska,** at 514 Lomen St., is an importer of art and other goods from the Russian Far East. Alaska Native art you find in Nome is likely to be authentic, but still ask; see "Native Art: Finding the Real Thing" (p. 36). International visitors should see chapter 2 to find out about the difficulty of carrying ivory out of the United States.

Venturing Beyond Town by Road

The modest attractions downtown would hardly justify a trip to Nome, but the city's surroundings do. The roads provide unique access to a large stretch of the Seward Peninsula. Unlike other Arctic Bush areas, where someone has to take you into the wilderness, in Nome all you have to do is rent a car and go. There are few cars in Nome (they have to be flown in or shipped by barge), so you won't see many other vehicles on a huge expanse of spectacular territory, with wildlife-viewing opportunities as good as anywhere in the state.

You could see moose, reindeer, foxes, or bears, and nowhere else in the world do you have a better chance of seeing muskoxen from a car. Wildlife sightings are possible anywhere you drive, but check in with the visitor center or the **Alaska Department of Fish and Game,** at 103 East Front St., at the intersection of Steadman Street (ⓒ **907/443-2271**), to find out the best locales to see animals and call ⓒ 907/443-5796 for fishing information in the summer only. They can also give you guidance on fishing along the roads and a "Nome Roadside Fishing Guide," or download it from www.alaska.gov/adfg (click on "Sport Fisheries," then "Interior," then "Northwest"). Check "Getting Around," above, to find a mode of transportation.

The best option for seeing the nature accessible via Nome's roads may be to join a ranger-guided hike offered by the Bering Land Bridge National Preserve. Call ahead to check on current offerings (see "Visitor Information," above).

ROAD HIGHLIGHTS   None of the three roads radiating from Nome has services of any kind—just small Native villages, a few dwellings, and some reindeer herders—so you must be prepared and bring what you need with you, including insect repellent and a good spare tire. The visitor center provides a road guide. Here are some highlights:

The **Nome–Council road** heads 72 miles to the east, about half of that on the shoreline. It turns inland at the ghost town of Solomon, an old

Teller.

Bristle-thighed curlew.

mining town with an abandoned railroad train known locally as the Last Train to Nowhere. The engines were originally used on the New York City elevated lines in 1881, then were shipped to Alaska in 1903 to serve the miners along this line to Nome. This is a scenic spot for bird-watching, and fishing is good in the Solomon River, all along the road. Council, near the end of the road, has a couple of dozen families in the summer. A 3-foot-deep river separates the road from the village.

The **Nome–Taylor road,** also known as the Kougarok Road, runs north of town 85 miles from Nome over the tundra and through the Kigluaik Mountains, eventually petering out and becoming impassable. About 40 miles out, you reach lovely Salmon Lake, with a lakeshore campground with picnic tables, grills, and outhouses. A few miles farther, a road to the left leads to the 125°F (52°C) Pilgrim Hot Springs. Access is limited to the hot springs, so check with the visitor center before going.

The **Nome–Teller road** leads 73 miles to the village of Teller, which has 260 residents and a store. It's an opportunity to see an authentic Arctic Native village.

BIRD-WATCHING　Bird-watchers will make many discoveries out on the Nome roads, turning to previously unused pages of their bird books. A bird list is available at the visitor center, and they post recent sightings and can tell you where to look—each of the three roads has a different habitat. The best time to visit for birding is Memorial Day through June and in early August. There's a chance to see Siberian birds, and you are likely to see bluethroats, yellow wagtails, wheatears, Arctic warblers, and Aleutian and Arctic terns. Nome is the only place to see a bristle-thighed curlew without chartering a plane (but be ready for a strenuous hike). You don't need a guide, although guided field trips do come to Nome (see "Bird-Watching," in chapter 11). National park rangers from the Bering Land Bridge National Preserve offers a Saturday bird outing during the migration in May and June; call ahead to check on current details (see "Visitor Information," above).

MOUNTAIN-BIKING　The roads of Nome are one of the world's great undiscovered mountain-biking destinations—where else can you bike past musk-oxen and reindeer? There is no bike rental in town, but for bike enthusiasts, it may be worth renting a bike in Anchorage or bringing yours from home. There is a bike-repair guy in town, Keith Conger, who is a good contact point for information or help with your bike, at **Bering C Bikes,** 500 Spinning Rock Rd. (© **907/443-4994**).

10

THE BUSH | Nome: Arctic Frontier Town

THE kotzebue OPTION

The Northwest Arctic's authentic Iñupiaq center of Kotzebue (*Kotz*-eh-biew) isn't our first choice for most visitors. Those interested in Iñupiaq culture should go to Barrow, while those looking for bird-watching or self-guided outdoor sightseeing should go to Nome. Kotzebue lacks activities or attractions geared to the typical tourist, and it doesn't make sense to go there just to walk around.

On the other hand, intrepid travelers seeking real adventure can use Kotzebue as a hub for a vast, spectacular area of Arctic wilderness. The **National Park Service** (P.O. Box 1029), Kotzebue, AK 99752 (© **907/442-3760** or 442-3890), manages an immense area of protected land in the region, including Kobuk Valley National Park, Cape Krusenstern National Monument, and Noatak and Bering Land Bridge national preserves (find websites to each through www.nps.gov). The **Northwest Arctic Heritage Center** offers classes on traditional Native crafts and medicinal plants, and employees will answer questions about the town as well as the public lands. The center is open June to September Monday to Saturday 8:30am to 6:30pm, the rest of the year Monday to Friday 8am to 12pm and 1 to 5pm. The Park Service is the best source of visitor information for Kotzebue and the region, especially since outdoor activities are essentially the only thing to do if you go there.

There are several remote rivers near Kotzebue with easy self-guided floating for experienced outdoors people. This is the best chance to get deep into the Arctic on your own. The great Noatak River originates in the Brooks Range and flows 450 miles through America's largest undisturbed wilderness in the impressive scenery of the Noatak National Preserve. The Selawik, Squirrel, and Kobuk rivers all have long sections of easy water. **Equinox Wilderness Expeditions** (p. 518) offers float trips in the area,

Seeing the Sights in the Air

Nome is a hub for bush plane operators. Flightseeing charters are available, or you can fly on one of the scheduled routes out to the villages and spend a couple of hours touring. The way to do it is to contact a flight service, explain what you have in mind, and follow their advice. Expect to pay $210 to $350. Don't plan to stay overnight in a village without advance arrangements, and don't go in bad weather—you'll see little and may get stuck in a tiny village. **Bering Air** (© **800/478-5422** in Alaska only, or 907/443-5464; www.beringair.com) has a long and illustrious reputation and serves 32 villages from Nome and Kotzebue. They offer flightseeing trips by fixed-wing aircraft or helicopter on hourly charter rates (expensive if there are just one or two of you along). Or they will sell you a seat on a scheduled loop flight that visits various villages, charging the fare only to the closest village on the trip while you enjoy the entire round-trip. They even offer charters across the Bering Strait to the Russian towns of Provideniya and Anadyr.

Where to Stay

There are several good B&Bs and motel rooms besides those listed below, including the **Nugget Inn** (© **877/443-2323** or 907/443-4189). Staying at a B&B makes sense, as your host can introduce you to the community in a less contrived although not necessarily every year. Expect to pay $4,500 per person. Most river running in the region is self-guided. Get details from *The Alaska River Guide,* by Karen Jettmar, director of Equinox (Menasha Ridge Press). Obviously, you should be experienced in the outdoors and in river floating before heading out for a multiday trip in the Arctic. And plan ahead, arranging details well in advance with the Park Service and your pilot. **Bering Air** (☏ **800/478-5422** in Alaska only, or 907/443-5464; www.beringair.com) is one good operator in Kotzebue. A popular way to take a float trip is to use scheduled service into a riverside village.

Kotzebue also offers curious travelers a chance to dig deep into the Iñupiaq way of life with **Arctic Circle Educational Adventures** (☏ **907/442-6013** in summer, or 907/276-0976 in winter; www.fishcamp.org). The adventure takes place at a fish camp similar to those where Native people spend the summer gathering food for the winter—you can participate in set-net fishing, fish cutting, food gathering, and other traditional subsistence activities, as well as hiking, town tours, and bird-watching. You are a participant rather than an observer and spend real, unmediated time with Native people. The camp on the beach 5 miles south of town is as simple as Bush life, but with a modern kitchen, dining room, shower, and sauna. Guests sleep in plywood cabins without plumbing. Rates are $150 per person per day for lodging, meals, and transfer from the airport, and an additional $100 per day for tour activities. The season is from late June to mid-August.

Alaska Airlines (☏ **800/252-7522;** www.alaskaair.com) offers daily jet service to Kotzebue. Lodging is at the **Nullagvik Hotel** (www.nullagvik.com; ☏ **907/442-3331**), a comfortable, modern hotel on the beachfront owned by the NANA regional Native corporation. High-season rates are $219 double.

way than a formal tour company. The visitor center and their website can provide information on them.

Aurora Inn Suites ★   Look here for the best traditional hotel rooms in town, in a mock country inn on the town's main street. They're nicely furnished and even have some style, a remarkable contrast to the other hotels in Nome. Another plus in this smoky town, there are lots of smoke-free rooms here. The same company, owned by the Bering Straits Native Corporation, owns a car-rental operation, which is on-site.

302 E. Front St. (P.O. Box 1008), Nome, AK 99762. www.aurorainnome.com. ☏ **800/354-4606** or 907/443-3838. Fax 907/443-6380. 56 units. $150–$250 double. Extra person 16 and older $10. AE, MC, V. **Amenities:** Sauna. *In room:* TV, hair dryer.

Sweet Dreams B&B   Convenient to the Iditarod finish line and across from good food at Airport Pizza, this B&B's best assets are the hosts, Erna and Leo Rasmussen, who are deep wells of Nome history and local knowledge. Leo is a former mayor and a personable and funny man. The two-story house has a rustic, old-fashioned feel, with lots of Alaskan memorabilia and a sun room on top. Two rooms share a bathroom, while a third has its own, but not attached. A full breakfast is served when Erna has time to prepare it, and they pick up and deliver to the airport.

406 W. 4th St. (P.O. Box 2), Nome, AK 99762. (☎ **907/443-2919.** 3 units, 2 with shared bathroom. $140 double. Rate includes full breakfast. MC, V.

Where to Eat

You might not go out of your way to dine at any of the restaurants in Nome, but once you're here, you can find an adequate meal at various establishments. Several are operated by immigrant families, who offer their national cuisine along with standard American-style fare. All tend to be open quite late and accept credit cards.

Probably the best place to eat in town is **Airport Pizza,** which no longer is at the airport—it is at 406 Bering St. (☎ **907/443-7992;** www.airportpizza.com). The restaurant, which tends to be noisy, serves breakfast, sandwiches, Tex-Mex, and pizza. It brews fancy coffee, has 15 microbrews on tap, offers free Wi-Fi, and is open long hours every day. But the delivery service is the biggest claim to fame: They package pizzas and put them on bush planes flying out to tiny villages.

Husky Restaurant, 235 Front St. (☎ **907/443-1300**), may not look promising from its street frontage, next to a couple of liquor stores, but inside the small dining room, it's very clean and quiet, and the service is friendly and efficient. The specialty is Japanese food, but you can also get a good halibut sandwich or various other American choices. Locals like the teriyaki chicken and the Philly burger.

Milano's Pizzeria (☎ **907/443-2924**), on 503 Front St. in the Old Federal Building, serves Italian and Japanese meals, as well as good pizza.

Twin Dragons, on Front Street near Steadman Street (☎ **907/443-5552**), serves Chinese food good enough to have kept them in business for many years, and also Vietnamese noodles and pizza.

BARROW: WAY NORTH

Half-liquid land comes to an arbitrary point at the northern tip of Alaska, Point Barrow, a long tendril reaching into the Arctic Ocean where bowhead whales pass close to shore during their annual migrations. The Iñupiat settled here more than a thousand years ago because it's such a good whale-hunting spot, and that's why they still live here today, dragging their skin boats miles out on the frozen ocean to wait for whales along the cracks in the ice pack. And, according to age-old tradition, they still share the whales they catch among the entire community. Indeed, even visitors who show up on a Saturday in late June, during the Nalukataq, may be offered a piece of maktak (whale blubber and skin) and a chance to bounce high in the air in the blanket toss.

Barrow is the northernmost settlement on the North American continent, above the 71st parallel, but that's not all that makes it unique. The town of 4,417 is a cultural treasure. It's ancient, but it's also the seat of the North Slope Borough, a county government encompassing an area larger than the state of Nebraska, in which lies North America's largest oil field. The borough has everything money can buy for a local government, yet the people still must contend with crushing ice, snooping polar bears, and utter isolation. From these ingredients, they have concocted an extraordinary mixture of sophisticated modernity and wise tradition. Alaska's largest corporation is based here; its top executives are also subsistence hunters. At the Iñupiat Heritage Center, it has been possible to see, on successive nights, traditional dance in the Iñupiaq language and avant-garde theater in the same language.

Natives prepare to whale hunt.

Geography and the natural environment also make the place interesting. This is the most heavily instrumented and intensively studied scientific site anywhere in the American Arctic. At the labs north of town, cutting-edge work on climate change takes place that could affect the whole world. The tundra around Barrow is dotted with lakes divided by tendrils of swampy tundra no more substantial than the edges of fine lace. On this haven for migratory waterfowl, the flat, wet land and the ocean seem to merge. Indeed, for all but a few months, it's a flat, frozen plain of ocean and land. For 65 days in the winter, the sun never rises. In the summer, it doesn't set. Ice recedes from the shore only for a few brief months. Such extreme geography is a magnet for visitors.

Essentials

GETTING THERE   **Alaska Airlines** (© **800/252-7522;** www.alaskaair.com) flies a couple of times daily to Barrow from Anchorage, by way of Fairbanks. The fare from Anchorage is $600 or $700. You can save by booking their 1-day and overnight tour packages, described in "Exploring the Town & Getting Outside," below. Book them through **Alaska Airlines Vacations** (© **866/500-5511;** www.alaskaairalaska.com).

VISITOR INFORMATION   The City of Barrow has a small **visitor center,** at Momegana and Ahkovak streets, near the airport and Wiley Post & Will Rogers Monument, with a guide to talk to, maps (including a numbered walking tour map), and other publications. Hours are changeable but have been daily, summer only, from 10am to 4:30pm. To obtain advance information, contact the City of Barrow, Office of the Mayor, P.O. Box 629, Barrow, AK 99723 (© **907/852-5211,** ext. 231; www.cityofbarrow.org).

GETTING AROUND   Facing the Chukchi Sea, Barrow has two sections, lying on each side of Isatkoak Lagoon. **Browerville,** to the east, has the Iñupiat Heritage Center and the Stuaqpak, or big store, which contains a small food

Nalukataq blanket toss.

court and many services. The old part of **Barrow,** with the hotels and airport, is to the west. The northern tip of Alaska, **Point Barrow,** is north of the town on a spit. The road leads 6 miles in that direction, but the absolute end is farther out, beyond the road. Other gravel roads lead about 10 miles out of town on the tundra.

The airport is right in town. Depending on where you stay and how much luggage you have, you may be able to walk to your hotel. Taxis are handy and come quickly, charging $6 or $7 in town, $10 beyond town ($5 for seniors), plus $1 for each additional passenger. **Arcticab** (© **907/852-2227**) and **Alaska Taxi** (© **907/852-3000**) are two of the four cab companies.

SPECIAL EVENTS The return of the sun after 2 months below the horizon is met by traditional celebrations on **January 21.** The **Piuraagiaqta,** a spring festival, takes place in mid-April and includes many fun events. In the tea-making contest, couples race to set up a camp stove and melt ice to make tea. If the traditional bowhead whaling season is a success, the **Nalukataq** takes place in late June, usually on a Saturday, but the actual date depends on the preference of the successful captain. It is his responsibility to feed the entire community. The Eskimo blanket toss is also a traditional element of the event (injuries are common, so don't take it lightly). In the fall, generally from early to mid-October, the whale hunt launches from the beaches of town (rather than the ice, as in spring). If you're lucky, you can be on hand as a whale is pulled ashore and butchered by the community. This usually occurs at the NARL runway, north of town; ask around, as everyone will know if a whale has been landed.

[FastFACTS] BARROW

Alcohol Legality The sale of alcohol is illegal in Barrow and importation for personal use in your luggage is limited and controlled by a permit system. Without going through the permit process, you can bring in 1 gallon of beer, 1 liter of distilled spirits, or 2 liters of wine. Violating these laws is bootlegging, a serious crime. For more information, call ahead to Barrow Alcohol Distribution (✆ **907/852-3788**) or the Office of the Mayor (✆ **907/852-5211,** ext. 231).

Bank **Wells Fargo** is at 1078 Kiogak St. (✆ **907/852-6200**), with an ATM.

Hospital **Samuel Simmonds Memorial Hospital** is at 1296 Agvik St. (✆ **907/852-4611**).

Internet Access Free at the **Tuzzy Library,** at the Iñupiat Heritage Center in Browerville.

Police Contact the **North Slope Borough Police Department,** 1068 Kiogak St. (✆ **907/852-6111**).

Taxes Barrow imposes **no sales tax. Room tax** is 5%.

Exploring the Town & Getting Outside

The **Iñupiat Heritage Center** (✆ **907/852-0422**) is the town's main attraction and one of Alaska's most remarkable cultural institutions. It is part museum, part gathering center, and part venue for living culture. Inside is a workshop for craftspeople where hunters build the traditional boats and tools they use and where drummers build their drums; during the summer, an artist is usually in residence for visitors. Storytellers and dancers have a performance space. In the museum area, displays of artifacts change regularly, while a permanent exhibit covers Eskimo whaling and the influence of Yankee whaling on it (the quiet pride here carries a real emotional wallop). Iñupiaq dancing and drumming demonstrations, a blanket toss, games, and a crafts sale happen every afternoon in the summer from 1:30 to 3:30pm; these are the same programs that are the highlight of the escorted tours. The center is open Monday through Friday from 8:30am to 5pm (to see the program on weekends, call ahead). Regular admission is $10 adults, $5 students, free for seniors and age 6 or younger, with an added fee of $7 for the dance program.

The other site that's worthy of a special trip is **NARL,** as the former Naval Arctic Research Laboratory is known. Now the nation's busiest year-round Arctic research site, NARL has interesting exhibits in the new Barrow Arctic Research Center, and the cafeteria in the Ilisagvik College building serves three good meals a day; it's open during normal business hours. The main tourism business in town is **Tundra Tours** (✆ **800/882-8478** or 907/852-3900; www.tundratoursinc.com). Arctic Slope Regional Corporation, a corporation representing the Iñupiat, owns the company and the Top of the World Hotel. Their tour introduces the town to visitors who arrive with little idea of what to expect. The 6-hour summer-only tour includes visits to an Eskimo skin boat, the cemetery, and the Arctic Ocean, for a dip of toes. The highlight is a visit to the Heritage Center with a cultural presentation, including Eskimo dance and a chance to buy crafts made by Native artists. The day-trip tour is $350 single occupancy, $505 double occupancy, for the tour and a night in Barrow at the Top of the World Hotel, giving you time on your own without the tour group; neither price includes airfare. Book the tour with Tundra Tours. If you buy the tour separately when you're already in Barrow, it's $135.

In season, during the spring and fall, Barrow is a good place to see polar bears. The bears are always around when the ice is in; they're dangerous and people take extreme care to avoid them. To find bears, you need a ride on an all-terrain vehicle with a guide beyond the end of the town's road system. There will probably be someone offering those tours when you arrive, but at the time of this writing, we couldn't find anyone. Call ahead to the visitor center or your lodgings to see if you can line something up. For an expensive and adventurous option, see "Polar Bear Viewing," below.

A polar bear.

Where to Stay

King Eider Inn ★★ The best rooms in town—indeed, some of the best in the Bush—are found in this clapboard building near the airport. They're crisp and airy, with faux rustic furniture, and kept up well. It surely helps that shoes are not allowed in the hotel—you have to take them off at the front door every time you come in. The halls and rooms are decorated with Native art. A room with a kitchenette is $10 more, and the enormous and luxurious Presidential Suite (where Barrow's honeymooners and visiting celebrities stay) is $297 summer, $269 winter. The lobby is comfortable, with a stone fireplace, and free coffee and other hot beverages are offered there around the clock. Bathrooms have large shower stalls, not tubs. Smoking is not permitted.

1752 Ahkovak St. (P.O. Box 1283), Barrow, AK 99723. www.kingeider.net. ℂ **888/303-4337** reservations, or 907/852-4700. Fax 907/852-2025. 19 units. Summer $189 double; winter $169 double. Extra person $25. AE, MC, V. **Amenities:** Sauna. *In room:* TV, Wi-Fi.

Top of the World Hotel ★ This is a good hotel with familiar standard rooms, worn in places but perfectly comfortable. The staff works to keep the place clean

---

Polar Bear Viewing

If want to be sure of seeing polar bears (weather permitting), **Alaska Air Expeditions** (ℂ **907/694-4294;** www.alaskapolarbeartours.com) offers the ultimate opportunity. Pilot Tim Cook takes just a few visitors a year: He contacts his Native village friends on the North Slope, finds out where the bears are, then flies there from Fairbanks with his guests. This is an authentic Arctic exploration, with prices and uncertainties to match, but he's never failed to find bears and, after landing, usually gets his guests within 100 feet of them. Prices start at $2,423 per person for an overnight, based on a group of five. Viewing is best mid-September through October.

and quiet. Rooms have light furniture and blue carpet, desks, and refrigerators. Those on the water side have remarkable views of the Arctic Ocean, and it's only a few steps to the beach and the heart of Barrow. The lobby is a place where people pass time, somewhat cluttered with a TV and a stuffed polar bear. The hotel is owned by the Native corporation that also operates Tundra Tours, and you stay here if you come on the package tour.

Agvik St. (P.O. Box 189), Barrow, AK 99723. www.tundratoursinc.com. © **907/852-3900.** 44 units. Summer $150–$220 double; winter $125–$155 double. Extra person $20. AE, DC, DISC, MC, V. *In room:* TV, fridge.

Where to Eat

There are several decent restaurants in Barrow. Generally, they stay open very late, always have a TV on, offer free delivery, and don't brew decaffeinated coffee—people around here run on lots of caffeine and sugar.

Adjoining the Top of the World Hotel, **Pepe's North of the Border,** 1204 Agvik St. (© **907/852-8200**), is the most famous place in town, thanks to an appearance owner Fran Tate made with Johnny Carson on *The Tonight Show* some 20 years ago. They serve large portions of familiar American-style Mexican food, steak, and seafood; lunch is $10 to $20, dinner $20 to $35. It's the only restaurant listed here that serves breakfast. The bus tours come here for lunch, and Tate hands out souvenirs.

Brower's Cafe, 3220 Brower's Hill (© **907/852-3456**), occupies the most historic building in town, the 19th-century whaling station and store built by Charles Brower, who introduced Yankee whaling techniques to the Iñupiat and sired one of its most illustrious families. The restaurant serves American and Chinese dishes, with a price range of $10 to $47. Big windows look out on the beach, and a famous whalebone arch is just outside.

Northern Lights Restaurant, in Browerville at 5122 Herman St. (© **907/852-3300**), has a very comfortable, clean dining room and is operated by a charming family. Their menu goes on and on, with the owner's own Chinese food, plus deli selections and burgers, and the best pizza in town. Prices range from $13 to $30.

PRUDHOE BAY: ARCTIC INDUSTRY

The Prudhoe (*Prew*-dough) Bay complex is more than a huge oil field—it's an amazing achievement. Massive, complex machinery must operate in winter's deep, dark cold, and in summer must avoid harm to a critical habitat for migrating caribou and waterfowl, on wet, fragile tundra that permanently shows any mark made by vehicles. Workers are forbidden even to set foot on the tundra. Most places, as you look from the edge of one of the gravel pads, the heathery ground looks as undisturbed as a calm sea.

But that doesn't make it a good place to go on your vacation. The grim town of **Deadhorse,** which serves the oil facility, is really more of an industrial yard, barely deserving to be called a town; it certainly isn't anything you'd travel to see. To get beyond it to Prudhoe Bay, you have to sign up for a tour. The tour has never gone inside the buildings, and under post-9/11 security measures, it doesn't even go close to the most interesting areas. Visitors do get to stop at the Arctic Ocean,

10

THE BUSH

Prudhoe Bay: Arctic Industry

A polar bear eyes a wolf at the Arctic National Wildlife Refuge.

the only way to the water for those who drive up on the Dalton Highway. That hardly justifies the trip, however, unless you are bent on driving the highway anyway (it is covered in chapter 9, in "The Dalton Highway"). Frankly, we can't recommend spending the time and expense required for a Prudhoe tour. If you're curious about the Arctic, a trip to Barrow or Nome makes more sense.

If you do go to Deadhorse with the objective of touching the Arctic Ocean, you must reserve at least 24 hours ahead and provide information to clear security for the ride. The tours are operated by the **Arctic Caribou Inn,** P.O. Box 340111, Prudhoe Bay, AK 99734 (www.arctic caribouinn.com; ✆ **907/659-2368**). They will need your name and identification information such as a driver's license or passport number to run a background check before allowing you on the oil field. The inn also offers the area's visitor services, including a hotel and cafeteria; although tours

---

📎 Seeing ANWR for Yourself

The decades-old national controversy about whether to open the Arctic National Wildlife Refuge to oil exploration created strong interest in seeing that extraordinarily remote northeast corner of Alaska, which is done best in summer on a float trip. While interest in these floats may have increased for political reasons, their reputation of beauty and adventure has made them an attraction in their own right. The best time to see caribou is in June. Jim Campbell and Carol Kasza's Fairbanks-based **Arctic Treks** has led float trips in ANWR for 3 decades (✆ **907/455-6502;** www.arctictreksadventures.com). They offer shorter base-camp trips in ANWR, as well as the long river floats and other arctic journeys, for $4,000 to $5,000 per person.

For those who simply want to see ANWR without a wilderness trip, it's possible to visit the Iñupiaq village of Kaktovik, which lies within the boundaries of the refuge. While we wouldn't recommend the journey for most visitors, those with strong interest in a Bush village sojourn and curiosity about ANWR may enjoy it. Lodging and meals in Kaktovik come from the **Waldo Arms Hotel** (✆ **907/640-6513**), a gathering place known for warm hospitality. Kaktovik is served from Fairbanks by **Era Alaska,** also known as Frontier Flying Service (✆ **800/478-6779** or 907/450-7200; www.flyera.com). On the schedule, the destination is listed as "Barter Island."

Caribous migrating.

operate only in the summer, the hotel and restaurant are open year-round. Rooms have two twin beds, and management asks that you call for prices on rooms and tours. The restaurant offers breakfast ($15), lunch ($18), and dinner ($20). No alcohol is for sale in the town, and it isn't allowed in the inn. The hotel is near the airport in Deadhorse and serves as the starting point for the tours. The tour itself lasts 2 hours. Visitors are carried by bus past the oil field to the shore, with a 15-minute stop at the Arctic Ocean. It costs $45. There is no other way to get from the end of the road to the water.

Alaska Airlines (© **800/252-7522;** www.alaskaair.com) has a couple of flights daily to Prudhoe Bay from Anchorage. A round-trip ticket costs around $800.

Several companies drive bus tours up the Dalton Highway all the way to Prudhoe, flying the other way. **Northern Alaska Tour Company** (© **800/474-1986** or 907/474-8600; www.northernalaska.com) offers these trips, with add-ons to make it more interesting: flightseeing stops, dayhikes, village visits, and other choices. The basic 3-day, 2-night tour is $989.

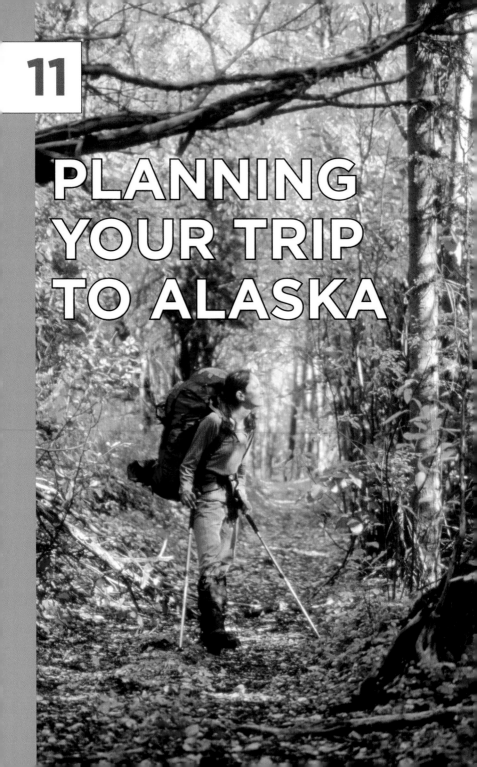

11

PLANNING YOUR TRIP TO ALASKA

P lanning a trip to Alaska can be a bit more complicated than traveling in the rest of the United States. Aside from the vast distances and range of climatic conditions, the best places book up quickly for the high summer season. This chapter provides general orientation information, gives advice on when to go and how much it will cost, and covers everything you'll need to plan a trip to Alaska.

GETTING THERE & GETTING AROUND

By Plane

CARRIERS Anchorage (ANC) is Alaska's main entrance and is served by numerous major carriers from the rest of the United States. A few flights arrive in Anchorage from Japan, Korea, or Germany, but the vast majority of international travelers arrive in the U.S. in another major city in the contiguous states and then take a domestic flight to Anchorage. It's also possible to fly into Fairbanks or Southeast Alaska. Most passengers come into Anchorage through Seattle, but for a bit more, you can fly nonstop to Anchorage from various major cities. There are far more choices in summer than in winter. **Alaska Airlines** (✆ **800/252-7522;** www.alaskaair.com) has more flights than all other airlines combined, with as many as 20 nonstops a day from Seattle in summer and daily summer nonstops from many cities around the country. Alaska Airlines is the only jet carrier with more than token coverage anywhere in the state other than Anchorage and has arrangements with commuter lines that fan out from its network to smaller communities.

FARES Fares vary wildly, especially in these days of economic instability and changing fuel costs. It's almost always cheapest to change planes in Seattle due to the competition on the Seattle–Anchorage route. Watching for sales can pay off. Summer sales sometimes hit in April. If you can make a last-minute decision, check for Web specials on the Alaska Airlines website and other airline sites, as there sometimes are bargains to be had you can't get any other way.

BUSH PILOTS To fly to a roadless village, or to fly between most towns without returning to a hub, you will take a small, prop-driven plane with an Alaska bush pilot at the controls. Small air taxis also charter to fishing sites, lodges, remote cabins, or anywhere else you want to go—even a sandbar in the middle of a river. An authentic Alaskan adventure can be had by taking a bush mail plane round-trip to a village and back. The ticket price is generally less than a flightseeing trip, and you'll have at least a brief chance to look around a Native village, although don't expect to find any visitor facilities without making arrangements in advance. It's cost effective to take

FACING PAGE: **Taking in a view from Wrangell–St. Elias National Park.**

these flights from towns that are relatively close to surrounding villages: Kodiak, Homer, Fairbanks, Nome, Kotzebue, and Barrow fit the bill. You will need to do some research, and not on the Internet; find the name of a local flight service that carries mail from the town visitor center, then call and explain what you have in mind. And wait for good weather.

By Ship

The most popular way to get to Alaska is on a **cruise ship** (chapter 4, "Cruising Alaska's Coast," provides an in-depth look at your options).

For an affordable, independent trip by sea, with a chance to stop as long as you like along the way, take the **Alaska Marine Highway System** (© **800/642-0066;** www.ferryalaska.com). It's our favorite form of public transportation. The big blue, white, and gold ferries ply the Inside Passage from Bellingham, Washington, and Prince Rupert, B.C., to the towns of Southeast Alaska, with road links to the rest of the state at Haines and Skagway. In summer, a ferry runs once or twice a month from that system across the Gulf of Alaska to the central part of the state. From there, smaller ferries connect towns in Prince William Sound and the Kenai Peninsula to Kodiak Island and the Aleutian Archipelago. For a complete discussion of the system and its intricacies, see "Getting Around by Ferry: The Alaska Marine Highway," in chapter 5.

By Rail

You can't get to Alaska by train, but you can get close. From the west coast of the U.S., you can take **Amtrak**'s Cascades train (© **800/USA-RAIL** [872-7245]; www.amtrak.com) to Bellingham, Washington; the dock for the Alaska ferry is quite close to the railroad station. From the east, it makes more sense to use Canada's **Via Rail** (© **888/VIA-RAIL** [842-7245]; www.viarail.ca). The transcontinental route starts all the way back in Toronto; you change in Jasper to end up in Prince Rupert, B.C., where you can catch the Alaska ferry north.

By Car

TIME & DISTANCE   We have included a description of the roads and average speeds you can expect (see "Alaska's Highways a la Carte," p. 406). Divide the distance you plan to drive by the expected speed to get the time it will take. Add some time for stops. For paved highways, you can count on averaging 50 mph. On some roads, you can go faster than 50, but you can't often drive at freeway speeds on these two-lane highways. Even when the surface is smooth—not always a given—the roads aren't designed for high speeds and are often clogged in summer with lumbering RVs. Besides, you need to be on the lookout for moose; hit one of those at 75 mph, and you both die.

The Cheapest Way to Alaska

Flying remains the cheapest and by far the simplest way to get to Alaska. Take other means only for the adventure, not for the savings. Round-trip train, ferry, and bus fare between Seattle and

Anchorage costs considerably more than a good airfare between the same cities. Driving is expensive, too, when you count rooms, food, and wear and tear on your vehicle.

ALASKA BY THE numbers

This chart shows some comparative indicators for 16 of Alaska's most popular destinations. The third column is the best season to visit—months at least part of which have enough going on and weather that is suitable (including weather that's good for winter sports). The fourth column lists modes of transportation to each community—in Alaska, you can't drive everywhere.

PLACE	POPULATION	SEASON	TRANSPORTATION	PRECIPITATION (IN.)	SNOW (IN.)
Anchorage	291, 826	May–Sept/Jan–Mar	Road, air, rail	16	71
Barrow	4,108	June–Sept	Air	4.5	30
Cordova	2,239	May–Sept	Air, ferry	93	119
Denali National Park	159	June–Sept	Road, rail	15	83
Fairbanks	97,581	May–Sept/Jan–Mar	Road, air, rail	11	68
Glacier Bay National Park	451	May–Sept	Air, ferry	70	117
Haines	1,713	May–Sept/Nov	Road, air, ferry	48	123
Homer	5,003	May–Sept/Mar	Road, air, ferry	25	55
Juneau	31,275	May–Sept	Air, ferry	56	99
Kenai	7,100	May–Sept	Road, air	19	61
Ketchikan	13,477	May–Sept	Air, ferry	151	37
Kodiak Island	13,592	May–Sept	Air, ferry	76	73
Nome	3,598	June–Aug/Mar	Air	16	61
Petersburg	2,948	May–Sept	Air, ferry	110	67
Seward	2,693	May–Sept	Road, rail	66	81
Sitka	8,881	May–Sept/Nov	Air, ferry	86	39
Skagway	920	May–Sept	Road, air, ferry	26	50
Unalaska and Dutch Harbor	4,376	June–Sept	Air, ferry	60	88
Valdez	3,976	May–Sept	Road, air, ferry	62	304

DRIVING TO ALASKA   Driving from any of the other states to Alaska is a great adventure, but it requires thousands of miles on the road and plenty of time. Allow at least a week each way. By car, Anchorage is 2,250 miles from Seattle and 3,400 miles from Los Angeles. By comparison, New York to L.A. is 2,800 miles. Traveling at an average of 50 mph, few vacationers will want to cover more than 500 or 600 miles a day, and that's a long day of nothing but driving. On such a plan, Seattle is 4 or 5 days from Anchorage without breaks.

Some of the 1,400-mile **Alaska Highway** is dull, but there are spectacular sections of the route, too, and few experiences give you a better feel for the size and personality of Alaska (and B.C. and Yukon). Putting your car on the ferry cuts the length of the trip considerably but raises the cost; you could rent a car for 2 weeks for the same price as carrying an economy car on the ferry one-way from Bellingham to Haines. Details on the Alaska section of the Alaska Highway, and other highways, are contained in chapter 9. The ferry is described in chapter 5. *The Milepost* (Morris Communications) contains good maps and mile-by-mile logs of all Alaska highways and Canadian approaches.

THE RENTAL OPTION   Renting a car is the easiest way to see the Interior and Southcentral parts of the state. All the major national car-rental companies are represented in Anchorage, as well as many local operators, which may have lower prices for older cars. In smaller cities and towns, there is always at least one agency; the town descriptions throughout this book provide details on firms in each. Base rates for major rental companies are in the range of $55 a day for an economy car. Weekly rentals equate roughly to 5 days' cost.

One-way rentals between Alaska towns are an attractive way to travel, but you generally pay steep drop-off charges, so a more popular plan is to fly into and out of Anchorage or Fairbanks and pick up and return the car there. A popular circular route from Anchorage or Fairbanks is through Denali and Fairbanks (or Anchorage) on the Parks Highway and back on the Richardson and Glenn highways. An Anchorage circle is to Valdez by ferry from Whittier and back on another part of the Richardson Highway and the Glenn Highway. See chapter 3 for more on routes. When comparison shopping for a car, consider taxes and fees, which can add 40% in Anchorage. Avoiding the fees can pay for an extra flight leg to start your trip in a community with lower car-rental taxes.

Here's a little-known tip for saving money if you want to use ground travel to get to Alaska. Avis car rental needs to get cars back from Haines and Skagway to Anchorage and Fairbanks in the fall. Take the ferry to those towns and rent after August 25, and the Alaska Avis franchise will charge a drop-off fee of only $50 (plus the daily rental). Find the special on the local website: www.avisalaska.com.

By RV

Touring Alaska in an RV makes a good deal of sense. The home on wheels offers spontaneity by freeing you from hotel reservations, and it gets you out of town and into the countryside, closer to the natural Alaska most visitors come for. At the same time, an RV is more comfortable than a tent in cool, unpredictable weather conditions.

Many retirees drive to Alaska in their motor homes, park the RV by a salmon stream, and spend the summer fishing. Sounds nice, but for most of the rest of us, with limited time, it makes more sense to rent an RV after flying to Alaska. Rental agencies are listed in Skagway (p. 200) and Anchorage (p. 217). The option of shipping your own RV to Alaska is also covered in the Anchorage chapter. Unless you have a large family, an RV rental saves little over traveling with a rental car, staying in hotels, and eating in restaurants (RVs rent for around $1,500 a week, plus gas and possibly mileage charges), so you make this choice to gain advantages, not avoid costs.

Alaska Highway Cruises (☎ 800/323-5757; www.bestofalaskatravel. com) offer the unique option of traveling one-way on a Holland America cruise ship, then picking up an RV for a land tour. You can choose a package that ends up back at Seattle by road or by air. The tours follow set itineraries with reservations along the way—the service is designed for first-time Alaska travelers and RV drivers who don't want to worry about the details—so some spontaneity is sacrificed. You get the security and simplicity of a package without being marched around in a group or cooped up in hotels. A cruise of a week followed by a week-long tour costs around $2,300 per person, double occupancy. There are various discounts, including for third and fourth passengers. Simple one-way RV rentals to Alaska are available, too, with, for example, an added drop-off fee of $1,000 to $1,200 between Seattle and Anchorage. See p. 216.

ESCORTED TOUR OR DO-IT-YOURSELF?

Hundreds of thousands of visitors come to Alaska each year on escorted package tours, leaving virtually all their travel arrangements in the hands of a single company that takes responsibility for ushering them through the state for a single, lump-sum fee. Many others cut the apron strings and explore Alaska on their own, in the process discovering a more relaxed, spontaneous experience. Each approach has advantages and disadvantages, of course, and which way you choose to visit depends on how you value those pros and cons.

An escorted package tour provides security. You'll know in advance how much everything will cost, you don't have to worry about making hotel and ground-transportation reservations, you're guaranteed to see the highlights of each town you visit, and you'll have someone telling you what you're looking at. Often a package price saves money over traveling at the same level of comfort independently. If there are weather delays or other travel problems, it's the tour company's problem, not yours. Everything happens on schedule, and you never have to touch your baggage other than to unpack. If you sometimes feel like you're a member of a herd on an escorted tour, you'll also meet new people, a big advantage if you're traveling on your own. Many passengers on these trips are retired, over age 65.

If you're short on time, escorted package tours make the most of it, as they often travel at an exhausting pace. Passengers get up early and cover a lot of ground, with sights and activities scheduled solidly through the day. Stops last only long enough to get a taste of what the sight is about, not to dig in and learn about a place you're especially interested in. On an escorted trip, you'll meet few, if any, Alaska residents, since most tour companies hire college students from "Outside" (a term Alaskans use to refer to anyplace other than Alaska) to fill summer jobs. You'll stay in only the largest hotels and eat in the largest, tourist-oriented restaurants—no small, quaint places loaded with local character. For visiting wilderness, such as Denali National Park, the quick and superficial approach can, in my opinion, spoil the whole point of going to a destination that's about an experience, not just seeing a particular object or place.

It's also possible for an independent traveler to obtain some of the predictability a package tour provides. You can reserve accommodations and activities and control your expenses by using a good travel agent experienced in Alaska travel. Some even offer fixed-price itineraries that allow you to travel on your own (see "Independent Travel Planning," at the end of this section). But independent travelers never have the complete security of those on group tours. Once you're on the road, you'll be on your own to take care of the details, and weather delays and other cancellations can confound the best-laid plans. If you can't relax and enjoy a trip knowing unforeseen difficulties could happen, then an escorted package tour is the way to go.

Large Tour Companies

A single cruise-ship company, Carnival, dominates the Alaska package-tour market operating under various brands. The "vertically integrated" operations allow the company to take care of everything you do while in Alaska with tight quality control. Holland America and Princess, both owned by Carnival, developed independently as the primary competitors in Alaska and still offer different brands, although the quality level is similar and the facilities are often in direct competition. With either, you can buy tours as short as a couple of hours or sign up for your whole vacation. All can be booked directly or through any travel agent. Other cruise lines also offer land tours, but typically only for their own passengers. If you will cruise to Alaska and want to add an escorted land tour, check for deals with your own cruise line first.

Holland America Line Tours   This giant company offers tours to more places than any other, including some excursions—on the Yukon River between Dawson City and Eagle, for example—that are entirely unique. The catalog covers just about anything in the state that could possibly be done with a group. Prices depend on a variety of factors, but in general, a tour of a week is about $1,400 per person. The operator of the motorcoach tours is called Gray Line, and the hotels are Westmark. The Westmark hotels, described in the appropriate sections of the book, are sometimes among the best in town, including those in Juneau (called the Baranof) and Fairbanks, while others are unremarkable. You'll find a description of the company's railcars on the Anchorage–Denali–Fairbanks run in chapter 8.

300 Elliott Ave. W., Seattle, WA 98119. ✆ **800/544-2206.** www.graylineofalaska.com or www. hollandamerica.com.

Princess Cruises and Tours   Princess built Alaska's best chain of hotels, reflecting a superior attention to quality. Two hotels are near Denali National Park, and one each is in Fairbanks, in Cooper Landing (on the Kenai Peninsula), and in Copper Center, near Wrangell–St. Elias National Park. Descriptions of each hostelry can be found in the appropriate chapter. The selection of tours has been more limited than Holland America's and has concentrated around Denali and the middle of the state.

800 5th Ave., Ste. 2600, Seattle, WA 98014. ✆ **800/426-0500.** www.princesslodges.com.

Independent Travel Planning

With this guidebook, you can book everything yourself, but for a long trip, it can get quite complicated to keep track of all the dates and deposits. If you're using a trusted travel agency to make trip arrangements, our reviews can help you make informed decisions. Read through the book, make your selections, and approach the agent with as detailed a plan as possible, derived from your own research. Then let the agent make the bookings you have chosen. Most agents who don't specialize in Alaska are aware of only the biggest attractions and best-marketed companies. Another option is to use a travel agency or trip planner based in Alaska. They'll know much more about the place and can help you more in picking out what you want to do.

Unfortunately, there are cautions to be offered in using the agencies. They work on commission, which means they're being paid by the establishments you're buying from. A good agent will disregard the size of the commission and really look out for you, but we've encountered too many visitors on poorly planned itineraries not to advise caution. Some travel agents book visitors on trips to far-flung corners of the state in quick succession, so they wind up staying only briefly in expensive places and then zoom off somewhere else, all with little concern for the visitors' true interests. Your best defense is to do enough research that you can actively participate in the planning.

Here we've gathered the names of some agencies that book Alaska trips. Expect to pay booking fees and to have the agent collect commissions from the businesses you use. Our knowledge of these agencies is limited to contacting them as a journalist, so a mention here is no guarantee; however, all of these have been around for several years, and we remove agencies from the list when we receive justified complaints.

Alaska Bound   This Michigan-based agency specializes in Alaska with a staff of former Alaskans. It started as a cruise planner, working primarily with Holland America, but now plans many independent trips, too, charging a per-person fee that depends on the length of the trip ($100 per person would not be exceptional).
116 Cass St., Traverse City, MI 49684. (✆ **888/ALASKA-7** (252-7527) or 231/439-3000. www.alaskabound.com.

Alaska Tour & Travel   Started in 1995 and steadily growing, this agency now claims to be the largest custom vacation company in Alaska. The same folks operate the Park Connection shuttle between Denali and Kenai Fjords national parks, and that central part of the state is what they know best and cover deeply. The website is remarkable, including a tool that allows you to build your own itinerary and a live availability-and-rate calendar for a range of Denali hotels. They also offer photos of destinations and a blog with planning tips.
P.O. Box 221011, Anchorage, AK 99522. (✆ **800/208-0200.** www.alaskatravel.com.

Alaska.org   This is a deep and well-built website that allows users to shop and customize tour packages or design their own vacations. The company produces an extraordinary amount of video and other material about destinations, including blog answers to user questions, so you can get a good idea of what you're buying. When you've seen enough, call the toll-free number for questions and booking. Or don't. You can use the site just to get information and call the listed businesses yourself, or even to request a referral via e-mail.
507 E St., Ste. 206, Anchorage, AK 99508. (✆ **888/ALASKA-8** (252-7528). www.alaska.org.

AskMatt Alaskan Adventures & Tours   Matthew Lowe is an energetic entrepreneur who has turned his encyclopedic knowledge of Southcentral Alaska travel into his own business. His strength is in activities, fishing charters, remote

A coupon book called **The Great Alaskan Tour Saver** (📞 907/278-7600; www.toursaver.com), which costs $100, is well worth the price if you plan on traveling as a couple, especially in the Southcentral region. The 130-plus coupons are two-for-one deals on some of the best activities, tours, train rides, flightseeing, fishing trips, and lodgings, valuable enough to pay for the book with just a couple of uses. Readers say they've saved a lot and it has become quite popular.

lodges, and winter trips, but he happily books travelers into budget B&Bs as well as more expensive lodges and resorts and charges no upfront fee.

P.O. Box 110261, Anchorage, AK 99511. 📞 907/868-1786. www.askmatt.com.

Sport Fishing Alaska   Choose this company to plan a fishing vacation. The owner, former lodge operator Sheary Suiter, knows where the fish will be week to week. That means SFA books clients at fly-in fishing lodges when and where the fishing is hot—a critical piece of information that can be difficult to obtain on your own. She charges a $95 upfront fee. (See "Fishing," below.)

9310 Shorecrest Dr., Anchorage, AK 99502. 📞 888/552-8674 or 907/344-8674. www.alaska tripplanners.com.

Viking Travel   Entrepreneurs in the small Southeast Alaska town of Petersburg built this agency, initially specializing in independent outdoor trips in their own area. Today, besides offering all the usual services of a travel agency, they plan trips for the whole state, offer money-saving airfare packages, and book all the region's ferries without surcharge. Get on their list, and they will book your cabins and vehicle reservations on the first day the system makes them available.

P.O. Box 787, Petersburg, AK 99833. 📞 800/327-2571 or 907/772-3818. www.alaskaferry.com.

PLANNING AN OUTDOOR VACATION

Most people visit Alaska to experience wilderness, so it's ironic that so many spend their time in crowded ships, buses, trains, and airplanes, the antithesis of a wilderness experience. You do need technology to get to the wilderness of Alaska, but unless you at least partly let loose of that umbilical cord, you'll never really arrive at your destination.

Every town in Alaska is a threshold to the wild. There's always a way to go hiking, biking, or sea kayaking, or to get on the bank of a stream or the deck of a boat to hook into a furiously fighting wild salmon—and end up in the evening back in a comfortable hotel room. Or take it a step further: Plan to go out overnight, perhaps with a friendly local guide at first, and then go out on your own. We've included lots of details on how to do this throughout the book. Scary? If it weren't a little scary, it would be Disneyland, and that it definitely is not. It's real, and that's why it's worth doing.

Use this section to learn about activities, outfitters, and wilderness lodges. The destination chapters cover outdoor options and practicalities in particular places.

Activities

BACKPACKING   Alaska's best country for trail hikes is in **Chugach State Park** near Anchorage (chapter 6), on **Chena River State Recreation Area** near Fairbanks (chapter 9), and in the **Chugach National Forest** on the Kenai Peninsula (chapter 7). For hiking beyond trails, go to **Denali National Park** or the **Denali Highway** (chapter 8), **Wrangell–St. Elias National Park,** or the **Dalton Highway** (chapter 9). Alaska trail hikes require the same skills as backpacking anywhere else, plus preparation for cold and damp (see "What to Wear," in chapter 2). Hiking beyond the trails is a glorious experience, but you need to know how to cross rivers and find your way—it's best if you have some outdoor experience. Or go with a guide; they're listed below. See "Health & Safety," later in this chapter, for some backcountry safety tips.

BIKING   Most every town in Alaska has a bike-rental agency. There are excellent bike routes all over the state and few restrictions on where you can ride. A bike is a great way into Denali National Park (see chapter 8), Anchorage has an extensive network of paved trails and many mountain-biking routes (see chapter 6), and guided biking is available in Haines and Skagway (see chapter 5). A couple that built an excellent reputation and a large business for more than a decade offering bicycle tours on Alaska's long, rural highways now operates **Alaskabike** (© **907/245-2175;** www.alaskabike.com), on its own from a home office. These are terrific vacations for avid cyclists. The 8-day tour over the spectacular Richardson Highway costs $2,995, inclusive. The schedule includes bike and kayak tours, too.

BIRD-WATCHING   In Alaska, birders can encounter birds in greater variety and greater numbers than they have seen before and add many new species to their life lists. We have listed birding groups and the best places to go in many of the sections on destinations. For marine birding, consider Sitka, Seward (Kenai Fjords National Park), Unalaska, and the Pribilof Islands (chapters 5, 7, and 10, respectively). Migratory bird festivals happen in May in Wrangell, Homer, and Cordova; Wrangell has the coastal marshes of the Stikine River Delta, Homer has handy sea bird colonies, and Cordova has the wetlands of the Copper River Delta, an accessible bird paradise of immense proportions (those towns are in chapters 5 and 7). Alaska's two

---

Keeping the Wilderness Clean

Human use shows up quickly in wild places. Even small signs can diminish the wilderness experience—trampled vegetation or charred wood from a campfire—and it's disgusting and disheartening to find toilet paper or human waste. The idea of Leave No Trace Camping, encouraged by Alaska's public land managers, is simple: Use the outdoors in such a way that no one would ever know you had been there. It's as important for rural highway driving and for dayhikes as for backpacking trips. The key is to plan ahead. For example, bring some kind of digging tool to bury feces, and sealable plastic bags with which you can pack out toilet paper and any other trash. To learn more, see the website of the Leave No Trace Center for Outdoor Ethics, www.lnt.org.

📎 A Guide to Guide Gratuities

As a general rule, tip fishing guides and outfitters $10 to $20 per person per day. For outings of less than a day, adjust the tip accordingly. At wilderness lodges, which normally have all-inclusive rates, it's often best to add the tip to your final payment when you leave and let the proprietor distribute it to the staff rather than try to do it at each meal. A blanket tip of $15 per person per day is acceptable.

largest cities have parks dedicated to inland birding and other bird resources as well: see the sections on Anchorage and Fairbanks for details (chapters 6 and 9). For Arctic birding, Nome is probably the best choice, thanks to the existence of roads that allow self-guided exploration (chapter 10). The very best bird and wildlife destination in Alaska, and surely among the best in the world, is the Pribilof Islands. You can sign up directly with the island's own Aleut residents for a tour there, described in chapter 10.

Serious birders with money to spend can dedicate an Alaska trip to some of the world's best and most famous remote bird-watching sites (those with milder or budding interest might better choose a less ambitious destination first, or make bird-watching only a part of an Alaska vacation). Learn about trips in birding magazines. *Bird Watcher's Digest* (www.birdwatchers digest.com) offers good, detailed advice on its website. Group trips are advertised in *Birders' World* (www.birdersworld.com) and *Birding* (www. americanbirding.org). Among the largest and most reputable operators coming to Alaska is Arizona-based **High Lonesome BirdTours** (© 800/743-2668 or 520/458-9446; www.hilonesometours.com), priding itself on relaxed trips for small groups. All-inclusive tours visit Kenai, Denali, Nome, Gambell, Barrow, Unalaska/Dutch Harbor, Adak, and the Pribilof Islands. Texas-based **Victor Emanuel Nature Tours** (© 800/328-8368; www. ventbird.com) counts well-known authors among its leaders.

CANOEING   Paddling a canoe on a remote Alaska lake or river is the best way to get into the wilderness without a backpack, a guide, or a great deal of expense. For beginners, it's easy to rent a canoe in Fairbanks (chapter 9) for a day trip. If you're ready to go overnight, the choices of routes are extraordinary, including the rivers of the Interior (chapter 9), the bird-watching country of the Copper River Delta near Cordova, or the supreme lake canoe routes of the Kenai National Wildlife Refuge (both in chapter 7).

CAR OR RV CAMPING   Campgrounds are almost everywhere in Alaska, many in extraordinarily beautiful natural places. Public campgrounds outnumber commercial ones. They're usually located where they are because there's something special about the place: a great view or beach, an exceptional fishing stream or trail head. Rarely will you find running water or flush toilets; most are seasonal, with hand pumps for water. (Alaska's public campgrounds fill up only in certain times and places, including weekend nights near Anchorage, fishing season on the Kenai River, and anytime in the summer at Denali National Park. Most other places, with little fear of finding a campground full, campers can be spontaneous, with flexibility other travelers can't share, able to stop when and where they like.

Even if you don't usually consider camping, think about renting a comfortable RV for a tour. One company offers these rentals as add-ons with cruise vacations, taking care of all the details for clients (that and other rental options are under "Getting There & Getting Around," earlier in this chapter).

If you fly to Alaska, car camping can be a bit complicated. Carrying a camp stove on an airplane is forbidden unless there is no attached fuel canister. Renting sleeping bags and other equipment in Alaska may be cheaper than bringing your own with airline baggage fees, though there is no charge on Alaska Air for up to three bags traveling in state. Rental agencies are listed with large towns in this book. You can also use the mail, sending packages to yourself care of general delivery at any post office.

We've mentioned some great campgrounds throughout the book, but there are many more than there is space to cover. A free map that lists all the public campgrounds along Alaska's highways is available from the Alaska Public Lands Information Center in Anchorage (p. 220). If you are planning to camp the whole way, get a copy of *Traveler's Guide to Alaskan Camping,* by Mike and Terri Church (Rolling Homes Press), which contains detailed reviews of virtually every public and commercial campground in the state.

FISHING Fishing in Alaska may spoil you for fishing anywhere else. The world's largest salmon and halibut were caught here in recent decades, and Pacific salmon are so plentiful that catching and processing them still provides one of the state's largest sources of employment. Fly-fishermen also come for thriving wild stocks of steelhead, cutthroat, and rainbow trout; Dolly Varden and Arctic char; and Arctic grayling.

There's no room here to tell you how to fish in Alaska—the best way is to pick it up from other anglers, most conveniently by going with a guide on your first outing. If you can afford it, a day of guided fly-in fishing to a remote stream is the ultimate (you can do it from virtually any town listed in chapters 5, 6, or 7). You can also study with a book; several are available, the best of which focus on individual areas of the state or particular fishing techniques rather than trying to cover everything.

The best all-around source of information is the **Alaska Department of Fish and Game Sport Fish Division** (www.sf.adfg.state.ak.us). Browse the website for run timing information and hot spots updated weekly, to learn generally about fishing in Alaska, and to obtain particulars about where to wet a line in different parts of the state (click "Publications" and then the region you are visiting). You can even buy a fishing license online. If you lack Internet access, the agency also produces printed guides and fields questions from the public, and they record the weekly local updates on telephone hot lines. Contact the office nearest where you will fish: We have listed the phone number for each in the town sections.

If fishing is the primary goal of your trip, think about booking time at a fishing lodge. The remote rivers of the Bristol Bay region have Alaska's most prolific salmon fishing, and the only way out there is to take a floatplane to a remote site. I recommend booking through **Sport Fishing Alaska,** described above under "Independent Travel Planning," p. 512. **AskMatt Alaskan Adventures & Tours,** in the same list, also specializes in booking trips to fishing lodges.

A salmon PRIMER

In Alaska, it's not so much where you wet your line, but when. The primary catch, Pacific salmon, lives in saltwater but spawns in freshwater, with each fish returning to the stream of its birth during a certain narrow window of time called a "run." When the salmon are running, fishing is hot; when they're not running, it's dead. And the runs change from day to day, typically lasting only a few weeks. (Halibut, on the other hand, are bottom-dwelling ocean fish; you can fish them from a boat every day when the tide is right.) You can fish salmon all over the state in fresh- and saltwater, but the closer you are to the ocean, the better the fish are. Salmon flesh softens in freshwater and the skin turns dull and red. Salmon right from saltwater that haven't started their spawning cycle are called silver bright—when you see one, you'll understand why. No Pacific salmon feeds in freshwater, but kings and silvers, meat eaters at sea, strike out of habit even in the river.

There are five species of Pacific salmon, each preferring its own habitat and, even when the habitat overlaps, each timing its run differently. Each species has two names.

King (or **chinook**) is the most coveted and best fighting fish, commonly growing to 20 to 40 pounds in 5 to 7 years at sea (the sport record, from the Kenai River, was 97 lb., and the largest ever, in a fish trap near Petersburg, was 126 lb.). It takes a lot of effort to hook and land a big king, but it's the ultimate in Alaska fishing. You also need a special king stamp on your fishing license from the Alaska Department of Fish and Game, which you can buy at the same time you buy your license. King runs come mostly from late May to early July.

The **silver** (or **coho**) is smaller than the king, typically 8 to 12 pounds, but it fights and jumps ferociously, making it nearly as big a prize. Silvers run mostly in the fall, beginning in August and lasting into October in some streams.

FLIGHTSEEING No one should come to Alaska without seeing the scenery at least once from a small plane. The most spectacular rides of all are the Mount McKinley flights from Talkeetna (chapter 8) and the Glacier Bay National Park flights from Gustavus, Haines, or other surrounding communities (chapter 5). But just about anywhere you go is worth seeing from the air; only then can you grasp how huge and complex the land is and how little changed it is by mankind. Fixed-wing flights give you the most time aloft for your money, with seats starting at around $100 for a brief flight.

RAFTING Letting an Alaskan river pull you through untouched wild country in a raft provides a unique perspective without the sweat and toil of backpacking. Alaska has many great rivers, virtually all undeveloped and, with few exceptions, never crowded. White-water guides operate on rivers all over the state, offering day trips in many towns. Outfitters also lead trips deep into Alaska, using the rivers to visit extraordinary places that can be reached no other way. Many companies offer floats; some are listed below and still others are in the destination chapters throughout this book.

SEA KAYAKING Just about every coastal town—from Kodiak east through Kachemak Bay, Prince William Sound, and the Southeast Panhandle—has at least one kayak outfitter taking visitors on day trips or expeditions. It is

Red (or **sockeye**) salmon, so named for their tasty red flesh, are the trickiest to catch. They usually weigh 4 to 8 pounds and can run in any of the summer months, depending on the region and stream. Reds feed primarily on plankton at sea, and when they strike a fly, it's out of an instinct that no one really understands; you need perfect river conditions to catch reds legally, because snagging anywhere but the mouth generally is not allowed in freshwater.

Pinks (or **humpies**) grow to only a few pounds and aren't as tasty as the other three species; their flesh lacks the fat that makes salmon so meaty in flavor, and it deteriorates quickly once the fish enter freshwater. Pinks are so plentiful that Alaska anglers usually view them as a nuisance to get off the line, but visitors often enjoy catching them: There's nothing wrong with a hard-fighting 4-pound fish, especially if you use light tackle, and a sliver-bright

pink salmon is tasty if cooked right.

Chum (or **dog**) salmon return plentifully to streams over much of the state but are rarely targeted by anglers. Yet a typical 5- to 10-pound chum hits and fights hard. Chums aren't prized for the table and are mostly used for subsistence by Alaska Natives, who smoke or dry the fish for winter use or freeze it to feed dog teams.

The gear you use depends on the species you are after and the regulations for the area you're fishing. You have to catch the fish in the mouth; snagging is allowed only in special circumstances. On saltwater, boats troll for kings and silvers with herring bait and gear to hold it down. Lures, salmon eggs, or flies will work on silvers and kings in the rivers, but regulations vary. Flies work best with reds. Most Alaska fishermen use spinning gear on the larger salmon species—landing such a large fish is iffy with a fly rod.

your best chance to get close enough to really know the wilderness and see whales, sea otters, seabirds, and marine life in an intimate way. Local guides are listed in each town section. Outfitters offering longer trips to a variety of places are listed below.

Outfitters & Outdoor Package Trips

Besides the outfitters and tour guides listed below, we've noted other operators in the destination chapters covering the towns where they are based. Browse through those chapters before deciding on a trip, as a trip with a small-town guide service can be wonderful.

Alaska Discovery   A local eco-tourism pioneer, Alaska Discovery was bought out by the famous Mountain Travel Sobek expedition company but still keeps local staff in Juneau and offers some of the best guided sea-kayaking trips in Southeast Alaska (sales staff is now in California). Glacier Bay and Admiralty Island outings cater to both beginners and the truly rugged. Their inn-to-inn trips are essentially outdoor-oriented package tours, taking groups to the best spots for day activities such as kayaking, rafting, or watching wildlife. Extended river trips float through the Arctic and on the Tatshenshini and Alsek rivers. They also offer outdoor packages for complete vacations. Check the website. A 3-day kayak expedition near Gustavus is $995, while 10 days in the Arctic is around $4,695.

P.O. Box 35003, Juneau, AK 99803. © **800/586-1911.** www.akdiscovery.com.

Alaska Wildland Adventures   This company specializes in outdoor vacations for those who want to be comfortable in the evening and aren't seeking strenuous physical challenges. The company concentrates on the Kenai Peninsula, where it operates three wilderness lodges, but also goes to Denali National Park. Most of its trips link a series of outdoor day activities, such as rafting, kayaking, hiking, glacier cruises, or wildlife-watching. Groups are small, and they also offer the lodges a la carte. An 11-day group safari is around $5,895; shorter trips, trips for families with kids, fishing trips, and other choices are available, too.

P.O. Box 389, Girdwood, AK 99587. © **800/334-8730** or 907/783-2928. www.alaskawildland.com.

Equinox Wilderness Expeditions   Karen Jettmar, author of *The Alaska River Guide,* the standard guidebook on floating Alaska's rivers, leads challenging rafting, sea-kayaking, and hiking trips and base-camp wildlife viewing each summer in some of the wildest and most exotic places around the state. Her groups are tiny, with five to eight members, and she offers custom coed, family, and women's trips. After 2 decades leading and teaching clients, Jettmar's firm was recently recognized as one of the world's best by *National Geographic Adventure.* A 10-day Arctic float trip costs around $4,200.

2440 East Tudor Rd., Ste. 1102, Anchorage, AK 99507. © **206/462-5246.** www.equinox expeditions.com.

Nova   These guys started commercial rafting on Alaska's rivers in 1975, but as the industry developed, they expanded only slowly, keeping their base in a tiny village on the Matanuska River, northeast of Anchorage, and primarily employing Alaskan guides. We like the fact that they don't minimize the hazards: They make it clear that these fast, cold waters aren't Disneyland rides. Their catalog covers longer expeditions on some of the state's wildest rivers, but also includes more affordable itineraries of 2 or 3 days. Two days on the Matanuska costs $349; 3 days on the Talkeetna, including 14-mile-long, class IV rapids of the Talkeetna Canyon, costs $1,350. Nova offers trips from Copper Center and Hope as well.

P.O. Box 1129, Chickaloon, AK 99674. © **800/746-5753** or 907/745-5753. www.novalaska.com.

St. Elias Alpine Guides   When you're ready for a real expedition, these are real professionals in real wilderness. Having given up on McKinley years ago as too crowded, they specialize in trekking, climbing, and floating the deep and rugged wilderness of Wrangell–St. Elias National Park. Theirs is the only trip catalog we know of that offers first ascents as part of the product line; so far, they've taken clients to the top of previously unclimbed mountains more than 45 times. For details, see p. 459.

P.O. Box 92129, Anchorage, AK 99509. © **888/933-5427** or 907/345-9048. www.stelias guides.com.

Multi-Activity Fly-In Wilderness Lodges

Any number of hotels use the word *lodge* in their names, but true wilderness lodges have unique qualities: They lie beyond the road system in places that are hard to get to but that are well worth spending some time in. These qualities also

You don't have to see Alaska only as an observer—you can be a participant. The **Iditarod Trail Sled Dog Race** (✆ 907/376-5155; www.iditarod.com), the 1,000-mile trek from Anchorage to Nome in March, uses volunteers at the start and finish and, for those who work their way up through the ranks, in the remote villages along the way. Visitors can be part of it, and become a part of the real Alaska, contributing only their time and travel to the state. Find the application on the website and act early; they get more volunteers than they can use. Other races and events also use volunteers but don't have a formal program like the Iditarod's.

Two facilities dedicated to study and rehabilitation of wildlife also take volunteers. You might not end up working directly with the creatures, but you can work behind the scenes and get much closer than a casual visitor—while contributing to a good cause.

In Seward, the **Alaska SeaLife Center** (✆ 888/378-2525; www.alaskasealife. org) studies, exhibits, and heals marine mammals, birds, and other wildlife and makes extensive use of volunteers (p. 302).

The **Alaska Raptor Center** in Sitka (✆ 800/643-9425; www.alaskaraptor. org) takes in injured eagles, owls, and other birds of prey and nurses them back to health in an impressive facility set along a rainforest stream. Volunteers work side-by-side with staff doing everything from selling T-shirts to working with birds (p. 144).

---

put wilderness lodges beyond most budgets. Getting there is expensive for guests and for operators; also, most lodges are small and have relatively large staffs to offer all-inclusive packages of rooms, meals, and guiding. For reasons explained elsewhere, we've generally excluded fishing lodges, concentrating instead on lodges that offer a variety of outdoor activities. Excellent lodges are described in the sections on Gustavus (p. 186), Homer (p. 339), and Denali National Park (p. 387). Here are three more that are so far from anywhere, we had no other place in the book to put them.

Caribou Lodge ★★ There's a lot to love about this place, south of Denali National Park: the location above the tree line, on its own alpine lake, miles from any other structure; the unlimited dry tundra hiking and views along the rounded ridge tops; the wildlife and the quiet. But what we love best, and what we suspect will matter most to visitors, is that it's real. This is home to Mike and Pam Nickols, the couple that personally hosts just three parties at a time, and for more than a decade they've lived out here in true bush style, year-round, far off the grid. They guide hiking, canoeing on the lake, and watching the wildlife; in the winter, they teach guests to drive a dog team over endlessly rolling hills of snow. Mainly, a visit is a chance to experience another way of life, one that exists in few places. The accommodations are simple but comfortable, each cabin with its own outhouse and a shared shower facility. Access is by small aircraft only, on skis in winter or floats in summer; in spring and fall, when the ice on the lake is soft, it's just about impossible to get there. For rough figuring, a plane from Talkeetna (p. 396) costs $165 to $210 per person, but inquire to get a more exact cost.

20 miles east of Talkeetna (P.O. Box 706), Talkeetna, AK 99676. www.caribboulodgealaska.com. ✆/fax **907/733-2163.** 3 cabins. $310 per person per day. Rates include all meals and guiding and

Using the Internet on the Road

If you decide to bring your laptop, you'll find that many hotels and even B&Bs have wireless Internet access for guests, usually for free, and there are numerous other free hotspots all over the state. If you leave the computer at home, you can stop in at an Internet cafe or the public library when you want to log on. Alaskans are the most Internet-connected population in the country, and there is access even in tiny villages where people live largely by hunting and gathering, so you can always count on finding a way of getting online with a little effort. We have listed Internet access for each Alaska community in the appropriate sections of the book. Coverage for wireless Internet technology, such as your BlackBerry or iPhone, is not universal, but the devices should work in the larger towns. Voice cellular coverage has spread to smaller communities, but even that remains spotty or nonexistent beyond city limits. Check on roaming with your own provider. For more on remote communication, see "Getting Lost/Wilderness Communications," p. 523.

are based on double occupancy, 2-day minimum. No credit cards. **Amenities:** Restaurant (family style, included in rate); guided activities included in rate; sauna.

Prince William Sound Lodge ★★ This comfortable, casual lodge sits on the beach of Tatitlek Narrows in the heart of Prince William Sound. Owner Chris Saal has been here since 1974, and he has built excellent accommodations. Activities are mostly self-guided or add-ons, although Chris does take guests on wildlife-viewing boat tours. You can also use the place like a beach house, enjoying walks and the marine environment, or arrange for fishing charters and more active pursuits. The food is terrific, too. A distinct advantage over other lodges: This one lies near the airstrip in the Chugach village of Tatitlek, where you can fly direct on a commercial flight from Anchorage, paying only for your seat rather than chartering the whole plane.

Ellamar (3900 Clay Products Dr., Anchorage, Alaska 99517). www.princewilliamsound.us. ✆ **907/440-0909** or 248-0909. 5 units. $325 per person per day. Rates include all meals and some guiding, 2-day minimum. No credit cards. **Amenities:** Restaurant (family style, included in rate); boat tour; sauna.

Winterlake ★★★ Among the best of Alaska's remote lodges, Winterlake earned its fame for its remarkable comfort, outdoor beauty, and extraordinary hosts. Carl Dixon is a classic Alaskan outdoorsman: hearty, cheerful, and most at home when working or traveling on the land. His wife, Kirsten, is a meticulous innkeeper, master chef, and cookbook author, trained at Le Cordon Bleu. A dog team is kept for guest instruction, and winter visitors also go snowmobiling and cross-country skiing. In the summer, guests enjoy the lake, float a river, hike trails from the lodge, or use the helicopter that is kept on-site for glacier or mountaintop excursions or remote fishing. Complimentary yoga, massage, and cooking classes are offered every day. Visitors get to the lodge by air from Anchorage with Rust's Flying Service; the fare is included in the lodge rates listed below, which vary according to how long you stay. We've given just two examples; use of the helicopter is extra. The Dixons also own the Tutka Bay Lodge, a short boat ride from Homer and the Redoubt Bay Lodge near Lake Clark Pass.

Mailing address: P.O. Box 91419, Anchorage, AK 99509. www.withinthewild.com. ℭ **907/274-2710.** Fax 907/277-6256. 5 cabins. 2 nights $2,130 per person; 4 nights $3,860 per person. AE, MC, V. **Amenities:** Restaurant (family style, included in rate); some guided activities, massage, yoga, and cooking classes included in rate; hot tub; sauna.

HEALTH & SAFETY
Crime & Emergency Services

CRIME   Sadly, crime rates are not low in Alaska's larger cities, although muggings are rare. Take the normal precautions you'd take at home. You're safe in daylight hours anywhere tourists commonly go, less so late at night leaving a bar or walking in a lonely place. Women need to be especially careful on their own, as Alaska has a disproportionately high rate of rape. The late-night sunlight can be deceiving—just because it's light out doesn't mean it's safe. Sexual assaults occur in towns big and small. Women should never hitchhike alone. If you are a victim of a crime, you can reach police from almost anywhere by calling ℭ **911** or, if it is not an emergency, by using the numbers listed under "Fast Facts" in each community section.

MEDICAL EMERGENCIES   You'll find modern, full-service hospitals in each of Alaska's larger cities, and even in some small towns that act as regional centers. There's some kind of clinic even in the smallest towns. Find medical facilities in each destination under "Fast Facts." Call those numbers, too, for referrals to a dentist or other health professional. In an emergency, call ℭ **911.**
  If health is a particular concern, consider joining **MedicAlert** (ℭ **800/ID-ALERT** [432-5378]; www.medicalert.org) and wearing its engraved bracelet, which will inform emergency medical personnel of a primary pre-existing medical condition and provide them with access to the organization's response center for your information on file, such as medications and emergency contacts. The cost is $40 for the first year, then $30 a year.

Outdoors Health & Safety

AVALANCHE   When snow sliding down a mountain comes to a stop, it hardens to a consistency that only metal tools can dig through. No one should go into the snowy backcountry without training in avalanche avoidance and recovery equipment, including locator beacons, probes, and shovels. Go with a guide if you are unsure.

BEARS & OTHER WILDLIFE   Being eaten by a bear is probably the least likely way for your vacation to end. More people die from dog bites than bear attacks. But it's still wise to be prepared for bears and to know how to avoid being trampled by a moose, which can be fatal.
  The first safety rule for bears is to avoid attracting them. Be tidy with your food and trash when you're camping, putting everything away in sealed containers. When backpacking, you can protect your food by hanging it from a long tree branch or, above the tree line, storing it in a bear-resistant canister (for rent or loan in Anchorage or at Denali or Wrangell–St. Elias National Park; see chapters 6, 8, and 9). Be careful not to spread food odors when you're cooking and cleaning up. Clean fish away from your campsite. Never keep food, pungent items, or clothing that smells like fish in your tent.

Make noise when walking through brush or thick trees to avoid surprising a bear or moose. Call out, sing, or carry on conversation. You might not scare a bear away this way, but at least you won't startle it. At all costs, avoid coming between a bear and its cubs or a bear and food (if a bear wants the fish you just caught, that's his food, too). Moose also are strongly defensive of their young, and a moose on its own can attack if it feels you're getting too close or if it previously has been stressed by contact with people or dogs. People are badly hurt every year trying to sneak by a moose on a trail. If you see a bear, stop, wave your arms, make noise, and, if you're with others, group together so you look larger to the bear. Avoid running, tempting the bear to chase (unless, of course, you can run a few steps to your car); depart by slowly backing away, at an angle if possible. If the bear follows, stop. Once in a great while, the bear may bluff a charge; even less often, it may attack. If you're attacked, fall and play dead, rolling into a ball facedown with your hands behind your neck. The bear should lose interest. In extremely rare instances, a bear may not lose interest because it's planning to make a meal of you. If this happens, fight back for all you're worth.

Many Alaskans carry a gun for protection in bear country, but that's not practical for visitors or for anyone not practiced in shooting. For most of us, a better alternative is a bear-deterrent spray. These are canisters that you fire to produce a burning fog of capsaicin pepper between you and a threatening bear. While less deadly than a gun, and with limited effectiveness in wind or rain, research shows they have a better overall track record against bear attacks than guns. You can't bring bear-deterrent spray on an airplane, even in your checked baggage, so if you fly, you will have to buy it on arrival and get rid of it before you leave, or ship it to yourself in Alaska. The product is easily available at Alaska sporting goods stores for about $45, or order direct from **Counter Assault** (✆ **800/695-3394;** www.counterassault.com). Whatever brand you buy, get a large canister, as this is one product you definitely don't want to run out of—sprays made for personal defense are not large enough. Also be sure to get a holster, as the spray is of no use buried in your backpack. If you do take a gun, it had better be a big one, such as a .300-Magnum rifle or 12-gauge shotgun loaded with slugs. No handgun is big enough to reliably stop a large bear bent on attacking.

BOATING SAFETY   Because of the cool temperatures, unpredictable weather, and cold water, going out on the ocean or floating a fast river is more hazardous in Alaska than in most other places, and you should go only with an experienced, licensed operator unless you know what you're doing. There's little margin for error if you fall into the water or capsize in this cold water. Always wear a life jacket. Always. If you do get wet, it is essential that you get warm and dry as soon as possible. The body temperature of a wet, cold person can easily sink so far he or she cannot get warm without external heating, a deadly condition called hypothermia. If you're sea kayaking or canoeing, always wear a life jacket, stay close to shore, and use rubberized dry bags (also called float bags) to pack everything you need to quickly warm a person who gets wet (see "Hypothermia," below). Having a way to get help in an emergency is also important (see "Getting Lost/Wilderness Communications," p. 523).

DANGEROUS PLANTS   Two shrubs common in Alaska can cause skin irritation, but there is nothing as bad as poison ivy or poison oak. **Cow parsnip,** also called pushki, is a large-leafed plant growing primarily in open areas, up to shoulder height by late summer, with white flowers. The celerylike stalks break easily, and the sap is highly allergenic for some people and has the quality of intensifying the burning power of the sun on skin for everyone. Wash it off quickly to avoid a rash or blisters. Never burn cow parsnip, as the smoke can be toxic. **Devil's Club,** a more obviously dangerous plant, grows on steep slopes and has ferocious spines that can pierce through clothing and cause infections. Also, don't eat anything you can't positively identify, as there are deadly poisonous mushrooms and plants.

DRINKING WATER   Unpurified river or lake water may not be safe to drink. Hand-held filters available from sporting-goods stores for around $75 are the most practical way of dealing with the problem. Iodine kits and boiling also work. The danger is a protozoan cyst called *Giardia lamblia,* which causes diarrhea and is present in thousands of water bodies all over the United States. If symptoms show up after you get home, tell your doctor you may have been exposed so that you can get tested and cured.

GETTING LOST/WILDERNESS COMMUNICATIONS   Even experienced people get lost outdoors. Hiking off trail or voyaging in a canoe, raft, or kayak, you quickly find that one mountain looks a lot like another. If you are unsure of your navigational skills, maps, or equipment, don't go. Beyond those basics, the most important safety precautions are to go with another person and to make sure someone knows where to look for you if you don't come back. For extended trips (more than a dayhike), leave a written trip plan with a person who will call rescuers if you are late. At the very least, leave a note in your car indicating where you are bound. Cellphones sometimes work near towns and highways, but not reliably, and there is little coverage beyond populated areas.

For serious outdoors people, technology can add an extra safety backup outdoors. Personal locator beacons with built-in GPS are the state-of-the-art solution. A range of units are available for $300 to $650 from outdoor and marine suppliers.

It is also possible to rent an Iridium satellite phone that will fairly reliably work outdoors anywhere on Earth, but you need to know where you are and whom to call at all times. A good rental firm is **RoadPost** (𝒞 **888/290-1616** or 905/272-5665; www.roadpost.com), based in Canada. Prices start at $9 a day, $1.80 a minute, plus a $30 delivery fee. The phone arrives with all needed accessories in an express package, which contains a prepaid return envelope to send it back.

HYPOTHERMIA   A potentially fatal lowering of core body temperature can sneak up on you. It's most dangerous when you don't realize how cold you are, perhaps in 50°F (10°C) weather on a damp mountain hike or rainy boating trip. Dress in material (whether wool or synthetic) that keeps its warmth when wet, choosing layers to avoid chilling perspiration. (See "What to Wear," p. 43.) Eating well and avoiding exhaustion also are important. Among the symptoms of hypothermia are cold extremities, being uncommunicative, displaying poor judgment or coordination, and sleepiness. A shivering victim still has the ability to warm up if better dressed; a lack of shivering means the body has gone beyond that point and warmth must be added from the outside or from warm drinks. Get indoors, force hot liquids on the victim (except if not fully conscious, which could cause choking), and, if shelter is unavailable, apply body heat from another person, skin on skin, in a sleeping bag.

INSECT BITES The good news is that Alaska has no snakes or poisonous spiders. The bad news is that Alaska makes up for it with mosquitoes and other biting insects. West Nile virus has not arrived here, so the mosquitoes are not dangerous, but they can ruin a trip. Effective insect repellent is a necessity, as is having a place where you can get away from them. We use shirts with hoods of netting when the bugs are at their worst. Mosquitoes can bite through light fabric close to the skin, which is one reason why people in the Bush wear heavy, baggy Carhart pants and jackets (made of canvas) even on the hottest days. Benadryl tablets or other antihistamines will often relieve swelling caused by mosquito bites.

RIVER CROSSINGS Hiking in Alaska's backcountry often requires crossing rivers without bridges. Use great caution: It's easy to get in trouble. Often the water is glacial melt, barely above freezing, and heavy with silt that makes it opaque. The silt can fill your pockets and drag you down. If in doubt, don't do it. If you do decide to cross, unbuckle your pack, keep your shoes on, face upstream, use a heavy walking stick if possible, and rig a safety line. Children should go in the eddy behind a larger person or be carried.

SEASICKNESS Most summertime visits to Alaska involve boat rides for fishing or sightseeing. Seasickness probably ruins more of these outings than any other cause. Avoid seasickness by abstaining from alcohol the night before, eating a light breakfast, limiting coffee, and sitting low and near the middle of the boat, away from odors and with your eyes on the horizon—no reading. While some swear by home remedies such as ginger or acupressure, the most reliable treatment is the scopolamine skin patch, available only by prescription, which lasts up to 3 days. The main choices for over-the-counter drugs are meclizine (brand names Bonine, Antivert, or Dramamine II) and dimenhydrinate (original Dramamine). Both are drowsiness-inducing antihistamines, but there's less of that side effect with the newer meclizine. To be effective, the drugs need at least 2 hours to get through your digestive system, so you must take the pill well before you get on the boat. For best effectiveness, take a tablet before bed and another on the morning of the outing. If you've taken nothing and feel yourself getting seasick, there is a last-minute cure that sometimes works: Chew up the tablets but don't swallow them, holding the mush under your tongue or against your cheek. The drug is partly absorbed through the lining of the mouth.

SHELLFISH Don't eat mussels, clams, or scallops you pick or dig from the seashore unless you know they're safe to eat. Generally, that means you need some specific and reliable local knowledge. There is a government program to ensure that commercial shellfish areas are safe, but the only easily accessible beaches it affects are on the eastern shore of Kachemak Bay. The risk is paralytic shellfish poisoning, a potentially fatal malady caused by a naturally occurring toxin. It can cause total paralysis that includes your breathing. A victim may be kept alive with mouth-to-mouth resuscitation until medical help is obtained. For more information, check the **Alaska Department of Environmental Conservation** website at www.dec.state.ak.us/eh/fss/seafood/psphome.htm, or go to www.alaska.gov and search for "PSP").

Driving Safety

ROAD REPORTS   The Alaska Department of Transportation has centralized highway reports with a handy toll-free phone and Internet system (*C* **511;** http://511.alaska.gov). Even in dry summer conditions, it is worthwhile to make the call or check the site before heading on an intercity drive, because road construction can cause long delays—at times, workers will close a major highway overnight for work. In winter, checking on conditions is a safety essential. Here are more seasonal tips.

SUMMER   Alaska's highways are two lanes except close to Anchorage and Fairbanks. Keep your headlights on all the time to help oncoming vehicles see you. Drivers are required to pull over at the next pullout whenever five or more cars are trailing them on a two-lane highway, regardless of how fast they're going. This saves the lives of people who otherwise will try to pass. When passing a truck going the other way on a gravel highway, slow down or stop and pull as far as possible to the side of the road to avoid losing your windshield to a flying rock. Always think about the path of rocks you're kicking up toward others' vehicles. Make sure you've got a good, full-size spare tire and jack if you're driving a gravel highway. For remote driving, bring along a first-aid kit, emergency food, a tow rope, and jumper cables, and keep your gas tank full.

WINTER   Drivers on Alaska's highways in winter should be prepared for cold-weather emergencies far from help. Take all the items listed for rural summer driving, plus a flashlight, matches, and materials to light a fire; chains, a shovel, and an ice scraper. A camp stove to make hot beverages is also a good idea. If you're driving a remote highway (such as the Alaska Hwy.) between December and March, take along gear adequate to keep you safe from the cold even if you have to wait overnight with a dead car at –40°F (–40°C; see "What to Wear," in chapter 2, and add blankets and sleeping bags). Never drive a road marked CLOSED or UNMAINTAINED IN WINTER. Even on maintained rural roads, other vehicles rarely come by in winter. All Alaska roads are icy all winter. Studded tires are a necessity. Also, never leave your car's engine stopped for more than 4 hours in temperatures of –10°F (–23°C) or colder. Virtually all vehicles in Alaska have electrical head-bolt heaters installed to keep the engine warm overnight; you'll find electrical outlets everywhere in cold Interior Alaska areas.

[FastFACTS] ALASKA

Alaskan Scheduled Flying Services   Companies include **Air Excursions** (www.airexcursions.com), **Bering Air** (www.beringair.com), **Era Alaska** (www.flyera.com), **Promech Air** (www.promechair.com), and **Wings of Alaska** (www.ichoosewings.com).

Area Codes   All of Alaska is in area code **907.** In the Yukon Territory, the area code is **867.** When placing a toll call within the state, you must dial 1, the area code, and the number.

Automobile Organizations   Motor clubs will supply maps, suggested routes, guidebooks, accident and bail-bond insurance, and emergency road service. The **American Automobile Association (AAA)** is the major auto club in the United States.

If you belong to a motor club in your home country, inquire about AAA reciprocity before you leave. You may be able to join AAA even if you're not a member of a reciprocal club; to inquire, call AAA (☎ **800/222-4357;** www.aaa.com). AAA has a nationwide emergency road service telephone number (☎ **800/AAA-HELP** [222-4357]).

Business Hours   In the larger cities, major grocery stores are open until late at night and carry a wide range of products (even fishing gear) in addition to food. At a minimum, **stores** are open Monday through Friday from 10am to 6pm and on Saturday afternoon, and are closed on Sunday, but many are open much longer hours, especially in summer. **Banks** may close an hour earlier, and if open on Saturday, hours may be short.

Car Rentals   Some small towns have only local car-rental agencies; details are listed in each section.

Cellphones   Pretty much every town that can be reached by road or ferry has cellular voice coverage, as well as some of the paved highways. That means the great majority of the people are covered and the great majority of the land is not. The largest provider is an Alaska company called ACS, which posts maps of its coverage area at www.acsalaska.com (click on "Wireless").

Crime   See "Health & Safety," earlier in this chapter.

Customs   **What Foreign Visitors Can Bring In**   Personal effects, which are items you use yourself, such as clothing, cameras, and fishing rods, are exempt from duties. In addition, every visitor over 21 years of age may bring in the following without paying duties: 1 liter of wine, beer, or hard liquor; 200 cigarettes, or 50 cigars for your own use and another 100 as gifts (but not from Cuba), or 2 kilograms (4.4 lb.) of smoking tobacco; and $100 worth of gifts. To claim these exemptions, you must spend at least 72 hours in the United States and cannot have claimed them within the preceding 6 months. The duty on goods exceeding these exemptions is 3% of the value on the first $1,000 (the flat rate); above that amount, it depends on the item. The flat rate applies only to items for your own use or gifts and can be used only once in 30 days. Importation of most raw food and plant material is prohibited or requires a special license. Foreign visitors may bring in or take out up to $10,000 in U.S. or foreign currency, traveler's checks, securities, and so on, with no formalities; larger sums must be declared to U.S. Customs and Border Protection (CBP) on entering or leaving, and paperwork must be filed. For more information, consult CBP's website (www.cbp.gov), contact a U.S. consulate or embassy, or call CBP officials in Anchorage (☎ **907/271-6855**).

Don't think about bringing **firearms** into the United States except for a hunting trip. Unless you are a U.S. citizen or permanent resident alien, you cannot bring in, buy, or even possess a gun without a permit from the **Bureau of Alcohol, Tobacco, Firearms, and Explosives** (☎ **304/616-4550;** www.atf.gov); these take up to 2 months to process (the application, Form 6NIA, is on the ATF website: www.atf.gov/forms/download/atf-f-5330-3d.pdf). The application must be accompanied by a valid hunting license (there are a few narrow exceptions, such as athletes involved in shooting competitions or visitors carrying certain invitations to qualifying events).

The **Alaska Department of Fish and Game** (☎ **907/465-6085;** www.alaska.gov/adfg) sells hunting licenses to nonresident aliens for $300 (tags are that much or more); however, aliens can hunt only with a registered guide. First find the guide, then let him or her help with the paperwork, but start many months in advance and be ready to pay.

Taking Home Wildlife Products   Authentic Alaska Native art and crafts made from protected marine mammals are perfectly legal to buy and own under U.S. and Alaska law, even though possessing marine mammal parts is not legal for non-Natives. Alaska Natives have used these materials for thousands of years, and their subsistence harvest is not a danger to the species. But some individual states have more restrictive laws (you may want to check), and generally marine-mammal products you buy made of any threatened or endangered species cannot be taken out of the country unless they're at least 100 years old. To leave the United States, including going through Canada, you will need a U.S. Fish and Wildlife Service declaration form (Form 3-177), and you may also need a wildlife export permit recognized by the Convention on International Trade of Endangered Species, known as CITES. These permits can be complicated to obtain and take 60 to 90 days for processing. For international visitors, the most practical advice is simply to avoid buying anything made from marine mammals or any other species requiring a CITES permit, including brown or black bear, wolf, lynx, bobcat, or river otter. Before you buy an item, make sure you can legally take it home, then have the shop mail it to you insured, and have them take care of the paperwork. If you carry it with you in your baggage or mail it yourself, perhaps because you bought it from someone who can't handle the paperwork, you'll need to get your own permits and clearance from Fish and Wildlife. For information, contact the **U.S. Fish and Wildlife Service** in Anchorage (☏ **907/271-6198;** alaska.fws.gov/law). Foreign visitors exporting wildlife may need to contact the agency's **Division of Management Authority** in Washington, D.C. (☏ **800/358-2104;** http://international. fws.gov), regarding permit requirements.

Drinking Laws   The minimum drinking age in Alaska is 21; ID is often checked, even for the elderly, and in many places every single customer making a purchase in a liquor store must show identification. Most restaurants sell beer and wine, while some have full bars that serve hard liquor as well. Packaged alcohol, beer, and wine are sold only in licensed stores, not in grocery stores, but these are common and are open long hours every day. Under state law, **bars** don't have to close until 5am, but many communities have an earlier closing, generally around 2am. Open containers of alcohol are not allowed in your car or, with few exceptions, in any public place outside a bar or restaurant. Don't even think about driving while intoxicated, which in Alaska carries mandatory 3-day jail time for the first offense. More than 100 rural communities have laws prohibiting the importation and possession of alcohol (this is known as being "dry") or prohibiting the sale but not possession of alcohol (known as being "damp"). Before flying into a Native village with alcohol, ask about the law or check a list online (go to www.dps.state.ak.us/abc and click on "Dry/Damp Communities"). Bootlegging is a serious crime, and serious bad manners, in Alaska Native communities that are trying to address the damage of alcohol abuse.

Electricity   As in Canada, the United States uses 110–120 volts AC (60 cycles), compared to 220–240 volts AC (50 cycles) in most of Europe, Australia, and New Zealand. Downward converters that change 220–240 volts to 110–120 volts are difficult to find in the United States, so bring one with you.

Embassies & Consulates   The following nations have consulates in Anchorage: **Canada,** 310 K St., Ste. 220 (☏ **907/264-6734;** www.anchorage.gc.ca); **Japan,** 3601 C St., Ste. 1300 (☏ **907/562-8424;** www.anchorage.us.emb-japan.go.jp); **Korea,** 800 E. Dimond Blvd., Ste. 3-695 (☏ **907/339-7955;** http://usa-anchorage.mofat.go.kr/eng/am/usa-anchorage/main/index.jsp); and **Mexico,** 610 C St., Ste. A 7 (☏ **907/334-9573**).

All embassies are in the nation's capital. If your country isn't listed below, call for directory information in Washington, D.C. (☏ **202/555-1212**), or check **www.embassy. org/embassies**.

The embassy of **Australia** is at 1601 Massachusetts Ave. NW, Washington, DC 20036 (☎ **202/797-3000;** http://australia.visahq.com). Consulates are in New York, Honolulu, Houston, Los Angeles, and San Francisco.

The embassy of **Canada** is at 501 Pennsylvania Ave. NW, Washington, DC 20001 (☎ **202/682-1740;** www.canadainternational.gc.ca/washington). Other Canadian consulates are in Buffalo (New York), Detroit, Los Angeles, New York, and Seattle.

The embassy of **Ireland** is at 2234 Massachusetts Ave. NW, Washington, DC 20008 (☎ **202/462-3939;** www.embassyofireland.org). Irish consulates are in Boston, Chicago, New York, San Francisco, and other cities. See website for complete listing.

The embassy of **New Zealand** is at 37 Observatory Circle NW, Washington, DC 20008 (☎ **202/328-4800;** www.nzembassy.com). New Zealand consulates are in Los Angeles, Salt Lake City, San Francisco, and Seattle.

The embassy of the **United Kingdom** is at 3100 Massachusetts Ave. NW, Washington, DC 20008 (☎ **202/588-6500;** http://ukinusa.fco.gov.uk). Other British consulates are in Atlanta, Boston, Chicago, Cleveland, Houston, Los Angeles, New York, San Francisco, and Seattle.

Emergencies   Generally, you can call ☎ **911** for medical, police, or fire emergencies. On remote highways, there sometimes are gaps in 911 coverage. If you can find a phone, dialing 0 will generally get an operator who can connect you to emergency services. To learn about equipment that can contact help beyond the reach of conventional communications, see "Getting Lost/Wilderness Communications," p. 523.

Family Travel   To locate accommodations, restaurants, and attractions that are particularly kid-friendly, look for the "Kids" icon throughout this guide.

Gasoline   The cost of gasoline changes too quickly to list in this book. You can find national and state price averages updated online daily at www.fuelgaugereport.com. Prices in Alaska range from a bit over the national average in Anchorage to much higher in rural areas, where they could be double or more. As elsewhere in the U.S., taxes are already included in the price quoted or on the pump. One U.S. gallon equals 3.8 liters or .85 imperial gallons. Fill-up locations are known as gas or service stations.

Insurance   Travelers from within the U.S. are often covered under their regular health insurance as long as they remain in the country. Take a minute to check your coverage, making sure it adequately covers emergency medical transportation and treatment, especially if you will be adventuring in remote areas. The cost of a medevac flight can easily be in the five figures. Check the coverage offered by your credit cards and, if necessary, buy a travel insurance policy to cover you just for the trip.

International visitors should certainly make health insurance arrangements before traveling to the U.S. Doctors and hospitals are expensive and often require proof of coverage before they render services (in an emergency, of course, you'll always get quick treatment, regardless of ability to pay). For advice on medical insurance while traveling, visit www.frommers.com/planning.

There are several kinds of travel insurance: for **trip cancellation or interruption,** for **medical costs,** and for **lost or delayed luggage.** Typically, they are sold together in a per-trip or annual comprehensive plan. Insurance for trip cancellation or interruption is a must if you have paid the large cash deposits demanded by many Alaska outfitters, fishing guides, wilderness lodges, package tour operators, and cruise companies. A premium of 5% to 7% of the cost of the trip is well worth the protection against the uncertainty of Alaska weather (most deposits are lost in case of weather delays or cancellations) or unexpected crises that might prevent you from being able to depart as planned. Interruption insurance will get you home under covered circumstances.

Major insurers such as those listed below offer policy holders access to 24-hour phone assistance to help handle crises. Read the policy carefully to find out when you are covered. Purchase your travel insurance directly from an insurance company not with the trip operator holding your deposit.

Insurance on your baggage is included in most travel insurance plans. If not, consider the pros and cons of a separate policy. Your baggage is often covered under your homeowners' policy or credit card benefits, but read the fine print. If an airline loses or damages your bags, they are usually responsible for up to $2,500 per passenger on domestic flights or, on international flights, up to approximately $635 per checked bag, excluding expensive items such as jewelry and cameras. Good luck getting an airline to actually pay in a reasonable period of time, however, as it is notoriously difficult. Travel insurance companies pay faster. Various companies sell travel insurance online, including **Travel Guard** (© **800/826-1300;** www.travelguard.com) and Access America (© **800/284-8300;** www.accessamerica.com).

Or look for the best deal around by going to **www.insuremytrip.com**. The site allows travelers to get instant quotes from many insurance companies at once by providing the dates of the trip, amount and type of coverage, and ages of the travelers.

With **rental cars,** you face a whole different set of insurance considerations. Most of these are the same as renting a car anywhere. You are likely covered by your own auto policy or credit card issuer, but do check before traveling. If you are not covered, do buy it: The potential costs you face are even larger than having a crash at home, because they include the rental company's lost business.

One special Alaska consideration: Ask the reservation agent or check the rental contract for rules about driving on unpaved roads, such as the Dalton, Denali, or Steese highways. We've listed two companies in Fairbanks that rent for use on unpaved highways (p. 419), and one in Anchorage (p. 218); very few others allow it. Cars do get damaged on these roads, and you may be setting yourself up for a real headache if you violate the rental contract and that happens. There are alternatives if you want to drive the Copper River Highway from Cordova (p. 358) or the McCarthy Road in Wrangell-St. Elias National Park (p. 456).

Internet & Wi-Fi See "Using the Internet on the Road" (p. 523) and the "Fast Facts" sections throughout the book for how to get online in each Alaska community.

Legal Aid If you are "pulled over" for a minor infraction (such as speeding), never attempt to pay the fine directly to a police officer; this could be construed as attempted bribery, a much more serious crime. Pay fines by mail or directly into the hands of the clerk of the court. If accused of a more serious offense, say and do nothing before consulting a lawyer; tell the police you want an attorney. Here the burden is on the state to prove a person's guilt beyond a reasonable doubt, and everyone has the right to remain silent, whether he or she is suspected of a crime or actually arrested. Once arrested, a person can make one telephone call to a party of his or her choice. International visitors should call your embassy or consulate.

Mail At press time, domestic postage rates were 28¢ for a postcard and 44¢ for a letter. For international mail, a first-class letter of up to 1 ounce costs 98¢ (75¢ to Canada and 79¢ to Mexico); a first-class postcard costs the same as a letter. For more information, go to **www.usps.com** and click on "Calculate Postage."

The locations of the post offices in each town in this book are listed in the appropriate "Fast Facts" sections. You can receive mail addressed to you at "General Delivery" at the post office. Always include zip codes when mailing items in the U.S. If you don't know your zip code, visit www.usps.com/zip4.

Maps   For most of the popular areas, there are excellent trail maps published by **Trails Illustrated,** part of National Geographic (✆ **800/962-1643;** www.natgeomaps.com). They're sold in park visitor centers, too. The maps are printed on plastic, so they don't get spoiled by rain; however, they don't cover the whole state. For detailed topographic maps covering all of Alaska, the U.S. Geological Service is still the only place to go. Their map sales office in Anchorage (a fascinating place for anyone interested in cartography) is on the campus of Alaska Pacific University, the **Earth Science Information Center,** at 4230 University Dr. (✆ **907/786-7011;** http://alaska.usgs.gov/science/esic/index.php).

Money & Costs   Alaska is an expensive destination any way you slice it. For the sake of consistency, regular rates are used throughout the book, but keep in mind that when tourism drops drastically, it is easy to negotiate breaks.

With the exception of rural highway motels, rack rates for standard motel rooms are rarely less than $140 in the high season. (We've rated them this way: inexpensive, less than $135; moderate, $135–$174; expensive, $175–$250; very expensive, more than $250.) Airfare from Seattle to Anchorage fluctuates wildly with competition among the airlines and fuel prices, with a round-trip with 14-day advance purchase currently about $600. (Flying is cheaper than the alternatives, driving or taking the ferry and bus.) Flights from Anchorage to Bush communities are that much again, and more. Even the train is expensive, with a one-way fare from Anchorage to Fairbanks (a 350-mile trip) costing $210. A couple ordering a good salmon dinner, appetizers, and wine will pay at least $100 in a fine restaurant, plus tip. One reason cruise ships have become such a popular way to visit Alaska is that, for the same quality level, they're less expensive on a daily basis than independent travel and offer the chance to see remote coastal areas that can be quite costly to get to for land-based visitors. (See chapter 4 for details on cruising.)

To travel at a standard American comfort level, a couple should allow $175 per person, per day, for room and board. The cost of an activity such as flightseeing, wildlife cruises, or guided fishing is typically $100 to $350 per person. Add ground transportation: A car is the best way to see much of the state, and you won't do much better than $55 a day for an economy model from the major national firms. Weekly rentals generally cost the same as renting for 5 individual days. You also may need train and ferry tickets.

You can trim your costs, however, by cutting your demands. You'll learn more about the real Alaska staying in B&B accommodations than in a standard hotel room. Expect to pay $100 to $125 for a nice room with a shared bathroom, $125 to $150 for a private bathroom (much more in a luxury B&B inn). The free breakfast cuts down on food costs, too. And there are plenty of family restaurants where you can eat a modest dinner for two for $50, with a tip and a glass of beer. Traveling in that style will bring down the cost of room and board to about $115 per person, per day for a couple.

You can save the most money by giving up a private room every night and cooking some of your own meals. Camping is a fun way to see Alaska and costs only $10 to $20 a night in state and federal government campgrounds. Hostels are available in most towns for around $25 a night.

Don't economize, however, when it comes to activities. Unlike other destinations, where relatively inexpensive museums or an interesting street scene take up much of your time, a trip to Alaska is all about getting outside and seeing nature. You can hike for nothing, but going sea kayaking, whale-watching, or flying out to see bears or to fish in a remote stream, you have to pay. Cut those expenses, and you cut much of the reason for coming in the first place.

You can save on activities, however, by traveling in the shoulder season, before and after the peak summer season. Hotel and guided activity prices drop significantly, typically 25% or more. May and September are solidly in the shoulder season, and sometimes you get bargains as late as June 15 or as early as August 15. Traveling in the winter is a whole different experience but certainly saves a lot of money—where hotels are open, you'll find their rates typically running a third to a half lower than their high-season levels. For other considerations on off-season and shoulder-season travel, see "When to Go," earlier in this chapter.

Carrying your money need not be a problem, regardless of your style of travel; those from the United States don't need to make any adjustments in their usual habits. Even Bush hub communities now have ATMs. The only places that don't usually have ATMs these days are remote outdoor destinations such as lodges or parks and tiny Native villages. You'll find ATM info in the "Fast Facts" section for each town in this book.

Every business you'd expect to take credit, charge, or debit cards at home will accept them here. Even bed-and-breakfasts and greasy-spoon diners take cards. Few businesses of any kind will take an out-of-state personal check. Traveler's checks are good just about anywhere, but there's no longer any reason to go through the hassle and expense.

Newspapers & Magazines   The state's largest newspaper is the *Anchorage Daily News;* you can find its content and a lot of information useful for visitors at www.adn.com. Seattle newspapers and *USA Today* are often available.

Packing   See "What to Wear" in chapter 2.

Passports   See "Embassies & Consulates," above, for whom to contact if you lose your passport while traveling in the U.S. For other information, contact the following agencies:

For Residents of Australia   Contact the **Australian Passport Information Service** at (C) **131-232,** or visit www.passports.gov.au.

For Residents of Canada   Contact the central **Passport Office,** Department of Foreign Affairs and International Trade, Ottawa, ON K1A 0G3 ((C) **800/567-6868;** www.ppt.gc.ca).

For Residents of Ireland   Contact the **Passport Office,** Setanta Centre, Molesworth Street, Dublin 2 ((C) **01/671-1633;** www.foreignaffairs.gov.ie).

For Residents of New Zealand   Contact the **Passports Office,** Department of Internal Affairs, 47 Boulcott St., Wellington, 6011 ((C) **0800/225-050 in** New Zealand, or 04/474-8100; www.passports.govt.nz).

For Residents of the United Kingdom   Visit your nearest passport office, major post office, or travel agency, or contact the **Identity and Passport Service (IPS),** 89 Eccleston Sq., London, SW1V 1PN ((C) **0300/222-0000;** www.ips.gov.uk).

For Residents of the United States   To find your regional passport office, check the U.S. State Department website (http://travel.state.gov/passport) or call the **National Passport Information Center** ((C) **877/487-2778**) for automated information.

Police   Dial (C) **911** in an emergency. Nonemergency phone numbers for local police departments are listed throughout the book.

Smoking   In Alaska's cities, smoking is prohibited in most indoor public places. In Anchorage and Juneau, smoking is prohibited even in bars. Smoking is more common in small towns, where rules are usually less strict, but virtually all hotels and B&Bs are smoke-free, so ask about smoking areas when you book your room if this is a concern.

Taxes   Alaska imposes no state sales tax, but most local governments have a sales tax and a bed tax on accommodations. The tax rates are listed in each town section throughout the book under its "Fast Facts." All prices and rates are listed without tax unless otherwise noted. The United States has no value-added tax (VAT) or other indirect tax at the national level.

Telephones   By-the-minute cards are often the least expensive way to call home for international visitors. They are sold in grocery stores and convenience stores. **Local calls** made from public pay phones usually cost 25¢, but in Alaska, you usually can't find one. The dominant phone company is trying to do away with them. Most long-distance and international calls can be dialed directly from any phone. **For calls within the United States and to Canada,** dial 1 followed by the area code and the seven-digit number. **For other international calls,** dial 011 followed by the country code, city code, and number you are calling. Calls to area codes **800, 888, 877,** and **866** are toll-free but won't work from outside the U.S. and Canada, and occasionally won't work from outside Alaska. For **local directory assistance** ("information"), dial 411; for long-distance information, dial 1, then the appropriate area code and 555-1212.

The least expensive way to call internationally is by Skype.com and other voice-over-Internet services, which work anywhere you have your computer and a broadband connection, but connection speed is spotty in places.

Time   Although the state naturally spans five time zones, in the 1980s, Alaska's middle time zone was stretched so almost the entire state would lie all in one zone, known as Alaska Standard Time (AST). It's 1 hour earlier than the U.S. West Coast's Pacific Time, 4 hours earlier than Eastern Standard Time. Crossing over the border from Alaska to Canada adds an hour and puts you at the same time as the West Coast. The balance of the continental United States is divided into **four time zones:** Eastern Standard Time (EST), Central Standard Time (CST), Mountain Standard Time (MST), and Pacific Standard Time (PST). When it's 8am in Anchorage, it is 9am in Los Angeles (PST), 10am in Denver (MST), 11am in Chicago (CST), noon in New York City (EST), 5pm in London (GMT), and 2am the next day in Sydney.

As with almost everywhere else in the United States, daylight saving time is in effect from 1am on the second Sunday in March (turn your clocks ahead 1 hr.) until 1am on the first Sunday in November (turn clocks back again).

Tipping   Tips make up a major part of the compensation for many service workers. To leave no tip in a restaurant is socially unacceptable and leaves your server unpaid. To leave a small tip is a powerful indication of displeasure for bad service; to leave no tip suggests you don't know any better. In restaurants, bars, and nightclubs, tip your server 15% to 20% of the check, depending on the quality of service. Tip **checkroom attendants** $1 per garment, and tip **valet-parking attendants** $1 each time you get your car. Tipping is not expected in cafeterias or fast-food restaurants where you order at a counter. In hotels, tip **bellhops** $1 per bag and tip the **housekeeper** at least $1 to $2 per day. Tip **cabdrivers** 15% of the fare, and tip **hairdressers** and **barbers** 15% to 20%. Do not tip gas-station attendants and ushers at movies and theaters.

See the box "A Guide to Guide Gratuities" (p. 514) for guidelines on tipping outdoor guides, outfitters, and employees at full-service wilderness lodges.

Toilets   You won't find public toilets, or "restrooms," on the streets in most U.S. cities, but they can be found in hotel lobbies, bars, restaurants, museums, department stores, railway and bus stations, and service stations. Large hotels and fast-food restaurants are often the best bet for clean facilities. It can be a long way between any toilets on rural Alaskan highways; see "Keeping the Wilderness Clean" (p. 513).

Visas   The U.S. State Department has a **Visa Waiver Program (VWP)** allowing citizens of the following countries to enter the United States without a visa for stays of up to 90 days: Andorra, Australia, Austria, Belgium, Brunei, Czech Republic, Denmark,

Estonia, Finland, France, Germany, Greece, Hungary, Iceland, Ireland, Italy, Japan, Latvia, Liechtenstein, Lithuania, Luxembourg, Malta, Monaco, the Netherlands, New Zealand, Norway, Portugal, San Marino, Singapore, Slovakia, Slovenia, South Korea, Spain, Sweden, Switzerland, and the United Kingdom. (**Note:** This list was accurate at press time; for the most up-to-date list of countries in the VWP, consult http://travel.state.gov/visa.) Even though a visa isn't necessary, in an effort to help U.S. officials check travelers against terror watch lists before they arrive at U.S. borders, visitors from VWP countries must register online through the Electronic System for Travel Authorization (ESTA) before boarding a plane or a boat to the U.S. Travelers must complete an electronic application providing basic personal and travel eligibility information. The Department of Homeland Security recommends filling out the form at least 3 days before traveling. Authorizations will be valid for up to 2 years or until the traveler's passport expires, whichever comes first. Currently, there is a $14 fee for the online application. Existing ESTA registrations remain valid through their expiration dates. **Note:** Any passport issued on or after October 26, 2006, by a VWP country must be an **e-Passport** for VWP travelers to be eligible to enter the U.S. without a visa. Citizens of these nations also need to present a round-trip air or cruise ticket upon arrival. E-Passports contain computer chips capable of storing biometric information, such as the required digital photograph of the holder. If your passport doesn't have this feature, you can still travel without a visa if the valid passport was issued before October 26, 2005, and includes a machine-readable zone; or if the valid passport was issued between October 26, 2005, and October 25, 2006, and includes a digital photograph. For more information, go to **http://travel.state.gov/visa**. Canadian citizens may enter the United States without visas but will need to show passports and proof of residence.

Citizens of all other countries must have (1) a valid passport that expires at least 6 months later than the scheduled end of their visit to the U.S.; and (2) a tourist visa.

Australian citizens can obtain up-to-date visa information from the **U.S. Embassy Canberra,** Moonah Place, Yarralumla, ACT 2600 (✆ **02/6214-5600**), or by checking the U.S. Diplomatic Mission's website at **http://canberra.usembassy.gov/consular**.

British subjects can obtain up-to-date visa information by calling the **U.S. Embassy Visa Information Line** (✆ **0891/200-290**) or by visiting the "Visas to the U.S." section of the American Embassy London's website at **www.usembassy.org.uk**.

Irish citizens can obtain up-to-date visa information through the **U.S. Embassy Dublin,** 42 Elgin Rd., Ballsbridge, Dublin 4 (✆ **353/1-668-8777; http://dublin.usembassy.gov**).

Citizens of **New Zealand** can obtain up-to-date visa information by contacting the **U.S. Embassy New Zealand,** 29 Fitzherbert Terrace, Thorndon, Wellington (✆ **644/472-2068; http://newzealand.usembassy.gov**).

Water   See "Drinking Water," p. 523, to learn about safe water in the outdoors.

USEFUL WEBSITES

MAJOR AIRLINES

Air Canada
www.aircanada.com
Alaska Airlines/Horizon Air
www.alaskaair.com
American Airlines
www.aa.com

China Airlines
www.china-airlines.com
Continental Airlines
www.continental.com
Delta Air Lines
www.delta.com
Frontier Airlines
www.frontierairlines.com

United Airlines
www.united.com

US Airways
www.usairways.com

LARGE ALASKAN FLYING SERVICES

Bering Air
www.beringair.com

Era Aviation
www.flyera.com

Penair
www.penair.com

Wings of Alaska
www.ichoosewings.com

MAJOR HOTEL & MOTEL CHAINS

Best Western International
www.bestwestern.com

Clarion Hotels
www.choicehotels.com

Comfort Inns
www.comfortinn.com

Courtyard by Marriott
www.marriott.com/courtyard

Days Inn
www.daysinn.com

Econo Lodges
www.choicehotels.com

Embassy Suites
www.embassysuites.hilton.com

Farfield Inn by Marriott
www.farfieldinn.com

Hampton Inn
www.hamptoninn1.hilton.com

Hilton Hotels
www.hilton.com

Holiday Inn
www.holidayinn.com

Howard Johnson
www.hojo.com

Hyatt
www.hyatt.com

InterContinental Hotels & Resorts
www.ichotelsgroup.com

Marriott
www.marriott.com

Motel 6
www.motel6.com

Omni Hotels
www.omnihotels.com

Quality
www.qualityinn.choicehotels.com

Ramada Worldwide
www.ramada.com

Red Carpet Inns
www.bookroomsnow.com

Red Lion Hotels
www.redlion.rdln.com

Residence Inn by Marriott
www.marriott.com/residenceinn

Rodeway Inns
www.RodewayInn.com

Sheraton Hotels & Resorts
www.starwoodhotels.com/sheraton

Super 8 Motels
www.super8.com

Travelodge
www.travelodge.com

Westin Hotels & Resorts
www.starwoodhotels.com/westin

CAR-RENTAL AGENCIES

Alamo
www.alamo.com

Avis
www.avis.com

Budget
www.budget.com

Dollar
www.dollar.com

Enterprise
www.enterprise.com

Hertz
www.hertz.com

National
www.nationalcar.com

Payless
www.paylesscarrental.com

Rent-A-Wreck
www.rentawreck.com

Thrifty
www.thrifty.com

Index

See also Accommodations index, below.

Photo Credits